ALSO BY JULES WITCOVER

85 Days: The Last Campaign of Robert Kennedy

The Resurrection of Richard Nixon

White Knight: The Rise of Spiro Agnew

*A Heartbeat Away: The Investigation and Resignation of
Vice President Spiro T. Agnew* (with Richard M. Cohen)

Marathon: The Pursuit of the Presidency, 1972–1976

The Main Chance (fiction)

*Blue Smoke and Mirrors: How Reagan Won and Why Carter Lost
the Election of 1980* (with Jack W. Germond)

Wake Us When It's Over: Presidential Politics of 1984
(with Jack W. Germond)

*Sabotage at Black Tom: Imperial Germany's Secret War
in America, 1914–1917*

*Whose Broad Stripes and Bright Stars?: The Trivial Pursuit
of the Presidency, 1988* (with Jack W. Germond)

Crapshoot: Rolling the Dice on the Vice Presidency

Mad as Hell: Revolt at the Ballot Box, 1992 (with Jack W. Germond)

The Year the Dream Died: Revisiting 1968 in America

*No Way to Pick a President: How Money and Hired Guns
Have Debased American Elections*

PARTY

OF THE

PEOPLE

PARTY
OF THE
PEOPLE

A History of the Democrats

Jules Witcover

 Random House · New York

Library of Congress Cataloging-in-Publication Data

Witcover, Jules.
    Party of the people : a history of the Democrats / by Jules Witcover.
        p. cm.
    Includes bibliographical references and index.
    ISBN 0-375-50742-6
        1. Democratic Party (U.S.)—History. I. Title.
JK2316.W735 2003
324.2736—dc21
        2003041269

Book design by Mercedes Everett

In memory of Paul Wellstone,
Democrat of the people

"I belong to no organized party. I am a Democrat."
—Will Rogers

PREFACE AND ACKNOWLEDGMENTS

The literature of politics in America includes hundreds of richly detailed, scholarly volumes by eminent historians. Not many, however, have focused on the conception, development, successes and tribulations of the world's oldest existing party. This book is an attempt to tell that story by presenting the perceptions and wisdom of past and present chroniclers of political history, then adding my own experiences and observations collected from Washington and on the presidential campaign trail across the country over the last half a century.

Most of my previous political books, including seven on presidential elections, have fallen into the category of contemporary history; that is, they were written as the events described unfolded and immediately thereafter. In preparing this volume, I have come to appreciate more than before the invaluable perspective afforded by the passage of time, well utilized by the professional historians on whose work much of this book is based, especially the early and middle chapters. Reinforced as well, however, has been my belief in the comparable value of firsthand observations from participants and witnesses to the events to be chronicled. Therefore, I have attempted to draw from the two disciplines of contemplative history and contemporary or "instant" history to produce an extensive, popular account of the birth and life of the Democratic Party over the more than two hundred years of its existence.

As a panorama of a party two centuries old, this account cannot hope to encompass all the detail and scholarship of the many excellent political volumes already written, or all aspects of the Democratic Party's history at every level. The objective is to present a sweep of the party's evolution from conception and first cries from the crib in 1792 to its current raucous yells in the competition of a lusty two-party system whose own stability and dominance nevertheless continue to be challenged.

I am first of all indebted to Arthur M. Schlesinger Jr., editor of the definitive four-volume *History of U.S. Political Parties,* the benchmark work that was my stepping-off point. He also thoughtfully alerted me to *The National Experience: A History of the United States,* edited by Professor John M. Blum of Yale University, which impressively presents a running account of American political and social history by an array of the most distinguished historians.

For the colonial and immediate post-colonial periods, I found particularly helpful the works of Noble E. Cunningham, Wilfred E. Binkley, Stephen G. Kurtz and Claude G. Bowers; for the Jeffersonian era, Cunningham, Thomas S. Pancake and Nathan Schachner; for the Jacksonian years, Schlesinger and Robert V. Remini; for the Civil War and aftermath, David M. Potter, Christopher Dell and Joel H. Silbey; for the Cleveland and Bryan era, Paolo Coletta, Allan Nevins and J. Rogers Hollingsworth; for the Wilson and World War I period, Blum, Ray Stannard Baker and Arthur S. Link; for the long FDR reign in peace and war, Schlesinger, Kenneth S. Davis, Frank Freidel, Nathan Miller and Sean J. Savage; for the Truman years, my old bureau chief and friend Robert J. Donovan, David McCullough, Merle Miller's oral history and HST's memoirs; for the JFK years, Theodore H. White, Schlesinger, Richard Goodwin, Theodore Sorensen, Lawrence O'Brien and William Manchester; for the LBJ years, Doris Kearns Goodwin, Joseph Califano, Robert Dallek and Johnson's memoir; on the Vietnam War and protest, Stanley Karnow, Tom Hayden and Todd Gitlin; on the civil rights movement, Taylor Branch and David L. Lewis; on Democratic Party reform, William J. Crotty; on development of the Democratic Leadership Council, Kenneth Baer, and interviews with Al From and Elaine Kamarck; and on the Clinton-Gore years, David Maraniss, Peter Baker, Martin Walker and Howard Gillman. Their specific works can be found in the bibliography along with all the other books on which I relied in various degrees.

Also indispensable were the Brookings Institution volume on national party conventions and voting records by Richard C. Bain and

Judith H. Parris; the two-volume *Running for President,* edited by Schlesinger; the presidential elections history by Eugene H. Roseboom; the Democratic National Committee's own history and *The Washington Post*'s book on the 2000 election.

I have profited as well from associations and friendships over the years with a range of Democratic national chairmen, especially Lawrence F. O'Brien and Robert S. Strauss, and also Henry M. Jackson, John Bailey, Fred Harris, Jean Westwood, John White, Charles Manatt, Paul Kirk, Ronald Brown, David Wilhelm and Donald Fowler; also many national committee staff workers and campaign managers, media consultants, pollsters and other players of the political game, including all the fellow reporters who have shared my learning experience about the Democratic Party on the campaign trail.

Of special assistance has been critical guidance on historical perspectives from Lewis L. Gould, Eugene C. Barker Centennial Professor in American History at the University of Texas in Austin and author of the Random House companion volume on the Republican Party, who reviewed this manuscript and offered invaluable counsel. I am grateful to Katie Hall for her concept of this history and to Matthew Thornton, Robin Rolewicz, and Steve Messina at Random House for their professional shepherding of the project. Finally, I am indebted as always to my longtime diligent agent and friend, David Black, and above all to my wife, Marion Elizabeth Rodgers, for her unflagging support even as she persevered on a very ambitious manuscript of her own, providing sustenance both material and emotional during the writing.

CONTENTS

PARTY

OF THE

PEOPLE

Alexander Hamilton, Thomas Jefferson's principal adversary as leader of the Federalists in the period leading up to formation of the original Republican Party, forerunner of today's Democratic Party.

Chapter 1

AN UNWANTED PREGNANCY,
1775–1792

THE DEMOCRATIC PARTY of the United States, the oldest existing in the world, was in a sense an illegitimate child, unwanted by the founding fathers of the American Republic. They had no intention of bringing about the birth of any such institution, and in fact the first president, George Washington, warned darkly against the conception of any political parties.

The American colonies had managed without them through their early political struggle for independence from the British, and in their first efforts to create governing mechanisms of their own in the newly declared independent states. The Continental Congress came and went without party structure, and the Articles of Confederation offered no provision for parties. They were widely regarded as hostile to the pursuit of a harmonious society and were seen as the agents of all manner of special interests. Thomas Jefferson once famously observed: "If I could not go to heaven but with a party, I would not go there at all."[1]

This attitude was not surprising in a young nation that was being shaped out of a European tradition that had also essentially shunned political parties—organizations created to embrace and advance common positions across a broad range of public matters. Rather, it had been the practice for like-minded individuals to come together temporarily to advance specific, narrow interests and to disband upon the success or failure of such alliances. They were usually called "factions" or "interests," never "parties." Americans of the time were conditioned less by internal political differences than by their opposition to the British crown that led to the American Revolution.

When independence was won, their most prominent political figures, largely patrician members of the landed and commercial gentry, found themselves engaged together in the heady and positive task of building a new government. Washington, the military hero of the Revolution, stood above politics and was universally recognized as the new nation's unifying figure.

But the fierce competition of ideas between two other brilliant men— Alexander Hamilton, the dashing, stylish aristocrat bent on shaping a national government of privilege based on the British model, and Jefferson, the unpretentious defender of the pioneer spirit determined to establish an unprecedented representative democracy—was at the core of the series of events that eventually led to the existence of parties and, ultimately, the Democratic Party of today. Many other men were involved in the fight, most notably James Madison, principal architect of the Constitution, as the chief ally of Jefferson. But in essence it boiled down to whether Hamilton or Jefferson would have his way.

Hamilton had a colorful if questionable pedigree. Derided by John Adams in his autobiography as "the bastard brat of a Scotch pedlar,"[2] Hamilton was born in 1755 on the island of Nevis in the Caribbean West Indies. His mother was a brilliant and attractive French Huguenot who recognized his talent as a writer as well as his industry and ambition. Sent to America at age fifteen to be educated, he attended King's College (later Columbia), fought in the Revolution, became an aide to Washington and a literary celebrity who gained entry into the world of aristocracy, of which he became an outspoken protagonist.

He was short and slender, with reddish hair on a large head of fair complexion. Historian Claude G. Bowers described him as "graceful and debonair, elegant and courtly, seductive and ingratiating, playful or impassioned, he could have fitted into the picture at the Versailles of Louis XV." But he also was, Bowers wrote, a vain egotist "singularly lacking in tact, offensively opinionated, impatient and often insulting to well-meaning mediocrity, and dictatorial. He did not consult—he directed. He did not conciliate—he commanded. . . . He was a failure in the management of men, and only his superior genius made it possible for him to dominate so long."[3]

Jefferson was a contrast to Hamilton in heritage as well as political creed. Born in 1743, his mother was a Randolph, an aristocrat, but his father was a middle-class farmer in frontier Virginia, and the son preferred to dwell on that lineage. Dismissively, he observed of his mother's family that it traced its "pedigree far back in England and Scotland, to which let everyone ascribe the faith and merit he chooses."[4] He started school with backwoods classmates, but adjusted easily to the aristocratic ways of the College of William and Mary, while still adhering to his frontier roots.

William E. Dodd, in *Statesmen of the Old South*, observed that it was not difficult "to see how the great principle of Jefferson's life—absolute faith in democracy—came to him. He was the product of the first West in American history; he grew up with men who ruled their country well, who fought the Indians valiantly. . . . Jefferson loved his backwoods neighbors and he, in turn, was loved by them."[5]

Jefferson was also a far cry from Hamilton, his junior by twelve years, in appearance, manner and style. He was tall and slender, with red hair tied in back, a man who, in Bowers's description, "dressed conventionally, because men must, and was careless of his attire." He had a look, Bowers wrote, "more of benevolence than force, more of subtlety than pugnacity. Nor, in that day of lace and frills, was there anything in his garb to proclaim him of the élite. . . . His tact was proverbial. He never sought to overshadow or overawe. . . . Considerate of his foes, he never hurt the sensibilities of his friends through offensive methods."[6]

Hamilton and Jefferson led the principal factions based on regional interests from which a party system would emerge. Although the party of Jefferson was not the first created—the short-lived Federalists of Hamilton preceded it—it would prove to be the most enduring. By the twenty-first century, it had survived with modifications for more than two hundred years, an existence unmatched anywhere in the world. In chronicling the birth and development of today's Democratic Party, however, it is essential at the outset to review the early dominance of the Federalist faction, opposition to which by Jefferson, Madison and others midwifed their new party and gave it its purpose and direction.

Long before the American Revolution, societal forces in the colonies had foreshadowed the existence of a two-party system. The earliest settlers in the piedmont locale of Virginia and other Eastern seaboard regions had established themselves not only in agriculture but also in commerce and trade, and took leading roles in what self-governing existed. Planters of tobacco were among the aristocrats of the time, tied closely to British tradition and lifestyle. Later arrivals, from Maine to Georgia, were obliged to move westward for land and a more primitive agrarian life, and were known—often disparagingly in the East—as backwoodsmen. In colonial affairs, they were underrepresented and overtaxed, more susceptible to Indian attacks and, saddled with debt, resentful of their more comfortable brethren often living in more favorable conditions under the Crown.

At first, these settlers of the Western regions were heavily Scotch-Irish who bought or squatted on land of Eastern speculators. They were practitioners of various Protestant religious sects outside the Congregational Church in New England and the Episcopal in the South, but often were taxed to support them, adding to their resentment of the older settlements of the East. The Scotch-Irish focused particularly on Pennsylvania. William Penn's secretary, James Logan, wrote in 1729 that "it looks as if Ireland is to send all its inhabitants hither, for last week not less than six ships arrived, and every day two or three arrive also."[7]

Soon German immigrants were also moving west and south into Maryland, the Shenandoah Valley of Virginia, the Carolinas and Georgia. Their commitment to the soil, and local life, and their hostility toward the aristocrats of business and commerce in the Eastern towns, made them natural recruits against any centralized government in the colonies, be it British or colonial.

A hundred years before Jefferson penned the Declaration of Independence, some Virginia backwoodsmen fell in behind Nathaniel Bacon, the owner of a frontier plantation ravaged by Indians, and rebelled against Virginia's royal governor, Sir William Berkeley, an exploiter of the Indian fur trade. The so-called Bacon's Rebellion produced more protection and forced some social reforms, but when Bacon died the rebels paid for their behavior at the hands of vengeful piedmonters. The clash between the established settlers and the frontiersmen, between the men of commerce and farmers, in many cases between the wellborn and well-educated and the toilers of the soil, was a forerunner of the eventual factional struggle that was played out in the writing of the Constitution, and in the subsequent evolution of bona fide political parties.[8]

Before that could happen, however, the oppression of both segments of the early American society by the British brought them together in the fight for independence. For the six years of the Revolutionary War,

1775–81, men of the seaboard and of the frontier joined forces against the foreign power that increasingly taxed them, intruded on their trade and on their liberties, until independence created the conditions wherein the old domestic factionalism inevitably reemerged.

A leading early defender of the backwoodsmen in that competition was William Findley of western Pennsylvania, a Scotch-Irish settler who challenged establishment in his state of the first Bank of North America in 1782, on grounds it benefited only the wealthy propertied class. A group of "Constitutionalists" gained control of the Pennsylvania assembly and threw out the bank. Similar clashes in other states heightened the interest of the propertied classes in establishing a national government that could check development in the states deleterious to them. The Articles of Confederation ratified in 1781 and the Continental Congress it created had proved in their eyes to be inadequate to the task, and pressure built for a stronger political framework among the states.

At the time, the new nation had a population of only about 5 million, of which nearly one person in five was black and in slavery. The bulk of all these new Americans lived along or near the Atlantic seaboard, overwhelmingly in rural towns and villages. The largest city was Philadelphia, with about 70,000 inhabitants, with New York next with 60,000 and Boston third with 25,000. Farming and shipping, over woeful roads, were the main occupations, and manufacturing was a minor undertaking. Schools were run by churches or the aristocracy, which also dominated politics.

In the 1780s, the Federalists (sometimes called the Nationalists) were the leading faction behind Hamilton, a patriot who nevertheless had a strong residual admiration for all things British, and John Adams of Massachusetts, a bald, portly, vain man of high temper twenty years his senior. The brilliance of Hamilton's mind and cunning compensated for the difference in age in establishing his dominance over Adams in the faction. The Federalists were propertied gentlemen of business and trade from seaboard New England, New York and other Eastern states, along with large landowners, all advocating a strong national government that would defend the caste system. Many had been officers in the Revolutionary army.

The Federalists were what the name implied—citizens who wanted greater concentration of power at the national level, with economic, banking, taxation and foreign policies controlled by the federal government, the better to protect their property and wealth. As their leader, Hamilton had what amounted to contempt for the basic concept of democracy, if that meant equality of rights and power between the aristocracy he represented and the common man, on the farm or in the town. He preferred a government on the model of the British monarchy, to the point of favoring a president-for-life with broad and arbitrary powers.[9]

The Federalists' opposite numbers, known simply at first as anti-Federalists, were men of agrarian interests largely from the backwoods South, as well as small farmers and business operators, all of whom favored decentralized government. Most foot soldiers in the Revolutionary army found their political home here. The anti-Federalists were more locally oriented farmers and townspeople, often debt-ridden, and defenders of individual and states' rights who looked to a central government as oppressive, much as they had viewed the British crown. They often referred to Federalists as "Tories," after the British party, and after fighting for and winning independence from England, they did not want to come under the thumb of any other national entity.

Although Jefferson was a champion of the interests of agriculture and the workingman, and was cool to any Federalist national government benefiting the wealthy and wellborn, he never cast himself as an anti-Federalist. Indeed, he took pains to dissociate himself from that faction, which he saw as merely reactive to the Federalists. He adopted a more positive posture, looking to the sort of democracy that he believed was the goal of revolutionists in France, where he had served with great personal relish as American minister. His purpose in public life, he wrote on one occasion, was to eradicate "every fibre of ancient or future aristocracy."[10] It was easy to see why Hamilton and Jefferson would soon find themselves on a collision course in charting the political framework of the new nation.

While Hamilton could be said to have fathered the Federalists as the first American political party, they did not survive as a real force beyond the early 1800s. As for the anti-Federalists, they were pathfinders for, but not the founders of, Jefferson's party, which in its evolution has far outlived not only the Federalists but also such other subsequent parties as the Whigs, the Know-Nothings, the Progressives and a host of lesser entities. By the time of the birth of the Republican Party of today in 1856, what by then had come to be known as the Democratic Party was already seventy-three years old.

The post-Revolution competition between the older, landed and commercial interests and the frontier agrarians was at times bitter and fierce. The seaboard mercantile class continued to impose harsh and unjust burdens on farmers, particularly in debt collection that brought with it the threat of squalid debtors' prison. In Massachusetts in 1786, a Revolutionary War officer named Daniel Shays led raids on state courts to disrupt debt judgments against farmers, and tried to seize arms from a Continental arsenal. The raid was put down but what came to be known as Shays's Rebellion did produce some reforms.[11]

In the late spring of 1787, both the Federalist and anti-Federalist factions—not yet organized parties in any real sense—became involved in the sensitive labors leading to the writing of the Constitution and its ratification by the original thirteen states. A convention for the purpose was called in Philadelphia with Washington as its president and delegate from Virginia. The Federalists greatly outnumbered the anti-Federalists and took the lead from the start. They had local chapters in key Eastern states, and were experienced in politics through colonial assemblies, state legislatures and town meetings, notably in New England.

By contrast, the anti-Federalists were loosely associated and generally cool or downright hostile to the notion of a constitutional convention that might intrude on local and states' rights. Indeed, one of the original thirteen states, Rhode Island, a seat of local agrarian interests, boycotted the Philadelphia deliberations. So did Patrick Henry of Virginia, a leader of the backwoodsmen who feared the establishment of a new government of aristocrats wielding intrusive powers who would merely replace the British. He declined appointment to the Virginia delegation.

The epic struggle between Hamilton and Jefferson did not come in the actual writing of the Constitution for two reasons. First, Hamilton's plans for doing away with the states and creating a government approaching a monarchy was rejected by the convention, and his influence in Philadelphia was modest. Second, Jefferson was serving as the United States minister in France at the time, hence he was not a delegate to the convention nor a signer of the finished product. Like Hamilton, he also had concerns about it, but of a different sort. For all the general concern among the delegates to the convention over the question of whether a strong central government should dominate (Hamilton's view) or the states should hold the upper hand in the new government (Jefferson's), the debate just as importantly dealt with protecting the economic interests of the seaboard and frontier regions. The aristocratic, propertied men of commerce and trade from the coastal areas largely got their way, so most of the support for the Constitution came from them, with the frontier agrarians for the most part reluctantly going along.

Madison, originally aligned with the Federalists in authoring the Constitution, was himself a landed aristocrat from the Virginia piedmont, a short, soft-spoken and rather weak-looking scholar of philosophy and political science trained at the College of New Jersey (later Princeton). In *Federalist Paper No. 10,* he cogently laid down why factionalism in the debate over the Constitution would inevitably set the young nation on the course of partisan alignment:

"The most common and durable source of factions has been the various and unequal distribution of property. Those who hold and those who are without property have ever formed distinct interests in society. Those who are creditors and those who are debtors fall under a like discrimination. A landed interest, a manufacturing interest, a moneyed interest, with many lesser interests, grow up of necessity in civilized nations and divide them into different classes actuated by different sentiments and views. The regulation of these various and interfering interests forms the principal task of modern legislation and involves the spirit of party and faction in the necessary and ordinary operations of government."[12] As we might say today, "class warfare" would unavoidably dictate the formation of parties of self-interest.

The focus on property as a determinant in the political equation raised questions about the edict in the Declaration of Independence that "all men are created equal" and endowed with the same rights. In the reality of the time, that meant adult white males only, and equality clearly also depended on their wisdom, their wealth and their education. These distinctions at once separated the new Americans, particularly the well-born and well-bred of the cities of the East, from the unschooled workingmen and farmers of the frontier West and South.

A significant portion of the "property" that determined social and economic status was in slave-owning. As early as 1619, black men, women and children, known universally then as negroes, were transported in bondage from Africa to the colonies, especially in the South, and retained by law in that condition. By 1770, black slaves constituted about one sixth of the entire colonial population; in South Carolina alone, about two thirds of all inhabitants were enslaved Africans laboring principally in agriculture.[13]

These slaves had no rights in law, yet were critical to the growth and prosperity of white-owned plantations and farms. And in time, three fifths of a state's slave population would be counted in determining that state's representation in the House of Representatives—without, of course, voting rights being afforded to slaves. Although not concentrated exclusively in the South, slavery became another important distinction between Southern agrarian and Northern commercial interests and a significant element in Southern political strength.

Jefferson, although a slave owner himself, was outspoken in opposition to the institution, seeking unsuccessfully to have it abolished in his native Virginia. He wrote in his autobiography: "Nothing is more certainly written in the book of fate that these people are to be free."[14]

After nearly four months of debate behind closed doors at the Constitutional Convention in Philadelphia, the differing views of the two main factions were delineated and where possible compromised. The delegates from the twelve original states participating signed the historic document on September 17, 1787, and submitted it to all thirteen for ratification. Most moved quickly to do so, but it was not until three years later that Rhode Island, after standing aside, became the last of the original thirteen to accept the Constitution—by only two votes in its legislature.

Most Federalists saw the Constitution as the salvation of the new Republic, providing the means by which the states would join together to guarantee the objectives of the Revolution. Most anti-Federalists viewed the new document as a threat to the democratic principles and individual liberty for which the Revolution had been fought. These basic differences assured continued conflict and factionalism, the seeds of eventual party birth.

Hamilton was the only delegate to the Constitutional Convention from New York who signed the finished document, though with great reservations. Addressing the convention, he had warned that a "republican" government would produce corruption and intrigue in the hands of the rabble. On another occasion, he acknowledged to Washington that he had "long since learned to hold public opinion of no value."[15] But along with Madison and John Jay of New York, he participated in authoring the eighty-five long articles in defense of the new Constitution that came to be known as the *Federalist Papers,* and worked for and finally achieved its ratification in his state. In what he later called, in a letter to Gouverneur

Morris, "a frail and worthless fabric,"[16] he saw, however, the only available vehicle for his elaborate plans to establish a government of the aristocracy he so desired.

In Jefferson's absence, key anti-Federalists as proponents of states' rights, though greatly outnumbered in Philadelphia, helped achieve compromises on such matters as the broader representation of small states in the House of Representatives and the electoral college, through which the nation's presidents were to be chosen. The Constitution also provided, in the event no presidential candidate received a majority of the electoral vote, that the choice would go to the House, weighted in favor of the smaller states.

At Jefferson's insistence from Paris, a bill of individual rights was included as the first ten amendments. On his return home in late 1789, he rallied to the Constitution's support, while continuing as a defender of agrarian interests concerned about the Federalists and their elitism based on wealth, education and social stature.

The Federalists emerged from the formative Philadelphia convention clearly the decisive faction in a young nation whose leaders were still antagonistic toward the divisive notion of party. As for the anti-Federalists, they were much weaker and disorganized as a faction and too alienated toward the idea of centralized government to endure and develop as a real party, as Jefferson realized.

Nearly sixteen months after drafting the Constitution, on February 4, 1789, George Washington was elected the first American president and John Adams his vice president, without the benefit or hindrance of a political party.[17] Though nominally a Federalist like Adams, Washington, only fifty-seven but already in physical decline and of unrelentingly sober mien, was the overwhelming choice of his countrymen of whatever faction. In a way his immense popularity served to postpone the formation of a true party system. Standing above factionalism and declining to campaign or even express a willingness to serve, Washington required no party apparatus to elect him, a circumstance he much preferred.

But the original manner set forth in the Constitution for electing the president would prove in time to be inadvertently instrumental in the creation of the party system. It provided that each state cast its electoral votes, based on its congressional strength, for two presidential candidates, only one of whom could come from the elector's home state, as a means of avoiding excessive parochialism in the choice. The candidate receiving the most votes would become president and the runner-up vice president.

With only ten states voting, Washington won easily, garnering 69 electoral votes to 34 for Adams, clearly understood to be his running mate, who became vice president. It was an arrangement arrived at by the Constitution's drafters without much thought that it could result in any partisan division of power, because parties simply were not envisioned by the founders. But before long such a division would surface to unmask the arrangement as an instrument of partisan mischief.

Adams, for one, clung to the abhorrence of party politics. As vice president, he observed: "There is nothing I dread so much as the division of the Republic into two great parties, each under its leader. . . . This, in my humble opinion, is to be feared as the greatest political evil under our Constitution."[18]

As long as Washington occupied the presidency, overt party structure and coordination were stymied. Nevertheless, Federalists formed the core of his administration, with Hamilton as secretary of the treasury, and of Congress. Jefferson as secretary of state upon his return from Paris was the outsider in the cabinet. In Congress, only ten anti-Federalists held seats in the House and only two in the Senate. According to Linda K. Kerber, a University of Iowa history professor, "Federalists thought of themselves as a government, not as a party."[19]

From the start Hamilton was by far the most influential voice in the cabinet, gaining the first president's acquiescence in imposing a sweeping national banking discipline on the states. He pushed through federal assumption and funding at face value of all public debt, including that incurred by the Revolutionary War. He established a national bank authorized to tax the citizenry of the states, float bonds and create currency, and constructed a tariff to protect young American industry.

All these actions concerned Jefferson as benefiting the merchant class at the expense of farmers and laborers, triggering his fight with Hamilton. Jefferson acceded for a time to Hamilton's view that such sweeping steps were required to preserve the Union by placing it on a sound fiscal footing. But Hamilton's Bank of the United States soon became a critical element in the opposition of Jefferson and his frontier followers, whose debt and tax obligations were deepened by such policies. Also, Hamilton's personal demeanor, overbearing and dictatorial, contributed to the developing rift. Henry Cabot Lodge, in *The Works of Alexander Hamilton,* observed that within the cabinet Jefferson was offended because Hamilton "could not rid himself of the idea that he was really the prime minister."[20]

In challenging Hamilton, Madison took the lead as a prominent and leading member of the House of Representatives. As such, he played a larger role than anyone except Jefferson in the events that gave birth to the new party of democracy, providing a focal point for organizing the faction that opposed the aggressive treasury secretary. In a speech from the House floor in February 1790, Madison fired the first salvo against Hamilton's grand scheme to assure and sustain the primacy of the aristocratic class in the young nation. He proposed that in the government's funding of the public debt, original debtors, especially poor farmers and backwoodsmen, be protected from exploitative practices by speculators and the propertied rich. Madison's proposal was voted down, but the effort had served to alert the working class to Hamilton's purpose.[21]

Hamilton moved on to seek congressional approval of his plan to have the federal government assume the states' debts—a further consolidation of power in the national administration. It meant, among other things, the federal taxation of citizens of relatively debt-free states of the South like Virginia to bail out Northern debt-ridden states like Massachusetts. This time the Hamilton initiative narrowly failed, but he turned cunningly to none other than Jefferson to achieve his end.

According to Jefferson, in June 1790 he encountered Hamilton by chance outside Washington's presidential office in New York, then the seat of the government. The secretary of the treasury told him that his whole bank plan was imperiled by Madison's opposition to the federal assumption of state debts, and that the Union would fall without it. Jefferson offered to host a dinner at his home for Hamilton and Madison, to try to achieve some understanding on the matter.[22]

The dinner ended, Jefferson later wrote, "in Mr. Madison's acquiescence in a proposition that the question should be again brought before the House by way of amendment from the Senate, that he would not vote for it, nor entirely withdraw his opposition, yet he would not be strenuous, but leave it to its fate."[23]

At the time, states of the North and South were arguing about the location of a permanent site for the American capital, with Philadelphia, where it was to be moved temporarily from New York, vying with a proposed new site at Georgetown on the Potomac River, preferred by the

South. Jefferson recalled that either Hamilton or Madison then observed "that as the pill [of the state debt assumption] would be a bitter one to the Southern states, something should be done to soothe them; and the removal of the seat of government to the Patowmac was a just measure."[24]

As Joseph J. Ellis pointed out in his book *Founding Brothers,* other meetings on both the assumption and the location of the permanent capital had been going on prior to Jefferson's dinner and continued afterward, casting doubt on whether the dinner was as pivotal in either decision as Jefferson claimed. In any event, Jefferson much later charged in a letter to Washington that he had been "duped" by Hamilton about the peril to the Union in the matter. Jefferson said he had been "made a tool for forwarding his [Hamilton's] schemes, not then sufficiently understood by me; and of all the errors of my political life, this has occasioned me the deepest regret."[25] But at the time, he wrote to James Monroe that until the matter was settled "there will be no funding bill agreed to, our credit will burst and vanish, and the States separate, to take care, every one of itself."[26]

While he preferred to have the states settle their own debts, Jefferson wrote, he could see "the necessity of yielding to the cries of the creditors ... for the sake of the Union, and to save it from the greatest of all calamities, the total extinction of our credit in Europe."[27] Madison went along on the grounds that "the crisis demands the spirit of accommodation,"[28] but he was aware the deal served to consolidate Hamilton's power.

The battle, however, had only begun. The assumption of states' debts not only gave Hamilton the rationale for increased federal taxation in the states, resisted bitterly in the South and the frontier regions of the West where Jefferson was their protector. It also loosed into rural regions a flood of speculators from Northern cities who induced unwary backwoodsmen to swap redeemable Revolutionary holdings for counterfeit stock or other worthless paper. "What must be the feelings of the widow and orphan," a contributor to the *Pennsylvania Gazette* asked, "when they find themselves thus defrauded of a great part of their little all, and that, not unlikely, the earnings of their late husbands and fathers who died in the service of their country, by these pests of society who ought to be despised?"[29]

As much as anything else, the argument between Hamilton and Jefferson over Hamilton's bank and tax policies was the real incubator from which Jefferson's new party would be born. It defined the sharp and basic differences between the existing ruling merchant class after the Revolution, led by Hamilton, and the underdog society of farmers and workingmen forged into a political force by Jefferson.

Furthermore, Hamilton, in the debate over creation of a national bank, brushed aside the fact that the Constitution had not provided any specific authorization for such an action and declared that such power was implied. It was a breathtaking grasp for unfettered authority that Madison challenged on the House floor. "The doctrine of implication is always a tender one," he said in a mild tone. "If implications thus remote and thus multiplied may be linked together, a chain may be formed that will reach every object of legislation, every object within the whole compass of political economy. . . . It takes from our constituents the opportunity of deliberating on the untried measure, although their hands are also to be tied by the same terms."[30]

Madison's distress was to no avail. The bank bill passed narrowly, with all but one of the votes against from Southern congressmen, who correctly saw the bank as much more advantageous to Northern commercial interests than to the agrarian South. Washington, however, was nervous about overstepping the Constitution. He called on Jefferson and the attorney general, Edmund Randolph, to write opinions, both of which sided with Madison. As Washington appeared to waver, he came under verbal assaults from Hamilton allies in New York, to the point, Madison wrote Jefferson, "the licentiousness of tongues exceeded anything that was conceived."[31] Washington, however, finally signed the bank bill.

The contention between the Hamilton and Jefferson camps was further inflamed in 1791 by a seemingly innocuous comment Jefferson made on the occasion of his sending to a printer a copy of Thomas Paine's pro-democracy essay *The Rights of Man*. In an accompanying note, he expressed his pleasure "that something is at length to be publicly said against the political heresies which have sprung up among us."[32] Unknown to Jefferson, the printer used the remark as the preface to the reprint, noting it came from the secretary of state.

Adams, who had been writing aristocratic Federalist essays under the pen name Davila, took the reference to "heresies" to mean his writings, and was said to be livid, assuming that Jefferson had put Paine up to penning his treatise. Soon a battle of newspaper columns was under way by anonymous authors on both sides. Jefferson sat back and enjoyed the tumult he had inadvertently triggered. He informed Washington that he had no intention of entering the war of the written word. Paine's critics, he suggested, feared "that this popular and republican pamphlet [would] wipe out all the unconstitutional doctrines which their bellwether, Davilla, has been preaching for a twelve-month."[33]

In this newspaper war, the Jeffersonians until late 1791 had no major journalistic mouthpiece to contest with the Hamiltonian paper, the *Gazette of the United States,* published in Philadelphia by John Fenno. Jefferson and Madison finally assisted the Revolutionary poet Philip Freneau to put out a new paper, *National Gazette,* in Philadelphia reflecting the Jeffersonian viewpoint. Through anonymous essayists and sometimes directly, they traded barbs: Freneau assailed the speculations by aristocrats taking advantage of inside information about Hamilton's bank operations; Fenno defended the treasury secretary and accused Freneau's paper of being supported by "a party." Freneau acknowledged the charge, if by a party Fenno meant "a very respectable number of anti-aristocratic and anti-monarchical people."[34]

Hamilton himself joined the fray under a pseudonym in Fenno's sheet, believing sharply critical letters about him were written by Jefferson, when they really were the work of Madison and other Jefferson supporters. Seeking to drive Jefferson from the Washington cabinet, Hamilton in one article asked: "Can he reconcile it to his own personal dignity, and the principle of probity, to hold an office under [the Washington administration] and employ the means of official influence in that opposition?"[35]

Jefferson held his tongue and pen, but Freneau identified Hamilton by name as the critic, observing that "all is not right with certain lofty-minded persons who fondly imagined their ambitious career was to proceed without check or interruption to the summit of their wishes.... The devil rageth when his time is short."[36]

In May 1792, Hamilton spilled out his bitter feelings toward Jefferson and Madison in a lengthy letter to his friend Edward Carrington of Virginia, accusing them of plotting against him on personal as well as policy grounds. He had become convinced, Hamilton wrote, "that Mr. Madison, cooperating with Mr. Jefferson, is at the head of a faction decidedly hostile to me and my administration [of the Treasury Department]; and actuated by views, in my judgment, subversive of the principles of good government and dangerous to the Union, peace, and happiness of the country." After all, he noted, "Mr. Jefferson, it is known, did not in the first instance cordially acquiesce in the new Constitution for the United States; he had many doubts and reserves."[37]

Hamilton charged that Jefferson had challenged the "constitutionality and expediency" of the Hamilton bank with "asperity and ill humor toward me. . . . When any turn of things in the community has threatened either odium or embarrassment to me, he has not been able to suppress the satisfaction which it gave him."[38]

Madison, he wrote, had as his objective Hamilton's resignation from the cabinet, and had "boldly led his troops" in Congress to that end, but had failed. In discussions of the public debt, Hamilton went on, "Mr. Madison dealt much in insidious insinuations calculated to give an impression that the public money, under my particular direction, had been unfaithfully applied to put undue advantages in the pockets of speculators, and to support the debt at an artificial price for their benefit. The whole manner of this transaction left no doubt in any one's mind that Mr. Madison was actuated by personal and political animosity." Hamilton saw it all as part of a scheme in which "Mr. Jefferson aims with ardent desire at the Presidential chair."[39]

While he was at it, Hamilton complained to Carrington that in foreign policy Jefferson and Madison were doing their best to make trouble with the English to the advantage of the French. "They have a womanish attachment to France and a womanish resentment against Great Britain," he wrote. "They would draw us into the closest embrace of the former, and involve us in all the consequences of her politics; and they would risk the peace of the country in their endeavors to keep us at the greatest possible distance from the latter. . . . Various circumstances prove to me that if these gentlemen were left to pursue their own course, there would be, in less than six months, an open war between the United States and Great Britain."[40]

Jefferson, Hamilton went on, was a hopeless Francophile. "In France, he saw government only on the side of its abuses," he said of Jefferson's tenure there leading up to the French Revolution. "He drank freely of the French philosophy, in religion, in science, in politics. He came from France in the moment of a fermentation, which he had a share in exciting, and in the passions and feelings of which he shared both from temperament and situation. . . . He came, electrified with attachment to France, and with the project of knitting together the two countries in the closest political bands."[41]

Hamilton unquestionably was correct in his assessment of Jefferson as pro-French, just as Hamilton himself was pro-British. Jefferson's observation of democracy in the making in Paris had clearly inspired and reinforced his pursuit of it at home. It was not long before Hamilton and other Federalists were referring to Jefferson and his cohorts as "the French party," just as they in turn often called Hamilton and his faction "the English party."

Furthermore, Hamilton mused, Jefferson probably returned from Paris "with the expectation of a greater share in the direction of our councils than he has in reality enjoyed," adding, "I am not sure that he had not peculiarly marked out for himself the department of the finances" given by Washington to Hamilton. In any event, he wrote, Jefferson and Madison had gotten their heads together upon Jefferson's return and "my subversion, I am now satisfied, has been long an object with them."[42]

In newspaper articles signed with a pseudonym, Hamilton essentially repeated the same allegations. Washington, distressed by this conflict between his two ranking cabinet members, wrote to both men in the summer of 1792 urging them to desist, even as he knew that Jefferson had not joined in the written fray. He wished, Washington said, "that instead of wounding suspicions, and irritable charges, there may be liberal allowances, mutual forebearances and temporising yieldings on all sides."[43]

Hamilton responded, however, that he could not desist, after having been "the object of uniform opposition from Mr. Jefferson" and "of unkind whispers and insinuations" from him. "I have long seen a party formed in the Legislature under his auspices," Hamilton said, "bent upon my subversion."[44] Freneau's paper, he charged, had been started by Jefferson to render him and all the objects connected with his administration odious.

In response to Washington's effort to cool tempers, Jefferson wrote the president denying Hamilton's allegations and defending his fealty to the Constitution. "No man in the U.S. I suppose, approved of every title in the constitution," he wrote; "no one, I believe approved more of it than I did: and more of it was certainly disproved by my accuser than by me, and of it's [sic] parts most vitally republican.... [M]y objection to the constitution was that it wanted [lacked] a bill of rights securing freedom of religion, freedom of the press, freedom from standing armies, trial by jury, and a constant habeas corpus act. Colonel Hamilton's was that it wanted a king and house of lords. The sense of America has approved my objection and added the bill of rights, not the king and lords."[45]

As for Hamilton's accusation that he tried to scuttle his plans to create a national bank, Jefferson wrote: "If it has been supposed that I have ever intrigued among the members of the legislatures to defeat the plans of the Secretary of the Treasury, it is contrary to all truth." He acknowledged, however, "that I have utterly, in my private conversations, disapproved" of Hamilton's bank scheme. He argued that the treasury secretary's plan "flowed from principles adverse to liberty, and was calculated to undermine and demolish the republic, by creating an influence of his department over the members of the legislature." The Hamilton plan was made possible, he wrote, "by the votes of the very persons who, having swallowed his bait, were laying themselves out to profit by his plans."[46]

Jefferson acknowledged, along with Madison, helping Freneau, a classmate of Madison's at Princeton, get his newspaper started in Philadelphia. But he told Washington: "I can protest in the presence of heaven, that I never did by myself or any other, directly or indirectly, say a syllable, nor attempt any kind of influence" over his paper, or write anything "to which my name was not affixed or that of my office."[47] He did, however, urge Madison at one point: "For God's sake, my dear sir, take up your pen, select the most striking heresies, and cut him to pieces in the face of the public."[48]

Jefferson said he welcomed the journalistic rivalry between Fenno and Freneau. "But is it not the dignity, and even the decency of government committed," he asked, "when one of its principal ministers enlists himself as any anonymous writer or paragraphist for either one or the other of them? No government ought to be without censors," he said, "and where the press is free no one ever will. If virtuous, it need not fear the free operation of attack and defense." He said he assumed Freneau would continue "to give free place to pieces written against the aristocratic and monarchical principles" of Hamilton and the Federalists.[49]

The clash between the two cabinet members was hardening. In private letters Jefferson charged Hamilton with endless meddling in the business of the State Department. As early as 1790, in the midst of a confrontation between Britain and Spain, Hamilton had injected himself into foreign policy by bringing directly to Washington without advising Jefferson a request from Major George Beckwith, an unofficial British emissary, for permission to move British troops through the Northwest Territory against what was then Spanish Louisiana. Hamilton urged that permission be granted; when Jefferson learned of the matter, he argued that the United States make no response at all. The matter blew over but Jefferson resented Hamilton's bypassing of his department. Other intrusions of State Department responsibilities followed, to Jefferson's further irritation.[50]

As for Hamilton's own department, Jefferson warned of the treasury secretary's use of his patronage power there to influence legislators "to get rid of the limitations imposed by the Constitution" so that he could "prepare the way for a change, from the present republican form of government, to that of a monarchy, of which the English constitution is to be a model."[51]

Washington abandoned his effort to quell the feud, and within days Hamilton resumed his anti-Jefferson assaults in Fenno's paper, finally calling on his foe to resign from the cabinet. Jefferson did not reply in public print, but in a letter to Edmund Randolph he wrote: "The indecency of newspaper squabbling between two public Ministers has drawn something like an injunction from another quarter." Every allegation against him, he wrote, "is false.... But for the present, lying and scribbling must be free to those who are mean enough to deal in them and in the dark."[52] Jefferson remained as secretary of state.

Meanwhile, Hamilton continued to consolidate the power of the aristocracy with his national bank. Amid more speculation about profiteering by members of Congress who had written the bank bill, at least ten of them were made bank directors. Their foes labeled them "a corrupt squadron,"[53] a phrase Jefferson himself began to employ. The bank had more to do than any exchanges of hot words with his growing determination to mobilize a new political force against the Federalists.

The second presidential election of the new nation was now at hand. The reelection of Washington as president in 1792 was a foregone conclusion, but the same could not be said for Adams as vice president. With Washington still regarded as above party, foes of Hamilton began to focus on Federalist Adams to express their disfavor. The mechanism in the Constitution for choosing both president and vice president without resort to party was about to be subjected to factional and personal animosities. Party politics without that label was knocking on the door.

Edmond (Citizen) Genêt, first embraced by Jefferson as the representative of the new French Republic to the United States, was later repudiated for blatant interference in American foreign policy.

Chapter 2

THE NEW PARTY IS BORN, 1792–1796

BECAUSE GEORGE WASHINGTON remained unassailable after his first term, it fell to his much less revered vice president, John Adams, to take the political brunt of the deep divisions in the country created by the banking policies of his fellow Federalist, Alexander Hamilton. Accordingly, in the 1792 election anti-Federalists and Jeffersonians moved to replace Adams as vice president with George Clinton of New York.

Just that spring Clinton had been elected governor of the state in a bitter campaign against Supreme Court Chief Justice John Jay, the Federalist candidate, in what was among the first major clashes of factional strength. Jay was a classic aristocrat who had written the New York Constitution that reserved the vote for the wealthy and propertied, and who memorably had said, "those who own the country ought to govern it."[1] Clinton, on the other hand, was a classic democrat and a favorite of the Sons of Tammany, an early republican political society of the sort that was emerging in a number of states.

Although conflict at the national level was the driving force moving toward party formation, other such rudiments of collective action at the state level were taking shape. John Beckley in Pennsylvania and James Madison and James Monroe in Virginia, as well as Aaron Burr in New York, rallied like-minded political activists against a second term for Adams.

Hamilton, while cool at best toward the Federalist vice president,

wanted no part of Clinton, nor of Burr. Hamilton described Burr in letters
to friends as an "embryo Caesar,"[2] who also was being mentioned for a
time as the possible anti-Federalist candidate. Hamilton's repeated derision of Burr, in public and in private, would in time precipitate the
famous duel that cost Hamilton his life and Burr his political career.
Hamilton suspected that Jefferson, "entertaining and propagating opinions inconsistent with dignified and orderly government,"[3] was behind
the Clinton candidacy. An anonymous contributor in the *Pennsylvania
Daily Advertiser* warned of a conspiracy against "the virtuous Adams" by
"the jacktails of mobocracy."[4] Thus for the first time was there a direct
election clash at the federal level between the two factions.

Again as in 1789, presidential electors each had two votes, with the
candidate receiving the most—it would clearly be the reluctant Washington—becoming president and the runner-up vice president. Adams's critics persuaded some Federalist electors to withhold their second votes
from him and give them instead to anti-Federalist Clinton. Had Clinton
then finished second to Washington he would have replaced Adams as
vice president, leaving a factional split at the highest levels of national
executive office. But Adams survived, though by an embarrassing vote of
only 77 electoral ballots to 50 for Clinton. Washington, never declaring a
candidacy and remaining above party or faction though nominally on the
Federalist ticket, again finished first with all 132 votes available to him.

A crisis of having a vice president of opposite ideology from the president was averted, but forces opposed to Hamilton gained strength in the
states, taking more seats in a Congress that had been overwhelmingly
dominated by the Federalists in Washington's first term. The work of Jefferson, Madison and allies to build a political vehicle that could make an
effective challenge to Hamilton and the Federalists was off to a good start.

By now the Federalists themselves had taken on most of the trappings
of party. Existing organizations like local chambers of commerce, the military officers' Society of the Cincinnati and rich men's clubs provided a
solid nucleus. Beyond that, political circumstances and the very size of the
new country were dictating the establishment of parties. For one thing,
the process of electing a national leader required organization on a grand
scale and a political network to support it, connecting the political committees and clubs that were springing up in the various states. Debates
and votes in Congress also required factional caucuses to develop strategy
and cohesion.

Arthur M. Schlesinger Jr., in his editor's introduction to *History of U.S. Political Parties,* observed: "It was soon perceived that parties could greatly facilitate the work of the national government by throwing links across the far-flung country, by providing means of eliciting and expressing public opinion and by introducing a measure of regularity and predictability into the conduct of public affairs."[5]

At the same time, however, the anti-Federalists, who had persevered as a faction against creating a dominant national government and had opposed much of the work of the Constitutional Convention, were becoming a shell. Jefferson recognized the need for a new agrarian-based democratic, or "republican," party capitalizing on the frontiersmen's hostility toward Hamilton and his pro-British reputation. Jefferson held with supreme conviction that "cultivators of the earth are the most valuable citizens"[6] and looked to them as the new party's core.

In the various states, Jefferson had found local political clubs with leaders who could be recruited as soldiers in a national "republican" movement: Samuel Adams, John Hancock, Ben Austen and Charles Jarvis in Massachusetts; Abraham Bishop in Federalist stronghold Connecticut; John Langdon in New Hampshire; Matthew Lyon in Vermont; Clinton, Burr, Robert Livingston and John Pintard of the Sons of Tammany in New York; Beckley, William Maclay and Albert Gallatin in Pennsylvania; John Francis Mercer in Maryland; Madison, Monroe and William Giles in Virginia; Willie Jones and Nathaniel Macon in North Carolina; Charles Pinckney in South Carolina; James Jackson in Georgia.[7]

If the Federalists had wealth, social standing and political sophistication on their side, Jefferson had the raw numbers. The young nation's tillers of the soil, its craftsmen, shopkeepers and enlisted men of the Revolution constituted more than 90 percent of the population, and were responsive to Jefferson's warnings of "monarchical" rule by the aristocracy. They were tinder for the fire of democracy that he sought singlemindedly to ignite, fanned by Hamilton's transparent affection for the British model and lifestyle.

The drawback for Jefferson was that so many of these foot soldiers in his army for democracy, being unpropertied, were unable to vote. In New England, only Vermont had no property requirement; in New Hampshire, tax-paying men could cast ballots. So it was Jefferson's task to take those relatively few political activists of standing in each state, and the strength and persuasive power of his democratic ideas, to generate and spread opposition to the Federalist vision sufficient to arrest its drive. Farmers and other workingmen had to be convinced of the importance of the vote and of their ability, acting collectively, to affect the conduct of government.

Absent a national party there emerged, starting in Pennsylvania, Democratic Clubs and Democratic Societies patterned on groups known as the Sons of Liberty as early as the 1760s, and the revolutionary Jacobin societies in France. The new clubs took a distinctly anti-British, pro-French posture that achieved such notoriety that in time even the supposedly nonpartisan Washington would feel obliged to attack them as subversive.

Jefferson steadfastly maintained that he abjured the practice of many other public figures of engaging in attacks on political rivals through newspaper essays written under pseudonyms. But he was an inveterate letter writer whose correspondence encouraged allies to do so, in the process attracting recruits to his standard. It was in this context that he famously wrote to Carrington: "If left to me to decide whether we should have a government without newspapers, or newspapers without a government, I should not hesitate for a moment to prefer the latter."[8]

The growth of newspapers in the states became a critical development in the communication of political ideas, through the Federalist organ edited by Fenno and the chief opposition sheet under Freneau. Of the latter, Madison, who was instrumental in persuading Freneau to launch his *National Gazette,* wrote: "I entertained hopes that a free paper, meant for general circulation, and edited by a man of genius of republican principles and a friend of the Constitution, would be some antidote to the doctrines and discourses circulated in favor of Monarchy and Aristocracy."[9]

Jefferson had first labeled his new political force the "Republican Party" in a letter to Washington on May 23, 1792,[10] but it soon came to be known, in turn, as the Democratic-Republican and finally, later, the Democratic Party. By some accounts, the original name "Republican" was chosen out of sentiment for the French Republicans and their own revolution.

The anti-Federalists, while forerunners of this new party, were not its direct antecedents. Jefferson as the founder did not share their abhorrence of all central government; in fact, he had been won over to the Constitution by the compromises accepted by the Federalists that were fashioned to accommodate the agrarian South and assure states' and individuals' rights.

In his letter to Washington, Jefferson made a point of characterizing the anti-Federalists as mere hangers-on to the new party. "The Republican Party who wish to preserve the government in its present form are fewer in number than the monarchical Federalists," he wrote. "They are fewer even when joined by the two or three or half dozen anti-federalists, who though they dare not avow it, are still opposed to any general government: but being less so to a republican than to a monarchical one, they naturally join those whom they think pursuing the lesser evil."[11]

Jefferson, in discussing the new party, drew a class distinction with the Federalists in what political scientists call the first party system. In referring to the Federalists as "monarchical," he sought to link their aristocratic membership, pointedly including Hamilton, with the British. In the same letter to Washington, Jefferson warned that Hamilton's objective was "to prepare the way for a change from the present republican form of government to that of a monarchy," while describing his new party as "of the people."[12]

But Jefferson and Madison themselves were aristocrats, elite members of the American society in terms of education, style, land and property ownership. It was their advocacy, Jefferson said, of an "increase in the direct popular control over the government, the widening of the right of suffrage, the limitation of the power of the Federal Government and the conservation of the powers reserved to the States by the Constitution"[13] that more accurately defined the new Republican Party. Madison became its leader in the House of Representatives.

In foreign policy, the pro-British Hamilton also had a critical role in an episode that underscored growing party factionalism, again with Jefferson and Madison as his leading adversaries. With the end of the French monarchy, the new French Republic in 1793 had sent to the United States a dashing young man named Edmond Genêt to be its minister. Although he was only thirty years old, he already had diplomatic seasoning in Prussia, Austria and Russia, where he had been thrown out for excessive expressions of enthusiasm for the American rebellion against monarchy. "Citizen Genêt" arrived amid a tumultuous reception in Charleston, a hotbed of revolutionary spirit that indeed had spread throughout the American states with the news of the success of the French Revolution. An immediate debate ensued about whether he should be officially received by President Washington, with Jefferson and Hamilton in the forefront.[14]

Genêt's arrival posed a dilemma, because the French Republic already was at war with England in a conflict that was shaking Europe, and many American farmers and other Revolutionary fighters wanted the United States to declare war on England in reciprocation for French aid in the American Revolution. In earlier treaties, the American government had pledged to support France, and the Federalists were in no temper to get involved in the European war. Hamilton, again moving in on Jefferson's territory as secretary of state, proposed to Washington that Genêt be received with the qualification that the gesture not be regarded as guaranteeing a binding effect of the treaty. The American treaty obligation, the Federalists argued, had been negated by the fact France had moved first in declaring war on England.

Jefferson counseled Washington to receive Genêt with no qualifications. "The reception of the Minister at all," he wrote, "is an acknowledgment of the legitimacy of their government; and if the qualifications meditated are to deny that legitimacy, it will be a curious compound which is to deny and admit the same thing."[15] He further argued that existing treaties were not with the deposed French monarch but between the two nations regardless of the government in power, "and the nations remaining in existence, though both of them have since changed their forms of government, the treaties are not annulled by these changes."[16]

The outcome was a proclamation of neutrality written by Randolph and approved by Washington and his cabinet that stated: "the duty and interest of the United States require that they should with sincerity and good faith adopt a course of conduct friendly and impartial toward the belligerent Powers."[17] Madison attacked the proclamation, saying it "wounds the national honor by seeming to disregard the stipulated duties to France" in their alliance and also "wounds the popular feeling by a seeming indifference to the cause of liberty."[18] In so saying, he put the Jeffersonians on the side of the same cause for which Americans had waged their revolution. So far so good in terms of party-building.

Meanwhile, Hamilton, under the pseudonym "Pacificus," launched a fiery defense of the proclamation of neutrality in Fenno's newspaper, as a means not only of guaranteeing American shipowners abundant cargoes but also of maintaining ties with the English. In the process, he argued that the United States was not bound to help France, minimized French aid in the American Revolution and even assailed the French revolutionists for having executed their monarch, Louis XVI.[19] At Jefferson's urging,

Madison replied, citing Hamilton's own comments on treaty obligations in his *Federalist No. 75.*

In the end, Washington agreed to receive the new French minister, and the hugely popular and personable Genêt proceeded to cut a wide swath through the pro-French republican camp on a month's journey from Charleston to Philadelphia to present his credentials to the American president. Genêt's presence provided the circumstance for a new outpouring of sentiment in support of the French Revolution and the new French Republic. Jefferson wrote to Monroe of the "old spirit of '76 rekindling the newspapers from Boston to Charleston."[20] On arrival in Philadelphia, Genêt was greeted enthusiastically by street crowds, wined and dined, and welcomed by Jefferson and Washington, but with a distinct coolness by the latter.

The heady reception in the streets, however, eventually proved to be too much for young Genêt. He became increasingly aggressive and strident in pushing his pursuit of American aid against the British, undercutting the spirit his arrival had first unleashed, and in which Jefferson had so reveled. Genêt proposed to Jefferson that the United States pay the balance of its Revolutionary War debt to the French Republic, then to be used to buy armaments, and that the Treaty of 1778 be renewed as a "true family pact" between two liberty-loving countries.[21] Jefferson rightly saw the proposal as counter to the proclamation of neutrality and stalled Genêt, who was now becoming a detriment to recruitment for the new party.

At this time, the British minister to the United States, George Hammond, protested the harboring of vessels in American ports captured by French privateers in American waters, and the enlisting of American sailors to man French warships, as counter to American neutrality. The cabinet determined that Hammond was right, and that such ships should be restored to their owners and recruitment of American sailors prohibited. Genêt was livid. He demanded that Washington reject "the cowardly abandonment of . . . friends in the moment when danger menaces them."[22] He said he would appeal to the American public, which had greeted him so effusively everywhere, to support him over Washington's head.

Jefferson was appalled. "I am doing everything in my power," he wrote to Monroe, "to moderate the impetuosity of his movements, and to destroy the dangerous opinion that has been excited in him that the people of the U.S. will disavow the acts from the Executive to Congress, and from both to the people."[23]

Nevertheless, Genêt, taking it upon himself to conduct French foreign policy from his quarters in Philadelphia, began talking openly of defying the neutrality proclamation by having one such seized British ship, the *Little Sarah,* anchored at Philadelphia, loaded with munitions and dispatched to France. Jefferson, learning of the report, went to Genêt and tried to talk him out of it, to no avail. With Washington out of town, his cabinet met and Hamilton, along with his ally, Secretary of War Henry Knox, proposed firing on the ship if it tried to break out. Jefferson objected to taking any warlike action without Washington's approval. On the president's return, the talks resumed, with Jefferson calmly counseling that the ship be required to remove any armaments before sailing. Washington agreed, but by this time the *Little Sarah* was already at sea and on its way.[24]

Genêt's behavior had turned his presence from a boon to the cause of democracy in the United States to one of embarrassment and discredit. Jefferson and Madison moved quickly to dissociate themselves and the Jeffersonian party from Genêt's rantings. "His conduct is indefensible by the most furious Jacobin," Jefferson wrote to Monroe. "I only wish our countrymen may distinguish between him and his government."[25] Madison, in a separate note to Monroe, said Genêt's behavior "has been that of a madman."[26]

Jefferson penned resolutions for several Virginia counties denouncing all actions (such as Genêt's) that might drive a wedge between the United States and France, then had them sent to Washington. He warned that the neutrality proclamation was a violation of the alliance with France and was "a leading step toward assimilating the American government to the form and spirit of the British monarchy." In this sense, Jefferson argued that the war in Europe, in illuminating the Federalist allegiance to the British as opposed to the Jeffersonian ties to France, had "kindled and brought forward the two parties with an ardor which our own interests merely could never excite."[27]

In the meantime, the question was: what to do about this loose cannon, Genêt? The cabinet—Jefferson, Hamilton, Knox and Randolph—met with Washington. Hamilton not only denounced Genêt but associated him with the rebelliousness of the Democratic Societies against the government. Jefferson warned against any harsh action that would do damage to America's friend, France, at its time of peril at the hands of the allied monarchs in Europe. It was Hamilton and the Federalist pro-British view against the Jeffersonian pro-democracy position once again.

Jefferson took it upon himself as secretary of state to write to the American minister in France, laying out the behavior of Genêt in temperate terms and urging his recall be requested, while eloquently expressing America's friendship toward the French Republic. He submitted the note to Washington and the cabinet, and it was approved by all with only one deletion insisted upon by Hamilton—a Jefferson condemnation of any war between the two countries as "liberty warring on itself."[28] Apparently it smacked too much of "democracy" to suit the treasury secretary.

Eventually Genêt was recalled, but the episode was another illustration of the civil war within the cabinet between the Federalist champion and the architect of the new party, first generally labeled "republican" in lowercase, loosely meaning "derived from the people," and only eventually in uppercase. The internal conflict continued as Hamilton and Jefferson each saw the question of American attitudes toward the war in Europe through the prism of his particular bias. The Genêt experience, which gave Hamilton much to gloat about, so wearied Jefferson in the summer of 1793 that he informed Washington that he intended to resign from the cabinet. The president persuaded him to stay through the year.

In January 1794, Jefferson did step down and returned to Monticello to take up domestic chores—and plan the development and mobilization of the party he was determined would one day wrest power from the party of Hamilton. He left leadership of the new party in the capable hands of Madison, who through his work in Congress became its public face, with Jefferson insisting he was in permanent retirement. Madison became so identified with the Republican leadership that the expression "Madison's party" came into vogue, and he was critically engaged in fashioning party identification and allegiance in the House behind his legislative agenda. So strong did party loyalty grow among many Republican members that a Federalist congressman from Connecticut, Zephaniah Swift, wrote to a friend: "There is no such thing as conciliation with them. They would not have any confidence in an Angel if he would not avow himself of their party."[29]

Jefferson himself, in a letter to William Giles from Monticello, defended the party solidarity mobilized by Madison. "Were parties here divided merely by a greediness for office, as in England, to take part with either would be unworthy of a reasonable or moral man," he wrote, "but where the principle of difference is as substantial and as strongly pronounced between the republicans and the Monocrats of our country, I hold it as honorable to take a firm and decided party, and as immoral to pursue a middle line, as between parties of Honest men, and Rogues, into which every country is divided."[30]

Through the summer and fall, Republican politicians made pilgrimages to Monticello to confer with Jefferson regarding the congressional elections and party organizational matters. In the November elections, the Jeffersonians successfully defended incumbents or ousted entrenched Federalists in New York, Philadelphia and other target cities. In Philadelphia, they defeated Thomas Fitzsimmons, a key Hamilton lieutenant in the House of Representatives in the bank debate, and in Boston they threw a scare into one of the Federalists' premier orators, Fisher Ames, with a strong campaign in behalf of Dr. Charles Jarvis.

So nervous were the Boston Federalists that they ran a newspaper advertisement listing the endorsements of a host of businessmen and other prominent Bostonians in what the *Independent Chronicle* called "a new practice" in politics. The newspaper asked editorially: "How many of the poor seamen or Captains are there among the signers who have lost their all? Not one—are they of no account in the estimate?"[31] Ames managed to win, but Madison wrote Jefferson that the outcome was due only to "the vote of negroes and British sailors smuggled in under the loose mode of holding elections" in Massachusetts.[32]

In the meantime, more foreign policy crises involving American relations with the French and British had been keeping the controversy between Jefferson and Hamilton well stoked. With Jefferson retired to his Virginia estate, Madison in the House took up the task of opposing Hamilton's pro-British positions. Jefferson had left Madison with a powerful weapon in a report to Congress on the state of foreign commerce and trade that demonstrated severe damage to American interests by British policies in conduct of the war against the French Republic.

In June 1793 the British had imposed a blockade of the coast of France, classifying grain as contraband as a way of starving the French into surrender. The move was a blow to American shipping that even Hamilton protested as "harsh and unprecedented."[33] In November the British had also invoked an old maritime law that barred American trade with the French West Indies, and then captured 250 U.S. merchant ships as violators.

In early 1794, armed with Jefferson's report, Madison proposed retaliatory legislation in the House that would impose higher duties on goods and ships of nations, especially England, that violated American maritime rights. Anti-British feelings rose ever higher, to the political embarrassment of Hamilton. Federalists also called for increased defensive fortifications on the American coast amid more talk of war, which neither Madison nor Hamilton wanted.

A stormy debate ensued, with Hamilton directing the pro-British argument behind the scenes and Madison and Giles on the House floor railing against the English seizure and searching of American vessels and other offenses, including continued British maintenance of outposts in the American West.

Congress escalated the situation by voting an embargo aimed principally at the British. Hamilton's world suddenly was crumbling, and with it the grip of the Federalist Party on the nation's politics, creating an opening for Jefferson's diligent efforts to give greater shape and strength to the new Republican Party.

As tempers mounted and a war fever climbed, a group of worried Federalists in the Senate urged Washington to send an emissary to London to quiet the fears and negotiate a treaty. They pushed Hamilton himself for the post, but Washington rightly deemed him too controversial by virtue of his conspicuous favoritism toward Britain. For the same reason, Jefferson, just as openly pro-French, was bypassed, and Washington—notably, at Hamilton's suggestion—put forward another pro-English Federalist, John Jay, even as he continued to serve as Chief Justice of the Supreme Court. The Jeffersonians, outraged, demanded an explanation from Washington. They were rebuffed.[34]

From the outset, Hamilton was deeply involved in formulating Jay's negotiating instructions. He realized that the outcome would be critical to the survival of the financial structure he had so carefully and forcefully crafted for the United States—and to the survival of the Federalist Party. Jay was told to insist on the British evacuation of the western forts it held, on the opening of British West Indies ports to American ships, and the settling of other outstanding differences while doing no damage to the American treaty with France.

But after five months of negotiations, in November 1794, Jay accepted terms so overwhelmingly favorable to the British that in effect they violated the American treaty with the French. Washington was so apprehensive of Senate approval of the treaty that he kept the details secret and held off signing it and submitting it for Senate ratification.[35]

At the same time, in the Western regions, events in late 1794 were conspiring to strengthen Jefferson's hand in rallying frontiersmen to his cause. Hamilton had pushed through an excise tax on whiskey, which in barter functioned as currency in many of the more rural regions. Poor farmers and grain growers in the West who manufactured the popular product at first evaded the tax and finally rebelled against it. In western Pennsylvania, poor small distillers made raids on more prosperous large distillery owners who could afford the tax, destroying their stills in what was called the "Whiskey Rebellion."

Hamilton persuaded Washington to send fifteen thousand militiamen to quell it and, with aspirations to be a military hero himself, rode out with the old general.[36] The rebellion fizzled, but docile prisoners were rounded up and brought to Philadelphia, humiliated in a march down Market Street and jailed. Such conduct only intensified Western hostility toward the seaboard—and toward Hamilton. Fears that the new government might become another repressive monarchy helped to solidify frontier dissent and bolster Jefferson's position as the leader of the young nation's backwoods interests.

In various states, Democratic Societies that had been springing up to protest the aristocratic direction of the new national government played an important role. They encouraged voter turnout for Jeffersonian candidates, publishing newspapers reflecting the Republican point of view in much the same way committees of correspondence had flourished in the Revolutionary period.

Washington, always on guard against the formation of parties, finally denounced strongly these "self-created societies"—a phrase that seemed to demean the right of groups of individuals to chart their own political course. Madison, in a letter to Monroe, called Washington's denunciation the "greatest error in his political career."[37] Jefferson, in a rare criticism of the president, said it was "one of the extraordinary acts of boldness of which we have seen so many from the faction of monocrats."[38] Washington's tirade persuaded many of the Democratic Societies to withdraw, demonstrating forcefully his continued immense influence on public affairs. But it also served to diminish the long-held perception of the president as above party, and to place him belatedly in the Federalist camp. Hamilton, for his part, never hesitated, as we would say today, to play the Washington card in rallying public support for Federalist policies and schemes.

In January 1795, Hamilton finally followed Jefferson into retirement from government service, but he, like Jefferson, had no intention of removing himself from political and party affairs. Remaining as always sympathetic toward the British, he played a key role in a long and bitter fight over the treaty—as usual, with Jefferson as his partisan adversary—that spilled out into the streets and villages across the young country.

Not surprisingly, Hamilton was willing to accept provisions that Jefferson and his associates considered humiliating and unacceptable. The British agreed to abandon their Western outposts but refused to pay compensation to American slave owners, mostly in the South, for indentured blacks they had seized, nor to end the impressing of American seamen for British ships. The treaty also gave the British preferential treatment on trade while imposing certain restrictions on what cargoes American ships could carry and where.

Jay's acceptance of all these terms outraged the Jeffersonians. The treaty was widely denounced as a refutation of America's treaty obligations with France and a new alliance with Britain against its old ally in the American Revolution against the English. The Senate debate on the treaty went on in secret for eighteen tumultuous days, after which the Federalists prevailed. But when the Senate voted to bar publication of the approved terms, the public was further inflamed.[39]

Nevertheless one opponent, Stevens Thomson Mason of Virginia, openly turned over the full text to the Jeffersonian paper, the *Aurora,* which published it, creating still greater uproar throughout the country as other newspapers also reprinted the document. The treaty to which Jay had agreed was blatantly favorable to the British and unfavorable to the French, and to the American South, which was further alienated from what was now seen as the Federalist administration and its pro-British proclivity. Was this, many men in the street and on the farms were asking themselves, what we had fought a revolution for?

Street protests sprang up everywhere, marked by burnings in effigy of "Sir John" Jay. In Boston, Samuel Adams presided at a rally at Faneuil Hall so large and heated that Hamilton contemplated the calling out of militia against the protesters. When Hamilton himself sought to speak to a mass meeting on the treaty in New York, he was shouted down.[40]

Anti-British sentiment was further fanned by more reports of English ships seizing American cargoes bound for France. But the capture by the British of a French ship bearing certain dispatches of the French minister to the United States, Joseph Fauchet, gave Washington reason to proceed with the treaty. The papers suggested that the French had conspired with Jefferson's successor as secretary of state, Randolph, to incite the Whiskey Rebellion. Randolph resigned and Washington, reacting against apparent French meddling, after wavering for seven weeks finally signed the treaty, in August 1795.

His standing in the nation made support of the treaty a test of loyalty to him. Hamilton unleashed his pen in defense of the treaty under the name "Camillus" and Senate foes labored to block it, but after another long debate it was ratified precisely by the two-thirds vote required in the Constitution.

The ratification of the Jay Treaty convinced the Jeffersonians, as historian Stephen G. Kurtz later put it succinctly, "that a government dominated by Alexander Hamilton could not be trusted to right America's grievances against England."[41] But as long as the deified Washington remained in the presidency, the security of his administration was insulated from challenge by his popularity. Therefore the possibility that he would accept a third term in 1796 hung like a dark cloud over opposition hopes of changing the course of the government, particularly in relation to Great Britain. Washington's expressed reluctance to serve even a second term was well known and the assumption was that he wanted to retire after it.

But the Federalists knew he continued to be their best bet to stay in power. Therefore many hoped that speculations about possible war with France, irate over the Jay Treaty, might in the end reach Washington's sense of public responsibility and persuade him to make himself available for a third term.

If Washington did not run again, however, some perceptive Jeffersonians began to feel that in some conditions of the Jay Treaty they had the elements with which to rally support for their cause, and for an electoral takeover of the government by their new party in 1796, behind Jefferson. The man of Monticello himself recognized the political potential in keeping the issue of the treaty's injustices alive beyond its ratification. In September 1795, aware of a Republican majority of more than twenty votes in the lower chamber of Congress, he predicted in a letter to Monroe in Paris that "the House of Representatives will oppose it as constitutionally void, and thus bring on an embarrassing and critical state in our government."[42] It was a reasonable prediction at the time, but one that did not take into account crafty Federalist maneuvers, Washington's resoluteness under pressure and unanticipated disunity in the Jeffersonian ranks.

In November, Madison met in Fredericksburg, Virginia, with Joseph Jones, the local party delegate, who proposed a clever scheme for keeping the debate on the Jay Treaty before the country.[43] The Virginia legislature would pass resolutions calling for a constitutional amendment giving the House of Representatives an equal voice with the Senate in the ratification of treaties. Other Southern states could be expected to sign on, and if the effort did not succeed entirely, it would provide the raw material for a later assault on the presidency once Washington had retired to Mount Vernon.

The political problem, obviously, was that as long as Washington did remain as president, continued criticisms of the treaty could easily be characterized by his supporters and those of the treaty as acts of ingratitude and disloyalty toward the hero of the Revolution.

When Republican John Taylor opened the debate in the Virginia legislature on what came to be known as the Virginia Resolves by charging that the treaty was unconstitutional, John Marshall for the Federalists defended its validity, moving against it would be "an unnecessary affront"[44] to Washington. Nevertheless, the legislature approved the proposals, which also included a call to cut terms of U.S. senators from six to three years, another move to enhance the power of the U.S. House, where congressmen served for only two years.

The Virginia Resolves were dispatched to Philadelphia, triggering legislative and public debates in the other states and underscoring once again the North-South division, and the conflicting attitudes regarding the British, that defined the Federalists and Jeffersonian Republicans. The Federalist legislatures in New Hampshire, Vermont, Massachusetts, Rhode Island, Connecticut, New York, New Jersey and Maryland all rejected the challenge to the treaty and to Washington. But in Pennsylvania, where a strong Republican Party was emerging in the wake of the federal repression of the Whiskey Rebellion, the proposals were defeated only after a vigorous debate in the lower house.

In Kentucky, South Carolina and Georgia, it was a different story; all their legislatures voted for the Virginia Resolves. The absence of a guarantee in the Jay Treaty that the British would compensate slave owners for hundreds of slaves taken in the Revolution further embittered South Carolinians particularly against the former colonial power. In Congress, however, the greater representation of Federalist Massachusetts, and the unwillingness in the North especially to administer any kind of criticism of the revered president, in the end defeated the Resolves. "The name of the president," Madison wrote to Edmund Pendleton, "is everywhere used with the most wonderful success by the treaty partisans."[45]

The Federalists were quick to see this latest assault on the Jay Treaty as a political ploy. "Is it not manifest," Massachusetts Federalist leader Fisher Ames asked, "that the violence of this storm springs from the anticipation of the Election of the Presidency? . . . These little whirlwinds of dry leaves and dirt portend a hurricane."[46] Ames feared an impending effort to impeach Washington. The president, however, astutely calmed the waters with cordial references to France—thus accommodating the Jeffersonians—in a speech to Congress in December and a New Year's greeting to the French minister. At the same time, Federalists warned of the likely consequence of rejection of the treaty—war with the English— that they then would lay at the door of the opposition.

Although the Virginia Resolves were rejected by Congress, they did serve the Jeffersonians' political objective of sustaining public concern over the Jay Treaty—and the pro-British proclivities of the administration still strongly influenced by Hamilton, operating through his ideological soul mates in the Washington cabinet.

In March 1796 some of the more resolute foes of the treaty in the House, led by Edward Livingston of New York, introduced resolutions demanding that Washington produce for its perusal all papers pertaining to the Jay Treaty. He argued that although the Constitution gave the Senate responsibility for treaty ratification, the House was empowered to provide the appropriations for implementation and hence was entitled to see the papers.[47]

Madison, apparently unaware of this tactic and uncertain of his party support in the matter, tried to water it down by giving Washington leeway to decide which papers should be produced. But a Republican congressional caucus, possibly the first to be held to decide on a specific party position on an important issue, declined. Party discipline in the caucus, Albert Gallatin reported afterward, was lacking. Attendees cool to the notion of forcing the president on the matter, he said, "were left at full liberty to vote as they pleased, without being on that account proscribed or considered as having abandoned the principles of the party."[48] Madison's ability to assert party control was limited at this early state of affairs.

Washington, who had so often held himself aloof from the partisan wrangles between the forces of Jefferson and Hamilton, this time saw his presidential prerogatives challenged frontally, and he responded with zest. He rejected the demand for the treaty papers with a stern lecture to the House on its limits and responsibilities. "The nature of foreign negotiations requires caution," he wrote, "and their success must often depend on secrecy.... The necessity of such caution and secrecy was the cogent reason for vesting the power of making Treaties in the President with the advice and consent of the Senate; the principle on which that body was formed confining it to a small number of members. To admit, then, a right in the House of Representatives to demand, and to have, as a matter of course, all the papers respecting a negotiation with a foreign power, would be to establish a dangerous precedent."[49]

Washington observed that "it does not occur that the inspection of the papers asked for can be relative to any purpose under the cognizance of the House of Representatives, except that of an impeachment, which the resolution has not expressed."[50] The comment seemed to imply with a certain defiance that such action might be what the petitioners had in mind. Furthermore, he reminded the House that he had been presiding officer of the Constitutional Convention and that a proposal before it to give the House a voice in the treaty process had been rejected.

The decision was a blow not only to the Republican Party but specifically to Livingston and Gallatin, who in effect had gone over the head of Madison as the party's leader in the House in pressing for the papers. They responded by pushing through a resolution requiring a full debate on the House floor on how Washington's decision should be answered. Madison was jolted by the president's action and immediately assumed Hamilton's hand in it. "The absolute refusal was as unexpected as the tone and tenor of the message was improper and indelicate," he complained to Jefferson. "There is no doubt in my mind that the message came from New York."[51]

Hamilton had indeed counseled the president in the matter, but before Hamilton's advice arrived Washington had already had his cabinet's agreement that the House had no claim on the papers under the Constitution. The president himself decided to put his prestige and standing with the country on the line.

Madison, fearing his party allies had overstepped their hand in even leaving the impression they might be considering impeachment, moved in to reassert his leadership role. As the chief architect of the Constitution, he made a convincing case for the House's right to pass on appropriations, and to have the required information on which to make its judgments. The House agreed.

Accordingly, debate on the appropriations began, with the Federalists energized by Washington's firm stand. One of their most outspoken firebrands, Robert Harper of South Carolina, charged that the Republicans were indeed out to impeach the president. At this point Hamilton stepped in. Through Senator Rufus King, he proposed a massive petition drive among merchants and others who would be damaged by a war with England for carrying out the treaty's terms. At the same time, he urged Washington to wait out the expiration of the terms of the House members and then go ahead with execution of the treaty, while privately apologizing to England.

Soon pro-treaty petitions were flooding Congress. In Massachusetts, the Federalist "Essex Junto" was particularly effective in demonizing the opposition, often focusing on the Swiss-born Gallatin, who spoke with a pronounced German accent, as a convenient whipping boy. His own constituents in western Pennsylvania eventually favored implementation of the treaty, convinced by Federalist pamphleteering that failure to approve it, and another treaty with Spain dealing with trade in the Western regions, would imperil their economic well-being. In the end, he voted for funding the treaty requirements. The Jeffersonian majority that had existed at the start of the confrontation was ebbing away.

Finally, the Federalists' greatest orator, Fisher Ames, was summoned from his sickbed to make the plea for the implementing money. In a masterful speech, he made a simple case—appropriate the necessary funds or the country itself would fall. He conjured up images of fearful Indian attacks on innocent backwoods wives and children in the West if the British frontier forts to be turned over to Union troops under the treaty were not so disposed.[52] Even Livingston, who had launched the Republicans' fight against the treaty, closed by suggesting that his colleagues make their best judgments on how to vote. That surrender may have been more effective in the end than all of Ames's dramatics. With the sudden disappearance of some Republican members, the decision to implement the treaty passed narrowly. "For the moment at least," Madison wrote to Monroe, "it presses hard on the republican interest."[53]

Thus was the Union "saved," but only by Washington's prestige and at a great cost to the friendship with France, and by public expressions of support for executing the treaty, generated by fears of war. Madison delivered the most lucid postmortem on the outcome in a letter to Monroe in Paris, writing that "it is to be ascribed principally to an appeal to petitions under the mercantile influence and the alarm of war. The people were everywhere called on to chuse [*sic*] between peace and war, and to side with the treaty if they preferred the former. This stratagem produced in many places a fever and in New England a delirium for the Treaty which soon covered the table with petitions. The counter petitions, though powerful from Philadelphia, and respectable from other quarters, did not keep pace."[54]

The Jeffersonians, who had earlier calculated that the fight over the controversial Jay Treaty could be their ticket to the presidency in 1796, underscoring the Federalists' continuing ties to the British, were disappointed by the outcome. "A crisis which ought to have been so managed as to fortify the Republican cause has left it in a very crippled condition," Madison confessed in another letter to Jefferson.[55] His own failure to keep control of his party in the House at a critical time had contributed to the defeat.

Washington, nearing the end of his second term, had by the Federalists' trading on public fealty toward him sacrificed much of his identity as nonpartisan. He had for a fact shared the Federalist position on most critical issues but was ready to retire. Yet he delayed an announcement through the summer of the election year, even as many presidential electors were being chosen in the states. The delay impeded the efforts of supporters of the expected nominees, Federalist Adams and Republican Jefferson, to organize campaigns. The Jeffersonians particularly could not launch criticisms of Adams as long as the untouchable Washington remained the possible Federalist opponent.

Washington's still-firm grip on the public frustrated Southern leaders. An editor in Savannah expressed his feelings in a play on the Lord's Prayer that went: "Our President which art in office, illustrious be thy name; thy election come, our will be done, resign for none on earth until thou art called to heaven—Vouchsafe us our peaceful bread; but forget not the trespasses against us, lead Jay not into temptation and deliver us from the evil which we suffer under the British treaty, for in thee is vested all constitutional power and glory. Amen."[56]

In John Beckley's view, the delay in Washington's declared retirement was a calculated move to undermine Jefferson's chances for the presidency. Somehow obtaining advance word of the decision, which was finally announced on September 19, Beckley wrote a friend: "You will readily perceive that this short notice is designed to prevent a fair election, and the consequent choice of Mr. Jefferson."[57] In any event, Washington's decision against a third term finally lifted the cloud that had shadowed the new party in its aspirations to national power. It was, in Fisher Ames's words, "a signal, like dropping a hat, for the party racers to start."[58]

In the president's Farewell Address of 1796, said to have been drafted in important parts by Hamilton but expressing Washington's own views, he sought—tardily, it turned out—to stifle all thoughts of party among his countrymen. Still regarding himself as above partisanship, he warned "in the most solemn manner against the baneful effects of the Spirit of Party." That spirit, he said, "serves always to distract the public councils and enfeeble the public administration. It agitates the community with ill-founded jealousies and false alarms; kindles the animosity of one part against another; foments occasionally riot and insurrection. . . . A fire not to be quenched, it demands a uniform vigilance to prevent its bursting into flame, lest, instead of warming, it should consume."

With the Republicans doubtless in mind, he called parties "potent engines by which cunning, ambitious and unprincipled men" would "subvert the power of the people" and were "truly their worst enemy." The "alternate domination of one faction over another," he warned, would result in "formal and permanent despotism," in time encouraging men "to seek security and repose in the absolute power of an individual."[59] The Farewell Address was probably remembered more famously for Washington's warning against foreign entanglements, but was more notable in terms of the development of parties for his seeming pox on both houses, when his intent probably was more the squelching of the opposition.

Nevertheless, Washington's decision to retire opened the door wide to the party system. With no constitutional mechanism for selecting candidates for the 1796 presidential election, like-minded political figures were obliged to caucus, however informally. With Washington gone, the Federalists were now free to assert themselves more effectively as a party, and almost at once the partisan mischief about which he had warned occurred.

Adams, not only as vice president but as one of the few remaining authentic heroes of the American Revolutionary movement, stood first in line among most Federalists to succeed Washington, and particularly those in his home state of Massachusetts, the party stronghold. A most important exception, however, was Hamilton, the party's acknowledged political leader. Adams had had differences with Washington's treasury secretary and was aware of Hamilton's scheming to replace him as vice president in 1792. Adams was too independent to suit Hamilton, determined to maintain his influence with the next president. He did not, however, attempt to buck Adams as one of the two Federalist names to be put forward for the consideration of presidential electors, knowing the man's entrenched position in Massachusetts. Rather, he focused on the second name to run with Adams, ostensibly for vice president but not necessarily so under the system in place that awarded the presidency to the highest vote-getter and the vice presidency to the runner-up.

It was a scheme that, unwittingly, would play a critical role in the eventual advancement of the Republican Party and the decline of the Federalists. It would, thanks in large part to Hamilton's plotting against fellow Federalist Adams, provide the opening by which Jefferson would be elevated to the vice presidency when his new party had barely learned to walk.

For a time, Hamilton and ally Rufus King of New York, the Federalist leader in the Senate, explored the possibility of getting the old and popular patriot Patrick Henry of Virginia to seek the presidency on their side. Such a coup, they reasoned, might have undercut Jefferson's electoral strength in Virginia. They persuaded John Marshall, then a congressman from Virginia, to sound Henry out, but he was happily retired and not interested.[60]

In the meantime, at the urging of Federalists William L. Smith and Robert Harper of South Carolina, King had proposed to Hamilton the name of former Governor Thomas Pinckney of South Carolina to run with Adams. Pinckney's state was regarded as the Federalists' best chance in the South and Pinckney himself had just returned from a highly successful diplomatic mission as minister to Spain. Hamilton and friends could argue that Pinckney would provide regional balance to the ticket, while they carried out a clever plot to use him to scuttle Adams and at the same time keep Jefferson from the first office.[61]

Behind the scenes, Hamilton and his allies lobbied among Federalist electors, North and South, to have them cast one of their two presidential votes solidly for Pinckney, while encouraging the withholding of votes for Adams in the North. Hamilton calculated, correctly, that Adams would not be able to crack Jefferson's immense popularity in the South and thought Pinckney, running well in the South, would finish ahead of Adams on second Southern votes and claim the presidency. By this means, Hamilton hoped, Adams would at best remain vice president for a third term and Jefferson would be denied either national office. The scheme would thoroughly serve Hamilton's objectives, since his first priority was to prevent the election of his arch-foe Jefferson, even more than his desire to see Adams defeated.

Jefferson, while reluctant to leave Monticello and continuing to insist that his decision to remain retired was "forever closed,"[62] was, in effect, drafted by party leaders to run for president under the Republican (or increasingly the Democratic-Republican) label. Aaron Burr, the crafty and effective party organizer from New York, became his running mate after an active courtship of party leaders in the Northeast, but only after an acrimonious caucus of Republican senators that was indecisive. The argument of regional balance also was advanced for Burr running with Jefferson. In the end, however, the calculating Burr was chosen, according to one report, out of concern that if he weren't picked he might defect to the opposition, and loss of his great organizing talents in New York could hurt Jefferson.

In the fashion of the day, neither Adams nor Jefferson campaigned, leaving electioneering to their supporters. For the first time in the young Republic, a serious contest unfolded for the national leadership between two identifiable parties, with distinct foreign-policy as well as domestic identifications. The Federalists, especially with the political departure of the above-politics Washington, became more associated with ties to England and the Jeffersonians with France, particularly in terms of continuing speculation about American involvement in another war. In the context of the first presidential campaign that was truly open and contested, partisan local and state committees worked diligently in behalf of their national standard-bearers.

With Jefferson by intent physically on the sidelines during the election and Madison also somewhat withdrawn, state party leaders stepped up. In places like Pennsylvania, where a committee of correspondence had kept like-minded Republicans in touch with each other, they nominated presidential electors who then were chosen by popular vote. In other states, partisans worked for the election of state legislators who chose electors favorable to their presidential candidate.

John Beckley, a Virginia intimate of Jefferson and Madison and later clerk of the U.S. House, played a key role for the Republicans in Pennsylvania with a clever strategy of wedding local political leaders to the campaign for Jefferson. Meeting in secret, he arranged to have some of the most prominent men in the state, including six present or former congressmen, a U.S. senator and members of leading families, placed on the slate pledged to Jefferson. The Federalists had assembled much lesser known elector candidates and the move caught them flat-footed, which enabled the Republicans to capitalize on the greater voter awareness and popularity of their slate.

With as yet no national party organization in place in any real sense, Beckley fostered optimism among his own forces by repeatedly inflating reports of Jefferson support in other states. He mounted a get-out-the-vote, straight-ticket voting effort that had all the trademarks of later campaigns, complete with extensive literature drops and distribution at the polls of a reported fifty thousand lists of the fifteen electors pledged to Jefferson, fourteen of whom won. The Pennsylvania vote would prove to be critical to Jefferson's strong showing nationally and mark Beckley as one of the party's most astute and valuable early organizers and strategists.[63]

Indeed, Beckley, a three-time mayor of Richmond, has been called the first national party chairman, although no firm party structure existed at the time. As early as 1791 he had made it a practice to go by horseback around New England, meeting with like-minded activists to counter the policies of the Federalists. He worked closely with Madison and Monroe in the earliest days of the new party. In their biography of Beckley, Edmund and Dorothy Berkeley wrote that he was "among the first to recognize that strong common financial interests were automatically drawing Hamiltonian supporters together, and that the opposing interests of the general public would not be effectively represented unless organized."[64] He was a leading critic of Hamilton's bank and of the man, leading the Berkeleys to observe that "he was as responsible as any one man for the overthrow of the federalist domination of the government and all it stood for, and for the destruction of Hamilton's ambition to be a presidential candidate"[65] (though Hamilton was foreign born and therefore ineligible). A man with little formal education and no wealth, Beckley eventually became chairman of a committee of correspondence linking state parties, and an architect of the new party at the side of Jefferson and Madison.

Arthur M. Schlesinger Jr., recalling Jefferson's earlier pointed aversion to party politics, has written: "The quadrennial presidential contest served, after Washington's retirement, both as an inescapable focus for national party competition and as a powerful incentive to national party organization. Even Jefferson soon decided that, with the right party, he would be willing to go, if not to heaven, at least to the White House."[66]

Jefferson, however, maintained to the last that he would have preferred to remain in retirement and have Madison as the new party's presidential candidate. He wrote to his close Virginia friend and protégé that "there is nothing I so anxiously hope, as my name may come out either second or third. These would be indifferent to me; as the last would leave me at home the whole year, and the other two-thirds of it."[67]

French enthusiasm for Jefferson led the next French minister to the United States, Pierre Adet, to inject himself into the American presidential campaign. He toured New England complaining openly about the Washington-Adams administration, praising Jefferson fulsomely and warning of war with France if he were not elected. Adet's conduct delighted the Federalists, who did their best to exploit the foreign interference.

Through all this, Adams remained confident that his home state and region would come through for him. "If Colonel Hamilton's personal dislike of Jefferson does not obtain too much influence with Massachusetts electors, neither Jefferson will be President, nor Pinckney Vice President," he wrote to his wife, Abigail. "I am not enough of an Englishman, nor little enough of a Frenchman to please some people. These would be very willing that Pinckney should become chief. But they will be disappointed. I find nobody here intimidated."[68]

In the end, Hamilton's ploy failed to give adequate weight to New England's loyalty to Adams, which proved decisive. In this election, the personal reputations of the candidates counted for more than specific issue positions they espoused, although representations—and misrepresentations—of those positions were circulated widely. Adams was labeled "an avowed monarchist" in one Pennsylvania flyer and it was reported outrageously in Philadelphia's *Gazette of the United States* that "President Washington loves a republican and hates a monarchist" and "therefore wishes that the republican Jefferson may be his successor."[69] Jefferson, for his part, was accused of misconduct as governor of Virginia during the Revolution. But regional loyalty to him did not waver either.

While New England held fast for its native son, the effort to boost

Pinckney fell short, and Jefferson, as expected, ran strongly in the South and made some Northern inroads. Hamilton succeeded neither in derailing Adams nor making Pinckney president. Instead, his conniving split Federalist ranks and contributed to Jefferson's finishing second to Adams, who narrowly won the presidency with 71 electoral votes to 68 for Jefferson, making the Virginian vice president in a Federalist administration, clearly signaling trouble ahead.

The New Englanders, who had gotten wind of Hamilton's plan and were fearful Adams would lose, gave all 39 of their first votes to him and only 22 of their second to Pinckney. New Hampshire and South Carolina gave enough second votes to Jefferson to move him ahead of Pinckney, who thus finished third with 59. Burr, the subject of some general distrust, especially in Virginia, trailed the others with only 30. He was left with the suspicion that he had been abandoned by the Republicans in deference to Jefferson's chances.

Stephen G. Kurtz, in *The Presidency of John Adams: The Collapse of Federalism,* observed: "Hamilton must be condemned as a strategist, because he failed to estimate the pro-Adams sentiment in New England correctly.... There was sufficient doubt about Adams' strength for the fear campaign [of a Jefferson presidency] to have worked efficiently. Doubtless many Federalists sincerely believed that Pinckney was their only bulwark against Jeffersonian victory. Had Hamilton not pushed the idea of a straight party ticket so often and so early honest doubts might have worked against Adams. Brilliantly conceived, the project of electing a dark horse candidate was miserably carried out and must take rank ... as a major cause of the Federalist party's collapse."[70]

For the first time, the United States found itself with a divided national administration—and the elements of a two-party system. In its very first bid to run the country, the new party of Jefferson and Madison had come within three electoral votes of success. Had Hamilton not meddled with the Federalist electors in his failed attempt to depose Adams and bring about the presidency of Pinckney, Jefferson and his new party may well not have achieved the electoral breakthrough they enjoyed in 1796. In addition to Jefferson's election to the vice presidency, his new party could claim political dominance in Virginia, the Carolinas, Georgia and Kentucky, congressional gains in Delaware and Maryland and important inroads in Pennsylvania and New York. Also, for the first time party tickets were formed in several states and advanced as such to voters.

While Adams managed narrowly to win the presidency, the closeness of the outcome was a blow to his prestige. Henceforth he was referred to by ridiculing foes as "President By Three Votes." He may have been saved by his opponents' blunder in challenging Washington's presidential prerogatives in carrying out the Jay Treaty, which gave the fading Federalists a temporary lease on life.

The Republicans' near-miss against Adams, however, was clear evidence that the new party behind Jefferson and Madison, fast developing in the various states, was the force of the future. At the same time, with the emergence of a party system, the constitutional provision for electors casting two ballots for president cried out for amendment to avoid the partisan split that had occurred with Federalist Adams as president and Republican Jefferson as vice president. Thanks to that provision and inadvertently to Hamilton's Federalist machinations, what eventually was to become the Democratic Party already had its foot in the door to national power.

Chauncey Goodrich of Connecticut observed that as a result "we must expect [Jefferson] to be the nucleus of a faction" that "will give him some greater advantage for mischief."[71] He was right. Jefferson, determined to impede Hamilton's concerted effort to secure the rule of the aristocracy over the new nation, was positioned instead, through his infant party, to intensify his efforts to install the rule of democracy as he wanted it to be.

Chapter 3

A HEARTBEAT FROM POWER, 1797–1800

THE SHOTGUN MARRIAGE between John Adams and Thomas Jefferson was an uneasy one. This was so in spite of the fact that they had been close colleagues in the Continental Congress and in drafting the Declaration of Independence, and had served in diplomatic posts in Europe at the same time. They had had their differences over the British, but even before the election of 1796 made Adams the next president by a mere three electoral votes, Jefferson had written him a letter saying he had not doubted for "one single moment" that Adams would win, and that outcome was perfectly agreeable to him.[1]

In fact, in anticipation of a possible tie vote between himself and Adams that would have thrown the election into the House of Representatives, Jefferson had written to Madison authorizing him, if that happened, to "solicit on my behalf that Mr. Adams be preferred."[2]

This spirit of good will may well have been tempered, however, by Jefferson's expectation of difficulties ahead, particularly in terms of possible war with France, which was still seething over the Jay Treaty, interpreted by many in Paris as an American alliance with the British against the French. In his expressions of relief at having had the presidential cup pass from his lips, Jefferson may have rationalized that it was the better part of politics to have Adams bear the brunt of the fallout from French ire.

On Washington's retirement, Jefferson wrote: "The President is fortunate to get off just as the bubble is bursting, leaving others to hold the

Albert Gallatin of Pennsylvania, Swiss-born leader of the Jefferson party in the U.S. House of Representatives upon the retirement from Congress of James Madison.

bag. Yet, as his departure will mark the moment when the difficulties begin to work, you will see that they will be ascribed to the new administration, and that he will have his usual good fortune of reaping credit from the good acts of others and leaving to them that of his errors."[3]

In any event, Adams expressed the highest hopes for a cooperative relationship with Jefferson, particularly because their mutual adversary, Hamilton, would not have the influence he had enjoyed in the Washington administration. "I feel no apprehension from Mr. Jefferson," Adams wrote Elbridge Gerry just prior to his inauguration. "The Cause of the irritation upon his Nerves [Hamilton], which broke out in some disagreeable Appearances a few years ago, is now removed.... I expect from his ancient friendship, his good Sense, and general good dispositions, a decorum of Conduct at least, if not as cordial and uniform a support as I have given my Predecessor, which is the Pride and boast of my life."[4]

In the first weeks of the new administration, Adams and Jefferson seemed to resume their own close friendship, even to the point of staying at the same boarding house. The chumminess led Justice William Paterson to write to a friend: "I am much pleased that Mr. Adams and Mr. Jefferson lodge together. The thing carried a conciliation and healing with it and may have a happy effect on parties. Indeed, my dear sir, it is high time we should be done with parties."[5] But it was already too late in the young nation's political development for that latter prayer to be answered.

At first, Jefferson's warm words of conciliation toward Adams created such a climate of mutual respect and accommodation between the two men as to raise concerns among Madison and other Jeffersonians that the new vice president might be falling into a political trap. An overly close association with the new Adams administration could compromise Jefferson's independence of political action and impede the quest of the Republican Party toward national power. If, for instance, war came against France and Jefferson was perceived as allied with, or at least conciliatory toward, Adams, the vice president and his own party would find themselves in a most untenable position.

Apparently on an impulse, Jefferson drafted a letter to Adams prior to his inauguration congratulating him on his election and implying cooperation in whatever was to be faced. Jefferson wisely decided to send the draft to Madison for perusal, noting that he would feel perfectly comfortable serving as Adams's vice president, particularly if he could be persuaded to follow a reasonable course. Besides, Jefferson added pointedly, "he is perhaps the only sure barrier against Hamilton's getting in."[6]

Jefferson and Adams shared a common antagonist in Hamilton. Adams knew all too well of Hamilton's failed efforts to prevent his election by lobbying for electoral votes for Pinckney, and the seeds were already deeply planted for an approaching split in the Federalist ranks over them. Jefferson also saw in Adams a comrade against the Hamilton bank, which Adams once called a "system of national injustice" that subordinated "public and private interest to a few aristocratic friends and favorites."[7]

When Madison read the draft letter, he urged Jefferson not to send it. It might well offend those who had worked diligently for his own election, and it would not be wise to place in Adams's hands a written endorsement that could be surfaced to Adams's benefit in some future adversity between them.[8]

Madison's caution led Jefferson to reflect and revise his approach. He expressed his good wishes to the new president but made clear he could not become an active party in his administration. Cleverly, he seized upon the Constitution and the separation of powers to justify his position. In his only constitutionally assigned function, as president of the Senate, he was part of the legislative branch and hence could not function with the executive. It was the perfect dodge—preserving good will with Adams but maintaining independence from him, for himself and his party.

As for Hamilton, the coziness between Jefferson and Adams was grating on him, and he suggested to Rufus King that the new president was himself being co-opted. "If Mr. Adams has vanity," he wrote, "'tis plain a plot has been laid to take hold of it. We trust his ready good sense and integrity will be a sufficient shield."[9] A breach in the Federalist ranks was becoming obvious. Those men including Hamilton who were seen as more pro-British and rigid in their politics than Adams came to be known as High Federalists. However, perhaps because Adams feared the dismissal of Washington's cabinet would be seen as a criticism of the great hero, he retained it, including three Hamilton courtiers: Timothy Pickering as secretary of state, Oliver Wolcott as secretary of the treasury and James McHenry as secretary of war. Henceforth all were conduits for the New Yorker's schemes, some in conflict with Adams's own plans and policies. It was a mistake that was to cause the new president considerable grief before he finally cashiered the trio.

At the same time, Jefferson's party, in its yet-unstructured infancy, had gained a toehold in the executive branch, modest as it was in those days of vice-presidential impotency. While serving uncomfortably as Adams's man-in-waiting, Jefferson addressed himself to rallying the young nation's agrarian and rural interests, which were largely ignored by a Federalist government driven by policies that favored men of commerce and banking. In this effort, Gallatin became his chief lieutenant in the House, Madison having retired in 1796. The Washington administration's muscular reaction to the Whiskey Rebellion had given Jefferson a powerful organizing message for a new party opposed to such "monarchical" tendencies and methods. He also mended fences early with Burr, who had felt ill served by Virginia in the 1796 election, receiving only one of its electoral votes.

The severe negative fallout from the Jay Treaty continued to dominate foreign affairs and fuel the political struggle between Jefferson and Hamilton. Jefferson and most other Americans had an emotional tie with France as their Revolutionary ally, but Hamilton and the Federalists had a commercial one with England, whose trade with its former colony eclipsed that of France with the young nation. Federalist hostility toward the French, building since the Adet interference in the 1796 presidential election, hardened in the wake of French seizures of American ships at sea, to the point that war with France seemed imminent, although the existing treaty between the two countries pledged otherwise. Only Monroe's determined efforts as minister to France to placate the French over their Jay Treaty objections gave any promise that peace could be maintained.

Washington had sent Monroe to Paris with that purpose in mind, but Federalists chafed at what they considered his excessive friendliness to the host country. When word reached Paris in January 1795 that the Jay Treaty had indeed been signed, the French government immediately pressed Monroe for details. He told the French leaders that Secretary of State Edmund Randolph had assured him that Jay had been "positively forbidden to weaken the engagements between this country and France,"[10] but he was unable to produce such details because of Washington's insistence on keeping the terms secret until they were presented to the Senate.

When the treaty's provisions finally became known in Paris in August, along with news that the Senate had ratified it and Washington had signed it, the French were irate. They declared that the alliance with the United States "ceased to exist" and their minister was being recalled.

Monroe, outraged that he had been kept in the dark, let it be known he favored the election of a Republican president in the election of 1796. The Federalists generally and Hamilton in particular demanded his recall, and Adams complied in the spring of 1797.

In Monroe's place, the new American president sent Charles Pinckney, another Federalist, but the French refused to accept him. There ensued a long debate within Federalist ranks on how to respond, with important Federalists in New England pressing for war. Adams finally decided to send a special three-man mission—Pinckney, John Marshall of Virginia and Elbridge Gerry of Massachusetts—to Paris to negotiate a way out of the morass.

At one point Adams considered including Jefferson, America's former minister to France. Jefferson declined, arguing again that as President of the Senate he was a legislative rather than an executive branch officer. Adams also finally thought better of the idea, writing later that to have sent Jefferson would have been akin to the King of England sending the Prince of Wales to Washington. Jefferson, he wrote in the terms of royalty, "is the first prince of the country, and the heir apparent to the sovereign authority [himself]."[11]

In some quarters, it was believed that disagreement over this matter and how it was handled was what chilled the warm feelings between Adams and Jefferson of the immediate post-election period. Jefferson wrote later that Adams had ruled him out for the Paris mission on Jefferson's own grounds but then asked him to sound out Madison for the post. When Jefferson reported that Madison was not interested, Jefferson wrote, Adams said it was just as well because objections had been raised to Madison. Adams himself later wrote that when he had proposed nominating Madison, Wolcott, the Hamilton acolyte Adams inherited as his treasury secretary from Washington, had killed the nomination by announcing for the cabinet: "Mr. President, we are willing to resign." Adams wrote that he and Jefferson "parted as good friends as we had always lived; but we consulted very little afterwards. Party violence soon rendered it impracticable, or at least useless." Jefferson, however, said he was never consulted at all after the episode.[12]

In any event, the breach was an important development in terms of the rise to national power of the Jeffersonian party. It confirmed the wisdom of Jefferson keeping his distance from the Adams administration and it provided the strongest personal justification yet for him to do so. It shattered the illusion that Jefferson could serve effectively in the councils of the opposition party and at the same time advance that opposition party's best interests. From this point, Jefferson was able to resume his party leadership role with a free hand, and increasingly so as point man against Adams's policies that threatened war with France. Jefferson believed it had to be avoided at all costs, for the sake of both the country and the party.

It so happened that at this time Jefferson made himself the brunt of attack and embarrassment, the victim of his own careless pen. A year earlier, he had written a letter to an old friend in Italy, Philip Mazzei, complaining in the heat of the Jay Treaty controversy of "an Anglican monarchical and aristocratic party,"[13] with a pointed and unflattering allusion to Washington as a pushover for the English. The letter found its way into public print as the nation's greatest hero was finishing his years in retirement at Mount Vernon. Federalist criticism rained down on Jefferson, who as was his custom suffered in silence, mortified that word of his comments had reached the great man, who never thereafter spoke to him.[14] It was not one of Jefferson's happiest times.

He may have been able to take some solace that summer, however, in the knowledge that his bitter foe, Hamilton, had suffered a much more personal and personally damaging embarrassment. Six years before, he had allowed himself to be duped by the beautiful wife of a small-time hustler who then in effect blackmailed the lofty secretary of the treasury for more than a year as the price of his silence. When the man himself ran afoul of the law and pressured Hamilton for help, he refused, whereupon the man spilled the beans to three members of Congress, including Monroe. They confronted Hamilton, who owned up only to a private indiscretion and won agreement of the three to remain silent about the matter.[15]

Nevertheless, the story got out and Hamilton asked the three to provide affidavits of his innocence as a public official. The other two complied but Monroe declined either to confirm or deny the story. Hamilton finally revealed the whole matter himself, which some observers suggested later removed any hope that Hamilton might be elected to public office.

After these two sagas of the weaknesses of the mighty, brought to the surface amid fierce political battle, a chagrined Jefferson wrote a friend: "You and I have formerly seen warm debates and high political passions. But gentlemen of different politics would then speak to each other, and separate the business of the Senate from that of society. It is not so now.

Men who have been intimate all their lives cross the street to avoid meeting, and turn their heads another way, lest they be obliged to touch their hats. This may do for young men with whom passion is an enjoyment. But it is afflicting to peaceable minds."[16]

It was not until the fall of 1797 that the three-man American mission to Paris finally set sail, and on arrival the reception was cold. The French Directory, as the revolutionary leadership was called under the Republic, had lost its most moderate members and was now in the hands of more anti-American men and, as was eventually revealed, were captives of personal avarice.

As Pinckney, Marshall and Gerry waited for months for negotiations to start, unofficial French agents approached them with what amounted to blackmail demands, including a $13 million loan to the Republic and, most astonishing, a $250,000 bribe to Foreign Minister Charles Talleyrand. As the demands continued, it was reported later, Pinckney finally declared to the agents: "It is no; no, not a sixpence!"[17] This declaration was later embellished by the Federalists as the famous "Millions for defense, but not one cent for tribute!"[18] The French officials, however, held fast and continued to stall on beginning negotiations.

The frustrated American mission sent dispatches to Adams in code that arrived in March 1798. The president, shocked by the French audacity, counseled with his cabinet members, who in turn consulted Hamilton. While not favoring a declaration of war, Hamilton did urge through his acolytes an extensive rearmament program for land and sea defense, manpower mobilization and abrogation of the old treaty with France. At the same time, he suggested negotiations with the British, seeking their support.

The next month, in exasperation, Pinckney and Marshall finally left Paris for home, leaving Gerry behind in his own hope to resolve the woeful situation. He too left several months later, by which time word of the secret French blackmail attempts had filtered back to officials in America, all but burying chances of further negotiation.

While calling for congressional approval of his defensive measures, Adams kept the dispatches secret, apparently leaving Jefferson and his allies to believe that the damage they would inflict on French-American relations had been exaggerated. Jefferson in effect accused Adams of warmongering and demanded, as had been done in the case of the Jay Treaty, that the papers from Paris be opened to scrutiny by Congress.

It was a major political blunder by Jefferson. Adams agreed and turned them over, after substituting the letters X, Y and Z for the actual names of the French agents. The Federalists immediately exploited the political opportunity to embarrass the Jeffersonians by pushing a resolution through Congress ordering publication and wide distribution of what now became known as the XYZ Papers.[19]

Disclosure of the French blackmail demands electrified the American public. The pro-French ardor born of the French assistance to the American Revolution and enthusiasm in the United States toward the French Revolution, first heightened by the Genêt visit and then deflated by it, collapsed. Madison wrote that he was astonished at Talleyrand's involvement not so much as a result of its "depravity" as of its "unparalleled stupidity."[20]

Federalist pressure for war against France soared, against the determination of the Jeffersonians to avoid it. In Federalist hands, Congress in May 1798 suspended the 1778 treaty with France, created a Navy Department to oversee shipbuilding and attacks on armed French ships, tripled the size of the provisional army and levied the taxes to pay for it. Adams called on Washington to oversee the army but objected when Hamilton lobbied hard through his cabinet cronies to be made second in command. Washington, however, given authority by Adams to pick his staff, insisted. Adams was dismayed at the way Hamilton had used Washington to compel him to promote "the most restless, impatient, artful, indefatigable and unprincipled intriguer in the United States if not in the world."[21]

These arrangements raised deep concerns among the Jeffersonians, who had long opposed a standing army, that the new military strength would be used not for defense against a foreign power but rather to suppress growing domestic dissent.

The XYZ affair triggered huge animosity between the two party camps—in street rallies and protests, in the warring factional press and in loud argumentation at the dinner tables of high society in Philadelphia and New York. Ugly insinuations began to be raised about lack of loyalty to the government. On the House floor in April, two Federalists, Francis Dana of Massachusetts and John Allen of Connecticut, had made slurring remarks about Gallatin, the Swiss-born Jeffersonian. Proposals were bandied about to bar all but native-born Americans from holding public office or even voting. Many immigrants from France left the country or considered doing so.

Americans sympathetic to the French Revolution had for some time been wearing red cockades—ribbon rosettes—as a sign of their support. Now Federalists urged supporters of the government to sport black cockades. When in May Adams declared a day of fasting and prayer in Washington, street clashes broke out between the reds and the blacks.

Jefferson, although keeping a low profile as was his wont amid all the furor, became the target of assaults from Federalist newspapers. One intoned editorially: "The Vice-President—May his heart be purged of Gallicism in the pure fire of Federalism or be lost in the furnace." And this: "John Adams—May he like Samson slay thousands of Frenchmen with the jaw bone of Jefferson."[22]

Abigail Adams, writing to her sister, observed that "the publick opinion here is changing very fast, and the people begin to see who have been their firm unshaken friends. . . . The common people say that if Jefferson had been our President, and Madison and Burr our Negotiators, we should all have been sold to the French."[23]

In the wake of the XYZ affair that had struck the Republicans low in their pursuit of peace with France, Fisher Ames, the Massachusetts Federalist leader, counseled finishing them off politically. If not, he warned, "they will soon rise from the mire, where they now lie, and attach themselves to any set of honest men, who in every question shall be for doing the least and latest. Thus a new party may be formed to paralyze and distract our measures."[24]

Another Federalist firebrand, Stephen Higginson, wrote bluntly of his proposed remedy: "Nothing but an open war can save us, and the more inveterate and deadly it shall be, the better will be our chance for security in the future."[25] And from George Cabot: "It is impossible to make the people feel or see distinctly that we have much more to fear from peace than war. . . . War, open and declared, would not only deprive our external enemy of his best hopes, but would also extinguish the hopes of internal foes."[26] All this while, hostilities continued on the high seas between French and American shipping, short of a declaration of war.

In the fever of patriotism and accusation that the crisis released, the Federalists, just as they were riding high with control of both the executive and legislative branches and the Republicans on the ropes, took a politically damaging misstep in the summer of 1798. They pushed three repressive laws through Congress, called the Naturalization, Alien and Sedition Acts. Jefferson moved deftly, using these blatant efforts to stifle political dissent to recruit more support for the new party, and to trumpet his view that the Federalists, with Hamilton still pulling the strings, were determined to impose a "monarchical" rule on the country.

The Naturalization Act increased the residency requirement for American citizenship from five years to fourteen, an obvious move against immigrants, thought generally to favor the Jeffersonians politically. The Alien Act empowered President Adams to deport any non-citizen deemed by him to be "dangerous" to the peace and safety of the United States.[27]

Jefferson, writing to Madison, called the bill "detestable" and Madison described it to Jefferson as "a monster that will disgrace its parents."[28] Edward Livingston, arguing against it in the House in behalf of the Jeffersonians, declared that Americans who submitted to its provisions "would deserve the chains that these measures are forging for them." He warned: "The country will swarm with informers, spies, delators, and all the odious reptile tribe that breed in the sunshine of despotic power." How could Americans "call ourselves free and enlightened," he posed, "while we advocate principles that would have disgraced the age of Gothic barbarity."[29] But the Alien Act was passed in the House, 46–40.

Although Adams never sent anyone packing, libertarians continued to decry the law, and Irish and French aliens critical of the administration's obvious pro-British posture saw it as a serious threat to them. Many of them went into hiding or fled the country.

The Sedition Act was even more blatant. It provided fines and imprisonment for anyone, alien or citizen, found guilty of encouraging disorder or rebellion, or who wrote or published "false, scandalous and malicious writing" defaming the president, his government or any member of Congress or bringing them "into contempt or disrepute."[30] Clearly the act was aimed at the Republicans, even to the point of specifying it would expire with the end of the sitting Adams administration. That way, if the Federalists were to lose power in 1800, they would be free to attack the new Republican administration. The Jeffersonians challenged the bill as a clear violation of the First Amendment protection of free speech and freedom of the press, but it also passed narrowly. Washington himself raised no objection, in the process earning increased recognition after all as a true Federalist.

Hamilton, now a private citizen, for his part professed to fear the Sedition Act went too far, writing to Wolcott that some of its provisions would "endanger civil war."[31] The serious breach in Federalist ranks was now threatening that party's future, after only a dozen years in power under Washington and Adams. That did not, however, stop the Federalist government from seeking and obtaining indictments, fines and jail for many opposition writers and publishers. Livingston himself was accused of sedition for his House speech against the Alien Bill. The Jeffersonians found themselves at the mercy of a judiciary in Federalist hands.

Jefferson wrote to Madison that the Sedition Act was "so palpably in the teeth of the Constitution as to shew [sic] that they [the Federalists] mean to pay no respect to it."[32] Recognizing that this was an issue that could reverse the Republicans' fortunes, he urged his friend and other leading Republicans to start bombarding the newspapers again with stinging criticisms. But it also came to Jefferson to offer calming counsel. "A little patience," he said, "and we shall see the reign of witches pass over, their spells dissolved, and the people recovering their true sight, restoring their government to its true principles."[33]

John Taylor of Virginia, a longtime critic of the Constitution, wrote to Jefferson proposing that the Union be dissolved and a new republic created by joining Virginia and North Carolina. Jefferson replied that "in every free and deliberating society, there must, from the nature of man, be opposite parties, and violent discussions and discords; and one of these for the most part, must prevail over the other for a longer or shorter time. . . . But if on a temporary superiority of the one party, the other is to resort to a scission of the Union, no federal government can ever exist. . . . Seeing, therefore, that an association of men who will not quarrel with one another is a thing which never yet existed, from the greatest confederacy of nations down to a town meeting or a vestry; seeing that we must have somebody to quarrel with, I had rather keep our New England associates for that purpose."[34]

Nevertheless, the three repressive acts compounded Jefferson's deep concern about the direction of the government under the Federalists. With the approaching 1800 election in mind, he intensified his efforts to shape and strengthen a political vehicle capable of challenging the ruling party's most oppressive tendencies and actions, and eventually of replacing it in power.

To this end, Jefferson, in collaboration with Madison, wrote a sharp indictment of the Alien and Sedition Acts and sent it to John Breckinridge in Kentucky, which had only recently been admitted to the Union. The idea was to rally the states to rein in the federal authority, not break with it. The criticism formed the basis of resolutions passed in the Kentucky legislature that same year declaring the Alien and Sedition Acts null and void on grounds they were unconstitutional infringements on individual rights.

The Kentucky Resolutions declared that the Constitution had been created as a compact among the states, hence the states had the right to intercede in this fashion when the federal government overreached its powers. They noted that powers not granted to the federal government were reserved to the states. Other states were urged to pass similar resolutions. Madison, returning to the Virginia General Assembly, persuaded his colleagues to approve somewhat milder resolutions protesting the repressive federal acts. But when others failed to follow suit, the Kentucky legislature passed a second round in 1799, also initiated by Jefferson and Madison, declaring the right of states acting in concert to reject "unconstitutional" laws passed by Congress. This time Jefferson first considered threatening withdrawal from the Union rather than surrender individual liberty, but Madison toned him down with a restatement of protest against laws violating the Constitution.[35]

The Kentucky and Virginia Resolutions signaled an intensification of Jefferson's drive for the presidency in 1800, and for years thereafter they were the cornerstones of the Jeffersonian party's preachings on individual and states' rights against the incursions of federal authority. Jefferson and Madison used the resolutions relentlessly to arouse public opinion against the Federalists and, in the process, to encourage wider support for the new opposition party.

Meanwhile, Hamilton continued to press his argument with France. But Adams had been receiving strong reports of conciliatory feelings in Paris, and in February 1799, without consulting his cabinet, he suddenly reasserted his authority. He nominated a new minister to France and implied that he himself would resign if the Senate balked at confirming the nomination. He got his way and the negotiations with Paris were resumed by a new three-man mission. The surprise action jolted High Federalist leaders, who were aware that their grip on national power was slipping and believed only a war could save them and the party. They intensified their pressure for the mobilization of a standing army and the taxes to support it. The Jeffersonians, in stiff opposition, took note that raising and maintaining an army ostensibly to fight a war would also give the government a powerful instrument to maintain domestic order, a purpose the Federalists denied.

Adams's decision to send a new mission to Paris, ignoring Hamilton and his allies in the cabinet, confirmed the seriousness of the split in Federalist ranks. In effect, Adams was flexing his muscles against the diminished influence of the man who had held such power in the Washington administration. At the same time, the matter of staffing a new provisional army drove an even deeper wedge in the Federalist Party when Adams sought to court key Republican leaders, particularly those with military experience in the Revolution, with offers of high army posts. Looking to the approaching 1800 election, he struck on the notion of including Burr and another important Republican, John Peter Muhlenberg of Pennsylvania, on the list of brigadier generals he would submit to Washington, who had agreed to lead the army on the condition that he would pass on all commissions. Hamilton and his friends in the Adams cabinet would not buy it, nor would Washington himself, who in retirement showed no reluctance to display his Federalist allegiance.[36]

"The heads of departments were exclusive patriots," Adams wrote later. "I could not name a man who was not devoted to Hamilton without kindling a fire. . . . I soon found that if I had not the previous consent of the heads of departments, and the approbation of Mr. Hamilton, I ran the utmost risk of a dead negative in the Senate."[37] Such was the state of internal division in the party as Adams approached a bid for reelection. If war was to come, it was to be a Federalist war led by Federalists. Even Washington, that legendary foe of partisanship, insisted that no Republicans be commissioned because, he said on one occasion, "you could as soon a scrub a blackamore [sic] white, as to change the principles of a profest [sic] Democrat."[38] The final officers' list included forty-nine Federalists and no Republicans. The decision to keep them from serving in the army added to the Jeffersonians' fear that the enlarged military force would be used to put down domestic dissent.

Adams himself was not in favor of a large army, particularly one led by Hamilton, whose acting command he swallowed under pressure from his cabinet and Washington. Adams preferred a naval buildup, creating another cause for dissension in the Federalist ranks. But by virtue of his military command, soon Hamilton was back in the administration's inner circle, taking over the duties if not the title of secretary of war from his hapless minion, McHenry, to Adams's severe consternation. He seemed to many a prisoner in his own administration, and damaged with the public as a result of the higher taxes required to prepare for the war so desired by the zealots in his party.

An anti-tax uprising in western Pennsylvania in 1799 led by John Fries drew federal forces to suppress it. Fries was arrested and convicted of treason but later pardoned by Adams, to the ire of the High Federalists. Such incidents as the Fries Rebellion, amid overwrought Federalist warnings of "civil war," further poisoned the agrarian population against the Federalists, and became recruiting tools for the new party in the hands of Jefferson and Madison.

Jefferson, who himself eschewed public debate, wrote Madison: "The engine is the press. Every man must lay his purse and his pen under contribution." He urged Madison to send him his efforts with the promise that "your name shall be sacredly secret."[39] In return, he sent various political pamphlets to Monroe for circulation among their friends, with the admonition: "Do not let my name be connected with the business."[40] At the same time, he held a series of dinner meetings with important Republicans in Congress to bring more cohesion to the party legislative program, including repeal of the Alien and Sedition Acts, under the leadership in the House of the energetic Gallatin.

Anti-tax sentiment naturally rose as peace negotiations continued, until the French revolutionary regime, now in the hands of Napoleon after a coup d'état, decided it did not want the distraction of trouble with America to continue. Harassment of American shipping ceased and the crisis was over, eliminating the need for a provisional army. Adams called on Congress to halt recruiting and, in his newly exerted independence, dismissed Hamilton's High Federalist cronies Pickering and McHenry from his cabinet.[41] Jefferson, who had championed the French Revolution as a European version of America's own, was able to use Napoleon's takeover as a rationale for getting off the pro-French bandwagon.

While Adams might benefit at the expense of Hamilton from the passing of the war cloud, the continuing public ire at federal taxes and the appearance of internal party disarray obviously imperiled his chances for reelection in 1800. With the prospect of peace, the Federalists did increase their majority in the House in 1798 with gains in surprising places like Virginia, but there was no doubt that Adams faced a tough fight to retain the presidency. In a letter to Rufus King, George Cabot described Adams's party plight as "two Federal parties" in Congress.[42]

With Adams and Hamilton splitting the Federalist ranks, what was now more formally known as the Democratic-Republican Party but still more familiarly as the Republican was poised to seize national power outright for the first time. It was not destined to happen, however, without a lengthy struggle within the new party to determine the identity of the next president. Jefferson was the party's clear preference, but the same constitutional shortsightedness of the founding fathers that had made him a stepson vice president under Federalist Adams in the 1796 election—two votes for each elector—was at work again to complicate his claim on the presidency.

Chapter 4

THE NEW PARTY TAKES OVER, 1800–1801

IN 1796, JEFFERSON had become vice president in part as a result of Hamilton's maneuverings to elevate Adams's ostensible running mate, Thomas Pinckney of South Carolina, to the presidency over Adams. Now, in 1800, another South Carolinian, Charles Cotesworth Pinckney, was on the Federalist ticket with Adams, in the hope that Pinckney's state could provide Southern support for the ticket. Although Adams, like Washington, was a sitting president seeking a second term, the split in the Federalist ranks brought another challenge to him, again engineered by Hamilton, to Jefferson's eventual benefit.

The Federalists' political leader imperiled Adams's chances for reelection by urging Federalist electors in South Carolina to cast one of their two votes for Pinckney and withhold the other from Adams. The gambit was defended on grounds that with Adams holding his strength in the Northern states, both Adams and Pinckney would be elected, thereby shutting out the Republican candidate, Jefferson, from both the presidency and the vice presidency. It proved to be a scheme too clever by half, but did achieve one of Hamilton's goals—denying Adams a second term.[1] Irate at his exclusion, and the firing of Pickering and McHenry, Hamilton made a complete break with Adams.

The election of 1800 was an unabashed two-party battle. Adams and Jefferson did not campaign in the modern sense of stumping openly for votes, although Adams did make an inspection trip from Philadelphia to

Aaron Burr of New York tied Jefferson for the presidency on their party's ticket in 1800, lost the contest between them in the House and became vice president.

the prospective new capital in Washington by a circuitous route that was much commented on by the Jeffersonian press. Both men made their views known in private letters, some of which found their way into print. Their supporters spoke for them, Adams presented as the caretaker of the policies of Washington, and Jefferson as the defender of states' rights and farmers and the foe of the Alien and Sedition Acts, of "monarchism" and of policies that would yet lead to war with France.

Views Jefferson had stated in 1799, including support for freedom of religion and the press, and opposition to a standing army, served as an unwritten platform for his candidacy. Before election day, they were included in a comparison of the Federalist and Republican "platforms" printed in the *Aurora*—in terms favorable, to be sure, to the Jeffersonians.

In their campaign speeches for their candidate, the Republicans hammered hard not only against the Alien and Sedition Acts but also at the Federalists' imposition of taxes to maintain an army and navy. Vice President Jefferson stood as the presidential candidate of the new party fashioned largely by himself and Madison, with Aaron Burr of New York as Jefferson's running mate, ostensibly for the vice presidency.

Interparty strife blossomed in the campaign as the Federalist camp preached the virtues of continuity and the Republicans argued it was time for a change. With party organizations now emerging more solidly in the states, and presidential electors still chosen by state legislatures in eleven of the sixteen states then in the Union, major political battles ensued in them well in advance of the presidential election balloting. With the method for selecting presidential electors left to the states, debates and contests went forward between Federalist and Republican forces to choose the method most advantageous to each side—popular vote, choice by the state legislature or some variation.

Although party politics was still in its infancy, the techniques, strategies and machinery that became commonplace in later years could already be found in embryo in various states. The Federalists, incumbents for twelve years, had patronage on their side as a tool for organization and voter turnout. The Republicans, as the outsiders striving to gain purchase in the political game, had to be, if anything, more industrious and innovative in developing apparatus to choose candidates and promote their chances for election. Committees at town and county levels wrote and circulated pamphlets boosting either their presidential electors or presidential candidate, or both—and attacking their opponents.

For example, in Virginia, where the electors were to be chosen statewide by popular ballot, an old accusation surfaced that Jefferson as governor of Virginia during the Revolution had been guilty of misconduct. A seven-page circular was prepared and distributed to county committees bearing ammunition to counter the allegation: "The General Committee having been informed that efforts were [being made] in many parts of the state to injure Mr. Jefferson and his friends, by the revival of an often refuted calumny, they have deemed it right to place in your hands the means of repelling the attack with success." Documents were supplied "sufficient to convince every candid and liberal mind that the conduct of Mr. Jefferson . . . was such as every wise and prudent statesman would have pursued in similar circumstances."[2]

In New Jersey, where the presidential electors were to be chosen by the state legislature, instead of promoting Republican legislative candidates on the basis of their local interests and agendas, the pitch was made for the choice of candidates pledged to vote for Jefferson and Burr. A campaign flyer said: "We ought to give our suffrages for those characters in nomination, who will vote for Electors that will join in placing at the head of the American Government, men who have distinguished themselves throughout life in advancing the rights of man, and particularly the preservation of our Republican government. Such men as Thomas Jefferson and Aaron Burr; the first penned our Declaration of Independence, and both fought during the revolutionary war in establishing it."[3]

As in Virginia, local committees were established throughout the state, though not as well coordinated. In one instance in Gloucester County, some Federalists showed up for a Republican meeting at a schoolhouse, whereupon it was called off and reconvened in the home of a Republican. From the earliest time, party gatherings, unlike open town meetings, were intended for the discussion of party nominations and other business by party loyalists, and were held in local taverns.[4] In South Carolina, self-selected candidates advertised in local newspapers their availability to be presidential electors or for election to Congress, specifying their party affiliation.

In Maryland, in a practice known as the canvass, candidates took advantage of all manner of public gatherings, from church services to sporting events, to address the crowds. Of one such meeting, the *Federal Gazette* of Baltimore reported that Colonel John Francis Mercer, "after panegyrising the character of Mr. Jefferson, and defending it against the charges of pusillanimity and deism, . . . discanted on the official conduct of Mr. Adams. He declared several acts of congress unconstitutional and offered himself as a member of the next assembly, to forward the election of the former and to oppose the reelection of the latter."[5] Clearly, such candidates were running not to advance local issues but as vehicles to express presidential preference.

The pursuit of public or legislative support in behalf of presidential candidates seriously undermined the traditional disinclination of candidates, especially in staid New England, to sell themselves to voters. A congressman in Connecticut warned of the dangers of such conduct: "In this state, no instance has ever been known where a person has appeared as a public candidate, and solicited the suffrages of the freeman, for a place in the legislature. Should any person have the effrontery or folly to make such an attempt, he may be assured of meeting with the general contempt and indignation of the people, and of throwing an insuperable bar in the way of attaining the object of his pursuit."[6] That attitude obviously was waning as local politics became national politics in the making of a president. The *Connecticut Courant* despaired that "the detestable practice of electioneering is . . . indirectly gaining ground in these states."[7]

Furthering the party spirit was the fact that men elected to Congress came from considerable distances to attend the sessions and often took rooms and meals in the same Philadelphia boarding house. "Jefferson lodges at St. Francis's hotel with a knot of Jacobins," South Carolinian Federalist William Smith reported to a friend.[8]

Another Philadelphia boarding house, Marache's, served as the Republican Party headquarters, and it was there congressional leaders caucused in 1796 and again in 1800 to consider the choice of a running mate for the obvious presidential candidate, Jefferson. On the first occasion they were unable to agree but Burr in effect had lobbied himself into the role. In 1800, Gallatin, as the Republican leader in the House and hence the caucus chairman, was delegated to determine the wishes of Republicans in New York, as a key to ticket balance and electoral success. When George Clinton declined, Burr was anointed by the caucus, with assurances from Southern Republicans that they would not desert him, as he charged Virginians had done in 1796.

The Republicans thought and hoped their caucuses could be kept secret, but the Federalists, who likewise were now holding party meetings and caucuses, found out about them and publicized them as somehow disreputable and even unconstitutional. The *Aurora,* the Republican Party organ in Philadelphia, turned the tables by printing an account of a Federalist caucus. "Here we see the consultation of all the members of the federalist party is confessed," it said, "and it is boasted of that this factious meeting, this self appointed, self selected, self delegated club or caucus, or conspiracy . . . unknown to the constitution or the law undertook to decide for the people of the United States who should be President and Vice President."[9]

Another critic of the congressional caucus, Benjamin Austen Jr., wrote: "If any thing will rouse the freemen of America, it must be the arrogance of a number of members of Congress to assemble as an Electioneering Caucus, to control the citizens in their constitutional rights. Under what authority did these men pretend to dictate their nomination? Did they receive six dollars a day [the congressional stipend] for the double purpose of caucusing and legislating? Do we send members to Congress to cabal once in four years for President?"[10]

Republican Party efforts did not go unnoticed by the Federalists. One leader, Theophilus Parsons, wrote to Jay: "The Jacobins appear to be completely organized throughout the United States. The principals have their agents dispersed in every direction; and the whole body act with a union to be expected only from men, in whom no moral principles exist to create a difference of conduct resulting from a difference of sentiment."[11] Indeed, the organizing and focus on national candidates encouraged the phenomenon of straight-ticket voting, which soon proved to be the backbone of party politics.

In this regard, the *Aurora* proclaimed that "every man who is not for the whole Republican Ticket, Regards the Public Good, Less than his Prejudices."[12] A Federalist flyer in New Jersey likewise preached: "Let no slight dislikes or preferences induce you to relax your efforts or break the ticket; if you are for President Adams, be wholly so; by omissions of any on the federal nomination, or taking up any of the other, we shall defeat our intentions, and we may . . . ruin our country!"[13] It was a sentiment not shared in this instance, obviously, by Hamilton.

The open declaration of party affiliation, and of collective political action among like-minded citizens, also was reflected in the growth of a partisan press among the more than two hundred newspapers, most of them weeklies, that now existed in the states, predominantly in Northern cities along the Eastern seaboard.

When editor Alexander Martin launched the *Baltimore American and Daily Advertiser* in 1799, he declared and justified his Republican preference: "The American people have long enough been imposed upon by pretended impartiality of printers; it is all delusion; every party will have its printer, as well as every sect its preacher; and it is as incongruous for a publication to be alternately breathing the spirit of Republicanism and Aristocracy as for a clergyman to preach to his audience Christianity in the morning and Paganism in the evening." Editors in this day, he wrote, had "too much at stake, in the contest of liberty against slavery, virtue against vice, and truth against sophistry, to admit of more than a limited impartiality. In supporting the principles of republicanism, the Editor is aware that he shall lay himself open to all the hatred, malice, slander and persecution, which form the leading policy of the advocates of toryism and royalty; but he pledges himself not to allow them a single inch."[14]

In some instances, declared Republican editors received financial support from party leaders. Jefferson himself sent money to a rabidly anti-Adams writer and editor, James Callender, when he was out of work and when he was planning a new publication. Callender, in turn, sent Jefferson galleys of his efforts, which Jefferson commended. Later, Jefferson sought to disavow any attempt to influence what Callender wrote, confiding to Monroe: "As to myself, no man wished more to see his pen stopped; but I considered him still as a proper object of benevolence. . . . He considers these [payments] as proofs of my approbation of his writings, when they were mere charities, yielded under a strong conviction that he was injuring us by his writings."[15]

It was a rather weak defense, and one not bought by Adams's wife, Abigail, who after the election excoriated old friend Jefferson with bitter accusations of anti-Adams bashing while professing to remain above the presidential election fray. Jefferson also came to Callender's defense when he was indicted and convicted under the Sedition Law, but failed to save him from a seven-month sentence.[16]

In the 1800 presidential election, no contest was more pivotal than the fight in late April and early May for control of the New York legislature. The state's electoral vote had been the key to Adams's election in 1796 and the Jeffersonians knew they needed it to win in 1800. Hamilton himself directed the Federalist campaign for state legislative seats, understanding he needed to control the state party to maintain his national influence. Burr, tapping into an already efficient network of ward committees in New York City, shrewdly led the Republican effort. First, he won Jefferson's agreement to bring about a change in state law to have the legislature pick the presidential electors. Then he outfoxed Hamilton in their choices of state assembly candidates.

Burr waited until the Federalist leader had chosen his local and little-known legislative candidates. Then he disclosed he had persuaded some of the most prominent New Yorkers to run for the state assembly, including former Governor George Clinton and General Horatio Gates. Voting took place over three days, with Hamilton and Burr electioneering at city polling places. The Republicans swept all New York City seats, all but assuring that Jefferson would capture every one of the state's electoral votes.

Once again the politically wounded Hamilton schemed to turn the tables. In a letter to Governor John Jay, he proposed to his fellow Federalist that a special session of the legislature be called to provide for selection of the state's electoral votes by popular vote in the legislative districts. Citing evidence of Federalist losses in the New York Senate, Hamilton wrote that unless his scheme was adopted: "The moral certainty therefore is, that there will be an anti-federal majority in the ensuing Legislature; and the very high probability is that this will bring Jefferson into the chief magistracy.

"I am aware that there are weighty objections to this measure," he went on, "but the reasons for it appear to me to outweigh the objections; and in times like these in which we live, it will not do to be over-scrupulous. It is easy to sacrifice the substantial interests of society by a strict adherence to ordinary rules." He wasn't suggesting doing anything illegal, he said, "but merely that the scruples of delicacy and propriety, as relative to a common course of things, ought to yield to the extraordinary nature of the crisis. They ought not to hinder the taking of a legal and constitutional step to prevent an atheist in religion, and a fanatic in politics, from getting possession of the helm of state."

What he called "the anti-federal party" was plotting to overthrow the government "by stripping it of its due energies," he wrote, or lead a "Revolution, after the manner of Bonaparte." If his scheme was to be implemented, he said, "the motive ought to be frankly avowed," declaring that if the step was not taken, "the executive authority of the general government would be transferred to hands hostile to the system heretofore pursued with so much success."[17]

Jay curtly dismissed the idea, scribbling on the back of Hamilton's letter that he was "proposing a measure for party purposes which I think it would not become me to adopt."[18] The governor didn't bother to respond to Hamilton, thus dealing him another stinging defeat in his stronghold. Burr wrote to Jefferson attesting to the honesty of the Republican campaign and the villainy of the Federalist effort. "On the part of the republicans there has been no indecency, no unfairness, no personal abuse," Burr wrote, "on the other side, the influence and authority of office have been openly perverted and prostituted and the town has been inundated with scurrility and ribaldry issuing from federal presses and circulated by federal runners."[19]

In a profession known for bad losers, Burr stuck out as a bad winner. In the wake of his success in the New York legislative elections and lobbying by New York allies, the Republican caucus in Congress gave him a place on the party's national ticket, reemphasizing the understanding that Jefferson was the presidential candidate and Burr his vice-presidential running mate.

Even in the Federalist stronghold of Massachusetts, the Republicans made an all-out effort. Fisher Ames, writing in the *Boston Gazette,* warned his fellow Federalists: "Here at last the jacobins have taken their post, and here they have entrenched themselves to assail our sober and orderly liberty. Here we see of late, indeed within a single year, an almost total change in the tacticks [sic], and management of parties. The jacobins have at last made their own discipline perfect: they are trained, officered, regimented and formed to subordination in a manner that our militia have never yet equalled. Emissaries are sent to every class of men, and even to every individual man, that can be gained. Every threshing floor, every husking, every party at work on a house-frame or raising a building, the very funerals are infected with bawlers and whisperers against government."[20]

In defense against this onslaught, the Federalist-controlled Massachusetts legislature, in a reverse of the abortive Hamilton strategy in New York, switched the choice of presidential electors from direct popular vote by district to the legislature, to eliminate the chance of the Republicans winning any of the state's electors.

When the Federalists in Congress caucused and chose Adams and Pinckney as their candidates, they agreed to give equal support to both men on the grounds that both then could be elected. The broad assumption was that Adams would be reelected president and Pinckney elected vice president. But that expectation did not factor in Hamilton's conniving against the president. "I will never more be responsible for him by my direct support, even though the consequence should be the election of Jefferson," Hamilton wrote Theodore Sedgwick after the calamitous New York vote. "If we must have an enemy at the head of government, let it be one we can oppose, and for whom we are not responsible, who will not involve our party in the disgrace of his foolish and bad measures. Under Adams, as under Jefferson, the government will sink."[21]

Hamilton's sentiments did not escape Adams's youngest son, Thomas, who wrote a friend: "The Feds have split. Some are resolved to abandon the present leader . . . Gen'l Pinckney will be run as V.P. in several Eastern States and as President in the Southern, which according to some calculations will put him into the [presidential] chair."[22]

During the summer, the campaign went forward with partisan appeals. The Virginia Federalist Committee defended the raising of an army and navy and the taxes to pay for them by reminding voters "that our government has preserved us from the two most powerful nations in the world [England and France] . . . and that we remain, if we will, free and independent. But the fleet, the army, taxes, all the little evils which were necessary to the attainment of these great and invaluable objects, make a strong impression, and are attributed as crimes to the government."[23]

The Republican *Aurora* warned, however, that a Federalist victory would bring war. "With Jefferson we shall have peace, therefore the friends of peace will vote for Jefferson," it proclaimed, "the friends of war will vote for Adams or Pinckney."[24]

Harsher words came from newspapers and pamphlets on both sides. A Jeffersonian sheet accused Adams and Hamilton of being members of "a monarchical party in the United States," and prayed that voters "will never permit the chief magistrate of the union to become a King instead of a president."[25]

In return, Jefferson was fiercely and repeatedly attacked as a "deist"— one who believed in the existence of a God but not supernatural revelation. As a champion of religious freedom, Jefferson chose not to explain his views, leading the Federalist *Gazette of the United States* in Philadelphia to insist that "the only question to be asked by every American, laying his hand on his heart, is 'shall I continue in allegiance to God—and a religious president; or impiously declare for Jefferson—and no God!' "[26]

Jefferson's staunch defense of religious freedom for all was interpreted by foes as being against religion itself. One pamphlet circulated by a New York clergyman charged that Jefferson's election would "destroy religion, introduce immorality, and loosen all the bonds of society. . . . The voice of the nation in calling a deist to the first office must be construed into no less than rebellion against God."[27]

Jefferson, however, with New York's electoral votes assured for him, continued to draw strength elsewhere, especially in Pennsylvania. By October it seemed clear the outcome of the election would be decided in South Carolina, where Hamilton had been at work in behalf of Pinckney. He wrote a fifty-four-page pamphlet bitterly attacking Adams that fell into Republican hands and set off sharp recriminations and disarray in Federalist ranks. Adams, he wrote, was inflicted with "disgusting egotism, untempered jealousy, and ungovernable indiscretion," among other things.[28] For his own intemperate words, Hamilton slipped further in the already eroded esteem of the country. In other correspondence, Hamilton also began to derogate Burr in extreme terms and prefer Jefferson, if it came to election of a Republican. "Burr will certainly attempt to reform the government à la Buonaparte," he wrote. "He is as unprincipled and dangerous a man as any country can boast—as true a Cataline [*sic*] as ever met in midnight conclave."[29] (Catiline was a scheming and despicable Roman villain.)

Adams scored solidly in New England, New Jersey and Delaware, and in critical South Carolina. Federalist candidate Pinckney rejected the pressures of the Hamilton camp to have the state abandon Adams and give its electoral votes to Jefferson and himself. If Adams were sacrificed, he said, he would withdraw. At the same time, Senator Charles Pinckney, Jefferson's campaign manager in the state, hurled allegations of voter irregularities benefiting state legislators in the Federalist stronghold of Charleston that are familiar today: "It is said several Hundred more Voted than paid taxes. The Lame, Crippled, diseased and blind were either led, lifted, or brought in Carriages to the Poll."[30]

On the night before the state legislature was to vote on the rival slates of presidential electors, the Republicans were to meet to finalize theirs. But they learned that the Federalists had plans to crash the meeting, possibly to play on state loyalties and urge Republicans to support Jefferson and Federalist Pinckney. The Republicans quickly canceled the meeting. In the end, South Carolina gave all its votes to Jefferson and Burr, sealing the Federalists' defeat. But the final electoral vote, dispatched by mail and messenger to the new capital in Washington by mid-December, signaled further dispute. With all Republican electors casting one vote for Jefferson and one for Burr, they wound up in a 73–73 tie. Adams with 65, Pinckney with 64 and John Jay with one vote trailed.

No precaution having been arranged in the Republican camp to cast one less vote for Burr to assure Jefferson's election as president, under the Constitution the election was thrown into the House of Representatives for resolution. Burr, feeling ill used by the party in 1796, especially in Jefferson's Virginia, and ever ready to exploit an opportunity, was not disposed to step aside and settle for the vice presidency. In fact, Burr had warned Virginian John Taylor in advance of the election that "after what happened at the last election [his winning only one Virginia electoral vote] ... I was really averse to have my name in question ... but being so, it is most obvious that I should not choose to be trifled with [in the 1800 balloting]."[31] Jefferson observed later, apparently in response to Burr's remarks, that he "had taken some measures"[32] to make sure Virginia's Republican electors voted unanimously for Burr with their second ballot. Madison, however, who also was an elector, wrote in his *Autobiography* that getting that unanimous Burr vote was almost upset by the concern of a staunch Jefferson voter who feared a strong Burr vote might jeopardize a Jefferson presidency.

Jefferson himself was under the impression in advance of the final tally that the fix was in for him, that "one vote should be thrown away from Colo. Burr" in South Carolina, he told Thomas Mann Randolph, his son-in-law, and "it is believed Georgia will withhold from him one or two. The votes will stand probably T.J. 73, Burr about 70, Adams 65."[33] For one reason or another, it didn't happen. The Republicans had just won a majority in the new House, but the election would be decided by the old, where the Federalists had a majority. The Constitution required, however, that the vote be taken by state delegation, with each state having a single vote, and neither party held a majority of the delegations, which a candidate needed to be declared the winner.

The Federalists, faced with being thrown out of power for the first time in the nation's brief history, took solace in the Republicans' dilemma. Connecticut Federalist Uriah Tracy chided them for being "in such a rage for having acted in good faith ... if they had not had full confidence in the treachery of others, they would have been treacherous themselves."[34] Jefferson wrote to Monroe: "The Feds in the legislature have expressed dispositions to make all they can of the embarrassment, so that after the most energetic efforts, crowned with success, we remain in the hands of our enemies by the want of foresight in the original arrangement."[35]

The congressional Federalists at first schemed for ways somehow to throw out the election and hold another. Jefferson, hoping to head off that outcome, wrote directly to Burr even before the final votes were in, observing that "several of the high-flying federalists have expressed their hope that the two republican tickets may be equal, & their determination in that case to prevent a choice by the H of R. (which they are strong enough to do) and let the government devolve on a President of the Senate [a Federalist]. Decency required that I should be so entirely passive during the late contest that I never once asked whether arrangements had been made to prevent so many from dropping votes intentionally, as might frustrate half the republican wish; nor did I doubt, until lately, that such had been made."[36]

Jefferson seemed to be assuming in all this that Burr understood he was intended to be no more than the vice-presidential nominee on the Republican ticket, although the selection process authorized two votes for president from each elector and none for vice president, that office going to the runner-up. In the most diplomatic language he could manage, Jefferson went on to suggest that Burr's occupancy of the vice presidency would deprive the new Jefferson regime of his service in a cabinet post—a hint that if he bowed out of the vice presidency there would be a place for him in it.

"I feel most sensibly the loss we sustain of your aid in our new administration," Jefferson wrote, dismissing the apparent likelihood that Burr would have an equal claim on the presidency. "It leaves a chasm in my arrangements, which cannot be adequately filled up. I had endeavored to compose an administration whose talents, integrity, names and dispositions should at once inspire unbounded confidence in the public mind, and insure a perfect harmony in the conduct of the public business. I lose you from the list & am not sure of all the others. Should the gentlemen who possess the public confidence decline taking part in their affairs, and force us to take persons unknown to the people, the evil genius of this country may realize his avowal that 'he will beat down the administration.' "[37]

The "evil genius" was, obviously, Hamilton, toward whom Burr shared

in spades Jefferson's disfavor. Burr's reply hinted of nothing but acquiescence in all of Jefferson's desires. He mentioned his own expectation that
the Rhode Island electors would withhold a Burr vote, adding that "I do
not however apprehend any embarrassment even in Case the Votes
should come out alike for us—my personal friends are perfectly informed
of my wishes on the subject and can never think of diverting a single Vote
from you—on the Contrary, they will be found among your most zealous
adherents. I see no reason to doubt of your having at least nine States [a
majority] if the business shall come before the H. of Reps."[38]

As for the possibility of serving in a Jefferson cabinet, Burr wrote that
he was sure there were plenty of good Republicans available, but "I will
cheerfully abandon the office of V.P. if it shall be thought that I can be
more useful in any Active Station. In short, my whole time and attention
shall be unceasingly employed to render your Administration grateful
and honorable to our Country and to yourself."[39]

There the matter between Jefferson and Burr rested. By the time the
House convened to break the tie in February 1801, the Federalists had
decided, to Hamilton's further dismay and humiliation, to back Burr, on
the broad theory that it would be better to deal with an ambitious
scoundrel than with a deeply committed ideologue opposed to the core
of Federalist beliefs. The decision triggered a flood of letters from Hamilton to party colleagues excoriating Burr as a "voluptuary" and a man
"without probity." If the Federalist Party chose to back Burr in preference
to Jefferson, he said, "it will have done nothing more or less, than place in
that station a man who will possess the boldness and daring necessary to
give success to the Jacobin system, instead of one who for want of that
quality, will be less fitted to promote it."[40] He suggested that Jefferson, if
supported by the Federalists, could be counted on to sustain the Hamilton bank, avoid any war in Europe and keep Federalists in lower government posts.

Hamilton's influence in his own party, however, was waning by the
day, and Federalist overtures to Burr were already under way. Although
Jefferson harbored suspicions that the New York Republican was conniving with the opposition, there was no evidence of it. In fact, Burr had written to General Samuel Smith, a Jefferson campaign lieutenant, in advance
of the vote that in the event of a tie "every man who knows me ought to
know that I would utterly disclaim all competition. Be assured that the
Federal party can entertain no wish for such an exchange. As to my

friends, they would dishonour my views and insult my feelings by a suspicion that I would submit to be instrumental in counteracting the wishes and expectations of the United States." He authorized Smith "to declare these sentiments if the occasion should require," and Smith readily obliged.[41]

Still, the supporters of Jefferson were mistrustful of their old adversaries. Some Southern states warned of armed intervention if their choice was frustrated by Federalist intrigue. One Republican leader, Joseph Nicholson of Maryland, warned that "Virginia would instantly proclaim herself out of the Union" if the state's native son were denied the presidency.[42] Republican strategists, while pursuing a timely vote in the House, considered other options. Madison proposed that Jefferson and Burr issue a joint statement calling the newly elected—and Republican-controlled—House into session to decide the matter, in Jefferson's favor, of course. But Gallatin, as the Republican leader in the House, opposed the idea as contrary to the Constitution. The Republicans in the House, he said, would just have to hold fast until the Federalists yielded. Another Republican, Hugh Brackenridge of Pittsburgh, called on Jefferson to proclaim himself president on inauguration day, March 4, with Burr's written assent, and start governing. Jefferson declined.

Congress finally met to vote on February 11, amid snow-covered mud paths in the barely settled new capital city. Crowds jammed the gallery as Jefferson as vice president and president of the Senate presided before the joint session for tabulation and announcement of the expected tie vote. The matter then went before the House, where by this time both sides had made accurate calculations of the support of the sixteen existing state delegations. Jefferson counted on eight, the Federalists six for Burr, with two divided, and nine required for election.

On the first ballot, as expected, Jefferson won eight: New York, New Jersey, Pennsylvania, Virginia, North Carolina, Kentucky, Tennessee and Georgia. Burr had six: New Hampshire, Massachusetts, Rhode Island, Connecticut, Delaware and South Carolina. The other two, Vermont and Maryland, were deadlocked so they cast blank ballots. More House members individually voted for Burr than Jefferson, 55–51, but it was the delegation count that mattered.[43]

The roll call resumed through the afternoon and night, as a snowstorm blanketed the city outside, until the twenty-seventh call of the states was completed without a single shift by any state. At eight o'clock the next morning, the House recessed to enable the members to eat and catch some sleep, then resumed the roll call at noon. Six more votes were taken, still with no break. Nicholson, suffering a high fever, plowed his way on foot to the Capitol to cast his vote for Jefferson. Failure to have done so would have swung the state, and the presidency, for Burr. The House suspended again for a day.

At this point, word came that James A. Bayard, the sole House member from Delaware who had been voting for Burr, was on the verge of switching to Jefferson. In any event, Jefferson was convinced the Federalists were beaten. He wrote Monroe that if they had the votes to put the government in the hands of the Senate president pro tem, they would have so voted by then. At the same time, he told Monroe that "many attempts have been made to obtain terms & promises from me. I have declared to them unequivocally, that I would not receive the government on capitulation, that I would not go into it with my hands tied."[44]

Nevertheless, Bayard, fed up with Burr after failed efforts to enlist him in winning over House members with various offers, tried to recruit a Virginian, John Nicholas, to sound out Jefferson on a deal whereby Bayard, two Maryland congressmen and the one from Vermont would vote for him in exchange for accepting the very terms Hamilton had laid down. Nicholas balked, but General Smith agreed to submit them to Jefferson. Smith informed the four congressmen the next day that Jefferson had authorized him to say that the terms "corresponded with his views and intentions, and that we might confide in him accordingly."[45] Later, Jefferson denied in the most strenuous terms that he had struck a deal, but Smith confirmed he had approached Jefferson and the Republican leader had said he "would conduct, as to those points, agreeably to the opinion I have stated as his."[46]

In any event, after six tense days of roll calls, on February 17, on the thirty-sixth ballot, the Federalists gave up. A pivotal Vermont elector absented himself, throwing the state to Jefferson, and four Maryland Burr electors cast blank ballots, also giving their state to Jefferson. Bayard also didn't vote, nor did the South Carolina delegation. Jefferson was elected president with ten states to four for Burr and two not voting. The Republicans also wound up with a thirty-three-seat majority in the House. Only twelve years after the nation's first presidential election, at which time no political parties were in existence, the Federalist Party was already out of power, crippled by its own extremism. The new national party constructed by Jefferson and Madison, with critically important allies in Congress and the states, had seized the moment and found itself in control of the American government.

Jefferson liked to call what had happened "the revolution of 1800." The Federalists were down, but not yet out. One New York Federalist, Francis Crawford, wrote a friend: "It has been vainly boasted that the Sun of Federalism was about to Set and that we were about to die, but Surely we are not dead yet and if it must be so let it not be without a Struggle— let us pray . . . that those men who are Stigmatizing us with the name of Tory and every other opprobrious Epithet might be once more Disappointed."[47]

One can only conjecture what the future of Jefferson's party might have been, or whether indeed it would have had much of a future, had the erratic and conspiratorial Burr become president instead of Jefferson. As it was, the new party found itself on the cusp of a twenty-eight-year occupancy of the White House, under four successive presidents of varying effectiveness and party leadership. The Jeffersonian era had begun. Before it ran its course, the nation's first two-party system would devolve, for all practical purposes, into the domination of a single party, itself rent by factions threatening its own survival.

The PRAIRIE DOG sickened at the sting of the HORNET —
or a Diplomatic Puppet exhibiting his Deceptions!

Top: Burr challenged Hamilton to a duel in 1804 over personal remarks the Federalist leader had made about him, and mortally wounded him. This painting portrays Hamilton firing into the air as Burr is shooting him.

Bottom: In 1804, President Jefferson undertook covert negotiations with Spain to buy West Florida. This cartoon shows him as a scrawny prairie dog stung by a hornet with Napoleon's head and coughing up $2 million in gold coins for the purchase.

Chapter 5

THE JEFFERSONIAN ERA BEGINS,
1801–1809

WHEN THOMAS JEFFERSON took the oath as the nation's third president on March 4, 1801, the first to do so at the unfinished Capitol in Washington, he immediately reached out to his political adversaries. Referring to past conflict, he observed that "every difference of opinion is not a difference of principle.... We are all republicans, we are all federalists."[1]

Now that the election was over, Jefferson assured the Federalists that while "the will of the majority is in all cases to prevail," he did recognize that "the minority possess their equal rights, which equal laws must protect, and to violate would be oppression." He went on: "Let us then, fellow citizens, unite with one heart and one mind, let us restore to social intercourse that harmony and affection without which liberty, and even life itself, are but dreary things."[2]

The Federalists, though defeated in 1800, remained strong in the New England states. James Monroe, from his office as governor of Virginia, cautioned Jefferson that "there is no political error more to be avoided than a step [that] gives cause to suspect an accommodation with that [Federalist] party.... Be assured, with the leaders of the royalist party you will never have a friend. With principles so opposite, it is impossible.... The way is to drive off the mass of the people by a ... firm yet moderate course, from those leaders, and leave them to the ignominy they deserve."[3]

That already was Jefferson's intent, but he also was aware that his margin of only eight electoral votes over Adams was a modest mandate. In a letter to General Horatio Gates, he explained: "I hope we shall make up an administration that will unite a great mass of confidence, and bid defiance to the plans of the opposition meditated by leaders who are now almost destitute of followers. If we can hit on the true line of conduct which may conciliate the best part of those who were called federalists, and yet do justice to those who so long have been excluded. . . . I should hope to be able to obliterate, or rather to unite the names of federalist and republican. The way to effect it is to preserve principle, but to treat tenderly those who have been estranged from us, and dispose their minds to view our proceedings with candour. This will end in approbation."[4]

Jefferson seemed still to hope that permanent party dichotomies could be avoided by merging the existing factions. "The people have come over in a body to the republican side," he wrote in his first days as president, "and have left such of their leaders as were incurable to stand by themselves, so that there is every reason to hope that the line of party division which we saw drawn here, will be totally obliterated." And shortly afterward: "The symptoms of a coalition of parties give me infinite pleasure. Setting aside only a few only, I have been ever persuaded that the great bulk of both parties had the same principles fundamentally, and that it was only as to our foreign relations there was any division. These I hope can be managed as to cease to be a subject of division for us. Nothing shall be spared on my part to obliterate the traces of party and consolidate the nation, if it can be done without abandonment of principle."[5]

Jefferson's soothing words did not, however, mean he would fail to take political advantage of the success that his new party had just achieved. Unlike Washington and Adams before him who had suffered members of their cabinets whose allegiances were elsewhere, Jefferson placed his chief party collaborators in the key posts—James Madison as secretary of state and Albert Gallatin as secretary of the treasury. For regional considerations he also chose three New England Republicans—Levi Lincoln of Massachusetts as attorney general, Henry Dearborn of the same state as secretary of war and Gideon Granger of Connecticut as postmaster general. He conferred regularly on party matters with Gallatin, whose residence became the focal point for meetings on party policy and strategy.

At lower levels of the federal bureaucracy, Jefferson permitted some Federalists to remain on the payroll. But he moved decisively to bring in many more loyal Republicans in adherence to accepted patronage practice, and to undo a slew of "midnight appointments" of Federalists by Adams, principally to the judiciary, the one branch still in Federalist hands, prior to Jefferson's inauguration. The appointments included the defeated president's assignment of his son John Quincy Adams to a desirable post, and Jefferson's countermanding of it was a cause of lasting friction between John Adams and Jefferson.[6] One nomination could not be undone—the lifetime appointment as Chief Justice of the Supreme Court of Virginian John Marshall, an arch-foe of Jefferson.

However, the new president did demonstrate his determination as head of the executive branch to assert strong political leadership of the legislature, now in his party's hands. He exerted his influence on the selection of party leaders in the House and Senate and, often in collaboration with Gallatin, presented drafts of desired bills to them. He took to inviting leading Federalists as well as Republicans to dine at the White House, always separate by party. Under his guidance, the Republican-controlled Congress made clear it would not extend the hated Alien and Sedition Acts slated to expire in 1801, and Jefferson issued presidential pardons to those convicted under them. Congress also repealed the Judiciary Act, under which Adams had packed circuit court benches with Federalists. It abolished the circuit court judgeships and, for good measure, undertook impeachment action against prominent Federalist judges.

Hamilton raged in print against many of these moves, but with severely diminished influence. Lamenting his own fate, he wrote to Gouverneur Morris: "Mine is an odd destiny. Perhaps no man in the United States has done more for the present Constitution [which he repeatedly demeaned] than myself; and contrary to all my anticipations of its fate, as you know from the beginning, I am still laboring to prop the frail and worthless fabric. Yet I have the murmurs of my friends no less than the curses of my foes for my reward. What can I do better than withdraw from the scene? Every day proves to me more and more that this American world was not meant for me."[7] It was a proposition that in a short time would prove to be all too true.

This self-pity did not, however, prevent Hamilton from proposing a radical restructuring of the Federalist Party, with an executive council of twelve members with a president in charge, and with each state having a vice president and twelve-member council, along with local branches. He floated the idea among fellow Federalists, but drew little interest. His day was past.[8] With Jefferson firmly in control, to Hamilton's dismay, the House voted impeachment charges against one district court judge, John Pickering, on allegations of incompetency based on his heavy drinking and evidence of mental instability. The Senate convicted and removed him. A second House impeachment, of Supreme Court Associate Justice Samuel Chase on grounds of political favoritism, failed, however, to muster the necessary two-thirds vote of the Senate for conviction. Such actions were not reassuring to the ousted Federalists. Adams, for his part, had left Washington in the early hours before Jefferson's inaugural address, thus beginning a long estrangement between the two old Revolutionary and diplomatic colleagues and friends.

The Federalists, however, clung to control of the judicial branch, cemented by Adams's appointment of John Marshall as chief justice. His ruling in the celebrated *Marbury* v. *Madison* case exasperated many Republicans by confirming the role of the judiciary in passing on the constitutionality of legislative acts.

Jefferson had not become president simply to purge Federalists from the government employment rolls and pad them with Republicans. When he spoke of the "revolution of 1800," he clearly had in mind steering the ship of state off the course set by the Federalists onto a less centralized path. He was determined, after more than a decade of Hamilton's banking policies, the Federalist focus on trade and commerce, and what he considered the pro-British, "monarchical" tendencies of the "federal party," to enhance the agricultural core of the economy. In his view, it remained the heart of the young nation, to be extended westward while opening overseas markets for its farm products.

The new president did not, however, turn his back on the more mercantile aspects of the economy. He told Congress the "four pillars of our prosperity" were manufacturing, trade and navigation, along with agriculture, and that he was "decidedly in favor of making all the banks Republican" and bringing them into the new party's orbit.[9]

Jefferson also made clear his intention to curb the power of the central government in defense of individual and states' rights. In his inaugural, he pledged "a wise and frugal government, which shall restrain men from injuring one another, shall leave them otherwise free to regulate their own pursuits of industry and improvement, and shall not take from the mouth of labor the bread it has earned."[10]

Under his close guidance, Congress repealed all internal taxes and approved a new plan by Gallatin to abolish the public debt by 1817, a policy close to Republican hearts. Of the tax repeal, he told Congress, "The remaining sources of revenue will be sufficient to provide for the support of government, to pay the interest on the public debts, and to discharge the principals in shorter periods than the laws or the general expectations had contemplated.... Sound principles will not justify our taxing the industry of our fellow citizens to accumulate treasure for wars we know not when."[11] The rhetoric was not unlike that employed in defense of severe tax cuts by leaders of another, yet unborn, Republican Party two centuries later.

Accordingly, Congress reduced military and naval spending. Jefferson remained firmly opposed to a standing army and took comfort in the fact that the United States was, as he also said in his inaugural address, "kindly separated by nature and a wide ocean from the exterminating havoc of one quarter of the globe."[12]

While the transition to Republican power went swimmingly at home, the geographic insulation of which Jefferson had spoken did not shelter the country from exigencies of the continuing conflict and competition of nations in Europe. His aspirations to focus inward and westward in support of agrarian interests encountered inhibiting foreign policy complications with Britain and France when they resumed their war in 1803. Once again, American trade on the high seas, and principally British interventions against it, antagonized relations with both countries.

There were rumblings within Jefferson's party as well. As long as the Federalist Party was a serious and threatening adversary, the Republicans enjoyed a high degree of cohesion. But with the Federalists now severely reduced in strength and influence, the new party became afflicted with internal squabbling and dissent. While the Revolutionary leaders of the party—men like Jefferson, Madison and Monroe—continued to provide its direction, voices of discontent were more loudly heard, and a generation of young political figures with new ideas began to emerge in party councils.

When Jefferson had been in the White House only five months, a warning of internal dissension came from the Republican governor of Pennsylvania, Thomas McKean. "When ever any party are notoriously predominant they will split," he wrote; "this is in nature; it has been the case time immemorial, and will be so until mankind become wiser and better. The Outs envy the Inns [*sic*]. The struggle in such a situation is only for the loaves and fishes."[13]

The immediate and most obvious cause of real or potential disunity was Vice President Aaron Burr. His actions, rather than his words, in permitting the long and contentious fight in the House between himself and Jefferson for the presidency had made him persona non grata not only with Jefferson but also with most other party leaders. In the first year of the new administration, as president of the Senate he cast a tie-breaking vote that had temporarily derailed Jefferson's efforts to repeal Adams's hated Judiciary Act. On the occasion of a Federalist dinner on Washington's birthday in 1802, he proposed a toast: "to the union of all honest men!" which was taken by some as a slap at Jefferson.[14]

Burr complained to his son-in-law of his isolation within the administration. "I dine with the President about once a fortnight, and now and then meet the ministers in the street," he wrote. "They are all very busy: quite men of business. The Senate and the vice-president are content with each other, and move on with courtesy."[15]

Leading Federalists observed the Burr freeze and considered the prospects of recruiting him to their side. Theodore Sedgwick wrote to Rufus King: "I have the best evidence that Burr is completely an insulated man at Washington—wholly without personal influence."[16] And Harrison G. Otis, with a thinly veiled reference to Burr's alleged untrustworthiness, asked John Rutledge: "Is he to be used by the Federalists, or is he a two-edged sword, that must not be drawn? I have sometimes inclined strongly to the opinion that you ought to make use of him . . . that you cannot so conveniently carry hostility into your enemy's camp under any other general."[17]

A prominent pro-Republican editor, James Cheetham of the *New York American Citizen,* reported to Jefferson of frequent contacts with Burr and the vice president's criticisms of the administration. "The end is obvious," he wrote. "It is to bring the present administration into disrepute, and thereby to place Mr. Burr in the Presidential Chair."[18]

Gallatin told Jefferson of his own concerns about Burr, while taking note of his political influence in the important state of New York. Jefferson nevertheless gave Burr short shrift, rejecting his appeals for federal patronage for fellow New Yorkers, while closely watching Burr's moves toward a candidacy for governor of his state. Burr's interest in the job clearly demonstrated that he knew his chances for a second term as vice president on the Republican ticket were slim to nonexistent.

Burr was as divisive a factor in the party politics in New York as he was in Washington. His bid for the governorship was challenged by moderate Morgan Lewis, and Burr's foes among the Clinton faction in the state conspired to destroy his political career. With Burr's reputation tarnished in the 1800 presidential standoff, Senator John Armstrong wrote to Governor Clinton's nephew DeWitt Clinton in the summer of 1802: "Can we look to any circumstances more auspicious to ourselves than the present? I think not. The cards are with us. . . . An unbroken vote from this State does not merely disappoint Mr. B—it prostrates him and his ambition forever, and will be a useful admonition to future schismatics."[19]

Gallatin, watching the situation, wrote to Jefferson: "Appearances are stormy in New York; the schism disgusts many Republicans [and] is fomented by the Federalists." The president, however, was loath to inject himself in the party division. "I see with sincere grief that the schism in New York is setting good republicans by the ears," he wrote to Granger, who had influential friends in the state. "It is not for me to meddle in this matter; but there can be no harm in wishing for forbearance."[20]

Burr himself met with Jefferson in January 1804, expressing a willingness to step aside if, as historian Noble E. Cunningham Jr. describes it in his book *Jeffersonian Republicans in Power,* "some mark of favor were bestowed upon him to show that he retired with Jefferson's confidence."[21] But Jefferson gave him no encouragement and in his notes on the meeting observed that he had "habitually cautioned Mr. Madison against trusting him too much."[22] Burr's friends chose to interpret Jefferson's neutral position as indicating he had no objection to Burr as governor of New York, but the notion had little credibility among most party activists.

With Burr in political eclipse and Hamilton, Jefferson's bête noire in his pre-presidential days, subdued by the change in political fortunes at the national level, a Republican congressman and fellow Virginian, John Randolph, emerged as the next political thorn in Jefferson's side. As the Republican House leader, he was more Catholic than the pope when it came to adherence to the new party's principles as laid down by Jefferson and Madison in the Kentucky and Virginia Resolutions of 1798. He saw Jefferson's reaching out to the Federalists as apostasy, and resented what he saw as the president's deep intrusion into the legislative business of Congress.

Randolph was a frail man of boyish face weathered by infirmity, with a high-pitched voice and an aristocratic, overbearing manner that turned off Federalists and many Republicans alike.[23] At twenty-eight, with only a single term in the House, he was appointed chairman of the House Ways and Means Committee by his friend Speaker Nathaniel Macon of North Carolina, and he soon replaced William B. Giles as the party's House leader, to Jefferson's unease. Randolph's demeanor led a Federal critic, Senator William Plumer, to write a friend: "His manners are far from conciliating. Many of the party dislike him—and on trifling measures they quarrel with him, but on all matters that are really important to the party they unite with him. . . . His ill state of health renders him fretful and peevish; his manners are haughty—and he often unnecessarily tramples on the pride and wounds the feelings of his adherents, by a constant display of his superiority."[24]

What first kicked off Randolph's criticism of Jefferson was an otherwise obscure 1795 deal in which a group called the Yazoo Land Companies had bribed the Georgia legislature for a grant of 35 million acres of Indian land in the state's western region, now part of Alabama and Mississippi. The state legislature subsequently rescinded the fraudulent deal and in 1802 the land was ceded to the federal government. By that time, however, much of it had been sold off, and in 1803 a Jefferson-appointed commission recommended setting aside 5 million acres in the Southwest for legitimate claimants. Randolph irately accused the administration of being involved in the fraud.[25]

When the commission report reached the House for approval in 1804, Randolph's rancor was fueled by the appearance on the House floor of the postmaster general, Gideon Granger, in support of the claimants. Randolph broke openly with Jefferson, offering several critical resolutions defending Georgia's right as a sovereign state to rescind the contracts and rejecting federal payment of the claims. "Asking one of the states to surrender part of her sovereignty," he argued at one point, "is like asking a lady to surrender part of her chastity."[26]

The matter was temporarily shelved but came up again in 1805, in a heated debate led by Randolph, who argued that the Republican Party in advancing a compromise had cast aside its constitutional principles. By five votes, the House voted for settling the claims despite opposition from seventeen of the nineteen members of the usually pro-Jefferson Virginia delegation.

Randolph, on the verge of a complete severance with the Jeffersonians, was obliged to stay his hand because he had been designated chief House prosecutor in the approaching Senate impeachment trial of Justice

Chase, which needed strong Republican Party support to win conviction. Focused as he was on the Yazoo controversy, Randolph failed to make a sufficiently convincing case against Chase, who was acquitted of all six articles of impeachment against him. Randolph's stock plunged in the party, especially in the North, and personally with Jefferson and Madison. But he was far from finished as an internal engine of party challenge and dissent.

Amid such distractions within his political family, Jefferson also invited criticism within party ranks with major gestures and actions that demonstrated a new strain of nationalism in his otherwise devoted pursuit of limited, decentralized government. Although on taking office he had pledged to pursue "peace, commerce, and honest friendship with all nations, entangling alliances with none,"[27] circumstances forced unforeseen and contrary involvements on him.

In his first year in the White House, he was obliged to send a naval force into the Mediterranean to defend American merchant shipping against the preying of pirates from Tripoli and other Barbary Coast states in Northern Africa. And the resumption of hostilities between England and France in 1803, on the heels of the peace treaty at Amiens in 1802, led him to warn Congress that with "the flames of war lighted up again in Europe ... the nations pursuing peace will not be exempt from all evil."[28] While he called on the combatants to respect the rights of American ships and sailors as neutrals, he was faced with greater need for a naval force he had long opposed. More significant in America's expanding role on the international stage was Jefferson's decision, driven by his determination to protect and expand the role of agriculture in the nation's society, to seek and achieve new territory in the American West. In 1803 he startled the country and critics with his purchase of the sprawling Louisiana Territory from Napoleonic France, in a single stroke doubling the size of the United States.

Shortly after Jefferson had taken office as president, word came from Europe that Napoleon, in the secret Treaty of San Ildefonso, had acquired from Spain rights to the Louisiana Territory, with actual possession delayed. When the Spanish administrator of the port of New Orleans disclosed in late 1802 that the French intended to restrict its use, Jefferson was obliged to consider his stricture against entangling alliances.

He wrote to Robert Livingston, the American minister in Paris, that while France had always been regarded as a "natural friend," there was "on the globe one single spot, the possessor of which is our natural and habitual enemy. It is New Orleans, through which the produce of three-eighths of our territory must pass to market." He warned that "the day that France takes possession of New Orleans" the United States would have to "marry ourselves to the British fleet and nation" to cope with the immense commercial threat.[29] At the same time, he alerted Congress to "the danger to which our peace would be perpetually exposed whilst so important a key to the commerce of the Western country remained under foreign power."[30]

Jefferson did not, however, allow himself to imagine that the whole of the immense Louisiana Territory would be up for purchase. He told Livingston to make an offer to the French for New Orleans and the territories of West and East Florida only, and obtained an appropriation of $2 million from Congress for general expenses. He dispatched Monroe to Paris in early April 1803 to help Livingston in the negotiations.

Two days earlier, however, Talleyrand had astonished Livingston by suddenly asking him whether the United States would care to buy all of Louisiana. Livingston, and Monroe on his arrival, seized the offer and negotiated a price of $15 million, along with a promise, sought by the French, to extend American citizenship as well as religious freedom to all Catholics living there. Talleyrand told the American negotiators: "You have made a noble bargain for yourselves and I suppose you will make the most of it."[31] It was the understatement of the age in diplomacy.

At home, however, the news was not greeted with universal approval. Settlers in the Western regions, mostly Republicans, delighted at the prospect of further westward expansion. But Federalists in New England viewed it as a political setback and accused Jefferson of unsavory action, inasmuch as Napoleon had promised Spain that France would not surrender Louisiana to another power. Nor was there any explicit provision in the Constitution for such a purchase. Federalists shortsightedly looked on the deal as an unwise extension of the public debt. Jefferson, knowing the Constitution's lack of authority for the purchase, considered seeking a constitutional amendment permitting the creation of new states out of the territory, but relented when Livingston warned him delay might lead Napoleon to change his mind.[32]

When some fellow Republicans argued that a president had the implied power to act (as Hamilton had successfully argued in defending establishment of his bank), Jefferson without reference to the point submitted the deal to the Senate, where it was easily ratified by a vote of

24–7. Before the year was out, a congressionally authorized exploration of the 828,000-square-mile territory was under way by Meriwether Lewis, Jefferson's private secretary, and Lieutenant William Clark, with a party of forty-five men. Jefferson proclaimed the new acquisition an "empire for liberty,"[33] justifying this distinctly nationalistic action as a guarantor against foreign threats to individual rights that were a foundation not only of the Constitution but of the Jeffersonian party as well.

The Louisiana Purchase, Jefferson and Madison argued, should include West Florida, an area known today as the Panhandle, since it once had been part of French Louisiana. But in a 1763 treaty, France had ceded the territory to the English, who after the American Revolution had in turn ceded East and West Florida to Spain. In 1804, however, France denied it had ever claimed West Florida as part of Louisiana, and Monroe was sent to Madrid to negotiate the American claim on it. The Spanish balked, leaving this aspect of the Louisiana Purchase in limbo.

Even without it, however, the huge Louisiana acquisition provided a most serendipitous prelude to Jefferson's decision to seek a second term in 1804. Like Washington before him, Jefferson waited until the election year to announce that in spite of his "decided purpose" to return to Monticello after one presidential term, "the unbounded calumnies of the federal party have obliged me to throw myself on the verdict of my country for trial."[34] After the successes of the first four years, both politically and diplomatically, he had every reason to expect the verdict to be positive. He had not fulfilled his claim that under his stewardship "we are all republicans, we are all federalists." Instead, the plight of the opposition party was sufficiently dire as to be approaching extinction. In the off-year congressional elections of 1802, the Jeffersonian party had increased its margin over the Federalists in the House from 33 seats to 64, and in the Senate from 5 to 16.

The only question for the Republicans in 1804 was the identity of Jefferson's running mate, since it was clear that the controversial Burr would not be offered a second term. By this time, the Twelfth Amendment providing separate voting for president and vice president to avoid the Jefferson-Burr electoral-vote deadlock of 1800 had been passed by Congress but not yet ratified. So the party had to lay plans in its choice of the second man on the ticket to assure there would be no repetition of that fiasco.

With no national political structure yet in place, it fell to the Republican caucus in Congress, in informal conversations with state party organizations, to function as a national party central committee in choosing the national ticket. It was taken as a matter of course that the caucus would anoint Jefferson for a second term, and its 108 members did so, unanimously, on February 25, 1804.

The group then cast ballots for Jefferson's running mate. Six Republicans got votes, led by Governor George Clinton of New York, who won sixty-seven, more than the majority required for nomination. The party's prime organ, the Philadelphia *Aurora,* reported afterward: "It is worthy of particular notice that the name of Mr. Burr was not introduced either in the meeting, or in a single vote."[35] Then, with the 1800 election controversy and the unratified Twelfth Amendment in mind, the caucus appointed a thirteen-member committee to consider how best to support Clinton "in such manner . . . as not to endanger the election of Mr. Jefferson."[36] Unlike the secretive caucuses of 1800, the Republicans met openly in 1804, thereby inviting criticism not only from Federalists but also from some Republican recalcitrants about the role party leaders in Congress were assuming for themselves in the absence of any more formal and democratic process.

A former Federalist member of the House, William Grove, complained to William Gaston of North Carolina: "I suppose it will become fashionable for the Members of Congress to Nominate all the Officers of the General and State Government by and by."[37] Republican Littleton Tazewell of Virginia, unhappy about the cavalier dismissal of Burr, complained to Randolph: "How fast is this government of ours settling into aristocracy; and into an aristocracy of the worst kind, the aristocracy supported by Intrigue. The people although nominally still possessed of the authority and power of the government, in fact have no interest whatever, except in Congressional elections. When these are made, they become a mere tool in the hands of their Representatives, compelled to execute whenever they decide. The manner of your late proceedings conclusively proves these positions. An unauthorized meeting undertake[s] to decide, that one of the old Servants of the people is no longer worthy of their confidence. . . . An intriguing character has nothing therefore to perform, but to secure the good will of a majority of the majority of the members of Congress, and his success is inevitable." The process, he charged, resulted in "burying thus all sort of responsibility in the secrecy and confusion of a ballot box."[38]

Randolph replied in effect that he agreed, "yet, as you cannot devise a remedy, it appears to be one of those inherent evils in our system . . . to which we must submit."[39] The *Aurora* was more positive about the process. In the past, it said, "the republicans had been willing to entrust the initiation of the important choice of president and vice president" to their congressional representatives, and "the persons recommended had in every instance been cheerfully supported by the electors, and we must continue in the same course if we desire to triumph; we must respect the recommendations, as long as we can discover no sinister motives in the conduct of those who recommend."[40]

Other forces were at work, however, to challenge the primacy of the congressional caucus. More and more states were turning away from selection of presidential electors by the state legislatures toward the popular vote. In 1800 only five of the sixteen states voting had the popular ballot; by 1804, eleven of the seventeen voting had it. Although Jefferson himself did not campaign for election, some men running to be presidential electors did. Monfort Stokes, a Republican in North Carolina, circulated flyers pledging his vote for Jefferson. Pressure for a similarly popular voice in the nominating process was inevitable.

At age sixty-seven, Clinton was not deemed a prospective presidential candidate for 1808, a factor in his support from Virginia, whose congressional delegation was already looking ahead to maintaining the "Virginia dynasty" with the prospective candidacy of Madison, assuming Jefferson would not seek a third term.

The conspicuous shunning of Burr by the party's congressional caucus did not, however, get him out of the party's hair. One outgrowth of the Louisiana Purchase was fear in the Northern states that their influence in the Union would be overwhelmed. Accordingly, Timothy Pickering and other New England Federalists of the so-called Essex Junto began entertaining the notion of breaking off from the Union and forming a new "Northern Confederacy" with Nova Scotia and other Canadian provinces, with Burr at its head.

In late 1803, Pickering had written fellow Federalist Stephen Higginson of Massachusetts: "Although the end of all our Revolutionary labors and expectations is disappointed, I rather anticipate a new confederacy exempt from the corrupt and corrupting influence and oppression of the aristocratic Democrats of the South. . . . There will be a separation. . . . The British provinces, even with the assent of Britain, will become members of the Northern Confederacy."[41]

They approached Burr, offering their aid in his campaign for governor of New York. Fearful that the Louisiana Purchase would result in more agrarian states whose voting power would further diminish the influence of New England in the Union, these would-be secessionists saw Burr as a possibly willing co-conspirator, military leader and even president of the new breakaway country. They even considered that if war broke out with the remaining Union states, Hamilton might agree to be commander of the new army, but he made clear from the start he opposed secession.

At a meeting of Federalists in Albany prior to Burr's nomination as the party's gubernatorial candidate, Hamilton took note of "the ill opinion of Jefferson and the jealousy of the ambition of Virginia" in Federalist ranks, and that "these causes are leading to an opinion that a dismemberment of the Union is expedient. . . . It would probably suit Mr. Burr's view to promise this result; to be chief of the Northern portion; and placed at the head of the State of New York"—an outcome as Burr's bitter critic he obviously did not favor.[42]

Senator Uriah Tracy of Connecticut, strenuously objecting to the provision in the purchase promising statehood and citizenship to residents of the territory without a constitutional amendment, revealed the basic political concern of the New England Federalists in the secessionist talk. "This would be absorbing the Northern States and rendering them as insignificant to the Union as they ought to be," he complained, "if by their own consent, the measure should be adopted."[43] Another Federalist congressman, the Reverend Manasseh Cutler, agreed. "The admission of the province [Louisiana] into the Union must throw New England quite into the background," he wrote. "Her influence in government from the rapid population of the southward and westward is naturally declining, and this must be nearly a finishing stroke. . . . The moment Louisiana is admitted to the Union the seeds of separation are planted."[44]

Oliver Wolcott, in a letter to Federalist Congressman Roger Griswold of Connecticut, wrote of the proposal that its advocates, fearing the subordination of Northern interests, "are determined at all hazards, to free this part of the Country at least, from the abhorred domination of the perfidious Virginians. It is of the utmost consequence, therefore, to ascertain whether the Northern Democrats in Congress have begun to open their eyes, on the degraded condition of the Northern States and whether a 'Union of Parties' is practicable with the view of opposing Virginia influence."[45] Griswold replied that it was doubtful such a union could be accomplished, but that the Federalists ought to support Burr in New York.

In any event, Griswold said, the other prominent New Yorker, Hamilton, would have to agree to put the new confederacy under Burr, and that was unlikely. Indeed, Hamilton, having gotten wind of the scheme, helped smash it by working for Burr's loss to Lewis for the governorship. According to the *Mirror of the Times* of Wilmington, Delaware, one Fourth of July toast in Philadelphia proclaimed: "The advocates of Burrism and third party principles—May they be speedily shipped on Board a British prison ship, and exported to the congenial regions of Nova Scotia."[46] Jefferson himself, aware of the secession conspiracy, expressed no concern. "It will be found in this, as in all similar cases," he wrote to a friend, "that crooked schemes will end by overwhelming their authors and coadjutors in disgrace."[47]

The consequences of Hamilton's role in Burr's New York defeat would soon be infinitely more deleterious to Hamilton himself. In February 1804 a New Yorker named Dr. Charles Cooper had heard Hamilton at some event launch a sharp verbal criticism of Burr as a candidate for governor. Two months later, in a letter to the *Albany Register*, Cooper made reference to, but did not quote, the attack, adding that "I could detail to you a still more despicable opinion which General Hamilton has expressed of Mr. Burr."[48] Another two months passed, at which point Burr, in a letter of his own, confronted Hamilton with the report, calling on him to explain or retract the use of the word "despicable."

Hamilton replied that the word was too ambiguous for him either to confirm or deny, and objected "on principle, to consent to be interrogated as to the justness of *inferences,* which may be drawn by *others,* from whatever I have said of a political opponent in the course of a fifteen-year competition."[49] In other words, Hamilton was tweaking Burr for rising to the bait on purely political, as opposed to personal, remarks that he couldn't clearly recall anyway. Burr insisted on an apology and withdrawal of the unspecified slander, not just for the alleged "despicable" allegation but for all past offenses. Hamilton went as far as saying the conversation in question "turned wholly on political topics and did not attribute to Colo [*sic*] Burr, any instance of dishonorable conduct, nor relate to his private character."[50]

But that didn't satisfy Burr either. Apparently further agitated by what he considered Hamilton's equivocating and seeking to raise the humiliation level, Burr said he required a flat retraction. Hamilton, now against the wall, replied that he couldn't be held responsible for "any *rumours* which may be afloat" over the course of their long acquaintanceship.[51] Burr finally cut off the exchanges with an invitation of a duel with weapons of Hamilton's choice, as the challenged party. He selected a pair of old family pistols, and on the morning of July 11, on a cliff overlooking the Hudson River at Weehawken, New Jersey, Burr fatally wounded Hamilton—and his own already evaporating political career.

Although the precise words that led to Hamilton's death at age forty-nine were never reported, there was ample slander of Burr by him on the record. Most prominent was the Hamilton assault during the post-election controversy resulting from the electoral vote tie between Jefferson and Burr in the 1800 presidential election. Hamilton wrote of Burr in part in a letter to James Bayard of Delaware:

> Be assured, my dear sir, that this man has no principle, public nor private. As a politician, his sole spring of action is an inordinate ambition; as an individual, he is believed by friends as well as foes to be without *probity;* and a voluptuary by system—with habits of expense that can be satisfied by no fair expedients.... No engagement that can be made with him can be depended upon; while making it, he will laugh in his sleeve at the credulity of those with whom he makes it;—and the first moment it suits his views to break it, he will do so. Let me add, that I could scarcely name a discreet man of either party in our State, who does not think Mr. Burr the most unfit man in the United States to run for the office of President. Disgrace abroad, ruin at home, are the probable fruits of his elevation.[52]

After the duel, Burr fled in the face of indictments on charges of murder in New York and New Jersey. Over the next three years, he was the subject of a series of bizarre reports that included leading a secession of the western part of the country and establishing a buffer state between Louisiana and Mexico with himself in command. In 1806 he led a force of about sixty men on flatboard boats down the Ohio and Mississippi Rivers on a mysterious mission. When a confederate informed Jefferson that Burr was intent on committing treason, Jefferson ordered him captured and, in 1807, Burr was indicted. In his trial, presided over by old Jefferson adversary John Marshall, Burr won acquittal on grounds his prosecutors failed to produce the constitutionally requisite "two witnesses to the same overt act" of treason or "confession in open court." He went to Europe for a time and returned home to practice law, discredited and destitute at the time of his death at age eighty.[53]

The death of Hamilton by Burr's hand removed one of Jefferson's foremost critics outside the new party and one of the major embarrassments to the Jeffersonians within it. Other sources of internal bickering thrived elsewhere, however, in the absence of serious competition from the Federalists. In Pennsylvania, squabbles abounded over patronage, and Jefferson in 1802 reassured Governor McKean that it was little more than Federalist troublemaking. "Despairing of success by their own strength," he wrote, "the only hope of the federalists is in dividing their opponents. This was to be expected and we must count on it's [*sic*] not being always unsuccessful."[54]

In 1803, to a concerned Gallatin, Jefferson wrote: "I have for some time been satisfied schism was taking place in Pennsylvania between moderates and high-flyers. The same will take place in Congress whenever a proper head for the latter shall start up, and we must expect division of the same kind in other States as soon as the Republicans shall be so strong as to fear no other enemy."[55]

John Beckley, the master Pennsylvania political organizer who now was clerk of the House of Representatives, added his voice to the concern that a serious breach was in the making. Jefferson took note that "the rudiments of such a third party were formed in Pennsylvania and New York has been said in the newspapers, but not proved. Although I shall learn it with concern whenever it does happen, and think it possibly may happen that we shall divide among ourselves whenever federalism is completely eradicated, yet I think it the duty of every republican to make great sacrifices of opinion to put off the evil day."[56] He declined to take sides, instead urging peace for the good of the party.

Fingers of accusation increasingly pointed at William Duane, editor of the *Aurora*, in a personal fight with Alexander Dallas, appointed federal district attorney by Jefferson. Dallas wrote directly to Gallatin, who found himself unappointed referee in the affair, complaining that "the violence of Duane has produced a fatal division. He seems determined to destroy the republican standing and usefulness of every man, who does not bend to his will."[57]

The split within the Jeffersonian party threatened the emergence of a real or potential third party. In 1804, Duane was among the first to use the term "Tertium Quid," meaning a third part of something, or just "Quids" to describe the dissidents. He said Tench Coxe, the Jefferson-appointed federal purveyor of public supplies in Pennsylvania, "may be emphatically called the head of the third party in this state, as Mr. Burr is that of the third party in the state of New York," claiming only minority support in the Republican Party and accepting backing from Federalists.[58] The Quids also fashioned themselves Constitutional Republicans, suggesting truer allegiance to the precepts of the founding fathers.

Although the disunity within the Republican Party in Pennsylvania and a few other states continued past the election of 1804, it did not affect the outcome. For all the internal party dissension, the general prosperity that reigned in Jefferson's first term, with American commerce greatly benefiting despite foreign interference on the high seas, and national pride in the Louisiana Purchase, assured his reelection. The Federalists put up feeble opposition in the presidential candidacy of Charles Cotesworth Pinckney of South Carolina, Adams's running mate in 1800, and Rufus King of New York for vice president. Jefferson won in an electoral vote landslide, 162–14, with Pinckney getting only a handful of votes from Connecticut, Delaware and Maryland and Jefferson sweeping the former Federalist stronghold of Massachusetts. Clinton also won 162 electoral votes, but with the Twelfth Amendment finally ratified, he became vice president without incident or argument.

John Quincy Adams, signaling his movement toward the Republican ranks, pronounced emphatic last rites over his father's Federalist Party in a letter to Rufus King, on the basis of the popular appeal of Jeffersonian democracy. "The power of the Administration rests upon the support of a much stronger majority of people throughout the Union than the former Administrations ever possessed since the first establishment of the Constitution," he wrote. "Whatever the merits or demerits of the former Administrations may have been, there never was a system of measures more completely and irrevocably abandoned and rejected by the popular voice. It never can and never will be revived. The experiment [of Federalism], such as it was, has failed and to attempt the restoration would be as absurd as to undertake the resurrection of a carcass seven years in its grave."[59]

Nevertheless, Jefferson's second term was fraught with difficulties, largely resulting from the continuing opposition of the Quids at home and the challenges to American shipping at sea. He struck an optimistic note in his second inaugural address, pledging to focus the nation's energies and resources on needed public works. "War will then be but a suspension of useful works, and a return to a state of peace, a return to the progress of improvement."[60] This promise caused some consternation among old Republicans, who wondered whether their leader might be straying from his conviction that smaller government was better government.

Some of them also were disturbed about his late interest in expanding the boundaries of the country. In mid-1805, Jefferson was said to have discussed with Gallatin a possible military occupation of Florida and Texas, but was dissuaded by a warning that such action could embroil him in a European war. In November the cabinet approved an offer of $5 million to Spain for the Floridas, and about the same time word came from Paris that Talleyrand had offered to use France's influence with Spain to strike a deal on Florida and Texas for $10 million. Although it smacked of Talleyrand's earlier bribery proposal in the XYZ affair, Jefferson decided to consider it, but for the original $5 million.[61]

At the opening of the Ninth Congress, Jefferson made a tough speech on foreign policy, mentioning Spanish provocations against the American Southwest and British hostility toward American neutral trade. He even called for increases in the army and navy—once anathema to him. But he backed off a few days later and suggested that the Florida issue could be settled by negotiation, without mentioning the Talleyrand proposal.

The abrasive Republican House leader, John Randolph, in a meeting with Jefferson, was told Congress would be asked for a secret appropriation of $2 million to buy Florida. When Secretary of State Madison told him the purchase was the only alternative to war with France and Spain over the territory, Randolph, with the XYZ affair obviously in mind, said he would not be party to bribery and loftily told Jefferson that he "had a character to support and principles to maintain."[62]

Randolph plainly was chagrined at the hold the president had on the legislative branch. "It is certainly a melancholy truth," he complained in writing to Monroe, "that . . . the only question which the major part of [the House] inquires into is, 'what is the wish of the Executive?' and an intimation of the pleasure of that branch of the government is of equal force with law." The development, he wrote, "is truly mortifying and distressing to the true republicans, the number of whom, it is to be feared, diminishes every day."[63]

When the appropriation request came before Randolph's committee, he managed to defeat it at first, but on a second go-around the $2 million was voted for negotiations on Florida. Randolph was unrelenting in his abuse of Jefferson and Madison, charging in the House that "most of the evils which the United States now [suffers] proceeded from the measures of the Executive—and from the weak and pusillanimous spirit of the keeper of the Cabinet—the Secretary of State."[64] The delays caused by Randolph's opposition, however, and Napoleon's focus on the war in Europe scuttled the West Florida deal for the time being.

The Florida question was soon overshadowed by the growing crisis over American shipping and British aggressive actions against it, including the impressment of English deserters serving on American merchant ships. Such ships were intercepted at sea and many American as well as British seamen were seized. By 1806, Jefferson could no longer tolerate the practice without some response. "The love of peace which we sincerely feel & profess," he wrote, "has begun to produce an opinion in Europe that our government is entirely in Quaker principles, & will turn the left cheek when the right has been smitten. This opinion must be corrected when just occasion arises, or we shall become the plunder of all nations."[65]

But he was not ready to accept that war with Britain was the only answer. Monroe, the U.S. minister in London, was instructed to pursue negotiations for relief from the English harassment, and a special emissary was sent to assist him. Randolph himself wanted the appointment but, not surprisingly, he was passed over in favor, of all people, of a Federalist, William Pinkney, a Baltimore lawyer with connections in London. Randolph was irate, and his friend Macon observed sarcastically of Pinkney: "He must therefore be a good republican, or we are all federalists and all republicans, or have the times changed?"[66]

Randolph expressed his disfavor in a letter to George Hay, Monroe's son-in-law. "The administration may do what it pleases," he wrote. "It favors federal principles, and, with the exception of a few great rival characters, federal men. Attack it on this ground, and you are denounced for federalism: are told by those, who agree with you in condemning the same measures, that you are ruining the republican party—that we must keep together, etc; the old republican party is already ruined, past redemption. New men and new maxims are the order of the day."[67]

Congressman John Smith of Virginia lamented: "I am sorry to say that there is not that harmony existing among the republicans in the House of

Representatives that could be wished; some of the members of which, it is said, have gone far towards denouncing the executive."[68]

Meanwhile, Jefferson's message to Congress on the British interference was referred to Randolph's Ways and Means Committee, stacked with his friends and supporters, where it was shelved for two months, until the House, under pressure from Jefferson, moved to bypass the committee. In late January 1806 a Pennsylvania congressman, Andrew Gregg, offered a resolution barring the importation of all British goods and products. A colleague, Joseph Clay of Philadelphia, proposed a milder version focused on the critical West Indies trade. Still another, more limited, resolution was introduced by Joseph Nicholson on behalf of the administration, calling for the exclusion only of materials the United States could "supply ourselves with our own industry, or obtain from other countries."[69]

Virginian Randolph saw all these resolutions as chiefly benefiting Northern commercial and trading interests at the expense of "the great agricultural interest" of the South, which was supposed to be at the heart of Jeffersonian policy. He saw them also as manifestations of executive branch domination of the legislative in the hands of Jefferson, Madison and other cabinet members. In House debate, he charged the proposals were "not of an open declared cabinet; but of an invisible, inscrutable, unconstitutional cabinet, unknown to the Constitution. I speak of backstairs influence—of men who bring messages to this House, which, although they do not appear on the journals, govern its decisions."[70]

Jefferson, on another occasion, seemed to make reference to Randolph's complaint of executive meddling in legislative affairs. In a letter to fellow Republican Congressman Barnabas Bidwell of Massachusetts, he wrote: "When a gentleman, through zeal for the public service, undertakes to do the public business, we know that we shall hear the cant of backstairs counsellors. But we never heard this while the declaimer was himself a backstairs man as he calls it, but in the confidence and views of the administration as may more properly and respectfully be said. But if the members are to know nothing but what is important enough to be put into a public message, and indifferent enough to be made known to all the world, if the Executive is to keep all other informations to himself, and the house to plunge on in the dark, it becomes a government of chance and not of design."[71]

The proposals for retaliation against England, Randolph also argued, would put the United States into alliance with a France that had moved from its admirable republican intentions in its own revolution to the despotism of Napoleon. "Gentlemen talk of 1793," he declared. "They might as well go back to the Trojan War. What was your situation then? Then every heart beat high with sympathy for France, for republican France! . . . Because she was fighting the battles of the human race against the combined enemies of liberty; because she was performing the part which Great Britain now, in fact, sustains, forming the only bulwark against universal domination."[72]

The vehemence of Randolph's assault led Senator Plumer to observe that he "has passed the Rubicon."[73] Jefferson's son-in-law, Thomas Mann Randolph, wrote a fellow Virginian that "it may be taken for granted in the country that Mr. R is the bitter and determined enemy of the present administration, and that he has resolved to fall himself or destroy it in the public sentiment."[74]

John Quincy Adams, son of the former president, speculated in his diary that Randolph was motivated by resentment and by concern that Jefferson was bent on positioning Madison, deeply disliked by Randolph, for the presidency in 1808. "He has been so exasperated at the attempts to take the management of the House from his hands," Adams wrote, ". . . that he has poured forth all the ebullitions of his resentment on this question. . . . It is said there is now very warm electioneering in the party for the next presidential election, and that Mr. Randolph's object in his present denunciation is to prevent Mr. Jefferson from consenting to serve again, and Mr. Madison from being his successor. Mr. Randolph's man is said to be Mr. Monroe."[75]

Randolph himself confirmed Adams's surmise in a letter to Monroe. "There is no longer a doubt," he wrote, "but that the principles of our administration have been materially changed . . . suffice it to say, that every thing is made a business of bargain and traffick, the ultimate object of which is to raise Mr. M—n to the presidency. To this the old republican party will never consent—nor can N.Y. be brought into the measure. Between them and the supporters of Mr. M there is an open rupture. Need I tell you that they (the old republicans) are united in your support?—that they look to you, Sir, for the example which this nation has yet to receive—to demonstrate that the government can be conducted on open, upright principles, without intrigue or any species of disingenuous artifice."[76]

In a direct attack on Madison from the House floor, Randolph read from a pamphlet on American neutrality rights by the secretary of state, ridiculed it and threw it to the floor. So poisonous in attitude had he become that he finally turned his wrath on the House of Representatives itself. What really was needed, he said, was an embargo on American shipping to England. But instead of supporting his plan, he said, "like true political quacks, you deal only in handbills and nostrums"—thus also dismissing the proposals of friends Clay and Nicholson.[77]

In the process, Randolph alienated many of his own followers, to the point that many who had voted with him against the Gregg resolution cast their votes against him in the subsequent passage of the more moderate Nicholson proposal. It won, 87–35, with only nine Republicans against, and was similarly cleared in the Senate. Jefferson applauded the vote, citing it as a rejection of Randolph. "I have never seen a H of Representatives more solidly united in doing what they believe to be the best for the public interest," he wrote to Monroe. "There can be no better proof of the fact that so eminent a leader should be at once and almost unanimously abandoned."[78]

Randolph attributed his failure to Jefferson's iron hand on the legislature. "If all, who talked with us by the fireside, had supported their own opinions," he complained later, "our numbers would have been very different."[79] But most counts of Quid strength in the House did not exceed thirteen members, including Randolph, Macon and Nicholson, among the most articulate and skilled of the old Republicans.

The Quid movement elsewhere, in Pennsylvania, New York, Rhode Island and even in Virginia, also was struggling. There was virtually no relationship among the state factions, and the notion that Randolph somehow was the leader of a third party was erroneous. Jefferson steadfastly declined to inject himself into the intraparty fights other than to express his fervent desire that fellow Republicans reconcile themselves for the good of the party and country.

Jefferson's prediction, after roundly defeating the Federalists in 1800, that the Republican Party would be plagued by internal division, certainly had been borne out. With Randolph's latest and open opposition, Jefferson moved quickly to consolidate his own strength within the party, particularly among Randolph's friends. He invited House Speaker Macon to the White House for a private talk and appointed Nicholson to a federal judgeship. Macon promised Jefferson only that he would not join forces with Randolph; others quietly responded favorably to the president's overtures.[80]

Randolph reached such a point of alienation that in April 1806 he declared himself to be no longer a member of the Republican Party but rather a "Quiddist." From the House floor, he declared that "relative to what is generally called quiddism," he was "willing to meet gentlemen on that ground. If we belong to the third party," he said, "be it so."[81] Unrepentant in his defiance of the Republicans, he explained: "I found I might cooperate or be an honest man—I have therefore opposed, and will oppose them."[82] But for all of Randolph's bombast, there never was a "Quiddist" party, and those separate Quid movements in a few states bore no discernible allegiance to him.

By this time, Randolph and his small band of Republican dissenters had lost any ability to function as a third party even in Congress. Their efforts to call the Republicans back to the purity of their original purpose as advancers of the agrarian interest and decentralized government had been overwhelmed by the practical opportunities and demands of a growing nation.

In the next Congress, Macon was replaced as speaker and Randolph as chairman of the House Ways and Means Committee. Randolph also was pushed aside as party leader in the House in favor of a new Jefferson favorite, Bidwell, joining Jefferson ally William Giles, the party leader in the Senate. The president defended his involvement in legislative affairs, and a cooperative posture toward Congress, as a legitimate part of his job, and most members willingly agreed.

John Quincy Adams observed in his diary during the second Jefferson term that the president's "whole system of administration seems found upon this principle of carrying through the legislature measures by his personal or official influence. There is a certain proportion of the members of both Houses who on every occasion of emergency have no other enquiry but what is the President's wish."[83] By this means did Jefferson foster in a practical way the sense of party against the efforts of such as Randolph to undercut it.

In the off-year congressional elections, in which the in-party normally lost strength, the Republicans actually posted modest gains. And when Jefferson in November 1807 declared he would not seek a third term, jockeying immediately began among the prospective successors—Madison, Monroe and aging Vice President George Clinton. Randolph and many Quids backed Monroe, but Madison from the start was the odds-on favorite.

Jefferson still had one major storm to weather before retirement. The ban on British exports proved ineffective, as the British, and to a lesser extent the French, continued their harassment of American shipping. By 1807, about fifteen hundred American merchant vessels had been seized. That summer, the British raised the stakes when their frigate *Leopard* fired upon, boarded and searched the American warship *Chesapeake* near the mouth of the Chesapeake Bay, impressing four of its seamen into British service. Halting and searching merchant ships for British deserters was one thing; seizing a warship was another; this was an act of war that demanded a muscled response.[84]

At the same time, western Indian tribes under the leadership of Shawnee chieftain Tecumseh and his brother Tenskwatawa, known as "The Prophet," were attacking white settlements in the Midwest with the assistance of British officials in Canada. Demands for war were heard throughout the North, demands that Jefferson resisted, contending that denying the British, and the French, all access to American foodstuffs and other raw materials could bring a halt to the intrusions. The answer was a full embargo in 1807 against all foreign trade.

It also failed to be effective, as British exports were smuggled into the United States from Canada, while at the same time American industry and agriculture suffered. A resulting depression struck hardest in New England, heavily dependent on the export of manufacturing goods. There were many illegal sailings from American ports, and widespread protests against an invisible monster known as "Ograbme"—embargo spelled backwards. Congress enacted a less severe Non-Intercourse Act, but domestic industry continued to suffer, with ominous signs for the Republican Party that only eight years earlier had taken power amid the highest hopes. Federalism in New England appeared to be on the verge of rising from the dead. Through Jefferson's last year in office, he managed to avert pressures for war against the British, but left the continuing prospects of it to his successor.

Jefferson looked forward to passing the presidency to his old friend and political partner, Madison, but Randolph and other dissidents continued to press Monroe as the Republican nominee. In addition, Vice President Clinton, at sixty-eight barely able to preside over the Senate but vocally opposed to the embargo, was advanced by some other embargo critics from New York, Pennsylvania and Maryland as an alternative. Once again, the choice fell to the party's congressional caucus, still functioning as the closest thing to a national party committee.

The supporters of Monroe and Clinton, aware that Jefferson's strong hold on Congress would in all probability result in Madison's nomination, raised objections to the right of the caucus to make the choice. But they were ineffective in joining forces, and in January 1808 the caucus met. Most of the opponents of Madison, notably including Randolph, boycotted it and Madison was overwhelmingly chosen, by a vote of 83–6. In an indication of how insignificant the vice presidency already was regarded, the caucus named the doddering Clinton for a second term in the post.[85]

Among those attending the Republican caucus was John Quincy Adams, heretofore a Federalist senator, confirming his conversion from his illustrious father's camp to the now-dominant party. Federalist Congressman Barent Gardenier of New York wailed to King: "Would you suppose it possible the scoundrel could summon impudence enough to go to their caucus? I wish to God the noble house of Braintree had been put in a hole and a deep one 20 years ago."[86]

Also notable was the adoption of a resolution by John Nicholas to establish a national campaign committee of correspondence with one member from each of the seventeen existing states—the first formal gesture toward creating a national party structure for the purpose of advancing the party's national ticket. Randolph assailed the selection of Madison in an "Address to the People" protesting the caucus action and signed by sixteen congressional Quids who had absented themselves from it. The campaign thus proceeded with a Madison-Clinton ticket and Randolph holding with Monroe in the hope that the Federalists, with no outstanding candidate of their own in sight, would fall in behind Monroe as preferable to Madison. Jefferson wrote to Monroe suggesting he might withdraw his name, to no avail.

Randolph and other Quids based their opposition to Madison on grounds that he had been an ineffective secretary of state, particularly in imposition of the embargo. Jefferson countered by dispatching a host of diplomatic correspondence and other papers to Congress that documented Madison's skill and firmness in dealing with foreign affairs. In Virginia, where the embargo had caused much difficulty and pain for planters, Randolph's personal behavior and harsh rhetoric canceled out whatever home-state benefit otherwise may have existed for Monroe, and Madison remained strong there.

At one point Jefferson wrote directly to Monroe suggesting the unwisdom of letting Randolph and other Quids function as his champions: "Some of your new friends are attacking your old ones out of friendship to you, but in a way to render you great injury."[87]

In the end, the Federalists gave up on thoughts of backing Monroe and in a late, secret conference of party leaders from eight states in New York, they settled once again on their weak 1804 ticket of Charles Pinckney and Rufus King. It was no contest. Madison won 12 of the 17 states and 122 electoral votes to 47 for Pinckney. New York gave its six presidential votes to its former governor, Clinton, who retained the vice presidency over King. There was, however, a ray of light for the Federalists in that Madison won 40 fewer electoral votes than Jefferson had received in 1804 and Pinckney won 33 more than he had four years earlier. Also, the Federalists made a comeback in their New England stronghold, winning every state except Vermont. Dissatisfaction with the embargo was responsible as well for a loss of 24 Republican seats in the House.

In March 1809, Jefferson finally got his wish to return to Monticello and permanent retirement. He had capped his eight years as president by seeing the reins of national and party power turned over to the man of his choice. At the same time, however, the Jefferson years had demonstrated that a political party without serious and challenging opposition was not necessarily in the most desirable of circumstances. Into the vacuum of Federalist decline came internal Republican disunity that made Jefferson reflect nostalgically about the days of fierce party competition. In a letter to fellow Virginia Republican Wilson Cary Nicholas, he observed: "I did believe my station in March 1801 as painful as could be undertaken, having to meet in front all the terrible passions of federalism. . . . But I consider that as less painful than to be placed between conflicting friends."[88]

It did not, however, come unexpected to him. He had written in 1798, after all, that "in every free and deliberating society there must, from the nature of man, be opposite parties and violent dissensions and discords; and one of these, for the most part, must prevail over the other for a longer or shorter time. Perhaps this party division is necessary to induce each to watch and delate to the people the proceedings of the other."[89]

Yet the party had held together, and state-by-state party organization advanced despite the internal squabbling in key states. Statewide elections strengthened the campaign machinery, organized from the top down, from the state level to the county and town, with public participation rising with the popular vote. The third-party threat had been turned away, and the party grew organizationally in New England, where Federalist opposition remained the strongest. There was still no national party organization worth the name—no national party committee other than the newly created committee of correspondence, and Republican leaders in Congress continued to dominate party affairs. The party mantle had been successfully passed from Jefferson to his most trusted lieutenant, and Madison now took power as the third member of the Virginia presidential dynasty.

The Federalists, meanwhile, were experiencing a transfusion of young blood as the older generation tried in vain to keep the waning party on the now-outmoded track of government by aristocracy that had brought it into and out of power, with the passing of giants like Washington, Hamilton and the senior Adams. The younger Federalists largely put aside lofty theory, rolled up their sleeves and began to emulate the Jeffersonians' success in party organizing. The Federalists were still down but not out, and with the harassment of American shipping unresolved, war clouds continued to gather as Madison contemplated his long-awaited turn at national and party leadership.

Chapter 6

THE PARTY STANDS ALONE, 1809–1827

THE LEADERSHIP OF the Republican Party that Madison assumed in 1809 had strong congressional strings tied to it. Unlike the two presidential nominations of Jefferson that were for all practical purposes by general party acclamation, Madison's had come in a contested caucus of Republican members of Congress. He knew, therefore, that he was in a sense their creature—an unjust circumstance, in that Madison as much as Jefferson had been an architect of the new party.

In any event, Madison, for all his own legislative experience, proved as president to be less assertive than Jefferson had been in giving effective direction to Congress. It was clear from the start of his presidency that he would not be afforded the same cooperative welcome from Congress or his own party that Jefferson had enjoyed.

At the same time, the intraparty factionalism that had complicated Jefferson's second term continued in Madison's first. Although Randolph's dissident voice within the party had become ineffective, the intensity of his dislike of Madison assured it still would be heard. Beyond that, congressional opposition barred Madison's desired selection of Gallatin, his trusted lieutenant, to be his secretary of state. The Smith brothers of Maryland, Robert and Samuel, William Giles of Virginia and Michael Leib of Pennsylvania, leaders of an anti-Gallatin clique known as "the Invisibles," ludicrously played on grounds of Gallatin's Swiss birth and accent to threaten Senate rejection of his nomination to State.[1]

In 1814, President Madison faced the threat of disunion from four New England states over the war with England and what they saw as their region's diminishing influence. Delegates from Vermont, Massachusetts, Rhode Island and Connecticut met at a Hartford Convention, but a peace treaty derailed their rebellious notions.

Gallatin then was serving admirably as secretary of the treasury, and Madison considered giving that job to the incompetent Robert Smith as a way of persuading the Smith brothers not to block Gallatin at State. The idea was that Gallatin could in effect handle both jobs, but he balked at the deal. He told Madison the new administration would be better off if he stayed at Treasury and put Smith at State, where the president himself could oversee foreign policy. "In making this arrangement," Henry Adams wrote much later, "Madison knew that he must himself supply Smith's deficiencies; but stronger wills than that of Madison had yielded to party discontent, and he gained much if he gained only time."[2]

So Madison appointed Robert Smith, who had been Jefferson's unimpressive navy secretary, as secretary of state. As predicted, Smith proved to be so unqualified that Madison was obliged to function essentially as his own foreign secretary, often personally redrafting papers and documents prepared by Smith. In time, he replaced Smith with the highly qualified Monroe. But at the outset, with the appointment of two nonentities as secretaries of war and navy, Gallatin clearly was the strength of a weak cabinet, though the circumstances that had denied him State compromised his influence. And in succumbing to the Invisibles on the matter of Gallatin, Madison signaled what would prove to be a congressional dominance that handcuffed him throughout his White House tenure. Presidential leadership of the party, so obvious under Jefferson, was more symbolic than real under his successor.

In the absence of an assertive executive, much of party legislative direction evolved on the congressional caucus, committee chairmen and the Speaker of the House. The congressional elections of 1810 brought a change of the Republican guard; nearly half the old party membership was replaced by a new generation whose roots were not nurtured in the Revolutionary soil that had brought forth the party's founders and earliest members. The new generation, with heavy representation from Southern and newer Western states, elected one of its own, thirty-four-year-old Henry Clay of Kentucky, as speaker. Other newcomers such as John C. Calhoun of South Carolina and Peter B. Porter of western New York joined him as leaders of a faction favoring expansion and a more nationalistic attitude. Clay appointed like-minded colleagues like Felix Grundy of Tennessee and fellow-Kentuckian Richard M. Johnson to committee posts. The emergence of a strong congressional wing of the party dominated by these younger Republicans inspired Randolph to observe that "the truth seems to be that [Madison] is President de jure only; who exercises the office de facto I do not know."[3]

Madison, like Jefferson before him, sought at the outset of his tenure to reach out beyond party in an effort to smother the ashes of Federalism. The party of Hamilton, while having essentially died in terms of mounting a presidential challenge, continued to smolder and even glow at the state and congressional levels, particularly in its old stronghold of New England. Federalist representation in Yankee state legislatures held firm or grew, and in New York, Pennsylvania and Maryland as well, isolated episodes of defiance of the federal government occurred. Still, according to Henry Adams, "the Union stood in no danger. The Federalists gained many votes; but these were the votes of moderate men who would desert their new companions on the first sign of a treasonable act, and their presence tended to make the party cautious rather than rash."[4]

The greater challenges now came not simply from the intraparty factionalism at home but also from the continuing threat of war raised by the abuses of England, and to a lesser extent France, against American neutrality and shipping at sea. By now, trade and commerce abroad had become a much more significant element in the American economy, with a growth in domestic manufacturing that increasingly met consumer demands at home and began to seek foreign markets as well. Britain's trade barriers damaged New England industry particularly, fueling Federalist distress.

The anti-British sentiment that had governed Jeffersonian attitudes from the earliest days continued to be reflected in Republican support for strong measures against England to lift its oppressive policies. The Clay faction, emboldened by the young nation's growing strength and sense of self, champed at its party's resort to diplomacy to reach accommodation and, soon known as the "War Hawks," pressed for more muscular action. Federalists in Congress, still exhibiting pro-British feelings, argued that war would be much more damaging to American trade than the offending abuses. Also, they noted that war with England would make the United States a de facto ally of France, which was no longer defended by the Republicans now that Napoleon was its dictator.

The American embargo, despised at home, had been repealed in the final days of Jefferson's administration but the abuses continued, leading to enactment in early 1809 of a Non-Intercourse Act. It permitted resumption of trade with all nations other than Britain and France as long as those two countries' abusive policies continued. When this measure proved fruitless, Congress enacted another that lifted the ban on these two with a stipulation that if either of them ended its hostile acts against American shipping, the ban would be imposed on the other. Napoleon promptly said France would comply (but didn't), whereby Madison reimposed the ban on the British.

In the meantime, fears that the English might move to take control of Spanish-held lands in the Southwest and especially West Florida, now heavily populated by Americans, led Madison to authorize use of militia forces to secure the region. In September 1810 local forces stormed a Spanish port at Baton Rouge, declared "this territory of West Florida to be a free and independent state," and asked the United States "to take the present Government and people of this State under their immediate and special protection, as an integral and inalienable portion of the United States."[5] Madison signed a secret proclamation directing American territorial officials to take control of the region on grounds it was part of Louisiana conveyed in the purchase of 1803.

When he revealed the move to Congress in December, it set the Federalist press to cries of protest. The *Columbian Centinel* of Boston attacked "the right and authority of Mr. Madison, in face of the Constitution, without any provision to that effect by Law, to order a forcible seizure of a part of the territory of a friendly state."[6] The Republican *Richmond Enquirer* responded: "We are proud to see such a man as Madison at the head of the nation, so clear in his views, so cool in his decisions, so firm and unshrinking in his purposes. Where is the being who will now complain of Madison's want of nerve?"[7] Subsequently, Madison secretly asked authority from Congress to extend protection to East Florida against any attempt by England or France to occupy the area, subject to any reclaim from Spain, which eventually relinquished it.

The pressure for war against England gained momentum in 1811 in light of alleged British encouragement of Indian hostility toward American settlers on the expanding frontier, by providing arms and other assistance from Canada. The Shawnee chieftain Tecumseh and his brother Tenskwatawa rallied their tribe against the encroachments of their land by the white men. Amid the ensuing terror, Governor William Henry Harrison of the Indiana Territory dispatched a thousand American troops to the Shawnee settlement near Prophetstown along the Wabash River at the mouth of Tippecanoe Creek. In the Battle of Tippecanoe, which made

Harrison a national hero, the Americans destroyed the town and kicked off a long and bloody war at home.

Abroad, months passed with the British orders to seize American ships and seamen still in place, and impatience rising in the War Hawks' camp. Madison recalled the U.S. ambassador and, in June 1812, under heavy pressure finally asked Congress to declare war. By this time, the English had agreed to modify their policy, but it was too late. Congress acted, with Republicans voting nearly five to one for the declaration and all Federalists against. Although the defense of trade and commercial interests was at the heart of the war decision, national honor and pride also were invoked by Madison and other Republicans as justification. Madison blamed America's resort to war on "the injuries and indignities which have been heaped upon our country" and British policies "hostile to the United States as an independent and neutral nation."[8]

Madison, spurred on by the War Hawks, also cited the accusation of British complicity in the Indian trouble as a factor in his action. Johnson of Kentucky proclaimed: "I can have no doubt of the influence of British agents in keeping up Indian hostility." He accused them of encouraging the Indians "to murder our citizens," and Grundy argued that the only way to ensure peace on the American frontier was to drive the British out of Canada.[9]

Largely unspoken was the evident desire of the War Hawks for further territorial expansion, including northward into Canada, as the spirit of nationalism continued to drive the nation, especially in the South and West. Andrew Jackson of Tennessee, writing of the causes of the War of 1812, said its objective was "to seek some indemnity for past injuries, some security against future aggression."[10] Clay, for his part, defended the war declaration on grounds that "Great Britain arrogated to herself the pretension of regulating our foreign trade . . . persisted in the practice of impressing American seamen [and] instigated the Indians to commit hostilities against us."[11]

Madison's personal motivation was widely questioned, then and later. Although his messages to the English leading up to the declaration were increasingly belligerent with warnings of war, what Henry Adams later called "a Federalist legend" suggested that he had been "coerced" by Clay and Grundy into seeking the war approval from Congress "by threats of opposing his renomination for the Presidency." However, Adams noted, "whatever were his private feelings, he acted in constant agreement with the majority of his party, and at most asked only time for some slight armaments."[12]

Madison himself later wrote to the South Carolina legislature in explanation of his war decision: "When finally and formally assured by the British government that its hostile measures would not be revoked, no alternative was left to the United States but irretrievable degradation, or the lesser calamity of a resort to arms."[13]

Supreme but unfounded optimism about the war's outcome from the War Hawks unrealistically fanned expectations. Clay assured Madison that "the militia of Kentucky alone are competent to place Montreal and Upper Canada at your feet."[14] Had the war been entirely a land affair, those expectations might have been realized. The British had fewer than 5,000 soldiers in Canada; most of their ground forces were otherwise occupied against Napoleon in Europe. Congress authorized an army mobilization of 25,000 volunteers for a five-year enlistment and 50,000 more for one year. The government also had the resource of an estimated 700,000 more in the state militias.

The war, however, importantly engaged the British navy, unequaled in the world, and the Americans were woefully unprepared to do battle with it. Congress moved slowly to build up the American navy and to raise the taxes and float the loans required to wage a winning fight. Hamilton's Bank of the United States had been abolished in 1811, so Gallatin was obliged to go to state banks ill equipped to meet the need.

Federalists and their allies, now often referred to as the "peace party," considered the president's decision precipitous. They labeled the conflict "Mr. Madison's war" and called the Republicans siding with him the "war party," and the erratic conduct of it rained much criticism down on him. Three land attacks toward Canada in 1812 ended ignobly in defeat or retreat, for lack of adequate strategy, planning, resources and coordination.

Nevertheless, Madison was unanimously renominated in 1812 by a Republican congressional caucus boycotted by Giles, Samuel Smith and other anti-Gallatin Invisibles, and reelected, but not without stiff opposition. Republicans in the New York legislature rebelled and put forward DeWitt Clinton to oppose him. His campaign was managed by a newcomer to the national political scene from the state legislature named Martin Van Buren, who struck an effective alliance with the Federalists. Clinton carried all of New England except Vermont and all the Middle

Atlantic States except Pennsylvania. He lost to Madison by only thirty-nine electoral votes in what was far from a ringing endorsement of the war policy. In the congressional elections, the Federalists rebounded in New England and New York, doubling their strength in Congress. One notable old Republican casualty was John Randolph, now a fierce opponent of "Mr. Madison's war," who lost his House seat from Virginia.

The Republican Party that had stood so united behind Jefferson when he entered the White House in 1801 remained unthreatened by the Federalists on a national level. But it found itself fractured as never before by factionalism—old Republicans against young, war adherents against those for peace and, increasingly, North against South and West. A political landscape that at first was marked by factions that did not consider or call themselves parties had developed into a two-party system that now was disintegrating into a splintering single party. Jefferson's 1801 declaration that "we are all republicans, we are all federalists" had turned out to be more than a clever phrase. The clear party lines that had emerged from the Hamilton-Jefferson conflict of the last decade of the 1700s were once again blurred, not by unification but by a general erosion of firm ideological positions, as the new country found itself in the grasp of the impulses and perils of nationalism.

The American cause in the war began to take a more positive turn in late 1813 with a victory by Captain Oliver Hazard Perry over the British fleet on Lake Erie, restoring U.S. control of the Great Lakes. General Harrison's subsequent defeat of the British, and the killing of Tecumseh, secured Detroit and the Northwest frontier and effectively ended the threat from the Indian confederacy, while failing to gain any ground in Canada.

By 1814, with Napoleon defeated and exiled to Elba, the British were able to focus on the American war. They sent their ablest troops to undertake invasions at Niagara and Lake Champlain in New York and at New Orleans, while making amphibious assaults on Atlantic Coast cities. In August they sailed up the Chesapeake Bay and the Potomac to Washington, where they torched the White House, the Capitol and other public buildings as Madison and aides fled to nearby Virginia.[15] The British tried but failed to capture Baltimore and withdrew, but left the administration, and Madison personally, humiliated. The Niagara and Lake Champlain engagements were repulsed, however, and American forces at Plattsburgh, New York, drove the British back into Canada.

Meanwhile, Andrew Jackson was in New Orleans, having already ended the major Indian threat in the Southwest by defeating the Creek tribes at the Battle of Horseshoe Bend and then taking Pensacola in Spanish West Florida to deprive the British of a base there. With a militia force, he routed the British in the final important battle of the war, in the process becoming a national hero and, soon, a political figure of great significance.

Madison and the Republican Party still were obliged to weather one more internal political challenge. Fiercely anti-war Federalists in Massachusetts and other New England states, strengthened in their home region by growing animosity toward the administration in Washington, were busy conducting town meetings in the various states. They considered acts of defiance against pursuit of the war as well as the possibility of disunion and a separate peace with England.

Federalist governors resisted call-ups of their state militias for war service and discouraged military enlistments, and New Englanders continued to trade with Canada. A young Federalist congressman from New Hampshire named Daniel Webster posed the question: "Where is it written in the Constitution that you may take children from their parents, and parents from their children, and compel them to fight the battles of any war in which the folly or the wickedness of government may engage it?"[16]

With the war still in stalemate in October 1814, the Massachusetts legislature called for a convention of New England states to consider a regional defense against British invasion and amendments to the Constitution. They wanted to strengthen the hand of states in the decision to make war and protect the voting power of the original states in the face of the expanding Union. In mid-December twenty-six delegates from Vermont, Massachusetts, Rhode Island and Connecticut met secretly in Hartford for three weeks. Although Timothy Pickering had been one of the prime initiators and most extreme war foes, he did not attend. The leadership was in the hands of moderate Harrison Gray Otis.

The group proposed, among other things, amendments requiring a two-thirds vote of both houses of Congress to declare war and admit new states, barring the foreign-born from holding federal offices, limiting the presidency to one term and prohibiting the successive election of two presidents from the same state—a slap at the "Virginia dynasty." It further said that if its recommendations were ignored and the war continued, another convention should be called and given "such powers and instructions as the exigency of a crisis so momentous may require."[17]

Representatives of this Hartford Convention were dispatched to Washington to deliver the ultimatum, but on arrival they encountered a capital city celebrating Jackson's triumph at New Orleans and the startling news that a peace treaty had just been signed at Ghent in Belgium. Suddenly their meeting and findings were deflated amid perceptions that they had acted in disloyal self-interest. Politically, the Hartford Convention drove yet another nail into the Federalist Party coffin.

Yet the War of 1812 itself on balance proved to be an economic boon to New England in the impetus it gave to the region's manufacturing industries. The British, well aware of the sympathies toward themselves in their former Northern colonies, largely spared the region a tight blockade for most of the war, with a resultant prosperity in comparison with other parts of the Union. Textile factories multiplied several-fold while Southern planters bore the brunt of the war's economic hardships. A new trade treaty negotiated in London by Gallatin and Clay in the fall of 1815 promised more prosperity, and in 1816 a Second Bank of the United States was authorized by Congress. The still-bitter Randolph wrote that the Madison administration "out-Hamiltons Alexander Hamilton."[18]

What some called "neo-Federalism" and Clay labeled "the American System" began to focus more on economic self-sufficiency, encouraging greater agricultural production including raw materials for domestic manufacturing and calling for more road-building. A reorganized militia and larger navy were approved. In 1816, to combat British dumping, the Northern and Western regions of the country backed enactment of a protective tariff. Once again, the discordant voice of Old Republican Randolph was heard, saying he would not agree "to lay a duty on the cultivator of the soil to encourage exotic manufactures." But fellow Southerner Calhoun rejoined by calling for American manufactured goods to "at all times, and under every policy . . . be protected with due care."[19] Support in Dixie for the tariff, however, was weak.

Surviving a war that had been so conspicuously mishandled and in the face of continued Republican factionalism, Madison managed to complete his second term with sufficient popularity that the contest to succeed him engaged three supporters—Monroe, Senator William H. Crawford of Georgia, his secretary of war, and Governor Daniel D. Tompkins of New York. With the Republican congressional caucus again voting on the nomination, Monroe and Crawford, better known to the federal legislators, were the serious contenders. Monroe barely won, with 65 votes to 54 for Crawford, and Tompkins was chosen to be his running mate. The forlorn Federalists again offered Rufus King, who never bothered to campaign.

The Republican Party that Monroe thus inherited was by now a much-changed entity. The structure remained and expanded, but its purpose was diffused by its more complex membership. Many of the old Republicans with whom Monroe had served were out of public life and young men like Clay and Calhoun owed no particular loyalty to him. Nor were they basically guided by the limited vision of Jefferson—an affinity to state and individual rights and tied to the agrarian lifestyle on which the party had been created and sustained until the appeals of nationalism intruded—ironically initiated by Jefferson himself with the Louisiana Purchase.

Election returns gave Monroe an overwhelming victory over King, 183 electoral votes to 34, and all states except Massachusetts, Connecticut and Delaware. The one-sidedness of the outcome suggested the impending end of the two-party system and evolution into a single party, or none at all. Even before Monroe had taken the oath of office, Andrew Jackson, commander of the federal army in the South, wrote to him recommending that he strike a lethal blow to party politics by disregarding factionalism in choosing his cabinet.

"Every thing depends on the selection of your ministry," Jackson wrote. "In every selection, party and party feelings should be avoided. Now is the time to exterminate the *Monster* called Party spirit. By selecting characters most conspicuous for their probity, Virtue, capacity, and firmness, without any regard to party, you will go far to eradicate those feelings which on former occasions threw so many obstacles in the way of government; and, perhaps, have the *pleasure,* and *honor,* of uniting a people heretofore politically divided. The Chief Magistrate of a great and powerful nation should never indulge in party feelings.... Consult *no party* in your choice."[20]

Monroe, however, continued to cast a wary eye toward the surviving Federalists. He replied to Jackson that for all the diminution of Federalist influence, "still, southern and eastern federalists have been connected together as a party, have acted together heretofore, and altho' their conduct has been different, of late especially, yet the distinction between republicans and federalists, even in the Southern and Middle and Western States, has not been fully done away.... To give effect to free government, and secure it from future danger, ought not its decided friends, who stood firm in the day of trial, to be principally relied on? Would not the association of any of their opponents in the Administration itself wound their feeling, or, at least, of very many of them, to the injury of the republican cause? My impression is that the Administration should rest strongly on the republican party, indulging towards the other a spirit of moderation, and evincing a desire to discriminate between its members, and to bring the whole into the republican fold as quick as possible."[21]

Monroe said the time had not yet arrived to write off the existence of parties, though that would be his eventual goal. His first task, he told Jackson, was to keep fellow Republicans united "by not disgusting them by too hasty an act of liberality to the other party" and doing nothing to assist a Federalist revival. "To accomplish both objects," he wrote, "and thereby exterminate all party divisions in our country, and give new strength and stability to our government, is a great undertaking, not easily executed. I am nevertheless decidedly of opinion that it may be done."[22]

The old party distinctions had become so blurred by now, however, that Monroe had no qualms in choosing the son of the most recent Federalist president, the converted John Quincy Adams, a man steeped in diplomatic experience, to be his secretary of state. And in light of Northern skepticism about continuation of the "Virginia dynasty," Adams's Massachusetts base recommended him as well. Surviving Federalists, putting the best face on things, argued that the Republican Party had become more Federalist in its policies than Jeffersonian. A French diplomat observed: "The government of his country, Federalist or Republican, moves with giant strides toward an extension of strength and power which insensibly changes its nature."[23]

With all the tribulations of party and country through the Madison years, the nation emerged with immense prospects for prosperity at home and new stature in the world. In that sense, Madison's tenure had led the way for what was soon to be called the "Era of Good Feelings" under Monroe. Soon four new states had entered the Union—Indiana, Mississippi, Illinois and Alabama—as settlers continued to move west and south. The nation's population approached 9 million, or more than double the number since Washington's first inauguration. Nearly half still lived in New England and the Middle Atlantic states, and New York was now the largest city. But the westward movement was increasing rapidly, keeping

America predominantly agricultural for all the industrial growth in the Northeast.

For two years, the nation enjoyed peace at home and abroad. With Federalism a spent force at the federal level, Monroe began to welcome other important Federalists into his government. He handed out patronage with little regard to party and generally deferred to the Republican congressional leadership in much the way Madison had done. This led Crawford in 1817 to write apprehensively to Gallatin: "It is certain that the great depression of the Federal party, and their apparent disposition to lose themselves for a time in the council of the nation by uniting in the measures of the Executive, cannot fail to relax the bonds by which the Republican party has been hitherto kept together. Should they pursue this course until the schism shall be completed, it is not easy to foresee the consequences to the Republican party."[24]

Rivalries bred of political ambition also caused friction within Monroe's cabinet. Adams obviously had hopes of following in his father's footsteps to the presidency, an objective also in the eyes of Crawford as treasury secretary and of Clay as House speaker. Clay particularly pushed for American recognition of emerging independent states in South America, to which Monroe was sympathetic but not yet ready to commit the nation.

In 1818, when Jackson, under orders from Monroe to put down hostilities from the Seminole Indians in Georgia, pursued them into Eastern Florida and seized Pensacola, Adams and Clay split on whether the general should be censured for exceeding his authority. But the matter passed without any reprimand, and in subsequent negotiations with Spain, the Adams-Onís Treaty of 1819, finally ratified in 1821, transferred all of Florida to the United States, which agreed to assume up to $5 million in claims of American citizens against Spain. At the same time, it was agreed that Texas would remain Spanish territory and the western boundary of the United States was set at the Pacific Ocean. The spirit and fact of American nationalism continued to flourish. Personal trips to the West by Monroe further encouraged the expansion.

The Era of Good Feelings, however, did not last. With prosperity came much land speculation, financed by state bank loans and eventually by the second federal bank. By 1819, a decline in the European market for American agricultural products and textiles led the Second Bank to start calling in loans and pressuring the state banks to do the same. The result was the panic of 1819, marked by falling commodity prices and depression in the factory system that had blossomed in New England after the War of 1812 with new methods of mass production and cheaper transportation.

For the Republican Party in the South particularly, there was also the entrenched and growing "peculiar institution" of human slavery to deal with. The slavery trade created not only unspeakable conditions for the black families in bondage but also increasing criticism and moral outrage from outside the South. A key to the economy in both North and South was cotton, the Deep South's major and most profitable crop, the harvesting of which was heavily dependent on the existence of slavery. Politically and morally, it would prove to be among the most pivotal issues ever to be faced in the evolution of the modern Democratic Party, and it came to a head in 1819 with the petition of the Missouri Territory to enter the Union as a state.

The Constitution specifically recognized slavery as an institution to be permitted or barred by decision of the individual states. The founders intentionally avoided the issue, specifying that the matter of the migration or importation of slaves should not be addressed at least until 1808. Jefferson was himself a slave owner but preferred not to raise the matter in terms of national policy. By the time Monroe was president, there were eleven slave and eleven free states, and the application of Missouri for admission as a slave state in February 1819 set off a political firestorm. Republican Congressman James Talmadge Jr. of New York proposed an amendment to Missouri's petition that would bar the introduction of additional slaves into the state and provide for the eventual emancipation of those already there.

Southern members of Congress argued, however, that it was within the sovereign rights of each state to decide the question. Northerners noted that the authors of the Constitution had treated slavery as a temporary institution with no indication they intended that it be spread to new states. Republicans, especially in the South, accused the Federalists in the North of stirring up conflict as a means of reviving their staggering party. Jefferson, who had on several occasions condemned human bondage, spoke out from retirement against the Talmadge amendment, charging that Federalist leader Rufus King was "ready to risk the Union for any chance of restoring his party to power and wriggling himself to the head of it."[25]

After much haggling, a compromise was struck in March 1820. Missouri would be admitted to the Union as a slave state and Maine as a free state.[26] Congress also voted that slavery would be "forever prohibited" in all remaining territory acquired in the Louisiana Purchase north of 36° 30' north latitude. John Quincy Adams wrote in his diary that he favored the Missouri Compromise, "believing it to be all that could be effected under the present Constitution, and from extreme unwillingness to put the Union at hazard."[27]

As a Northerner, Adams saw the compromise as fostering more division in the country along sectional lines, noting that the emancipation of all slaves would result in "threatening in its immediate effect that Southern domination which has swayed the Union for the last twenty years."[28] From Monticello, Jefferson wrote ominously: "This momentous question, like a fire-bell in the night, awakened and filled me with terror. I considered it at once as the knell of the Union. It is hushed, indeed, for the moment. But this is a reprieve only, not a final sentence."[29] And later: "All, I fear, do not see the speck on our horizon which is to burst on us as a tornado, sooner or later. The line of division lately marked out between different portions of our confederacy is such as will, never, I fear, be obliterated."[30]

Thus was the first important step taken by a contentious Congress to deal with the one issue that forty years hence was destined, as Jefferson predicted, to split the nation and its politics along sectional lines and threaten its very existence.

Monroe was so secure as the end of his first term approached that a caucus call to all Republican members of Congress to consider the party's 1820 presidential and vice-presidential candidates drew attendance of only about forty. The caucus was adjourned with unanimous approval of a decision in effect not to bother with nominations. By now, more and more states were turning to the popular vote to select presidential electors anyway. Opposition slates for presidential electors were put forward in New York and Pennsylvania, reflecting displeasure with the Missouri Compromise, but Monroe electors prevailed in both states. In the electoral college, he won all but one of the 232 electors, the other going to the junior Adams. His Federalist father, the first Adams president, was among the electors voting for Monroe in what was now essentially a one-party system at the federal level.

That diminution of party competition was fine as far as Monroe was concerned. "Surely our government may get on and prosper without the existence of parties," he wrote to Madison as late as 1822. "I have always considered their existence as the curse of the country." He continued, however, to make important appointments only to fellow Republicans as a demonstration of his own fealty. "The charge of amalgamation is not correctly levelled at me," he wrote.[31] Yet the absence of a strong party leadership hand diminished his influence and leverage with Congress, in Republican control but factionalized. The House more and more looked to the speaker, Henry Clay, for party guidance, in the formulation of his American System and even in foreign policy.

Monroe's second term was marked chiefly by his determination, pushed vigorously by Clay, to support the newly declared independence of Spanish and Portuguese colonies in Latin America and discourage further European colonization in the Western Hemisphere. Adams as secretary of state informed France, Russia, Spain and its allies that the United States opposed any further colonization in the hemisphere. At the same time, the British foreign secretary, George Canning, concerned that Spain might attempt to reassert territorial claims in the New World, proposed that Britain and the United States jointly declare their strong opposition to any such future moves while declaring no designs themselves on Spanish territories.

Adams balked at any such restriction, and also at any joint declaration. He convinced Monroe that an American position standing alone was required in keeping with the young nation's new stature in the hemisphere and the world. What came to be known as the Monroe Doctrine basically told Europe to take care of its own affairs; the Western Hemisphere, backed by the United States, was henceforth off limits to outside colonization. Monroe warned the European powers that "we should consider any attempt on their part to extend their system to any portion of this hemisphere as dangerous to our peace and safety."[32]

Politically, Monroe's eight-year presidential tenure, while it marked the further disintegration of the Federalist Party as a national force and the passing of the first party system, also saw more erosion of presidential leadership in Republican Party policies in favor of congressional influence in them. At the same time, however, the role of Republicans in Congress over the party's presidential nomination waned, with the party congressional caucus only sparsely attended in 1824. Greater attention was paid to the voices of the party in the state legislatures and, in the election itself, of the expanding universe of eligible (white male) voters.

The election of 1824 produced chaos in the Republican ranks. The weakened congressional caucus nominated Crawford, Monroe's secretary of the treasury, to be the party's presidential candidate, giving him 64 of 68 votes, but nearly 150 Republicans in Congress didn't attend. Three other prominent Republicans entered the race on the basis of endorsements from state legislatures or mass meetings of voters. John Quincy Adams, the nationalist and converted Federalist from Massachusetts, was put forward by New England legislators and other supporters; Clay became the candidate of proponents of his American System; Jackson, sent to the Senate by the Tennessee legislature in 1823, rode his popularity as a military hero into the fray, although he himself earlier observed that he was not qualified to be president. A laudatory biography by John Eaton helped recast Jackson as the champion of "the common man," and glowing comments from visiting Revolutionary War hero the Marquis de Lafayette also aided his cause. Calhoun, another presidential candidate for a time, bowed out and became the party's nominee for vice president.

In all this, there was little semblance of party cohesion, discipline, organization or party machinery to advance any candidate in the resulting free-for-all. In addition to the aforementioned candidates, even old Federalist warhorse Rufus King in New York flirted for a time with a candidacy. Adams, adhering to the old tradition of declining to campaign, dismissed reports of the electioneering of others by aloofly declaring, "I only want what is freely bestowed."[33] He pointedly said he didn't want to be obligated to support positions not his own, and he responded to complaints from supporters by saying he was adopting a "Macbeth Policy," quoting Shakespeare from Act 1, Scene 3: "If chance will have me King; why, chance may crown me. Without my stir."[34] Monroe, for his part, declared his neutrality.

Except for the Crawford backers, the congressional endorsement was much demeaned as an elitist "King Caucus" futility amid the expanding public franchise. Some states like Maryland passed resolutions against the caucus and the Western states wanted no part of it, preferring to appeal directly to the voters. In any event, the caucus choice, Crawford, soon saw his candidacy set back when he suffered what first was diagnosed, erroneously, as a paralytic stroke, but he remained in the running.

In New York, supporters of the various candidates connived to bring about results most advantageous to them. Aware that the full field would likely throw the election into the House of Representatives because no one candidate would achieve the majority of electoral votes required by the Constitution, Adams and Crawford backers focused on undercutting Clay, wary of his popularity and political dominance as House speaker. His failure to win sufficient support in New York doomed his chances.

Nationally and in the states, the disintegration of party commitment and electioneering produced an abysmal election turnout of only 25.5 percent, driven mostly by partisan press accounts and harangues and by the personal and sectional appeals of the candidates, most notably Jackson. He ran first in both the popular and electoral votes, but his 99 electoral votes were only a plurality, forcing the election into the House. Adams was second with 84 electoral votes, Crawford third with 41 and Clay fourth with 37. The Constitution having stipulated that only the first three finishers would be eligible for House consideration, with each state delegation casting a single vote, Clay was out in the cold. With Crawford still ailing, the practical choice came down to Jackson or Adams. Meanwhile, Calhoun was elected vice president.

Although Clay had been eliminated from the presidential contest, he remained influential with the electors he had won in three states and found himself aggressively courted by the Jackson and Adams camps. Jackson supporters argued that their man, as the plurality winner of both the popular and electoral votes, deserved his backing. In addition, the legislature of Clay's home state of Kentucky told him to throw his support to Jackson. But Clay saw Jackson as a political rival in the Western states, had questions about his qualifications to be president and doubted his commitment to his American System.

Several times in the weeks before the House convened for the fateful vote on the presidency, Clay met privately with Adams for hours on end, giving rise to speculation that a deal was in the works—most prominently that Adams would make Clay his secretary of state in return for Clay's support in the House vote. Clay, also privately, indicated to friends that his political positions were closer to those of Adams than of Jackson, and that he could not support a military man for president, especially one whose abilities and judgment he questioned.

Jackson supporters could see the handwriting on the wall. The pro-Jackson *Columbian Observer* of Philadelphia ran an anonymous letter in which the writer declared he was "of opinion that men, professing any honorable principles, could not, or would not be transferred, like the planter does his negroes, or the farmer does his horses" for political favor.[35]

On the night before the House was to vote, Adams and Jackson encountered each other at Monroe's last reception as president, and the climate was distinctly cool. Jackson, with a woman on his right arm, said, according to witnesses, "How do you do, Mr. Adams. I give you my left hand, for the right, you see, is devoted to the fair; I hope you are very well, sir." Adams stiffly replied: "Very well, sir; I hope General Jackson is well."[36]

In the end, while steadfastly denying any deal, Clay finally threw his support to the son of the former Federalist president. In the House vote, Adams won 13 state delegations to 7 for Jackson and 4 for Crawford, and was proclaimed the new president. Adams accepted the verdict almost apologetically, saying he would have been willing, indeed would have preferred, another election under the circumstances if the Constitution had so provided, especially because another—Jackson—had been "further recommended by a larger minority of the primary electoral suffrages than mine."

When a House committee of notification led by Daniel Webster brought Adams the news, he handed Webster this long-winded reply in writing: "Could my refusal to accept the trust thus delegated to me give an immediate opportunity to the people to form and to express a nearer approach to unanimity the object of their preference, I should not hesitate to decline the acceptance of that eminent charge and to submit the decision of this momentous question again to their determination."[37]

Jackson was hardly mollified by the observation. The cry of another "corrupt bargain" erupted when, in one of Adams's first presidential actions, he did indeed appoint Clay as his secretary of state. No amount of denials of a deal could quiet the Jacksonians, who already felt they had been robbed of the presidency by a disregard in the House of the demonstrated popular will. Jackson himself raged: "Was there ever witnessed such a bare-faced corruption in any country before?"[38] Jackson said later he had believed before the appointment that Adams was a "virtuous, able and honest man," but "when these strange rumours [of Clay's selection] become facts ... from that moment I withdrew all intercourse with him."[39] Thus did Jackson launch a political war against the new president that would continue for four years, until the next presidential election.

Almost from the start of the presidency of the second Adams, it functioned under a cloud that grew only darker as he encountered congressional resistance and more factionalism in what was left of his adopted party. In his inaugural address, Adams pledged to disregard party differences by "embracing as countrymen and friends" all who could serve with distinction rather than simply "those who bore the badge of common party."[40] And again he made reference to his awareness that he was not the people's popular choice. "Less possessed of your confidence in advance than any of my predecessors," he said, "I am deeply conscious of the prospect that I shall stand more and oftener in need of your indulgence."[41] (It was an acknowledgment not uttered 176 years later when another son of a president also took the oath of office as the choice of fewer voters than cast for another candidate.)

Adams decided to keep all Monroe cabinet ministers who wanted to stay, writing later that to do otherwise "would make the government a perpetual and intermitting scramble for office."[42] He retained an outspoken Jacksonite, John McLean, as postmaster general and even appointed old Federalist Rufus King as ambassador to London. In his first annual address to Congress, Adams set out to put the federal government on a course of greater economic growth with the internal improvements to facilitate it. He also urged Congress to support more exploration of Western territories and, in general, advance Clay's concept of a self-sufficient American System. He suggested creation of a national university and federal support of the arts, literature and science, implying the United States was lagging behind England and France and admonishing Congress, in an infelicitous phrase, not to be "palsied by the will of our constituents."[43]

Such comments drew accusations that the former Federalist was revealing the old traits of aristocracy. Even Jefferson charged Adams with wanting "a single and splendid government of an aristocracy ... riding and ruling over the plundered ploughman and beggared yeomanry."[44]

As time went on, the rhetoric between the Adams camp and its foes became increasingly sharp and personal. Senator Martin Van Buren of New York, now a key Jackson political adviser, was in the vanguard of Adams's critics in Congress, along with Calhoun and the irrepressible and vitriolic John Randolph. Randolph became so abusive of Clay in one speech that Clay challenged him to a duel. Their honor was satisfied when each fired at the other and the only damage inflicted was a bullet hole in Randolph's coat. Adams, for his part, observing Van Buren's behavior, wrote harshly that "he is now acting over the part in the affairs of the Union which Aaron Burr performed in 1799 and 1800: and there is much resemblance of character, manners and even person between the two men."[45]

In the congressional elections of 1826, old Republicans lost ground and foes of Adams gained control of both the House and Senate. His outlook for reelection in 1828 against Jackson, the man who had outdistanced him in popular and electoral vote in 1824 and had not stopped reminding voters of it since then, was grim, and he knew it. In the final year of his term, Adams's foes in Congress, led by Van Buren, pushed through protectionist legislation favorable to Northern manufacturers but also with some provisions damaging to the region. At the same time, it was so hostile to cotton growers in the South dependent on foreign markets that they dubbed it "the tariff of abominations." Adams, loyal to his native North, signed it and thus incurred the wrath of many in both regions, to the political advantage of Jackson.

The second Adams's presidency would prove, indeed, to be only an interim in what soon would be known as the Age of Jackson, marked by the splitting in two of the Republican Party and the development of a second party system. In one camp would be the Clay generation and old party followers under the name National Republicans; in the other, the Jacksonians calling themselves Democratic-Republicans, or just plain Democrats—the direct descendants of the party of the same name today.

President Andrew Jackson's reforms encountered opposition even within his own ranks. This 1831 cartoon shows (left to right) four cabinet members, Secretary of War John Eaton, Secretary of the Navy John Branch, Secretary of State Martin Van Buren and Secretary of the Treasury Samuel Ingham, seeking to desert him.

Chapter 7

JACKSONIAN DEMOCRACY, 1828–1836

ANDREW JACKSON, MILITARY hero turned politician, was of no mind after the 1824 election to accept quietly the decision of the House to ignore the popular will by making John Quincy Adams, converted Federalist, the first minority American president. Returning home by carriage in early 1825 from Washington to Nashville, Jackson had repeatedly been greeted along the way by supporters expressing their ire over the "corrupt bargain" between Adams and Henry Clay they believed had denied Jackson the White House. He assured his followers that the deed would be reversed in the election of 1828.

To that end, the Tennessee legislators who had launched Jackson's political career in 1823 by sending him to the United States Senate, and a year later advanced his first presidential bid, now found themselves with many high-powered political volunteers ready to take over a second Jackson candidacy.

Foremost among these "Jackson men" was Van Buren, who headed the Albany Regency in New York and had organized Crawford's presidential campaign in 1824. As a first critical step, Van Buren in 1827 entered into an alliance with Calhoun, who was still serving as vice president under Adams, to bring together what the New Yorker called "the planters of the South and plain Republicans of the North"[1] to deny Adams a second term. Beyond that, however, Van Buren was out to create a party based more on principle—the old Jeffersonian ideas of liberty and equality—than on personality, one that would last beyond Jackson's presidency. In a sense, this was the embryo from which today's Democratic Party was born.

The phenomenon of Adams's vice president joining the Jackson camp reflected not only Calhoun's disaffection from Adams but also his own political ambition and the shrewd maneuverings of the Jackson managers. Calhoun had given up his own presidential bid in 1824 and settled for the vice presidency, but saw his future going down with Adams in 1828, so he began casting his eyes elsewhere. At the same time, the Jackson camp, concerned that Calhoun might also run against Adams, won Jackson's cooperation in luring the South Carolinian to his own campaign. Jackson, now sixty-one years old, helped float rumors that he was in ill health and if elected would in any event serve only a single term. Calhoun, seeing the possibility of elevation to the presidency as Jackson's vice president or succeeding him as the Jacksonian candidate in 1832, agreed to run for the vice presidency again, on the Jackson ticket.[2]

Van Buren then toured several Southern states enlisting other prominent political figures, including a recuperating Crawford, to the Jackson banner. Also involved were Thomas Hart Benton, a barrel-chested Senate orator from Missouri, Senator John Eaton of Tennessee and some influential newspaper editors, most notably Amos Kendall of Kentucky.

Meanwhile, Adams and Clay, importantly supported by Daniel Webster, were attempting to strengthen their own collaboration looking to the 1828 election. Adams, having left his father's old Federalist Party behind, had now assumed the leadership of the old Republicans, championing central government, a national bank and protective tariffs favored in his native New England. Clay, the leading figure among the younger generation that had come to dominate congressional politics, continued to push his American System, described by Arthur M. Schlesinger Jr. in *The Age of Jackson* as "rebaptized Federalism."[3]

The resultant dichotomy between the "Jackson men" and the "Adams men" was not generally regarded at first as the start of a new two-party system. The principals in both camps all considered themselves Jeffersonian adherents to the same Republican Party that had reduced the Federalist Party to scattered, regional impotency.

However, Van Buren, declaring his intent to achieve "the substantial reorganization of the old Republican party," convened a central committee in Nashville in mid-1827 "for the purpose of corresponding with other

Jackson committees in the different sections of the country."[4] It was can-
didate-oriented, however, rather than ostensibly focused on creating a
new party, although what Van Buren really had in mind was just that.

Adams, as in 1824, shunned personal involvement in the 1828 campaign, continuing to honor the tradition of the previous presidents
against active electioneering in their own behalf. "If my country wants my
services," he observed haughtily, "she must ask for them."[5] Jackson professed to honor the tradition as well, but in the hands of his astute campaign managers he did put in an appearance at a celebration in New
Orleans on the thirteenth anniversary of his victory over the British there,
under the guise of attending a patriotic, rather than a political, affair.

Jackson's public appeal had been amply demonstrated in 1824, and
Van Buren did not hesitate to capitalize on his candidate's standing as a
national military hero, augmented now by his near-successful first venture into presidential politics. In a campaign relatively devoid of lively
issues and with the Jackson camp willingly engaging its man in a popularity and personality contest with the aloof Adams, the competition
proved to be one-sided. Also, taking advantage of Jackson's image as a
rough-hewn backwoodsman—one that his wealth and erudition defied
but did not seem to diminish—his managers broke new ground in dramatic vote-seeking while offering him in a vague way as a reformer.

Even as Van Buren diligently sought support for Jackson from political leaders, he never lost sight of the imperative of rallying the voters as
well. "Those who have wrought great changes in the world," he wrote
later, "never succeeded by gaining over chiefs; but always by exciting the
multitude. The first is the resource of intrigue and produces only secondary results, the second is the resort of genius and transforms the face
of the universe."[6]

Van Buren and associates seized upon Jackson's nickname, "Old Hickory," to construct a campaign built on that image, dubbing local political
organizations Hickory Clubs, raising "Hickory poles" and planting hickory trees at rallies and barbecues. One anti-Jackson newspaper complained: "Planting hickory trees! Odds nuts and drumsticks! What have
hickory trees to do with republicanism and the great contest?"[7]

But the Jacksonians were undeterred in pressing the theme. Soon
drawings of hickory branches and leaves, and likenesses of Jackson himself, were adorning all manner of campaign souvenirs, from badges,
plates, pitchers, even snuffboxes and ladies' hair combs. Inspired by the

popular war hero, the campaign was awash in songs, parades and other hoopla as Jackson's strategists played relentlessly on their man's personal appeal and celebrity.

Adams, even as president, was no match for him with the widening popular electorate, especially as the Jackson camp, reminding voters that Adams once had been a Federalist, tagged him as a "monarchist" and cast the election as a fight between democracy (Jackson) and aristocracy (Adams). It was a pitch that had great resonance now that the decision-making on the presidency was passing from state legislatures to (white) manhood suffrage. With 24 states now in the Union and 18 of them choosing presidential electors by popular vote, and with the population having increased from 5.3 million in 1800 to 12 million, campaigners if not the candidates themselves going directly to the voters was an inevitable development.

In a greater sense than before, citizens felt a larger personal stake in the presidential election, especially with Jackson's own well-promoted appeal as a man of the people amid what came to be called "the rise of the common man."[8] All the new trappings of the campaign also gave it an entertainment quality that captured public attention, and an increased sense of nationhood along with already developed sectional outlooks.

Part of the attraction for citizens as the Adams and Jackson forces reached out to this expanding universe of voters was an unprecedented level of mudslinging and scandal-mongering on both sides. An epidemic of partisan newspapers appeared and entered the fray, particularly in behalf of the Democratic candidate. Adams was accused, for example, of having procured, while he was minister in Moscow, a young American girl for the czar. It turned out that the young woman was the maid to Adams's wife and nurse to his son Charles, and had been routinely introduced to the czar. The Democrats nevertheless dubbed Adams "The Pimp of the Coalition"[9] and also accused him of having had premarital sex with his wife.

One National Republican newspaper, the *Cincinnati Gazette,* topped those allegations with charges that Rachel, the woman who lived with Jackson as his wife, actually was not, and he had lured her away from her legal husband. She had, in fact, been found guilty in a Kentucky court of desertion and adultery some thirty-five years earlier. Jackson's committee in Nashville provided documentation that the woman believed at the time her husband had obtained a divorce, and that she and Jackson had then wed, and had remarried legally after the husband's divorce had been granted. Still, the publisher, Charles Hammond, asked voters: "Ought a convicted adultress and her paramour husband to be placed in the highest offices of this free and christian land?"[10]

Hammond continued his pounding at Jackson, at one point publishing an editorial that said: "General Jackson's mother was a COMMON PROSTITUTE, brought to this country by the British soldiers! She afterward married a MULATTO, with whom she had several children, of which number General JACKSON IS ONE!!!"[11]

Another editor, John Binns of the Philadelphia *Democratic Press,* had circulars printed that bore drawings of six coffins representing militiamen Jackson allegedly had put to death for seeking to return home after their enlistments had been completed. This "Coffin Hand Bill" also had a sketch purporting to show Jackson running a sword cane through the back of a man picking up a stone with which to defend himself, in an incident in which Jackson successfully pleaded self-defense. The handbill observed: "Gentle reader, it is for you to say whether this man, who carried a sword cane, and is willing to run it through the body of any one who may presume to stand in his way, is a fit person to be our President."[12]

Despite all this and more, including charges that Jackson was a heavy-drinking gambler and slave trader, his backwoods Carolina and Tennessee roots, his military record and rough-and-rugged yet dignified appearance won him strongest support in the South and West, and also with factory workers and craftsmen in the East. The Van Buren organization, structured down to the state and local levels as the popular vote now dominated the election of all manner of public offices, overwhelmed the effort on the opposition side. Adams swept his native New England, but it was far from enough. Jackson won every other state except New Jersey, Maryland and Delaware in a turnout of only half the eligible electorate. He captured 56 percent of the popular vote and the electoral college by a margin of 178–83 over Adams.

Yet Jackson entered the presidency as a largely unknown political quantity. His impressive showing in reaching for the White House in 1824 and his success in achieving it in 1828 rested essentially not on any detailed political platform. Rather, what carried the day was his celebrity as a war hero and the personal popularity that stemmed from it, and his colorful résumé. The son of Scotch-Irish immigrants born in poverty in backwoods Carolina, a boy-soldier in the now-distant Revolution with little formal education, he was the first American president not from a genuinely aristocratic family. As such, he was a truly self-made man, lifting himself to considerable wealth as a lawyer, planter, slave owner and land speculator in Tennessee. He owned and lived in a great mansion near Nashville, The Hermitage, and for all his image as a Western frontiersman was a most imposing figure, standing tall and carrying himself almost regally.

At the same time, however, he managed to convey to ordinary Americans in all parts of the expanding country that he was in full concert with "the common man." What soon came to be known as Jacksonian Democracy reflected not only the old Jeffersonian reverence for the agrarian life and those who led it, but also a perception of the people as honest, hard-working, moral and self-reliant. Jackson wrote admiringly of "the real people" whose "success depends upon their own industry and economy," city artisans as well as rural farmers and backwoods hunters, who understood "that they must not expect to become suddenly rich by the fruits of their toil."[13] While lauding all the American "laboring classes" for their "independent spirit, their love of liberty, their intelligence, and their high tone of moral character," he singled out agriculture as "the first and most important occupation of man," contributing "that enduring wealth which is composed of flocks and herds and cultivated farms."[14]

In all this, Jackson pointedly excluded labors focused exclusively or primarily on the making or manipulation of money as opposed to the production of goods by the sweat of the common man's brow. This perspective helped explain his vehement animosity toward the Second National Bank, whose destruction he set out to achieve in 1832 as perhaps the major policy initiative of his presidency.

Opponents saw in Jackson's policies toward the bank and other business and corporate interests the enthroning of a "King Mob" personified in himself. This posture made him loved by one segment of the electorate and hated by the other, in part, as one observer has noted, because "his blunt words and acts assumed the character of moral gestures which forced men to declare themselves, for or against."[15] But Daniel Webster of Massachusetts commented: "People have come five hundred miles to see General Jackson, and they really seem to think that the country has been rescued from some dreadful danger."[16]

While Jacksonian Democracy was a coalescing force among the nation's workingmen, at the same time it was a divisive one, recruiting support through the device of fear of a dominating aristocracy. In later times, what he waged would be called "class warfare," but Jackson seemed to see himself speaking not for a class of Americans but for the whole upstanding populace against a small but erosive cancer on the body politic.

The tactic was politically disarming to the National Republicans, who also had Jeffersonian roots but recognized that the nation had become more complex in terms of its economy and the interrelationship of the states than was true in Jefferson's time. They, too, may have longed for the simpler good old days. But they saw the virtues in Clay's American System, which sought to accommodate the old agrarian strengths and lifestyle of the South, maintained and extended in the frontier West, along with the inevitable development during and after the War of 1812 of the manufacturing economy of the East.

Although Jackson came into the presidency on the strength of his celebrity as the liberator of New Orleans and his personal magnetism rather than any clearly defined agenda, his ingrained Jeffersonian views and his concern that mercantile considerations were a peril to the country inevitably reinforced the new party alignment. Determined to put more of the federal government in the hands of "the real people," he set out to "reform" the civil service by instituting a rotation of bureaucrats that would root out corruption and incompetence—and also political opponents—and substitute party loyalists for jobholders who had a "habit of looking with indifference upon the public interest" or regarded their posts "as a species of property" and "a means of promoting individual interests."[17]

Opponents labeled Jackson's purported cleansing "the spoils system," turning the civil service into a vehicle for the reward of party support and an ongoing means of recruitment for and fealty to the Democratic Party. In fact, during Jackson's eight years in the White House, about 80 percent of federal officeholders kept their jobs, and some of those who lost them were truly incompetent. At the highest levels, he did make Van Buren his secretary of state and relied on other members of his "kitchen cabinet" for advice, although as a strongly opinionated man he essentially made up his own mind on major policies.

In so doing, Jackson did not feel obliged to look to the Democratic-controlled Congress for counsel and support to the degree that most of his predecessors had. One reason was that the congressional caucus no longer was the key to presidential nomination now that the popular vote held sway. Another was that Jackson had been elected with broad support in the various states; many men who came to Congress under his umbrella of popularity did not share all his views as they became known. Sectional and economic differences drove some of these men into the arms of the Adams/Clay camp or, as Jacksonians preferred to think, their leader's strong views helped purify their own ranks.

On one matter, however, Jackson had a free hand because all sections of the white-dominated country favored his action—repressing the Indian tribes who often hindered the Western expansion of white settlers. The Indians, politically powerless in the new nation thrust upon them, posed no political risk to Jackson as he confronted the question of their removal to lands west of the Mississippi more forcefully than any of his predecessors. To the great pleasure of whites in the South and West, Congress in 1830 passed an Indian Removal Act, and Jackson defended the undertaking in rhetoric that sought to soften the insensitivity of his implementation.

Five tribes—the Creeks, Cherokees, Chickasaws, Choctaws and Seminoles, known as the "Five Civilized Nations"—were relocated, with Jackson telling Congress at year's end that "the benevolent policy of the Government ... is approaching a happy consummation. . . . Toward the aborigines of the country no one can indulge a more friendly feeling than myself, or would go further in attempting to reclaim them from their wandering habits and make them a happy, prosperous people."[18] The removal, however, was physically and psychologically brutal to the tribes pulled from their ancestral homes and burial grounds. In 1832, Chief Black Hawk and about a thousand of his tribesmen returned to Illinois and had to be driven back across the Mississippi by soldiers and militiamen.

The Seminoles in Florida behind Chief Osceola also rose up later with assistance from runaway black slaves and had to be suppressed. In Georgia, the Cherokees took legal action and won support from the Supreme Court, but Georgia officials simply ignored the decision and the Cherokees eventually moved west also. Jackson, retaining his "benevolent" rhetoric, was able to inform Congress near the end of his presidency that the removal was nearly completed. "I feel conscious," he proclaimed, "of having done my duty to my red children."[19]

In other matters, however, the pull of sectional interests created political challenges for him. One was the pressure from Western supporters for road construction and other internal improvements, and the opposition to them from Northern urban dwellers and Southern planters who saw little benefit for themselves and resisted paying for them. The matter came to a head in 1830 when Jackson vetoed a bill that would have provided federal money for a sixty-mile road from Maysville, Kentucky, on the Ohio River, to Lexington. If such roads of local rather than national import were to be built, he argued, a constitutional amendment should be required. The veto amounted to a shot across the bow of the National Republicans favoring the road; Jackson had made his point, and later did permit some local construction bills to become law while detouring a potentially major federal intrusion.

A much more critical crisis for the Democratic Party and the nation arose in Southern opposition to the tariff of 1828, which sought to protect Northern manufacturing, as discriminatory against the region. Cotton growers in the South, which had little manufacturing itself, exported two thirds of their crop to Europe and depended heavily on European consumer imports that were subject to high tariffs. This opposition was strongest in South Carolina, where the economy was hard hit by the panic of 1819 and by weakened cotton prices in the face of new competition from Western growers. In addition, in a state in which the black population far exceeded the white, slavery was the key to profitable farming. The heavy hand of the federal government, in this case in imposing the tariff, always fanned fears that the South's "peculiar institution" would be undercut or destroyed altogether. It was a concern that had been heightened in the row over slavery in Missouri and the compromise that had followed, and made South Carolina perhaps the firmest remaining bastion of states' rights.

Into the equation stepped a prominent son of South Carolina, Vice President Calhoun. As an early supporter of protectionism when he was vice president to John Quincy Adams, Calhoun recognized that he was increasingly out of step with his home state. By the time the tariff of 1828 was enacted, he had broken with Adams and had agreed to seek another term as vice president on the Democratic ticket with Jackson. At the same time, obviously with an eye to bolstering his political position in South Carolina and the South generally, he injected himself more forcefully into the tariff debate with an essay called "The South Carolina Exposition and Protest." It appeared with anonymous authorship, but its writer soon became known.

Calhoun boldly proposed the right of nullification, or "interposition," by a state of any federal statute that it regarded to be discriminatory against its people or unconstitutional. The remedy to the oppressive tariff was intended by Calhoun as a step that his and other Southern states might take that was short of secession from the Union. He took as his inspiration the Virginia and Kentucky Resolutions of 1798 penned by Madison and Jefferson, which defended the sovereignty of the states as a protest against the Alien and Sedition Acts that had created such havoc when enforced by the first President Adams.

Calhoun recycled the argument that the states had entered a "compact" in creating a federal government with limited powers, and had not surrendered their sovereignty in the process. To seek nullification of a federal law, he suggested, the people of any state could elect delegates to a state convention that could in turn determine that the law was unconstitutional and thus declare it null and void within its boundaries. Congress then would be faced with the options of agreeing with the nullification or passing a constitutional amendment bestowing power upon the federal government to enact the questioned law, subject to ratification by three fourths of the states.[20]

Early in 1830, with Calhoun silently presiding, the Senate debated his idea. His fellow South Carolinian Robert Y. Hayne presented the argument for nullification, urging Western senators to join him and reminding those from New England that they themselves had considered nullification and even cessation during the War of 1812. But Webster strongly disputed the argument. The federal government, he said, was not a mere agent of the states, but of the Union that had created them, and the arbiter of federal law was the Supreme Court of the land, not any state. Any attempt by a state to put itself above the Union, he warned, would be an act of treason and lead to civil war.[21]

As had also happened in the attempt by Jefferson and Madison to use state sovereignty to trump the Alien and Sedition Acts, other states in the South declined to back Calhoun. Jackson also made his feelings known about the radical proposal. At a dinner commemorating Jefferson's birthday attended by Calhoun soon after the Hayne-Webster debate, Jackson rose and, looking directly at his vice president, offered the famous toast: "Our Federal Union: it must be preserved."[22] Calhoun had gambled and lost; with the secretary of state, Van Buren, himself coveting the presidency and encouraging the rift between Jackson and Calhoun, it was only a matter of time before Calhoun was pushed aside. Jackson subsequently learned that Calhoun, as a member of Monroe's cabinet, had attacked Jackson's military action in Florida in 1818, and he cut Calhoun cold.

Van Buren, witnessing the Jackson-Calhoun split and himself hoping to replace Calhoun as Jackson's running mate in 1832, cleverly proposed his own resignation from the cabinet as part of a shake-up that would also take with it friends of Calhoun. Jackson agreed and proposed to send Van Buren to London as the American ambassador, pending the 1832 election. Calhoun, outraged at Van Buren's maneuvering and distressed about his own sinking political star, got his revenge. With Van Buren already in London, his ambassadorial nomination came before the Senate over which Calhoun presided. Somehow, a tie resulted that Calhoun triumphantly broke, rejecting Van Buren and forcing him home. According to Thomas Hart Benton later, Calhoun declared: "It will kill him, sir, kill him dead. He will never kick, sir, never kick." But Benton happily told him: "You have broken a minister, and elected a Vice President."[23]

Benton proved to be correct. With the congressional grip on presidential nominations greatly weakened and state legislatures also yielding to choices by popular vote, a new mechanism—the national convention—appeared on the scene at which Jackson easily worked his will to obtain Van Buren as his 1832 running mate.

The convention device was first introduced, however, not by the Jackson Democrats nor by the National Republicans, but rather by the nation's first notable third party, calling itself the Anti-Masons. It was born of a case of the suspected murder of one William Morgan, of Batavia, New York, a former member of the secret Society of Freemasons who disappeared as he was about to publish an exposé of the society. Attempts to block its publication created demands for an investigation and ultimately a clamor against Masons in public office, culminating in a call for a convention to nominate a presidential candidate. Delegates from thirteen states met on September 26, 1831, in Baltimore, where former Attorney General William Wirt of Maryland was chosen, despite disclosing that he himself once had been a Mason! The group was largely opposed to Jackson, who also was a Mason, as was Clay for that matter.

The Anti-Masons proved ineffective as a party, with many of its leaders eventually joining the National Republicans against Jackson's reelection; their historical significance rested largely on their role of introducing the national convention as a vehicle of presidential candidate selection. In December 1831 the National Republicans followed the example with their own nominating convention, also in Baltimore, where 168 delegates from 18 states and the District of Columbia unanimously chose Clay to head their ticket and John Sergeant of Pennsylvania as his running mate.

Five months later, 334 Democrats from every state except Missouri met in the same city, merely to concur in the renomination of Jackson by a host of state conventions, and to anoint his handpicked choice for vice president, Van Buren. "The Little Magician," intensifying his efforts to resurrect the old Jeffersonian principles in the party, now had a personal as well as an ideological stake in succeeding.

The nullification issue reached a crisis point in 1832 after Jackson, who had supported some protectionism on taking office, began to soften his position in response to Southern opposition to the high tariffs of 1828. He proposed a new, reduced tariff bill that was designed more to raise federal revenue than to shelter Northern industries, warning manufacturers not to expect the people to "continue permanently to pay high taxes for their benefit."[24]

But the Southerners, and Calhoun in particular, were not placated. He declared he would seek nullification by South Carolina, and was supported by the state legislature. In October it met and called for election of delegates to a state convention in accordance with Calhoun's plan. In late November the convention overwhelmingly declared the tariffs of 1828 and 1832 "unauthorized by the Constitution" and thus "null, void, and no law, nor binding upon this State, its officers or citizens."[25] The state ordinance barred enforcement of the tariffs in South Carolina starting in February 1833, as well as any appeals to federal courts. Any federal attempt to intervene, it said, would bring about the state's secession from the Union. Hayne thereupon resigned from the Senate to become governor of the state and Calhoun quit the vice presidency and accepted appointment to Hayne's seat to lead the nullification fight from the Senate floor.

Jackson was confronted with a crisis of immense proportions, but he had the nation on his side. No other Southern state backed South Carolina's bold and radical action, and Jackson quickly and forcibly threw himself and the power of his office against Calhoun. He declared his readiness to "die with the Union," dispatched a warship and other naval vessels to the Charleston harbor, said he would lead an army against the state himself if necessary, and threatened to have Calhoun hanged for treason.[26] He sent a proclamation to the people of South Carolina declaring "the power to annul a law of the United States, assumed by one State, incompatible with the existence of the Union, contradicted expressly by the letter of the Constitution, unauthorized by its spirit, inconsistent with every principle on which it was founded, and destructive of the great object for which it was formed."[27]

The state legislature defiantly replied with a resolution declaring "that the opinions of the President, in regard to the rights of the States, are erroneous and dangerous, leading not only to the establishment of a consolidated government ... but to the concentration of all powers in the chief executive." It warned "that each state of the Union has the right, whenever it may deem such a course necessary for the preservation of its liberties or vital interests, to secede peaceably from the Union, and that there is no constitutional power in the general government ... to retain by force such state in the Union."[28]

Jackson turned up the heat by calling on Congress to enact a "force bill" that would authorize use of the military to oblige compliance with federal law in any resisting state. South Carolina, finding itself standing alone against Jackson, sought an out and found it in a compromise proposal by Clay in consultation with Calhoun. The tariff schedules so despised by the state would be reduced over a nine-year period until none was higher than 20 percent. Jackson could live with that approach, and when Congress passed the compromise in early March 1833 he signed it.

Two weeks later, the South Carolina convention withdrew its nullification ordinance, but in a final act of meaningless bravado declared the force bill null and void. Jackson ignored the action; he had won the day and in the process set down an important marker regarding the preeminence of the Union. At the same time, Calhoun's departure from the ranks made it easier to sustain the Jeffersonian philosophy of liberty and equality in the Jackson party by weakening the voice for the defense of slavery within it.

The failure of the South Carolina nullification nevertheless drew a battle line of sectionalism on the national map. While the tariff issue did not directly relate to the question of slavery, the South Carolina position was importantly determined by the economic ramifications of the "peculiar institution" throughout the slave-owning Southern states. "It is useless and impracticable to disguise the fact that the South is a permanent minority," Chancellor Harper of South Carolina wrote, "and that there is a sectional majority against it—a majority of different views and interests and little common sympathy.... We are divided into slave-holding and non-slave-holding states and ... this is the broad and marked distinction that must separate us at last."[29] It was a prescient and ominous observation that held dire consequences for the Democratic Party not far down the road.

Meanwhile, Jackson's hostility toward the Second National Bank saw no diminution, especially in the hands of its president, the aristocratic and often contemptuous Nicholas Biddle of Philadelphia, since 1823. Under his stewardship, the bank was extended to twenty-nine branches until it dominated the banking and business communities of the nation. It became the prime depository of government money, issued sound paper currency and kept state banks on a tight rein, controlling 20 percent of all bank notes and one third of all bank deposits and specie.

Jackson's argument against this economic powerhouse was that the bank and Biddle saw as their masters not the public but its big investors, and that both the reality and the potential of corruption were inherent. For just one example, Webster borrowed heavily from the bank while serving as its legal counsel. The bank also had its critics among advocates of both hard money (gold and silver coinage) and soft money (more fluid state bank notes). Understandably, land speculators favored paper money and laboring men distrusted it because of its constant fluctuations, and old Democrats like Jackson and Benton were antagonistic toward both the state and national banks. Jackson once told Biddle point-blank: "I do not dislike your Bank any more than all banks."[30]

Jackson, in his first address to Congress, had already indicated his severe doubts about "both the constitutionality and the expediency of the law creating this bank,"[31] and had figured in the calling of an investigation of the bank by the House. When the inquiry cleared the bank in 1830, Jackson nevertheless resumed his attack, and in 1831, amid talk of rechartering the bank whose mandate was to expire in 1836, Benton took the Senate floor and lashed out at the idea. He opposed rechartering, he said, "because I look upon the bank as an institution too great and powerful to be tolerated in a Government of free and equal laws.... It tends to aggravate the inequality of fortunes; to make the rich richer, and the poor poorer; to multiply nabobs and paupers."[32]

Biddle, however, decided to apply for a new charter in 1832, egged on by Clay, already nominated for president by the National Republicans and seeing it as an issue on which to throw Jackson on the defensive in the election. Webster, who was profiting personally from the bank's existence, also encouraged Biddle. When one House member from Massachusetts sought to modify the charter to assuage Jackson, Clay intervened. "Should Jackson veto it," he proclaimed, "I shall veto him!"[33]

Jackson kept a low profile on the matter as it moved through Congress and finally passed in early July. Van Buren, just returned from London and distressed over the news, rushed to Jackson's bedside, where the president was confined at the time. He was relieved when Jackson took his hand and firmly declared: "The bank, Mr. Van Buren, is trying to kill me, *but I will kill it!*"[34] Thereupon he promptly vetoed the recharter bill in a stinging rebuke written by Amos Kendall and other advisers. The so-called Bank War was on and Clay had his issue.

"The bank is, in fact, but one of the fruits of a system at war with the genius of all our institutions," Jackson wrote during the Bank War, "a system founded upon a political creed the fundamental principle of which is a distrust of the popular will as a safe regulator of political power, and whose ultimate object and inevitable result, should it prevail, is the consolidation of all power in our system in one central government." He deplored "the means by whose silent and secret operation a control would be exercised by the few over the political conduct of the many by first acquiring that control over the labor and earnings of the great body of the people. Wherever this spirit has effected an alliance with political power, tyranny and despotism have been the fruit."[35]

Jackson thus interpreted the bank controversy for the voters in terms of good versus evil, and rallied the masses of them to his banner. The bank seemed to represent to him the worst example of federal intervention into the affairs of the people to the advantage of the already advantaged few. While recognizing that "superior industry, economy and virtue" warranted their rewards," he argued that "when the laws undertake to add to these natural and just advantages artificial distinctions . . . and exclusive privileges to make the rich richer and the potent more powerful, the humble members of society—the farmers, mechanics, the laborers—who have neither the time nor the means of securing like favors for themselves, have a right to complain of the injustice of their Government."[36]

Jackson charged that foreign holders of stock, along with a small number of rich Americans, sought "grants of monopolies and special privileges" that had set "section against section, interest against interest, and man against man, in a fearful commotion which threatens to shake the foundations of the Union."[37]

Biddle, in turn, complained to Clay that Jackson had unleashed "a manifesto of anarchy," and Webster said the veto "manifestly seeks to influence the poor against the rich. It wantonly attacks whole classes of the people, for the purpose of turning against them the prejudices and resentments of other classes."[38] They saw class warfare declared in the veto, although Jackson would insist his views reflected concern for the well-being of the nation at large.

With the bank question thus cast in terms that inflamed the working classes and infuriated defenders of the bank, the presidential campaign between Jackson and Clay became another boisterous affair as in 1828, with all the "Old Hickory" trappings, parades, barbecues and rallies. This time, the Jackson campaign, led by Amos Kendall at the head of a central committee in Washington, brought new coordination to the effort. The Jacksonians charged the National Republicans with corrupting the political process with money supplied in quantity by bank interests; the Clay campaign countered with widely circulated cartoons casting Jackson as "King Andrew I" and decrying "executive usurpation" in his extensive use of the presidential veto.

In the end, however, his opponents were no match for the Jackson personality and image as the protector of the common man. The president was reelected with 55 percent of the vote to only 37 percent for Clay and 8 percent for the Anti-Mason candidate, Wirt. Jackson won 219 electoral votes to 49 for Clay and 7 for Wirt. The Bank War, which might have been Jackson's demise, instead helped deliver him another four years in the presidency.

The Democratic Party was in the van, no longer a splinter of the Jeffersonian Republican Party known formally as the Democratic-Republican Party with the National Republican Party as its rival splinter. With Jackson at the helm as the choice of "the real people," and apostles of democracy like Benton sounding the clarion call against the special interests, the Democratic Party, to Van Buren's delight, took on the egalitarian identity that would mark its character from then on. The National Republicans were left to flounder as essentially an anti-Jackson force, joined in defeat by the remnants of the Anti-Masons and other ineffective minor factions.

Jackson, in his second term, set out to finish off the national bank, whose survival remained the fierce objective of Biddle, who was utterly contemptuous of the president. "This worthy President," Biddle declared at one point, "thinks that because he has scalped Indians and imprisoned judges, he is to have his way with the Bank. He is mistaken."[39] But it was Biddle who had it wrong.

Jackson stopped using the bank for federal deposits, paying government bills out of deposits already made and shifting federal funds to a great number of state banks, soon known as "pet banks." To achieve his destruction of the bank, Jackson had to remove two balking secretaries of the treasury, putting a compliant Roger Taney in the job of withdrawing the federal deposits and shifting them to the favored state banks.

Biddle defensively called in bank loans and pulled back credit. Complaining businessmen who appealed to Jackson for relief were told to "go to Biddle."[40] The battle killed any chance of rechartering the bank, forcing Biddle to seek and obtain a charter from Pennsylvania, but only until 1841, when the bank died, to Jackson's great pleasure.

Businessmen, investors and other anti-Jackson men who had gone down to defeat as National Republicans in 1832, along with remnant Anti-Masons, finally banded together to resist "King Andrew I," the dictator they saw as throttling their credit and choking their prospects for greater growth and profit. They took the name "Whigs" after the British who opposed their monarch in the eighteenth century, but Jackson was no king, and his followers no Tories. He had the great mass of the people behind him, believing him to be their champion against aristocracy and, in the case of Biddle, presumptions of monarchy.

The Whig movement grew rapidly in New England, where the industrial revolution was producing more big manufacturers in the region's shift from its old dominance by shipbuilders and commercial men. Many Southern planters concerned about the threat to slavery inherent in Jackson's successful throttling of nullification in South Carolina also shifted toward the Whigs.

Yet except for a relatively brief time during the fight with Biddle, the Jackson years were marked by lively economic expansion. In the South, cotton prices were high and markets eager to absorb the production. Planters accompanied by their slaves ventured west to new towns and cities that began to develop their own commerce and manufacturing. Land speculation, boosted by Benton's campaign to put public lands within reach of "the common man," and the building of new roads and canals to open the interior all pronounced the prosperity of the Jackson stewardship.

But without a national bank, and with so many state banks issuing paper money, trouble was around the corner. Late in Jackson's second term, he tried to apply a brake by requiring that all federal land purchases be made in gold or silver, a move that arrested sales and caused a sharp drop in inflated land prices. By this time Jackson had made good his promise to wipe out the national debt, and Congress launched a major internal improvements effort through the states. But federal deposits were withdrawn from the pet banks, obliging them to call in their own loans from borrowers. At the same time, an economic downturn in England reduced the demand for cotton and other American crops and products. Jackson was getting out of the presidency just in time.

This outlook, not so apparent at the time, did not diminish the desire of Vice President Van Buren to succeed Jackson, nor the retiring president's wish to have his trusted and effective political strategist do so. The political landscape, at least, looked secure for Jackson's heir apparent, with the newly forming Whig Party nowhere ready to make a serious and coordinated challenge in 1836. But there was one problem: "The Little Magician," not called that in a complimentary sense, was among the most unpopular politicians on the scene at the time.

As the leader of the Albany Regency, what magic he performed was in his ability to survive in the rough-and-tumble of New York politics, combining affability with steely determination and more than a touch of unscrupulousness. He was known for keeping his own counsel, a talent that made him seem remote to many as he rose from the humblest beginnings to state and then national power.

Van Buren, born in the Dutch village of Kinderhook in old New York in 1782, was the son of a tavern keeper who helped his father on the premises and kept his eyes and ears open among the drinking customers. After some formal teaching in a local academy, he joined two local law offices and at his father's side plunged into work for what was then the Republican Party. He climbed rapidly and was elected to the state Senate, where within ten years he gained control of the state party organization. He was regarded as a genius of political strategy but at the same time a man of caution who did not commit himself, perhaps the better to preserve his maneuverability.

His appearance—he was a relatively short, compact man with a high forehead and sandy hair—made him the subject of some chiding. Calhoun, for one, said Van Buren was not "of the race of the lion or the tiger; he belonged to a lower order—the fox; and it would be in vain to expect that he could command the respect or acquire the confidence of those who had so little admiration for the qualities by which he was distinguished."[41] He was, in fact, often also called "the Red Fox of Kinderhook" in recognition of his craftiness.

In New York, Van Buren in short order became the leader of the so-called Bucktail faction of the state party, bent on wresting control from the forces of Governor DeWitt Clinton, still retaining traces of Federalist roots. In 1812 the Bucktails achieved a rewriting of the state convention that brought greater democratic practices to New York politics at the expense of the old aristocratic ways. They swept the Clintonians aside and ensconced the Albany Regency in their place.

Van Buren, elected to the United States Senate, left in the Regency a firm organization fine-tuned to do his bidding, and to keep a strong hold on the Democratic politics of the state at every level. A governing council in Albany of his most trusted associates—men like Silas Wright Jr., William L. Marcy, Edwin Croswell, Benjamin F. Butler and Azariah C. Flagg—directed party politics and doled out patronage to maintain discipline as well as reward the most loyal and effective subordinates.

The domain included the state's judiciary, whose members were appointed through the Regency, and the legislature, where the Regency caucus controlled the timing of bills and their fate. Wright's order to the flock was that "they are safe if they face the enemy, but that the first man we see step to the rear, we cut down."[42] The Regency also financed and controlled the *Albany Argus,* edited by Croswell as the party organ.

Long afterward, Van Buren in his autobiography wrote of the Regency: "I left the service of the State for that of the Federal Government with my friends in full and almost unquestioned possession of the State Government in all its branches, at peace with each other and overflowing with kindly feelings towards myself, and not without hope that I might in the sequel of good conduct be able to realize similar results in the enlarged sphere of action to which I was called."[43]

It was this strong-willed and strong-armed discipline that Van Buren also had brought to directing the election and reelection machinery of Jackson, and was now poised to employ in his own behalf. Jackson almost certainly could have had a third term had he wanted it, but he decided to adhere to the tradition set by Washington. Instead, running Van Buren was widely equated with a bid for a third term for the Jacksonian Democracy.

Van Buren approached the 1836 presidential election with the Democratic nomination already in hand. Jackson had seen to that by calling the party's nominating convention in May 1835, again in Baltimore. Van Buren was chosen unanimously on the first ballot, despite considerable dissatisfaction with the way his nomination had been jammed down the delegates' throats. After all, Jackson had emphasized from the beginning of his own party leadership that its power derived from the will of the people, and that the convention was intended to be a vehicle to hear and implement the people's choice. Van Buren hardly fit that description, as the head of a New York political machine and as a somewhat cloaked figure behind the Jackson throne.

One outspoken and ambitious but singularly unimpressive critic of Van Buren, Richard M. Johnson of Kentucky, whose main claim to fame was that he shot Tecumseh in the War of 1812, was removed from presidential contention by the expedient of making him Van Buren's running mate. John Catron of Tennessee told Jackson that Johnson's fathering of two daughters by a mulatto mistress made him "affirmatively odious" to the South. The man, he said, "wants capacity, a fact that is generally known and universally admitted. . . . I pray you to assure our friends that the humblest of us do not believe that a lucky random shot, even if it did hit Tecumseh, qualifies a man for Vice President."[44] But Johnson could be sold as a military hero in the Jackson mode. Such was the state to which the vice presidency had already sunk in the judgment of the ticket-makers.

For all of Van Buren's ambitions to head a party of principle rather than of personality, the convention approved an address to the people, in what later would be called a party platform, that was a paean to the recent Jackson and past Jeffersonian years, with eighteen mentions of Old Hickory and a total of twenty-six of the Virginia dynasty of Jefferson, Madison and Monroe. In a confirmation that the convention had been obliged to swallow a distasteful pill, Van Buren was mentioned only once, in urging fellow Democrats to put aside "personal animosities or personal preferences" and accept him as "a lesser evil."[45]

The anti-Jacksonian forces, not yet effectively coalesced into what came to be the Whig Party in the second party system, thrashed about in their opposition. Daniel Webster entered the lists as the nominee of a

Massachusetts convention. Two others, John McLean of Ohio and Clay, awaited a public clamor for their candidacies that never came. A Tennessee senator, Hugh Lawson White, who had broken with Jackson, was advanced by a group of home-state congressmen but declined to take the Whig label, finally winning the endorsement of the Tennessee legislature but little else.

Practically from nowhere came another prospective candidate from Ohio who, like Johnson, had a military background that would enable him to appropriate the Jackson image. Indeed, General William Henry Harrison had been commander at the Battle of the Thames in which Tecumseh was shot by Johnson, and he publicly expressed displeasure with the way Johnson sought to magnify his role in the fight. Harrison, a former Indiana territorial governor and Ohio congressman and senator, was more in the hero tradition of Jackson than Johnson was, and soon a groundswell developed in Ohio for him as a presidential candidate.

Before long, Harrison became the subject of political parades and rallies throughout the Midwest, and groups of Whigs and Anti-Masons endorsed him in New York, New Jersey, Pennsylvania, Delaware, Maryland and even Vermont. He spurned an overture to be Webster's running mate and became part of a disorganized anti-Jackson strategy to deny Van Buren an electoral vote majority and throw the election into the House. No national nominating convention was held; no vice-presidential nomination was made. Instead, Webster in New England, White in the South and Harrison in the East and West ran as sectional candidates with little to no coordination.

John Quincy Adams, for one, washed his hands of the mess. "The remarkable character of this election," he said, "is that all the candidates are at most third-rate men." He called White and Harrison "men of straw" for sacrifice "as the Israelites set up a calf, and as the Egyptians worshipped oxen and monkeys."[46]

As in the past, the candidates eschewed personal campaigning as such, but they took advantage of invitations to fund-raising dinners to make speeches outlining their positions. In the wake of Jackson's success as a candidate of the "real people," the others also took on the trappings of their champion while political committees in the various states organized diligently in their behalf. Harrison for one declared that "I did not bring myself forward; my friends did not bring me forward. I was brought forward by the Spontaneous Will of the People."[47]

Van Buren, laboring under the reputation of excessive ambition, stayed home, but Jackson campaigned for him, thereby reinforcing the impression that a Van Buren presidency would, in effect, be a third term for Jackson. One young Whig leader, William H. Seward of New York, tried to use it against Van Buren by describing him in print as "a crawling reptile, whose only claim was that he had inveigled the confidence of a credulous, blind, dotard, old man."[48] But it was to no avail.

In the end, Van Buren won a bare majority of the popular vote—50.9 percent to 49.1 percent for the others combined. His electoral vote, however, was decisive—170 to 73 for Harrison, 26 for White and a pathetic 14 for Webster, isolated in Massachusetts. South Carolina, still irate over Jackson's stiff rejection of tariff nullification, gave its 11 electoral votes to Senator Willie P. Mangum of North Carolina.

Yet Jacksonian Democracy without Jackson was not the same for the voters. With a scattershot strategy, and against the vaunted Jacksonian organization, the still-forming Whigs had come within an eyelash of forcing the election into the House, where they hoped Van Buren's unpopularity would keep him from the White House. The Whigs—and the invigorated Harrison—looked ahead to the 1840 election as their chance to end the Age of Jackson.

Chapter 8

JACKSONIANISM WITHOUT JACKSON, 1837–1844

THE DEMOCRATIC PARTY that Van Buren inherited from Jackson was to a considerable degree of his own making, in the formative stages at least. But it was Jackson's firm stewardship and broad appeal that had made it into a truly national party. Through the mechanism of the national convention, he had taken away the dominant role of the congressional party caucus in choosing candidates and placed it in the hands of a broader collection of politicians at the local and state as well as federal levels. The state legislatures, too, had to take a back seat in the process to the will of the "real people," at least as expressed through convention-going party leaders.

Jackson had also taken advantage of the expanded electorate that resulted from immigration, a widening of voter eligibility in many states and the growth of the Union to twenty-four states by 1824. Just as Jefferson in his day had labored, amid a much more restrictive electorate, to rally farmers against the Federalist aristocracy, Jackson had enlisted the discontented against the comfortably entrenched. He had successfully pitted the poor against the rich, the immigrants and other workers against the entrepreneurs, the debtors against the speculators and bankers, the farmers of the South and the frontiersmen of the West against the established power-wielders of the East.

In waging and winning the Bank War, Jackson also left Van Buren a federal government that, while continuing to espouse the Jeffersonian

A DEMOCRATIC VOTER

In 1836, Democratic factions in New York vied for the Irish immigrant vote. This cartoon shows Tammany Hall and Locofocos soliciting an Irishman who says, "As I'm a hindependent Helector, I means to give my Wote according to conscience and him as Tips most!"

ideal of states' rights, emphatically declared its responsibility to intervene in behalf of the common good when the forces of privilege overreached acceptable bounds. "It is the duty of every government," Jackson wrote in his Farewell Address, "so to regulate its currency so as to protect this numerous [working] class as far as practicable from the impositions of avarice and fraud," and to bar "the paper money system" from functioning as "an engine to undermine your free institutions."[1]

The question was, however, whether Van Buren, the calculating Easterner, lacking the trust and support Jackson had enjoyed inside and outside the now-bolstered party, could use his fabled political skills to rally these forces behind himself in place of the Scotch-Irish military hero turned populist champion. This test came early in his new administration as his fiscal policies, amid rampant speculation in the absence of a national bank system, threw the country into new economic turmoil.

During Jackson's last year in office, he had issued a so-called Specie Circular in which he ordered federal land offices to accept only gold and silver in payment for public lands—a severe blow to land speculators, causing sales and prices to tumble. At the soon-to-retire president's urging, Congress also had voted distribution of millions of federal dollars to the states for internal improvement, encouraging them to initiate projects that exceeded their own abilities to finance. Meanwhile, hard economic times in England led to curtailed British investment in America, especially in the importing of cotton.

Only weeks after Van Buren was sworn in as president, New York banks halted specie payments and curtailed loans, triggering similar action by other banks across the country and runs on them that culminated in the panic of 1837.[2] By 1839 the country was in its worst depression ever, with banks, businesses and factories closing their doors amid soaring unemployment. The funds to the states for internal improvements were cut off and Van Buren continued the hard-money policy embraced by Jackson, refusing new demands for chartering a new national bank.

In so doing, Van Buren allied himself with the most radical anti-bank forces of the time in New York, known as "Locofocos." The name came from an incident in which the radicals, faced with the threat of having a meeting thrown into darkness by political opponents, struck friction matches—known as Locofocos—to resume their meeting.[3] They wanted federal deposits barred from all private banks, and in 1840 Van Buren obliged. He got Congress to pass an Independent Treasury Act creating state depositories for federal money and "free banks," as distinguished from the powerful private interests of the Eastern states.

In short order, the political advantage that had accrued to Van Buren from his close association with Jackson was sharply eroded by the economic distress, and by a much more organized and determined Whig opposition. It was now led by a crafty New York political operative, Thurlow Weed, whose skills had been honed by battles against Van Buren's Albany Regency.

Van Buren also encountered trouble in foreign policy. A rebel insurrection in eastern Canada in 1837, aided by Americans along the border, brought a Canadian response that led to one American death and the burning of an American steamer, the *Caroline,* carrying supplies to the rebels. The U.S. demand for reparations was ignored by the British, and a year later a boundary dispute between Maine and Canada briefly flared into violence.

The Whigs took to calling the beleaguered president "Martin Van Ruin."[4] And, encouraged by the 1836 showing of General Harrison against him, by 1839 they had struck on the idea of remaking Harrison more in Jackson's image, taking a page from the Jacksonians' political playbook of turning a military hero into a president.

In the first Whig national convention, in Harrisburg, Pennsylvania, in late 1839, the party through the machinations of Weed and allies shunted Henry Clay aside and nominated Harrison, the hero of the Battle of Tippecanoe over the Indians and of the Battle of the Thames over the British. When a Democratic editor in Baltimore mockingly wrote that Harrison, who was descended from an old aristocratic Virginia family and had settled into the life of a country squire in Ohio, would be happy sipping hard cider in a log cabin, the Whigs seized on the caricature. Soon he was being offered as "Old Tippecanoe" and contrasted with an aristocratic, dandified, well-manicured Van Buren, who had come from beginnings much more humble than Harrison's.

The 1840 presidential campaign went downhill from there, with log cabins and jugs of hard cider advanced as symbols for Harrison in torchlight parades, rallies and barbecues across the land. Another Harrison motto, stamped on bronze and copper medallions, proclaimed: "He leaves the plow to serve the country."[5] The old general was even persuaded at occasional public appearances to lift a cider jug and take a gulp or two for the edification of his audience.[6] If the nation was experiencing the rise of the common man, Weed was determined to have his candidate seen as one himself.

Nominated as Harrison's running mate was a recently converted Democrat, John Tyler of Virginia, a close friend of Clay chosen in part to assuage the disappointed and irate loser. Tyler had opposed Jackson on nullification and bank policy, and was seen as a magnet for Southern support to the ticket. With the Virginia dynasty of presidents frustrated by the anticipated Democratic renomination of New Yorker Van Buren, the Democratic Richmond Junto split off and threw its weight behind Tyler as Harrison's partner on the Whig ticket. The slogan became "Tippecanoe and Tyler Too,"[7] with the Whigs also singing, "Van, Van is a used up man."[8]

The Democratic convention in Baltimore in May 1840, at which the party's name was formally changed from Democratic-Republican, unanimously put Van Buren at the top of its ticket again. But it pointedly nominated no vice-presidential candidate, avoiding official embrace of Richard Johnson, who had conspicuously been subordinate to Harrison on the battlefield that was Johnson's main claim to fame.

Taking another page from the Democrats' book, the Whigs established a national campaign headquarters in Washington. It sent out reams of Harrison propaganda to local Tippecanoe Clubs, which in turn dispatched coonskin-capped surrogate speakers to the hinterlands, preaching the folksy new party line. Even Clay was induced to tell voters their choice was "between the log cabin and the palace, between hard cider and champagne."[9]

There was no end to the gimmicks dreamed up by the heretofore staid Whigs, now liberated by having their own "common man" at the head of their ticket. In Cleveland, they assembled a thick ball of tin and pushed it from town to town to a Whig convention in the state capital of Columbus, singing as they went: "As rolls the ball, Van's reign does fall, And may he look to Kinderhook."[10] The Democrats unwisely kissed off the barrage as transparent hokum. Jackson himself in retirement observed: "The Log Cabin hard cider and coon humbuggery is doing us a great service."[11]

Amos Kendall, running Van Buren's campaign, turned out lofty statements about the perils of hard money and the private banks, but they floated harmlessly above the low-denominator rhetoric of what henceforth would be known as the Log Cabin Campaign. Jacksonianism without Jackson was dealt a crushing defeat at the polls: Harrison received 234 electoral votes to only 60 for Van Buren. The popular vote, however, was much closer—Harrison 52.8 percent, Van Buren 46.8 percent, in a record turnout. Although Van Buren lost, he amassed half as many votes again as he had won in 1836. Indeed, the Democratic Party star was hardly in eclipse; in the next congressional elections, the party won a majority of nearly two to one in the House.

More than demonstrating the appeal of the Whig Party or the death of Jacksonianism, the huge turnout of nearly 80 percent of all eligible (white male) voters was a commentary on the effectiveness of political electioneering as public entertainment. This was particularly so as the franchise shifted more from the landholding gentry to that common man first identified by Jackson and adopted, at least for election purposes, by the Whigs.

Not reflected in the results of the presidential election of 1840, but surfacing for the first time as a factor that before long would come to dominate and then imperil the very life of the Democratic Party, was the issue of slavery. A relatively small but intense group of abolitionists, formed into a Liberty Party, nominated James G. Birney of Michigan, a onetime Southern slaveholder, for president. He received only 2.3 percent of the popular vote and no electoral votes, but his candidacy was the political embryo of a movement in the North that was destined to shake the Democratic Party to its core.

Since the days of the founding fathers the thought of abolishing slavery in America had been submerged out of an obvious recognition of its political sensitivity, and its predictable economic impact on the South. Jefferson himself, while continuing to be a slave owner, spoke and wrote of it as an evil and even, as already noted, sought unsuccessfully to have the "peculiar institution" banished in his own state of Virginia. But as a national issue, he and most other major political figures after him recognized the explosive nature of abolitionist talk and determined that it was prudent if not morally justifiable to avoid it.

Nevertheless, certain religious groups like the Quakers pursued antislavery activities, achieving abolition widely in the North and agitating for such remedies as emancipation accompanied by forced colonization of the freed blacks back to Africa. In 1817 abolitionists in the North and South formed the American Colonization Society, and five years later the first settlement of freed blacks from the United States was created in Liberia.[12] Eventually, however, the notion of colonization faltered because of the unwillingness of many blacks to emigrate, and because it was seen by many abolitionists as no more than a safety valve for an unacceptable abomination in Dixie. Among those who continued to favor the idea, however, was a young Whig from backwoods Illinois named Abraham Lincoln.

One of the first important voices for emancipation and colonization was that of a Quaker from New Jersey, Benjamin Lundy, who organized anti-slavery groups in several Upper South states and edited a newspaper called *The Genius of Universal Emancipation* in Baltimore, with William Lloyd Garrison of Boston as a crusading writer. One Garrison editorial got him arrested and briefly imprisoned, after which he returned to Boston and began a weekly paper, *The Liberator,* that called for complete abolition without colonization. "I *will* be as harsh as truth, and as uncompromising as justice," he wrote in its first issue. "On this subject, I do not wish to think, or speak, or write with moderation. . . . I am in earnest—I will not equivocate—I will not excuse—I will not retreat a single inch—AND I WILL BE HEARD."[13]

In 1832, Garrison organized the New England Anti-Slavery Society and the next year joined in creating the American Anti-Slavery Society. Other staunch abolitionists, including Theodore Dwight Weld, joined the effort and in time Garrison, who pushed for full participation by women and was committed to nonviolent protest, withdrew and formed his own society. Also prominently participating were free blacks, including Frederick Douglass, an escaped Maryland slave who became the most outspoken leader of American blacks of the time.[14]

Anti-slavery efforts in Southern states were largely futile and became principally a Northern undertaking. The expansion of slavery into the West fueled the intensity of the crusade, especially among Northern white farmers who feared increased competition from slave labor in the Western states. The growing controversy over slavery put a severe strain on the North-South alliance that Van Buren had so diligently put together. Consequently, he labored throughout his administration to reassure Southern Democrats that their way of life built on the "peculiar institution" was best protected within the party.

When abolitionists in 1834 and 1835 began to petition Congress to abolish slavery in the District of Columbia, and to blanket the South with abolitionist literature, Van Buren was involved in gaining congressional adoption of a "gag rule" requiring the immediate tabling of all such anti-slavery petitions.[15] In 1835, when Jackson's postmaster general, Amos Kendall, ordered his subordinates in the South to seize all abolitionist literature, Van Buren as vice president cast the deciding vote in a Calhoun resolution that required such seizure.

But other developments kept the slavery issue in the forefront. In 1836 settlers in Texas, many of them transplanted Americans, declared their independence from Mexico, defeated the Mexican army in the Battle of San Jacinto and proclaimed a new Republic of Texas. Its president, Sam Houston, began negotiations for annexation by the United States, but Jackson, though he heartily approved, held off completion of the deal in deference to President-elect Van Buren, who thereupon declined to proceed. The pertinent question was whether Texas, where slavery existed, would trigger with an application for statehood a major controversy over extending the "peculiar institution" into new American territory.

The core of the opposition to the abolitionists, however, beyond the economic rationalizations, was blatant racial prejudice. In the North as well as in the South, mobs persecuted militant abolitionists and free blacks, and in Alton, Illinois, in 1837, an anti-slavery editor, Elijah Lovejoy, was murdered by a mob.

Defenders of slavery in the South offered apologist arguments, such as the observation in 1837 by Senator Calhoun: "I hold that in the present state of civilization, where two races of different origin, and distinguished by color and other physical differences, as well as intellectual, are brought together, the relation now existing in the slaveholding states between the two is, instead of an evil, a good—a positive good."[16]

Another defender from the floor of the Virginia legislature had this to say on the matter in 1832: "We have no hesitation in affirming, that throughout the whole slaveholding country, the slaves of a good master are his warmest, most constant, and most devoted friends; they have been accustomed to look up to him as their supporter, director and defender. Every one acquainted with southern slaves, knows that the slave rejoices in the elevation and prosperity of his master. . . . [We] have no doubt that they form the happiest portion of our society. A merrier being does not exist on the face of the globe, than the negro slave of the United States. . . . Why, then, if the slave is happy . . . should we endeavor to disturb his contentment by infusing into his mind a vain and indefinite desire for liberty—a something which he cannot comprehend, and which must inevitably dry up the very sources of his happiness? . . . Let the wily philanthropist but come and whisper into the ears of such a slave that his situation is degrading and his lot a miserable one . . . and that moment, like the serpent that entered the garden of Eden, he destroys his happiness and his usefulness."[17]

The chief argument of most abolitionists, aware that the Constitution made no provision for ending slavery, was that slavery was a sin against morality and a denial of the "unalienable rights" endowed by the Creator on all men according to the Declaration of Independence. To obtain them, many advocates frustrated by the limited effectiveness of moral suasion eventually turned to political action.

In January 1837 former President John Quincy Adams, now back in the House of Representatives, sought to contest the "gag rule" passed the previous year in the House barring consideration of any matter whatever relating to slavery or its abolition. Armed with a host of petitions from his Massachusetts constituents to end slavery in the District of Columbia, Adams was first voted down, but he proceeded to defy the gag by reading the language of one of the petitions as part of his motion.

Ignoring orders from the speaker, James K. Polk, to desist and be seated, Adams, over roars of objection from Southern colleagues, declared that he did "most earnestly petition your honorable body immediately [to] abolish slavery in the District of Columbia—" Polk interrupted: "Take your seat!" Adams, as he sat down, continued reading: "and to declare every human being free who sets foot upon its soil."[18]

Adams was ruled out of order and his petitions were tabled in keeping with the gag rule. But his gesture confronted the House not only with the slavery issue but also with the right to petition, in an embarrassing episode for the federal legislature. Later, when Adams resumed his call for abolition in the nation's capital, Southern members walked off the House floor. Calhoun offered a series of resolutions declaring slavery to be a state matter under the Constitution and leaving to Congress the matter of slavery in the District, and then forbidding it.

Van Buren, pressed to take a position on the subject, concluded that states could decide on the fate of slavery in their own borders only, and that under the Constitution Congress had no power to interfere there or in the District. He thus put himself in alliance with Calhoun in their mutual desire to keep slavery off the party and national agendas.

By 1840, however, the American Anti-Slavery Society had about 2,000 local branches in the North with nearly 200,000 members, even as the Liberty Party was formed and ran Birney as its presidential candidate. The society provided an outlet for abolitionist sentiment, though not yet a politically effective one. Nevertheless, as Ralph M. Goldman observed in *Dilemma and Destiny: The Democratic Party in America*, in the early efforts to end slavery in the District of Columbia, "the abolitionist camel was poking its nose under the tent."[19]

To Van Buren, architect of the North-South alliance that brought Jacksonian Democracy into political reality, the camel was an unwelcome intruder. It underscored a basic split among the Jacksonians between those, mostly in the North, who looked upon black slaves as human beings not to be held in bondage forever and those, mostly in the South, who saw them as property and a basic ingredient in the Southern economic and social way of life. The split had the practical effect over the next two decades of producing Democratic presidential candidates known as "Northern men with Southern principles," or "doughfaces," who could straddle the sectionalism and the ideology that threatened to destroy the party.[20]

Van Buren's defeat at the hands of Harrison and the Whigs after "Jackson's third term" appeared at first to signal the end of Jacksonianism, but fate and the residual Democratic sentiments of John Tyler proved otherwise. The sixty-eight-year-old Harrison, plodding bareheaded through an inaugural address of nearly two hours on a chilling, wind-blown day, contracted pneumonia and died exactly one month later, elevating Tyler, the former Democrat, to the presidency.

Tyler was at his home in Williamsburg at the moment of Harrison's death and did not learn of it until the next morning. He headed off to Washington, where two days later he was sworn in as president by a U.S. District Court judge, rendering moot a potential question as to whether the Constitution meant for an ascending vice president to become president or just acting president. Article II, Section 1 said somewhat ambiguously only that in the event of a president's "death, resignation, or inability to discharge the powers and duties of the said office, the same shall devolve on the Vice-President."[21] Did the words "the same" refer to the office itself or simply the powers and duties?

Tyler allowed no time or opportunity for debate. Having already taken an oath to uphold the Constitution as vice president, he asserted to the judge that he was qualified to assume the presidency with no additional oath. Nevertheless, he asked that the oath be readministered "as doubts may arise, and for greater caution."²² The judge signed an affidavit to that effect in case anyone challenged Tyler's legitimacy as president. Because Harrison at the time of his inauguration had pledged to serve only one term, other Whig leaders like Clay had been looking ahead to making another presidential bid themselves four years down the road. Now, suddenly, that road appeared blocked by Tyler, only recently a Whig.

Clay set out to jump-start his American System agenda, introducing legislation to sell public lands to finance internal improvements and offering squatters cheap prices. Tyler, who was not about to let Clay set policy for his administration, used the presidential veto to reject much of Clay's agenda, demonstrating that he had not completely abandoned his old Democratic–and Jacksonian–principles. When Clay pushed restoration of a national bank through the Senate, Tyler wasted no time vetoing the attempt. Clay tried again and Tyler used his veto again. Efforts by Clay to pass a constitutional amendment restricting the president's veto power failed, and in 1842 the frustrated Kentuckian resigned from the Senate with his eye on the Whig presidential nomination in 1844. The Whigs were beside themselves with the turn of destiny that had, in their minds at least, put another Democrat in the White House.²³

The turmoil created by Tyler's independence and Clay's frustration gave the Democrats a foothold for regaining national power in 1844. Whigs in Congress declared Tyler persona non grata in their party and most of his Whig cabinet resigned, except for Secretary of State Daniel Webster, who was engaged in critical negotiations with the British over their interference with the American slave trade.

In 1841 slaves being transported from Virginia to New Orleans aboard the American brig *Creole* mutinied and sailed the ship to the Bahamas, where the British let them go free. Webster, at the insistence of Southern slave owners, demanded their return. The controversy ended in the Webster-Ashburton Treaty of 1842, with the British expressing regret for not having offered an immediate explanation and apology for the incident, but not returning the mutineers. The treaty itself settled disputes on the border between Maine and Canada. That done, Webster also quit the Tyler cabinet and was replaced by Abel P. Upshur.

Thomas Hart Benton accurately described Tyler as "the president without a party," but Tyler pressed on to salvage some achievement in his troubled presidency. When Upshur was killed in an explosion at sea, he was replaced as secretary of state by Calhoun, who was instructed to achieve the annexation of Texas before Tyler's term expired in 1845. It was an order to which Calhoun wholeheartedly responded, seeing Texas as the next slave state. The new Republic of Texas, frustrated by Van Buren's unwillingness to address the matter, in 1838 had turned to the British for recognition as an independent nation and ally in the Western Hemisphere. That initiative gave Tyler a special incentive to negotiate on annexation and statehood, and with it the question about the further extension of slavery.

More than territorial expansion was in Tyler's mind as he looked toward Texas. Hopelessly alienated from the Whigs and the Van Buren wing of his old home, the Democratic Party, Tyler began to shore up his cabinet with Democrats and to lure more popular Southern Democratic support with the promise of Texas annexation. Two important allies, Robert J. Walker, "The Wizard of Mississippi," and Henry Wise of Virginia, obtained a secret letter from Jackson calling for annexation. Meanwhile, Tyler was reported to be planning a convention of his own in Baltimore in 1844 at the same time as the Democratic convention, to persuade his old party to make him its nominee, with the Jackson letter as his trump card.

In April 1844, Calhoun finally reached agreement with Texas on an annexation treaty and Tyler submitted it to the Senate for ratification. But Calhoun, in his determination that Texas be a slaveholding state, wrote the British minister implying that annexation was essential to the preservation of slavery. When abolitionists learned of the note, they bitterly opposed the deal, as did Van Buren, trying to assuage Northern Democrats. In what amounted to a stop–Van Buren strategy by Walker, the fate of Texas became a political football and, added to fears that annexation might bring war with Mexico, the Senate killed ratification, 35 of 51 senators voting against it.[24]

By now, the nose of the abolitionist camel was much deeper into the Democratic Party tent. Van Buren strained to maintain the North-South alliance in the face of increasing Southern concern that the party of Jackson and Van Buren was surrendering to the abolitionist sentiment of the North. In 1842 the Supreme Court had ruled that the Fugitive Slave Act of 1793 was constitutional, but that states could prohibit their officers from enforcing it within their boundaries. Several Northern states passed "personal liberty laws" that said individuals could not be forced to assist in the capture and return of fugitive slaves.[25]

While most Northerners accepted the idea that no federal action could abolish slavery in states where it already existed, they agreed with the abolitionists that it should not be spread to new states and territories. They were motivated, however, as much by a desire to protect the new Western regions for free white farmers as out of concern about the exploitation of the black slaves. The feeling was intensified as the American frontier also moved onward toward the Rocky Mountains, Oregon and California, spurred by an eager migration of farmers, fur trappers, panners for gold and religious missionaries, and driven by an intensified American nationalism called Manifest Destiny.

The regions of the Northern Rockies and Oregon, explored by Lewis and Clark in the early 1800s, and California, home of a Spanish network of Franciscan missions even earlier, offered another vast expanse for American settlement—and possible slavery. What was known unofficially as the Oregon Territory was the subject of competing claims by the British on the basis of Sir Francis Drake's discovery of the Oregon coast in 1579 and later land explorers, and the Americans. Protestant and Catholic missionaries in the 1830s and early 1840s made the long trek from the East in covered wagons, bent on bringing Christianity to the native heathens in the whole Far West region.

Included were the Mormons, who had left their original base in upstate New York in the early 1830s under the leadership of Joseph Smith and had settled by turns first in Ohio, Missouri and then Illinois. In 1843, Smith reported a revelation instructing his people to practice polygamy, causing a split in the Mormon Church and his arrest and jailing. The next year, he was pulled from the jail and murdered by an anti-Mormon mob, and Brigham Young assumed control, leading most of the Mormon community across Iowa and eventually to the Great Salt Lake in quest of religious and political freedom, in a separate nation to be called Deseret.[26] While Mormons did not practice slavery, they did exclude blacks from their church.

As the 1844 election approached, the growing pressures for the abolition of slavery and the pursuit of Manifest Destiny posed a dilemma for both Democrats and Whigs, striving to hold together their shaky sectional and philosophical coalitions. Van Buren, though defeated for reelection in 1840, remained the titular head of the Democratic Party and was considered the clear favorite to be chosen his party's standard-bearer again. The same was true for Henry Clay as the Whig candidate. Rejected in 1840 in favor of his party's infatuation with military hero Harrison, Clay represented a return to the true Whig faith after the party's unhappy experience with Tyler, who had reverted to his Democratic ways upon inheriting the presidency after Harrison's untimely death, and had lost all chance of nomination. Clay, betrayed once by his party, was deemed entitled to his chance.

Having resigned from the Senate to focus on the next Whig presidential nomination, Clay openly bucked the old admonition against campaigning for himself by making a trip in late 1843 and early 1844 through Virginia, North and South Carolina and Georgia, accepting speaking engagements along the way. He talked up his American System, including advocacy of another national bank, higher tariffs and internal improvements, but said nothing about the annexation of Texas. Van Buren, too, avoided the sectionally divisive matter.

In late April 1844, however, as Tyler continued to seek annexation in the final year of his presidency, Clay and Van Buren suddenly sent letters to Washington newspapers laying out their opposition. They apparently hoped to keep the controversial issue out of the approaching campaign in which they expected to face each other.

Both parties held their conventions in Baltimore in May, with the Whigs first. Clay being the obvious choice, the party that had made Harrison into a Jackson clone with his log cabin and hard cider campaign did the best it could with the erudite Kentuckian by adding to his usual nicknames, "Prince Hal" and "Harry of the West," a new monicker: "The Old Coon." Caged live raccoons and "coon" dolls populated the city, just as Hickory poles had adorned Jackson rallies. Clay was nominated by acclamation and a platform was approved that made no mention of Texas. His late declaration against annexation seemed not to deter the enthusiastic convention delegates, sensing victory at last for him in his third presidential try. Chosen as his running mate was former Senator Theodore Frelinghuysen of New Jersey, a Protestant activist of nativist sentiments, a move that would prove to be very damaging to the Whig ticket.

In the last days of the month at the Democratic convention, Van Buren was not so fortunate regarding his letter against bringing Texas into the American fold. Jackson, strongly in favor of that step, loudly declared his opposition to his old political strategist. Other party leaders, especially in the South where annexation was seen as adding another slaveholding state, joined the revolt, and the pull of Manifest Destiny also worked against Van Buren. As the titular party leader, a majority of the delegates were pledged to him, but as the previous election's loser, he did not inspire great enthusiasm and his opposition to Texas annexation gave them a justification for wavering.

The only rival for the Democratic nomination with much support going into the convention was Lewis Cass of Michigan, a former general and territorial governor who had been Jackson's secretary of war and a minister to France. Into the breach stepped Robert Walker of Mississippi, a transplanted Yankee who was a vocal advocate of annexation as a means of protecting the voting strength of the "peculiar institution" in Congress.

Determined to block Van Buren, Walker capitalized on the concern of Van Buren delegates over his opposition to admitting Texas. He deftly engineered restoration of the convention rule requiring a two-thirds majority for presidential nomination that had applied in 1832 and 1836 but had been dropped in 1840.[27] The move was Van Buren's undoing. He received 146 of the 266 votes cast on the first ballot to only 83 for Cass, but he needed 177 under the reinstated rule. In six more ballots, Van Buren's total steadily faded while no other candidate threatened. Tyler, who had hoped his old party might turn to him, got nowhere, and the first deadlocked convention resulted. A motion to nominate Jackson convulsed the floor, but was ruled out of order, and the convention adjourned for the night in an uproar.

Word spread during the adjournment that Richard Johnson, holding a small number of delegates, had released them to Cass. The Van Buren camp, concerned that a Cass stampede would be started, realized that Van Buren was finished and began casting about for an alternative. Benjamin Butler of New York held a secret letter from Van Buren offering to yield his delegates to his highly esteemed New York colleague Silas Wright, but Wright had already indicated he did not wish to be considered. George Bancroft, the Democratic leader in Massachusetts, then hit upon the one man who could unite the convention.

It so happened that the former Speaker of the House and governor from Jackson's home state, Tennessee, James K. Polk, had been engaging in the first serious campaign for the vice-presidential nomination, backed enthusiastically for that little-esteemed post by Jackson. Polk had declared firmly for the annexation of Texas and Bancroft now proposed him as the best compromise. Jackson had raised the possibility earlier with Polk, who had decided to lay back and wait, lest he alienate the Van Buren forces he would need if a deadlock did occur. The strategy turned out to be a fortuitous one.

With the wily Walker also in Polk's corner, the delegates overwhelmingly smitten by Manifest Destiny turned to the Tennessean. The next morning, he had forty-four votes on the eighth ballot, and on the ninth, the Van Buren votes from New York swung to him, creating a tide that, eventually by unanimous vote, made him the first dark-horse Democratic presidential nominee. One Whig newspaper ominously declared: "This nomination may be considered as the dying gasp, the last breath of life, of the 'Democratic Party.' "[28]

To conciliate the rejected Van Buren, the convention nominated his popular friend Wright for vice president, but Wright quickly declined and the convention settled on George M. Dallas of Pennsylvania as Polk's running mate. Wright, after a term as governor in New York, was defeated for reelection in 1846 and died the next year, regarded at the time as among the ablest Democratic politicians and public servants. John Greenleaf Whittier in his poem "The Lost Statesman" wrote of his passing:

> *Man of the millions, thou art lost too soon!*
> *Who now shall rally Freedom's scattering host?*
> *Who wear the mantle of the leader lost?*
> *Who stay the march of slavery?*[29]

As a result of Polk's nomination in 1844, the Democratic Party leadership of Van Buren, Thomas Hart Benton and Francis P. Blair, editor of the *Washington Globe,* was out in the cold, replaced by new masters of party rules manipulation. The convention demanded and got a platform that reiterated support for Jacksonian principles and reforms, and asserted "our title to the whole of the Territory of Oregon is clear and unquestionable, that no portion of the same ought to be ceded to England or any other power." Therefore, it went on, "the re-occupation of Oregon and the re-annexation of Texas at the earliest practicable period are great American measures, which this convention recommends to the cordial support of the Democracy of the Union."[30] The language conveyed the Democratic Party position that the United States had been entitled to claim both territories from the start.

Taking back the page from their own playbook that had been lifted by the Whigs in creating Harrison as a carbon copy of military hero Jackson, the Democrats introduced Polk as "Young Hickory," a chip off the old Tennessee frontier block. The Whigs responded with a smear campaign against a man they painted as an obscure nobody, and the Democrats hit back against Clay, a known quantity whose record of switched votes in the Senate gave his opponents ample ammunition.

So did the choice of Frelinghuysen as his running mate. His reported nativist and anti-Catholic views, circulated by the Democrats among immigrant Irish and Germans, rallied these growing constituencies to the Polk camp. Martin John Spalding, a prominent Catholic cleric in Baltimore from Kentucky, declared that he would vote for Clay but not Frelinghuysen. When informed he could not thus split his vote, he said he would vote for neither man.[31] At the same time, misguided Whig reports that Clay supported more restrictive laws against immigration and naturalization, aimed at exploiting conservative sentiment toward the newly arrived foreign populace, backfired.

Clay himself was nothing if not what another of the descriptive names proclaimed him: The Great Compromiser. Aware of the allegations of nativism against his running mate and of his own opposition to liberal naturalization, he sent a letter to the *New York Courier and Enquirer* that transparently sought to assuage all critics. "Every pulsation of my heart is American and nothing but American . . . I am in favor of American industry, American institutions, American order, American liberty," he wrote, then added: "Whilst I entertain all these feelings and sentiment, I wish our Country, forever, to remain a sacred asylum for all unfortunate and oppressed men whether from religious or political causes."[32]

More notable was a perceived flip-flop over the annexation of Texas. During the pre-convention period when Clay was under the impression that Van Buren would be his Democratic opponent, he had shared Van Buren's position against bringing Texas into the Union. But after the pro-annexation Polk had been nominated instead, Clay wrote to the editor of the Tuscaloosa, Alabama, *Monitor* saying he "personally" had no objection to annexation as long as it didn't imperil the Union. Cries of rank expedience filled the air as critics saw the letter as a crass effort to compete with Polk for abolitionist support.

Clay compounded the deed with a second letter of "explanation" saying if elected he would accept annexation of Texas "without dishonor—without war, with the common consent of the Union, and upon just and fair terms."[33]

His waffling gave birth to a Democratic jingle:

> *He wires in and wires out,*
> *And leaves the people still in doubt,*
> *Whether the snake that made the track*
> *Was going South, or coming back.*[34]

Conscience Whigs—men opposed to slavery—fled party ranks to support Birney, the Liberty Party nominee.

The Democrats also resurrected the old charge from Jackson's own lips of the "corrupt bargain" whereby Adams had become president in 1824 and Clay his secretary of state. As a demonstration of Polk's own limited appetite for power, he announced he would seek one term only. The move, while risking diminished influence were he elected, brought encouragement to men like Van Buren, Cass and Calhoun who could look to 1848 with hope for their own nomination—and their support in the meantime. At the same time, Jackson helped dissuade Tyler, disowned by the Whigs, from seeking a second term as an independent, a move that could have undercut Polk fatally in the South.

The combination of unexpected Democratic unity behind the first dark-horse presidential nominee and Clay's circumlocutions on Texas annexation, as well as the fact that as a three-time candidate Clay was seen by many as old goods, brought Polk the presidency and leadership of what still considered itself the Jacksonian party. At forty-nine, he was the youngest man elected to the highest office up to that time. For all of Clay's missteps, he trailed Polk by only 1.5 percent in the popular vote, 38,181 ballots out of about 2.7 million cast. The electoral vote was a bit more decisive: Polk 170, Clay 105.

Birney, as the categorical abolitionist candidate, won 62,300 popular ballots, more than the Clay deficit. Clay's late switch on Texas was not enough to turn the tide for him. In critical New York, which Clay lost by only 5,106 votes, Birney got 15,812, three times what Clay had needed to carry the state and win the election. He was also undone there by what was reported to be extensive illegal voter registration of immigrants strongly opposed to the nativist sentiments attributed to Clay's running mate, and by this time to himself as well.

As for the retiring Tyler, he was not quite finished. After the election, he proclaimed the outcome had confirmed that the voters wanted Texas brought into the Union. He called on Congress to approve a joint resolution approving annexation, a tactic that would permit passage by a simple majority rather than the two thirds required for Senate ratification of a treaty. After vigorous debate, the resolution passed in the House, 120–98.

In the Senate, Van Burenites resisted, fearful that vast Texas would be carved into four separate slave states and any Democrat who had voted for annexation would be punished by Northern voters in the next election. The Van Burenites hoped a compromise might be struck whereby a portion of yet-to-be-settled Texas would be admitted as free territory, but Tyler and Calhoun refused. Northern Whig opposition, however, helped force another compromise whereby the president, who they believed would be Polk, could accept the House bill or negotiate a new treaty. The Senate narrowly passed the compromise, 27–25.

Tyler, however, upon quickly signing the bill, asked Texas to accept the House version, which it did, only days before he left the presidency. The Van Burenites considered Tyler's conduct a supreme act of treachery. Polk had already promised Benton and other leading anti-slavery Democrats in Congress that he would indeed renegotiate, and they still counted on him doing so, as the legislation provided, once he took office.

Also on Polk's plate as he embarked on his presidency was the question of Oregon. With Manifest Destiny well advanced, the Democratic Party now had the chance to complete an America that would stretch from sea to shining sea.

In the 1852 presidential campaign, Democratic nominee Franklin Pierce was haunted by opposition allegations of alcoholism. This cartoon shows him clinging to a tree and holding up a bottle to a passing Quaker preaching temperance, as championed by Maine liquor laws.

Chapter 9

MANIFEST DESTINY, WAR AND COMPROMISE, 1845–1852

WITH JAMES POLK in the White House, the Jacksonian Democrats were back in control. The interruption caused by the 1840 election of Whig William Harrison and the succession upon his death of the independent-minded John Tyler had proved to be only a brief hiatus in Jacksonian policies.

Tyler, the Virginian who had left the Democratic Party in disagreement with Jackson's squelching of Calhoun's nullification doctrine, had never found an accommodating home among the Whigs. Once the converted Democrat assumed the presidency, he began wielding his veto power against key aspects of the Clay American System. It was almost as if Tyler had never left his old party, and the Democrats had not been out of the presidency at all.

Polk, nominated and elected as a dark-horse candidate and supposedly handicapped from the start by his announcement that he would serve only one term, nevertheless strongly asserted himself. With critics like Van Buren on the left and Calhoun on the right, Polk straddled his own party, steering a centrist, hard-driving course. He ignored some of Jackson's recommendations for cabinet posts, and the demands of New York Van Burenites, or "Barnburners," for the top positions.

Polk made James Buchanan of Pennsylvania his secretary of state and Robert J. Walker, the man who had manipulated Van Buren's convention rejection and was a powerful representative of the Southern interests, treasury secretary. He fired Francis Blair and closed his paper, the *Globe,* making Thomas Ritchie and his *Washington Union* the party's mouthpiece in their place. "I must be the head of my own administration," he wrote to Jackson at the time, "and will not be controlled by any newspaper."[1]

The anti-slavery Barnburners were so called because they were said to be willing to burn the barn to get rid of the "rats," the rival "Hunkers" who hungered, or "hunkered," after victory so much that they would at all costs accommodate the South on slavery.[2] The Barnburners were further incensed when Polk appointed as secretary of war William L. Marcy, a onetime Barnburner who had become a Hunker leader.

Jackson, at first modestly promoting his fellow Tennessean for the vice presidency, was delighted when political lightning struck down Van Buren and Polk was elected president. Polk, like Jackson, was a wholehearted advocate of Manifest Destiny, the annexation of the newly independent Republic of Texas and the vast open territories of Oregon and California. Tyler having already achieved congressional approval of adding Texas, it was only a matter of working out details with the new republic. In December 1845 the vast new state was admitted, though not without ominous ramifications involving a spurned and agitated Mexico.[3]

Upon the annexation, the government of Mexico immediately broke off diplomatic relations with the United States.[4] However, serious differences carried over from the new state's boundary claims had to be resolved, as well as personal claims of American citizens against their southern neighbor. Texas insisted that its southern border with Mexico was at the Rio Grande; the Mexicans, going back to old Spanish exploration days, put it at the Nueces River farther north.

In the summer of 1845, Polk ordered General Zachary Taylor to move fifteen hundred American troops into the contested region between the two rivers. They located at Corpus Christi at the mouth of the Nueces, and in early 1846 advanced south to the Rio Grande. Mexico, still smarting from the loss of Texas, erupted with talk of war.

Mexican officials agreed to meet with an American negotiator over the dispute. Polk sent John Slidell of Louisiana, armed also with authority to press earlier American bids to purchase California and New Mexico as well. Polk reasoned that Mexico, in dire financial straits, might be willing to make a deal for lands it found difficult to hold and defend. But the Mexican officials became irate over the effrontery of the American scheme.

The shaky Mexican government collapsed and was replaced by a revolutionary regime that vowed to defend Mexican integrity and honor. Slidell was turned away, told that only the question of Texas had been open to negotiation and until it was resolved there could be no other discussion. Writing of the impasse, Slidell heatedly informed Polk: "Be assured that nothing is to be done with these people until they shall have been chastised."[5]

Polk apparently agreed, and in early May 1846 he readied a belligerent message to be presented to Congress. But before it could be delivered, word reached Washington that about two weeks earlier, Mexican troops, goaded by the American presence, had crossed the Rio Grande and engaged the Americans in the disputed region, killing or wounding sixteen of them.

That was the last straw for Polk; he informed Congress: "The cup of forbearance had been exhausted even before the recent information from the frontier. . . . But now, after reiterated menaces, Mexico has passed the boundary of the United States, has invaded our territory and shed American blood on American soil. . . . War exists, and, notwithstanding all of our efforts to avoid it, exists by the act of Mexico herself."[6] Two days later, Congress formally declared war on Mexico.

At the same time, the Oregon question had been casting another heavy shadow over American diplomacy. The Oregon Territory had been jointly occupied by the British and Americans since 1818 and Polk wanted it all. He had declared in his inaugural address that he intended "to assert and maintain by all constitutional means the right of the United States to that portion of our territory which lies beyond the Rocky Mountains. Our title to the country of the Oregon," he said, "is clear and unquestionable, and . . . those rights we are fully prepared to maintain."[7]

Polk, however, did not relish the thought of waging war against the British when armed conflict against Mexico also was possible. So in mid-1845, to the outrage of Lewis Cass and others in the settled Northwest, he informed the British through their minister in Washington, Richard Pakenham, that he was willing to divide "the Oregon country" along the 49th parallel, considerably farther south than a line at the 54th parallel, then its northern border with Russian Alaska. Pakenham summarily rejected the offer on his own, leading Polk to withdraw it, declaring that "the only way to treat John Bull was to look him straight in the eye" and hold "a bold and firm course."[8]

In December 1845, Polk obtained congressional approval to give England a year's notification of intent to terminate joint occupation of the territory. American supporters of Manifest Destiny like Cass raised cries of "All of Oregon or none" and "Fifty-four forty or fight"—after the map designation of the northern border of the territory.[9] The British Foreign Office, also not relishing another war in the New World, finally agreed in 1846 to a treaty that gave the harbor of Puget Sound to the United States and Vancouver Island to England, along with navigation rights on the Columbia River. By the time the Senate ratified the treaty, on June 15, the United States was at war with Mexico, and all but the most vehement expansionists were content that the Oregon dispute had been settled peaceably.

Polk and the Democratic Party, with the annexation of Texas and the Oregon settlement, had already greatly increased the landmass of the country. But Polk, in pursuing the Mexican War, also had his eye on New Mexico and California. Many Whigs, caring less about this expansion because they did not see in it the same peril of slavery that caused them to oppose Texas annexation, suggested that Polk had provoked the war with Mexico, or had not done all he could have to avert it.

Northern (Conscience) Whigs argued that by sending General Taylor into the region between the Nueces River and the Rio Grande, Polk had put American troops at risk in what was not undisputed American territory. The Massachusetts legislature in 1847 approved a resolution declaring that the war had been "unconstitutionally commenced by the order of the President" and was being conducted with "the triple object of extending slavery, of strengthening the slave power, and of obtaining the control of the free states."[10]

Despite this lack of unanimity on the home front about pursuit of the war, superior American armaments, equipment and generalship enabled a force of eight thousand soldiers, bolstered quickly by sixty thousand volunteers, to defeat the larger but inferior Mexican army. Taylor crossed the Rio Grande and captured the Mexican garrison at Monterey in September 1846, becoming yet another American military hero with politics in his future. But he let the Mexicans withdraw and Polk, lacking confidence in him, cut his force in half. Yet Taylor won again in the Battle of Buena Vista and reinforced his reputation as "Old Rough and Ready."

Meanwhile, a small force of seventeen hundred men under Colonel Stephen W. Kearny captured Santa Fe and proclaimed the annexation of

New Mexico. Then they moved westward and joined American settlers under Captain John C. Frémont, who had already staged the Bear Flag Revolt and declared the independence of California. Frémont, too, would have politics in his future before long. Finally, General Winfield Scott, still another future political candidate, landed near Vera Cruz in March 1847, captured the city and doggedly led his forces toward Mexico City. He defeated Mexican leader Santa Anna at Cerro Gordo in mid-April, reached the fringes of the capital in August and the Mexican forces surrendered soon after.[11]

Polk sent the chief clerk of the State Department, Nicholas P. Trist, to negotiate a peace treaty, but when little progress was reported, Polk ordered Trist back to Washington. The diplomat, convinced he was on the verge of a satisfactory outcome, ignored the president's orders and on February 2, 1848, signed the Treaty of Guadalupe Hidalgo. The United States obtained California, New Mexico and the boundary on the Rio Grande it had claimed for a payment of $15 million and the assumption of American citizens' claims against Mexico.

Trist's achievement was impressive, but on return Polk declared him an "impudent and unqualified scoundrel"[12] for having disobeyed the president's orders, and fired him. Yet Polk submitted the treaty to the Senate, which approved it by 38–14 in March, thus adding more than half a million square miles to the Union. Along with Jefferson's earlier acquisition of the huge Louisiana Territory, what was now the Democratic Party could justly lay claim to making the United States a colossus astride a continent.

The new acquisitions did not meet with universal approval because they came in the context of the continuing debate over the extension of slavery into new territories. Southern Whigs generally saw the developments favorably as an expansion into the Southwest and West of their region's way of life. Easterners, especially Northern Whigs, saw them in terms of a growing rival political and economic base, and Southern dominance of the party. Poet James Russell Lowell of Massachusetts, married to a prominent abolitionist, wrote:

> *They jest want this Californy*
> *So's to lug new slave-states in*
> *To abuse ye, an' to scorn ye*
> *An' to plunder ye like sin.*[13]

Even before the start of the war with Mexico, Van Buren had warned the Democratic Party against giving the Whigs the opportunity "to charge with plausibility, if not truth, that it is waged for the extension of slavery."[14] Such an allegation, he believed, would drive Northerners out of the party and mean certain defeat in 1848. When, shortly after the shooting began, Polk urged Congress to appropriate $2 million as an inducement to Mexico to sell New Mexico, the Van Burenites charged he was out to buy more slave territory. The move led a Northern Democratic congressman, David Wilmot of Pennsylvania, to introduce a resolution in 1846 stipulating "an express and fundamental condition to the acquisition of any territory" be that "neither slavery nor involuntary servitude shall ever exist in any part of said territory."[15]

This Wilmot Proviso, which split the Whigs and the nation North and South, passed the House twice but each time failed in the Senate. The proviso demonstrated how the slavery issue was marching hand in hand with the doctrine of Manifest Destiny, deepening the breach between North and the Old South even as the nation was bursting from its old boundaries. Jackson, just before his death, warned that if the Union were destroyed in the process, it would take "oceans of blood and hundreds of millions" of dollars to restore it.[16]

The focus on slavery shaped by the abolitionists as a moral issue often overshadowed the economic and racial aspects of the opposition in the North to its westward extension. Wilmot himself insisted that his object was the defense of "the rights of white freemen. I would preserve for free white labor," he said, "a fair country, a rich inheritance, where the soils of toil, of my own race and own color, can live without the disgrace which association with negro slavery brings upon free labor."[17]

The Wilmot Proviso drove a deep wedge in the Whig Party, but as long as the Mexican War was going on, the Democrats sought to avoid further party division by limiting discussion of the slavery issue. They rationalized at the time that no new territory had yet been integrated into the Union and therefore a resolution could be put off.

Polk, himself a slaveholder in Tennessee, was accused by Northern Whigs of having started the war to acquire more territory open to slavery. He denied it and expressed impatience and dismay at the way both sides on the slavery issue sought to use it for political advantage. "What connection slavery had with making peace with Mexico is difficult to conceive," Polk wrote later.[18] Well before Mexico had surrendered and ceded the California and New Mexico territories, however, the proviso split the Democrats as well as the Whigs along sectional lines.

Increasingly, the debate over extending slavery was taking on a moralistic, crusading tone, especially in the North. The anti-slavery New York Barnburners, having lost control of the state Democratic Party to the Hunkers at its 1847 convention in Syracuse, seceded at a convention in Herkimer outside of Utica in October and endorsed the Wilmot Proviso. But many Northern Democrats, such as Cass, opposed the proviso in the hope of keeping Southern Democrats aboard for the 1848 presidential election.

Calhoun resisted the courtship. In 1847 he had proposed Senate resolutions declaring the territories belonged collectively to the states and therefore no citizen of any state could be barred from moving into a territory with his slaves. Under the Constitution, only when a territory became a state, he argued, could it prohibit slavery within its borders. Thus slavery would be legitimate in all the territories, in conflict with the Missouri Compromise of 1820.[19]

In the summer of 1847, Calhoun had also launched a Southern Rights Movement outside the Democratic Party to pressure it to pay more attention to Southern interests. But many Dixie Democrats continued to see their interests best protected within a national party that sought to finesse the slavery issue. Later that year, Cass and his fellow Democratic senator, Stephen A. Douglas of Illinois, joined forces behind another compromise whereby it would be left to the settlers in any territory whether or not to permit slavery. Called "squatter sovereignty" by Cass and "popular sovereignty" by Douglas, it had some appeal in the South by taking the decision out of the hands of Congress and giving the region a fair shot at determining the outcome.[20]

Calhoun, however, dug in with compatriots from the Old South states. Known as the Chivalry, they banded together in Virginia, Georgia and Alabama, pledging to support no presidential candidate who endorsed the Wilmot Proviso and, with Florida, adopting an Alabama Platform that challenged any congressional or territorial right whatever to exclude slavery. The signers said their delegates to the 1848 Democratic national convention would vote against any candidate who backed either the proviso or popular sovereignty.[21]

With Polk a self-declared lame-duck president leaving a splintered Democratic Party with uncertain leadership and growing sectional divisions, the continuation of Jacksonian Democracy was imperiled as the 1848 election approached. The turmoil in Democratic ranks, more than any impressive unity and purpose among the also divided Whigs, threatened Democratic retention of the White House.

When the party's national convention opened in Baltimore, three factions vied for party leadership: anti-slavery, led by Van Buren, nominated in advance by the rump Barnburners convention; pro-slavery, led by Calhoun; and popular sovereignty, led by Cass. Van Buren and the Barnburners were hampered by their split with the Hunkers in New York, and when the national convention sought to divide the state delegation between the two factions, they walked out. Calhoun's unyielding posture on the central issue was too extreme for many Southerners and he had little support in the North. That left Cass and two other candidates for the nomination, James Buchanan of Pennsylvania and Levi Woodbury of New Hampshire.

Cass had proved too weak to best Van Buren in 1844 and had been obliged to give way to dark-horse Polk in that stalemated convention. But he was a Northerner and his stand on popular sovereignty offered the Democratic Party a way to placate the South while not committing itself in the party platform to any equivocal stand for or against slavery in the territories. With the New York delegation not voting, Cass was declared nominated on the fourth ballot as the preference of the Northwest who was tolerable to the South, having opposed the Wilmot Proviso. His total of 179 votes was actually 15 short of the two thirds of the 290 eligible votes required under the convention rule, but because New York's 36 votes were not cast, the base without challenge was reduced to 254, putting him 9 votes over.[22]

Notable at the Baltimore convention was a decision to establish a formal Democratic National Committee, with one member from each state to help coordinate activities among the state party committees. Benjamin F. Hallett of Massachusetts, a Hunker, was chosen as the first national chairman. He also served as chairman of the platform committee that did its best to avoid the slavery issue, in keeping with his own Hunker sentiments. The new national committee was to meet during congressional and presidential election years to coordinate political activities. The convention also ruled that each state was entitled only to seats equal to its electoral vote "and no more," a caveat that was more often than not honored in the breach at future conventions.[23]

Van Buren and the Barnburners, dismayed at the choice of Cass,

whom they regarded as a "doughface," a "northerner with southern principles," left the party they now derided as the "Slavocracy."[24] They formed
a new one of their own in Buffalo in August, calling it the Free Soil Party.
The party, in an almost religious fervor, nominated Van Buren as its presidential candidate and Charles Francis Adams, a Conscience Whig and
son of John Quincy Adams, as his running mate.

Using the motto "Free Soil, Free Speech, Free Labor, and Free Men,"
the new amalgam of Barnburners, abolitionists, Conscience Whigs and
advocates of free land to settlers wrote a platform opposing any slavery in
the territories. It also called for federal aid for internal improvements and
a homestead act that would bestow farms without cost to settlers on public lands.[25] The new party's most vigorous and effective spokesman was
John Van Buren, the nominee's son, who stumped the country in the
cause. It was driven by idealism, but the practical effect was to help defeat
Cass, as the Whigs once again played the military hero card by selecting as
their nominee one of the prime figures in the Mexican War, General
Zachary Taylor.

The Whigs' nomination of Taylor was one of the factors that led to
the Free Soil Party, because many Conscience Whigs fled their own party
and joined the Free Soilers rather than back Taylor, a Virginia native who
was a major slaveholder in Louisiana. "Old Rough and Ready" was a lifetime soldier of no discernible political ties or principles, including any
active advocacy of slavery. When first approached about the possibility of
running for president, Taylor expressed amusement about the prospect of
a man who had never even voted for the office, and owned up to no political affiliation. Pressed on the matter, he would say only that had he voted
in "the last presidential election, it would have been for Mr. Clay."[26]

Taylor said he would not campaign for the presidency, so that he
could accept the job "untrammeled" by commitments and serve only as "a
president of the nation and not a party."[27] A series of political celebrations
in his honor starting in early 1848 warmed him, however, to the possibility, while old Whigs like Horace Greeley cringed at the thought. Clay, running again and commenting on Taylor's qualifications, quipped: "I wish I
could slay a Mexican,"[28] and Webster, also a candidate again, called him
"an illiterate frontier colonel."[29]

While avowing to follow George Washington's tradition against campaigning for the office, Taylor did permit himself a letter to his son-in-law
Captain John Allison, in advance of the Whig convention, confessing, "I

am a Whig, but not an ultra Whig," and huffily adding, "I trust I will not be again called on to make further explanations."[30] That seemed to satisfy the great majority of Whigs, who were more interested in his electability than his principles. They nominated him on the fourth ballot in Philadelphia over the hapless Clay and General Winfield Scott, with Millard Fillmore of upstate New York as his running mate. Clay refused to campaign for the ticket, saying pompously that "self-respect, the consistency of my character and my true fame require that I should take no active or partisan agency in the ensuing contest. The Whig party has been overthrown by a mere personal party."[31]

In Taylor, the Whigs indeed had a winner of personal appeal, even to the point of cutting into the immigrant vote that normally flocked to the Democratic nominee. The Democrats were obliged to run two sectional campaigns, in the South against the Wilmot Proviso and in the North touting popular sovereignty for the territories as an effective way to exclude slavery there. Hammered by the Free Soilers, Cass was whipsawed while Taylor rode the same wave of patriotic adulation that had brought battlefield heroes Jackson and Harrison to the White House before him.

In the first presidential election in which all states voted on the same day, Taylor was narrowly elected in what would prove to be only another interruption in the Jacksonian Democracy. He won 47.4 percent of the popular vote to 42.5 percent for Cass and 10.1 percent for Van Buren, and captured the necessary majority of the electoral vote, winning 163–127 for Cass and none for Van Buren.[32] The Democrats retained a numerical edge in both the House and the Senate, indicating that Democratic Party ties remained strong and that Taylor's celebrity was as much a factor in his election as the Democrats' split over slavery. Importantly, the voice against human bondage was growing louder.

One policy result of Cass's loss was a strengthening of the anti-slavery cause among Northern Democrats who believed that pandering to the South on the issue had cost Cass the election. At the same time, Southern Democrats feared that their party was no longer a dependable protector of the "peculiar institution." The matter of the territories splitting into new states, and whether they would be admitted to the Union as slave or free, became ever more critical to the survival of the Democratic Party, and of the Union itself.

At the time Taylor took office in March 1849, California and New Mexico still were territories run by military governments reporting to the president. The discovery of gold along the American River in January 1848 had triggered the famous California gold rush of 1849 when eighty thousand "Forty-niners" poured into the territory from the East, the Midwest and abroad, operating individually and out of miners' camps, many riddled with crime and violence.

With Congress immobilized by the slavery controversy and failing to authorize civil government in the territories, Taylor moved in himself, calling on the settlers in California and New Mexico to write constitutions of their own and apply for statehood. By October 1849, Californians had held a convention and drafted a constitution barring slavery in the proposed new state. Voters in the territory ratified it the next month and elected state officials to whom civil authority was swiftly turned over by the military.

In the New Mexico Territory, the same process went forward a bit more slowly, but by May 1850 a constitution also would be drafted and ratified prohibiting slavery in the new state. Without waiting for New Mexico to complete its work, in December 1849, Taylor asked Congress to approve California's application for statehood and New Mexico's as soon as it was ready.[33]

But if Taylor thought the worst was over, he was woefully mistaken. Southern Whigs felt betrayed by his support of admitting California as a free state. Calhoun, laboring to rally his Southern supporters against any hindrance to slavery's extension, talked darkly of secession if thwarted, or if California and New Mexico were admitted with a prohibition against slaveholding. Abolitionists resumed and intensified their demands that slavery be banned in the District of Columbia. Southerners wanted a tougher fugitive slave law. And amid all this, Texas and New Mexico were embroiled in a boundary dispute of their own.

The dire situation cried out for a voice of compromise, and once again it came from Henry Clay, now seventy-two and all dreams of achieving the presidency behind him. On January 29, 1850, he proposed to the Senate a complex series of resolutions that he hoped would avert dissolution of the Union. His proposals offered something for everyone.

First, Clay recommended that California be given its request to enter the Union as a free state. Then territorial governments would be created from the remaining land obtained from Mexico, leaving the slavery question to the settlers there. Texas would give up its boundary claim against New Mexico in return for assumption by the federal government of

Texas's national debt incurred before joining the Union. Slavery would be abolished in the District of Columbia subject to local approval, with compensation given to slave owners, and the slave trade ended there. A tougher fugitive slave law would be enacted along with a declaration by Congress not to interfere with interstate slave trade.[34]

The Clay compromise, joined by Democrat Stephen Douglas, launched an intensive congressional debate over the next seven months. Clay spoke first, and for two days pleaded for the compromise to preserve the Union. A few weeks later, Calhoun, near death, sat in the Senate as a colleague read his rebuttal. The only solution, he pleaded, was for the stronger North to yield on the slavery issue and what he called the restoration of equal rights for the South in dealing with the territories.

In his speech, Calhoun flatly warned of peaceful secession or war. If the North could not settle its differences with the South "on the broad principle of justice and duty," he said, "say so; and let the States we both represent agree to separate and part in peace. If you are unwilling we should part in peace, tell us so; and we shall know what to do, when you reduce the question to submission or resistance."[35] For Calhoun personally, the threat proved empty; before the end of March, he was dead.

Three days after Calhoun's final speech, Webster took the Senate floor in his most famous oration of an illustrious career. A free-soiler before now, he rejected abolitionist arguments and, while rejecting Calhoun's allegations against the North, weighed in to support the compromise. He urged an end to anti-slavery agitation and approval of a stronger fugitive slave act, again to mollify the South and thus preserve the Union. Senator William H. Seward of New York, speaking for the Conscience Whigs, rejected the compromise and argued that the only solution was for the South to yield "to the progress of emancipation."[36]

While such yielding was not in the cards, the cause of compromise was advanced by moderates gaining control of a Southern convention in Nashville and indicating willingness to accept a just deal. A major roadblock now was Taylor himself, who was bitter over Clay's dismissal of his own proposal on California and New Mexico. In the event of congressional approval of the Clay proposals, it was feared Taylor would exercise his veto in spite of statements that he would not use that power. But fate stepped in when, at a Fourth of July celebration, Taylor in the hot sun consumed a quantity of iced drinks, suffered cramps and an attack of gastroenteritis that killed him five days later.

Vice President Fillmore, a Conscience Whig, on taking office as president sided at once with Clay and Webster, and joined them in working for the compromise. More haggling followed, but by September the main features proposed by Clay were adopted and signed by Fillmore. California was admitted as a free state; two new territories, New Mexico and Utah, were to be created, with the slavery issue to be decided by popular sovereignty; the Texas–New Mexico border was ironed out with the agreed compensation to Texas; slave trade (but not slavery itself) in the District of Columbia was ended and a stronger fugitive slave act promised.[37]

The compromise, like bad-tasting medicine that's good for the patient, did not go down easily in many quarters, North or South, or within the Democratic Party. Southern Democrats opposed in vain admitting a slave-free California that gave the free states a 16–15 edge over the slave states. Northern Democrats deplored the notion of a fugitive slave act that would facilitate returning to their Southern owners slaves who had escaped to the North. Moderate Democrats in both sections strove to calm tempers in the interest of the Union, with the harder task below the Mason-Dixon line.

House Speaker Howell Cobb, a Georgia Democrat, joined with Whigs in creating a new Constitutional Union Party in his state that accepted the compromise with what came to be known as the Georgia Platform. It included the caveat that any congressional move to restrict slavery anywhere, or any backsliding in the North on enforcement of the stronger fugitive slave law, would be vigorously opposed, "even (as a last resort) to a disruption of every tie which bounds [Georgia] to the Union."[38] The new party elected candidates in local and state elections in 1851, and the movement spread to Alabama, Mississippi, Florida and South Carolina. But the development did more damage to the Whig Party than to the Democrats, signaling a coming Whig disintegration nationally.

Broadly speaking, however, there was a feeling of relief across the land that the slavery issue had achieved a final solution. The business community saw the compromise as a harbinger of less contentious times and dealings between North and South. As historian Eugene H. Roseboom wrote, "The booming prosperity of the early fifties, an excellent sedative for sectionalist nerves, was a great factor against radicalism in both North and South."[39]

Fillmore told Congress he considered the compromise "a final settlement of the dangerous and exciting subjects which they embraced."[40]

Some forty-four Democratic and Whig congressmen signed a pledge never to support any candidate who threatened to overturn the agreement.

Emerging from the whole compromise was a new Democratic leader in Stephen Douglas, the five-foot, four-inch "Little Giant" from Illinois. His oratorical and negotiating skills had supported and later supplanted Clay in achieving the plan designed to head off Southern secession on terms acceptable to the North. He resolved "never to make another speech on the slavery question,"[41] but it soon became clear that he hoped to use his role in the debate to put himself in the White House.

When the Democratic Party gathered in Baltimore in June 1852, Douglas joined Cass, Buchanan and Marcy as contenders for the presidential nomination. Many wandering Democrats had by now returned to the party fold from the Free Soil and other adventures, including the New York Barnburners and other Van Burenites. A sentiment was growing among many free-soilers that in all the furor over slavery extension, the Democratic Party had lost sight of its basic Jeffersonian and Jacksonian principles, which pointedly included individual freedom.

Therefore the party was obliged, it was argued, to address slavery more in moral than in economic terms, and thus needed to be led by a true believer. But the senior Van Buren had at last retired and Silas Wright was dead. That pointed, in the minds of many, to Thomas Hart Benton, who in 1850 had lost his Senate seat in the slave state of Missouri but not his strong opposition to slavery. Benton, however, rejected entreaties to seek the presidency, having already thrown himself energetically into writing a history of his times. The party would have to look elsewhere, and the prospects were not exciting. Before choosing a presidential nominee, the convention adopted a platform endorsing the compromise and vowing to "resist all attempts at renewing in Congress, or out of it, the agitation of the slavery question, under whatever shape or color the attempt may be made."[42] The driving motivation was party unity to assure victory at the polls.

With the two-thirds rule again applying, the field of four active contenders led to another deadlocked convention, and another dark-horse nominee. On the forty-ninth ballot, the party turned to a little-known former senator from New Hampshire, Franklin Pierce, whose views on slavery were sufficiently subdued to avoid dissension. His service as a general in the Mexican War also enabled the party to play the military hero card once again, even to labeling him as yet another "Young Hickory."

Among the Whigs, President Fillmore wanted a term in his own right and Webster also sought the nomination, but when the party also met in Baltimore two weeks after the Democratic convention, it too stalemated, rejecting both men closely associated with the Clay compromise, in which the Whig platform merely "acquiesced." Instead, the Whigs also once again bought into the military hero worship. Fillmore led on the first ballot, only two votes ahead of another Mexican War leader, General Winfield Scott of Virginia, a rather pompous man known as "Old Fuss and Feathers," many of whose delegates opposed the compromise. Webster was third, far behind. Efforts to pool the Fillmore and Webster support failed and on the fifty-third ballot Scott finally reached the required two-thirds majority.

The new Georgia party nominated Webster, thus undercutting Scott in that state, and in the general election other Southern Whigs simply did not vote. Many Irish, German and others of immigrant stock, of growing importance in American elections, rejected Scott on the basis of reports circulated by the Democrats that he was biased against "foreigners." The Whigs, in turn, accused Pierce of cowardice in the Mexican War and drunkenness in what degenerated into an ugly, dull campaign. In an important sense, the election was a referendum on the Clay compromise, embraced by Pierce and the Democratic Party, and tolerated by Scott and the Whigs. Pierce won by 6.8 percent in the popular vote, but swamped Scott in the electoral college, 254 votes to 42. The free-soilers, running John P. Hale of New Hampshire under the new label of the Free Democratic Party, got only 5 percent of the popular vote and no electoral votes.

Jacksonian Democracy had another lease on life, but the Whig Party was all but destroyed on the national scene, with sectional sentiment toward slavery overruling its philosophical tenets. The second American party system was at an end. The Democratic Party had demonstrated a surprising unity in light of the deep divisions that had been laid bare by the debate on the slavery question. Democrats North and South hoped the Compromise of 1850 had indeed brought a finality to the troublesome issue. That unity and that hope, however, would soon prove to be ephemeral.

Top: In 1860, Senator Stephen Douglas of Illinois was chosen in Baltimore over President Buchanan as the Democratic nominee. The cockfight cartoon also depicts the candidacy of Vice President John C. Breckinridge of Kentucky by defecting Southern Democrats.

Bottom: In 1861, Governor Francis Pickens of South Carolina, a leading secessionist in his state, called on lame-duck President Buchanan to remove the federal forces at Fort Sumter in Charleston harbor. This cartoon depicts Buchanan hoping to hold off action until the inauguration of Republican Abraham Lincoln.

Chapter 10

THE PARTY SELF-DESTRUCTS, 1853–1860

PRESIDENT PIERCE'S INAUGURAL pledge that he would "unhesitatingly" implement the Compromise of 1850 gave confidence to many that the Democratic Party under his leadership would survive the sectionalism that had decimated the rival Whigs. But others were not so sure. Many old Jeffersonians and Jacksonians were chagrined that their old party, in the desire to keep the South aboard, was embracing candidates who, in the disparaging phrases, were "Northerners with Southern principles," or "doughfaces." Pierce himself drew the admonition from anti-slavery stalwarts in his own party, especially when he selected Jefferson Davis of Mississippi to be his secretary of war.

While this strategy served its purpose, recruiting old Southern Whigs as their own party crumbled, it was not without loud objections from old Democratic loyalists. Francis P. Blair, back in the fold after having joined Van Buren in the Free Soil experiment, complained: "Who are the leaders in the South who make such loud professions of Democracy?... Men who never were Democrats, but abhorred the name when it rallied the country around an Administration that was true... to the cause of free government.... Where did they study for their Democratic diploma? In the school of every opposition that ever assailed the party re-established by Jackson."[1]

Northern Whigs, too, were being lured into the Democratic Party by the strategy. One wealthy New York businessman, James W. Gerard, explaining his move, said: "If my party gives itself up to leaders who will betray its principles...I will go over to the old Democratic party."[2] Another Whig, Rufus Choate, was asked later about his switch: "But, Mr. Choate, what becomes of your long cherished Whig principles?" Choate replied: "Whig principles! I go to the Democrats to find them. They have assumed our principles, one after another, till there is little difference between us."[3]

In an effort to placate all elements of the party, the new converts as well as the old faithful, Pierce ran into a buzz saw over patronage that only intensified the troublesome animosities. In the South, he split federal appointments between so-called Southern Rights Democrats like Davis and Union Democrats and antagonized both. In the North, he outraged party regulars by choosing Caleb Cushing of Massachusetts, a former Tyler Whig, to be his attorney general. And he stirred up a hornet's nest among the Hunkers in New York by making returned Barnburner Marcy his secretary of state. The Hunkers themselves were now split into Hard-shells, favoring no patronage to the Barnburners, and Softshells, who were willing to have them back in the Democratic fold. The Hunker factions nominated separate tickets in 1853 and threatened to block the Pierce appointments in Congress.

While the old party lines were blurring, the sectionalism would not fade so easily. The Clay compromise had left burrs in the hides of Southerners and Northerners alike. The admission of California as a free state, having broken the parity of fifteen slave and fifteen free states, dismayed the South. It gave the North a new advantage in the Senate, and the more rapid population growth in the North as a result of industrial expansion brought the region increased membership in the House of Representatives as well. Railroad construction opening the West to greatly expanded commerce also made the South feel threatened by Northern and free-state domination.

At the same time, enforcement of the new Fugitive Slave Act specified in the compromise, the bone given to the South, roiled the North. Seized blacks were brought before federal commissioners without a trial by jury or the right to testify. If a commissioner determined the defendant was a slave to be returned to his owner, the commissioner received $10, but only $5 if he freed the accused. The arrangement not only encouraged convictions to line the pockets of commissioners but also raised suspicions that commissioners were being bribed by slave traders seizing free blacks. The law also required white citizens to assist federal marshals in capturing runaways, making them unwilling accomplices. The passage of personal liberty laws challenging enforcement, in the face of a continuing Underground Railroad assisting Southern blacks to escape to Canada, further agitated Southern slaveholders.[4]

All this unfolded as a new novel was published that rallied support for abolition—Harriet Beecher Stowe's *Uncle Tom's Cabin*. The story of human bondage in the South first appeared in serial form in an abolitionist weekly paper but came out in novel form in 1852, selling 300,000 copies in the first year, and soon was brought to the stage. Its impact was startling and far-reaching, North and South, reigniting the flame of sectional hostility that the Clay compromise was designed to snuff out, or at least reduce to smoldering.

When Congress reconvened in December 1853, separate Democratic factions in the Senate, one Northern and Western, the other Southern, set out to give the party the leadership both thought Pierce was failing to provide. The first, led by Douglas, strove to get past the patronage fights and focus on territorial expansion, which inevitably would raise the slavery question anew. The other, led by a group of Southern senators who roomed together in a boarding house on Washington's F Street, set about picking up the mantle of the departed Calhoun to defend the Southern "way of life" by opposing confirmation of appointees identified as antislavery.[5]

In early 1854, Douglas as chairman of the Senate Committee on Territories introduced a bill to organize the Nebraska Territory, part of the Louisiana Purchase, whose land had been declared off limits to slavery in the Missouri Compromise of 1820. Immediately what was called the "F-Street Mess," led by R.M.T. Hunter and James M. Mason of Virginia, Andrew P. Butler of South Carolina and David R. Atchison of Missouri, declared the bill would be scuttled unless slavery was allowed in the territory—in other words, unless the Missouri Compromise was repealed.

Douglas of Illinois had more in mind than western expansion. As part of his plan for gaining the presidency, he wanted to remove Indian tribes to make way for white settlers who would help build a transcontinental railroad on a northern route from Chicago to the Pacific Coast. Opening the Nebraska Territory to civil government would facilitate the effort. But the route starting in his home state, making Chicago the mid-American metropolis, had rivals who preferred the railroad to run west from New Orleans or St. Louis. The matter of slavery became a central element in the competition, with Atchison at one point declaring he would see Nebraska "sink in hell" before he would agree to it becoming anything but a slave state.[6]

Douglas, who cared more about western expansion than he did about slavery, attempted various language to satisfy the Southern bloc and finally agreed to the outright repeal of the Missouri Compromise. The result was the Kansas-Nebraska bill, which stipulated that popular sovereignty would determine the slavery question in the two would-be new states. Douglas tried to placate outraged anti-slavery Northern Democrats by assuring them settlers in both Kansas and Nebraska would opt against slavery. They were not convinced; they did not want to rely on the settlers' judgment and sentiment. Nebraska, neighbor to free Iowa, was not considered a problem, but Kansas, bordering on slave-state Missouri, was another matter. Southerners in Congress, figuring Kansas would become a slave state and offset free Nebraska, were willing to settle for that.

Pierce, always striving for intraparty comity, went along. The Senate passed the bill in March 1854 and the House three months later. The president signed it despite fierce demonstrations in opposition in New England and the Northwest. Many white settlers who were planning to move across their state borders into the two territories and abolitionist Northerners saw the bill as evidence of what was called Slave Power muscling the Democratic Party and Pierce into submission.

Even before passage of the Kansas-Nebraska Act, the controversy had been instrumental in generating a new political movement of immense significance. A pamphlet called "Appeal of the Independent Democrats in Congress to the People of the United States" by Senator Salmon P. Chase of Ohio assaulted Douglas and his bill as "a gross violation of a sacred pledge; as a criminal betrayal of precious rights; as part and parcel of an atrocious plot to exclude from a vast unoccupied region immigrants from the Old World and free laborers from our States." It warned that the West faced becoming "a dreary region of despotism, inhabited by masters and slaves."[7] The statement became a rallying cry of "anti-Nebraska men" against a Democratic Party under Southern dominance.

In Ripon, Wisconsin, in February 1854, a group of Conscience Whigs, Free Soilers, abolitionists and anti-slavery Northern Democrats, led by one Alvan E. Bovay, joined forces and, calling themselves Republicans, began organizing. About five months later, after Pierce had signed the bill, a similar group met in Jackson, Michigan, identified itself as the Republican Party,[8] and the third party system, midwifed by the slavery issue, emerged. The founders deliberately took the name of the old Jeffersonian party but welcomed all comers into a fusion effort to express their opposition and contempt for a Democratic Party that in their view had become captive of the Southern "Slavocracy." In some states they called themselves the People's Party. The anti-Nebraska movement demonstrated its clout in the congressional elections that fall. Free-state Democratic members of the House lost 66 seats, reducing them from a dominating 93 to only 27. A new, major rival to the shaken Democratic Party was already making its presence felt.

The Kansas-Nebraska bill was not, however, the only spark that fired the rebellion against the Democrats. New economic and social developments that Pierce failed to address adequately drove wedges between the old party and its traditional constituencies. Demands for land grants to help states build railroads and make waterway improvements, and appeals for a new homestead act, either were ignored or vetoed by Pierce, driving off Westerners particularly.

Significantly also, the flood of immigration from Ireland, Germany and other European countries brought changes that generated suspicion and hostility toward the newcomers. They were blamed for everything from job losses among the American-born to depressed wages, crime, slums and drunkenness, with the prime target members of the Catholic Church, which experienced a growth of nearly 40 percent from 1850 to 1854. And because, preyed upon and prodded by local party organizers, they voted overwhelmingly Democratic, apprehension among Protestants was predictable. The arrival of a papal nuncio in the United States in 1853 stimulated talk of Vatican influence, seemingly confirmed by pressures for aid to parochial schools. Pierce's appointment of an Irish Catholic as postmaster general was taken by concerned non-Catholics as additional evidence.[9]

All this fed a movement of nativism and temperance that Horace Greeley dubbed the Know-Nothings, seeking to keep the foreign-born from holding public office and inhibiting their ability to vote by extending the time required before applying for citizenship. Their aggressiveness eroded Democratic support in many cities but did solidify Catholic support in others for the party, viewed by the harassed immigrants as a shield against such hostility.

The Know-Nothings, first called the Native American Party in Louisiana, had moved north, electing a mayor of New York and six members of Congress in 1844. They held a national convention of sorts in Philadelphia in 1847, backing Taylor for president, and another in Trenton in 1852 nominated Webster, who ignored the compliment and died a few months later. From the secret Order of the Star-Spangled Banner came the name Know-Nothings because members, when asked about its activities, replied: "I don't know."[10]

Essentially more nativist than anti-slavery, the movement that eventually called itself the American Party seemed to be riding a tide of popularity with hopes of capitalizing on Democratic disorder in the 1856 presidential election. But it erred at its national convention when Southern members forced through some pro-slavery resolutions, causing a major walkout of Northern delegates and sending it skidding toward eventual oblivion. Reduced to a Southern party with a narrow, negative appeal, it could not long survive.[11]

As expected, the trouble in implementing the popular sovereignty ordered in the new expansionist legislation was not in Nebraska, but in Kansas. Free-soil advocates encouraged settlers to move into the state in advance of any vote on slavery, but not enough arrived to counter overwhelmingly pro-slavery sentiment, bolstered by illegally voting Missourians. The result was the election of a pro-slavery territorial delegate to Congress and a pro-slavery legislature. It expelled anti-slavery members, ordered the death penalty for anyone aiding a fugitive slave and made it a crime to express abolitionist views.

The free-state forces organized a shadow government in Topeka and drew up a constitution of their own that called for an end to slavery in the state by 1857 and demanded new elections.[12] Over the next year, as armed terrorists attacked free-soil settlers, Pierce declared the Topeka constitution illegal and did nothing. When the free-state capital was moved to Lawrence, the attacks shifted there. It was left to John Brown, a dedicated and driven abolitionist, to respond, and on the night of May 24, 1856, he and several of his sons attacked a small sleeping community, killing five pro-slavery settlers who were not, however, slaveholders. Outraged Missourians hit back, burning another town and killing one of the sons as Brown himself went into hiding.[13] The plague called "Bleeding Kansas" claimed more than two hundred lives in the first year.

In the Senate, Charles Sumner of Massachusetts denounced the violence and called for admission of Kansas under the Topeka constitution, attacking the Pierce administration for tolerating the "rape" of Kansas. In the process, he made a personally disparaging remark about a stroke-induced infirmity of Senator Andrew P. Butler of South Carolina. A few days later, a young nephew of Butler, Congressman Preston Brooks, strode onto the Senate floor and caned Sumner into a state of unconsciousness that kept him out of the Senate for several years. Brooks was censured by the House and obliged to resign, but was then reelected, demonstrating the deep hatred that opposition to slavery had engendered at the highest governmental levels.

As the 1856 presidential election approached, the involvement of Pierce and Douglas in the Nebraska-Kansas bill and its brutal fallout compromised their chances for the Democratic nomination. But they sought it anyway, along with two other past losers, Cass and Buchanan. Cass, now seventy-four, was also tarnished by the same brush, having voted with Douglas to repeal the Missouri Compromise against the position of many fellow Northern delegates. However, Buchanan, Polk's secretary of state, had been in London as minister to England during the Pierce administration and uninvolved in any aspect of "Bleeding Kansas."

The party met in Cincinnati in early June and approved a platform that specifically endorsed "non-interference by Congress with slavery in state and territory, or in the District of Columbia," reflecting the theme of limited federal power and retention of all unspecified powers by the states.[14] In other words, the convention reaffirmed popular sovereignty, then being tested to the fullest in Kansas. On the first ballot, Buchanan, whose campaign was managed by Senator John Slidell of Louisiana, led with 135½ votes to 122½ for Pierce, 33 for Douglas and 5 for Cass. Pierce's support gradually eroded until the fifteenth ballot, when the count was Buchanan 168½, Douglas 118½, Cass 4½, Pierce 3½. After one more roll call, with Buchanan still about 28 votes short of the two-thirds majority, Douglas instructed his manager to withdraw his name in favor of the man who was twenty-two years his senior. Douglas would have another chance later. John C. Breckinridge of Kentucky was named Buchanan's running mate.[15]

The newly formed Republicans had met in Pittsburgh in the previous February and authorized a call for a nominating convention that pointedly did not use the word "Republican." Instead, it summoned all those opposed to repeal of the Missouri Compromise and extension of slavery into the new territories, and in favor of admitting Kansas as a free state and restoring the action of the federal government "to the principles of Washington and Jefferson."[16]

The first Republican National Convention met in Philadelphia in June, eleven days after the Democratic convention, with all the Northern states and the Territory of Kansas represented, plus four slaveholding states. With a plea for sectional conciliation, it nevertheless demanded admission of Kansas as a free state and declared that Congress held full sovereignty over the territories with the right and duty to bar slavery and polygamy from them. Opponents of slavery did not have to guess which party best represented them.

In a roll call described as informal, Colonel John C. Frémont of California, yet another Mexican War hero and Western explorer known as "The Pathfinder" who had served one term in the Senate, received 359 votes to 190 for John McLean of New Jersey, an associate justice of the Supreme Court and formerly a conservative Whig. On the next, formal vote, Frémont was nominated with 520 votes to 37 for McLean.

The Know-Nothings, now badly split into North and South factions, saw their Northern segment also back Frémont, and the Southern nominated former President Fillmore. Neither man was a nativist, indicating the Know-Nothings at least did know that they had no chance whatever unless they tried to expand their base beyond a core of hate-mongers against foreigners and Catholics.

The three-sided race among Buchanan, Frémont and Fillmore raised again the potential of another presidential election being thrown into the House of Representatives. Democratic Party loyalties had suffered serious defections, and the other two new parties had little pedigree on which to rely. Thus the candidates and their supporters were obliged to make their case in terms of sectional and philosophical appeal. For the Democrats, it was preservation of the party and the Union by somehow holding North and South together. For the Republicans, it was to Northern voters ridding the nation of the evil of slavery and to Westerners opening the territories to free labor and opportunity. Fillmore, attempting to accentuate the positive at the head of a negative party, avoided the nativist theme and tried to take a high road unfamiliar to many of those who marched uncertainly behind him.

The Know-Nothings, however, could not hold that course for long, charging erroneously that Frémont, an Episcopalian, was really a Catholic, a claim in which many Democrats willingly joined, hoping to keep Northern Protestants in their own camp. In the end, Buchanan's distance from involvement in the Nebraska-Kansas mess saved him from attacks from both rival parties that surely would have come against either Pierce or Douglas. And the well-established Democratic Party organization, in Buchanan's home state of Pennsylvania especially, carried him through. He won 45.3 percent of the popular vote and 174 electoral votes, to Frémont's 33.1 percent and 114 electoral votes and Fillmore's 21.6 percent and 8 in the electoral college.

The Democratic Party, for all its difficulties over slavery and territorial expansion, had again managed to survive. The Know-Nothings were finished, but the new Republican Party was just getting started. With little organization and support only in the North, it had served notice of greater political peril ahead to a Democratic Party increasingly perceived as controlled by a South that was clinging to its immoral "peculiar institution."

Buchanan himself did little to counter that perception, appointing a cabinet that was more sympathetic toward slavery than any in the past. He chose Cass, who had opposed the Wilmot Proviso, to be his secretary of state and Georgia's Howell Cobb to head Treasury.

More important, the new president, in his inaugural address, sought to defuse the slavery issue by directing public attention to a critical case concerning the matter before the Supreme Court, whose nine justices included five from slaveholding states and four Democrats. Buchanan had been in conversation with two of the justices and apparently had reason to believe the Court would rule in a fashion favorable to the South. Aware that the new Republican Party's serious challenge to his election had been based on the single issue of slavery, he hoped the Court would hand down a definitive decision that would take the issue off the table once and for all, and thus nip the new party in the bud.[17]

The case concerned a former slave named Dred Scott, originally owned by an army doctor named John Emerson in Missouri, a slave state, who had taken him into free Illinois, then on into the Wisconsin Territory and back into Missouri. Upon Dr. Emerson's death, Scott in 1846 had sued for his freedom in the state court, arguing that having lived in free territory qualified him. He won, but the Missouri Supreme Court reversed the ruling on appeal. The case then slowly worked its way to the U.S. Supreme Court, posing whether a black person was a citizen of the United States with legitimate access to its highest court.

The decision, written by Chief Justice Roger B. Taney, declared that blacks, seen historically in the country as "beings of an inferior order," had "no rights which any white man was bound to respect."[18] The ruling, as noted in one dissent, ignored that free blacks were entitled to vote in four of the original states. Taney and the Court also took it upon themselves to rule on the constitutionality of the Missouri Compromise of 1820, repealed in 1854, which barred the holding of slaves in territory of the Louisiana Purchase outside of Missouri. They found that the Fifth Amendment, requiring due process of law to deprive anyone of property, rendered it unconstitutional.

Rather than burying the slavery issue as Buchanan had hoped, the case only inflamed anti-slavery forces in the North. Former slave Frederick Douglass joined the outcry, and Republican leaders suspected a conspiracy between Buchanan and the Court's majority to put the issue to rest once and for all. In New York, William Seward raised the threat of reorganizing or packing the Court. J. S. Pike, Washington correspondent of the *New York Tribune,* ridiculed the majority as "five slaveholders and two doughfaces upon a question where their opinion was not asked," whereby the Court "draggled and polluted its garments in the filth of pro-slavery politics."[19]

The Dred Scott decision, instead of immobilizing the Republican Party, gave it strong new ammunition for arguing that the Democratic Party and now the Supreme Court were captives of the South, bent at all costs on extending slavery to the territories and making it a permanent national shame. Stephen Douglas particularly saw the decision as undermining the whole argument for popular sovereignty in the territories. If Congress could not vote to keep slavery out, how could territorial legislatures do so, even if so inclined? Douglas saw the issue as critical to his own presidential ambitions and to loosening the stranglehold he saw the South administering to his party.

The viability of popular sovereignty had its acid test in Kansas. Buchanan, disturbed by the furor kicked up in the Scott decision, decided to send Robert Walker, the transplanted Pennsylvanian who became "The Wizard of Mississippi," to Kansas as territorial governor. Buchanan instructed him to achieve a fair election on a constitution that would enable Kansas to apply for statehood. Walker attempted to use his political wizardry to conciliate pro-slavery and free-soiler settlers at a constitutional convention in the town of Lecompton, but their differences proved too great to overcome. When the pro-slavery territorial legislature set about planning for the election of delegates, the free-soilers balked, alleging unfairness, and refused to participate.[20]

The constitution produced by the participating pro-slavery men, which among other things called for barring free blacks from Kansas and reaffirming the slave status of some three hundred blacks already there, was summarily opposed by the free-soilers. The drafters would allow no votes on the constitution's individual provisions, permitting only an up-or-down vote on the whole. With the anti-slavery settlers boycotting, it was easily ratified. In a new election for members of the territorial legislature, however, Walker persuaded the free-soilers to take part and they won control by a comfortable margin. The new legislature ordered a referendum on the Lecompton constitution; this time the pro-slavery forces refused to participate and it was voted down.[21]

In the meantime, seeking to assuage his Southern-dominated cabinet, Buchanan had proceeded against Walker's protest to ask Congress to admit Kansas as a state under the Lecompton constitution. Walker resigned, whereupon Douglas injected himself into the fight, personally confronting Buchanan with allegations of surrender to the Southern wing of their party. The split between the Democrats who clung to the old North-South alliance and those who wanted no more of it was now open and deep.

When the Lecompton constitution itself finally went before Kansans for their yes-or-no vote on slavery, the anti-slavery settlers once again refused to take part and the pro-slavery forces prevailed. Buchanan seized on the vote to press his call on Congress to admit the territory as a slave state. Douglas fought the bill in the Senate, but only three Democrats joined him along with the Republican minority, and it passed. A compromise version offering Kansas a land grant if it accepted went before the voters, but they turned down what many construed to be a bribe, and Kansas continued as a territory until 1861, when it finally was admitted to the Union as a free state. All that was achieved before then was confirmation of slavery's potency as a Democratic Party divider—and Douglas's determination to resist it, and in the process advance his own pursuit of the White House.

The North-South dichotomy in the party was further widened by another economic panic in 1857, as land speculation, reckless investment and credit, spurred in part by the California gold rush, plunged the

Northeast into depression. The South, where the cotton crop continued to be robust and find ready European markets, largely escaped. The region's advocacy of low tariffs that hurt Northern manufacturers increased their hostility toward Dixie, as did its harboring of low-cost slave labor. Old Democrats in the North abandoned their former party and joined the new Republicans.

As a result, the congressional elections of 1858 offered a significant measure of the relative strengths of the new party rivalry between the Democrats and Republicans. No contest drew more attention than Douglas's defense of his Senate seat in Illinois against a Springfield lawyer and former Whig named Abraham Lincoln. Douglas's breach with Buchanan widened that summer as a result of a speech the fiery senator made in Chicago in which he denounced the Lecompton constitution as a "swindle."[22] Buchanan purged Douglas supporters from his administration and had his political lieutenants work for Douglas's defeat in his reelection bid, even to the point of bolting the state Democratic convention and naming a rival slate against the incumbent senator and his allies. Douglas lobbied Republican leaders in the hope of heading off an outside challenge, but the prospect of having Buchanan as an ally in defeating him was too appealing for them to turn down.

This man Lincoln who challenged Douglas was little known outside Illinois but was no political neophyte. He had served one term in the House of Representatives during the Mexican War, which he strongly opposed. In 1852 he ran and narrowly lost for the Senate and was trying again. At forty-nine he was an odd-looking yet imposing man, a gangling six feet four inches tall with the rugged appearance of an outdoorsman. His physical contrast with the stocky, diminutive Douglas could not have been sharper. The central issue in their campaign was whether slavery should be extended into the territories; at that time neither man opposed its existence in the established Southern states. In contrast to Douglas's advocacy of popular sovereignty to resolve the question, Lincoln flatly opposed extension of the "peculiar institution."

This difference provided the heart of the famous debates between the two men across the breadth of Illinois in the summer of 1858. The critical moment came in August in their debate at Freeport, where Lincoln posed a question that proved pivotal not so much in their contest for the Senate, but ultimately in their more important rematch in the presidential election two years later. With the backdrop of the Dred Scott decision holding that slaveholders could not be barred from bringing their "property" into the territories, Lincoln asked Douglas if there was any way territorial settlers could block slavery in advance of achieving statehood.

The question pointed up how the Scott decision had undermined Douglas's concept of popular sovereignty, and Douglas responded in a manner that directly challenged the Supreme Court's ruling. "It matters not what way the Supreme Court may . . . decide as to the abstract question whether slavery may or may not go into a Territory," he proclaimed. ". . . The people have the lawful means to introduce or exclude it as they please."[23] Douglas explained that a territory could keep slavery out by refusing to enact a local slave code required to enforce the institution. Clearly, the answer was not what Southern Democrats wanted to hear; Douglas had said much the same on other occasions but not under the spotlight of the celebrated debates.

Douglas tried to shore up his support in the South in another debate at Alton in mid-October, wherein he painted the North, and inferentially the Republican Party, as seeking to ride roughshod over Dixie in the matter. If each state would "mind its own business, attend to its own affairs, take care of its own negroes, and not meddle with its neighbors," he declared, "then there will be peace between the North and the South, the East and the West, throughout the whole Union." But, he went on, "The moment the North obtained the majority in the House and Senate by the admission of California, and could elect a President without the aid of Southern votes, that moment ambitious Northern men formed a scheme to excite the North against the South, and make the people be governed in their votes by geographical lines, thinking that the North, being the stronger section, would outvote the South, and consequently they, the leaders, would ride into office on a sectional hobby."[24]

Lincoln denied any interest in splitting North and South, saying the real issue was whether slavery as a practice was right or wrong. "The sentiment that contemplates the institution of slavery in this country as a wrong is the sentiment of the Republican party," he said at Alton. But that did not mean, he added, that his party was bent on ending it; merely on holding it in check where it already existed. While considering slavery to be wrong, he added, Republicans "nevertheless have due regard for . . . the difficulties of getting rid of it in any satisfactory way . . . they insist that it should, as far as may be, *be treated* as a wrong: and one of the methods of treating it as a wrong is to *make provision that it shall grow no larger.*"[25]

Lincoln's condemnation of slavery on moral grounds underscored the new Republican Party's identity as a Northern creature willing to achieve success or suffer failure on, as Douglas pointed out, a sectional argument.

Douglas managed to win reelection to the Senate by a narrow margin, but his Democratic Party lost control of the House. Furthermore, his break with the South-appeasing Buchanan over the Kansas constitution row and his refusal to accept the Dred Scott decision as the final answer on the extension of slavery into the territories confirmed him as persona non grata in his own party, still heavily dependent on Southern support. Heading toward the presidential election of 1860, with the beleaguered Douglas determined to be the Democratic nominee, the party of Jefferson and Jackson faced a severe moment of truth.

At the same time, violence mounted with a raid in October 1859 by abolitionist John Brown, still a fugitive from justice after the Kansas killings, on a federal arsenal in a firehouse at Harpers Ferry, West Virginia. With a band of eighteen white and black men, Brown held the firehouse for two days, allegedly in an attempt to provoke a slave uprising, during which many of his men were killed or wounded by U.S. Marines under the command of General Robert E. Lee. Captured, tried and hanged for murder, Brown predicted before mounting the gallows that "the crimes of this guilty land will never be purged away, but with Blood."[26]

Amid a resulting hysteria in the South about a rumored black insurrection, North-South animosity mushroomed in Congress, with the Democratic Party now in the minority in the House. A few days after Brown's execution, the Democrats, with the help of Know-Nothings and surviving Whigs, thwarted the election of Republican John Sherman of Ohio to be speaker, on grounds he had endorsed a new book by a white North Carolinian, Hinton Rowan Helper, critical of slaveholding as poisonous to the interests of all whites. In the heat of the debate, some members of Congress began toting pistols onto the House floor.[27]

In the Senate soon after, Jefferson Davis of Mississippi introduced a series of resolutions calling for a national code to protect slave property and the barring of state personal liberty laws designed to shield captured blacks from the fugitive slave law, so despised in the North but insisted upon in the South. Davis's objective was at least in part to complicate Douglas's bid for the next Democratic presidential nomination. In a direct slap at the Little Giant, the resolutions were endorsed by the Democratic caucus in the Senate.

Unsurprisingly, the Democratic Party was deeply and bitterly divided as it held its national convention in Charleston in April 1860. The South Carolina site had been chosen as a gesture of good will toward Dixie, but it was a fruitless one. Douglas was the clear choice of Northern Democrats, with others favoring no specific candidate and motivated only by the desire to deny him the nomination. Buchanan and his associates threw in with firebrands from seven Southern states—Alabama, Georgia, Florida, Mississippi, Louisiana, Texas and Arkansas—who consulted beforehand on bolting the convention unless the platform included a federal guarantee of slavery in the territories, a provision they knew Douglas could not accept.

The anti-Douglas forces proposed a platform that incorporated many of the Davis Senate resolutions, including the poison-pill provision. The Douglas forces opposed it, insisting on popular sovereignty in the territories, and after seven bitter days of argument forced through a compromise that did little more than acknowledge the deep divide over slavery. The bombastic William L. Yancey of Alabama demanded that the party stop pandering to the North and take a categorical stand in defense of the "peculiar institution." The floor leader for Douglas, Senator George Pugh of Ohio, replied: "Gentlemen of the South, you mistake us—you mistake us—we will not do it!"[28] Thereupon a host of Deep South delegates walked out behind the Alabama delegation led by Yancey.

An attempt to nominate Douglas under the two-thirds rule of the total convention, not those still present, then slogged through fifty-seven ballots without success. The convention finally was forced to adjourn with plans to reconvene in Baltimore in June, and all delegations were urged to come at full strength. The Southerners who had walked out held their own convention and adopted the platform based on the Davis resolutions, but took no action then on a presidential nominee.

Meanwhile, also in Baltimore, a group of old Whigs sought to revive their near-comatose party in conjunction with moderate Southerners who abhorred secession, former Know-Nothings and even some Republicans who were not as strident against slavery as their brethren. They formed a new Constitutional Union Party whose objective was the preservation of the Union at all costs. They nominated the moderate former Senator John Bell of Tennessee, an opponent of the Nebraska and Lecompton bills, on the second ballot over Sam Houston of Texas, and unanimously picked Edward Everett of Massachusetts as his running mate.[29] Their platform essentially held that the right of property could not be denied either by Congress or a territorial legislature, and that it was the federal government's obligation to protect that right.

A week later in Chicago, at a Republican National Convention devoid of the sort of fireworks that were tearing the Democratic Party apart, the delegates nominated Lincoln on the third ballot over William H. Seward of New York, managed by Thurlow Weed and regarded by many of the delegates as too stridently anti-slavery. Senator Hannibal Hamlin of Maine was nominated for vice president. The Republican platform, seeking to reaffirm the party's stand against slavery without excessively trumpeting it, included a strong states' rights plank that by implication criticized the Dred Scott decision supporting slavery in the territories. The platform also courted Westerners with advocacy of internal waterways improvements and a transcontinental railroad, and it sought to assuage German immigrants led by Carl Schurz, now a key Northern voting bloc, by calling for a new homestead law and opposing some Northern state efforts to tighten naturalization laws.[30]

When the Democrats reconvened in Baltimore on June 18, the North-South hostility of the Charleston meeting reconvened with them. Some delegates who had walked out of the Charleston convention showed up, as did newly named delegates from states that had withdrawn from the previous meeting. It took three days to work out procedures, and even then the convention work was delayed by a portentous collapse of a temporary floor constructed over the hall's orchestra pit, with delegates sent sprawling and retreating as repairs were made. Hours of more haggling went on over the admittance or barring of delegates from the Southern states who had walked out at Charleston. The Douglas forces agreed to the readmission of all such delegates except those from Alabama and Louisiana, but Virginia in protest led another walkout, joined by other Southern delegations as well as Oregon and California.

The remaining delegations proceeded with the first roll call for the presidential nomination. Douglas received all but six votes cast, but as a result of the walkout nearly 40 percent of the total eligible ballots were not cast, keeping him short of the required two-thirds majority. He picked up eight votes on the second ballot but still was far short. Thereupon a resolution was offered and passed by the delegates present proclaiming that Douglas, "having now received two thirds of all the votes given in the Convention," was unanimously declared the nominee.[31]

In a gesture to the South, the choice of a running mate was left to a caucus of the Southern delegates who had not departed, and they selected Benjamin Fitzpatrick of Alabama. The convention unanimously accepted the recommendation and adjourned, but Fitzpatrick declined and the Democratic National Committee subsequently filled the vacancy by choosing Herschel V. Johnson of Georgia as the vice-presidential nominee. The platform on which he and Douglas would run stipulated that the question of slavery in the territories would be left to the Supreme Court— yet another finesse designed not to alienate the South beyond repair.

On June 28, 115 Southern Democrats who had walked out at the original Charleston convention and a like number who withdrew from the Baltimore meeting convened once more in Charleston. There, dubbing themselves National Democrats, clearly a misnomer, they selected a nominee of their own, Vice President John C. Breckinridge of Kentucky, with Senator Joseph Lane of Oregon as his running mate. Their platform provided for protection of slavery by Congress.[32] The united Democratic Party of Jackson was no more; if Douglas the popular-sovereignty candidate was to be elected, he was going to have to accomplish it largely without the South.

With four candidates vying for the presidency, the election of 1860 became two contests, one in the North between Douglas and Lincoln, the other in the South between Breckinridge and Bell. The Democratic Party ran two separate candidates and two separate campaigns out of separate national party committees in Washington, resulting in an impossible schism that assured Lincoln's election unless Douglas, Breckinridge and Bell together could win enough votes to force the contest into the House of Representatives. Efforts to fuse the three anti-Lincoln candidacies were futile. Jefferson Davis proposed that the three withdraw in favor of Horatio Seymour of New York, but Douglas refused, contending the action would only drive his supporters into the Lincoln camp. Buchanan, openly opposing Douglas, launched the Breckinridge campaign with a speech at a massive rally in Washington.

The main concern for the Republicans was that the Democrats would succeed in convincing voters that Lincoln's election would mean the destruction of the Union, as a result of Southern secession over fears that he would kill the "peculiar institution." Accordingly, while holding to their position against extension of slavery into the territories, Lincoln surrogates—he did not campaign or make a single speech himself—

emphasized other proposals including homestead legislation for farmers and settlers, a protective tariff in the manufacturing states and internal improvements including the transcontinental railroad to the Pacific Coast.[33]

The Lincoln camp aggressively touted its candidate as a rugged frontiersman, identifying him as "The Railsplitter," with paintings, cartoons and gold coins depicting his reported earlier ax-wielding in the construction of railroad lines. Soon Lincoln Rails became a campaign symbol in the tradition of Jackson's Hickory Clubs. Marching clubs called Wide-Awake Societies proliferated throughout the North, members often wearing special uniforms, chanting and singing the virtues of "Honest Abe."

In contrast to Lincoln, Douglas campaigned broadly himself, North and South, continuing to promote popular sovereignty as the only way to bring Northern and Southern Democrats together, prevent secession and preserve the Union. He spoke in twenty-three states in all regions of the nation, including the Deep South in the final weeks when defeat stared him in the face, pleading for preservation of the Union. He warned the North that secession could result if a purely sectional candidate like Lincoln were elected, but he also left in the South no doubt that as president he would not stand by idly if any Southern state were to try to secede. In response to a question at Norfolk, he replied that as president, "I, as in duty bound by my oath of fidelity to the Constitution, would do all in my power to aid the government of the United States in maintaining the supremacy of the laws against all resistance to them, come from whatever quarter it might."[34]

Douglas's straightforwardness did him no good. Lincoln won 39.8 percent of the popular vote to 29.5 percent for Douglas, 18.1 percent for Breckinridge and 12.6 percent for Bell. The four-man race did not prevent Lincoln from winning a clear majority of the electoral vote, carrying all of the free states except for three of seven New Jersey electors. Douglas was severely damaged by his loss of the South, winning only Missouri and the three electors lost by Lincoln in New Jersey. Bell won Tennessee, Kentucky and Virginia and Breckinridge the rest, all in the Deep South, plus Delaware and Maryland. The final electoral totals were Lincoln 180, Breckinridge 72, Bell 39, Douglas a mere 12. The result was a clear message to the South: it no longer had the political power to impose its will on the slavery question.

The region's response to that reality was not long in coming. South Carolina and other states throughout the Deep South began weighing the necessary formal steps for secession. Buchanan, in effect repudiated by not being given a second nomination and his candidate and party also rejected, considered his powers limited in the four months remaining to him in office. Only Congress could mend the breaches inflicted by the stormy political events culminating in Lincoln's election, he argued, and with both House and Senate out of session in November on the heels of the election, a long lull occurred in which the threat of secession was not taken seriously at first. As for Lincoln, he remained in Springfield, determined not to involve himself until national power came to him on the first Monday in March. Northern politicians assumed that the South's talk of secession was bluff.

Buchanan, however, did meet with his cabinet three days after the election to consider a critical matter that could not be put off. The newly built Union garrison of Fort Sumter in the harbor at Charleston, South Carolina, protected by fewer than a hundred men and designed to defend against a foreign foe, now had to contemplate a threat from the rear by secessionists. Buchanan decided to change fort commanders and ordered the transfer of a Southerner, Major Robert Anderson of Kentucky, from nearby Fort Moultrie, while he considered a compromise move.

It came in his annual address to Congress on December 3. Warning of a possible slave insurrection, he urged the calling of a constitutional convention to resolve the slavery question. He suggested amendments that would assuage the South by securing the practice of slavery where it already existed and assuring the return of fugitive slaves seized in the North.

"The incessant and violent agitation of the slavery question throughout the North for the last quarter of a century," he said, "has at length produced its malign influence on the slaves and inspired them with vague notions of freedom. Hence a sense of security no longer exists around the family altar. This feeling of peace at home has given place to apprehensions of servile insurrections.... Should this apprehension of domestic danger, whether real or imaginary, extend and intensify itself until it shall pervade the masses of the Southern people, then disunion will become inevitable."[35]

Buchanan, while denying South Carolina's right to secede, indicated he lacked the power to use force to prevent it, thereby encouraging other Southern states to believe they could also withdraw from the Union with impunity. At the same time, he blamed the North, observing that the impasse had resulted from "the long-continued and intemperate interference of the Northern people with the question of slavery in the Southern states."[36]

President-elect Lincoln, for his part, was careful not to make any public gesture or statement toward heading off the Union breakup that would be seen as a presumptuous and premature act of leadership. To give the South any hope that he would go back on his stated principles against slavery, he said from Springfield, "would make me appear as if I repented for the crime of having been elected, and was anxious to apologize and beg forgiveness. To so represent me would be the principal use made of any letter I might now thrust upon the public."[37]

Some sentiment appeared in the North at first to permit the Southern states, in the words of Horace Greeley's *New York Tribune*, to "go in peace."[38] Thurlow Weed's *Albany Evening Journal* proposed reenactment of the Missouri Compromise. Republican Congressman John Sherman suggested dividing the remaining Western territories "into states of convenient size, with a view to their prompt admission into the Union" as a way to dodge the issue of slavery expansion into them.[39] Special committees were created in the House and Senate to consider the options, which basically narrowed down to peaceful separation of the South, some compromise not likely to be accepted by the North, or war.

On December 11 the Louisiana legislature called for a state convention to consider secession, and on December 20, South Carolina was the first state to take the fateful step, with expectations that others would follow soon. Only two days earlier, in an effort at conciliation and compromise in the spirit of Henry Clay, Senator John J. Crittenden of Kentucky had introduced resolutions to reinforce a federal slave code and repeal of all personal liberty laws. Another would have protected slavery south of the boundary of the old Missouri Compromise extended westward to the Pacific, and in any territory "hereafter acquired."[40] The language suggested encouragement to expanding slavery into the Caribbean, the aspiration of some Southern slaveholders.

With the persevering Douglas futilely laboring for compromise as part of a special Senate "Committee of Thirteen," this and other subsequent efforts to avert secession, including an offer to admit New Mexico as a slave state, all went for naught. Lincoln, saying nothing publicly, was reported privately to have told his supporters: "Entertain no proposition for a compromise in regard to the extension of slavery. The instant you do, they have us under again; all our labor is lost, and sooner or later must be done over . . . have none of it. The tug has come, and better now than later."[41]

The Republicans agreed and stood fast, and as the end of the momentous year approached, Buchanan and his defeated party found themselves at rock bottom, soon to relinquish national power in the most decisive and definitive fashion since the Democratic Party had been reconstituted by Andrew Jackson. Some Southern members of the Buchanan cabinet bailed out, including Cass of Michigan, the infirm secretary of state, when Buchanan failed to send requested reinforcements to Anderson at Fort Sumter. At year's end, however, he relented and on New Year's Eve of 1860, rebuffing a delegation from South Carolina that demanded withdrawal of all Union troops from Charleston, he authorized the dispatch of a relief ship to Sumter.

The Democratic Party was broken in two, at last succumbing to the reality that it was split between a Southern wing that clung to slavery and insisted on imposing it on the whole party, and a Northern wing that would no longer permit the South to do so. The Union itself was impaled on the division between North and South, with brutal and bloody ramifications hardly imagined yet ahead.

THE SMELLING COMMITTEE.

In 1868, after Radical Republicans had successfully brought impeachment charges against President Andrew Johnson, pictured on the far right in this Currier and Ives cartoon, Democratic senators, joined by seven Republicans, acquitted him, leaving impeachment as a rotting horse carcass.

Chapter 11

CIVIL WAR AND PEACE DEMOCRATS, 1861–1868

AS 1861 BEGAN, lame-duck Democratic President Buchanan showed some backbone against the first actions of secession. Upon the resignation of Southern members of his cabinet, he filled the vacancies with strong Union defenders. He told Congress that the Union was "a sacred trust" and that he was committed to collecting federal taxes and protecting federal property everywhere. That included Fort Sumter at the mouth of Charleston harbor, which he finally reinforced after a first ship was fired upon from secessionist shore batteries.

Meanwhile, thirty Southern members of Congress sent word to their districts that "the argument is exhausted," and most Deep South congressional delegations headed for home.[1] Senator Crittenden tried a last-ditch effort to hold them off by proposing a referendum to the nation on his resolutions. Douglas, in the spirit of his earlier advocacy of popular sovereignty to determine the slavery question in the territories, enthusiastically embraced the idea, asking, "Why not give the people a chance?"[2] But the Republicans, following Lincoln's advice, blocked it. By the first of February, Mississippi, Florida, Alabama, Georgia, Louisiana and Texas all had followed South Carolina into secession. Delegates from these seven states met in Montgomery, Alabama, and on February 7, 1861, adopted their own provisional constitution for the new Confederate States of America.

There remained one last attempt to avert an open clash. With Virginia still holding back from secession, seventy-one-year-old former president John Tyler, the Democrat turned Whig who had returned to his old party allegiance upon ascending to the presidency, called for a peace conference of a dozen border states, six free and six slave. The Virginia legislature sponsored it, inviting all states North and South to meet in Washington on the same day of the convention in Montgomery launching the Confederacy.

The Deep South states boycotted the peace conference at Willard's Hotel, and those from the Far West could not get there, so it was dominated by Northern and border-state Democrats. Some 132 representatives from twenty-one states attended, with the venerable Tyler of Virginia as chairman, and fashioned proposed constitutional amendments that got nowhere. The conference's recommendations finally came before the Senate on the final night of the Buchanan administration and were rejected. Buchanan had somehow managed to complete his presidential term, going out with a whimper, and the Democratic Party with him.

When President-elect Lincoln finally arrived in Washington days before his March 4 inauguration, Douglas, the Democrat he had defeated, called on him to adopt a conciliatory attitude toward the South. Lincoln edited his inaugural address, first drafted in Springfield, to reflect that advice. He softened earlier language suggesting coercion to assure compliance with Union laws and pledged Union troops would not invade the South. He intended to act, he said, "with a view and a hope of a peaceful solution of the national troubles, and the restoration of fraternal sympathies and affections."[3] But he was firm about his position that no state had a right to secede and that it was a president's obligation "to administer the present government as it came to his hands, and to transmit it, unimpaired by him, to his successor."[4]

Lincoln said he would "hold, occupy and possess" federal property including Fort Sumter in seceded states, would collect import duties due the United States and deliver mail throughout the country "unless repelled."[5] He pleaded that "though passion may have strained, it must not break, our bonds of affection" and predicted all Americans would be guided "by the better angels of our nature."[6] Douglas, who in a symbolic gesture of solidarity reached out and held Lincoln's hat as the new president began his address, called the speech a "peace offering." But the London *Times* pronounced it "neither more nor less than a declaration of civil war."[7] Yet the words of this first Republican president, by Buchanan's reckoning later, conveyed a policy, including Union retention of Fort Sumter, not far from his own.

The day after Lincoln's inauguration, however, grim news came from Major Robert Anderson, the commanding officer at Sumter. He informed the new president that he would need at least twenty thousand troops and did not believe he could hold the fort for more than four to six weeks. Cabinet members urged evacuation of Sumter and also Fort Pickens in Florida, and Douglas and other Northern Democrats agreed. But Lincoln wrote Anderson promising to send relief and notified the governor of South Carolina he would be delivering provisions only, not men or ammunitions.

Rather than waiting for the arrival of the relief ship, the new Confederate government in Montgomery demanded the evacuation of Sumter. Anderson refused, at the same time lamenting that he was close to being starved out without any such demand. At 4:30 a.m. on the morning of April 12, 1861, the shelling of Sumter began, and thirty-three hours later Anderson was forced to evacuate. Somehow, not a single man died on either side, but the Civil War was under way.

The conflict between North and South had already split the Democratic Party, with hordes of members in Dixie transferring their allegiance to the new Confederacy. With the outbreak of hostilities, Northern Democrats with varying degrees of enthusiasm pledged support to the war effort under Lincoln. In a gesture of unity, the Republican Party changed its name to the National Union Party and many Democrats, including Douglas, joined with it in what proved to be an essential ingredient for a Union victory in the war. Many others, however, while avowing support of the fight to save the Union, continued under the tattered Democratic banner as the loyal opposition, challenging Lincoln on a range of domestic issues and, in time, on his conduct of the war.

The first group came to be known as the War Democrats, the latter as the Peace Democrats, each with factions of its own depending on the vigor with which they criticized the war effort and pushed for peace negotiations. Before long, however, moderate and radical Democrats alike were lumped together by many Unionists. The Republican *New York Tribune,* for example, confidently dismissed the Democratic Party as "a myth, a reminiscence, a voice from the tomb, an ancient, fishlike smell."[8]

At the outset, the public mood cried out for the abandonment of partisan politics. "Whoever is not prepared to sacrifice party organizations and platforms on the altar of his country," Douglas proclaimed to the Illinois Assembly in Springfield, "does not deserve the support or countenance of honest people."[9] In Chicago, he told a huge crowd: "Every man must be for the United States or against it. There can be no neutrals in this war; only patriots or traitors."[10]

Peace Democrats, distressed at the change in Douglas's posture from that of a strong pleader for peace with the South before the outbreak of the war, urged him to restate his position to clarify the apparent contradiction. In response, he wrote a long letter dated May 10, 1861, that gave them no comfort. "One of the brightest chapters in the history of our country," it said, "will record the fact that during this eventful period the great leaders of the opposition, sinking the partisan in the patriot, rushed to the support of the government and became its ablest and bravest defenders." In what amounted to a credo for the War Democrats, Douglas observed that "if we hope to regain and perpetuate the ascendancy of our party, we should never forget that a man cannot be a true Democrat unless he is a loyal patriot."[11]

The letter was his last political testament. Less than a month later, six weeks after the fall of Sumter, Douglas's voice was silenced by death at the age of forty-eight, and the Democratic Party—and the War Democrats—suddenly found themselves with a vacuum of leadership. Douglas men in various Northern states surfaced, including West Point graduate George B. McClellan, a close friend of Douglas who was then a military engineer in Illinois. He took command of the Ohio militia, and other War Democrats received similar posts in other Northern states. When Congress met for a special war session in July, the War Democrats' leader in the House was another Douglas man, John A. McClernand of Illinois. So was James A. McDougall of California, the Senate leader of the War Democrats. But none of them approached Douglas's stature and influence.

Kate Sprague, daughter of Lincoln's treasury secretary, Salmon P. Chase, was said to have observed about the Democrats that "when the South seceded the brains of the party went with it,"[12] and that comment was all the more pertinent with the passing of the Little Giant from Illinois. His tenacious pursuit of popular sovereignty as the solution to the slavery question had not prevailed, but it had injected into the debate a much-needed reasonableness, always expressed with an inspiring vigor and forcefulness.

Many of Douglas's followers joined him in embracing the war effort and Lincoln under the new National Union Party banner, while not completely severing their Democratic affiliation. The new president appointed more of these War Democrats than Republicans to ranking military posts and spread patronage among all those now declaring themselves to be Unionists. At the same time, Lincoln called up 75,000 members of the militia over the next three months as both sides girded for the unimagined slaughter to come.

In the organization of the thirty-seventh Congress, the Democrats eschewed a caucus of their own, demurred on nominating a candidate for House speaker and joined the Republicans in support of Lincoln's war legislative agenda. Many regular Democrats, however, seeing their party facing extinction, soon determined that party tradition and principle required that they remain a viable alternative. Ignoring the new Union Party label of the opposition, some took to referring to the Lincoln party as the Black Republicans. They sought to keep fellow Democrats in the ranks by arguing it was motivated less by zeal to preserve the Union than to impose the abolition of black slavery, to the detriment of the white population. Lincoln's aggressive assumption of war powers not granted by the Constitution or Congress, notably his suspension of the writ of habeas corpus providing protection against illegal seizure and imprisonment, confirmed to the Democrats the wisdom of their persevering as an opposition party.

The most vociferous of these Peace Democrats, derisively called Copperheads by the Republicans after the treacherous snake, clung to the view that the North had been unduly harsh toward the South and aggressive in pursuing abolition, precipitating secession. They were increasingly convinced that the South could not be brought back into the Union by force of arms, and they pushed for a negotiated settlement. Their slogan became "the Constitution as it is, the Union as it was," and, some added, "and the Negroes where they are."[13]

The Peace Democrats were led by Ohio Congressman Clement L. Vallandigham and Mayor Fernando Wood of New York. Vallandigham was a bombastic speaker in support of national unity who aroused deep animosity among Unionists with fiery allegations that their pursuit of abolition destructively took precedence over the preservation of the Union. He rallied like-minded Democratic congressmen and issued a ringing call for the party not only to keep its principles alive but also, looking down the road, eventually to provide the only political vehicle that could win the war.

Democrats, he wrote to party colleagues, had an obligation to support the Lincoln administration "in all constitutional necessity, and proper efforts to maintain its safety, integrity and constitutional authority." But, he said, they were being asked to go well beyond that, "to give up your principles, your policy, and your party, and to stand by the Administration in all its acts." This they could not do, he declared, because the Democratic Party was "the only party capable of carrying on a war; it is the only party that has ever conducted a war to a successful issue, and the only party which has done it without abuse of power, without molestation of the rights of any class of citizens, and with due regard to economy.... If success, then, in a military point of view be required, the Democratic Party alone can command it."[14]

Wood, a onetime Tammany stalwart who managed to regain the office of mayor against the machine, argued that the Democratic Party could not be "an abolition war party. There can be no such thing as a War Democrat, because when a man is in favor of the war, he must be in favor of the policies of the war as it is prosecuted by the party in power, with its unavoidable tendency to destroy the Constitution and the Union." He added: "With our aggrieved brethren of the slave states, we have friendly relations and a common sympathy."[15] Charges of treason were heaped on both Vallandigham and Wood by the Republicans and some War Democrats.

In Lincoln's conduct of the war, he sought in the beginning to downplay abolition as a motivation and elevate saving the Union. He did so in deference to Unionist slaveholders in the border states and Northerners who continued their denigration of blacks as racially inferior and feared their competition with whites in the labor market. Black abolitionist leader Frederick Douglass, however, applied unrelenting pressure for an end to slavery. "The American people and the Government at Washington may refuse to recognize it for a time," he said in May, "but the inexorable logic of events will force it upon them in the end; that the war as waged in this land is a war for and against slavery."[16]

Concern that the view expressed by Douglass was correct increasingly mobilized the Peace Democrats' opposition to Lincoln. So did certain actions by the Unionist-controlled Congress, which in August 1861 and again the following July passed laws authorizing the confiscation of Southern slaveholders' property, including the slaves themselves, who were to be set free. While the North was in no position to implement the laws effectively, they reinforced the impression that ending slavery was the North's goal, beyond saving the Union.

So did actions by Congress barring the return of runaway slaves and the freeing of all slaves in the District of Columbia, with compensation to their owners. A similar offer to pay border-state slaveholders for their slaves if they would release them was rejected, however. This impression that the slavery issue was becoming the North's prime motivation in pursuing the war was, indeed, an important catalyst among Democrats in their determination not to permit the extinction of the party of Jefferson and Jackson. They clung to the notion that it was the only vehicle through which North and South could be brought together again in what came to be called "peace without victory"—that is, without forcing abolition on the South.

Also persuading the Democrats to keep their party in active opposition was the fact that congressional Republicans under the new Union Party label were continuing to press other aspects of their party's old agenda. In 1861, after Democratic legislators from the secession states left Capitol Hill, the Republicans won admission of Kansas as a free state, and the new party scored heavily in Northern state elections that fall. The Unionist Congress in 1862 also passed a homestead act that awarded 160 acres of undeveloped farm land to squatters and set aside other tracts for the creation of sixty-nine land-grant colleges. High tariffs were enacted and a new national bank was established that served to solidify the Democratic opposition.

At the same time, these moves had only limited political influence in shoring up Lincoln's public support. His forces in the field suffered setbacks that in turn intensified criticism by the Peace Democrats and sentiment in the North to let the South "go in peace." The commanding general of Lincoln's Army of the Potomac, George McClellan, was so cautious in moving against the Confederate army in Virginia that the president at one point wrote to him: "If you do not want to use the army, I would like to borrow it for a few days."[17]

He finally relieved McClellan of command, replacing him with General John Pope, who marched his army into Virginia but also was repulsed. When Confederate General Stonewall Jackson seized Harpers Ferry, West Virginia, in September and marched on Hagerstown, Maryland, near the Pennsylvania border, Lincoln restored McClellan to his old command. The outlook for the North was glum.

The president finally concluded that his war effort required a bold psychological stroke. The mounting cost in human terms demanded that abolition of slavery be acknowledged as a cause worth the huge sacrifice. But Lincoln did not want to act from a losing military posture, so he waited for a more favorable moment.

It came on September 17, 1862, when the Union forces under McClellan turned back General Robert E. Lee's Confederate army at Antietam, Maryland, in the most costly single day's fighting of the war to that time— about four thousand men killed. Five days later, Lincoln issued his Emancipation Proclamation, declaring that all slaves in the rebellious states were after January 1, 1863, to be "forever free."[18] The announcement energized the North and brought strong approval from Europe, particularly among workers' groups, undercutting the South's cotton trade.

The proclamation cost Lincoln some support from War Democrats and was seized by the Peace Democrats as evidence of hypocrisy on his part. A taunting poem was soon in circulation:

> *Honest old Abe, when the war first began,*
> *Denied abolition was part of his plan;*
> *Honest old Abe has since made a decree,*
> *The war must go on till the slaves are all free.*
> *As both can't be honest, will some one tell how,*
> *If honest Abe then, he is honest Abe now?*[19]

The Antietam battle, which blunted a threatening Confederate march toward Washington, was not decisive, however, and many Peace Democrats only intensified their calls for a negotiated peace that would leave "the Constitution as it is and the Union as it was." In the congressional and state elections in the fall of 1862, the Democrats picked up thirty-two seats in Congress, a traditional gain by the out-of-power party in an off year, and several governorships and other statewide offices in key states. They read the result as meaning voters would back the war to preserve the Union but not to end slavery. While the election still left the Democrats as the minority, they hoped the result might cool Lincoln's commitment to emancipation, which only hardened Southern resistance.

But it did not. The Democrats increasingly protested against what they saw as the president's abuse of civil liberties in the arbitrary arrest of war critics. In return, the Unionists denounced them as traitors, though the Democrats insisted it was Lincoln and his conduct of the war they were against, not the war itself or the objective of preserving the Union. The Peace Democrats drew much of their public support from the Midwest, especially in the Ohio Valley, where small farmers of Southern origin suffered from lack of transport and feared a postwar influx of blacks, based on both racist and economic concerns. German, Irish and other ethnic communities shared these fears and longed simply for the prewar status quo of the Union as it was—and the blacks as they were.

As 1862 ran its course, the battle of arms seemed mired in stalemate. Once again, Lincoln removed McClellan from command, this time replacing him with General Ambrose Burnside, who engaged Lee at Fredericksburg, Virginia, with more heavy casualties and no decisive result. Meanwhile, an invasion of northern Mississippi by General Ulysses S. Grant was blunted and his forces driven back to Memphis at Christmastime.

Among the Copperheads who lost a bid for reelection in 1862 was Congressman Vallandigham. His defeat did not silence his opposition to the war; rather, he intensified it as a public speaker and crusader. Back home in Ohio, he began to attack the Lincoln war policy, in the wake of the Emancipation Proclamation, as an effort not to free blacks but rather to erode the power and influence of whites. In January 1863, as Lincoln signed the proclamation, Vallandigham on the House floor declared the war should continue "not a day, not an hour.... Stop fighting. Make an armistice" with the South, he demanded. "If, to-day, we secure peace and begin the work of reunion, we shall yet escape; if not, I see nothing before us but universal political and social revolution, anarchy, and bloodshed, compared with which the Reign of Terror in France was merciful visitation."[20]

After the Fredericksburg stalemate, a frustrated Lincoln changed commanding generals once again, replacing Burnside with Joseph Hooker of Massachusetts, an outspoken soldier with an autocratic reputation who had boldly said the army needed a "dictator." The president wrote him: "Of course it was not for this, but in spite of it that I have given you the command. What I now ask of you is a military success, and I will risk the dictatorship."[21] But Hooker also was battered by Lee's forces at Chancellorsville and had to withdraw, setting the stage for a major offensive by the Confederate army.

As Lee crossed into Pennsylvania and marched toward Harrisburg,

Lincoln again made a change, placing General George Meade of Pennsylvania in command. The opposing forces met at Gettysburg, where the Union army threw back the famous charge of General George Pickett, and after a bloody day of fighting sent Lee into retreat on July 3. The next day—Independence Day—a long siege of Vicksburg, Mississippi, by Grant brought surrender by the Confederate forces and Union control of the Mississippi River. For all practical purposes the Southern rebellion was broken, though not yet abandoned.

That same critical month, riots broke out in Northern cities in protest against a new military draft law that included a provision whereby a man could avoid being called up by hiring someone to serve for him, or by paying the federal government $300. Many blacks donned the Union uniform, raising complaints among Democrats fearful that their service would enhance their status as equals with whites—precisely what the war was now about.

Poor whites, especially the Irish, took to the streets, focusing their anger not so much on the rich who could buy their way out as on blacks who were to be the beneficiaries of the fighting. The New York *Daily News* asked editorially: "Why should a worker leave his family destitute while he goes out to war to free a Negro who will then compete with him for a job?"[22] A black children's orphanage in New York was burned and seventy-four people died and hundreds of others were beaten. All this fed the Peace Democrats' argument against the war and against Lincoln, while at the same time raising more questions about their loyalty to the Union.

At the Democratic state convention in Ohio in July, Vallandigham said Democrats could reasonably join the fight against secession but should also "fight the unarmed, but more insidious and dangerous Abolition rebels of the North and West, through the ballot box."[23] Later, in August, Vallandigham in Dayton emphasized that he was for preservation of the Union but not for abolition of slavery. "I am for suppressing all rebellions," he said, "both rebellions. There are two—the Secessionist Rebellion South, and the Abolition Rebellion, North and West. I am against both; for putting down both."[24]

Such declarations led General Burnside, then commanding what was called the Department of the Ohio, to arrest and detain him for military trial, charging him with a violation of an army general order stating "declaring sympathy for the enemy will no longer be tolerated." Anyone convicted, the order said, would be tried "or sent beyond our lines into the lines of their friends."[25] The arrest disturbed not only the Peace Democrats but also fellow Ohio Congressman Samuel S. Cox, known as a "conditional" War Democrat, and others supporting the Unionist position.

Vallandigham refused to enter a plea and the military court sentenced him to close confinement for the duration of the war. He appealed for a writ of habeas corpus but the judge refused, ruling that Burnside had acted within his power. The opinion dismissed the Peace Democrats as "a class of mischievous politicians [who] had succeeded in poisoning the minds of a portion of the community with the rankest feelings of disloyalty," further describing them as "artful politicians, disguising their latent treason under hollow pretensions of devotion to the Union."[26] Such comments hurt the whole Democratic Party in the 1863 elections. "We are making a fierce fight," Cox wrote that summer, "but we carry weights," meaning Vallandigham and other Peace Democrats.[27]

The decision against him created an uproar among Democrats of all shades in Ohio and other Union states and Lincoln set it aside, directing instead that Vallandigham be given over to the Confederacy. After a brief stay in the South, he boarded a ship that ran the Union blockade and took him to Windsor, Canada, just across the boundary from Detroit. The Peace Democrats immediately trumpeted the case as illustrative of the civil liberties abuses of which they accused Lincoln. They called on War Democrats to join with them in protest. Such War Democrats as Cox did, while other "conditional" War Democrats now embraced the war policy even more wholeheartedly.

Vallandigham, more than ever a hero in the eyes of Ohio Peace Democrats when he was sent South, was nominated for governor in his home state as a symbol of their fight in behalf of First Amendment rights, but was soundly defeated. From Canada, he later made his way back home and rejoined the movement.

Meanwhile, the Union armies drove on in pursuit of elusive victory. In the fall of 1863, Grant defeated the Confederate forces at Chattanooga, leading Lincoln to put him in command of all Union forces. Through the winter and into 1864, Grant marshaled a massive force that finally met Lee in May in the Virginia Battle of the Wilderness. Despite taking huge losses at Spotsylvania and Cold Harbor, Grant moved on to Petersburg and more stalemate as Lee dug in for the defense of Richmond.

At the same time, Grant sent his chief lieutenant, General William Tecumseh Sherman, toward Georgia and his famous march to the sea. As the 1864 presidential election approached, however, with victory in the war not in sight, Lincoln's reelection prospects seemed imperiled, and the Democratic Party's hopes were on the rise.

Lincoln did not have the political luxury of a six-year term, as did Confederate President Jefferson Davis, although he too was being widely criticized for his conduct of the war. In Lincoln's own cabinet his secretary of the treasury, Salmon P. Chase, resigned and sought to rally support for the National Union nomination, but was seen as a spoiler. General John C. Frémont, the Republican Party's first presidential nominee in 1856, was nominated again at an anti-Lincoln rump convention in Cleveland in late May. But he got nowhere at the National Union convention in Baltimore in June and withdrew. Lincoln was renominated on the first ballot, and only a protest vote by the Missouri delegation in favor of Grant deprived the president of unanimous endorsement. The name "Republican" was seldom heard as the party emphasized national unity in recognition of the support of many War Democrats. Indeed, *Harper's Weekly,* noting the amalgam of factions under the Union banner, observed: "We are at the end of parties."[28]

In a gesture to the War Democrats, one of them, Andrew Johnson of Tennessee, son of a poor tailor, former senator and then military governor of the state, was chosen as the vice-presidential nominee under the National Union banner. With Lincoln's approval, he replaced incumbent Hannibal Hamlin of Maine, creating a backwoods ticket that might appeal to the voters. Nevertheless, the president was pessimistic about his chances. In August, with the Democrats gathering in Chicago for their own nominating convention, he called on his cabinet members to cooperate with "the President-elect to save the union between the election and the inauguration; as he will have secured his election on such ground that he cannot possibly save it afterwards."[29]

The Democrats were correspondingly optimistic. No president had been elected to a second term since Jackson. They were buoyed by their off-year congressional and gubernatorial successes in 1862 and their perception of a severely weakened and compromised Lincoln. Although Sherman was now on the outskirts of Atlanta, the Democratic platform castigated Lincoln's conduct of the war and alleged abuse of civil liberties, along with his Emancipation Proclamation as elevating the end of slavery over preservation of the Union. The platform attacked the use of blacks in the Union army and embraced the idea of "the Union as it was" in a negotiated "peace without victory," suggesting that slavery could survive the war after all. It called for "a cessation of hostilities with a view to an ultimate convention of the States, or other peaceable means" to restore the Union.[30] Among the platform shapers was Vallandigham, back from Canada and a convention delegate from Ohio.

The party nominated for president the still-popular Union general demoted by Lincoln, George McClellan, a war candidate running on a peace platform, and Congressman George Pendleton of Ohio, a Peace Democrat, as his running mate. Under pressure from War Democrats and party national chairman August Belmont, McClellan in effect repudiated a key part of the platform by declaring he would pursue the war to victory, stating that "the Union is the one condition for peace. We ask no more."[31] As a soldier, he said, "I could not look into the face of my gallant comrades of the army and navy who have survived so many bloody battles and tell them that their labors and the sacrifice of so many of our slain and wounded brethren had been in vain; that we had abandoned the Union for which we have so often periled our lives."[32]

Among the attacks on the president was a "Lincoln Catechism" circulated in New York that went like this:

> What is the Constitution? A compact with hell—now obsolete.
>
> By whom . . . ? By Abraham Africanus the First.
>
> To what end? That his days may be long in office—and that he may make himself and his people the equal of the negroes. . . .
>
> What is Congress? A body organized for the purpose of taxing the people to buy negroes, and to make laws to protect the President from being punished for his crimes. . . .
>
> What is the meaning of the word "patriot"? A man who loves his country less and the negro more.
>
> What is the meaning of the word "traitor"? One who is a stickler for the Constitution and the laws.
>
> What is the meaning of the word "Copperhead"? A man who believes in the Union as it was, the Constitution as it is, and who cannot be bribed with greenbacks, nor frightened by a bastile.[33]

Although the Democratic Party had survived the split that assured its defeat in 1860, it remained no match for the Union Party in power, bolstered as it was by the presence in its ranks of the War Democrats—and, more importantly—a change in the war's fortunes, even as the Unionists continued to tar the Democrats as the party of treason. Only days after the Democratic convention, Sherman took Atlanta, and in the fall a thrust toward Washington by Confederate cavalry was turned back into Virginia and then defeated in the Shenandoah Valley. The developments sharply undercut the Democrats' criticism of Lincoln as a wartime president and were instrumental in his solid reelection. He won 55 percent of the popular vote to 45 percent for McClellan and routed his foe in the electoral college, 212 votes to 21, the Democrat carrying only New Jersey, Delaware and Kentucky. Furthermore, the Republicans/Unionists increased their control of the Senate to 42–10 and the House to 145–40.[34]

Still, McClellan's 45 percent demonstrated that the Democratic Party was far from decimated. It had strong organizations in many of the larger key states and a growing political apparatus under national chairman August Belmont to coordinate party activities. A new Society for the Diffusion of Political Knowledge served as a vehicle for the writing and distribution of political tracts and speeches by Democratic leaders around the country. A strong party press functioned in support of Democratic candidates and policies, and in 1863 a group of party leaders led by New York financier Samuel L. Barlow bought the *New York World* and converted it into the leading Democratic newspaper. The problem was marshaling these resources to rehabilitate the party on the national stage, which was proving to be a very difficult task, with Republican/Union President Lincoln embarking on a second term amid ever more encouraging news about the war.

A week after the election, Sherman burned Atlanta and began his scorched-earth march toward Savannah and Charleston and into North Carolina. Lee, now appointed by Davis as commander of all Confederate forces, did his best to hold out, but finally at Appomattox on April 9, 1865, surrendered to Grant. The end of the war left the Democratic Party in the unhappy position of being widely seen as on the outside looking in. Credit for the victory went to Lincoln's Union Party, with those War Democrats aligned with it bringing little or no glory to their old political affiliation. In Congress at the time, the Democrats held less than a third of the seats. They controlled only one Northern state administration, in New Jersey, and they lost that in the fall election.

Only five days after the surrender at Appomattox, the euphoria over the end of the war was interrupted by tragedy. President Lincoln was shot by John Wilkes Booth, a wrathful actor, at Ford's Theatre in Washington as he watched a play with his wife, and perished hours later. Suddenly, Vice President Andrew Johnson, an old Democrat, was president at the head of what, with the war over, would soon resume its identity as the Republican Party. Both War and Peace Democrats hoped at this point that his elevation would be a vehicle for the restoration of his old party.

Johnson came into office with the unearned burden of a public reputation for drunkenness. It stemmed from a rambling, at times incoherent speech he had made in March 1865 upon taking the oath of office as vice president to preside over the Senate. The truth was that he had been recovering from a bout of typhoid fever and departing Vice President Hamlin had given him some whiskey as a bracer before the speech. Johnson apparently drank more than he should have considering his condition. Although there was no evidence of his having a drinking problem thereafter, the accusation clung to him.[35]

Many Radical Republicans in the National Union Party who were dissatisfied with what they saw as Lincoln's conservative, accommodating attitude toward the now-defeated South were hopeful at first at the advent of Johnson as president. But he disappointed them in keeping members of Lincoln's cabinet and continuing, in a general sense, the slain president's reconstruction aims of bringing reformed Confederate states back into the Union, while on his own firmly opposing black suffrage. This restoration of the Southern states, permitting white suffrage only, delighted the Democratic Party. To regain admission, they had formed new state governments in convention, had repealed secession, abolished slavery and elected members of the House and Senate, who came to Washington in December 1865 to take their seats.

The threat these restored states posed to the Radical Republicans was obvious if they were to team with the conservative Republicans and those Northern Democrats sympathetic to the South on the slavery issue during the war. Beyond that, passage of the Thirteenth Amendment barring slavery in all states also wiped out the old "federal ratio" calculation of counting only three-fifths of all blacks in each state in determining congressional apportionment. Now all blacks would be counted, a change likely to increase Southern—and Democratic—clout in Congress and in the electoral college as well.

At a time when hostility toward the South remained high in the North, the Democrats preached forgive and forget, no doubt with such political calculations in mind. Charles Mason, chairman of the Democratic National Committee at the time, wrote: "The erring members of our political family are now anxious to resume their wonted places in the social circle. Let them be welcomed as was the prodigal son in the parable and received back with all their rights and privileges unabridged. Let the promptings of resentment or revenge meet no favor from those who may perhaps feel that they need some forgiveness themselves."[36]

The radicals, however, blocked the seating of the Southern Democrats and established a Joint Committee on Reconstruction that challenged Johnson's conservative implementation of the Lincoln policy. Soon Congress was divided between the Republican/Unionist radicals on one side and the conservative Republicans, War Democrats, Peace Democrats and Southern Democrats on the other. The radicals' best hope of countering this coalition was to give the vote to the new freedmen, the Southern blacks who they hoped would flock to the radical camp in appreciation of its wartime commitment to abolition. The idea was to confront the Southern states with the choice of black enfranchisement or loss of strength in Congress and the electoral college, a key provision of the Fourteenth Amendment.

Forcing black suffrage on the South, however, was anathema to many Northern Democrats. They assured their Southern brethren that they had supported the war to preserve the Union only, not to give blacks equal rights with whites. A Union general, George W. Morgan, made the point graphically in a Fourth of July speech, saying Northern Democrats had agreed "to sacrifice life and limb in defense of the Constitution and Union, but not for the nigger."[37] Johnson himself shared that view, although not publicly in such terms. As a Jacksonian and the product of a poor, rural white childhood hostile to Southern slaveholding aristocracy, he supported abolition of slavery as a way to undermine it. Giving blacks the vote was another matter to him, as a defender of white laborers against the competition of free blacks.

For the radicals, recruiting newly enfranchised black voters in the South had the added appeal of making the postwar Republicans less vulnerable to the old accusation of being a Northern sectional party. At the same time, however, the radicals recognized the possibility that Southern Democrats could contrive to deny blacks the franchise but still use their numbers to increase Southern representation in Congress and the Dixie states' electoral vote. No issue grated more on Northern Democrats than the extension of the vote to blacks.

Johnson was confronted with both a challenge and an opportunity. The radicals in Congress and in the Union Party had no intention of allowing this accidental president to take the party and the country down Lincoln's path to reconstruction. To their thinking, they had been on the winning side in the war and had the right to call the tune in ways that would enhance, not diminish, their political power. Contrary to some opinion, Lincoln did not leave a well-honed reconstruction plan for Johnson to implement, but Johnson did embrace the basic notion of a conciliatory posture toward the Confederacy in the interest of restoring the Union.

Many more moderate Republicans were willing to go along with Johnson's reconstruction policy at the outset in their understanding that it was an "experiment" only in how to deal with the South. Charles A. Dana, the assistant secretary of war, wrote he was "quite willing to see what will come of Mr. Johnson's experiment. And I think it desirable to keep with him as far & as much as possible. I don't want to see the Democrats coming back into power through any unnecessary quarrel among ourselves."[38] In this he seemed to regard Johnson as a Republican in spite of his previous Democratic affiliation. As long as the new president's plan was viewed only as an experiment, many Republicans who favored black suffrage, for example, could go along in the hope or expectation that modifications would meet their concerns about how far conciliation with the South should go.

Democratic leaders, for their part, seeing this argument as a means by which Republicans sought to keep their members in line behind Johnson, disputed the idea that his plan was in any way merely experimental. The Democratic leader in Illinois, John A. McClernand, wrote Johnson's son-in-law, David Patterson, that the Republicans were "disparaging everything he does as an 'experiment.' "[39] Montgomery Blair of Maryland, Lincoln's postmaster general now allied with Johnson, wrote to Jeremiah S. Black, secretary of state under Buchanan: "Johnson told you in my presence that his action in relation to reconstruction was not an *experiment* to be abandoned but based on the constitution to which he was sworn to adhere!"[40]

With the various political camps that emerged during the war years,

Johnson had the chance to remake the Democratic Party from which he had come. He could pull together Lincoln Republicans and War Democrats, Peace Democrats to whom restoration of the Union was more important than the slavery issue and former Confederates opposed to the imposition of stern measures desired by the radicals as the cost of their states' reentry into the Union.

Many Democrats eagerly embraced Johnson in the belief that as an old Democrat he would convert the Lincoln administration he inherited into a springboard for their party's return to power, and they rushed to gain entry into his inner circle. "The faces in the ante-chamber of the President look very much as they would if a Democratic administration were in power," one visiting Democratic congressman, Adam Glossbrenner of Pennsylvania, wrote to a colleague. He mentioned seeing there fellow Democrats "said to be entirely with the President on negro suffrage in the reorganized or reorganizing states—and scores of others who are 'of us.' "[41] National party chairman Mason, addressing "the National Committee to the Democracy of the United States" in July, declared of Johnson: "It is hardly a superstitious fancy which regards him as having been specially ordained for this great and glorious mission. The designs of Heaven begin now to be visible throughout."[42]

At the same time, however, Democratic Party rehabilitation was hindered by differences between those party members who believed accommodations had to be made to broaden its base, and those who insisted the party could survive only if it adhered strictly to its traditional principles going back to Jefferson and Jackson.

The first group held that the Democrats of the future had to avoid at all costs being seen as anti-war, pro-slavery Copperheads, as the Union Party had often cast them. The second group argued that they needed to stick to their guns across the board, implying a rejection of the War Democrats who had thrown in with the Republicans during the war. That was the only sensible course, said the last previous Democratic president, James Buchanan. "I have never known any good coming to the Democratic party from hiding or suppressing their principles for the sake of expediency," he observed. "Drop the principles and the name of Democracy and our cause would be hopeless." It was preferable, Buchanan said, to be "an honest minority than a dishonest majority," and "a small party of convictions than a large party of accidents." To hold otherwise, he said, would be "treason to the party."[43]

Democratic leaders like Governor Horatio Seymour of New York optimistically saw the end of the war as the salvation of the party. He publicly declared that the "war issue is dead; the slavery issue is dead, and on all living issues the Democratic party are united."[44] McClellan's 45 percent of the vote in the 1864 election appeared to support the contention that the party retained a strong base. At the same time, Seymour said, the factions of the Republican Party "were necessarily kept together by the pressure of a great national trial and emergency during the war, but the war once over, what is still to keep them together?"[45]

The question of Johnson's leadership as a Democrat heading a Republican/Unionist administration had its first major confrontation with the radicals in Congress over his vetoes of two bills. The first was an extension of the life of the Freedmen's Bureau, an agency for the protection of the newly emancipated blacks against "black codes," abusive measures adopted by Southern states at war's end. Johnson, an old champion of states' rights, vetoed extension on grounds that states affected by it had not been represented in Congress at the time of passage. The veto was sustained by the Senate. He also vetoed a civil rights bill granting citizenship and equal protection of the laws to blacks in every state, again on grounds that it was an infringement of state powers. This time, the radicals applied sufficient pressure in the Senate to override.

In addition, Johnson opposed the new Fourteenth Amendment providing federal protection of due process of law in the states and barring certain former Confederate loyalists from federal office. It passed over his opposition, which only hardened radical sentiment toward him, as did his opposition to black suffrage, authorized later by the Fifteenth Amendment.

These clashes convinced Johnson and Northern Democratic allies that a more coordinated stand against the radicals was required. When a special National Union Convention was called for the summer of 1866 in Philadelphia, in advance of the congressional elections, conservatives of all stripes attended, including many leading War Democrats, prominent old Republicans like Thurlow Weed and Montgomery Blair and even Copperhead leaders Vallandigham and Wood. The convention endorsed Johnson's call for the restoration of elected Southern members of Congress who had been barred by the radicals. The convention turned out to be more a Democratic than Unionist affair; in fact, it was the first serious step in rehabilitating the Democratic Party after the Civil War. It was somewhat compromised by the presence of Vallandigham and Wood, who finally were asked to leave, but that didn't hinder the Republicans in dismissing the convention as a collection of "rebels."

Party distinctions were blurred in 1866, as several other factional and war veterans' conventions were held to mobilize support for or opposition to the Radical Republicans, who viewed Johnson as falling under the domination of a Democratic Party unduly influenced by the wartime Peace Democrats. Increasingly alienated from the party that had made him vice president and then president, Johnson did indeed look to his old political brethren for his future. But as time went on, developments cast him as political goods too damaged to give him any great optimism that the Democratic Party would make him its presidential nominee in 1868.

Amid all this political turmoil, an outbreak of race riots in New Orleans and Memphis brought support to radical demands for federal protection of freedmen and repressive measures against resisting Southern whites. Some Johnson supporters counseled soft-pedaling Southern reconstruction problems in favor of less controversial matters as a means of sidestepping radical confrontations against him. But he was determined to resolve the Southern issues first. In September, in advance of the 1866 congressional elections and against the advice of political advisers, Johnson undertook a rare presidential speechmaking tour of a dozen major Eastern and Midwestern cities called a "swing around the circle," defending his Reconstruction policies, often in bombastic terms. Radical foes challenged him everywhere, using his conduct on the stump to resurrect the drinking rumor against him and fueling his reputation as "the drunken tailor."[46]

In the elections, the radicals dealt Johnson a stinging defeat, casting the voters' choice as one between Radical Unionists and Copperhead Democrats, and electing a Congress strong enough to override his vetoes. The War Democrat president and the War Democrats as a force were demolished; the outcome opened the way for enactment of the radicals' harsh program toward the South. In March 1867 they established military control over the defeated region and required states seeking readmission to the Union to give the vote to blacks and ratify the Fourteenth Amendment. With blacks voting strongly with them, the radicals in Congress now dominated the government, holding Johnson hostage to their will. The most anti-Johnson of them sought whatever grounds they might find to remove him. A House investigating committee during the 1866–67 session picked through his record but found nothing they could use as a credible pretext.

The opportunity finally came in August 1867 when he suspended his scheming and disloyal secretary of war, Edwin M. Stanton, while Congress was out of session. The Tenure of Office Act required senatorial consent of removing officers it had confirmed, but in practice presidents had routinely fired men they didn't want. When Congress reconvened, it refused to endorse Johnson's suspension and Stanton resumed his office. Johnson fired him again in February 1868, but the secretary barricaded himself in his office with military guard, as the House voted articles of impeachment against the president. Most concerned the Stanton removal but one charged Johnson with bringing "the high office of the President of the United States into contempt, ridicule and disgrace" for having delivered "with a loud voice certain intemperate, inflammatory and scandalous harangues" during the much-criticized 1866 Western campaign "swing around the circle" that were "peculiarly indecent and unbecoming in the Chief Magistrate."[47]

The Senate tried him on the articles of impeachment in spite of the fact that Stanton, as a Lincoln holdover, was not subject to the law. With 36 votes needed to convict on the key ballot, the Senate fell one vote short, 7 Republican/Unionist senators having joined with the 12 Democrats to save not only Johnson but the Republic from further congressional usurpation.

Johnson obviously realized that his future in the Union Party was past. At the party convention in Chicago in May, he was denounced in the National Union platform that upheld the radical reconstruction he had fought. Instead, he entertained the hope that he might garner enough support in his old party to be its nominee in 1868. Although he had served in the White House more as a Democrat than a Unionist, he had been ineffective as president in restoring his Democratic credentials, sticking essentially with the Lincoln cabinet of conservative Republican/Unionists rather than bringing in prominent Democrats.

That the Democratic Party would be cast at the Unionist convention as the party of treason in the approaching campaign became immediately clear in the keynote address of German-American journalist and reformer Carl Schurz. "I spurn the idea," he declared, "that the American people could ever so forget themselves as to throw their destinies into the hands of men who, but yesterday, strove to destroy the Republic, and who, today, stand ready to dishonor it."[48] Nominated unanimously for president was the latest national hero, General Grant, who had been considered a Democrat and a Johnson ally until they had a falling-out over the Stanton affair. House Speaker Schuyler Colfax of Indiana was named his running mate.

In advance of the Democratic National Convention at the new Tammany Hall in New York opening on Independence Day, an early favorite was Salmon P. Chase of Ohio, appointed by Lincoln from his cabinet to be Chief Justice of the Supreme Court. Chase had presided with impartiality over the impeachment trial of Johnson, thus winning Democratic gratitude and Radical Republican ire, at the cost of any chance for the Republican presidential nomination. So he focused on the Democratic nomination but did not mount an overt campaign, keeping a low profile as friends in the New York delegation awaited an opportune time to advance him.

The front-runner when the convention opened was the 1864 vice-presidential nominee, George Pendleton, champion of the "Ohio Idea" of paying off war bonds and other debts with paper "greenbacks," much favored by farmers and other debtors. Johnson, elected with Lincoln on the National Union ticket but still essentially a Democrat, entered his old party's presidential contest with the backing of his home state of Tennessee and some other Southern delegations. On the first ballot he had 65 votes, placing him second behind Pendleton with 105. Another popular general, Winfield Scott Hancock, was third with 33½, with a field of favorite sons trailing.

Johnson started fading on the second roll call, however, and was never in contention thereafter. By the eighth ballot, Pendleton approached a majority (with two thirds required for nomination), but he too then fell back, with Hancock moving up. Senator Thomas A. Hendricks of Indiana took the lead on the twenty-second ballot, at which point the Ohio delegation, with Pendleton now out of the running, suddenly switched to the reluctant convention chairman, Governor Horatio Seymour of New York. He, in turn, tried to nominate Chase, but was pulled forcefully from the rostrum by supporters and out of the hall. The scene produced a stampede for Seymour and the nomination, amid raucous celebrating. Johnson and Chase both were alienated, creating an early rift in party ranks that was closed too late to rescue Seymour.

The vice-presidential nomination, to the party's eventual regret, went to General Francis P. Blair Jr., son of Andrew Jackson's strong "kitchen cabinet" member. He became somewhat of a loose cannon, and his letter to a Unionist in Missouri, James Broadhead, caused an uproar. "There is but one way to restore the Government and the Constitution," he wrote, "and that is for the President-elect to declare these acts null and void, compel the army to undo its usurpations at the South, disperse the carpetbag State governments, allow the white people to reorganize their own governments and elect Senators and Representatives."[49]

The Republican *New York Tribune* jumped on him: "Americans! If you want another civil war vote the Blair ticket."[50] Demands that Blair be dropped from the Democratic ticket were soon heard. Seymour was forced into a defensive posture and, against his wishes, onto the stump in October, to no avail. Although the Democratic platform embraced Pendleton's greenback policy, Seymour clung to his longtime hard-money position, making his task all the more difficult.

The Republicans also hammered at him for having made what they touted as a subservient speech to draft rioters in 1863. They "waved the bloody shirt" of the war against the "Copperheads," tarring all Democrats with the label. Republican Governor Oliver P. Morton of Indiana reduced the election choice to its starkest element:

> Every unregenerate rebel ... every deserter, every sneak who ran away from the draft calls himself a Democrat.... Every man who labored for the rebellion in the field, who murdered Union prisoners by cruelty and starvation ... calls himself a Democrat. Every wolf in sheep's clothing who pretends to preach the gospel but proclaims the righteousness of manselling and slavery; every one who shoots down negroes in the streets, burns up negro school-houses and meeting-houses, and murders women and children by the light of their own flaming dwellings, calls himself a Democrat.... In short, the Democratic party may be described as a common sewer and loathsome receptacle, into which is emptied every element of treason North and South, every element of inhumanity and barbarism which has dishonored the age.[51]

The Democrats, for their part, played the race card relentlessly in their own way, charging that the radicals' Reconstruction policies were designed to elevate former slaves above whites. The *New York Herald* bluntly insisted that "Universal Nigger Suffrage is the Great Issue of the Campaign . . . the whole campaign turns purely and simply upon this point of the political status of the nigger in Southern States, and the right of the States themselves to regulate that status."[52]

Grant stayed home and simply declared, "Let us have peace." He sloughed off Democratic characterizations of him as a heartless military brute and prevailed on election day. A strong Democratic showing of 47.3 percent of the popular vote to 52.7 percent for Grant amid such difficulties was generally lost in Grant's electoral college sweep by 214 votes to 80 for Seymour. The extension of suffrage to blacks in the South was critical in Grant's popular vote, which could have fallen behind Seymour's had the blacks not turned out. The Union general's electoral college margin, however, probably would not have been threatened, what with heavy support among white voters in the more populous Northern states.

In the first national election after the Civil War, the Republican victory assured continuation of the radical Reconstruction of the South without an accompanying acceptance among many in the Democratic Party. This was especially so of the Peace Democrats, who persevered in pursuing the goal of a more conciliatory policy toward the defeated Confederate states, though without the political clout required to achieve that goal. The party was not, however, entirely barren of public support. Although a war hero had headed the opposition ticket, the Democratic Party had still managed nearly half the popular vote. Nevertheless, it had lost its third straight presidential election, and the end of the drought was not nearly in sight.

The Republican Party, resuming its original name, continued to reap the political rewards for suppressing the Southern rebellion and preserving the Union, while reminding voters of Copperheads indifferent to slavery who would have settled for "peace without victory" over the great moral question of the day. For the Democratic Party, there was much repair work to be done.

Chapter 12

THE WILDERNESS YEARS,
1869–1880

THE DEMOCRATIC PARTY that survived the Civil War found itself without strong national leadership or any clear sense of direction. With war hero Grant in the White House as a Republican in 1869 and the Radical Republicans firmly in charge of Congress, the Democrats were well into a twenty-four-year presidential drought that would not end until 1885. Over that period, they would be in the minority in the House two thirds of the time and for all but two years in the Senate.

Grant chose several old War Democrats for his cabinet, including John A. Rawlins of Illinois as secretary of war, Adolph Borie of Pennsylvania as secretary of the navy and, when Rawlins fell ill and resigned, General William W. Belknap of Iowa as his replacement. Another War Democrat, Senator John B. Henderson of Missouri, a Lincoln disciple, was the principal author of the Fifteenth Amendment extending suffrage to all (males) without regard to "race, color, or previous condition of servitude"—anathema to Democrats generally and particularly to formerly slaveholding Southern whites.

Most War Democrats, however, eventually returned to the party fold. At the same time, the party benefited from growing support among Midwestern farmers, especially those of German ancestry and foreign-born Catholics. In the industrial states, poor white immigrants from Ireland and Germany filled the factories and voted Democratic, many of them alienated by the Republican pursuit of civil rights for black Americans, who were seen as competition in the job market.

DAVID AND GOLIATH.

Top: The Democratic nominee for president in 1872, *New York Tribune* editor Horace Greeley, is depicted in this cartoon as the biblical David about to slay Goliath—Republican President Ulysses S. Grant—with a quill pen and inkwell in his slingshot. Instead, Greeley suffered the worst Democratic defeat of the century in a two-man race.

Bottom: In 1876, Democratic presidential nominee Samuel J. Tilden of New York won the popular vote over Republican Rutherford B. Hayes by about 250,000 votes, but was one vote short of an electoral college majority. Twenty votes were in dispute; a special commission awarded all of them to Hayes, denying Tilden the White House.

But the Democratic posture of opposition to equal rights and opportunities for all cast the party as a defensive, negative force in these post–Civil War years. The Democratic candidate for governor in Wisconsin, General H. C. Hobart, warned in the late 1860s that the party would "always be in the minority if [it] sympathizes with the oppressors of mankind."[1] The war fought over slavery as well as secession had ended and all Democrats had to face that fact.

In Texas, Mississippi, Tennessee and Virginia in 1869, Democratic efforts were undertaken to create a "new movement" by defusing the main issues of Reconstruction and thus attracting support from moderate Republicans in various degrees of political fusion. In many states in the South, however, the old "Bourbon" Democrats believed they were strong enough to recover on their own without resorting to this approach. The party did make some gains in the congressional elections of 1870 but remained far from having a real prospect of becoming the majority in either house.

It fell to the old leader of the Peace Democrats, the indefatigable Vallandigham, to seek a more radical route out of the wilderness. He drafted a manifesto for local party organizations in his home state of Ohio that he labeled a "New Departure." It called on the party to "accept the natural and legitimate results of the war so far as waged for its ostensible purpose to maintain the Union and constitutional rights and powers of the Federal Government." Party members, he went on, should also accept the Thirteenth, Fourteenth and Fifteenth Amendments designed to erase the worst legal depredations of slavery "as a settlement in fact of all the issues of the war, and acquiesce in the same as no longer issues before the country."

Furthermore, the edict pledged to uphold "the absolute equality of each and every State within the Union" and denied that the federal government had any "power to expel a State from the Union, or to deprive it, under any pretext whatever, of its equal rights therein," specifically including "full and complete representation in Congress and in the electoral college." It said the party was "unalterably opposed to all attempts at centralization and consolidation of power in the hands of the General Government" and for "a perfect independence" among its legislative, executive and judicial branches. Finally, it called for "a universal amnesty" for all who fought for or aided the Confederate cause.[2]

This New Departure, soon applied on a national scale, sought not only to put the war behind the Democratic Party once and for all. It was also designed to welcome Southern Democrats back into the fold and lure newly enfranchised blacks in the South with an eye to the next presidential election. The gesture toward the blacks had only modest results at best. It met with stiff resistance and even hostility from whites in several Southern states, notably North Carolina, Georgia and Alabama. Traditional Democrats argued that breaking so sharply with the old racial arrangement in the South would only undercut the party's residual strength among white voters who still constituted a majority in most states in the region.

"The road to redemption is under the white banner," said John Forsyth of the *Mobile Register,* a leading Bourbon.[3] "Our Southern stake is so enormous that it begets timidity. We walk fearfully, as if treading on eggs; and long suffering and adversity have taught us to be distrustful of the very principles in which alone we can find our political redemption and salvation. . . . Great parties are founded on great ideas, and are not to be patched together with the putty of expediency."[4]

Another Bourbon, former Governor John A. Winston of Alabama, agreed that "an open out-and-out White Man's Ticket" was the only answer, because "the gray-eyed, straight-haired men of destiny must govern the earth among civilized nations," and "any entanglement with the negro must but result in embarrassing us."[5]

As other Democrats who were former slaveholder office seekers nevertheless set about persuading or cajoling their former slaves to vote Democratic as part of this New Departure, their efforts were inhibited by the emergence of the Ku Klux Klan terrorizing the black community. A leading New Departure proponent in Alabama, Albert Elmore, wrote a friend: "It is of the utmost importance to the democracy, & the country, that lawlessness and outrage, be put down. Let the democratic party move heavily in that direction."[6] A congressional investigation finally led to enactment of the Ku Klux Klan Acts of 1871, designed to give prosecutors in the Southern states a freer hand to cope with the intimidation of, and violence toward, blacks by white-hooded racists.

In the North, meanwhile, the party's image was being tarnished by major scandal in New York, where William M. Tweed, leader of Tammany Hall, and associates had taken control of the city government on the strength of the votes of easily manipulated immigrants. The Tweed Ring bilked as much as $200 million from the city through kickbacks and other schemes. A prominent Democrat, Samuel J. Tilden, played a major role in bringing Tweed to book, but the party paid a price in public esteem nonetheless.[7]

The ultimate measure of how deeply the Democratic Party had sunk came the next year when its 1872 national convention in effect abdicated the choice of the Democratic presidential nominee to a faction of the rival Republicans. Within the Republican Party, a serious split had developed between an already corruption-riddled Grant administration and its liberal critics. Taking advantage of Grant's inexperience in the world of finance, speculators in the gold market culled important advance information on administration policies from members of the president's family and cashed in on it handsomely. Corruption was also rife on other fronts, as railroad construction pushed the frontier westward, opening new opportunities that were rapidly exploited by men with inside information, including Vice President Schuyler Colfax.

The liberals, led by Senator Carl Schurz and Governor B. Gratz Brown of Missouri, were determined to challenge the usurpers. They had already begun the party break in their state in 1870, also charging the administration with abuse of patronage and opposing the continued presence of military governors in the Southern states to enforce Reconstruction edicts. They called themselves the Liberal Republicans and proposed a more conciliatory posture toward the South, amnesty for former Confederates, universal suffrage and civil service reform. Missouri Democrats joined them and together they drove the regular Republicans from control of the state government.

This success inspired similar cooperation on the national level. Democratic leaders reasoned that if their party again joined forces with the Liberal Republicans in 1872 they could take advantage of the Republican split, defeat Grant's reelection bid, enfranchise and bring more Southern Democrats to the polls, and resurrect the battered Democratic Party as a national force. The Liberal Republicans, calculating along parallel lines, sought to find a presidential nominee who would be acceptable to the Democrats and then form a winning coalition.

Schurz would have been their obvious presidential candidate, but having been born in Germany he was not eligible. Thinking in terms of requiring a Northern candidate who could counter the regular Republican strength in the postwar South, they considered such men as Charles Francis Adams of Massachusetts, Supreme Court Justice David Davis of Illinois, Senator Lyman Turnbull of Connecticut and others who either had been Democrats at one time or were considered acceptable to the other party.

Davis, who had received, and declined, the nomination for president of a new National Labor Reform Party, had considerable support going into the Liberal Republican national convention in Cincinnati in May. But he was strongly opposed by Schurz and a group of influential newspaper editors known as the "Quadrilateral" who favored Adams. At a critical point, Brown of Missouri and Francis P. Blair of Maryland, chagrined at the role these nonpoliticians were playing, rallied party professionals. Astonishingly to many delegates and to the consternation of many Democrats, they turned to the eccentric editor of the New York Tribune, reformer Horace Greeley. He was nominated on the sixth ballot, with Brown quickly chosen to be his running mate.[8]

The Democratic Party leaders were in shock over the selection. Their 1868 nominee, Horatio Seymour, had run a reasonable race against Grant, winning 47.3 percent of the popular vote, but there was little sentiment to go with him again. Indeed, no Democratic leader made any serious bid for the 1872 nomination, and with the Democratic National Convention opening in Baltimore only two months after the Liberal Republican choice of Greeley, there was insufficient time to rally support for an alternative.[9]

When the regular Republicans met in Philadelphia in June, they routinely renominated Grant and chose Henry Wilson of Massachusetts as his running mate, replacing Colfax. The convention's temporary chairman, Morton McMichael of Pennsylvania, recognized and castigated the opposition coalition in the making. "The malcontents who recently met in Cincinnati were without a constituency; the Democrats who are soon to meet in Baltimore will be without a principle," he declared in his opening speech. "The former, having no motive in common but personal disappointment, attempted a fusion of repelling elements, which has resulted in explosion; the latter, degraded from the high estate they once occupied, propose an abandonment of their identity, which means death."[10]

An early indication of what would happen in Baltimore a month later came in the Democratic convention's adoption, word for word except for a brief separate preamble, of the exact platform approved by the Liberal Republican convention. A vigorous protest from Senator Thomas F. Bayard of Delaware against having the Democratic leadership "force down our throats without mastication or digestion the action of other men who have not been called into our councils" got nowhere.[11]

By this time the convention delegates full well understood that the leadership had engineered a deal with the Liberal Republicans and was not to be turned aside. Any nominations for president from the floor were ruled out of order and the roll call of the states began. Alabama voted for Greeley and the convention greeted the action with loud approval. In the end, the New York editor had 686 votes to 21 for Jeremiah Black of Pennsylvania, 15 for Bayard, 2 for William S. Groesbeck of Ohio and 8 cast for nobody as a protest. Brown was similarly steamrollered through as the vice-presidential nominee and the convention was adjourned after only six hours.[12]

As in 1868, Grant sat out the campaign in near-silence, enjoying the view of the Atlantic Ocean from his cottage at Long Branch, New Jersey, and smoking cigars as party officials once again "waved the bloody shirt" of the Democrats' wartime "treason." Greeley, however, stumped energetically, preaching a message of racial and sectional reconciliation in opposition to the more radical aspects of the Reconstruction. His pledge of "full amnesty" for all former Confederate soldiers was the centerpiece of his vigorous but essentially hopeless campaign.[13]

Greeley—white-whiskered, often wearing a long duster over a rumpled suit and an oversized white hat over his bald pate—was a caricaturist's delight. Cartoonist Thomas Nast of *Harper's Weekly* relentlessly lambasted him with such brutal representations as one showing him shaking hands with John Wilkes Booth across the late President Lincoln's grave amid waving Confederate flags.[14] Greeley's abundant writings as editor of the *Tribune* also provided much fodder for criticism, and ridicule.

He turned out to be an effective campaigner, however, but the ordeal of his tireless effort—two hundred speeches in one stretch of eleven days—took a heavy toll on him, as he was already suffering from chronic insomnia and other ailments. On top of that, a week before the election his wife, also long ill, died. The election result was yet another blow: Grant won 55.6 percent of the national vote to only 43.9 percent for Greeley, with small labor and prohibition candidates sharing less than one percent. Greeley lost all but five former slave states, a measure of the failure of the party's attempt to draw Southern black voters from their perceived Republican benefactors. It was the worst Democratic defeat of the century, not counting the party split of the election of 1860. Three weeks later Greeley died, and with him the party's national experiment with fusion politics.[15]

All, however, was not lost for the Democrats. The second Grant administration, like the first, was riddled with scandal and corruption. In September 1873 the roof fell in on the era of financial irresponsibility and excess that had marked Republican rule since the end of the Civil War. The postwar boom of railroad construction and westward expansion collapsed, resulting in plummeting stock markets, thousands of bankruptcies, closed banks, strikes, unemployment and falling farm prices. The panic of 1873, ushering in a six-year depression, robbed the Republican Party of its reputation as the party of prosperity and paved the way for a Democratic comeback in the congressional elections of 1874.[16]

The Democrats seized upon the action of the Republican-controlled Congress in voting itself $5,000 in back pay for each member, calling it a "salary grab." They also castigated Grant for vetoing an expansion of paper money to help Americans in dire financial straits. The result was Democratic control of the House for the first time since the Civil War, doubling the party's membership, and also capture of governorships in New York, Pennsylvania, Massachusetts and other ordinarily Republican states.

The Democratic election success at the congressional level demonstrated the diminution of the bloody shirt as an effective political device in Republican hands. With the war amendments against racial servitude and subjugation now in place North and South and accepted by both parties, the Republican hold on Dixie was loosening, opening the way toward a Democratic Solid South in the not-too-distant future. The oppressive hand of federal—that is, Republican—enforcement, along with disgust over the corruption in the Grant cabinet, drove white landowners back toward their old party home. The old general's own ineptness made a joke of his "willingness" to serve a third term, which the House in 1875 scotched with a resolution declaring that breaking the Washington two-term tradition would be "unwise, unpatriotic, and fraught with peril to our free institutions."[17]

For all the damage done by the widespread corruption, however, the Republican Party retained its base with business and banking. In early 1875 the lame-duck Republican Congress, to the satisfaction of that base, enacted a Resumption Act reducing the amount of issued paper money and issuance of new bank notes along with the eventual retirement of all greenbacks.[18] The Democrats protested in behalf of greenback holders and a new Greenback Party surfaced, later reorganized as the Greenback-

Labor Party. By 1878 it would poll more than a million votes and elect fourteen members of Congress.

At the same time, still more corruption during the Grant administration put Republican members of Congress under the expanding cloud and raised Democratic hopes that at last, after sixteen years out of national power, the drought might soon be over. The wish was almost realized in 1876, but for one of the most bizarre and questionable outcomes of any American presidential election up to that time.

With the corruption issue certain to be the cornerstone of the next Democratic effort to win the presidency, the Republicans were in need of a nominee untainted by the Grant years, which now faced even more intense scrutiny from investigators of the Democratic-controlled House. Three distinct groups sought control of the national convention in Cincinnati in mid-June. The Radical Republicans were led by Roscoe Conkling of New York and Oliver P. Morton of Indiana, both of whom coveted the nomination but were too closely associated with the Grant administration. The so-called Half-Breeds passionately backed House Speaker James G. Blaine of Maine. The Reformers gave most but not all of their early support to Secretary of the Treasury Benjamin H. Bristow of Kentucky.

Blaine, a former newspaper editor with a flair for self-promotion, was regarded as the front-runner at the outset, but prospects of accommodations among the three factions were dim. Blaine was a bitter enemy of both Conkling and Bristow, and himself under a cloud when letters surfaced earlier suggesting improper use of his office in a Union Pacific railroad scandal. His chances slipped badly when he collapsed three days before the convention opened, a fact that a Conkling supporter did not overlook in addressing the assemblage. Nevertheless, Blaine was extolled by a fiery supporter, Colonel Robert G. Ingersoll, as "an armed warrior, like a plumed knight," and the description stuck.[19] Two governors, Rutherford B. Hayes of Ohio and John F. Hartranft of Pennsylvania, were put forward as favorite sons, with Hayes men from Ohio already conspiring with Bristow to stop Blaine.

Blaine led on the first six ballots and was only seventy votes short of nomination when Conkling and Morton, obviously to stop him, switched to Hayes. Bristow followed suit, giving Hayes the nomination on the seventh roll call. Congressman William A. Wheeler of New York was chosen as his running mate. Hayes, a Union general in the Civil War with a record clear of scandal or corruption and a hard-money advocate, was a safe if not exciting Republican choice. As a reform candidate, however, all Joseph Pulitzer could say in the *New York World* was, "Hayes has never stolen. Good God, has it come to this?"[20]

Eleven days later the Democrats met in St. Louis, their first such national convention west of the Mississippi. Their platform demanded repeal of the Resumption Act in behalf of greenback supporters, and three men were placed in nomination for president: Governors Samuel J. Tilden of New York and Thomas A. Hendricks of Indiana and Union General Winfield Scott Hancock of Pennsylvania. Tilden's path to quick nomination was blocked by his bitter New York foe, John Kelly, leader of Tammany Hall, who loudly denounced him and insisted that Tilden could not carry the Western states. The governor, however, was easily nominated on the second ballot and Hendricks then chosen as his running mate, with Kelly pledging to work for the ticket.[21]

Tilden, famous as the successful prosecutor of the Tweed Ring, was a wealthy corporate lawyer and speculator in land and stocks, which earned him a nickname of questionable political value, "the Great Forecloser."[22] Because he was a hard-money man like Hayes, the greenback question was shunted aside to be taken up with little support by the new Greenback Party. Neither man campaigned. Tilden, a reclusive bachelor who was in frail condition, remained in New York. He was committed generally to "a revival of Jeffersonian democracy," emphasizing decentralization and, obviously with the Grant era of corruption in mind, "high standards of official morality."[23] Hayes ventured only to Philadelphia to attend that year's Centennial Exhibition, where it was said he was recognized only when he signed a pavilion register.

In the extremely close election, Tilden had the advantage of an innovative and energetic national party chairman in New York Congressman Abram S. Hewitt. He organized a new literary and speakers' bureau to compile and distribute campaign literature and recruit prominent surrogates to carry the party's message. That message paid little note of Hayes, whose clean record offered no target, and focused on the Grant administration scandals, contrasting them with the political purity of "Honest Sam Tilden."

Republicans, in turn, cited Tilden's earlier political ties to Tammany in calling him an "eleventh-hour reformer" and, unable to run on the Grant record, unfurled the bloody shirt one more time. Colonel Robert

Ingersoll, who had immortalized Blaine as the "plumed knight" at the Republican convention but was now campaigning zestfully for Hayes, charged at a convention of the Grand Army of the Republic: "Every man that tried to destroy this nation was a Democrat. Every man that loved slavery better than liberty was a Democrat. The man that assassinated Abraham Lincoln was a Democrat. . . . Soldiers, every scar you have on your heroic bodies was given to you by a Democrat."[24]

Tilden was painted as an unreconstructed Democrat who would scrap the war amendments providing rights to freedmen. He was also personally assailed as a wealthy skinflint in the pocket of business, anti-Catholic and soft on the rebellious South. Veiled expressions of concern about his health were made to hard-money proponents, reminding them that soft-money man Hendricks would become president if Tilden were elected and failed to finish his term.

On election night, early returns pointed to a Tilden victory, and the *New York Tribune's* headline proclaimed "Tilden Elected." He won about 250,000 more popular votes than Hayes and appeared to sweep the Reconstructed South and border states, along with the key Northern states of New York, New Jersey, Connecticut and Indiana. But the electoral college vote was another matter. Tilden had 184, Hayes 165, with 185 required and 20 in dispute in four states—South Carolina, Florida and Louisiana in the South, and a single disputed elector in Oregon. Still, with Tilden needing only one electoral vote of the 20 and Hayes needing all 20, Tilden seemed certain to be elected.[25]

But the staunchly Republican *New York Times,* unlike the *Tribune,* held off declaring a Tilden victory. In the early morning hours, Democrats at the state party headquarters, uncertain about the outcome, called the *Times* for its electoral college vote. Surmising that the Democrats were in doubt, the managing editor of the newspaper, John C. Reid, hurried to the headquarters of Republican national chairman Zach Chandler, the manager of the Hayes campaign, at the Fifth Avenue Hotel. Accompanied by New Hampshire national committeeman William E. Chandler, they convinced the chairman to dispatch telegrams to Republican Party leaders in the three Southern states to challenge the votes there and to rush party aides and money to them. Later in the day, Zach Chandler audaciously announced: "Hayes has 185 electoral votes and is elected."[26]

In all three states, the Republican Party controlled the state governments and election machinery. The party had relied on aggressively induced black votes and habitual practices of fraud to turn out the Republican total. Countering such activities were widespread Democratic threats and acts of intimidation and violence in black communities and at the polls, also habitual. It was no secret that both parties had worked diligently and without restraint to carry these states in an exercise of mutual corruption. It was now a question of which party could manipulate the deplorable situation to its advantage.

In Florida, where Tilden had a small popular majority, the Republican-controlled board of elections certified the Hayes electors. In South Carolina, where Hayes had the popular vote edge, the Democratic-controlled board certified the Tilden electors. In Louisiana, election officials took testimony regarding padded registration rolls and intimidation of black voters. A member of the election board reportedly offered to hand the election to Tilden for one million dollars but was turned down. Money in support of Hayes changed hands and after the election three members of the board received federal appointments. In the end, two sets of certifications were given in each of the three Southern states, one set for each candidate. In Oregon, Hayes carried the state but one of his electors was a postmaster, a federal official barred by the Constitution from serving as an elector. The disputed Hayes elector, after much maneuvering, finally was certified.[27]

The dispute continued when, as provided in the Constitution, the two sets of certifications went before the president of the Senate to be opened and counted before both houses, the Senate controlled by the Republicans, the House by the Democrats. There being a vacancy in the vice presidency since the 1875 death of Henry Wilson, Senate President Pro Tem Thomas Ferry, a Republican, presided. Under an 1865 rule adopted by both houses, the electoral vote of any state would be rejected if opposed by either house. After the 1872 election, the votes of Louisiana and Arkansas, and three from Georgia, had indeed been thrown out. But in early 1876 the Republican Senate refused to readopt the rule because the House was then in Democratic hands. Had the rule still been in effect in late 1876, the House would have rejected the votes from the disputed states and Tilden would have been elected.[28]

To resolve the dilemma, a joint committee of the two houses produced a plan for an electoral commission of five senators, five congressmen and five Supreme Court justices. The Democratic House was to pick three Democrats and two Republicans; the Republican Senate was to choose three Republicans and two Democrats; four justices, two from each party, were to be designated and the fifth would be a man whose party affiliation was considered uncertain. By general agreement, that fifth man would be Justice David Davis of Illinois. The commission's findings would be final unless both houses agreed to overrule them. Confident Democrats figured the commission would not be so blatantly partisan as to award all twenty of the disputed electoral votes to Hayes. The plan was approved by large majorities in each house, but with the Republicans less enthusiastically in light of the seemingly favorable odds for Tilden. Hayes reportedly was against the arrangement because his old rival, Conkling, was an architect of it.[29]

On the same day the commission was approved, however, startling news came from the Illinois state capital in Springfield. The previous day, a coalition of Democrats and independents in the state legislature had elected Davis to the United States Senate, obliging Congress to replace him on the commission. Now more than ever, the fifth justice certainly would appreciate the imperative of impartiality from him. The other four justices on the commission chose as Davis's replacement Justice Joseph P. Bradley, who appeared to the Democrats to be the most independent of the remaining Supreme Court justices, all of them Republicans.[30]

The official electoral count began before a joint session on February 1, as a huge crowd jammed the House chamber. When the roll call reached Florida and both the Republican and Democratic electors were challenged, the issue went to the commission, sitting in the original Supreme Court chamber at the Capitol. Lawyers on both sides debated whether the commission should consider evidence relating to allegations of fraud by state election boards in deliberating or simply decide on the regularity and validity of the certifications presented. By a straight party vote of 8–7, with Bradley voting in the majority, the commission awarded Florida's votes to Hayes. Similar 8–7 outcomes occurred as the votes of the other three states were considered, delivering all twenty disputed votes to Hayes and making him president.[31]

Hewitt, the Democratic national chairman, later reported that Bradley had written a favorable opinion for the Democrats in the Florida dispute, but had been talked into rewriting it the other way by political associates and his wife. Bradley later insisted he had written two opinions and then chose the one favoring the Republicans.

When the final state case, South Carolina, was being considered, some disgruntled Democrats in the House considered a filibuster that would prevent a joint session and completion of the electoral count past March 4, when the new president was to take office. The prospect of deadlock, violence or both seemed real. Hewitt later wrote: "Business was arrested, the wheels of industry ceased to move, and it seemed as if the terrors of civil war were again to be renewed . . . to this dread issue we were much nearer than was even at that time supposed."[32]

But behind the scenes, negotiations over the next few weeks, later known as the Compromise of 1877, were already well under way between friends of Hayes and Southern and other congressional Democrats. With Hayes's acquiescence, the Republicans promised to bring railroad construction to the South and, more important, remove the remaining federal troops there enforcing the Reconstruction laws, including the three war amendments providing civil and voting rights to freedmen. The Democrats, for their part, would guarantee those rights in the South and lift the threat of filibuster so that the electoral count declaring Hayes the winner could be completed.

On the night of February 26 at the Wormley Hotel in Washington, Hayes's friends passed the word that he would take the federal troops out of Dixie, appoint a Southerner to his cabinet, and undertake new economic development and more aid to education for the region. Tilden, apprised of the development, declined to fight this "intrigue," telling friends that another such clash would "end in the destruction of free government."[33]

Some House Democrats wanted to continue the battle, and House Speaker Samuel J. Randall considered a legislative proposal to make the secretary of state the acting president until a new election could be held. But when one of the Wormley Hotel negotiators, Congressman William Levy of Louisiana, reported that he had received "solemn, earnest, and, I believe, truthful assurance" that the federal forces would be removed from the South, the opposition crumbled.[34]

One eminent historian, C. Vann Woodward, noted, however, that the chief elements in the compromise were in place before the talks at the Wormley Hotel. "A week before these negotiations opened," he wrote, "a means had been devised to insure the removal of the troops in case Hayes forgot his promises or was unable to carry them out. At a Democratic caucus, a majority of the members voted for a resolution to write into the army appropriations bill . . . a clause forbidding the use of troops to support the claims of any state government in the South until it should be recognized by Congress. . . . When the Republican Senate refused to accept the clause the House stood its ground and adjourned without making any appropriations for the army whatever."[35]

As a result, Woodward went on, Hayes was faced with the prospect of governing without an army; besides, lame-duck President Grant had already pledged to remove the federal troops from the South upon completion of the electoral count. Although he did not do so, Woodward concluded, "Grant deserves much of the credit or blame that has been assigned to Hayes for initiating the new Southern policy" that marked the end of Reconstruction. Hayes's negotiators, he wrote, "were giving up something they no longer really possessed in exchange for something that had already been secured by other means."[36]

In any event, at four in the morning of March 2, crowds packed the galleries as the certified electoral votes were delivered to the House chamber and read by Ferry, declaring Hayes and Wheeler elected. Hayes, on a train en route to Washington, was awakened and handed a telegram confirming that he had at last been certified as president-elect.

The Democratic Party had been tantalizingly close to its goal of recapturing the White House. It was indisputable, as the pre–Civil War formulation of the two-party system had asserted itself, that the party had at last regained parity with the Republicans. At the grassroots level, the Democratic Party not only was strong again, but with the prospect of a South without the politically oppressive presence of federal troops, the reemergence of a Solid South seemed ever closer.

Once Hayes took office, House Democrats, still smarting over what they considered a stolen election, repeatedly used parliamentary procedures to frustrate him and tied hostile riders to appropriations bills that Hayes vetoed. The result was more support for the new president from a public that saw the Democrats as sore losers. For his part, Hayes reached out to Democrats, even appointing a former Confederate soldier, David M. Key, as his postmaster general.[37]

In keeping with the promise he had made in the Wormley Hotel negotiations, Hayes withdrew federal troops from South Carolina and Louisiana, leading the way to termination of the two remaining carpetbagger governments in the South and their replacement with Democratic officials who pledged equal rights to all citizens, black and white.[38] It wasn't long, however, before Bourbon Democrats were, in effect, nullifying the Fifteenth Amendment, introducing discriminatory policies against blacks in attempts to restore and secure white supremacy in the South. With the disappearance of the federal forces and carpetbag Republican state administrations, and consequent strangulation of the black vote in Dixie, the Democratic Solid South of the eleven states of the Confederacy had become a reality again.

Meanwhile, congressional hearings into the disputed election had disclosed evidence of fraud on both sides. Tilden himself appeared before a House committee, and his evasive answers to accusatory questions left him and his party tarnished. The Democratic-controlled committee nevertheless concluded later that Tilden had been unfairly denied the presidency. But coded telegrams discovered by a Republican-controlled Senate committee implicated a Tilden nephew in apparent schemes to buy the electoral votes of South Carolina and Louisiana.[39] In any event, the election was over and Hayes sat securely in the Oval Office.

Elected as a reformer, Hayes sought extensive civil service reform but was heavily occupied in his first year with domestic strife, seen in violent railroad and other labor strikes. They brought sufficient strength to the new Greenback-Labor Party that in the congressional elections of 1878 both major parties lost seats in the House. The Democrats retained control, however, and picked up seven seats in the Senate, giving them control of both houses of Congress for the first time since the Civil War.

Once more, as in 1876, Democratic hopes were high for breaking the Republican hold on the executive branch in 1880, this time with the South appearing to be once more a dependable source of political strength. On the Republican side, Hayes had pledged as the GOP nominee in 1876 to serve only a single term, and he was true to his word. His decision facilitated plans of Grant supporters to run him again, and he was willing—a circumstance many Democrats would have relished, enabling them to remind voters of the corruption and scandals of his previous two terms.

At the party's national convention in Chicago in June, however, the third-term issue generated opposition to Grant and support for Blaine and for Hayes's secretary of the treasury, John Sherman of Ohio. Sherman's campaign was deftly managed by Congressman and Senator-elect James A. Garfield of the same state, who incidentally had served on the elections commission that had put Hayes in the Oval Office. Garfield outmaneuvered Conkling, the caustic manager for Grant and leader of the old-guard Stalwarts wing of the party in New York, in getting the convention to drop the unit rule for state voting on the presidential nomination, thus undercutting the Grant strength.

Grant led Blaine and Sherman on the first ballot, and after thirty-five ballots the order remained the same, with Grant still sixty-six votes short of the required majority. On the thirty-sixth roll call, Blaine and Sherman supporters suddenly swung to Garfield, also a former Union general, and he was nominated. A bone was then thrown to Conkling and New York in the vice-presidential nomination of Chester A. Arthur, an obscure deposed collector of the Port of New York.[40]

The Democratic convention met two weeks later in Cincinnati. Tilden's near-miss in 1876, and the wide Democratic belief that the White House had been stolen from him, might ordinarily have assured him renomination. But the disclosures of questionable conduct in that disputed election, as well as frail health and opposition from Tammany Hall in his own state of New York, all obliged him to bow out. His supporters lined up behind House Speaker Samuel J. Randall of Pennsylvania in a large and undistinguished field that also included General Winfield Scott Hancock of the same state. Hancock's appeal consisted of his Mexican and Civil War record, which countered that of Garfield, coupled with a reputation as a fair military governor after the war in Texas and Louisiana, giving him support North and South. He was nominated on the second ballot, after a flood of vote switches. Former Congressman William H. English of Indiana was named his running mate.[41]

With Congress in Democratic hands, and the party's dominance in the South restored with federal troops now out of the region, its best opportunity for the White House in two decades seemed to have arrived. But Hancock was inexperienced in politics and became the subject of much ridicule as an uninformed novice in Nast cartoons. His letter accepting the Democratic nomination was rated so vapid that *Harper's Weekly* remarked on its "certain childlike innocence," and *The Nation* observed that "no one but a scoundrel or a person of defective understanding would dispute a single proposition contained in it."[42]

Not subjected to such comments, Garfield confidently and securely ran a front-porch campaign from his home in Mentor, Ohio, drawing large crowds daily. Meanwhile, Hancock stumbled over such issues as the protective tariff, which the Democratic Party supported for revenue purposes only, and the Republicans attacked on grounds it would hurt American manufacturing and thus cost American jobs. He called it "a local issue," and one Nast cartoon showed him asking a prominent Democratic senator: "Who is Tariff, and why is he for revenue only?"[43]

Democrats in the key state of Indiana struck back with well-founded allegations that the Republicans were buying votes at an unprecedented pace and shipping Southern blacks there in "a scheme to Africanize our state for political purposes." The Republicans replied with this ditty:

> Sing a song of shotguns, pocket full of knives;
> Four and twenty black men running for their lives;
> When the polls are open, shut the nigger's mouth.
> Isn't that a bully way to make a solid South?[44]

More significantly, intraparty trouble in New York severely sabotaged Hancock's chances. In 1879 a split between the Tilden-controlled state organization and Tammany Hall under boss John Kelly had lost the governorship for the party. In 1880 a disgruntled Kelly sent a rival New York delegation to the national convention, which rejected it.

Kelly, more interested in electing a Tammany man as mayor of New York than Hancock for president, chose William Grace, a Catholic, whose presence on the ticket in a city that had not nominated a non-Protestant in two hundred years probably cost Hancock the state. Garfield won it by 20,000 votes, contributing what he needed for a minute 9,457-vote victory nationally and the 35 electoral votes that put him over the top. Garfield had 48.5 percent of the popular vote to 48.1 percent for Hancock, who carried every former slave state, and 3.4 percent for James B. Weaver, the Greenback-Labor nominee. Once again the Democratic Party had knocked on the front door of the White House and had been turned away, even with the Solid South marching in lockstep.

However, while Garfield's election signaled at least twenty-four straight years out of power for the national party, Democrats at the local level were building fortresses of political clout in the larger cities. Kelly's self-centered behavior in New York had demonstrated in a perverted way the growing power of the big-city boss. But population increases from European immigration, especially among Irish and Italians, and the development of urban political machines that recruited them with all manner of favors and services, gave the Democratic Party reason to believe that deliverance from the dark years was finally at hand, looking to the election of 1884.

In the election of 1884, Democratic Governor Grover Cleveland of New York was plagued by news that he had once fathered a child out of wedlock. He openly acknowledged the fact, noting he had assumed financial responsibility for his son's upbringing, and rode out the storm.

Chapter 13

ON THE ROAD TO PARTY RECOVERY, 1881–1896

ONLY FOUR MONTHS after the inauguration of new Republican President Garfield, destiny seemed to enhance the Democrats' long-frustrated drive for a return to national power. On July 2, 1881, as he was preparing to leave Washington for a commencement speech at Williams College in Massachusetts, Garfield was shot by a mentally unbalanced man named Charles J. Guiteau. He died two and a half months later.[1] The Republican Party found itself in sudden turmoil, especially in New York, always critical in presidential elections.

Little-known Vice President Chester A. Arthur, regarded as a political hack who had been made Garfield's running mate as a party sop to New York Stalwart boss Roscoe Conkling, now sat in the Oval Office. Almost immediately, Arthur stirred up intraparty dissension by dismissing most of Garfield's cabinet, including Blaine as secretary of state. At the same time, he ignored "Lord Roscoe" for a cabinet post and left untouched Garfield's appointment of William H. Robertson, one of Conkling's archenemies, as collector of the Port of New York, Arthur's old job.[2]

The Stalwarts, expecting that their old retainer would open the floodgates of patronage to them, instead were disappointed to find he had turned over a new leaf. As president, Arthur was determined to be his own man, and he found a new ally in the recently organized National Civil Service Reform League.

The latest accidental presidency was complicated, however, by continuing investigations of Republican corruption during the Grant years, especially after the Democrats gained seventy House seats in 1882 and won control of that body. With their help, Arthur defeated much pork-barrel legislation, reduced high tariffs and successfully sponsored reform creating a Civil Service Commission, to the chagrin of the Stalwarts. Meanwhile, the Republican Party split between the conservative Stalwarts and reformist Half-Breeds intensified, despite Arthur's surprising efforts to be even-handed.

This and other developments further encouraged Democratic hopes of regaining the White House two years hence. The Solid South was reemerging and Democratic governors including Grover Cleveland in New York were elected in several states. Big-city political clubs, increasingly active and powerful, were culling more and more votes through services and favors to the immigrant poor.

At the same time Arthur, for all the commendable reform of his personal politics, had succeeded mainly in undercutting his own chances for presidential nomination in his own right in 1884. The Stalwarts felt betrayed over patronage; the rival Half-Breeds sulked when Blaine was abandoned as secretary of state and favored him for the nomination; party reformers preferred Senator George F. Edmunds of Vermont.[3]

In advance of the Republican convention in Chicago in early June 1884, Blaine was the front-runner on grounds it was "his turn." He led Arthur on the first ballot and achieved the nomination on the fourth.[4] General John A. Logan of Illinois, head of the Grand Army of the Republic veterans' lobby, was named his running mate. Blaine's selection was popular with most of the party, except for the self-styled independents, or "Mugwumps," who questioned his integrity in light of his involvement in an Arkansas railroad land and bond deal, first aired in his failed bid for the presidential nomination in 1876.

A Massachusetts Reform Club met in Boston immediately after the Republican convention. An executive committee was appointed and held a conference in New York shortly afterward, led by reformers Carl Schurz and G. W. Curtis, urging the Democrats to nominate a reform candidate they could support. This breach in Republican ranks pumped up Democratic expectations even higher as the party met in Chicago in early July, attracting the largest convention crowd up to that time, estimated at 12,000. With Tilden aged and in ill health and Hancock out of favor for having narrowly lost the 1880 election he might have won, the only credible candidates were former Senator Allen G. Thurman of Ohio, Thomas A. Hendricks of Indiana, Thomas Bayard of Delaware—and Cleveland.[5]

The governor of New York, the portly former mayor of Buffalo, derided as "the Buxom Buffalonian" and among his own nephews and nieces as "Uncle Jumbo,"[6] was a comfortable, conservative fit for the Democratic Party. He was a booster of civil service reform and tariff reduction. A reputation for integrity, incorruptibility and an unshakable inner conviction of what was right and wrong had been manifested in his ready use of the veto power both as mayor and governor. Backed by Tilden and acceptable to the Mugwumps, he was a logical choice, being from the largest of the closely contested states.

But once again the assertiveness of Tammany Hall complicated the situation. As a minority faction in the New York delegation, the Tammany leadership sought a convention rules amendment abolishing the unit rule in voting on the presidential nomination. It was rejected, with all seventy-two of New York's votes cast against it under the very unit rule being challenged. The Tammany faction continued to object to its use, to no avail. Its members, more irate by the hour at the treatment they received, channeled their anger into a floor attack on Cleveland as unelectable.

First, however, other candidates had their names placed in nomination—except Hendricks. In an apparent skirting of the tradition against a presidential candidate addressing the convention, let alone appearing in the hall prior to selection of the nominee, Hendricks's name was not offered by his home state of Indiana. Instead, one of its former senators, Joseph E. McDonald, was submitted for nomination. This procedure then permitted Hendricks to make the nominating speech for McDonald, which ascribed to him all the qualifications that Hendricks himself conspicuously met.[7]

When the time came for the New York delegation to offer Cleveland's name, no reference was made to the anti-Cleveland sentiment in the delegation. During seconding speeches, however, Thomas F. Grady, a Tammany leader, took the occasion to tell the convention why his state's governor could not be elected. Shouts filled the hall demanding that Grady be declared out of order because he was not making a seconding speech. He was permitted to continue when a member of the Cleveland faction in the delegation generously offered a motion to that effect. The galleries erupted in disapproval, but Grady finished his harangue over the din.[8]

Another Tammany man, Bourke Cockran, also rose ostensibly to make a seconding speech but instead continued the attack on Cleveland. He said he was "too warm a friend of his to desire his promotion to an office for which I do not believe he has the mental qualifications."[9] After delving into the complications of New York politics for a time, still in a negative vein, Cockran finally seconded the nomination of Thurman.

The next morning, after more nominating and seconding speeches for minor candidates, General Edward S. Bragg of Wisconsin, in seconding Cleveland's nomination, memorably observed of the New Yorker's supporters: "They love him, gentlemen, and they respect him, not only for himself, for his character, for his integrity and judgment and iron will, but they love him most of all for the enemies he has made."[10] Grady jumped to his feet and responded: "Mr. Chairman, on behalf of his enemies, I reciprocate that statement, and we are proud of the compliment."[11]

As the roll call on the presidential nomination began, the split in the New York delegation remained front and center. On the first ballot, the New York chairman cast all 72 of the state's votes for Cleveland while announcing, apparently to try to placate the Tammany crowd, that only 49 of the delegates actually supported him. Cleveland led after the first roll call with 392 votes to only 170 for the next candidate, Bayard.

The convention adjourned and reconvened the next morning, at which time the Hendricks supporters made their move. He had received a solitary vote on the first ballot and McDonald 56. An Illinois delegate now rose to say one of his state's votes also was cast for Hendricks, setting off a floor demonstration. The head of the Indiana delegation announced his state was withdrawing McDonald's name with the intention of casting all its votes for Hendricks "at the proper time."[12]

On the next ballot, with Cleveland gaining 83 votes, Hendricks moved into third place behind Bayard. Before the results were announced, however, North Carolina switched all its votes from Bayard to Cleveland, and Virginia and other states began falling in line, putting Cleveland well over the top. Hendricks, proposed for vice president as a soft-money man from the West, authorized the Indiana chairman to say he would not accept. But after state after state voted for him, he relented and was declared nominated unanimously.

Cleveland was supported in critical New York by the state party leader, Daniel Manning, who became his campaign manager, and by Carl Schurz heading a band of independents and defecting Republicans, as well as a host of academic and literary celebrities and most of the New

York newspapers. On the Republican side, most leaders rallied, if somewhat reluctantly, to Blaine, except Conkling. Asked whether he would support his party's nominee and his old enemy, the always acerbic Lord Roscoe replied: "I do not engage in criminal practice."[13]

The Mugwumps, meanwhile, doing their bit for Cleveland, made the most of a resurfacing of that earlier shady deal first examined in 1876 in which Blaine had helped an Arkansas railroad obtain a land grant renewal, then collaborated in selling off its all but worthless bonds at exorbitant prices. The deal was outlined in letters supplied to a House committee by one James Mulligan, bookkeeper for the broker in the deal, Warren Fisher of Boston. But Blaine had skillfully talked his way out of the charge at the time. Now, in the 1884 campaign, more "Mulligan letters" incriminating Blaine were discovered, including a draft of a letter exonerating him that Blaine had written himself and sent to Fisher with a request written in Blaine's own hand: "Burn this letter when you have read it."[14] Editorial writers, cartoonists and pro-Cleveland political operatives had a field day with the incident.

Republican forces retaliated with a story they were confident would kill Cleveland's chances of election. Ten days after his nomination, the *Buffalo Evening Telegraph* trumpeted the news that the Democratic presidential nominee had fathered a son out of wedlock. A woman named Maria Halpin, who had worked in a shop in Baltimore, owned up to having had several intimate male friends, including Cleveland. She reported that she had borne the child ten years earlier and that Cleveland was the father. The Democratic nominee, rather than denying the whole matter as a political smear, accepted responsibility for the boy, named Oscar Folsom Cleveland, and reported he had provided support for him. Sometime after the child's birth, judging that the mother was unfit to raise him, Cleveland had arranged to have him placed in an orphanage, from which an upstanding family adopted him.[15]

If the Republicans thought the revelation would trump the negative Democratic attacks on Blaine for his shady railroad deal, they were mistaken. Although the news generated much preaching from pulpits on moral behavior from public officials, Cleveland's straightforward admission was an effective counter to it. Two prominent Protestant ministers of the day, James Freeman Clarke and Henry Ward Beecher, defended Cleveland. His openness contrasted with Blaine's evasions about the Mulligan letters. One anonymous Mugwump offered a solution: "We are told that

Mr. Blaine has been delinquent in office but blameless in private life, while Mr. Cleveland has been a model of official integrity, but culpable in his personal relations. We should therefore elect Mr. Cleveland to the public office which he is so well qualified to fill, and remand Mr. Blaine to the private station which he is admirably fitted to adorn."[16]

Throughout the fall campaign, the two parties matched attacks. The Democrats declared, "Blaine, Blaine, James G. Blaine, continental liar from the State of Maine!" and "Burn this letter!" The Republicans countered with "Ma, Ma, Where's my pa? Gone to the White House, Ha! Ha! Ha!"[17] When newspaper stories alleged that Blaine's wife was already pregnant at the time of their marriage and Cleveland received letters damaging to his opponent, he destroyed them, vowing he would not stoop to such tactics. But others on both sides had no such compunctions in what became one of the dirtiest presidential campaigns up to that time.

As Democrats Stephen Douglas and Horace Greeley had done before him, Blaine took to the stump for six intensive weeks, defending the protective tariff, decrying low wages for workers and railing against the perils of turning the country over to the party of rebellion. For the most part, Cleveland stayed in Albany, leaving campaigning and electioneering to strong Democratic organizations in the states. Once again, New York was pivotal. There the Blaine-Cleveland fight was complicated by the presence of two other contenders—John P. St. John, former Republican governor of Kansas running as the candidate of the Prohibition Party, and Benjamin F. Butler, nominee of the Greenback-Labor Party. Butler was secretly financed by the GOP to undercut Cleveland and, it was widely suspected, also backed by Tammany boss John Kelly, arch-foe of Cleveland.

Blaine, born of a Roman Catholic mother and of Irish descent, also looked to New York's large Irish population, traditionally Democratic, for backing against the governor, who as a free trader found himself being derided by the Republicans as the "British candidate."[18] It so happened that on the morning of October 29, as election day approached, Blaine spoke to a gathering of Protestant ministers at the Fifth Avenue Hotel. A Presbyterian clergyman named Samuel D. Burchard filled in for an absent preacher and uttered a phrase destined to live thereafter in the annals of political folly. "We are Republicans," he intoned, "and don't propose to leave our party and identify ourselves with the party whose antecedents have been rum, Romanism and rebellion."[19]

Blaine didn't appear to grasp what Burchard had said, and he made no comment. But a shorthand reporter wrote it down and turned it over to the Democratic Party. When the Democrats flooded the country with flyers trumpeting the phrase, Blaine finally disavowed it as an "unfortunate and ill-considered expression" and insisted he was "the last man in the United States who would make a disrespectful allusion to another man's religion."[20] But it was too late. There, apparently, went much of the Irish-Catholic vote, and with it the votes of "wets" and sons of the old Confederacy as well.

To complicate Blaine's problem, that night he dined at Delmonico's stylish Manhattan restaurant with such business multi-millionaires as John Jacob Astor and Jay Gould, discoursing on foreign trade before adjourning to a private room to discuss contributions to his campaign. When workingmen read of the meeting in the next morning's newspapers, and saw cartoons ridiculing "The Boodle Banquet" celebrating prosperity for the rich and poverty for the poor, there also went much of the labor vote.[21]

On election night, New York indeed was the key. Cleveland had the electoral votes of Connecticut, New Jersey, Indiana and the Solid South, for a total of 183. Blaine had the rest, except New York's 35, for 182. Thus the winner in New York would be the next president. Of the state's total of 1,167,169, Cleveland had a plurality of 1,149. Nationally, his popular-vote margin over Blaine was a mere 23,006 out of slightly more than 10 million ballots. Democrats jubilantly chanted: "Hurrah for Maria! Hurrah for the kid! I voted for Cleveland and I'm damned glad I did!"[22]

Blaine blamed his defeat on "rum, Romanism and rebellion" and rainy weather in Republican upstate New York on election day, along with the 25,016 votes won in the state by Prohibition candidate St. John. He wrote later: "As the Lord sent upon us an ass in the shape of a preacher and a rainstorm to lessen our vote in New York, I am disposed to feel resigned to the dispensation of defeat which flowed directly from these agencies."[23] But other factors such as the Mugwump effort in behalf of Cleveland and the high unemployment and economic doldrums accompanying Republican rule played a strong hand as well.

For the first time in nearly a quarter of a century, the Democratic Party no longer had been punished for the breakup of the Union with denial of the presidency. However, Cleveland's election, and a second, nonconsecutive election eight years later, would make him the only Democratic president in a fifty-two-year span that covered from 1860 to

1912. For thirty-two years, though, from 1865 to 1897, the Democrats did control at least one house of Congress. That condition put considerable power in the hands of party bosses, often United States senators who exerted great influence in the budgetary process.

Much of the party's presidential comeback in 1884 was attributable to the development of party organization, with a stronger national committee at the top and equally important state, county and local party structures that increasingly recruited workers down to the precinct level. The effort was particularly aggressive and successful in the cities, where immigration swelled the pool of prospective Democratic voters, especially among Catholics, Irish and Central European working-class arrivals. The task of reaching and providing various political services to this pool in return for reliable party support stimulated the development of a professional cadre manifested in the creation of party "machines" and "bosses" that brought both humanitarianism and exploitation to the business of grassroots politics.

The political life offered tangible benefits to the recipients of party services and new careers to those who devoted themselves to the disposition of those services. The product was both good and bad, with the blatant corruption of such entities as the Tweed Ring and Tammany Hall in New York creating more notoriety about the bad. In the climate of fast bucks and overnight success that marked what became known as the Gilded Age, machine bosses like John Kelly took on the trappings and approached the influence of some of the most prominent captains of business and industry.

If the spoils in political combat went to the victor, in the age of the political machine those spoils were dispensed to the loyal by the bosses in the manner of feudal baronies of old. Reform advocates of good government, derided by the machine leaders as "goo-goos," fought an uphill battle to rein in the power of the bosses, more often than not in futility.

Cleveland, while a recipient of the growth in Democratic Party organization in New York and other urban centers particularly, was no reflection of the shady side of politics that was so often personified in bossism. As governor, he had taken on Tammany, Kelly and Conkling, and had made bitter enemies of all three. His adopted motto was "Public office is a public trust,"[24] and as president his adherence to that belief frustrated bosses who found their access to federal patronage restricted after the twenty-four-year drought of national party power.

Democratic politicians, eager to get their hands on jobs held by Republicans, generally champed at Cleveland's political piety in insisting that GOP appointees who were carrying out their duties fairly and efficiently should remain to finish their terms. In 1885, of the 126,000 federal employees, only 16,000 held classified jobs to 110,000 available through political appointment. Cleveland, determined to resist pressure, declared he would interview no office seekers and send all applications to the department involved, observing that "this dreadful, damnable office-seeking was a nightmare."[25] But he did personally and meticulously review many job recommendations and eventually yielded regarding a majority of such appointees, particularly in the Post Office Department. By 1887 about 40,000 of 52,000 postmasters were removed, and about 77,000 of the inherited political appointees. At the same time, Cleveland nearly doubled the number of classified posts. Also, in a fight with the Republican majority in the Senate, he beat back an attempt to force him to share the power to replace incumbents, enabling him to clear out many holdover Republicans for whom he found cause.

At first, the new president pleased his Mugwump supporters with notable civil service reforms and continued his use of the veto power, especially against private veterans' bills he considered fraudulent or undeserving. Such vetoes brought particular criticism inasmuch as he had taken the not uncommon route in the Civil War, with two brothers already in Union uniforms, of buying a substitute to serve for him while he stayed at home to support his mother and sisters. He also got into political hot water by approving what proved to be the illegal return to the Southern states of Confederate flags captured in battle, further enraging Union veterans and supporters. He was obliged to rescind the order.[26] His appointment of two Southerners to his cabinet and one of them to the Supreme Court assuaged some resentment, but Cleveland often found himself whipsawed by sectional differences among his constituents.

In his resistance to rampant allocation of political spoils, there was considerable feeling within his party that he carried rectitude too far. As the party leader, many thought, he failed to grasp the realistic aspects of the role. He shied from initiating legislation, preferring to focus on the more passive aspects of the executive function. Meanwhile, after a lifetime of bachelorhood, forty-nine-year-old Cleveland, in June 1886, married twenty-two-year-old Frances Folsom. The marriage was well received by

the public after the earlier revelation of his fathering a son out of wedlock. It provided him, he acknowledged, a congenial buffer against the
endless bombardment of special patronage pleaders that continued to
plague his days.[27]

Cleveland's sense of leadership responsibility finally persuaded him
in 1887 to take on the touchy issue of tariff reduction in spite of deep divisions over it among his supporters. With Treasury surpluses and public
tax burdens piling up, he decided against the wishes and advice of many
Democratic leaders to challenge Republican protectionist interests in his
bid for reelection in 1888. While he was only modestly informed in the
intricacies of finance, he was repulsed by the specter of protected industrialists reaping huge rewards from government intrusion, and in his State
of the Union address in December 1887, he declared his intention to
revise the tariffs. A relatively modest bill passed the House but was
rejected by the Senate as Republicans seized the issue as a political winner
for them. They pushed through even more protection, confident that the
argument that the sheltering of new American job-producing industries
would mean victory in 1888.

Cleveland's renomination in St. Louis in early June was routine and
unanimous by acclamation, the first time since Van Buren's in 1840 that
no roll call was required, and the first time since then that a Democratic
incumbent had been renominated. Vice President Hendricks had died less
than nine months after taking office, and the Democratic convention
chose former Senator Thurman of Ohio, who had sought the presidential
nomination against Cleveland in 1884, as his running mate. In the wake of
Hendricks's death, some concern was voiced about Thurman's age, seventy-five, but he was chosen anyway. (Because the passing of Hendricks
had put a Republican, the Senate president pro tem, next in line of succession to the presidency, Congress in 1886 passed a new succession act
that placed members of the president's cabinet in line after the vice president, starting with the secretary of state. That order remained until 1947,
when Congress restored the old system but inserted the Speaker of the
House behind the vice president.)

The party platform endorsed Cleveland's recommendations on tariff
reduction. The only other matter of interest at the convention was a
speech on woman suffrage by Mrs. E. A. Merriwether of St. Louis, after
which she tried to offer a sarcastic resolution noting the refusal of Democratic men to grant it:

> Resolved, that we, the Democratic men of America in Convention assembled, advise and urge the Legislature of every State in this broad Union to enact such laws as will forever put a stop to the education of the women of this land, and thereby put a stop to the clamor for equal rights, as will forever close the doors of every school, public or private, to the female children of this country; we advise and urge that it be made a penal offense, punishable by fine and imprisonment, to teach any girl or child the letters of the alphabet; and that any woman convicted of reading a newspaper or book, or entering lecture halls, whether as a listener or speaker, be severely punished by law.[28]

The male conventioneers repeatedly shouted their disapproval and derision until she stopped, whereupon this portion of her remarks was stricken from the formal record.

Twelve days later the Republicans convened in Chicago and in their platform took up the Cleveland challenge, declaring, "We are uncompromisingly in favor of the American system of protection. We protest against its destruction, as proposed by the President and his party. They serve the interests of Europe; we will support the interests of America."[29] More than a dozen worthies were nominated for president, and it took eight ballots to settle on another former Union warrior, Benjamin Harrison of Indiana, grandson of President William Harrison. Blaine, who had narrowly lost to Cleveland in 1884, declined to run again and sat out the convention in Scotland, but influentially made known his preference for the cold and aloof Harrison. Levi P. Morton of New York, a former minister to France and heavy party financial supporter, was chosen on the first ballot to run with him.

Cleveland once again eschewed the campaign trail, leaving his bid for a second term in the hands of aging Senator William H. Barnum of Connecticut, co-chairman of the Democratic National Committee, Ohio railroad executive Calvin Brice and Senator Arthur P. Gorman of Maryland. Unfortunately for the support of lower tariffs, all three had long protectionist track records. Thurman was barely able to carry the campaign burden for the Democratic ticket. At one major rally at New York's Madison Square Garden, he took the podium only to declare that he was too ill to address the crowd. Known as "the noble old Roman," Thurman was famous for brandishing a large red bandanna that he used after applying

a pinch of snuff. Soon replicas of the bandanna were appearing everywhere, and a campaign ditty ended with the confident assertion that "The
Red Bandanna will elect two honest men I know: The noblest Roman of
them all and the Man from Buffalo."[30]

In his campaign, Harrison enlisted the considerable organizational
and political talents of the Republican boss of Pennsylvania, Senator
Matthew S. Quay. He raised millions of dollars from the business community and other supporters of protectionism, enabling him to flood the
North and West with campaign literature and all manner of flags, pins and
other paraphernalia. In New York in particular, again pivotal to the election's outcome, he challenged the registration rolls and went after the
large Irish-American vote, pouring "street money" into Irish precincts.
There and elsewhere, a campaign song reminded veterans and other voters of Cleveland's avoidance of service in the Civil War and his vetoes of
pensions for them:

> For when the strife was raging
> A substitute he found.
> If all had done as Grover
> Sent substitutes moreover,
> They all could live in clover
> And none want pensions now.[31]

Harrison himself daily addressed large crowds of supporters making a
political pilgrimage to his home in Indianapolis. Campaign strategists
reminded voters of his distinguished lineage, revamping the slogan of the
1840 presidential campaign featuring his war-hero grandfather and running mate, John Tyler, to read "Tippecanoe and Tariff Too."[32] And Blaine,
back from Europe, weighed in aggressively on the stump for Harrison.

Meanwhile, Cleveland's camp sought to stir up the Irish with accusations of scurrilous Harrison talk about their shiftlessness, which he
denied. A few days before the election, the Democratic *Indianapolis Sen-
tinel* published a copy of a letter allegedly signed by the Republican Party
national treasurer instructing party leaders in Indiana to hire "floaters" to
cast Harrison ballots. "Harrison has for years consorted with the worst
gang of political prostitutes that ever disgraced an American state," the
paper charged. "He has never disavowed, repudiated, denounced or even
mildly criticized a Republican rascal or a Republican fraud. . . . This talk of

Benjamin Harrison's spotlessness and purity is disgusting in the extreme."[33] On election day, there were widespread accounts of such floaters dutifully trooping to the polls.

In the end, Quay's focus on Indiana and New York made the difference. Harrison squeezed through in Indiana by a mere 2,348 votes. In New York, with neither Governor David Hill, who was focusing successfully on his own reelection, nor Tammany making any appreciable effort for Cleveland, Harrison captured the Empire State's 36 electoral votes, giving him 233 to Cleveland's 168, and the White House. Harrison was said to have gratefully observed that "providence has given us the victory," to which Quay, perhaps in reference to the votes of the Indiana floaters, reportedly commented, "Providence hadn't a damn thing to do with it,"[34] and that his candidate "would never know how close a number of men were compelled to approach the penitentiary to make him President."[35]

The Republicans also captured both houses of Congress for the first time since 1875. But for the second straight election, Cleveland won the popular vote, by 100,476 ballots, reaffirming that the Democratic Party had reestablished itself on the national level. Of his decision to fight the campaign over the tariff issue, he wrote later: "They told me it would hurt the party; that without it I was sure to be re-elected, but that if I sent in that message to Congress it would, in all probability, defeat me; that I could wait until after the election and then raise the tariff question. The situation as it existed was, to my mind, intolerable, and immediate action was necessary. Besides, I did not wish to be re-elected without having the people understand just where I stood on the tariff question and then spring the question on them after my re-election. Perhaps I made a mistake from the party standpoint; but damn it, it was right. I had at least that satisfaction."[36]

Others in the party agreed that the fight for tariff reduction and other reforms was worth waging. "We would rather fall with you fighting on and for a principal [sic] than succeed with the party representing nothing but an organized appetite," a young lawyer from Nebraska named William Jennings Bryan wrote to him. He consoled the defeated president that "your position was so wisely and bravely taken that I believe the party will look back to you in after years with gratitude and not reproach." He suggested that "if you would only move to Nebraska and run in '92 as a Western man with the friends you have in the East, we can elect you. Why not come to Omaha or Lincoln?"[37] It was an invitation from Bryan that would soon turn cold, when the party split over the issue of currency reform. Bryan championed the Western states' cause of free silver while Cleveland sided with the party Easterners who feared it would undermine gold and lead to a financial crisis.

The defeated president decided instead to practice law in New York and for the first time in his life make some money. He joined a Wall Street firm handling interests of the J. P. Morgan empire and soon became relatively wealthy through stock speculations. He began to develop more of a business outlook than was customary for a Democratic leader, and powerful financial figures in New York took a new interest in returning him to the White House in 1892.

In addition, Harrison appeared to be vulnerable. Republican platform pledges of 1888 were fulfilled with passage of the Sherman Anti-Trust and Silver Purchase Acts of 1890, but the latter was abhorrent to defenders of the gold standard and alienated the most conservative elements in his own party. Republican leaders also were soured by Harrison's personal coldness; New York party boss Tom Platt said he was "as glacial as a Siberian stripped of his furs."[38] And many voters disliked his profligate award of veterans' pensions. He appointed as pensions commissioner a lobbyist, James "Corporal" Tanner, who thereupon revealed his intention by shouting, "God help the surplus!"[39] Reduced revenues under the new McKinley Tariff Act of 1890 also swallowed up much of the federal surplus, and what came to be known as "the Billion Dollar Congress" of pork barrelers took care of the rest.[40]

In spite of the fact that Republican strength in the Senate was boosted in 1889 and 1890 by the admission of six new states—Wyoming, Idaho, North and South Dakota, Montana and Washington—the GOP in the 1890 congressional elections suffered one of its most devastating defeats as a result of its spendthrift behavior. Republican Senate control was cut to 8 seats and only 88 House members survived to face 235 Democrats and 14 Populists.[41] William McKinley, author of the new tariff act, himself lost his House seat and returned to Ohio, where he was elected governor the next year.

The emergence of populism among farmers, labor and others up in arms over falling agricultural prices, high transportation costs and currency policies about which they had little say was threatening, meanwhile, to change the whole political equation in the country. A farmers' Grange from the early 1870s and a number of other later populist groups were making inroads into Democratic Party strength. A new farmers' organization called the National Alliance achieved substantial gains in 1890 state elections, especially in the South.

A convention of the Southern Alliance met and formed a People's Party in Cincinnati in May 1891. A conference then was called for St. Louis in February 1892, attended by members of the National Alliance, Greenbackers, Prohibitionists, Knights of Labor, Nationalists and other small political groups. A platform was drafted, and in Omaha in July the new party's first national convention nominated General James Weaver, the 1880 Greenback nominee, for president and James G. Field of Virginia, a former Confederate general, for vice president.[42] Their objective was nothing less than to unite elements of all parties, sections, races and classes into a new political force.

"Free silver"—the federal purchase of the metal and its use as legal tender along with the traditional gold strongly favored in the East—was a Western cornerstone of the party's platform, along with demands for the nationalization of railroads, award of federal lands to citizen settlers only, a true merit system in federal employment, a graduated income tax and election reforms.

Cleveland's political instincts and urges were reawakened by the high-tariff policies under Harrison, the Democratic successes in the 1890 elections and the encouragements of his new law and business associates, and he began to consider a comeback. And with Senate rejection in 1890 of a Republican federal elections reform or "force" bill designed to counter Democratic-backed literacy tests and poll taxes inhibiting black suffrage, the Solid South remained a dependable source of Democratic votes.

But although Cleveland had been the popular-vote winner two times running and his popularity was still high, the Democratic presidential nomination was hardly his for the asking. One of his old rivals in New York, Governor David Hill, also had his eye on the White House, and as a stepping-stone toward it he ran for and won a Senate seat. Cleveland also encountered vigorous opposition from Charles A. Dana of the *New York Sun*, who chided him as "the Stuffed Prophet" and dubbed him "the Perpetual Candidate."[43]

In addition to Tammany, Hill had the backing of strong Eastern and Southern protectionists. In February 1892, amid bitter winter weather that kept many pro-Cleveland Democrats away, Hill abruptly called a "snap convention" of the state party attended mostly by his allies.[44] Pro-Hill delegates were chosen to the national party convention under the unit rule that had been so vociferously opposed by Tammany in the past. Cleveland backers held a quick convention of their own in New York and chose a rival delegation pledged to him and geared to fight the Hill group for the state convention credentials.[45]

The Republicans, for all their reservations, renominated President Harrison on the first ballot in Minneapolis in early June, after a weak challenge in behalf of old warhorse Blaine. He had served as Harrison's secretary of state but had resigned just before the convention in implied criticism of his boss. After nominating and seconding speeches praised Blaine for his leadership of the nation's foreign policy, Chauncey Depew of New York took the podium for Harrison and said: "I am tempted seriously to inquire, who, during the last four years, has been President of the United States anyhow?"[46] In the only roll call, Harrison got 535 $\frac{1}{6}$ votes to 182 $\frac{1}{6}$ for Blaine and 182 for McKinley, who really was being groomed for 1896 by his astute manager, Marcus Hanna. For vice president, the New York delegation passed over incumbent Levi Morton in favor of Whitelaw Reid, editor of the *New York Tribune* and, at the time, U.S. minister to France. Reid was nominated by acclamation. On the currency question, the party endorsed a bimetal policy, keeping silver and gold in parity.

The Democrats met in Chicago eleven days later in a makeshift structure called the Wigwam, plagued by strong winds and storms that pounded the tin roof as speakers sought to be heard over the din and water leaks dripped on them. With the New York delegation that was committed to Hill seated rather than the Cleveland group, bedlam reigned. The Cleveland forces, confident they had enough delegates from other states to give their man a first-ballot nomination, did not contest the granting of credentials to the Hill group. An estimated six hundred pro-Hill Tammany forces crowded the gallery and engaged in a shouting match with nearly twenty thousand other spectators, most of them for Cleveland.

Offered in nomination in addition to Cleveland and Hill was Governor Horace Boies of Iowa. Tammany firebrand Bourke Cockran, who had questioned Cleveland's "mental qualifications" in his attack on him at the 1888 convention, resumed his assault by challenging Cleveland for his acceptance of Mugwump support. "The Democratic Party cannot fuse with the party that despises it," he said; "... with the Mugwump there can be no treaty of peace nor implied faith. He has no weapon but slander and abuse. He does not want to enter the Democratic Party; he wants to own it. He wants you to lend him this party organization to accomplish his own purposes, and not for the good of the Democratic Party."[47]

The harangue was to no avail. On the first and only roll call, Cleveland was renominated with 617⅓ votes to only 114 for Hill, 103 for Boies and the rest scattered among eight other candidates. For vice president, the convention chose Adlai E. Stevenson of Illinois, a silver advocate and assistant postmaster general in Cleveland's first term who had deftly dealt with the party patronage matter that so distressed his superior. One delegate, in seconding Stevenson, declared: "I support Illinois' candidate because I understand he is a Democrat who believes that to the victor belong [*sic*] the spoils. Because he believes further that there are honest and competent men enough in this Democratic Party to fill all the offices, and I make the assertion that if he is placed in this high position, Mugwumps and Republicans will receive no quarter at his hands."[48]

Cleveland again campaigned on tariff reform, as rising prices at home were laid to Harrison and the high-protectionist McKinley Tariff. Vicious labor strikes over wages at the Carnegie steelworks in Homestead, Pennsylvania, and mines in Coeur d'Alene, Idaho, and Tennessee, made the argument that high tariffs might be fine for large industrial monopolies but not for the workingman.

Boss Quay and the other Republican professionals who had put Harrison in the White House in 1888 were disheartened and much less effective this time around. Hanna was more interested in setting up McKinley for 1896 than reelecting Harrison. And Blaine, ill and still grieving over the sudden death of his son, did the best he could as a Harrison surrogate on the stump, but he was exhausted and within three months he was dead.

Cleveland also had the advantage of fusion arrangements with the new Populist Party in particular states, where the Democrats and Populists shared the same presidential electors and the Populists ran their own local candidates.

With New York again a key, Cleveland's campaign manager, William C. Whitney, implored him to make his peace with David Hill and Tammany. He got Cleveland to take an old Tammany foe, Lieutenant Governor William Sheehan, as his state campaign committee chairman, and the two men met for dinner in early September with another old Tammany hack,

Richard Croker. When the former president asked how the campaign was faring in New York, Sheehan told him that pro-Cleveland newspapers were attacking Tammany and demanded that Cleveland stop them.

Further, when Sheehan asked for a pledge of increased federal patronage in a second Cleveland term, the Democratic nominee snapped back: "I will appeal from the machine to the people. This very night I will issue a declaration to the electors of the state telling them the proposition you have made to me and the reasons why I am not able to accept it. I will ask them to choose between us. Such is my confidence in the people that before the week ends, I believe that your machine will be in revolution against you."[49]

Sheehan and the Tammany organization backed off. Hill made one of several public appearances for his old New York enemy in Brooklyn a week or so later and Tammany went to work for him, concluding with a huge New York rally. In the South, meanwhile, the Democrats warned Southern whites of a Republican election proposal, called a "force" bill, designed to protect the voting rights of blacks. Racial mixing in schools and intermarriage surely would result, the Democrats suggested. Fanning such white fears, and the Tammany support in New York, effectively assured Cleveland's reelection in an expensive but relatively uneventful campaign. The popular vote was fairly close—Cleveland 46.1 percent, Harrison 43 percent—but the electoral vote was a landslide—Cleveland 277, Harrison 145. Weaver had 8.5 percent and 22 electoral votes.

Cleveland soon may have wondered why he wanted to return to the White House. Early in his second term he secretly underwent serious surgery to his upper right jaw and palate, and went into seclusion for more than a month, as economic decline seized the country. In fact, only days before he took office the panic of 1893 had begun, and within two months the stock market collapsed. Banks and railroads failed, and by the end of the year some fifteen thousand businesses were in bankruptcy. Cleveland's answer was to blame it all on the Silver Purchase Act, seek its repeal and return to the gold standard. This view put him on a collision course with all the free-silver forces in the Democratic Party who argued just the opposite—that divesting silver in 1873 had been the culprit.[50]

The cry went up again for unlimited coinage of silver as the answer of farmers and other creditors to crippling deflation. Perhaps more available money would bring higher prices. But Cleveland clung to his argument and, with Republican support, got Congress to repeal the Silver Purchase

Act, at the cost of further dividing his own party. A young firebrand from Nebraska in the House named William Jennings Bryan led the losing fight against the repeal and began to make a name for himself. Only thirty-three years old, he cast the battle over silver as a struggle against the president for the party itself.

"Today the Democratic party stands between two great forces, each inviting its support," he proclaimed in what proved to be a three-hour speech. "On one side stand the corporate interests of the nation, its moneyed institutions, its aggregations of wealth and capital, imperious, arrogant, compassionless. They demand special legislation favors, privileges, immunities. . . . On the other side stands the unnumbered throng which gave a name to the Democratic party and for which it has assumed to speak. Work-worn and dust-begrimed, they make their mute appeal, and too often find their cry for help beat in vain against the outer walls, while others, less deserving, gain ready access to legislative halls."[51]

When the repeal of the Silver Purchase Act failed to arrest the economic collapse or a drain on the gold reserves, Congressman Richard Bland, a free-silver advocate known as "Silver Dick," pushed through another silver coinage bill, but Cleveland vetoed it. He initiated several bond sales to fortify the gold standard, including a huge private sale to J. Pierpont Morgan that further alienated suspicious silverites. The fiery Bryan was moved to remark that "Cleveland might be honest, but so were the mothers who with misguided zeal threw their children into the Ganges."[52] Still the depression went on. Factories as well as farms were devastated, railroad building halted and investment dried up, and in 1894 nearly three million Americans were unemployed, many of them going hungry.

Soup kitchens were nicknamed "Cleveland's Cafes" and tales of the president's heartless indifference spread. One had him finding a man eating grass on the White House front lawn and Cleveland telling him: "Why don't you go around to the back yard? The grass is longer there."[53] It was the worst depression in the nation's history up to that time. South Carolina Governor "Pitchfork Ben" Tillman, campaigning for the Senate in 1894, declared: "When Judas betrayed Christ, his heart was not blacker than this scoundrel Cleveland, in deceiving the Democracy. He is an old bag of beef and I am going to Washington with a pitchfork and prod him in his old fat ribs."[54] The upshot was Coxey's Army, a march of about five hundred jobless on Washington on May 1, led by a wealthy Populist businessman, Jacob S. Coxey of Massillon, Ohio, who proposed a work relief project to build roads that Congress rejected. "We will send a petition to Washington with boots on," Coxey proclaimed,[55] and he did, and all he got for his trouble was arrest and about fifty of his marchers beaten.

Strikes broke out all over, notably one outside Chicago in July when the maker of Pullman railroad cars cut pay sharply and fired union leaders. Cleveland, claiming disruption of the mails, called out federal troops to suppress the strike, leading to more violence and a deepening rift in the Democratic Party between its business interests and labor. The governor of Illinois, Peter Altgeld, who earlier had pardoned as victims of unfair trials three anarchists imprisoned in the notorious Haymarket riot of 1886, tried to stay Cleveland's hand, but the president ran roughshod over him. Altgeld, his eye on a party kingmaking role, joined a growing sentiment to wrest party control from the president and his conservative ways.

Cleveland did get through the House the modest tariff reform he had promised, but Republican protectionists in the Senate restored many of the rates he had cut, and he let the bill become law without his signature. The defeat, together with the depression and the labor violence, set the stage for a huge Republican victory in the 1894 congressional elections, led by the protectionist champion, McKinley. The Republicans won control of both Houses, and in twenty-four states no Democrat was elected to Congress and in six others, only one.[56] It was among the darkest of hours for the Democratic Party, and for the now widely despised Cleveland. Perhaps a consolation was the defeat of Bryan for renomination to his House seat from Nebraska in which Cleveland was believed to have had a hand through connections in the state party.

Within the party, the split now was not between North and South but Northeast on one side, South and West on the other, the farm against the factory, debtors against creditors, silver Democrats against gold. It was a sorrowful legacy left to his party by the man who only twelve years earlier had led it out of the long post–Civil War political wilderness. Cleveland avoided talk about seeking a third term, but in any event neither his party nor the country was in a mood to entertain the idea. He was a gold standard man at a time the free and unlimited coinage of silver was being seized upon, especially in the Democratic South and West, as the party's and the nation's salvation.

All through 1895 the message of free silver was spread in these sections. "We believe that a large majority of the Democrats of the United

States favor bimetallism," a group of thirty-three silver Democrats wrote in a declaration of policy dissenting from the Cleveland position, "... and we assert that the majority have and should exercise the right to control the policy of the party and retain the party name."[57] In August, free-silver Democrats met in Washington and created a number of pro-silver state party organizations with an eye to taking over the national convention the next summer from the gold-standard allies of Cleveland. The president, for his part, recognized the stakes. "Disguise it as we may," he said, "the line of battle is drawn between the forces of safe currency and those of silver monometallism."[58]

Over the rest of the year and into 1896, Cleveland soldiered on, against increasing abuse within his own party, to promote inclusion of a gold-standard plank in the party platform at the approaching national convention. But it was an exercise in futility. The case for free silver as the policy by which the Democratic Party would be wrested from the rich and powerful and given back to "the people" was irreversibly on the rise. And a new leader to make that case would soon be thrust to the fore in one of the most dramatic convention scenes in the history of the party.

William Jennings Bryan of Ohio, defeated Democratic presidential nominee in 1896 and 1900, gained the party's nomination a third time in 1908 amid a weak crop of prospects. He became the first Democratic three-time loser in history.

Chapter 14

THE BRYAN ERA, 1896–1912

IT WAS NO wonder that Grover Cleveland called his second presidential term "the luckless years."[1] The depression, the strikes, the party defections to the Populist movement and especially the internal split over currency policy brought him to the Democratic National Convention of 1896 as a leader who had worn out his welcome. His position as defender of the gold standard was now distinctly out of step with the majority of party delegates, as demonstrated in an early vote as the convention opened at Chicago's Coliseum.

Senator David Hill of New York, another gold-standard man who had fought so vigorously against Cleveland's nomination in 1892, offered a resolution commending "the honesty, economy, courage and fidelity of the present [Cleveland] Democratic National Administration."[2] It was soundly defeated, 564–357.

That embarrassing vote followed the convention's rejection of Hill himself as the national committee's nominee to be temporary chairman, in favor of a free-silver advocate, Senator John W. Daniel of Virginia, in the first indication of silver strength. The outcome, by a vote of 556 for Daniel, 349 for Hill, marked the first time a national committee recommendation had been turned down, and made clear that the convention's presidential nominee would also be a champion of free silver.

The next important vote came on the platform plank on currency policy. The silver plank, with Senator Pitchfork Ben Tillman the opening speaker, said: "We demand the free and unlimited coinage of both silver and gold at the present legal ratio of 16 [parts silver] to one [gold].... We demand that the standard silver dollar shall be a full legal tender, equally with gold, for all debts, public and private, and we favor such legislation as will prevent for the future the demonetization of any kind of legal-tender money by private contract."[3]

Hill and Senator William F. Vilas presented the gold proposal: "We insist that all our paper and silver currency shall be kept absolutely at a parity with gold. The Democratic party is the party of hard money, and is opposed to legal-tender paper money as a part of our permanent financial system." Their proposal called for "the gradual retirement and cancellation of all United States notes and Treasury notes under such legislative provisions as will prevent undue contraction."[4]

Other delegates spoke on both sides, until only one remained to be heard—the former two-term congressman from Nebraska, William Jennings Bryan. He had been importantly involved in rallying Democratic state conventions to the cause of free silver in advance of the Chicago convention, but was little known in the East. Originally from Salem, Illinois, Bryan had moved in 1887 to Nebraska, where he practiced law in Lincoln and won a seat in Congress in 1890 at the age of thirty, just as the campaign for silver currency was blossoming in the state. Starting out as a dynamic speaker for the cause of lower tariffs, he soon gauged the growing political power of the currency issue and switched his emphasis accordingly. "I don't know anything about free silver," he said in 1892, but "the people of Nebraska are for free silver, and I am for free silver."[5]

When the Silver Purchase Act was repealed, Bryan labeled the action "the Crime of 1893" and predicted it would ruin Cleveland and the Democratic Party in the 1894 congressional elections, and he was right. He predicted the next presidential election would be waged "between the capitalists of the Northeast and the rest of the people of the country,"[6] and that the Democrats needed a presidential nominee from the West and unity between West and South to survive.

It fell to Bryan to reduce the complex currency issue to terms readily understandable to the common man. The "cheap money" represented by silver, he said, would benefit hard-pressed debtors; on the other hand, the gold standard would strengthen the oppressive hand of the already wealthy creditors. If, he said, a farmer "should loan a Nebraska neighbor a hog weighing 100 pounds and the next spring demand a hog weighing 200 pounds, he would be called dishonest, even though he contended that he was only demanding one hog—just the number he loaned.... The poor man is called a Socialist if he believes that the wealth of the rich should be divided among the poor, but the rich man is called a financier if he derives a plan by which the pittance of the poor man can be converted to his use. The poor man who takes property by force is called a thief, but the creditor who can by legislation make a debtor pay a dollar twice as large as he borrowed is lauded as the friend of sound currency."[7]

Bryan was reelected to his House seat in 1892, becoming one of the Democratic Party's strongest spokesmen in defense of the free coinage of silver. But he could not survive two years later in the Republican landslide that resulted from the depression under Cleveland. He ran for the Senate in 1894 but was defeated, whereupon he broke from the president of his party, telling the Nebraska state convention that continued to back Cleveland and the gold standard: "[If] the Democratic party, after you go home, endorses your action and makes your position its permanent policy, I promise you that I will go out and serve my country and my God under some other name, even if I have to go alone."[8]

The new People's Party would have been a natural home for him, but that, however, was never necessary, as his oratory in the cause of free silver brought an army of supporters within his own party. Out of elective office, young Bryan turned to journalism, becoming a writer and editor for the *Omaha World-Herald*. But he never surrendered his political ambition, which was much higher than a career in Congress. His clarion voice demanded attention, and it came to him in a measure unimagined by anyone else on July 8, 1896, in that great convention hall in Chicago.

Bryan wore that ambition on his sleeve, telling everyone he encountered that he intended, despite his age and inexperience, to become his party's next presidential nominee on the wings of the silver issue. Governor Altgeld, a man of equal political ambition whose German birth made him ineligible for the presidency, counseled him: "You are young yet. Let ["Silver Dick"] Bland have the nomination this time. Your time will come."[9] But Bryan refused to be put off. Covering the Republican National Convention for the Omaha paper in St. Louis in June, where Senator Henry Teller of Colorado bolted the GOP over the currency issue, a man hailed Bryan on the street. "We are going to Chicago to nominate Senator Teller [as a Democrat]; you had better come and help us." Bryan reportedly replied: "I can't do it. I am going to be nominated at Chicago myself."[10]

From the press box at the Republican convention, Bryan had observed the overwhelming first-ballot nomination of Governor William McKinley of Ohio over House Speaker Thomas B. Reed and several weak favorite sons. The feat was expertly engineered by industrialist Marcus Hanna, the grandfather of the later cadre of political managers and consultants who were in time to dominate American presidential politics.

McKinley, as author of the highly unpopular Tariff Act of 1890, had been defeated for reelection to the House, but under Hanna's management went on to win the Ohio governorship as the Democrats felt voter wrath for the depression under Cleveland. Garret A. Hobart of New Jersey was chosen as McKinley's running mate on a platform that declared the Republican Party to be "unalterably opposed to every measure calculated to debase our currency or impair the credit of our country." It insisted that "the existing gold standard must be preserved [and] all our silver and paper currency must be maintained at parity with gold" until an "international agreement with the leading commercial nations of the world" could be reached on "the free coinage of silver."[11]

Bryan also had a close-up view, standing on a desk in the press section, of the boisterous bolting of the convention by Teller and other Western silver men upon the adoption of the gold-standard plank. Permitted by the convention chairman to explain their departure, they were repeatedly interrupted by boos and catcalls from the floor, as Bryan had the unexpected reward of seeing onetime Republican loyalists embark on an exodus that would soon bring many of them into his own campaign army.

With the gold-standard plank firmly nailed into the GOP platform, Hanna anticipated the nomination at the Democratic convention of Missouri's Congressman Bland, co-author of watered-down silver coinage legislation and up to this time the most prominent but hardly dynamic advocate of free silver. This was the setting in Chicago three weeks later as Bryan rose on the convention floor to conclude the debate over the Democratic plank on currency policy.

It was only by fortuitous events that he found himself thus situated. Because his Nebraska delegation had come to Chicago contested, he had not immediately been seated as a delegate and hence could not be selected, as his supporters wanted, as keynote speaker. It was only when Senator James K. Jones of Arkansas, chairman of the convention resolutions committee, developed a sore throat and asked Bryan to take his place in the platform debate that the Nebraskan had his chance. But he obviously came well prepared.

His deep baritone voice reverberating through the hall, Bryan sounded an opening note of humility soon challenged by his own oratory. "I would be presumptuous, indeed," he began, "to present myself against the distinguished gentlemen to whom you have listened if this was a mere measuring of abilities; but this is not a contest between persons. The humblest citizen in all the land, when clad in the armor of a righteous cause, is stronger than all the hosts of error. I come to speak to you in defense of a cause as holy as the cause of liberty—the cause of humanity."

Reviewing the efforts of silverites over the previous year to build the convention strength now being displayed, Bryan waxed poetic about the labors of the farmer, miner and small-town lawyer who opened the West. He proclaimed them as equally entitled to the name "businessman" as the bankers, stock traders and corporate giants of the East, and just as deserving of the fruits of their labors. "What we need," he went on, "is an Andrew Jackson to stand, as Jackson stood, against the encroachments of organized wealth." He spoke in defense of the income tax as a device for redistribution of that wealth, and he chided the Republicans for even entertaining acceptance of bimetallism on condition of an international agreement if they truly believed that maintaining the gold standard was "a good thing."

The question, he said, was "upon which side will the Democratic Party fight; upon the side of 'the idle holders of idle capital' or upon the side of 'the struggling masses'...who have ever been the foundation of the Democratic Party." Speaking for the rural America from which he came and championing as well the cause of the Populist movement that saw silver currency in terms of agrarian salvation, Bryan warned: "Destroy our farms and the grass will grow in the streets of every city in the country."

Then, standing tall and with arms outstretched as if enduring crucifixion himself, he defiantly concluded his ringing advocacy of free silver with one of the most famous lines in American political history: "Having behind us the producing masses of this nation and the world, supported by the commercial interests, the laboring interests, and the toilers everywhere, we will answer their demand for a gold standard by saying to them: You shall not press down upon the brow of labor this crown of thorns; you shall not crucify mankind upon a cross of gold."[12]

Bryan stood there, arms still outstretched, head hung down in eerie silence, until the hall suddenly erupted. A *Washington Post* reporter described cheers "so deafening that only at irregular intervals could the music of the noisy band be heard, the stamping of feet was as the roll of thunder."[13] Bryan himself observed later: "The audience seemed to rise and sit down as one man. At the close of a sentence it would rise and shout, and when I began upon another sentence, the room was as still as a church. . . . The audience acted like a trained choir—in fact, I thought of a choir as I noted how instantaneously and in unison they responded to each point made."[14]

The roll call on the gold plank, shortly after Bryan's dramatic speech, brought overwhelming rejection, 626–303, after which the silver plank was adopted, 628–301. With this one oration, Bryan at once eclipsed Bland, now in his sixties, as silver's champion, as "the Boy Orator of the Platte." Because of commitments made to Bland before Bryan's electric speech, the Missourian led through three ballots. But Bryan passed him on the fourth and was nominated on the fifth, with 652 of the 930 delegates present and voting, with many gold delegates abstaining. Notably in the context of the fight between silver and gold, Bryan got only 22 votes from the Northeast. He threw the choice of his running mate to the convention, and several candidates were offered for the role, including Bland. But he withdrew his name after the third ballot and on the fifth roll call Arthur Sewall of Maine, a shipping executive and strong Eastern silverite, was chosen.

The gold-standard Democrats, recognizing early that they were beaten, had not challenged Bryan with a serious candidate of their own. But they were not going quietly. A group of national committeemen from forty-one states and three territories calling themselves National Democrats met in Indianapolis in early September and nominated a former Union general, John M. Palmer of Illinois, for president and a former Confederate general, Simon B. Buckner of Kentucky, as his running mate. They did so, arguing that a majority of the delegates in Chicago had been Populists more than Democrats, and that the real party "could not survive a victory won in behalf of the [free silver] doctrine and policy proclaimed in its name at Chicago."[15] Many Cleveland Democrats and other Democratic regulars endorsed the ticket. Senator Hill did not, preferring to hold his grip on the party organization in New York. "I am still a Democrat— very still," he quipped.[16]

The People's Party, meanwhile, had met in St. Louis in July and reluctantly endorsed Bryan only to maintain a solid front against the Republicans in behalf of free silver. In a show of independence, however, they nominated Thomas E. Watson of Georgia to be his running mate on what came to be called the Popocrat ticket. Also falling in line behind Bryan and silver were the bolting silver Republicans when the defecting Teller failed to get consideration on the Democratic ticket. A separate National Silver Party sponsored by the American Bimetallic Union joined the coalition for Bryan as well.

Thus was the presidential campaign of 1896 aptly called "The Battle of Standards." The hope of Hanna and the Republicans to elect McKinley simply by playing on the disappointments of the Cleveland administration was foiled by the Democratic rejection of the departing president in favor of the young, dynamic champion of free silver, who immediately began an energetic cross-country campaign by whistle-stop train. Hanna decided not to have the older McKinley imitate him. "I might just as well put up a trampoline on my front lawn and compete with some professional athlete as go out speaking against Bryan," McKinley himself said. "I have to think when I speak."[17]

Instead, he undertook a front-porch campaign with a vengeance. Hanna arranged a daily schedule of delegations to McKinley's hometown of Canton, where he met them on his bunting-draped porch and delivered well-crafted speeches. Under Hanna's strong hand, the McKinley campaign left nothing to spontaneity and the risk therein. There would be no chance encounters when supporting delegates arrived. The group's leader was required to submit his remarks in writing in advance; there would be no "rum, Romanism and rebellion" to upset the applecart.

By one estimate, McKinley spoke to 750,000 voters in Canton, more than a tenth of all those who voted for him. With currency the issue, McKinley's preference to trumpet his own high-tariff policy had to be subordinated to a defense of gold, about which he had been somewhat ambivalent, having voted for bimetallism in Congress.

While he was on record for the gold standard, McKinley also pledged to seek an international agreement on silver, to the consternation of pure gold advocates. Speaking to a Pennsylvania delegation, he finally took a categorical position. "Our currency today is good—all of it as good as gold—and it is the unfaltering determination of the Republican Party to so keep and maintain it forever," he said.[18] Grateful supporters began to

sport gold-bug pins, and most of the large Eastern newspapers that traditionally backed the Democratic candidate followed their perceived economic interest and went with McKinley, the candidate of "sound money."

Bryan, whose campaign finances were undercut by the defection of
the gold Democrats, had to compete against a $10 million campaign trea-
sure chest built by Hanna as he tapped into the fear of big business
toward Bryan and his populist message. Their money paid for the dispatch of as many as fourteen hundred McKinley surrogate speakers, some
of whom followed the Bryan train responding to his pro-silver speeches.
Most major Democratic newspapers, with the exception of William Randolph Hearst's New York Journal, backed McKinley. The McKinley campaign effectively courted labor by promising "A Full Dinner Pail" while
warning that a Bryan victory would mean retrenchment by business, wage
reductions and job cutbacks. Teller, the silver Republican leader who had
joined the Bryan camp, candidly observed: "If I were a working man and
had nothing but my job, I am afraid when I came to vote I would think of
Mollie and the babies."[19]

From the outset, McKinley denigrated Bryan for waging what later
was known as political class warfare. "All attempt to array class against
class, the classes against the masses, section against section, labor against
capital, poor against rich, or interest against interest," he charged, "is in
the highest degree reprehensible."

But Bryan cast the effort in terms of social justice. He waged a tireless
effort, whistle-stopping 100 days across 16,000 miles making 600 speeches
heard by an estimated 5 million people. Using the 16:1 silver-to-gold ratio
as his trademark, Bryan rode at the head of some of the most spectacular
torchlight parades ever. In one he sat in a carriage drawn by sixteen white
horses and a single horse of yellow. In others, sixteen young women
dressed in white were accompanied by one in yellow. But in the end, free
silver succumbed to the fear that it would reduce property values in the
East and to the fact that wheat prices were finally rising without free silver,
indicating an end to the depression blamed on the departing incumbent
Democratic president.

McKinley won 51.1 percent of the vote to 47.7 percent for Bryan, a
margin of more than half a million ballots, and a more emphatic 271–176
victory in the electoral college. Still, Bryan's highly emotional campaign
did put the Democratic Party back on track as the vehicle for the rural,
agrarian interests of the South and West against the power of Eastern

money. But industrialization continued its movement westward, and Bryan's failure to carry the labor vote, especially in New England, was his undoing. Yet he persevered as the man of the people, anointed in the press as "The Commoner."

Nannie Lodge, wife of Senator Henry Cabot Lodge of Massachusetts, author of the Republican gold plank, wrote of Bryan after the election that the Democrats were "a disorganized mob at first, out of which burst into sight, hearing and force—one man, but such a man! Alone, penniless, without backing, without money, with scarce a paper, without speakers, that man fought such a fight that even those in the East can call him a Crusader, an inspired fanatic—a prophet!"[20]

Bryan had, indeed, albeit in a losing cause, given the Democratic Party a new populist identity and installed himself as the unquestioned new leader of the class war against the moneyed interests. At the same time, however, he reduced the party to a sectional one of South and West that undermined its strength as a national force, facilitating the resumption of Republican power. Hitherto Democratic states like New York, New Jersey and Delaware went Republican as did the border states of Maryland, West Virginia and Kentucky, all previously won by Cleveland, offsetting Western state gains. Most of the Midwest and most major cities also went Republican. In his quest to return the Democratic Party to its Jeffersonian and Jacksonian roots, Bryan unwittingly risked miring it into minority status in the country, and at the same time he sapped the support of the Populist Party and left it dying on the vine.

The cause of the Democratic Party was further hampered by the fact that McKinley proved to be a deft and popular politician as president, and he benefited from an economic recovery resulting from the rise in wheat prices even before his election. When Europe's wheat crop dropped by 30 percent in 1897, American exports doubled, filling the gap and further enhancing the recovery.

Meanwhile, discoveries of gold in Australia, Alaska and South Africa increased its influx into the United States and helped bring the recovery that free-silver advocates claimed would result from their metal, diminishing the argument for silver coinage. The Republicans increased their majorities in Congress, and in 1899, with the sentiment for silver fading, McKinley sought adoption of the gold standard, and legislation was passed the following year. The centerpiece of Bryan's 1896 takeover of the Democratic Party had suddenly lost its political potency when Bryan couldn't continue to offer free silver as the answer to an economic turn-around that was under way without it.

At the same time, he did not abandon the cause of bimetallism. He took to addressing state legislatures on this and other aspects of the 1896 platform, calling on them to rewrite their state constitutions to incorporate direct elections and other progressive measures. He maintained his dominance of the party and demanded that his followers continue to support the platform that had contributed to his defeat.

Still a young man at thirty-seven, Bryan was looked upon by many within the party as a savior. He had rescued its soul from the business dominance that had marked the second Cleveland administration and reminded fellow Democrats of their egalitarian traditions. He was obliged, however, to shift his emphasis from the currency question to the mushrooming influence of industry, augmented by the development of powerful corporate trusts. Amid the prosperity they brought to the country, though, it was extremely difficult to make the argument that they were detrimental to the nation and its working classes.

Intruding on the rosy picture was an unanticipated McKinley adventure in the realm of foreign policy. Even before he took office, leading American editors including Hearst and Joseph Pulitzer of the *New York World* were agitating for intervention in Cuba against Spanish colonial rule. Bryan was among those leading the call for a "free Cuba," and when McKinley launched the Spanish-American War in 1898, Bryan raised a regiment to fight there. In this regard, though, he was eclipsed by the governor of New York, Theodore Roosevelt, who famously led his Rough Riders' charge up San Juan Hill and into the history books. The "splendid little war" was over in two months and with its end came new American colonies in Puerto Rico and the Philippine Islands.

Bryan, while supporting the eventual peace treaty in order to put the war behind the United States, opposed the acquisition of the Philippines as American "imperialism" and sought to make it an issue in the presidential election of 1900. But the effort was in vain, as the economy hummed. A farmer who heard Bryan rail against McKinley's adventurism reportedly commented: "Price of hogs is 60 cents a pound. Guess we can stand it."[21]

Politically, the most significant aspect of the war may have been the prominence it gave to Roosevelt. In 1899, Vice President Hobart died in office, requiring McKinley to choose a new running mate for his 1900 reelection bid. The choice was the only major issue before the Republican National Convention in Philadelphia in mid-June. Confident of McKinley's reelection, the delegates renominated him unanimously under the benign slogan "Let well enough alone."[22]

For reasons known only to himself, the president expressed no preference on a running mate and threw the decision open to the convention, specifically telling Hanna not to try to influence the choice. It so happened that Senator Thomas Platt, the Republican boss of New York State, was unhappy with the independence of Roosevelt as his governor but realized the man's popularity made him invulnerable for renomination. Supported by Pennsylvania boss and Mark Hanna foe Matthew Quay, Platt rallied big-city Republican bosses to a scheme to get Roosevelt out of New York politics by putting him on the national ticket, knowing as well that the choice would infuriate Hanna, who hated the bombastic Roosevelt.

Roosevelt, then only forty-one, preferred being reelected governor and saw serving as vice president as being prematurely put out to pasture. He wrote to Platt: "I would a great deal rather be anything, say professor of history, than vice president."[23] But Platt was determined to have his way, and the delegates were behind him. "Roosevelt might as well stand under Niagara Falls and try to spit water back," he said at one point, "as to stop his nomination by this convention."[24]

At the start, Roosevelt was equally determined to avoid the nomination. He sent a friend, Professor (later President) Nicholas Murray Butler of Columbia University, to inform Hanna he didn't want the job. But with McKinley pointedly instructing an aide to wire the convention that he had no preference and "any of the distinguished names suggested would be satisfactory,"[25] the die was cast. Possibly concerned that Platt could be a barrier to his renomination for governor, Roosevelt decided to attend the convention, thus giving further impetus to the vice-presidential stampede. Hanna became desperate. "By God, Teddy," he told the governor directly at one point, "you know that there is nothing in this country which can compel a man to run for an office who doesn't want it."[26] But by now Roosevelt was playing coy.

Hanna, after a frustrating phone conversation with McKinley, exclaimed to Wisconsin National Committeeman Henry Payne, a Roosevelt enthusiast: "Do whatever you please! I'm through! I won't have anything more to do with the convention! I won't take charge of the campaign!" Payne, startled, asked what the matter was. "Matter!" Hanna barked back. "Why, everybody's gone crazy! What is the matter with all of you? Here's this convention going headlong for Roosevelt for vice president. Don't any of you realize there's only one life between that madman and the presidency? Platt and Quay are no better than idiots! What harm can he do as governor of New York compared to the damage he will do as president if McKinley should die?"[27]

In the end, Roosevelt "reluctantly" notified the convention that "I cannot seem to be bigger than the party" and therefore would accept. Hanna told McKinley: "Now it is up to you to live."[28]

Even before Roosevelt had been placed on the Republican ticket, the Democratic outlook was not promising, and there was no keen competition for the party's presidential nomination as the party prepared to meet in St. Louis in July in recognition of growing Democratic strength in the Midwest. Tammany and other Eastern party factions focused on Senator Arthur P. Gorman of Maryland and Judge Augustus Van Wyck of New York, but their appeal rested mainly in not being Bryan. Admiral George Dewey, the hero of the battle of Manila Bay, briefly offered himself for the nomination but withdrew when it was clear that Bryan again was the party's preference. He insisted that the silver plank remain in the platform, even to the point of threatening to step aside if it was not, but the issue of imperialism dominated. Bryan was unanimously renominated after even his 1896 foe, David Hill of New York, conceded there was no alternative. Lauding Bryan's "impression upon the minds, and hearts and conscience of the American people," Hill acknowledged that "from the closing of polls four years ago until this very hour there never was a possibility of any other nomination being made."[29] In the interest of harmony, Bryan devoted his acceptance speech to attacking the foreign adventurism of McKinley. Nominated to be Bryan's running mate was Cleveland's vice president, Adlai E. Stevenson of Illinois, an able campaigner, after Hill declined to have his name considered.

But with Roosevelt taking to the stump as if he and not McKinley were the head of the Republican ticket, with McKinley again hewing to his front porch in Canton and with free silver undermined as an issue, Bryan was again outgunned. A poorly attended Populist convention at Sioux Falls, South Dakota, nominated Bryan once more, as did another Silver Republican group at Kansas City, but neither was of much help. A second Populist faction nominated Wharton Barker of Pennsylvania for president. Finally, a growing Social Democratic Party held its first national convention and nominated Eugene V. Debs as its standard-bearer.

This time around, with Bryan preaching not free silver but anti-imperialism, he asked whether Americans wanted "Republic or Empire." He called for independence for the Philippines under American protection and, with religious overtones that became increasingly part of his oratory, declared: "The command 'Go ye into all the world and preach the Gospel to every creature' has no Gatling gun attachment."[30] But his sermons to well-fed Americans in behalf of far-off natives did not strike much of a chord, and eventually he switched his campaign pitch to attacks on the corporate trusts that victimized workingmen at home. He even took his campaign into the Northeast, which he undiplomatically called "the enemy's country." Finley Peter Dunne's Mr. Dooley wrote: "All ye can say about Willum Jennings Bryan's rayciption is that he got by Wall Sthreet without bein' stoned to death with nuggets fr'm th' goold resarve."[31]

At the same time, the retention of a free-silver plank in the Democratic platform kept Gold Democrats from rejoining the party fold. In the colorful oratorical battle between Bryan and Roosevelt, Bryan's Bible-quoting proved no match for Roosevelt's flag-waving. The Republican vice-presidential nominee repeatedly referred to Bryan as "my opponent," as if Roosevelt was the head of his ticket, while McKinley contentedly observed from Canton. As for Hanna, he swallowed his distaste for Roosevelt and whistle-stopped himself through the West in search of populist votes for the Republican ticket, reminding crowds that the "full dinner pail" promised by McKinley in 1896 remained full.

The result was a worse defeat for Bryan than four years earlier, yet not a totally humiliating one considering the expanding prosperity. McKinley raised his share of the popular vote slightly to 51.7 percent to 45.5 percent for Bryan, a margin of nearly 900,000 ballots. The electoral vote, however, was more emphatic, 292–155. The Solid South again provided the core of Bryan's support, but he slipped in the West, even losing his own state of Nebraska. The sectional coalition he had forged on the issue of free silver had collapsed, his switch to anti-imperialism had fared no better, and two successive presidential defeats appeared to end his White House ambitions.

But Bryan was only forty years old, an age when most presidential aspirants only began to consider reaching for the prize. One thing was certain: he was far from ready to retire from a leadership role in the struggle for the resurrection of the Democratic Party. Three former Cleveland cabinet members, however, John G. Carlisle, Hoke Smith and J. Sterling Morton, left little doubt that they felt both Bryan and his populist, pro-silver agenda had run their course and a thorough housecleaning was required. "In order to achieve success," these so-called reorganizers wrote, "the Democracy must abandon all dead issues and return to the true principles of the party."[32] Other, younger Democrats like Mayor Tom Johnson of Cleveland didn't want a return to the Grover Cleveland Democrats either, and strove for entirely new, more progressive leadership.

With the crown of gold he so despised now placed firmly on the nation's brow, Bryan turned his focus to a progressive agenda that included election and campaign finance reform, abolition of child labor, railroad and stock regulation, and new food and drug protection laws. Through his newly founded weekly journal, *The Commoner,* he preached morality and redemption along with his political views, but was aware that his opponents in the party were on the verge of reasserting their claim to leadership.

Only six months after the McKinley-Roosevelt team was inaugurated, the political world was again turned on its head. While outdoorsman Roosevelt vacationed in the Adirondacks, McKinley was shot by an anarchist at the Pan-American Exposition in Buffalo and died eight days later. Hanna was said to have remarked to an associate: "Now look, that damned cowboy is President of the United States."[33]

In short order Roosevelt was co-opting some of Bryan's best political alarums, waging war on corporate wealth, trusts and political bossism, and in time leaping to the head of a reformist, progressive parade, offering a "Square Deal" to all. He asserted himself boldly in foreign affairs by intervening in the Panamanian revolt of 1903 and thus acquiring land for a Panama Canal, and at home as a conservationist. As a zealous trust-buster, Roosevelt thoroughly eclipsed the whole Democratic Party, assuring a continuation of the long era of Republicanism broken since before the Civil War only by the two separate terms of Cleveland, and destined to continue for more than a decade.

Bryan aggressively fought the return to party control of what he called "the Cleveland element," and he taunted the former president himself to run again, confident he would be defeated in 1904. "Cleveland represents as no one else does the plutocratic element of the party," he said at one point, "and is the logical candidate if the party returns to its wallow in the mire." He said he had "a right to speak of Grover Cleveland's Democracy, for I have borne his sins in two national campaigns."[34]

Roosevelt's dynamism in the White House assured his nomination in his own right when the next Republican National Convention met in Chicago in late June 1904. His only possible challenge, from his old enemy Mark Hanna, disappeared with Hanna's death in 1904. Senator Charles W. Fairbanks of Indiana was picked to run with Roosevelt.

Remarkably, in Democratic ranks, the name of Cleveland resurfaced. His resistance to Bryan's siren song of free silver and his own stubborn advocacy of the gold standard seemed in retrospect to have been warranted. And the party, after its two flirtations with a Prairie candidate, was ready to return to a dependable Easterner, and to staple together the combination that had won twice with Cleveland and gold.

Cleveland, however, decided in spite of Tammany support to stay on the sidelines. Hill, still in control of the party machinery in New York, put forward another New Yorker, Alton B. Parker, chief justice of the New York Court of Appeals. His emergence underscored the poverty of Democratic candidates, since there was no sufficiently appealing governor or senator from the East on the scene. Publisher William Randolph Hearst, now a New York congressman and would-be reformer of great personal wealth, made an earnest bid, but had been a Bryan supporter and had made many enemies in the party.

The convention opened in St. Louis in early July and Bryan was there, not as a candidate but as a determined opponent of Parker's nomination. The Commoner waged a sixteen-hour battle in the convention platform committee against a plank that said in effect the recent new discoveries of gold made moot any discussion of the currency. To placate both sides, Ben Tillman and other Southerners proposed that the platform remain silent on the issue of currency, but Bryan reacted by vehemently hurling insults at his opponents.

When he accusingly asked one elderly delegate whether he was acting "as the representative of the trusts" or in "the interest of the Democratic Party," the man calmly replied: "I was a Democrat before you were born. . . . I voted for you, sir, when to do so meant almost social and commercial ostracism. . . . My personal integrity has never been questioned." Thereupon Tillman confronted Bryan, telling him: "You are simply a damn fool! Silver is dead and you know it. You may dearly love your grandmother, but if she has lain in the grave for eight years, you surely will not insist on digging her up ... for the edification of your friends."[35]

On some other planks, Bryan was placated by Cleveland conservatives lest another of his emotional appeals from the floor get out of hand and somehow resurrect the fortunes of the man himself. The final platform bore distinct marks of Bryan's hand in statements against American imperialism, protective tariffs and "executive usurpation," and for Philippine independence, direct election of U.S. senators and other liberal causes.

In a failed bid to derail Parker's nomination, Bryan rose after four in the morning to second the nomination of Senator Francis M. Cockrell of Missouri. He railed against the militarism of Roosevelt and the wealthy interests behind Parker, asking at one point, "Must we choose between a god of war and a god of gold?"[36] Nevertheless, Parker was nominated easily on the first ballot with Hearst a distant runner-up. Senator Henry Gassaway Davis of West Virginia, a wealthy octogenarian, was chosen to be his running mate.

Parker went out of his way to show disdain for Bryan by dispatching a telegram to the convention, at a time Bryan was ill and in bed, stating flatly, "I regard the gold standard as firmly and irretrievably established,"[37] and if that didn't suit the convention, he would decline the party nomination. Bryan left his sickbed to lead the debate triggered by the Parker wire, but once more lost. In the process, however, he demonstrated his determination to remain a key player in the party. Ten days before the election that Parker was certain to lose, Bryan in his personal publication, *The Commoner,* served notice that he intended to reorganize the entire party "along radical lines."[38]

Bryan did campaign for the Democratic ticket, but more to reinforce his own support in the party than to elect Parker, who was no match for Roosevelt's appeal, even when the old Rough Rider played the incumbent and remained largely off the campaign trail. The only quiver in Parker's bow was a charge that the Republican National Committee had blackmailed wealthy industrialists to bankroll Roosevelt's campaign even as he railed against the power of the trusts. TR brushed aside the allegation as "monstrous" and "unqualifiedly and atrociously false"[39] and it failed to sully him in voters' eyes. He beat Parker by a record 2.6 million popular votes, the Democratic nominee winning only 37.6 percent to 56.4 percent for Roosevelt, and only 140 electoral votes from the South to 336 for Roosevelt—the worst Democratic defeat to that time.

On election night, Roosevelt astounded the country by announcing that "the wise custom which limits the President to two terms regards the substance and not the form, and under no circumstances will I be a candidate for or accept another nomination."[40] He was only forty-six at the time and had just been elected to his first full term in his own right, so the two-term tradition did not prohibit him from seeking another. The decision immediately cast him as a lame-duck president and made his second term captive to resentful Republican congressional leaders with commitments to special interests. A financial panic in 1907 compounded his difficulties, encouraging the defeated Democrats to think their chance to end another long White House drought might be only four years off, since he clearly was the most popular politician in the land.

At the same time, Bryan began to see the possibilities of a resurrection of his own at the head of a revitalized, reformed party. After a world tour in 1905–1906 that kept him in the public eye, however, Bryan made a tactical misstep by calling for government ownership of the railroads when they were just coming under federal regulation. Conservatives leaped on him, branding him a socialist. It was a charge that would resonate against him and the Democratic Party in the approaching presidential election of 1908. Cleveland professed to see "symptoms of Bryan insanity," but Roosevelt wrote to a friend: "I don't believe we have heard the last of him. His party is dreadfully hard up for Presidential timber."[41]

Bryan's hopes for a comeback were reinforced when in 1908 Roosevelt anointed as his successor his secretary of war, William Howard Taft of Ohio, a former federal judge and first civil governor of the Philippines who had never held elective office and clearly did not have the campaign skills of Roosevelt. But suspicions surfaced early in the press that Taft was merely a cover for a later convention stampede for Roosevelt's renomination in spite of his disavowals of availability. Sensitive to allegations of hypocrisy, Roosevelt openly espoused the Taft candidacy and in spite of an attempted push for the incumbent at the Republican convention in Chicago in June, Taft was overwhelmingly nominated on the first ballot. Congressman James S. Sherman of New York was chosen as his running mate.

Two weeks later in Denver, the Democrats did indeed resurrect Bryan, politically reborn by the party's failed return to conservatism behind the dismal Parker candidacy and strongly affected by the movement for progressivism sweeping the West. Bryan's credentials had regained their luster amid another weak Democratic field of presidential prospects. There was no Democratic governor or senator from an important doubtful state outside the secure South. Cleveland warned the party that Bryan would lead it to defeat for a third time, but his voice was stilled by death before the convention opened.

This time around, Bryan wooed labor by agreeing to an anti-injunction plank sought by union leader Samuel Gompers. With a progressive, populist platform in place and running on the slogan "Shall the People Rule?" he swept to an overwhelming first-ballot nomination. A like-minded former Indiana gubernatorial candidate, John Worth Kern, was picked to run with him. Once again, an array of third parties offered candidates, the most prominent of whom were Debs again by the Socialists and Tom Watson by the Populists. As matters turned out, what they took from Bryan still would not have been enough to elect him.

Bryan, with his brother Charles as campaign manager, sought to organize Bryan Clubs and a Democratic newspaper in every county and to enlist or at least neutralize the party's bosses in the major cities and states. But he was no match for the Roosevelt appeal in behalf of Taft and Republican money. A dull Bryan-Taft campaign was enlivened somewhat when Roosevelt launched a written debate with Bryan over the propriety of campaign finance dealings, to which Bryan responded in kind. But voters were not treated to the sort of face-to-face contest that could have ignited the race. Roosevelt's co-opting of the trustbusting issue and his public perception as a reformer of liberal cast cut the ground from under the Commoner. Beyond that, Bryan's performance on the stump had grown familiar to American audiences and Roosevelt dismissed him as "the cheapest fakir we have ever had proposed for President."[42]

Bryan's high-mindedness was seriously undercut in mid-September when the Hearst newspapers charged that his campaign treasurer, Governor Charles N. Haskell of Oklahoma, had blocked an anti-trust suit against Standard Oil in return for party contributions and had engaged in shady railroad dealings. When Haskell denied the allegations, Roosevelt pushed Taft to escalate the charges, and Haskell finally resigned. Bryan countered with charges that Roosevelt had similarly engaged in unsavory business deals, but Roosevelt cited his record as a crusader against "malefactors of great wealth" and lit a bigger fire under Taft to attack Bryan as a demagogue.

In the end Bryan was undone by his own familiarity and public acceptance of Taft as Roosevelt's surrogate, although Taft was a restrained conservative not at all in Roosevelt's mold. Bryan ran 1.2 million ballots behind him, winning only 43.1 percent of the popular vote to Taft's 51.6 percent, and 2.8 percent for Debs. Taft's electoral college margin was 321–162, almost as great as TR's over Parker four years before.

But the repudiation was more a personal one of Bryan as a candidate running once too often than of the Democratic Party or the progressive agenda he now embraced. The party did better outside the Solid South than it had in the previous two elections, Democratic governors were elected in five states won by Taft, and the progressive movement continued to spread rapidly in the East and West. Western farmers were demanding more favorable tariff rates for their produce and tighter federal regulation of railroads and the trusts that were squeezing them. If the Democrats, after nearly a quarter of a century with Bryan on center stage, could find a new leader to ride that progressive tide, and with Roosevelt gone from the Republican equation as they expected, they might be ready to claim the White House again in 1912.

As matters turned out, however, Roosevelt was not out of the equation, to the eventual good fortune of the Democratic Party. Taft proved much too conservative for Roosevelt's liking, or for party progressives who supported Roosevelt's reform initiatives, and he tangled with the conservative Republican congressional leadership on everything from protective tariffs to government regulation of business.

Taft threw in with the conservatives and launched an aggressive effort to purge the party's progressives in the congressional elections of 1910, even as the progressive movement was catching fire across the Midwest. His effort failed, and Roosevelt, returning from a highly publicized African safari that served to enhance his swashbuckler image, began to press for such reforms as a graduated income tax, inheritance taxes and stiff laws against child labor, to the great consternation of Taft and his allies in Congress.

Roosevelt embarked on a speaking tour proclaiming a "New Nationalism" of social welfare, election reform, federal regulation of big business and progressive labor legislation that drove a deep wedge in the Republican Party. This development gave the Democrats an opening in the 1910 elections, and they won control of the House of Representatives for the first time in sixteen years. A Bryan progressive, Champ Clark of Missouri, was elected speaker. In the Senate, the Democrats made enough gains to forge a working coalition with progressive Republicans, and they elected a new crop of attractive state governors, including an unlikely politician in New Jersey named Woodrow Wilson who had been president of Princeton University.

The Democratic off-year victory confirmed that the party had not gone down with Bryan two years earlier. "For the first time since Jackson's administration," the *New York World* said, "the Democratic party is emancipated and master of its own destiny. All the shackles have been struck off. There is no load of sectional issues or dead issues or economic fallacies for [it] to struggle under. As secession followed slavery to the grave . . . so the Bryan socialism has followed silver, and the Democratic slate is wiped clean. The party is back to first principles again, under leadership that is fit to lead."[43] That leadership, however, had yet to be determined.

At the same time, Taft's conservative foreign and anti-trust policies dismayed Roosevelt. After having made a show of renouncing nomination for a second full presidential term after his election in 1904, he decided in early 1912 that he had made a serious mistake in leaving the Republican Party in Taft's conservative hands. He rocked the GOP by declaring his intention to seek the party's presidential nomination against the man he had handpicked as his successor four years earlier. Suddenly, the Democratic outlook brightened with the prospect of the deepest split in Republican Party ranks since its formation fifty-six years earlier, when the nation had stumbled toward civil war.

Chapter 15

WILSON AND THE NEW FREEDOM,
1912–1915

AFTER A SIXTEEN-YEAR drought, three strong Democrats emerged in pursuit of the unexpected presidential opportunity created by Theodore Roosevelt's challenge to the incumbent Republican. All three were born in the South—House Speaker Champ Clark of Missouri, Congressman Oscar W. Underwood of Alabama, chairman of the House Ways and Means Committee, and native Virginian Woodrow Wilson, now governor of New Jersey.

Wilson was the least known nationally of the three and, unlike the other two, he had no background in national politics nor, until about two years earlier, in politics at any level. The son of a Presbyterian preacher and schooled at Davidson College, Princeton, the University of Virginia Law School and Johns Hopkins, he was a certified academic. He taught history and government at Bryn Mawr, Wesleyan and then law and political economics at Princeton. After a dozen years on the faculty he rose to the presidency of the prestigious university, observing all the while the tribulations of the Democratic Party marching frustratingly behind the silver banner of Bryan.

The Commoner's style did not sit well with this cerebral man and it was not long before Wilson began entertaining thoughts of forgoing the ivory tower of the college campus for more lively public endeavors. At the same time, he found himself embroiled in wearisome internal politics at the university that were causing him to consider his options, and

Bryan, appointed secretary of state by President Woodrow Wilson, committed himself to the cause of peace. When Wilson took harsh measures against Imperial Germany in response to her submarine warfare, Bryan resigned his post.

indeed may have forced him out of the presidency had he not taken one of them.

One of Wilson's friends was George Harvey, editor of *Harper's Weekly,* who began to tout the Princeton president as a potential president of the United States down the road. As early as 1906, Harvey featured a picture of his friend on the magazine's cover, and as head of the Harper's publishing house put out Wilson's controversial *A History of the American People.* A university presidency, however, hardly seemed a realistic stepping-stone to the White House. Harvey set his sights a bit lower for Wilson and settled on a United States Senate seat from New Jersey in 1906 as a prelude to running for governor in 1908.[1]

Democratic politics in the state was notoriously corrupt, in the hands of machine bosses in its leading cities and counties. Undeterred, Harvey approached the Democratic boss of Newark and Essex County, former U.S. Senator James Smith Jr., with his idea, and persuaded Smith that backing the upright if rather stuffy Princeton president for the Senate, and later for governor, would add considerable luster to the state party's tarnished image. Smith instructed the delegates from Essex County to put Wilson's name before the state legislature, which at that time chose members of the U.S. Senate. Wilson considered accepting the Democratic nomination but withdrew in deference to an old Princeton classmate, Edwin A. Stevens, who was also seeking the Senate seat.[2] Harvey, however, had achieved his objective of advancing Wilson's name as a prospect for future high political office.

The spotlight stayed on Wilson over the next few years as he spoke out for academic reform at Princeton. But as he suffered continued setbacks on this front, he paid more attention to the exhortations of Harvey and his dreams of parlaying a career in New Jersey politics into a Wilson presidency. By 1910, Wilson was looking for a respectable way out of academia, and Harvey was there to grease the route for him. At a lunch at the stylish Delmonico's in New York, Harvey met again with Smith, who had aspirations of returning to the Senate, and convinced him that Wilson would make an ideal front man for the party machine at the top of the Democratic state ticket.[3]

Harvey went to Wilson and informed him that if he wanted the nomination for governor, it could be arranged. All he had to do was agree that if elected he would make no effort to break up or hinder the Smith organization. In spite of the shady reputation of Smith and his machine, Wil-

son convinced himself that as one who preached the virtues of public service to his students, he could hardly say no to running, so he agreed to the
condition.[4]

From the start, all parties in the Wilson candidacy understood that
the governorship was to be a stepping-stone to the White House. In June
1910, with the gubernatorial election only half a year away, Wilson wrote
to a close Princeton friend, David B. Jones: "It is immediately as you know
the question of my nomination for the governorship of New Jersey, but
that is the mere preliminary of a plan to nominate me in 1912 for the presidency."[5] That was fine with Smith, who viewed Wilson's higher ambition
and plans as assurance of his own continued running of the politics of the
state, including the overseeing of patronage.

Despite opposition from some liberal Democrats that was easily overcome by the Smith machine, Wilson was nominated on the first ballot at
the party convention in Trenton. With an eye to adding the party's liberals to his following, he told the party at the Taylor Opera House that "I
did not seek this nomination" and would enter office "with absolutely no
pledges of any kind to prevent me from serving the people."[6] The Smith
organization saw the political value in such a declaration, but Wilson
meant what he said.

In the campaign that fall against Republican Vivian M. Lewis, a conservative former state banking and insurance commissioner, Wilson managed to benefit from the backing of the Smith machine while selling
himself to the voters as a reformer who would not be subservient to the
bosses. He proposed anti-trust legislation and regulation of the railroads
and utilities, and met the obvious suspicion that he would be the dupe of,
or willing collaborator with, the corrupt Democratic machine by pointedly pledging he would root it out, in contradiction to his pledge to
Smith.

When the confident Wilson offered to debate Lewis or any other
Republican on the issues of the campaign, one of the state GOP's most
prominent leaders, George Record, accepted. They agreed to a written
exchange of questions and answers in which Record hammered at Wilson's support from Smith and other Democratic bosses. Asked whether
"you admit that the boss system exists" and "if so, how do you propose to
abolish it," Wilson replied in writing: "Of course I admit it: Its existence is
notorious. I have made it my business for many years to observe and
understand that system, and I hate it as thoroughly as I understand it."

Wilson went on to note the system was "bipartisan" and that "it constitutes the most dangerous condition in the public life of our state and nation today; and that it has virtually for the time being destroyed representative government and in its place set up a government of privilege. I would propose to abolish it by the reforms suggested in the Democratic platform, by the election of men who refuse to submit to it, and who will lend their energies to breaking it up by pitiless publicity."[7]

When Record asked specifically whether he meant Smith and other prominent Democratic bosses, Wilson flatly said yes, adding only that they differed from the Republican bosses in "that they are not in control of the government of the state, while the others are, and they will not be and cannot be if the present Democratic ticket is elected." The Democratic bosses could only marvel at Wilson's cleverness.

They could only smile too when asked by Record, "what will be your attitude, if elected, toward the bosses who had brought forth your nomination?" Wilson wrote: "If elected I shall not either in the manner of appointments to office, or assent to legislation, or in shaping any part of the policy of my administration, submit to the dictation of any person or persons, 'special interests,' or organizations. I will always welcome advice and suggestions from any citizens ... but all suggestions and all advice will be considered on their merits, and no additional weight will be given to any man's advice because of his exercising, or supposing that he exercises, some sort of political influence or control. I shall deem myself forever disgraced should I, in even the slightest degree, cooperate in any such system."[8]

Wilson went on to win election in November with the second largest plurality for governor ever achieved in New Jersey. What's more, he unexpectedly carried with him a Democratic legislature. Almost at once, Smith and the other New Jersey Democratic bosses learned that the governor-elect was not just talking in his remarks about taking on bossism. It so happened that Smith, who had told Wilson earlier that to save the new governor from embarrassment he would not seek the U.S. Senate seat, changed his mind and passed the word to the new Democratic legislature, demanding the appointment. An obscure, oft-defeated Democrat named James Martine was the only man running in the state party primary for the Senate seat, and Wilson in his own campaign had called for direct election of U.S. senators. He went to Smith and urged him not to reach for the Senate seat, but Smith refused.

Wilson decided he would have to fight Smith on the matter or the integrity of his governorship would be discredited from the outset. "I am very anxious about the question of the senatorship," he wrote to Harvey a week after the election. "If not handled right it will destroy every fortunate impression of the campaign and open my administration with a split party." While saying he had "learned to have a very high opinion for Senator Smith" and believed he would do a good job in the Senate, he observed that his selection "would be intolerable to the very people who elected me and gave us a majority in the legislature."[9]

Besides, Wilson reasoned that as governor he would also be the leader of his party and he could not, for all his promise to Smith, leave its direction and control to somebody else. Smith, however, began to round up the support of other Democratic county bosses. Wilson decided he had no choice but to build an organization of his own, drawing on party liberals and local opponents of the bosses in Essex, Hudson and other key counties.

In this effort, he recruited Joseph Tumulty of Jersey City, leader of a group of Democratic legislators in Hudson County, to be his private secretary—the start of a long and significant political partnership. At a huge rally of liberal Democrats in Jersey City, Wilson made his pitch for the obscure Martine in the name of reform. The day before the new senator was to be chosen, Smith yielded to superior political power and withdrew in favor of Martine. All at once, Wilson had shaken the taint of bossism that had threatened to stifle his political career in its crib.

In his first year as governor, Wilson followed through on his reform agenda, bolstered by the bipartisan progressive majority in the state legislature that his own election had been instrumental in creating. His proposals for a corrupt practices act, a new public service commission to set utility rates, workmen's compensation, the commission form of government for the state's cities and several election reforms immediately propelled the governor of New Jersey into presidential speculation for 1912—just as Harvey had earlier hoped and planned.

With the larger ambition of the presidency clearly acknowledged, Wilson spent much of his second year as governor openly working toward that goal, traveling extensively around the country and touting his ideas. His focus on the state and his effectiveness as its chief executive diminished as his reformist inclinations hardened and became more obvious, causing him loss of support among many of his earlier conservative backers. By now Smith had achieved a degree of revenge in helping the Republicans regain control of the state legislature in 1911, and in 1912 his allies in the legislature turned a cold shoulder to many of Wilson's proposals.

Wilson himself was becoming ever more progressive, even to the point of seeing virtue in Bryan, about whom in 1907 he had injudiciously written in a private letter: "Would we could discover something at once dignified and effective to knock Mr. Bryan once and for all into a cocked hat."[10] When the *New York Sun* in January of 1912 published the offending letter, Wilson ate crow by telling a Jackson Day dinner that the time had come not only for the party to return to the principles "of good Irish hickory" but also to proclaim "the steadfast vision" and "the character and the devotion and the preachings of William Jennings Bryan."[11] Bryan was pleased and forgiving.

It was against this background of effective political positioning that Wilson approached the 1912 presidential election on an unabashedly fast track toward the Oval Office. The two other chief Democratic contenders, however, Clark and Underwood, had been aroused to challenge him. Clark, a big, easy-going man affectionately known as "Ol' Hound Dog," had heavy support in the West and the backing of William Randolph Hearst. As an old Bryan supporter, Clark hoped to inherit the dominant progressive wing of the party. Bryan, favorably disposed to him at first, took approving note of Wilson's dealings against the bosses in New Jersey and, while remaining neutral, began to express reservations about Clark's commitment and toughness. Clark showed no aversion to party machines that Wilson so conspicuously disdained. The Missourian diligently mined state primaries in the Midwest for convention delegates, as Underwood did the same in state conventions in the South, with much success. Another aspirant, Governor Judson Harmon of Ohio, and several favorite sons made up the Democratic field.

With convention delegates selected in several state primaries for the first time, Clark bested Wilson in California, Illinois, Massachusetts and Maryland, and Wilson defeated the Missourian in Wisconsin, South Dakota and Oregon, and also claimed the delegates in his own New Jersey. It was clear by June that Clark would arrive at the national convention in Baltimore with a clear delegate lead, though well short of the nomination.

The Republican convention in Chicago came first, in mid-June, and what happened there later in the month, with Bryan again covering it as a reporter, made the Democratic meeting seem all the more optimistic. The progressive revolt against President Taft, led in person by his former benefactor Teddy Roosevelt, was in full swing. The popular leader of that revolt in the Senate, Robert La Follette of Wisconsin, had already seen his chances for the presidential nomination all but destroyed by Roosevelt's decision to reclaim the party leadership; even with Roosevelt, the progressives faced an uphill fight to overcome the incumbent president's delegate strength. Through the spring, Roosevelt had also resorted to the state primaries to mine his popular appeal, and had won three times as many delegates in the contested races as Taft and La Follette combined. But the primary states provided only about 20 percent of the total, leaving Roosevelt well behind Taft. Nevertheless, he told a reporter: "I'm feeling like a bull moose," and that became the symbol of his campaign.[12]

On the convention floor and in committee meetings, the Roosevelt forces waged organizational and credential challenges to contested seats, to no avail. They announced that while they would not bolt the convention they would not participate in the voting. As they sat in silent protest, the convention renominated Taft on the first ballot, giving him 556 votes to 107 for Roosevelt in spite of the silent protest, and only 41 for La Follette. Sherman was renominated for vice president.

An outraged Roosevelt immediately held a protest meeting elsewhere in the convention hall, where supportive delegates formed a committee and declared they would conduct a convention of their own in early August, also in Chicago. Thus was born the Progressive Party, soon to be known more popularly as the Bull Moose Party, to oppose what Roosevelt considered forces of reaction behind Taft leading the country to perdition.[13] The resultant split in Republican ranks assured the defeat of the incumbent and, for all practical purposes, even before the new party met to nominate Roosevelt, turned the 1912 fight for the presidency to one between him and the Democratic nominee.

As the Democratic convention opened in Baltimore, Clark was far from the two-thirds majority required for the nomination, but he had just received what could have been a significant boost with the endorsement of the Tammany organization in New York. It turned out, however, to be less than a blessing. It led Bryan, who had been publicly neutral to this point and remained the hero of many delegates, suddenly to offer an anti-Tammany resolution. It called on the convention to stand "opposed to the nomination of any candidate for President who is the representative of or under obligation to J. Pierpont Morgan, Thomas F. Ryan, August Belmont or any other member of the privilege-hunting and favor-seeking class."[14]

Bryan's resolution threw the hall into an uproar. After angry declarations against him, it passed by a resounding vote of more than four to one, with the Wilson forces throwing in with Bryan. The overwhelming vote underscored the progressive temper of the convention. But if, as some suspected, Bryan thought the delegates might be moved to demand that he be the party's standard-bearer for a fourth time, there was no such groundswell. When the first roll call on the presidential nomination took place the next morning, Clark was ahead with 440½ votes to 324 for Wilson, 148 for Harmon, 117½ for Underwood and the rest scattered—including a solitary ballot for Bryan.[15]

After nine more ballots, a break for Clark came when New York boss Charles Murphy switched the state's 90 delegates from Harmon to the speaker, giving him a majority, which traditionally had a bandwagon effect. Not since Van Buren had so failed in 1844 had it not happened. But the supporters of Wilson and Underwood agreed to hold the line against Clark. On the fourteenth ballot, Bryan once again thrust himself onto center stage, saying he would withhold his vote from Clark rather than support anyone under obligation to Murphy and the New York delegation. Nebraska followed its leader and switched its votes to Wilson, with more derision voiced in the hall against Bryan. When the convention adjourned for the night, Wilson had moved within 58 votes of Clark.[16]

What the Bryan move had done was effectively challenge once again Clark's claim to be a logical successor to the progressive leadership with the backing of Wall Street interests. With Roosevelt having already declared the formation of the Progressive Party, and his nomination at its approaching convention a certainty, the prospect of Clark rather than Wilson challenging him for the progressive mantle seemed increasingly unpromising.

Telegrams demanding Wilson's nomination engulfed the Baltimore convention. On the twentieth ballot, Wilson reached one third of the total, enough to block Clark on his own, and on the twenty-eighth, he passed Clark, but the calls of the states droned on for another day. On the forty-second, the Illinois party boss, Roger Sullivan, broke for Wilson and on the next ballot he reached a majority. On the forty-fifth, Underwood withdrew, and on the forty-sixth, Wilson achieved the two thirds needed and the nomination. Governor Thomas R. Marshall of Indiana, a progressive and a Wilson supporter, was selected to be his running mate.[17]

In early August the Progressive Party convention in Chicago anointed

Roosevelt as its candidate amid heavy religious overtones, the singing of "Onward, Christian Soldiers" and "Battle Hymn of the Republic" and a score of female delegates. In keeping with the atmosphere, he delivered what he called his "Confession of Faith" in the new party as a vehicle of reform against the entrenched political establishment. Governor Hiram Johnson of California was nominated to be vice president.[18]

Although the fall campaign was a three-sided affair among Taft the Republican, Wilson the Democrat and Roosevelt the Progressive, for all practical purposes Taft was undone from the start by Roosevelt's insurgency, splitting the Republican vote. Taft found himself revealed as an old conservative in a new progressive tide. He did little active campaigning, and it became clear at an early stage that the presidency would go either to Roosevelt or Wilson. The campaign became a contest between the two to claim the progressive mantle, and each had a distinct approach and agenda.

For more than a year Roosevelt had been advocating what he called the "New Nationalism"—the use of federal power to promote, monitor and regulate corporate affairs and excess for the national well-being. "We must have complete and effective publicity of corporate affairs, so that people may know . . . whether the corporations obey the law," he said in one early speech. "We must have government supervision of the capitalization, not only of public service corporations . . . but of all corporations." He called for, among other things, laws "to prohibit the use of corporate funds directly or indirectly for political purposes," and in general a governmental oversight role to see that the fruits of the industrial age reached every American family.[19] In effect, Roosevelt's plan cast the federal government as a partner with corporate America.

Wilson, in consultation with Louis D. Brandeis, a prominent liberal lawyer and intellectual from Massachusetts, countered with a progressive program of his own called the "New Freedom." It accepted the Roosevelt premise that the corporate world required monitoring by government in the public interest, but went well beyond it in remedy. The Wilson/Brandeis approach disagreed that oversight was enough in cases where corporate wealth, power and resources destroyed or hindered fair competition. Excessive power, as in industrial trusts, had to be broken up and competition from small businesses and farms enhanced by "a body of laws which will look after the men . . . who are sweating blood to get their foothold in the world of endeavor."[20] By regulating the free market, Wilson argued, the little man could compete in it on more equitable terms. He wanted "regulated competition," he said, not "regulated monopoly."[21]

Roosevelt deplored the New Freedom as "rural Toryism." In turn, Wilson called the New Nationalism a "partnership between the government and the trusts," and declared that "free men need no guardians."[22] Acting on the issue of corporate money controlling campaigns raised by Roosevelt, Wilson eschewed contributions from corporations, and the Democrats conducted "dollar drives" among small contributors, but in the end had to rely on wealthy givers. In all this, Taft's conservatism was overwhelmed, and Debs, again the Socialist nominee, drew surprising support amid the prevailing atmosphere of reform.

The differences in substance and style of delivery made for a combative and exciting fall campaign. The old front-porch tradition of stay-at-home candidacies fell away as both Wilson and Roosevelt whistle-stopped across the country and back, speaking several times a day. Sometimes they got off their campaign trains for rallies and lengthy speeches before huge crowds in convention halls and at ballparks and local fairs. Other times they spoke more briefly and frequently from the platform of the rear car as crowds stood on and alongside the railroad tracks, until the train pulled off to the next town.

Roosevelt's bombastic oratory was contrasted by the measured lecturing of the academic Wilson, but generally speaking they were respectful toward each other. Roosevelt questioned his opponent's late journey to progressivism; Wilson harped on the split in the Republican Party and gently chided Roosevelt's soaring ego. At one point he observed dryly that if Roosevelt were elected he would be lonely, but would survive because "he finds himself rather good company."[23] Notable among Wilson's supporters was Samuel Gompers, lured not only by the Democratic plank against anti-labor injunctions but also by the Wilson personality and style.

The competition and the travel were wearing each man down when one of those frightening events all too frequent in presidential campaigns and politics took place in Milwaukee on October 14, less than a month before the election. Roosevelt had just emerged from his hotel en route to the municipal auditorium when a shot rang out, fired by a fanatic. The bullet hit Roosevelt in the right side of his chest and lodged in a rib, but was somewhat deflected by his eyeglass case and the text of the speech in his coat pocket he was about to make. In characteristic form, he proceeded to the hall and addressed a shocked and rapt audience. "Friends," he said, "I shall have to ask you to be as quiet as possible. . . . I have been shot . . . the bullet is in me now, so that I cannot make a very long speech. . . . [But] I can tell you with absolute truthfulness that I am very much uninterested in whether I am shot or not."[24]

He then spoke for more than an hour before going to a hospital for treatment. The wound turned out not to be serious, but he spent ten days there, while Wilson suspended his own campaign awaiting Roosevelt's ability to continue.

Even this demonstration of bravado, however, failed to win the support TR needed for victory. With Wilson and the Democratic Party successfully selling their new identity as progressives, Roosevelt was unable to bring enough like-minded Republicans to his new party to carry the day in the multi-candidate race. Wilson capitalized on the Republican split to fashion his election from only 41.9 percent of the vote, with Roosevelt winning 27.4 percent and Taft 23.2 percent. Debs won a surprising 6 percent and the Prohibition candidate, Eugene W. Chafin, had 1.5 percent.

Wilson's 6.3 million popular vote, to 4.1 million for Roosevelt and 3.5 million for Taft, was actually less than Bryan had received four years earlier, and the Democratic Party remained in minority status. But Wilson's electoral college vote was a landslide: 435 in 40 states to 88 for Roosevelt in 6 and only 8 for Taft in 2, with the South reasserting itself as a dominant force in the party. The Democrats also won control of Congress, narrowly in the Senate but with a comfortable majority in the House. Perhaps best of all, Wilson would take office unencumbered by major political obligations to anyone; he would have a free hand to implement the New Freedom on which he had based his campaign.

Wilson's election marked the end of the Bryan era, but the Great Commoner could take considerable solace in the fact that his party had become the vehicle for many of the progressive ideas he had espoused for most of two decades. In recognition of his service and loyal following in the party, Wilson made Bryan his secretary of state, despite the Nebraskan's relative lack of experience in foreign affairs.

The role of the new president's chief adviser fell to a recent but close friend from Texas, Colonel Edward M. House. Wilson instructed House to scout for other members of the cabinet. The Democratic national chairman, William F. McCombs, produced his own list of worthy applicants for a host of federal jobs, but Wilson put his main reliance on the wealthy and worldly House, who was a sort of soul brother to him in spite of sharply different backgrounds. House wrote later in his memoirs: "Almost from the first our association was intimate; almost from the first, our minds vibrated in unison. When we had exchanged thoughts with one another he translated our conclusions into action without delay. Nine times out of ten we reached the same conclusions."[25] Others, however, believe House greatly inflated his influence on Wilson and the importance of his role.

Another of Wilson's key aides was Joe Tumulty, the veteran of the New Jersey wars with bossism, who brought an astute understanding of the ways of politics as the president's personal secretary and general political adviser. From the outset, Wilson made clear that he would be an activist in office; he would be all business, directly and personally involved in the conduct of government. He dispensed with the traditional inaugural ball, called a special session of Congress to deal with tariff revision and for the first time since John Adams, a president went to Capitol Hill himself to present his legislative agenda. He met committee chairmen and took optimum advantage of the partisan advantage the congressional elections of 1912 had bestowed upon him.[26]

In short order, tariff reduction was enacted and before two years were out, Wilson, with counsel from Brandeis, had also achieved labor law reform, an income tax authorized by a new constitutional amendment and reform of banking and currency practices under a new Federal Reserve Act. Also, Congress put teeth in his proposals for regulated business competition with enactment of the Clayton Anti-Trust Act and creation of the Federal Trade Commission. These steps did not satisfy everyone, but they provided a certain momentum for a president who was setting out to be an achiever on a broad front.

Although Wilson did not like and was not skilled in the personal persuasion of members of Congress, he assigned able aides to perform the function, and accepted his role as leader of the Democratic Party as well as president. Both House and Bryan assisted him in this effort, and he took an active part himself in reform of the party to bring it more in line with his progressive ideas. He understood he had to be a Democratic president more than a progressive president to move his agenda through a Congress under the party's control. When stymied, Wilson did not hesitate to appeal to the voters for support, and his first two years were a marked success.

Meanwhile, Bryan, taking enthusiastically to his duties as the presi-

dent's right-hand man on foreign policy, and sharing Wilson's deep religious sentiments for world peace, busied himself negotiating a series of
treaties between the United States and other nations wherein both sides
agreed to cooling-off periods at times of tension and crisis. Wilson set a
high premium on morality in government and in the dealings between
governments, proclaiming at one point that "the force of America is the
force of moral principle."[27]

At home, however, Wilson's acquiescence in racial segregation among
federal employees, especially in the Post Office under Albert Burleson and
the Treasury Department under William G. McAdoo, brought charges of
moral indifference or worse from black leaders. He lamely argued that a
more formal segregation was in the best interest of blacks, raising questions about Wilson among Northern progressives.[28]

Nevertheless, he found his administration embroiled in various disputes with Japan, Haiti and other small Caribbean states, Colombia over
the taking of Panama, and Mexico. American business interests and Wilson's own sense of moral obligation in the face of perceived injustice prodded him on. A revolution in Mexico in 1911 had overthrown the dictatorial
regime, but in 1913, General Victoriano Huerta restored it in a coup d'état
and the major European powers recognized it, even as the Constitutional-
ist revolutionaries under Venustiano Carranza controlled much of the
country. Wilson refused to follow suit or appoint an ambassador, and
when Huerta declared himself military dictator, Wilson demanded that he
step aside. American encouragements to Carranza to depose Huerta got
nowhere, and on April 10, 1914, Wilson seized on the arrest of some American sailors ashore at Tampico to move against Huerta himself.

The sailors were released with apologies, but on another pretext Wilson ordered the navy to prepare to seize Veracruz, Mexico's most important port, and sent it in to bar a German merchant ship from unloading
arms there. A bloody fight ensued, with some American deaths. Amid
much mediation, Huerta finally abdicated power in July and the next
month Carranza marched into Mexico City and took over, with resentment against American interference still smoldering and more trouble
still brewing ahead. Wilson found himself embroiled in what came to be
called "missionary diplomacy."

If before all this Wilson had hoped and expected to be able to focus
all his attentions and efforts on his New Freedom agenda at home, he was
further disabused of the notion in August. The assassination of Austro-

Hungarian royalty at Sarajevo, Serbia, provided the fuse for the outbreak of World War I in Europe. The existing network of entangling alliances brought Germany in on the side of Austria-Hungary and Turkey against France, England, Russia and soon after Italy, in what in the summer of 1914 seemed a fearful but remote clash of honor and territorial demands that had nothing to do with America.

Wilson declared at the outset that the United States would maintain a policy of strict and unwavering neutrality toward all combatants. He offered to play "a part of impartial mediation" and called on all Americans to be "neutral in fact as well as in name."[29] It was a commitment that would become increasingly difficult to keep, particularly among Americans of German and Irish descent and those from various Eastern European countries embroiled in the war pitting the Central Powers against the Western Allies.

These were sorrowful and trying times for the Democratic president. His devoted and supportive wife, Ellen, died suddenly in August, in the midst of the Mexican controversy and the turmoil in Europe, leaving him in dismal isolation in the great house despite all those around him. And with the outbreak of hostilities in Europe, Roosevelt was nipping at his heels to rev up the country for war. The United States had no standing army to speak of, but Wilson, opposed to one, declined to panic. As Roosevelt peppered him with newspaper articles demanding greater preparedness, Wilson dismissed his admonitions as "good mental exercise" and told Congress in his annual message: "We shall not alter our attitude . . . because some amongst us are nervous and excited."[30]

Unbeknownst to Wilson at the time, however, Germany, in anticipation of likely American assistance to the Allies, had already set in motion plans to establish a sabotage operation in the United States under the oversight of none other than the German ambassador in Washington, Count Johann von Bernstorff. Von Bernstorff had been recalled to Berlin in July and given funds with which to impede the expected flow of munitions sold by neutral America to Britain and France on a come-and-get-them basis, practical only for the Allies with their control of the seas. At the same time, the ambassador was instructed to do all he could to keep the United States out of the war—a bizarre dual responsibility.[31]

Although the United States was neutral at the outset and for a considerable time thereafter, German behavior, as well as longtime American cultural affinity with Britain, complicated von Bernstorff's task. The German invasion of Belgium in violation of treaty obligations, and reports of German brutality and atrocities, conditioned an anti-German attitude that German propaganda had difficulty rebutting. Many German-Americans, however, including the prominent newspaper writer H. L. Mencken, retained strong sympathy for the cause of the old fatherland.

On the political front at home, a creeping recession, along with the uncertain outlook stemming from the war in Europe, produced some Democratic setbacks in the congressional elections of 1914, although the party did retain control of Congress, with the Democratic margin in the House cut by about two thirds. Republican gains in New York, Pennsylvania, Ohio, Illinois and Wisconsin all hinted at a GOP recovery in 1916 and a resumption of the dominance only recently broken by Wilson's election. The disintegration of the Progressive Party and Roosevelt's return to the Republican fold darkened the Democratic picture more. The threat triggered an intensified and generally successful effort by Wilson to complete enactment of the rest of the progressive Democratic platform of 1912 while the party still controlled Congress and the White House.

In 1915 the revolution in Mexico continued to vex Wilson as a distraction from the situation in Europe, and he finally recognized Carranza and his Constitutionalists as the de facto government. But it was the war in Europe that dominated his time and energy as he strove to remain neutral in the face of troublesome behavior by both the Germans and British. The German killing of civilians in the town of Louvain, Belgium, was documented in a report by a special commission under his friend James Bryce; at the same time, the British abused American shipping and the mails with a tight naval blockade of Germany.

Sentiment in America in support of the Allies grew steadily, however, and with the constant agitation of Roosevelt, Wilson finally agreed to major loans to Britain and France without which they would have been severely strained to buy the American armaments essential to their pursuit of the war. Not incidentally, the transactions sparked both American industry and agriculture. Meanwhile, the British blockade prevented Germany from buying such armaments that technically were available for its purchase as well under international neutrality rules.

Faced with this impasse, Berlin ordered the dispatch of German submarines, or U-boats, to disrupt not only enemy shipping but that of neutral America as well. Therein was the development that eventually was to strain Wilson's neutrality to the breaking point and bring the United

States into the war. Surprise being a key element in submarine warfare, traditional rules at sea of warning a target ship to permit the removal of crew and passengers were ignored. Wilson protested vehemently against surprise attack as "wanton" and "a flagrant violation of neutral rights." When Germany declared a zone around England in which merchant ships would be sunk on sight, Wilson declared that it would be held to "strict accountability" for such acts.[32]

Mindful that the policy risked outcomes that could involve American lives and possible U.S. entry into the war on the side of the Allies, Berlin decided it had no alternative if Germany was to be able to carry on with the war. In April an American perished in the sinking of a British ship; several days later an American ship was torpedoed. Then, on May 7, the huge British passenger liner *Lusitania,* which only four months earlier had brought Colonel House to Europe with offers to serve as a mediator between the warring sides, was sunk with the loss of 1,201 men, women and children, including 124 Americans.[33]

It so happened that on May 1, the day the *Lusitania* left New York harbor on its fated last voyage, von Bernstorff had run a paid notice in the shipping columns of the *New York Times.* "Travellers intending to embark for an Atlantic voyage are reminded that a state of war exists between Germany and her Allies and Great Britain and her Allies," it said, and those "sailing in the war zone in ships of Great Britain or her Allies do so at their own risk."[34] Von Bernstorff said later he had no foreknowledge that the *Lusitania* would be targeted, but his denial did not stem the flood of anger from American shores. "Our propaganda has completely collapsed," he cabled Berlin. "Another event like the present one would certainly mean war with the United States."[35]

Roosevelt called the sinking "murder" and advocated the immediate breaking off of diplomatic relations with Germany.[36] But Wilson, with the peace-loving Bryan in support, shied from precipitous action. Although Americans were shocked by the *Lusitania* sinking, they were not yet conditioned to be committed to war. In a speech in Philadelphia three days after the ship went down, Wilson argued that "there is such a thing as a man being too proud to fight. There is such a thing as a nation being so right that it does not need to convince others by force."[37] Such comments led Roosevelt to brand him as "yellow,"[38] and to taunt him unmercifully with references to "the shadows of men, women and children risen from the ooze of the ocean bottom."[39]

Bryan tried to discourage Wilson against fueling the situation with strong demands that Germany end its submarine warfare against merchant ships, but Robert Lansing, State Department counselor under Bryan, pushed the president to take the hard line. When further sinkings with American losses occurred, Wilson went ahead with his demand, calling for an apology and reparations in a stern note that Bryan refused to sign. Instead, he resigned as secretary of state and was replaced by Lansing.

Thus Wilson was whipsawed between Bryan, now a rallying point within the Democratic Party for all those in Congress who wanted to avoid war at almost all costs, and Roosevelt and other Republicans questioning the Democratic president's patriotism and manhood. As 1915 approached an end, Wilson's expectations of a presidency devoted to domestic tranquility and prosperity through fair and honest competition, as envisioned in his New Freedom agenda, were buried in a harsher reality.

Chapter 16

THE GREAT WAR TESTS THE PARTY,
1916–1920

AMID ALL THE turmoil around Wilson as he strove to maintain American neutrality in a Western world at war, he found some respite in a fast-moving courtship and then marriage in December 1915 to Edith Bolling Galt, a woman of considerable strength who henceforth played a dominant role in the president's life, public and private. The second Mrs. Wilson lightened his burden with her presence and provided a protective shield against unwanted intrusions, particularly those she herself did not like, including those of the ambitious Colonel House. But the developments in Europe and at sea, and the carping of Roosevelt, could not be put aside.

They finally obliged Wilson to make some gestures toward preparedness, though nothing approaching what Roosevelt was demanding. The president called for creation of a volunteer army of 400,000, serving part-time only, and proposed a "navy second to none," with new taxes levied to foot the bill.[1] He justified such steps in terms of staying strong enough to keep the peace, not wage war. House was dispatched to Europe again in early 1916, seeking negotiations while holding out the threat of America joining the war on the side of the Allies if talks were refused. At one point Germany offered an apology and an indemnity for another sinking, and tried to get the Allies not to arm their merchant ships as a way of dissuading German attacks on them, but the British declined.

When, without warning, a German submarine torpedoed the unarmed French steamer *Sussex* in March 1916, Wilson sent Berlin an ultimatum.

President Wilson, upon reelection on the slogan "He Kept Us Out of War," encountered a Democratic Party that was resistant to intensified military preparedness for World War I—as was Bryan (encircled in this cartoon).

Unless Germany desisted from the practice he would sever diplomatic relations. Convinced the higher priority was keeping the United States neutral, Germany agreed for a time, with intermittent violations. As a result, Wilson was able to seek reelection later in the year as the candidate of peace.

Remaining neutral continued to be Wilson's focus, except for another diversion in Mexico when he sent a military expedition across the border in early 1916 to deal with the renegade Pancho Villa, who had pulled Americans from a train and killed them, and conducted raids into New Mexico and Texas. American troops remained in Mexico for nearly a year before Wilson called them home.

Wilson approached the election of 1916 with a solid record of achievement, bringing regular Democrats along with him when strategy so served, building a progressive coalition when circumstances and opportunities so dictated. The Progressive Party's atrophy under Roosevelt's neglect and his return to the Republican fold provided for a clearer political landscape than in 1912. Wilson made the most of it with a rush of progressive legislation, including liberal workmen's compensation for federal employees and a strong child labor law. Differences over the degree of war preparedness required further delineated the parties.

The Republicans, still striving to recover from their 1912 split, recognized they would have to seek a presidential nominee who was not closely identified with either 1912 faction. This consideration clearly ruled out Taft and such prominent allies as Elihu Root and Henry Cabot Lodge, and on the progressive side Roosevelt and his 1912 running mate, Hiram Johnson, although Roosevelt clearly tried to put himself in contention. To find a politically untarnished candidate, they turned to Supreme Court Justice Charles Evans Hughes, who by the nature of his position had been insulated from that unhappy political turmoil. In keeping with that position, Hughes declined to permit his name to be entered in any state primaries (except in Oregon, where state law required it). Roosevelt was not enthusiastic about him, referring to him as "a Wilson in long whiskers,"[2] but had no substantial alternative to offer.

The Republican convention in Chicago in early June, and a Progressive convention in the same city at the same time, tried to reach a consensus on a single candidate, but the Republicans wanted no part of the obvious Progressive choice, Roosevelt, and the Progressives were not going to buy into Hughes. As a condition of support for Hughes, Roosevelt demanded that he make clear his position on key issues, but the

Supreme Court justice declined on grounds it would be improper as long as he remained on the bench. The Progressives went ahead and nominated Roosevelt, but he said he would decline the nomination if Hughes satisfied him on certain policy questions—an apparent effort to pressure the prospective Republican nominee.[3]

Meanwhile, the Republicans underwent two roll calls, with favorite sons who had no chance of nomination trailing Hughes badly. The Roosevelt floor leader then declared for Hughes and he was nominated by near-unanimous vote on the third ballot. Roosevelt's vice president in his second administration, Charles W. Fairbanks, was given the nomination again. Roosevelt, after a meeting with Hughes, eventually backed him, but without accustomed zest, signaling the collapse of the Progressive Party.

At the Democratic convention a week later in St. Louis, only Wilson's name was offered in nomination and only a single voice of objection blocked his selection by acclamation. He then won the one roll call by 1,092 votes to one, and Vice President Marshall was renominated. The convention's permanent chairman, Senator Ollie James of Kentucky, summed up the choices by asking: "Who would say that we can afford to swap horses while crossing a bloody stream?"[4]

The only other noteworthy oratory came from Martin H. Glynn of New York, the temporary chairman, who methodically called out the names of past presidents who had faced international problems that could have led to armed conflict, calling out after each one, "But we didn't go to war!" With succeeding names he asked the convention: "What did he do?" and the same reply came back. From this recitation came the Wilson slogan: "He Kept Us Out of War."[5] Attending the convention as a reporter, Bryan requested speaking time and stoutly endorsed Wilson as the candidate of peace.

The fall campaign was a battle to claim the banner of "Americanism." Although Hughes before his Court appointment had been elected governor of New York twice, his antiseptic dullness as a campaigner was a weak contrast to the crisp and image-inducing oratory of Wilson. Hughes stumped diligently, while Wilson demonstrated his leadership by staying home and running the country. A severe railroad strike broke out during the summer, and after several weeks the president summoned labor and management leaders to the White House, where, in effect, he jammed through a settlement creating an eight-hour day for railroad workers.

Wilson and Hughes fought for the support of the shattered Progressive Party constituency that had delivered 4 million votes to Roosevelt in 1912 and the Socialists who had given 900,000 to Debs. In this regard, Wilson's achievement of the eight-hour day for railroaders carried weight—Hughes, who opposed it, still sought to sell himself as a progressive as well. "I would not be here," he contended, "if I did not think of the Republican Party as a liberal party."[6] But he hurt himself with progressives in California when, during a visit there, he dealt mostly with party conservatives and gave short shrift to progressive icon Hiram Johnson.

As Wilson toured late in the campaign as the peace candidate, Hughes was somewhat undercut by the bellicose manner and words of Roosevelt in his behalf. A couple of weeks before the election, German Ambassador von Bernstorff cabled Berlin: "If Hughes is defeated he has Roosevelt to thank for it."[7] But the president also had some uneasy moments regarding the war. In August a German U-boat surfaced in the Newport, Rhode Island, harbor, the captain went ashore, returned and then sank six Allied ships in the next two days. Wilson was reduced to calling in von Bernstorff and protesting. There had been no violation of international law, but it was an embarrassment to the president.

Nevertheless, election day approached and the United States was still at peace. The Hughes campaign had a large advantage in money, but the Wilson forces had that dominant issue. One campaign poster showed a mother and children amid a war scene, bearing the caption: "He has protected me and mine."[8] Another bore this legend: "You are working, not fighting! Alive and happy, not cannon-fodder! Wilson and peace with honor? Or Hughes with Roosevelt and war."[9] Bryan, back in good party graces, was enlisted to stump the West preaching Wilson and peace. Meanwhile, Hughes was embarrassed elsewhere by strong support in German-American communities and their newspapers.

For all of Wilson's impressive first term—his flood of progressive legislation and the maintenance of American neutrality—the election nevertheless proved to be a cliffhanger. As expected, the South remained strongly Democratic, as were the border states, but Wilson carried only Ohio in the Midwest. With Minnesota and California not yet decided, Wilson retired for the night thinking he had lost the presidency. California finally went for him and narrowly assured his reelection, with 277 electoral votes and 9.1 million ballots to 254 electoral votes and 8.5 million popular votes for Hughes. The election, however, was a mixed bag for the Democratic Party. It held the Senate but lost three seats and the House was almost evenly split, with a handful of Progressives and Independents holding the swing votes.

In this face-off between the North, the Midwest and business and industry on one side, and the South, the Plains states, the Far West, and labor, farm and peace interests on the other, the Democratic Party behind Wilson had forged a winning combination. As the party of peace, progressivism and preparedness, it could look forward to a Democratic era approaching that enjoyed by the Republicans in the long period since the Civil War—if Wilson somehow could really keep the country out of war.

The election soon brought deceptively hopeful news from Berlin. In December, Germany, confident that the war in the East was going its way, said it was ready to negotiate for peace. The long stalemate had forced both sides to consider extreme military measures to end the conflict, with the Germans stepping up submarine activity and the British tightening their economic blockade. Wilson was more determined than ever to find a way out, and was about to launch a peace offensive when Berlin made its offer to talk. As an opening step, Wilson called for both sides to spell out their objectives. However, the Allies balked, and it soon became clear that Berlin wanted Wilson only as a facilitator of talks, not as a party to them.

Nevertheless, on January 22, he went before the Senate and delivered an appeal for "peace without victory," contending that only a "peace among equals" based on self-government, freedom of the seas and an end to massive standing arms could endure. He claimed to be speaking "for the silent mass of mankind everywhere who have as yet had no place or opportunity to speak their real hearts out concerning the death and ruin they see to have come already . . ."[10]

These were hopeful but unrealistic words. At the time Wilson uttered them, the Germans were secretly planning to resume all-out submarine warfare if the British would not come to the negotiating table for direct talks, without Wilson. They were also prepared to demand preposterous terms including territorial claims on the Baltic states, Belgium, Luxembourg and France, as well as the return of former German colonies. But Wilson knew nothing of all this and remained determined to take the lead in bringing about negotiations, whether the Germans wanted him involved or not.

On January 31, Berlin burst Wilson's balloon by announcing that on the following day unrestricted submarine warfare would resume. The declaration provided an exception of one American passenger ship on the Atlantic each month, to be conspicuously painted and bearing no contraband. But the exception was another way of saying all other American ships would be sunk on sight. A reluctant Wilson, after further consultation with House and Lansing, went before a joint session of Congress on February 3 and announced, almost apologetically, that he was breaking off diplomatic relations with Germany. Declaring American friendship toward the German people and the desire to remain at peace with them, he said: "We shall not believe that they are hostile to us unless and until we are obliged to believe it."[11]

It was not much longer before Wilson was so obliged. Although peace groups sharing the president's hopes staged rallies around the country at which Bryan orated enthusiastically, the proof Wilson required had already been obtained. On January 17, British intelligence had intercepted a telegram from the foreign minister in Berlin, Arthur Zimmermann, to the German minister in Mexico, Heinrich von Eckhardt, that when finally decoded a month later and sent to Washington awakened the American president to any illusions he had.

"We intend from the first February unrestricted U-boat war to begin," it said. "It will be attempted to keep United States neutral nevertheless. In the event that it should not succeed, we offer Mexico alliance on following terms: Together make war. Together make peace. Generous financial support and understanding our part that Mexico conquer back former lost territory in Texas, New Mexico, Arizona. Settlement in the details to be left Your Excellency."[12] Zimmermann also told von Eckhardt to press Mexico to persuade Japan to join in the war against America.

The brazen scheme to make a war ally of Mexico and reward it in victory with parts of the United States so jolted the president that he again appeared before Congress on February 26 and, not mentioning the Zimmermann telegram, requested authority to arm American merchant ships and use "any other instrumentalities or methods" to protect U.S. shipping.[13] But when Republican and other opponents of intervention balked, Wilson instructed Lansing to leak the telegram to an Associated Press reporter, and it appeared in newspapers across the country on March 1. Questions about the telegram's authenticity from the Hearst newspapers and others were dispelled with a startling confirmation from Zimmermann himself of its contents. Still, the peace forces in the Senate led by La Follette managed to filibuster the arms ship bill to death, leading Wil-

son to declare, in words usually associated with the Senate's later opposition to the League of Nations, that "a little group of willful men, representing no opinion but their own, have rendered the great Government of
the United States helpless and contemptible."[14]

American entry into the war was now inevitable. The sinking without
warning of three American merchant ships on March 18 prompted Roosevelt to demand a declaration of war, and still Wilson resisted that
inevitability. On the evening of April 2, however, he again addressed Congress, justifying his reluctant call to arms on the lofty grounds that "the
world must be made safe for democracy," declaring "its peace must be
planted upon the tested foundations of political liberty."[15] The Senate
approved the declaration, 82–6, and the House by 373–50, but the conduct of the war was not without partisan clashes, often involving Roosevelt.

In a personal vein, though growing old and with eyesight failing, the
former president, nearly two decades after charging up San Juan Hill to
glory, insisted on forming his own volunteer division and leading it into
the fight against Germany. Senate Republicans rallied around him, arguing that Roosevelt's very presence at the front would have a psychological
impact on both American and German troops. But Wilson wanted professional, not political, soldiers leading the American forces. Congressional
passage of a military draft left the decision on use of volunteers in his
hands, and he chose not to put them in the aging Roosevelt's care. In June,
9 million men registered, a figure that rose to 24 million by war's end,
with 3 million inducted into the army, joining 2 million volunteers.

The American entry was just in time, because the eastern front collapsed in the fall with the November Revolution in Russia and put the
exhausted Allied troops on the western front under extreme pressure
amid dire field conditions. Wilson's field commander, General John J. Pershing, declined, however, to send his troops into battle without essential
training, and it was not until the spring of 1918 that they arrived to reinforce the French and British. Once in place, they helped drive back German thrusts aimed at ending the war before the American resources could
be brought fully to bear. In the relatively short time during which Americans were deployed in the grim four-year war, more than 50,000 Americans nevertheless were killed. At sea, U.S. warships were so effective in
providing patrol and convoy duty for merchant ships and transports that
not one American soldier was lost en route to Europe.[16]

At home, Wilson hoped for an end to political partisanship. But Republicans were not willing to have the Democrats cement their political strength by taking credit for the war's successes and home-front prosperity, so they kept up a steady stream of criticism of his stewardship. A major Wilson administration failure was the erosion of civil liberties in the process of fostering positive public opinion toward the war. A week after the American entry, Wilson appointed a former journalist, George Creel, as chairman of a Committee on Public Information to drum up popular support in what became a massive propaganda campaign.

In selling the war, the Creel Committee became a sort of thought police that cast honest dissent as lack of patriotism or even treason. It focused on German-Americans and all things German, frowning on the speaking and teaching of German and even listening to German music. At Wilson's request, Congress passed an Espionage Act in 1917 establishing jail terms of up to twenty years and fines for anyone who consorted with the enemy or in any way hampered the war effort.[17]

The attorney general, Mitchell Palmer, declared open season on Socialists and other radicals, leading to the jailing of Debs for expressing his opposition to the war. Congress passed a Sabotage Act and a Sedition Act authorizing the government to move against anyone who uttered "disloyal, profane, scurrilous or abusive" remarks against it.[18] The conduct of the Creel Committee became a blemish on the Wilson years that in the end did damage to the Democratic Party. The president himself was so focused on ending the war and concluding a just peace that he seemed to block out the abuses of Creel and Palmer.

In January 1918, Wilson presented Congress with his formula for peace, known as the Fourteen Points. The main ones called for the evacuation of German troops from foreign territories and the restoration of old boundaries, and also creation of a League of Nations to guarantee and secure the integrity of borders and the maintenance of peace. This last was at the heart of Wilson's dream of a world at last living in mutual respect and security. This was to be "the war to end all wars," and as American strength began to assert itself, Wilson increasingly concentrated on the achievement of that world.

But the war dragged on through the spring and summer of 1918 before American reinforcements finally turned the tide on the battlefield. German soldiers began deserting in droves, and as a result, the German high command persuaded Berlin in October to propose an armistice using

Wilson's Fourteen Points as a framework. The Allies were agreeable to exploring it with pointed reservations, but Pershing wanted unconditional surrender. With House mediating with the Allies, the terms were somewhat hardened to require further German withdrawals.

Nevertheless, Roosevelt and fellow Republicans attacked the Wilson foreign policy as weak and ineffective in ending the war with a clear Allied victory. With the next congressional elections only weeks away, Wilson was persuaded by political advisers to make the voting a referendum on his conduct of the war and his quest for peace. Although he still hoped to avoid partisan politics in wartime, he yielded and on October 25 called on all Americans to express their support of the war effort by voting Democratic, giving his blanket endorsement to all Democratic candidates.[19] The move angered Republicans, gave them a late campaign issue and risked backfiring on the party of Wilson.

During all this time, the president's political situation at home had been disintegrating. The two major parties fought in Congress over tax policy to finance the war, which ultimately cost more than $33 billion. Progressive Democrats favored higher taxes on income, inheritance and excess profits to put the greater burden on those who received the greatest financial gains from the war; conservative Republicans favored more borrowing, sales and excise taxes to spread the debt more widely. Even with the Democratic formula winning out, the rich got richer and the middle class expanded, creating new recruits for the Republican Party.

Farmers in the Midwest also moved toward the Republican camp when wheat came under administration price controls while cotton prices were unregulated to the benefit of the Democratic South. Even there, defections resulted from Wilson's veto of a bill imposing a literacy test on immigrants, which Congress subsequently overrode on the strength of Dixie votes. Adoption in late 1917 of the constitutional prohibition on the manufacture and imbibing of liquor, favored in the religious South, had alienated laboring men in the North, and especially hard-drinking Americans of Irish, German and Scandinavian descent. And Palmer's assaults on civil liberties offended Northern liberals. The grand coalition of progressivism and peace that had delivered Wilson's 1916 reelection was becoming unglued.

On election day in November 1918, the voters demonstrated their impatience and disfavor. The Republican Party gained clear control in the House and a working control in the Senate, further complicating Wilson's quest for peace. He now knew that even if an armistice were achieved, a hostile Senate would stand as a prospective roadblock to the peace treaty he was so fervently contemplating. Only days later, on November 9, German resistance crumbled and the kaiser abdicated, and on November 11 the long-sought armistice was reached.

Wilson announced on November 18 that he would attend the peace conference in Paris himself, a declaration that further irritated the Republicans, who saw it as an effort to gain partisan advantage. He raised their irritation to rage when he announced the American team to accompany him. It included Lansing and House—and not a single member of the United States Senate.[20] The Republicans in particular smoldered over what they saw as a colossal affront to the Senate's constitutional advisory role in foreign policy.

Wilson was the first American president to go abroad on a diplomatic mission. The only Republican he took along was a nominal one, former ambassador to France Henry White. Along with Mrs. Wilson, the president and his party sailed on the S.S. *George Washington* on December 4. Prior to the opening of the peace conference, he made a triumphant tour of Europe, but the cheers he heard did not reflect any groundswell for his vision of a League of Nations to preserve the peace. The French, the most imperiled of the Allies during the war, wanted terms that would eradicate Germany as a military power forever. The British were after huge reparations, and the Italians and Japanese, as junior allies in the war, hoped for territorial rewards. The United States alone, under the altruistic Wilson, sought no material return for this moral investment in peace.

After much disputatious consultation, the Allies meeting at Versailles agreed to a Covenant of the League of Nations, based largely on Wilson's proposals. Its heart was Article 10, which called on the signatories "to respect and preserve against external aggression the territorial integrity and . . . political independence of all members of the League."[21] Member nations would be required to submit disputes to investigation by an executive council of Britain, France, Italy, Japan and four other states to be chosen by the full membership, or arbitration by a Permanent Court of International Justice to be created by the council. Beyond the restoration of borders, a system of mandates was called for to administer former German colonies abroad.

After the writing of a draft, Wilson returned home and ran into a buzz saw of questions and resistance from key members of Congress, especially

Republicans. They were still smarting at his partisan appeal to the voters in the November elections and his exclusion of senators generally and Republicans particularly from the peace conference team. Voices on the left, notably Debs, complained that no efforts had been made to bring in the Russians, who by now were well on the road to establishing a communist state. Leading the opposition to Wilson was Senator Henry Cabot Lodge, who organized what was known as a "Round Robin" signed by thirty-seven Republican senators and two senators-elect.[22] They protested particularly the notion of American troops serving as part of an international army to enforce Article 10, and argued that the Covenant should be set aside for consideration after the signing of the peace treaty. But Wilson insisted that it had to be included to ensure keeping the peace.

On his return to Paris, the president was met with intensified demands by the French for reparations from Germany for war damage to land and property, and various territorial demands from France and other Western powers, essentially pushing Wilson's Fourteen Points to a back burner. Wilson finally gave in on the key territorial and reparation demands while winning French acquiescence in a finite occupation of Germany and thereafter a British-American guarantee to defend France against future German attack. On May 7 the Treaty of Versailles was dispatched to Berlin and on June 28 it was signed by all parties. Much of this time, Wilson was in failing health. He had suffered a series of mild strokes as far back as 1896 and a more serious one in 1906 at Princeton, and his condition later raised questions about his effectiveness in the treaty deliberations.[23]

Accordingly it was a weary and ill Wilson who returned to Washington, where he was again met with heated debate over the terms he had helped to fashion. Under the leadership of Republican Senator William E. Borah of Idaho, a group of about a dozen "Irreconcilables" fought against all aspects of the treaty. A larger group headed by Lodge as chairman of the Senate Foreign Relations Committee undertook to attach amendments, or "reservations," to the treaty aimed mainly at Article 10 and the League. Amid increasing partisan wrangling, Wilson met with members of the committee in mid-August but refused to budge on Article 10. "It seems to me," he said, "the very backbone of the whole Covenant. Without it the League would be hardly more than an influential debating society."[24]

The struggle between Wilson and Lodge was not without its personal dimension. They came to despise each other, but beyond that Lodge truly believed that America should entrust its own security to its own military power, a view he shared with his old party compatriot, Theodore Roosevelt, who had died in January. And looking ahead to the next presidential election in 1920, Lodge also saw in his opposition a means of giving the Republican Party a rallying point. Wilson contended that any reservations would require renegotiation of the treaty, a claim disputed by the Republicans and others.

All this wrangling confused and eventually seemed to bore the American public, whose support Wilson had coveted to win over the opposition to the treaty in the Senate. To stimulate enthusiasm in the country for the treaty and the League, in September 1919 he undertook an ambitious cross-country speaking tour by train. As if he were campaigning once again for election, he traveled eight thousand miles and halted his whistle-stop train thirty-seven times to address the crowds that gathered at railside. But his Senate foes would not budge. On September 25 at Pueblo, Colorado, he was afflicted with a tremendous headache and exhaustion. His traveling physician, Dr. Cary Grayson, ordered cancellation of the rest of the trip and Wilson was brought back swiftly to Washington.

At the White House, the severe headaches continued and on October 2 he collapsed with a stroke, a blood clot on his brain that left him paralyzed on his left side. His thinking process was not impaired, however, and he continued his fight for the League from the White House, where his wife kept him in isolation. Professing to act on the advice of Dr. Grayson that the president must be relieved of as much stress as possible, Edith Wilson interposed herself between her husband and his cabinet. She took it upon herself to screen all papers coming to the presidential desk, while insisting later that "I, myself, never made a single decision regarding the disposition of public affairs." All she did decide, she said, was "what was important and what was not" to be seen by him, a not inconsequential function.[25]

Some Republicans were outraged at the situation. Senator Albert Fall of New Mexico complained: "We have petticoat government! Mrs. Wilson is president!"[26] Lansing finally went to Tumulty and, raising the question of Wilson's inability to carry out his presidential responsibilities, proposed that Vice President Marshall be so notified. When Lansing suggested that Tumulty or Grayson could certify Wilson's inability to function in the job, Tumulty replied, "You may rest assured that while

Woodrow Wilson is lying in the White House on the broad of his back, I will not be a party to ousting him," nor would Grayson.[27]

For the next months, Lansing, as the senior cabinet member, took it upon himself to conduct the cabinet meetings, until Wilson got wind of what was going on and wrote to his secretary of state inquiring whether it was true. Through all this, Marshall remained in the dark about Wilson's true condition until some White House intimates enlisted a reporter, Fred Essary, the *Baltimore Sun's* White House correspondent, to inform him privately, swearing Essary to secrecy. Upon learning the truth, Marshall reluctantly tried to discuss the matter directly with the president, but Mrs. Wilson barred him from the sickroom.[28]

The impasse left the treaty languishing in the Senate. Attempts between supportive Democrats and moderate Republicans to work out a compromise with the Borah and Lodge groups in mid-November got nowhere without the hand of the League's architect brought directly to bear, and the treaty was rejected, to the dismay of a host of peace organizations. They petitioned Congress to try again for agreement, but a bitter and rigid Wilson would accept no concessions. On January 8, 1920, he wrote fellow Democrats not to buck the will of the American people, who, he insisted, wanted Senate ratification without change. If it was not done, he said, the election of 1920 would be "a great and solemn referendum" on the treaty.[29]

Some Democrats, like Senate Minority Leader Gilbert Hitchcock, refused to give up and still sought to find a solution, but neither Lodge nor the Irreconcilables would yield, and Wilson again told Senate Democrats to hold firm. When some of the Lodge reservations were approved with a degree of Democratic assistance, the treaty came up again for one final vote on March 19. Along with twelve Irreconcilables, twenty-three Democrats, twenty from the South, stayed with Wilson and the treaty fell seven votes short of the two-thirds majority required for ratification. American participation in the Versailles Treaty and the League Covenant within it were dead. When Tumulty brought the news to Wilson at the White House, the stricken president's only comment was: "They have shamed us in the eyes of the world."[30]

As Wilson's second term drew toward a sorrowful close, the Democrats despaired about holding on to the White House in the approaching November election. The end of the war, rather than bringing good times, instead unleashed economic and social distress in the form of inflation, unemployment among returning veterans, race riots and mounting labor strife. Strikes at shipyards, steel plants and coal mines, even among the police in Boston, undermined organized labor's confidence in the Democrats. Lynch mobs and a revitalized Ku Klux Klan terrorized parts of the South. Along with all this, bombs mailed by extreme radicals to prominent business leaders and public officials led to witch-hunts by Attorney General Palmer and his infamous Red Scare.[31]

Civil liberties were stomped underfoot as Palmer fanned fears that the communist revolution in Russia, now proclaimed as a world movement by Lenin, was coming to America. Although the Communist Party here was insignificant, Palmer conducted widespread roundups of radical suspects among immigrants, aliens and organized labor. In one such raid on New Year's Day of 1920, some six thousand people were arrested without warrants and jailed. Palmer agitatedly warned the country about a major Red plot to unfold in May, but when it didn't happen, his scare tactics finally began to lose much of their steam. However, a lingering nativism from the war manifested itself in attacks on aliens as radicals, as seen in the Sacco-Vanzetti case. Two confessed Italian anarchists were tried and convicted of the murder of two shoe company employees during a 1920 payroll robbery despite inconclusive evidence, arousing wide protest in the civil liberties community.[32]

Through Wilson's second term, buoyed by his 1916 campaign pledge to support women's suffrage, the movement's female leaders pressured the president to fight for a constitutional amendment. Earlier he had been hesitant, but after their participation in the war effort he cited it as justification for extending the vote to them. In June 1919 it finally cleared both houses of Congress, and ratification by the states was completed in August 1920, in time for women to vote in that fall's election.

The immediate postwar period left an aching national hangover that added to the public disillusionment over the Wilson years and the Democratic stewardship of the country. Wilson's declaration that the election of 1920 would be a referendum on the League of Nations was wrong. Rather, it was the Wilson coalition, progressivism, and stability of the Democratic Party that were now on trial, with the jury of American voters in a very negative mood.

In 1924, Governor Al Smith of New York, an outspoken opponent of Prohibition, sought the Democratic presidential nomination over the opposition of "drys," including Bryan. He lost the nomination to John W. Davis but was nominated in 1928, the first Catholic to be so chosen.

Chapter 17

THE SIDEWALKS OF NEW YORK, 1920–1933

WILSON'S FAILURE TO win Senate approval of the League of Nations was not the only cause for the pessimistic outlook that faced the Democratic Party as the next presidential election approached. The rapid disintegration after the war of the New Freedom—his effort to achieve more equitable competition in commerce and industry through government regulation—again put private profit above public well-being. Corporate gouging together with striking labor eroded the cooperative spirit engendered by the war and intensified partisan rhetoric and behavior.

At the same time, falling prices for agricultural goods and a declining foreign market led many farmers to desert the Wilson coalition. And many Republican progressives, following Roosevelt, were returning to the party fold. With the Democratic president in solitary incapacitation in the White House, though still entertaining thoughts of a third term, the prospects for continuing the party in power in the 1920 presidential election were dim from the outset.

Yet, that election was destined to mark the emergence in the Democratic Party of the singular personality who before long would dominate it through its most challenging period at least since the Civil War— Franklin Delano Roosevelt. Together with another New Yorker, Alfred E. Smith, the pair would give the party a new and more vibrant identity that was to endure for two tumultuous decades.

Roosevelt's entry onto the national stage was in a distinctly secondary role. By the time the Democratic convention met in San Francisco in late June to pick its national ticket, the Republican leaders had already gathered in the infamous "smoke-filled room" in Chicago and anointed Senator Warren G. Harding of Ohio, a handsome, pleasant and pleasure-loving nonentity, as their nominee, and Governor Calvin Coolidge of Massachusetts, a prim and tight-lipped Yankee, for vice president. Harding was conspicuously fond of alcohol, women, golf and cardplaying, a combination that did not seem to give offense to an electorate primed for change from the troubled and sober years of Woodrow Wilson.

The Democrats, quickly discouraging any talk of Wilson seeking a third term in spite of his infirmity, took a long look at his son-in-law and secretary of the treasury, William G. McAdoo, and at his controversial attorney general, A. Mitchell Palmer. Neither one was endorsed by Wilson nor mustered sufficient convention enthusiasm, and on the forty-fourth ballot the party finally turned to Governor James M. Cox of Ohio. As his running mate, Cox chose the thirty-eight-year-old assistant secretary of the navy, Franklin Roosevelt, whose only previous experience with elective office had been as a New York state senator from 1910 to 1913. He was thought to bring strength to the Democratic ticket as a genial, patrician New Yorker with a reputation as a reformer and a famous political name as a distant cousin of the former Republican president.

Shortly after their nomination, Cox and FDR called on Wilson at the White House and assured him that they would not abandon the fight for the League. Then the two took to the campaign trail in an energetic but futile effort to sell it, and the rest of the progressive Wilson agenda, to an electorate eager to leave the war behind, and with it the tattered final years of a Democratic administration in economic distress and collective weariness.

On top of that, the Republican political organization outperformed the Democratic and outspent the Democratic National Committee by nearly four to one. Cox and young Roosevelt, for all their strenuous morning-to-night stumping across the country, were no match for the polished Republican campaign led by GOP national chairman Will Hays, a skillful organizer, with strong assistance from Albert Lasker, an early master of the political advertising art.

By contrast, Cox dropped Democratic national chairman Homer Cummings, who had been a key figure in the Wilson victories and had liquidated the 1916 Democratic campaign debt, and never found his organizational equal. Harding got away with a mostly front-porch campaign from his home in Marion, and Coolidge made only periodic speaking trips to his neighboring Yankee states and a few in the South. In an early speech, Harding urged a return to "not heroism, but healing, not nostrums but normalcy," and that appeal squared perfectly with the public mood.[1]

The Republican nominee, who in the Senate had voted for the League with the Lodge reservations, waffled his way through the campaign on the subject. Meanwhile, others of his party categorically pounded the Wilson brainchild and capitalized on hostility toward a world organization among various European ethnic groups and Southern isolationists. In a whispering campaign against Harding, it was widely rumored that he had Negro blood, an allegation that Wilson, Cox and Roosevelt all disowned. In any event, the rumor had no notable impact on the outcome.

Although Cox and Roosevelt were the Democratic candidates, the target of the Republican campaign was Wilson and his League. Near the end of the campaign, Cox began to trim his support of the League, indicating he would accept reservations to it that could lead to its acceptance by the Senate, but it was no use. In October, Hiram Johnson observed that if the election were a prizefight, "the police would interfere on the grounds of brutality."[2] The voters administered the worst popular-vote defeat yet suffered by the Democrats, giving Harding and Coolidge more than 16 million votes, or 60.4 percent, to only 9 million, or 34.2 percent, for Cox and FDR.

The electoral college result was just as bad: Harding/Coolidge 404, including the entire North and West; Cox/Roosevelt 127. As Joe Tumulty put it, "It wasn't a landslide, it was an earthquake."[3] Roosevelt, however, worked loyally for the ticket and benefited from the national exposure. He seemed to have a future in the party, but few imagined at the time how immense it would be.

Eugene Debs, running as the Socialist nominee from prison, polled a surprising 919,000 votes. In the congressional elections, it was another landslide for the Republicans, giving them a majority of 167 seats in the House and 22 in the Senate. Buried in the debris was the cause of progressivism, as control of the nation went back to the conservative Republicans who had held sway before Theodore Roosevelt had pushed and pulled the party on the progressive path. The long Republican reign in the White House since the Civil War, broken only by the presidencies of Cleveland and Wilson, was now resumed.

Still another casualty was the Democratic governor of New York, Al Smith, who had been elected two years earlier after an impressive career in state legislative politics. Unlike the aristocratic Franklin Roosevelt, Alfred Emanuel Smith was literally a kid from the sidewalks of New York. Born of a poor family in the shadow of the Brooklyn Bridge on Manhattan's Lower East Side, he became a family breadwinner when his father, a truckman, died while young Al was still in school. He swam in the East River with other tenement-dwelling boys, served as an altar boy at the local Catholic church, toiled as a peddler at the famous Fulton Fish Market, as a truckman's helper and a shipping clerk. He joined the Tammany Hall organization at age twenty-two and rose steadily as the urban immigrant's friend and defender.

In 1903 at thirty, the Irish Catholic Smith was elected to the New York State Assembly, where he served for twelve years, eventually as a reform majority leader. He then won election as sheriff of New York County (Manhattan), president of the New York City Board of Aldermen and, in 1918, governor of the most powerful state in the nation. But the Harding landslide of 1920 brought him down, seemingly short-circuiting another promising political career.

So, too, it was thought, did FDR's tragic affliction with poliomyelitis the next year, leaving his legs paralyzed. But Roosevelt, through grit and determination, carried on, with the help of crutches, leg braces and a conspiracy of silence about the degree of his motor debility that enabled him to continue in politics, eventually to unpredicted heights.

The eclipse that enshrouded the political fortunes of FDR, Al Smith and the Democratic Party as a result of the 1920 election soon vanished in the glare of the foibles of the unambitious and derelict Harding, and an administration of embarrassing corruption. The new president made clear in his inaugural address that Wilson's dream of American leadership in a postwar collaboration for peace was dead, declaring, "we seek no part in directing the destinies of the world."[4] In July, Congress passed a joint resolution ending the war with Germany and thereafter signed separate peace treaties with Germany, Austria and Hungary that declared the United States free of the obligations of the Versailles Treaty.

Within a short time, Harding proved to have neither the talent for the presidency nor sufficient interest in it to be taken seriously. His crony-filled staff ran roughshod over him, using their own governmental prerogatives and advantages of office to enrich themselves. He named his campaign manager, the unsavory Harry Daugherty, his attorney general, and Daugherty quickly made the Justice Department a clearinghouse for all manner of graft and corruption for what came to be known as the Ohio Gang of Republican and corporate operatives.[5]

Daugherty's roommate at a Wardman Park hotel apartment, Jess Smith, presided over the Ohio Gang's headquarters in a small house on K Street that doubled as a speakeasy and brothel, and provided a convenient poker table for Harding. Another crony, Colonel Charles Forbes, was installed as head of the Veterans Bureau and proceeded to milk it for millions in rakeoffs from the purchase of hospital supplies and hospital construction. Harding's secretary of the interior, Albert Fall, leased government oil reserves at Teapot Dome, Wyoming, and Elk Hills, California, to corporate oil interests to the tune of millions more. Both Forbes and Fall later wound up in prison, Jess Smith committed suicide and Daugherty eventually was forced to resign.

None of their misconduct was publicly known in Harding's first two years in the presidency. But farm discontent, resulting from high interest rates, heavy taxes and other factors, hurt the Republicans at the polls in the 1922 congressional elections. The Democrats, only two years earlier given up for dead, with their growing urban strength cut deeply into the GOP majorities in both houses, defeating seventy-eight House Republicans without the loss of a single Democratic seat. At the same time, disillusionment with Harding and his cronies among La Follette and other liberals denied him a working majority in the Senate. Soon congressional investigators were looking into the abuses of the Ohio Gang.

More significant for the Democratic Party in the elections of 1922 was Al Smith's return to Albany as governor. Smith's embodiment of the hardworking, hard-drinking ethnic city dweller who was coming to be the backbone of the party, along with his jovial and optimistic manner, was already propelling him into prominence as a presidential prospect for 1924.

Furthermore, his outspoken opposition to prohibition made him a favorite among fellow Irish-Americans and other voters of immigrant stock. He signed the first state law restraining prohibition enforcement and didn't hide his own drinking. He asked a group of reporters on one occasion in 1923: "Wouldn't you like to have your foot on the rail and blow the foam off some suds?"[6]

Smith signed another law in 1923 that went a long way toward outlawing the Ku Klux Klan in New York. That racist organization was already strenuously opposed to Smith as a Catholic. His stand against both prohibition and the KKK put him squarely in the camp of urban Democrats in a growing intraparty struggle with Democrats of rural America, many of whom were "dry," anti-Catholic, anti-black and anti-Semitic, especially in the South.

Meanwhile, Harding seemed blissfully unaware or unbelieving about the swindles perpetrated under his nose by his good friends. He confessed in one speech that his own father had once told him, concerning his good nature, "It's a good thing you wasn't born a girl. Because you'd be in the family way all the time. You can't say, 'No.' "[7] And he confided to his friend Nicholas Murray Butler: "I am not fit for this office and should never have been here."[8]

Fate may have heard this last remark. In August 1923 Harding, still shaken by Jess Smith's death, was returning from a trip to Alaska and winding up a speaking tour in the Pacific Northwest. Drinking and smoking to excess as usual, he was stricken with a cerebral embolism at his hotel in San Francisco and died on the spot, making Coolidge president.

Free of responsibility for the Harding administration scandals, the prudish and proper Yankee nevertheless had to oversee the extensive investigations into them. At the same time, he continued the reverence for business and corporate interests that had marked the brief Harding tenure. Coolidge's famous pronouncements that "the business of America is business" and that "the man who builds a factory builds a temple . . . the man who works there worships there"[9] assured corporate America that the nation remained in reliable hands—for the entrepreneurial interests.

The latest accidental president proved to be an adherent to the normalcy that Harding had avowed, but had failed to achieve for want of sufficient oversight of the larceny of his opportunistic administration pals. With productivity climbing in the wake of new industrial developments, of which Henry Ford's automobile assembly line was among the most significant, prosperity thrived in the business community, if not on America's farms. For the first time in the nation's history, the rural population dropped below 50 percent of the national total. An inexorable shift to urban America was well under way, and with it higher hopes in the Democratic Party that its strong appeal to immigrant voters bunched in the cities might put one of its sons back in the Oval Office in 1924.

In February of the election year, death finally claimed Woodrow Wilson, but the quest for new Democratic leadership had long before moved on. After the Republicans in Cleveland had routinely nominated the incumbent president for a term in his own right under the apt slogan, "Keep Cool with Coolidge,"[10] the Democrats met at Madison Square Garden in New York in June. Although Coolidge's skirts were clean regarding the Harding scandals, the Democrats still entertained the notion that the mess could be exploited to their political advantage. But voters had put it behind them under the soothing serenity of Harding's successor.

Whatever chances the Democrats had were severely compromised by their own disastrous convention. The long-existing conflict within the Democratic Party between its Eastern urban and Southern and Western rural interests and lifestyles bubbled over, this time in the context of a new issue—how to cope with the controversial Ku Klux Klan. It had been steadily growing in the South and parts of the West and gaining influence in the party there, preaching under the guise of American patriotism its venomous message of hate against foreigners, immigrants, blacks, Catholics and Jews. Eastern Democrats like Al Smith were determined that their party make an unequivocal declaration against the KKK in its 1924 platform.[11]

The sectional split also manifested itself in relation to prohibition. Smith led the opposition as the new spokesman not only of the cities but also of the hard-drinking Irish and other Americans of immigrant stock. Rural fundamentalists saw the Volstead Act barring manufacture, transport and consumption of alcohol as a centerpiece of their war against sin, and hence saw Smith, a Tammany man to boot, as the political Mephistopheles leading the enemy charge.

As governor of New York for nearly four years, Smith had built a record of progressivism while remaining personally conservative in his devotion to self-reliance, warning at one point during the Coolidge presidency of "the dangerous overcentralization of federal power."[12] He was the obvious candidate of the Eastern big-city forces despite the equally obvious political problem of his Catholicism, which was active and conspicuous. One of Smith's principal political lieutenants was a woman, Belle Moskowitz, chief publicist for the Democratic National Committee, who was instrumental in having the committee enlarged to accommodate female members. But Smith himself was cool to women's suffrage, even after the Nineteenth Amendment had been ratified in 1920, another element in his conservatism.

Emerging as his chief rival in a second presidential try, this time as a Westerner, was William McAdoo, who had moved from New York to California in 1922. McAdoo was now assuming the mantle of Bryan as a "dry" champion of agrarian America, professing hostility toward Wall Street although he himself was a corporation lawyer, and looking the other way on the KKK issue. He appeared to be operating on the premise that the old Bryan pitch would still work in a party in which the Bryan base was but a shell of what it had been. The Great Commoner himself waged war against the demon rum. So contrite was McAdoo in pursuit of the dry vote that at one point he apologized for once having eaten cake soaked in sherry.[13]

Backed by many old Wilsonian progressives, McAdoo appeared to be making strong headway toward the Democratic nomination when it was revealed that he had been on legal retainer from Edward L. Doheny, a wealthy oil tycoon who had passed on a "loan" of $100,000 in cash to Harding's interior secretary, Albert Fall, in the oil exploitation swindles. McAdoo's own hands apparently were clean, but the association left him politically scarred. A third candidate, Senator Oscar Underwood of Alabama, had two strikes against him in his own region, being anti-Klan and a "wet"—against prohibition.

Holding the convention in New York assured a raucous affair, as the galleries were packed with Smith supporters. Several favorite sons were nominated, but the most effective speech came from Franklin Roosevelt, leaning on crutches after his polio attack, in behalf of Smith, his fellow New Yorker. Roosevelt's clear and ringing voice filled the hall in a preview of many memorable orations to come and brought deafening cheers from the pro-Smith galleries, especially when he dubbed Smith "the Happy Warrior of the political battlefield."[14]

McAdoo found himself thrown on the defensive by his Doheny connection and on the KKK issue. On arrival in the convention city, he complained of the "sinister, unscrupulous, invisible government which has its seat in the citadel of privilege and finance in New York City."[15] But he continued to waffle on denouncing the Klan, and Bryan rose to his defense, declaring in his famous voice, amid hoots from the Tammany-packed gallery, that "it requires more courage to fight the Republican Party than it does to fight the Ku Klux Klan."[16] In the end, the resolution to castigate the KKK by name failed by a single vote, but the debate itself had taken a severe toll, the convention being aired to much of the nation on radio for the first time.

At the outset of the call of the states, McAdoo had a clear majority but was well short of the two thirds required for nomination, with Smith holding more than enough delegates from urban strongholds to block McAdoo. Both sides of this urban-rural struggle dug in for the long haul, and that was what it became. On and on the fight went, through an incredible 103 ballots over nine days in the steamy New York summer, as America listened and wondered about these bull-headed Democrats.

After the eighty-second ballot, the convention passed a resolution releasing pledged delegates to vote as they chose, but the deadlock continued. Nevertheless, both McAdoo and Smith did begin to lose strength, and on the 101st ballot Underwood and John W. Davis of West Virginia, who practiced law on Wall Street, moved ahead of them. On the 103rd, the weary delegates turned to Davis, who also had been Wilson's ambassador to Great Britain, nominating him by acclamation. Governor Charles W. Bryan of Nebraska, younger brother of the Commoner, was named Davis's running mate. When a reporter congratulated Davis, he replied: "Thanks, but you know how much it is worth."[17]

The nominee understood all too well that the marathon balloting had only widened the breach between the urban North and rural South and West, between Catholics and Protestants, between wets and drys, between bitter foes of the Klan and its fainthearted apologists. And the divisions were on open display over the airwaves, compounding the political damage. As for Davis himself, as a Wall Street lawyer he was not ideally suited to carry the Democratic message against special interests or to counter Coolidge's stolid defense of business as the business of America.

Davis attacked the Klan by name, as did the Progressive Party nominee, La Follette. But Coolidge simply rode out this and all other contentious issues by saying little about anything while carrying out his presidential duties with a minimum of energy and publicity. He made no secret of his fondness for sleeping and his philosophy that many problems would take care of themselves if one just let them sit undisturbed for a while.

The result in November was another huge Democratic defeat, with Davis's 28.8 percent of the vote (8.4 million ballots) to Coolidge's 54 percent on 15.7 million votes, the lowest ever for a nominee of the modern Democratic Party. La Follette received 16.6 percent on 4.8 million votes. The electoral college vote was Coolidge 382, Davis 136, La Follette 13. Yet in the congressional elections the Republicans made only modest gains, indicating that the Democratic Party's problem was coping with the sectional differences that came into conflict primarily when it sought to elect a national candidate.

Smith and Roosevelt saw another handicap to success—the Democratic National Committee itself, which was little more than a makeshift apparatus that for all practical purposes was thrown together in election years rather than as a permanent, continuing operation. With the advent of women's suffrage in 1920, the national committee had been enlarged to a hundred members, making it unwieldy and rife with internal frictions. What organizational strength the party had was often at the local and state levels. Smith observed at one point that "it has been the habit of the Democratic party to function only six months in every four years."[18]

In December 1924, Roosevelt circulated a letter to delegates proposing a gathering of "the common meeting points of Democratic minds from the North, South, East and West." The purpose would be to establish a national party machinery that would meet between presidential elections and achieve closer cooperation with state party organizations, and to provide a financial base for such a continuous operation.[19] The letter unearthed the usual regional and cultural disagreements, but brought hundreds of replies. Roosevelt called for a conference in Washington but the incumbent national committee chairman, Clem Shaver of West Virginia, balked and the meeting never took place. At one point the committee's office furniture and records were put in storage. Roosevelt's initiative as a private citizen revealed his own growing interest in political involvement, in spite of his serious infirmity. He continued to have individual meetings with other Democrats concerned about the lack of party organization and direction.

Meantime, Roosevelt kept writing. The party, he argued, had to make itself "by definite policy, the Party of constructive progress, before we can attract a larger following." Since Wilson had left the White House, Roosevelt wrote in 1925, "we have been doing nothing—waiting for the other fellow to put his foot in it."[20] The Republicans had accommodated with the Harding scandals, but the Democrats had failed to capitalize on them with an appealing agenda. In a review of *Jefferson and Hamilton* by Claude Bowers for the *New York World* in 1925, Roosevelt compared Hamilton's support from the moneyed and aristocratic classes of his time with Jefferson's reliance "on the scattered raw material of the working masses, difficult to reach, more difficult to organize." He wondered "if, a century and a quarter later, the same contending forces are not again mobilizing. . . . Hamiltons we have today," he observed, in apparent allusion to the Republicans, then asked: "Is a Jefferson on the horizon?"[21]

Coolidge's overwhelming election was deflating for Democratic visions of better days. McAdoo and Bryan continued to wage the sectional battle of South and West against the domineering East, and Smith went back to Albany, with his eye on a rematch against McAdoo four years hence. Bryan returned to the speaking stump as a religious fundamentalist and to Florida as a real estate dabbler, with a notable—and fatal—detour to Dayton, Tennessee, in the summer of 1925. There he took on the prosecution of a young schoolteacher named John Scopes, on trial for violating a law against the instruction of human evolution.

Pitted against the famed defense lawyer Clarence Darrow in the notorious "Monkey Trial," Bryan was called to the stand as an expert on the Bible. Darrow proceeded to make a fool of him by drawing admissions from him that his previous insistence that everything in the good book could be taken as literally true could not be so. Scopes was convicted of violating the local law, but the decision was later reversed, and Bryan, under severe physical and emotional stress, collapsed and died in Dayton only days after the trial.

The death in 1925 of another gallant political warrior, Senator La Follette, marked the effective end of his Progressive Party, though his namesake son sought to carry on from the Wisconsin base. The senior La Follette's death, however, enhanced the prospect for progressive Democrats to bring this small but energetic political force into their camp with an agenda appealing to its members.

In 1926, Smith was elected to his fourth two-year term as governor of New York and the Democrats further reduced the Republican majority in the House and gained near-parity in the Senate. But Coolidge kept cruising along, retaining his personal popularity in the country and especially within the business community. He was expected to be renominated easily, but on August 3, 1927, he jolted the political world by issuing a brief and simple message from his summer home in South Dakota's Black Hills: "I do not choose to run for president in 1928."[22] True to form, "Silent Cal" had consulted no one but his private secretary, Everett Sanders. Efforts to get him to elaborate or change his mind got nowhere.

The startling announcement opened the door for Coolidge's secretary of commerce, Herbert Hoover, whose work as food administrator during the world war and as overseer of Belgian relief had earned him a reputation as a master organizer. He proceeded to collect convention delegates at a great clip into 1928 but got no support from Coolidge, which caused some uneasiness in the Hoover camp. The president maintained his stony silence, and in June in Kansas City, Hoover was overwhelmingly nominated on the first ballot. Senator Charles Curtis of Kansas was chosen to run with him.

The Democrats, aware of what deep and prolonged division had wrought four years earlier, this time around made a swift and clean choice. McAdoo, at age sixty-four, and without the prod of Bryan to push his candidacy, did not contest for the nomination. And Smith, after four more years of highly visible public exposure as governor of New York in an electorate increasingly urban, did not seem quite so alien to rural America as he did in 1924. Yet he was still a "wet" Catholic of Irish stock, a Tammany man, a bit too jaunty, cocky and "common" for the liking of many non-city folk. His New York accent and "ain't" and "woik" pronunciations offended many ears in the boondocks.

All this was swept aside, however, as Smith carefully presented himself as a solid citizen concerned about the public welfare, the rights of workers and farmers, but no radical. He even chose as his campaign manager a prominent Republican industrialist, John J. Raskob, in a move seen as an effort to reassure businessmen and conservatives. But Raskob was also a "wet" Catholic, which was not reassuring to many conservatives, and certainly not to "dry" Southerners. Raskob and other millionaires who were brought in helped contribute more than $7 million to Smith's campaign treasury, compared to about $9 million spent for Hoover.

Roosevelt, for one, expressed fear that the Raskob appointment would "permanently drive away a host of people in the south and west and rural east who are not particularly favorable to Smith, but who up to today have been seeping back into the Party." And shortly afterward: "Frankly, the campaign is working out in a way which I, personally, should not have allowed and Smith has burned his bridges behind him."[23]

The Smith camp well remembered the riotous convention fiasco of 1924 and spread the word that there was to be no repetition this time around. Smith's delegates arrived, on their best "dry" behavior, at the Democratic National Convention in Houston, the site itself projecting a more conservative, calming mood than that of the political circus in Madison Square Garden four years earlier. The platform was moderation itself, with no references to the KKK or other divisive issues and even an uncharacteristic bow to higher tariffs. Regarding prohibition, the plank criticized the Republicans for waffling and promised "an honest effort to enforce the Eighteenth Amendment"[24] in spite of Smith's well-known opposition to it.

Once again, Roosevelt placed Smith's name in nomination as "the Happy Warrior" against a field of favorite sons. On the first roll call, Smith won 724⅔ votes, only ten short of the required two thirds. Ohio immediately switched its votes and other states quickly followed suit, finally giving Smith 849⅔ votes, to only 55½ for the next candidate, Senator Walter F. George of Georgia. Senate Majority Leader Joseph T. Robinson of Arkansas was named Smith's running mate as a conciliatory gesture to the South.

All seemed sweetness and light until Smith shook the convention by firing off a telegram to the about-to-depart delegates stating his belief that there should be "fundamental changes in the present provisions for national prohibition."[25] While such changes should be decided through the democratic process, he said, he felt a responsibility to provide leadership in the matter—an observation that outraged drys as a repudiation of the platform on which he would be running.

Smith wanted to be elected, but once nominated he was not about to trim his sails. He often demonstrated a certain disdain for his critics that delighted his followers but only intensified the vehemence of those opposed to him. He made little effort to counter the anti-Catholic argument against him by, for instance, recruiting prominent Protestants onto his campaign committee. He was also parochially disdainful toward parts of the country with which he was unfamiliar. When a reporter asked him his plans to address the states west of the Mississippi, he replied: "What are the states west of the Mississippi?"[26]

As a lively and entertaining campaigner, the loquacious, witty and warm scrapper from the sidewalks of New York left Hoover in the dust. But the election would not be decided on which of them was the more effective stump speaker. Hoover's delivery was humorless and boring, but his message was upbeat in a period of prosperity. "We in America are nearer to the final triumph over poverty than ever before in the history of any land," he proclaimed. "Given a chance to go forward with the policies of the last eight years, we shall soon with the help of God be in the sight of the day when poverty will be banished from this nation."[27] And the way things were going in the country, who was to say he was wrong?

Smith, whistle-stopping across the country and speaking from notes jotted on the back of an envelope, sought to counter this bright outlook with remarks tailored for local audiences, as a loudspeaker blared "The Sidewalks of New York." He touted repeal of prohibition in beer-making Milwaukee, farm relief in the Plains states and pleaded for religious tolerance in the Bible Belt. He made regular use of the radio, which he pronounced "raddio." It gave his rasping voice wider dissemination but also accentuated his New York accent, confusing or even annoying to many listeners. Those who only heard him on the radio missed the dynamic of the man in person—brown derby rakishly tilted, big cigar being constantly waved as he talked, almost in the manner of a vaudevillian of the day.

In all this, however, Smith managed in his courting of business to project a more conservative image than his New York background and record had suggested. He observed at one point, for instance, that "government should interfere as little as possible with business."[28] His message was lively in delivery but tame in substance at a time practical politics required that he draw the sharpest contrast with the incumbent Republican president.

Roosevelt was disappointed with the Smith strategy of trying to cut into the business vote, but played the good soldier. At campaign headquarters, he put his name to letters to businessmen observing that while "some of Mr. Hoover's regulatory attempts are undoubtedly for the good of our economic system . . . I think the policy of Governor Smith to let businessmen look after business matters is far safer for our country."[29]

In the end, Smith's overtures to business, and his magnetism and energy, could not compete with the prosperous times—nor counter the negative reactions that continued to find roots in the New Yorker's Tammany connection and provincialism, his "wetness" and, most important, his Catholicism. Well-financed Protestant movements against him, such as one led by Bishop James Cannon Jr. of the Methodist Episcopal Church South, and other attacks against him from the Anti-Saloon League, the Ku Klux Klan, the Woman's Christian Temperance Union and others did their work effectively.

Beyond these aboveboard assaults on him, preposterous rumors spread that nevertheless took their toll. One reported plans to bring the pope from Rome to live in the United States to facilitate counseling of the would-be Catholic president. Pictures of Smith standing at the entrance to the Holland Tunnel, connecting Manhattan with New Jersey under the Hudson River, were accompanied with the straight-faced explanation that if Smith were elected it would be extended under the Atlantic Ocean into the basement of the Vatican! There were also numerous undocumented accounts of a drunken Smith at public events. The *Fellowship Forum,* a fundamentalist publication, ran a cartoon showing Smith behind the wheel of a beer truck with the sign "Make America 100 Per Cent Catholic, Drunk, and Illiterate."[30]

The result in November was again predictable. While Smith nearly doubled the popular vote given to Davis in 1924, he fared even more poorly in the electoral college. Hoover was elected with 21.4 million ballots and 444 electoral votes to Smith's 15 million and only 87 electoral votes. Socialist Norman Thomas drew only 267,000 popular votes, the weakest showing by a third-party candidate since 1900. For all this, Smith still received the highest vote ever recorded by a Democratic nominee, win or lose, and he carried the dozen largest cities, all of which had gone Republican in 1924. Probably no Democratic candidate could have been elected in 1928, Catholic or Protestant, wet or dry, but the myth was established that these factors had brought Smith down. In losing, he did give the party a strong base in the urban North, but at a price in Dixie. The challenge for any succeeding Democratic nominee was to retain that new base while recapturing the old.

Despite another resounding Democratic defeat on the national level in 1928, one cause for celebration was the election of Franklin Roosevelt as governor of New York. His charismatic personality and grit had overcome his physical disability and placed him on the cusp of larger goals in the party and the country. His outspoken support of Al Smith in 1928 as in 1924 had given him the visibility he needed to embark successfully on an elective career on his own.

Hoover was the epitome of optimism as he was sworn in on March 4, 1929. "I have no fears for the future of our country. It is bright with hope," he said, with the country flying high and the stock market with it.[31] He retained Coolidge's esteemed secretary of the treasury, Andrew Mellon, in that key post. He promptly removed or lightened federal regulations on many private companies, and left to the states control of public lands, irrigation and reclamation projects. He called Congress into special session to raise tariffs to help American farmers and to aid them in other ways in marketing their products. But such moves were not much help, and farmers remained unhappy, unlike many others who were benefiting from the booming economy.

The stock market continued to climb in early 1929, so much so that many conservative financiers alerted the new president to the dangers of excessive speculation. He urged the New York Stock Exchange privately to try to put a lid on it, but without success, and he declined to call on Congress to intervene, saying he "had no desire to stretch the powers of the Federal Government" to that extent.[32] Despite other economic warnings, the speculation continued and the market continued to rise with it. Even as industrial production, employment and commodity prices began to fall steadily, the boom went on, with speculators refusing to acknowledge the signs of impending disaster. But on October 24 security prices nose-dived, panic selling set in, and in the next two weeks the market collapsed.

Hoover's optimism about the end of poverty being in sight was pathetically off the mark. Even after the crash, prominent industrial leaders continued to delude themselves. In December the head of Bethlehem Steel proclaimed that "never before has American business been as firmly entrenched for prosperity as it is today."[33]

Mellon's advice was to do nothing and let the economy right itself. However, Hoover urged captains of industry to keep wages and prices up, and called on Congress to cut personal and corporate taxes to spur revival. But it was all to no avail as private investment, spending and employment retracted defensively. Matters went from bad to worse, even as Hoover announced in May 1930 that "we have now passed the worst" and matters were bound to get better.[34] But he was dead wrong, and the public saddled him with the blame. He became the subject of ridicule, much of it of Democratic origin. As more and more men slept on park benches, a newspaper came to be called a "Hoover blanket," and an empty pocket turned inside out was dubbed a "Hoover flag."[35]

All this left the Democrats relieved that the great stock market crash had not occurred on their watch. At first, party leaders in Congress supported the Republican president in the atmosphere of crisis, but as it dragged on they took a more critical posture. In the congressional elections of 1930, amid rampant disillusionment with Hoover and the Republicans, the Democrats won a five-seat majority in the House and trailed the Republicans by only one seat in the Senate. Farmers joined city immigrants in helping to elect new Democratic governors in key states. And in

New York, Franklin D. Roosevelt was reelected by the largest margin in the state's history. Republicans who painted FDR as soft on Tammany undercut him with liberals but thereby improved his troubled relations with the machine.

John Raskob, Smith's campaign manager in 1928, had taken over as Democratic national chairman and proceeded to raise the necessary funds to accentuate the negative in laying the Great Depression at Hoover's feet. Under the direction of a former writer for the *New York World,* Charles Michelson, the party propaganda machine spewed out a steady stream of anti-Hoover editorial comments and speeches for Democratic candidates.

But it was Roosevelt at the state level who focused on imaginative responses to the depression. He launched programs for workmen's compensation and other labor benefits, backed a bond issue for relief for the unemployed, and spoke out for public power, reforestation and other policies that soon cast him as the party's most progressive voice, even as Smith took more conservative positions. At the same time, Roosevelt moved cautiously to a more accommodating posture on prohibition and distanced himself from Tammany Hall. All this underscored his independence from Smith, whose presidential candidacies he had twice vigorously supported. Smith seethed as Roosevelt failed to consult with him on his policies in Albany.

In Congress, Democratic efforts to fund federal public works, relief for the unemployed and other anti-depression measures were rejected by Hoover. He continued to preach self-reliance and local response to the crisis while looking for signs of recovery that did not come. When the depression hit Europe, the Republican president placed the blame there. And when he finally concluded that a balanced budget could not withstand the strains of the economic collapse, his approach was to use federal funds to prop up banks, insurance companies and other lending institutions rather than provide direct relief to the mushrooming army of American jobless and homeless.

This decision produced obvious partisan battle lines in the depression war. Democratic Senator Edward P. Costigan of Colorado declared that "nothing short of federal assistance [to the jobless] . . . can possibly satisfy the conscience and heart and safeguard the good name of America."[36] He joined with the younger La Follette to sponsor a $375 million relief bill, but the administration shot it down. Hoover insisted on channeling any relief through loans to states and localities from a newly created Reconstruction Finance Corporation, and only in cases of "absolute need and evidence of financial exhaustion."[37] When the Democrats offered more relief legislation through the RFC, Hoover vetoed it on grounds it was more than the agency needed or could efficiently dispense. Meanwhile, across the country, "Hoovervilles" of the unemployed blossomed along railroad tracks and near city dumps.

Such was the public climate and mood as the nation's two great parties prepared to address their quadrennial task of selecting their presidential nominees for 1932. And with Hoover grappling with the worst economic crisis the nation had yet seen, the Democrats believed they saw at last the light at the end of the dark tunnel that had kept them out of national power for a decade. Finally they had in Hoover's conservative response to the crisis the issue that would emphatically showcase their own progressive approach, which saw the depression in terms of human suffering rather than business downturn.

Inevitably, most Democratic eyes turned to the man in the wheelchair in Albany, who had easily survived the Hoover landslide of 1928. Roosevelt's diligent and shrewd labors in the political vineyards in behalf of other Democrats, most notably Smith in 1924 and 1928, looked brilliant in retrospect, and his anti-depression policies in his own state thereafter added to his luster. Most important, all this drew attention to his physical and mental vitality—and his political availability—at a moment of supreme opportunity for the Democratic Party, and for him.

In 1931, Roosevelt's chief political adviser, New York State Democratic chairman James A. Farley, undertook a political prospecting trip through eighteen Western states to sound out support for a Roosevelt presidential bid. He urged fellow state chairmen and governors to commit early to FDR as the likely party nominee. He reported to Roosevelt: "Have indicated that they must get away from the 'favorite son' idea, on the theory that it is only used for the purpose of tying up blocks of delegates to be manipulated," possibly for the vice-presidential nomination.[38]

Not everyone was bowled over by Roosevelt. Columnist Walter Lippmann was cool to the notion of rounding up delegates before spelling out an agenda. In a column in the *New York Herald-Tribune* on January 8, 1932, in an observation he lived to regret, Lippmann described Roosevelt as "a highly impressionable person, without a firm grasp of public affairs, and without very strong convictions." He called FDR "an amiable man with many philanthropic impulses, but he is not the dangerous enemy of anything. He is too eager to please." The New York governor, he went on, "is no crusader. He is no tribune of the people. He is no enemy of entrenched privilege. He is a pleasant man who, without any important qualifications for the office, would very much like to be President."[39]

Two weeks later Roosevelt announced his presidential candidacy by authorizing the state party in North Dakota to enter his name in its presidential primary, which he thereupon won. In March he won in New Hampshire, and in April in Wisconsin and Pennsylvania. Along the way, he also captured Democratic delegate contests in Alaska, Georgia, Washington, Iowa and Maine.

But by this time, an angry Smith had reneged on an earlier pledge not to run again and was in the thick of a stop-Roosevelt movement. With Tammany backing Smith against him, FDR lost more than half of his own state delegation. In Massachusetts, opportunistic Boston Mayor James M. Curley climbed on the Roosevelt bandwagon but botched his state's primary, to Smith's advantage. In May, FDR ran second to House Speaker John Nance Garner of Texas, the favorite of publisher William Randolph Hearst, in California. Still, he had beaten Smith in four of six direct primary clashes and heading into the national convention had the delegates of thirty-four states and six territories. However, he was short of the two-thirds majority needed for nomination, keeping alive the hopes of the stop-Roosevelt "Allies."

While limiting himself mostly to generalities in discussing what as president he intended to do about the depression, Roosevelt struck a distinctly populist chord. In a radio talk, he observed: "These unhappy times call for the building of plans that rest upon the forgotten, the unorganized but the indispensable units of economic power, for plans...that build from the bottom up and not from the top down, that put their faith once more in the forgotten man at the bottom of the economic pyramid."[40] Smith seized on the "forgotten man" theme to reinforce his own more conservative posture. "I will take off my coat and vest and fight to the end," he huffed, "any candidate who persists in a demagogic appeal to the masses of the working people of this country to destroy themselves by setting class against class and rich against poor."[41]

Roosevelt ignored him, while wishing Smith would not paint his old friend as a radical. Nevertheless, Roosevelt hinted at a risk-taking, innovative presidency. At a commencement at Oglethorpe University in Georgia, he declared: "The country needs and, unless I mistake its temper, the country demands bold, persistent experimentation."[42]

The Republicans, meanwhile, were well aware of their precarious position. Hoover's unpopularity, with the public and Congress alike, bred a joke in the Senate that he had been kidnapped with a ransom note that warned if half a million dollars wasn't delivered "within two hours, we'll bring him back."[43] Still, the party's national convention, meeting in Chicago in mid-June, after writing a platform that laid much of the blame for the continuing depression on Europe, routinely renominated Hoover and Curtis. Many Republicans expressed the hope that the Democrats would select Roosevelt, believing he would be the easiest to beat.

Later in June, also in Chicago, the Democrats at their convention accommodated their rivals, but only after surviving the lively stop-Roosevelt movement led by Smith. In 1928, when Smith left the New York governorship, he had strongly backed Roosevelt as his successor, deflating allegations that FDR's physical infirmity would prevent him from serving effectively. "You don't have to be an acrobat to be governor," Smith had said then of the man who was confined to a wheelchair.[44]

But now the more conservative Smith, piqued at Roosevelt for shunting aside old Smith advisers in Albany, became a rallying point for Democrats like Governor Joseph Ely of Massachusetts and Mayor Frank Hague of Jersey City, who saw Roosevelt as too liberal for their tastes. Many others looked to Smith as a way station only, preferring Wilson's secretary of war, Newton D. Baker, if Roosevelt could be stopped. Others joined Walter Lippmann in questioning FDR's intellectual heft. Chicago's Democratic boss, Ed Kelly, saw to it that the convention galleries were packed with Smith men.

Roosevelt, however, entered the fray with an impressive mix of deep thinkers and political professionals. His closest adviser, Louis Howe, had already put in place machinery to publicize FDR's virtues and raise money for him. Samuel Rosenman, Roosevelt's counsel in Albany, pulled together a brain trust of Columbia University professors including Raymond Moley, Adolf Berle and Rexford Tugwell. Hugh Johnson, a former army general turned businessman who was close to Bernard Baruch, was added to lend practicality to the academics. Jim Farley ran the political operation. Of the division of labors, Farley told Moley at one point: "I'm interested in getting him the votes—nothing else. Issues aren't my business. They're yours and his. You keep out of mine, and I'll keep out of yours."[45]

The convention platform, one of the shortest in memory, called for repeal of prohibition, a cut of at least 25 percent in operations costs of the federal government and a balanced budget. Narrowly averted was a row over the Democratic convention rule requiring a two-thirds majority for nomination, a major hurdle for the FDR forces. They made a brief effort to provide for nomination by simple majority, with the flamboyant Senator Huey P. Long of Louisiana, the notorious Kingfish who was in FDR's corner, offering without prior notice a resolution demanding the change. But the surprise attempt aroused such opposition, especially in the South where the two-thirds rule was seen as a protection against Yankee dictation, that it was abandoned.

Roosevelt, who had been part of the strategy to change the rule, extricated himself by noting its tardy presentation and saying he declined "to permit either myself or my friends to be open to the accusation of poor sportsmanship or to the use of methods which could be called, even falsely, those of a steamroller."[46]

Beyond Smith, the leading active opponent to Roosevelt was House Speaker John Nance "Cactus Jack" Garner of Texas, pushed by the Texas delegation, William Randolph Hearst and delegates from California. There were sufficient delegates for Garner and other candidates to block the front-running FDR's nomination.

That fact became clear on the first roll call, in the early hours of July 1 after interminable nominating speeches and backroom wheeling and dealing to bring about delegate switches for the New York governor. He received 666¼ votes, 102¾ short of the required two thirds, and after two more ballots, he had only 682 to 190¼ for Smith and 101¼ for Garner. Roosevelt still lacked 87 to go over the top, and panic began to set in among the FDR strategists; the pressure was on Farley. The convention recessed until that night, triggering more frantic efforts by the Roosevelt managers during the day to make up the deficit.

Howe and Farley went directly to Texas Congressman Sam Rayburn, leading his state delegation, arguing that no Southerner was going to be the nominee in any event. At the same time, other Roosevelt backers including financier Joseph P. Kennedy appealed to Hearst, warning him that a continued deadlock could lead to the renomination of Smith or the nomination of Baker, who as a supporter of the League of Nations was anathema to Hearst. The publisher finally agreed to urge Garner, who controlled all of California's forty-four votes by virtue of his primary victory, to bow out in favor of Roosevelt.

Garner, who was content in having achieved a lifelong ambition to be Speaker of the House, was willing, but members of the Texas delegation wanted the vice-presidential nomination for their man. Still, the reluctant Garner acquiesced, observing to Rayburn, "Hell, I'll do anything to see the Democrats win one more national election,"[47] and apparently the deal was struck. That night, when California was called on the fourth ballot, William McAdoo rose and announced: "California came here to nominate a President of the United States. She did not come here to deadlock this convention or to engage in another disastrous contest like that of 1924."[48] Whereupon he switched the delegation vote to Roosevelt. Texas followed suit, as did other states. A bitter Smith held his delegates, making a call for a unanimous decision impossible, but FDR wound up with 945 of the convention's 1,154 votes and was the nominee.

In a dramatic gesture, Roosevelt broke with tradition and the next morning took a chartered plane from Albany to Chicago to accept the nomination in person. The long and bumpy flight, arranged well in advance in a calculated move to project the nominee as a man of action in times demanding action, captured the public's imagination. So did an expression he used in his acceptance speech: "I pledge you, I pledge myself, to a new deal for the American people."[49] Thus was a name attached to an unprecedentedly progressive agenda for the Democratic Party whose details were to be spelled out later. The next day, cartoonist Rollin Kirby showed a farmer looking up at an airplane marked "New Deal," and the label stuck.[50]

Even before the general election began in earnest, more woes descended on Hoover. The convergence on Washington of as many as fifteen thousand jobless military veterans demanding immediate payment of a promised bonus put the capital under a state of siege. When the Senate voted down a bonus bill before it, many petitioners in this "Bonus Expeditionary Force" gave up and went home, but the rest dug in. They set up a shantytown of tents near the Capitol or slept in vacant government buildings and demanded to see President Hoover. He declined, but got Congress to pass legislation enabling the camping veterans to draw against their expected bonuses for fare to go home. Still, most refused to budge.

In July the administration ordered all squatters to clear out, and when violence erupted, two veterans were killed and several police were wounded. The incident provoked Hoover's secretary of war, Patrick Hurley, to call in cavalry and four infantry companies armed with tanks, machine guns and tear gas. Under the direction of General Douglas A. MacArthur, with junior officers Dwight D. Eisenhower and George S. Patton participating, the army burned down the shanties and drove the veterans and their families out. MacArthur characterized the petitioners as a "mob" animated by "the essence of revolution,"[51] and government officials labeled them criminals or communists, or both. But many average citizens were appalled at the veterans' treatment, further undermining support and respect for the president. The *Washington News* proclaimed editorially: "What a pitiful spectacle is that of the great American Government, mightiest in the world, chasing unarmed men, women and children with Army tanks. . . . If the Army must be called out to make war on unarmed citizens, this is no longer America."[52]

Roosevelt, meanwhile, spent the rest of the summer addressing internal campaign problems, one of which was concern within the party that he was ducking a serious matter of corruption within his own state involving New York Mayor Jimmy Walker. Harold L. Ickes, later a cabinet member, warned FDR that "while many independents and Republicans are favorably inclined toward you at this time, I find that they are not prepared to make up their minds finally until you have passed upon the case of Mayor Walker."[53] In a public hearing, Roosevelt personally grilled Walker relentlessly, and the beleaguered mayor finally resigned. FDR's aggressiveness caused resentment in Tammany circles, but met with wide approval elsewhere.

Organizationally, Roosevelt installed Farley as chairman of the Democratic National Committee. He ran the campaign from a New York headquarters that essentially bypassed county and state party committees, and made direct contacts with some 140,000 local party workers who had early identified themselves as Roosevelt men and women.

As the fall campaign began, Roosevelt was counseled to speak essentially on radio to conserve his strength, and let the public disenchantment with Hoover do the rest. Garner offered some pithy advice to his ticket mate against extensive travel: "All you have to do is to stay alive until election day."[54] But Roosevelt elected to demonstrate his vigor by first whistle-stopping to the Pacific Coast and then in the South, hobnobbing with

Democratic congressional leaders whose support he would need once elected. He spoke several times a day standing from the rear platform of the last car of his train, gripping the rail or his son James by the arm for balance. He thus projected an image of a robust man in sturdy good health, combating Republican whispers about his physical handicap to the point of obliterating it as a campaign issue.

On the stump in forty-one states, Roosevelt spoke in broad generalities about a progressive agenda that would pull the nation out of the economic morass into which it had fallen under Hoover. But his message was not a defined program and hardly a heralding of any liberal revolution. To mollify conservatives he proposed cuts in government spending to achieve a balanced budget, to the dismay of liberal brain trusters like Tugwell. At the same time, though, he hinted in general terms of the use of economic and social planning to cope with the country's ills and the needs of individual American workers.

Hoover, wrestling with the task of pinning down his evasive opponent, frustratingly labeled him "a chameleon on plaid."[55] Meanwhile, the incumbent was left to thrash about in defense of his stewardship of the depression years and in warnings of FDR's ideas as risky in perilous times. The "new deal" about which his rival spoke, he said, was no more than a "new shuffle" of old cards by a Democratic dealer.[56] At the same time, Hoover perhaps unwittingly warned of drastic change if Roosevelt was elected. At a late-campaign rally in Madison Square Garden, the Republican president prophetically cautioned his followers that the approaching election was "not a mere shift from the ins to the outs. It means deciding the direction our Nation will take over a century to come."[57]

Smith, for all his unhappiness toward FDR, eventually played the good soldier, finally campaigning energetically for the Democratic ticket in Massachusetts, one of his own strongest states, and Connecticut. On election day, another long Democratic drought came to an end. Roosevelt was elected with 22.8 million votes (57.4 percent) and 472 electoral votes from 42 states, to 15.75 million (39.7 percent) and 59 electoral votes in only 6 states for Hoover. Socialist nominee Norman Thomas wound up with 884,781 votes (2.2 percent) and no electoral votes.

With four months to go before he would take the oath of office, FDR essentially hunkered down, continuing to speak only in generalities of his plans and giving little suggestion of the dynamic leadership that would be unleashed then. He resisted efforts by Hoover to bring him into shared responsibility for the economic collapse. When the defeated president invited FDR to the White House, the president-elect merely listened to Hoover's proposals without associating himself with them. When Hoover sent Roosevelt two letters urging him to buy into eleventh-hour proposals to keep the ship of state afloat, Roosevelt held to the position that Hoover remained the president until a new one was inaugurated, and that he himself had no constitutional authority to exert executive power.

The arrival of the new year of 1933 brought both sad and ominous news, with the death of former President Coolidge and, on January 30, FDR's fifty-first birthday, the appointment by aging German President Paul von Hindenburg of a man named Adolf Hitler as chancellor. Hitler promptly dissolved the Reichstag and ordered elections, at the same time arresting opposition leaders. On the other side of the globe, Japan found itself censured by the League of Nations for aggression against Manchuria and withdrew from the League. But it was the grim domestic situation that commanded Roosevelt's attention as he planned for his own presidency.

The most disconcerting development before Roosevelt's inauguration occurred in Miami on February 15, little more than two weeks before he was to take the oath of office. He had just finished a speech in a park when a man named Giuseppe Zangara, standing only about ten yards away, jumped on a bench, pulled out a cheap revolver and fired five shots at the president-elect. A woman standing next to Zangara pulled at his arm, throwing off his aim, and Chicago Mayor Anton Cermak, FDR's host, was hit instead. Roosevelt put Cermak into a car and rushed him to a hospital, but the mayor died a few weeks later.[58] Zangara eventually was convicted and executed.

FDR's close call came amid more worsening economic news, as public panic produced an intensification of runs on the nation's banks. On inauguration eve, he took two more phone calls from Hoover seeking his successor's view on demands for immediate emergency action to shut down the banks. Roosevelt again reminded the man spending his last night in the Oval Office that he was still president. The Democratic president-elect calmly awaited the approaching moment when national power would finally and incontestably be passed to him, and it then would be his sole responsibility to meet the awesome rescue task that lay ahead.

In 1937, President Franklin D. Roosevelt, frustrated by U.S. Supreme Court rulings against seven New Deal programs, asked Congress for a Court reorganization that would add six more justices. The proposal caused chaos with the Democratic-controlled Congress and FDR was rebuffed.

Chapter 18

FDR AND THE NEW DEAL, 1933–1939

THE DEMOCRAT WHO took the presidential oath of office on Saturday, March 4, 1933, did not have pure party bloodlines. It was not only that his most illustrious relative, distant cousin Teddy, had been a Republican; his maternal grandfather, Warren Delano, a lifelong Republican, was fond of expressing his opinion that while not all Democrats "are horse thieves . . . it would seem that all horse thieves are Democrats."[1]

Young Franklin's father, James, nevertheless supported Democratic presidential nominee Grover Cleveland before helping to elect Teddy governor of New York in 1898. Franklin himself from all accounts virtually stumbled into politics and into the Democratic Party in 1910 when a leading Democrat in Dutchess County, aware of an expected open seat in the state assembly from the district, invited him to seek it. When it turned out that the incumbent decided to run for reelection after all, the twenty-eight-year-old Roosevelt decided he would try for the state senate from roughly the same district, even though the Senate seat there had gone Democratic only once in the previous forty-four years. It included Hyde Park, the Roosevelt ancestral home.

The Democratic leadership greased the nomination for young Roosevelt, and in the general election he capitalized on the fact that the Republican incumbent was a disreputable local political boss. As an upstate Democrat, FDR had nothing to fear from Tammany Hall's dominance in New York City and therefore ran against bossism in both parties.

With the Republican Party split locally as well as nationally between the conservative Taft forces and progressives, he deftly appealed to the latter while playing down his Democratic affiliation. On election day the Democratic Party scored heavily in Congress and the legislature in Albany, and Roosevelt won the Senate seat by 1,140 votes out of about 30,300 cast.

Almost at once, he made a name for himself by taking on the Tammany boss, Charles F. Murphy, in his attempt to install one of his organization hacks, William F. "Blue-eyed Billy" Sheehan, as United States senator, chosen at that time by the state legislature. "There is no question in my mind," Roosevelt wrote in his diary, "that the Democratic Party is on trial, and having been given control of the government chiefly through upstate votes, cannot afford to surrender its control to the organization in New York City."[2]

In the end, after a long and rancorous fight, Roosevelt helped to derail Sheehan, but another Tammany leader was chosen. Still, the young Roosevelt won national attention with his willingness to take on bossism, just as Woodrow Wilson in New Jersey was doing en route to the governorship there.

The fight with Tammany was only the first of several Roosevelt undertook, and not the only one he lost. Murphy also survived another insurgent group led by Roosevelt in 1912 known as the Empire State Democracy, and in 1914 FDR's thoughts of seeking the New York governorship were discouraged by President Wilson, who wanted Tammany support for his own reelection bid in 1916. Instead, Roosevelt decided to run for the U.S. Senate, whereupon Boss Murphy recruited James Gerard, the American ambassador to Germany, himself a Tammany man cleared by Wilson, to run against him. With Murphy handling the Gerard campaign while the ambassador stayed at his post in Berlin, Roosevelt was snowed under by nearly three to one in the Democratic primary. Gerard then lost the general election, but Murphy had another triumph over the rebellious Roosevelt.

Thereafter, FDR quietly made his peace with Tammany, helping its leaders with patronage matters in Washington as assistant secretary of the navy under Wilson, and he even spoke at the organization's Independence Day affair in 1917. When Democratic presidential nominee James Cox favored him as his running mate in 1920 and cleared the choice with Murphy, the Tammany boss reluctantly acceded and saw to it that Roosevelt was nominated to be vice president on the first ballot. And later, after FDR's enthusiastic support of Tammany man Al Smith for president in 1924 and 1928, he was able to balance his upstate backing and a truce with Tammany to be elected and reelected governor. By the time of his successful presidential candidacy, FDR had pretty much made a paper tiger of the once-fearsome New York machine.

In crowning his climb to power with the presidency, Roosevelt had rendered Hoover, the Republican he defeated, a lame duck for his remaining four months in the Oval Office. The departing president had soldiered on to the end, trying in vain to persuade Roosevelt to buy into his failed nostrums. Only days before FDR's swearing-in, Hoover forlornly lamented in a private letter to a Republican senator: "I realize that if these declarations be made by the President-elect, he will have ratified the whole major program of the Republican Administration."[3]

Now, having taken the oath, Roosevelt was empowered to apply his own remedies, and he left no doubt in his inaugural address that he would waste no time doing so. In words that would be among the most remembered of his unprecedentedly long presidency, FDR counseled the American people in that perilous hour that "the only thing we have to fear is fear itself—nameless, unreasoning, unjustified terror which paralyzes needed efforts to convert retreat into advance." He assured them he would not be so paralyzed. "This nation asks for action, and action now," he said. "Our greatest primary task is to put people to work," if necessary by "direct recruiting by the Government itself."[4]

He would work with the legislative branch, he said, calling on Congress for "the measures that a stricken Nation in the midst of a stricken world may require." And if that wasn't enough to lift the country from its economic morass, he said, "I shall not evade the clear course of duty that will then confront me. I shall ask the Congress for the one remaining instrument to meet the crisis—broad Executive power to wage a war against the emergency, as great as the power that would be given to me if we were in fact invaded by a foreign foe."[5]

Beaming confidently, the new president made clear from the very start that his would be no stand-pat administration. He had his cabinet sworn in as a unit in the Oval Office immediately after his inaugural parade, and in other ways the contrast with the floundering departed Hoover was electrifying. FDR at once issued a presidential proclamation declaring a four-day national bank holiday, closing every bank in the land, embargoing all shipments of gold and silver, and providing stiff fines and possible jail terms for hoarders.

Americans suddenly found themselves only with the cash they happened to have in their wallets or under their mattresses. If they ran out, they simply stopped buying or gave shops their IOUs. Some used postage stamps for currency and, in New York, subway tokens. Humorist Will Rogers declared: "This is the happiest day in three years. We have no jobs, we have no money, we have no banks; and if Roosevelt had burned down the Capitol, we would have said, 'Thank God, he started a fire under something.' "[6]

Governors of Michigan and other states had already ordered their banks closed, and Hoover had sought FDR's support in such a move. But Roosevelt's swift and dramatic step on his own clear and solitary authority to act gave force to his aggressive words, with powerful psychological effect on the public. He followed it quickly by summoning Congress into special session, during which an emergency banking act was rushed through, providing the liquidity that enabled most banks to reopen. Even the Republicans jumped aboard; the GOP floor leader, Bertrand Snell of New York, declared: "The house is burning down and the President of the United States says this is the way to put out the fire."[7]

Roosevelt addressed the nation via radio on Sunday night with his first "fireside chat" as president, with a refreshing directness. "I want to talk for a few minutes with the people of the United States about banking," he began. "... I want to tell you what has been done in the last few days, why it was done and what the next steps are going to be."[8] For the next twenty minutes he explained how the banks would be strengthened and deposits guaranteed. He called on his fellow Americans to return their savings to the banks when they reopened the next morning, assuring them that "it is safer to keep your money in a reopened bank than it is under the mattress."[9] On Monday morning, depositors rushed to the banks and followed their president's advice. Although many had been without cash for days as a result of the bank holiday, more money was deposited than withdrawn.

The stampede of the First Hundred Days was on. In rapid order over the next weeks, Roosevelt bombarded Congress with emergency legislation—on government spending cutbacks; on modification of the Volstead Act to permit sale of beer and light wines, with federal taxes applied; on farm relief and credit; on creation of a Civilian Conservation Corps; on jobless relief to the states; on federal oversight of securities sales; on creation of the Tennessee Valley Authority; on protections against small home mortgage foreclosures; on ending the gold standard; on railroad reform; on creation of the Federal Deposit Insurance Corporation and the National Industrial Recovery Act. In three months' time, all this and more—fifteen major pieces of legislation—had been signed into law.

In the process, Roosevelt kept the American people apprised of what he was doing in a series of radio fireside chats and press conferences that kept up their spirits and enthusiasm, even as the economy continued to drag. The theme song of the FDR campaign, "Happy Days Are Here Again," may technically have been premature, but it captured the upbeat mood that Roosevelt was bringing to the nation by force of action and personality. In the pursuit of recovery, he pushed progressive reforms that gave an identity to the New Deal that clung to it long thereafter, and played the central role in cementing the Democratic Party's claim to be the party of the people, especially the "little people."

The program was long on ambition and improvisation and short on long-range planning, and mistakes were often made along the way. But overall it projected a sense of vitality and movement in contrast to the recollections of Hoover inertia and drift. The members of the campaign brain trust played key roles, with Louis Howe as FDR's closest aide, Harry Hopkins as federal relief administrator and Lewis Douglas as budget director, charged with keeping the federal books balanced amid the mushrooming of new federal initiatives and agencies. Also influential was the new president's wife, Eleanor, who became a personal emissary around the country for her husband, in the process building an impressive following in her own right.

Patronage and politics were placed in the experienced hands of Jim Farley, essentially running the Democratic National Committee out of the office of postmaster general. In terms of ideology and structure, the party for years had been disjointed and directionless, after the almost unbroken drought of national power since the Civil War. In spite of FDR's own efforts in the 1920s to bring about some national cohesion among the freestanding state party organizations, the national committee had remained a physical shell, propped up once every four years for the purpose of running a national ticket. Now, with an energetic president at the helm and a philosophy of governing, however loosely conceived and articulated under the New Deal label, the Democratic Party had an opportunity to redefine itself, especially in a crisis atmosphere of new hope.

New agencies like the Agricultural Adjustment Administration (AAA), National Recovery Administration (NRA), Civil Works Administration (CWA) and Public Works Administration (PWA) were created to spur governmental-entrepreneurial cooperation, limit farm production and raise prices, wages and employment. Others provided mechanisms for refinancing homes and farms and warding off foreclosures, for fostering organization of trade unions and collective bargaining by their members. While these, taken together, did not lift the nation out of depression, they demonstrated government in action to seek solutions. And in all this, Roosevelt managed for a considerable period of time to act in the trappings of bipartisanship.

Nothing in all this frenzy of activity more epitomized the New Deal than the work of the Tennessee Valley Authority in mobilizing the natural resources of an entire region to bring electricity and power to its inhabitants. Yet it, too, was born of the same trial and error that marked the various other undertakings of the First Hundred Days. When progressive Republican Senator George W. Norris of Nebraska once asked FDR, "What are you going to say when they [Congress] ask you the political philosophy behind TVA?" Roosevelt was said to have replied: "I'll tell them it's neither fish nor fowl, but whatever it is, it will taste awfully good to the people of the Tennessee Valley."[10]

Roosevelt's message in introducing the experimental policies of the New Deal was that he intended to be the president of all the people, espousing actions that would benefit all segments of the society without regard to class or political affiliation. On one speaking tour in Wisconsin, he said his approach sought "to cement our society, rich and poor, manual worker and brain worker, into a voluntary brotherhood of freemen, standing together, striving together, for the common good of all."[11]

When he was approached early in 1934 to attend a Jefferson Day event in honor of the Democratic Party's founder, FDR declined. "Our strongest plea to the country in this particular year of grace," he explained, "is that the recovery and reconstruction program is being accomplished by men and women of all parties—that I have repeatedly appealed to Republicans as much as to Democrats to do their part." Rather, he suggested, "nonpartisan Jefferson dinners" would be a better idea.[12]

The question, however, was whether Roosevelt truly wanted nonpartisanship over the long haul or merely was courting all Republicans as a means of weaning away progressives in GOP ranks and bringing about a liberal-conservative realignment. According to Arthur M. Schlesinger Jr. in *The Coming of the New Deal,* Roosevelt in 1932 had observed to Tugwell: "Rex, we shall have eight years in Washington. At the end of that time we may or may not have a Democratic party; but we will have a Progressive one."[13]

As FDR saw it, the New Deal concept was not a war on American business but rather a partnership with it, supported at the outset by the likes of the U.S. Chamber of Commerce, and certainly not socialism. But as Roosevelt initiatives required more deficit spending and involved more and more academics and liberal thinkers, a conservative core in both major parties began to grumble about the Grand Experiment that was taking over the government and lives of the people.

Of all the FDR programs, the NRA, which called on business to draw up codes to ensure fair competition and provide for collective bargaining, maximum hours and minimum wages for labor, became the principal opposition target, and drew internal criticism as well. If a code could not be agreed upon in any industry, one could be imposed by the government. Businesses in compliance displayed a blue eagle symbol on their premises that soon came to be recognized as the mark of the New Deal.

The codes were complex, often overly favorable to big business and resulting in price fixing that hurt small entrepreneurs. Employers also resisted the labor provisions that to Roosevelt were core elements of the program. General Hugh Johnson proved to be an ineffective administrator and Roosevelt finally enlisted Clarence Darrow to head a board to investigate the NRA. Darrow's report criticized the agency's failures and Johnson eventually resigned.

The forces against the Roosevelt agenda first mobilized in a significant way in the summer of 1934, when wealthy Republicans including members of the duPont family and such prominent Democrats as Al Smith, John W. Davis, Jouett Shouse and John J. Raskob joined to form the American Liberty League. Its stated goal was to "teach the necessity of respect for the rights of persons and property"[14] and insist on the government's duty to protect private business against the intrusions of social experiment.

According to Schlesinger in *The Coming of the New Deal,* when Shouse called on Roosevelt and told him of the league's purpose, "Roosevelt suavely commented that every American citizen could subscribe to these objectives." But later at a press conference, he observed: "An organization that only advocates two or three out of the Ten Commandments may be a perfectly good organization, but it would have certain shortcomings in having failed to advocate the other seven or eight Commandments."[15]

Nevertheless, the League set itself up as the guardian of the Constitution, alleging that FDR's liberal, freewheeling ideas often abused it. But he continued to claim he was following a legitimate nonpartisan if innovative course. In frustration, the Liberty League and particularly the Republican Party looked to the approaching congressional elections of 1934, and to the tradition that the party in control of the White House customarily lost strength to the outs.

Roosevelt dealt in stride with the carpings of his conservative critics that his policies were undermining individual rights and freedom. In one fireside chat, he said: "Plausible self-seekers and theoretical diehards will tell you of the loss of individual liberty. . . . Have you lost any of your rights or liberty or constitutional freedom of action and choice?" He called on his listeners to reread the Bill of Rights "and ask yourself whether you personally have suffered the impairment of a single jot of these great assurances."[16] The stand-pat policies of his predecessors toward the depression, he emphasized, had gotten the country nowhere. It was time for the government to act, and act boldly.

When Hoover came out with a book, *The Challenge to Liberty,* in 1934, his friend Supreme Court Justice Harlan F. Stone advised against its publication. "The country is convinced that the time has come for sweeping reforms," he told Hoover, "and that these are being, and will be, resisted for selfish reasons by those who have an excessive stake in things as they are. . . . Even the man in the street is aware that every important reform in the past 75 years has been resisted and assailed as an infringement of individual liberty."[17]

While continuing to preach cooperation between the business community and workers, Roosevelt seemed to be losing patience with the criticisms on the right of his economic recovery efforts. "Now that these people are coming out of their storm cellars," he observed at one point, "they forget that there ever was a storm."[18]

The president escaped the growing complaints of businessmen in early summer by taking a long cruise on a navy ship through the Caribbean, the Panama Canal and on to Hawaii. But on return the gripes had grown even louder, from labor as well as business. Strikes broke out; FDR's budget director, Douglas, resigned over spending that threatened a balanced budget; some 150 prominent industrialists met secretly and castigated most of the New Deal legislative agenda. Roosevelt's efforts to assuage business leaders by having leading administration figures meet with them, and doing so himself, only incurred the disapproval of his younger liberal advisers. The president himself came away from the experience not only impatient toward the business community but also with distrust of it as a dependable partner in his hopes for cooperative efforts for recovery.

In another fireside chat well before the November elections, Roosevelt posed a series of questions to his listeners that nearly half a century later in the opposite context would prove politically advantageous to a presidential nominee of the opposite party: "The simplest way for each of you to judge recovery," he said, "lies in the plain facts of your individual situation. Are you better off than you were last year? Are your debts less burdensome? Is your bank account more secure? Are your working conditions better? Is your faith in your own individual future more firmly grounded?"[19]

Still later, in one more fireside chat, FDR countered the criticism of the Liberty League and Hoover's book by observing: "In our efforts for recovery we have avoided, on the one hand, the theory that business should and must be taken over into an all-embracing Government. We have avoided, on the other hand, the equally untenable theory that it is an interference with liberty to offer reasonable help when private enterprise is in need of help."[20]

As the off-year elections approached, Roosevelt hewed to his nonpartisan posture. He basically refrained from participation in the fall campaign and ordered his cabinet, except for Farley, to make no speeches in behalf of Democratic candidates. If this step did little for party development, his own standing with the voters remained remarkably high, insulated from partisan attack. Once, in Wisconsin, a Republican candidate for the U.S. House called him "a man who can't stand on his own feet without crutches." The Republican crowd objected, and the party's candidate for the Senate walked off the platform in protest.[21]

The voters' answers to FDR's questions about whether they were better off came emphatically in the off-year elections. The Democrats picked up nine seats in the House, giving them a whopping three-to-one advantage, and nine in the Senate, for a forty-four-seat margin over the Republicans there. The total Democratic vote for Congress rose and Democrats at the end of the day had thirty-nine governorships to only seven for the Republicans and one each for the Progressives and Farmer-Laborites. The Democratic Party was riding high behind a president who seemed just to be getting started with his grand plan, all the while insisting he was operating on a nonpartisan basis. The Republicans seemed lost for a strategy to combat it, especially as FDR continued his bipartisan rhetoric.

Roosevelt headed into the second half of his first term with a strong head of steam. Still, although he had made strides toward recovery, the nation was far from it. By 1935, some 4 million more workers were employed than in 1933, but 9 million remained jobless. In two years, the gross national product had grown nearly $20 billion, but was still far below the $50 billion of 1929, before the crash. Organized labor got a boost from the administration's support for collective bargaining, but the resultant added strength brought louder protests against unrealized workplace opportunity.

Aware of this rising discontent, Roosevelt in his State of the Union address to Congress in January 1935 stepped up his embrace of social reform, generating new concern in the business community. He called for enactment of a social security system and public housing, observing that "in spite of our efforts and in spite of our talk, we have not weeded out the overprivileged and we have not effectively lifted up the underprivileged."[22] This was the sort of talk guaranteed to raise cries of "class warfare" from Republicans in the first category. When that spring he sought $5 billion from Congress for relief programs, the Chamber of Commerce and the National Association of Manufacturers parted ways with the administration and the New Deal.

Opposition also was surfacing on the political left on grounds that the New Deal was not doing enough for the man in the street. It came most visibly and noisily from Democratic Senator Huey Long of Louisiana, "The Kingfish," whose freewheeling program of "Share Our Wealth" called for heavily taxing the rich and generous payments to the poor. As governor, Long had pumped millions into roads and public schools for his state and ruled Louisiana with an iron and corrupt hand, before moving to the Senate in 1933 with his eye on national power. But an assassin's bullet cut him down in September 1935, leaving extremist opposition to FDR to the likes of the Reverend Gerald L.K. Smith, Father

Charles E. Coughlin, a Detroit radio priest, and Dr. Francis E. Townsend, whose plan for monthly payouts to the aged to pump-prime the economy mobilized local Townsend Clubs of the elderly around the country. Smith and Coughlin, while presenting themselves as defenders of the downtrodden, traded in racism and anti-Semitism, and joined Townsend in creating a Union Party to fight the New Deal.

At the same time, as Roosevelt continued to press his New Deal agenda, the Supreme Court began to respond to questions about the constitutionality of important components, and especially the business community's pet hate, the NRA. On May 27, 1935, known thereafter among New Dealers as Black Monday, the Court struck down the NRA and two other Roosevelt programs by 9–0 decisions. The emphatic action against "the blue eagle" came in a case involving allegations that Brooklyn live poultry dealers were violating NRA codes by selling diseased chickens and not following wage and work hour regulations.

The Court held that Congress had gone too far in authorizing the president to establish codes for businesses not sufficiently engaged in interstate commerce to be covered under the commerce clause of the Constitution. FDR's solicitor general, Stanley Reed, argued unsuccessfully to the Court that the codes applied because 96 percent of the live poultry came from outside New York State. The dealers in question had sold thousands of pounds of the "sick chicken" below the market price, he complained, thus depressing the price elsewhere and infecting purchasers, predominantly poor blacks, with tuberculosis.

Chief Justice Charles Evans Hughes held that the NRA's code-making authority amounted to an "unconstitutional delegation of legislative power."[23] The decision rocked the Roosevelt administration, particularly because it was unanimous, with liberals Louis Brandeis and Benjamin Cardozo joining in. Almost at once, price wars broke out, and many employers began to cut wages and increase employee work hours. At first the president said nothing, sidestepping the issue in one press conference, but two days later called another at which he unloaded on the justices. He said the implications of the NRA decision were probably more important than those of any other since the Dred Scott case, and the justices had relegated the Constitution to "the horse-and-buggy definition of interstate commerce."[24]

For nearly an hour and a half, under ground rules that at the time barred direct quotation, he read a host of complaining telegrams sent to him and questioned whether the federal government henceforth was to "have no right under any implied power or any court-approved power to enter into a national economic problem.... Shall we view our social problems ... that the Federal Government has no right under this or following opinions to take any part in trying to better national social conditions?"[25]

An outraged Roosevelt met the challenge with another burst of legislation, much of it designed to fill the void created by the demise of the NRA, especially in the field of labor relations. He pushed through Congress the Wagner Labor Relations Act governing the right to organize and bargain collectively and a tough tax bill on the nation's wealthiest, and, above all, the Social Security Act. Earlier FDR had instructed his secretary of labor, Frances Perkins, to cover every American, farmers and their families as well as industrial workers. "From the cradle to the grave they ought to be in a social insurance system," he informed her.[26] When finally enacted in August 1935, conservative opposition had pared the objective back to about half the work force, and the aged benefits provided were meager. But the cornerstone had been set in place for the most famous and important of all New Deal programs.

By this time, Roosevelt's early aspirations for government to work in partnership with business in a nonpartisan atmosphere had largely eroded. Replacing them was a determination that government weigh in on the side of the workingman against the dominant influence of business, especially big business, in the workplace and in the society. And with the Supreme Court's decision in the NRA and other New Deal cases seemingly imperiling his agenda, FDR adopted a more aggressive posture in what was called by many the Second New Deal. Unlike the first, motivated as it was by a desperate drive for economic recovery, the second was more pointedly reformist, though the country was not yet out of the woods economically. Roosevelt continued to pay lip service at the altar of the balanced budget, but it became increasingly clear that in a showdown he was moved more by the plight of the workingman.

As the presidential election of 1936 approached, the business community found itself more often than not on the outside looking in at a national administration that had organized labor as a powerful political ally. Business saw the Supreme Court as its own ally against a Roosevelt program it deemed an unconstitutional threat to the American capitalist system under which business had prospered relatively unfettered for so long. More Court decisions voiding New Deal programs such as the AAA reinforced the view, as did Hoover's declaration that the New Deal was an assault on "the whole philosophy of individual liberty."[27] Others implied that the New Deal was somehow subversive and nurtured by foreign influences such as socialism and communism.

Roosevelt's personal popularity in the country, however, led prudent Republicans to question the political wisdom of waging the fight against his reelection on such premises. They had enough on their hands to come up with a candidate who could hope to compete with the beaming, optimistic Democratic incumbent. Hoover, though said to be interested in a return match, was too scarred by the depression. The more spirited, progressive members of the party, including Bob La Follette Jr. and Senator George Norris, were considered off the reservation, and Senator William E. Borah had declined to campaign for Hoover in 1932 and was in bad odor with party conservatives.

That left weak pickings as the GOP approached its national convention in Cleveland in June. Chicago newspaper publisher Frank Knox put himself in the running, and the small pool of Republican governors offered only Styles Bridges of tiny New Hampshire, a rock-ribbed conservative, and the congenial Alfred E. Landon of Kansas, who was more middle-road. Hoover's appearance drew a long demonstration in the hall, and his speech led the party's indictment of the New Deal, Roosevelt and "passage of laws contrary to the Constitution,"[28] but he stepped aside thereafter. In the end, only Landon's name went before the convention and he received all delegates' votes, except for nineteen from Wisconsin that went for Borah. Knox was selected as his running mate.

The Democratic convention in Philadelphia later in June was so routine that the most notable outcome was not the renomination of Roosevelt and Garner without debate or roll calls, but the revocation of the two-thirds majority rule for nomination that had assured the marathon conventions of the past. Farley as the party's national chairman posed the basic issue for Democrats: "Shall we continue the New Deal ... or shall the Government be turned back to the Old Dealers who wrecked it?"[29] Scrapping of the two-thirds rule was accompanied by orders to the 1940 convention to revise the system of delegate apportionment to give Southern states more say as compensation for the virtual veto power they had over presidential nominations under the two-thirds rule.

The campaign itself was a Democratic triumph from the start. Roosevelt's mastery of radio at a time when it was becoming the dominant communications vehicle in politics gave him a huge advantage over Landon, a colorless sort who spoke with a dull twang. While Roosevelt boasted of the virtues of the New Deal that had plucked the country from economic disaster, Landon at first offered a milder version, only in the campaign's latter weeks attacking the New Deal out of desperation. The Kansas state flower, the sunflower, was Landon's symbol, but that was about all that was sunny about his message or his campaign.

Roosevelt continued his homey fireside chats well into the campaign, still getting free airtime from the networks and local stations until the Republicans demanded the same for their man. Both campaigns then bought radio time, but the GOP essentially wasted its money on the uninspiring Landon. Harold Ickes, FDR's secretary of the interior, observed after hearing him on the air: "If that is the best that Landon can do, the Democratic committee ought to spend all the money it can raise to send him out to make speeches."[30]

Political poll-taking also made an appearance in the 1936 campaign, with a pioneer pollster, Emil Hurja, surveying voters for the Democratic National Committee not simply on their candidate choices but on their views of FDR's programs, the better to design effective radio and other voter contacts.[31] Other pioneers, including George Gallup and Archibald Crossley, tested public opinion as well, as did the *Literary Digest,* ultimately with disastrous results. It sent postcards only to its own heavily Republican readership, names in phone books and on auto registration lists, and predicted a Landon landslide. The campaign also marked the early use of other campaign professionals in the communications and voter turnout arts. A strong cadre of women political operatives, importantly including Molly Dewson, director of the Democratic Party Women's Committee and a friend of Mrs. Roosevelt, played a key role both at the convention and in the fall campaign.

Organized labor, too, weighed in importantly for the Democratic ticket in response to Roosevelt's strong efforts to spur union organizing and better working conditions, first through provisions of the NRA and, after its demise, of the Wagner National Labor Relations Act. The Democrats also were notably effective with black voters, having seated blacks as full-fledged convention delegates for the first time. A new Democratic organization, the National Colored Committee of the Good Neighbor League, turned out sixteen thousand black voters for a Roosevelt rally at

New York's Madison Square Garden. The party trumpeted the thousands of jobs given to blacks in the New Deal's Works Progress Administration (WPA).

Well-financed competing activities of the Liberty League were no match, however, and often turned moderates who saw good in the New Deal against the Republican ticket. Knox waged a futile effort to make an issue of the new social security law, charging it "puts half the working people of America under federal control."[32] They didn't seem to mind.

Roosevelt basically ignored Landon, preferring to remind voters of Hoover and what he called the "economic royalists" in control of the GOP. At the same time, he seldom invoked the Democratic Party, preferring to run as a reformer appealing for support from all voters. In his final campaign speech in New York, FDR cited the opposition's hate for him and said he welcomed it: "I should like it said of my first Administration that in it the forces of selfishness and lust for power met their match. I should like to have it said of my second Administration that in it these forces met their master."[33]

On election eve, Farley predicted to FDR that he would carry every state except Maine and Vermont. Farley was on the money, with Roosevelt winning by a record of nearly 11 million votes and all electoral votes except the eight from those two small New England states. The Democrats widened their majorities in both houses of Congress. Union Party nominee William Lemke drew 892,000 votes and the party was not heard from again.

The Democratic Party could honestly claim to have reached majority status in the land in a truly realigning election. For the first time since emancipation during the Civil War, blacks voted solidly Democratic and the Solid South held firm. Farmers believed they were being helped and voted accordingly. In the cities, the major Democratic bosses were marching in lockstep with the man who had cut his political eyeteeth fighting Tammany Hall in New York—Ed Flynn in New York, Ed Kelly in Chicago, James Curley in Boston, Frank Hague in Jersey City, Ed Crump in Memphis, Tom Pendergast in Kansas City. To the boss-led Irish of the Northern and Midwestern cities and liberal intellectuals now had been added the blue-collar organized labor vote and the unemployed new immigrants of all stripes and, most notably, blacks, often heretofore gratefully wed to the party of Lincoln, the great emancipator.

Ever since the Civil War, the party that had ended slavery had held their allegiance, and the limited black political leadership routinely had done the bidding of white Republican politicians. To counter the pattern, Democratic organizations such as Tammany Hall in New York as early as 1912 had courted black leaders through patronage appointments, and big-city Democratic leaders in Chicago, St. Louis and elsewhere were soon doing the same.[34] But it was not until 1934 that Arthur W. Mitchell in Chicago, who had campaigned for Roosevelt in 1932, became the first black Democrat elected to Congress, defeating a black Republican, Oscar DePriest.

After FDR's election, a "black cabinet" of mid-level administration officeholders met periodically to raise concerns of particular interest to the black community. It had no official standing but provided an outlet for those concerns, with an energetic, aggressive and independent woman, Mary McLeod Bethune, bringing the cabinet's views directly to Eleanor Roosevelt and eventually to the president. Members of the cabinet campaigned diligently for FDR in 1936 and were considered important in achieving the heavy black voter turnout.

The National Association for the Advancement of Colored People (NAACP) also became an FDR political ally despite perceived shortcomings in his support of its interests. The organization, which had long investigated lynching of blacks in the South and after World War I had pushed for federal anti-lynching legislation, won House approval for the anti-lynching bill in 1922, but it fell to a Southern filibuster in the Senate. In late 1933, Walter White, executive secretary of the NAACP, persuaded two liberal Democrats, Senators Edward P. Costigan of Colorado and Robert F. Wagner of New York, to reintroduce the legislation. It was reported out of the Senate Judiciary Committee in 1934, but the Senate's Democratic leadership declined to bring it to the Senate floor for a vote. White sought to meet with Roosevelt to enlist his help, but although the president condemned lynching and called on law enforcement agencies to suppress it, he essentially gave White a runaround on supporting federal anti-lynching legislation.

Next, White turned to the president's wife, urging her to intercede. She did her best, believing from the first in the justice of the legislation, but it was not until early 1936 that she was able to arrange a meeting for White with her husband. White later said that FDR was cordial but pleaded the need to get other vital bills through Congress as his rationale for not being willing to face a long Senate filibuster over the anti-lynching proposal. The president, White reported later, also swallowed the argument of Southern Democratic senators that such a law was unconstitutional. When the Senate's Democratic leadership continued to block consideration by the full Senate on grounds it would create a legislative logjam, Roosevelt silently, and no doubt relievedly, made no objection.

In April of 1937, a version of the anti-lynching bill was passed in the House by a vote of more than two to one, over the wishes of the Democratic leadership of Speaker John H. Bankhead of Alabama and Majority Leader Sam Rayburn of Texas, and with virtually no support from the White House. In June, the Senate Judiciary Committee reported the bill favorably, but again the Southern leadership kept it from the floor by threat of filibuster. FDR either yielded to or embraced this result, depending on whether one thought he really wanted an anti-lynching bill or didn't.

In this and other ways, Roosevelt demonstrated that while he may have been generally sympathetic to the cause of civil rights for black Americans, he was not going to go out of his way for them when to do so would jeopardize other of his objectives. Yet, for all that, blacks saw in his smiling countenance, in his empathetic and helpful wife and in the social welfare agenda of the early New Deal a general concern for their well-being, and they voted accordingly for his reelection. As Kenneth Clark put it, "It was an indication of the folk wisdom on the part of Negroes that they worshipped the Roosevelts in spite of the fact that FDR never clearly defined civil rights goals."[35]

Although the two most recent Democratic presidents, Wilson and FDR, had been at best indifferent to the racial discrimination that continued in the land, the economic benefits of the New Deal trumped that fact. As blacks along with other low-income Americans saw their lives improved by Roosevelt's new social programs, they responded at the ballot box. As Nancy J. Weiss put it in her book *Farewell to the Party of Lincoln: Black Politics in the Age of FDR,* "the struggle to survive took precedence over the struggle for equality." Or, in the more succinct words of a WPA worker in 1936: "I don't think it is fair to eat Roosevelt bread and meat and vote for Governor Landon."[36]

Through all this, Eleanor Roosevelt remained a staunch and empathetic lifeline to White, finally in 1939 coming out publicly in support of the bill, while her husband continued to express encouragement to the black leadership to maintain its efforts—without his help. Indeed, as

Nancy Weiss noted, it was Eleanor Roosevelt's open concern for the extension of all civil rights to blacks that provided a positive veneer over FDR's broad expressions of sympathy but general indifference. In her book, Weiss quoted Roy Wilkins of the NAACP as observing: "Mr. Roosevelt was no friend of the Negro. He wasn't an enemy, but he wasn't a friend." And this: "The personal touches and the personal fight against discrimination were Mrs. Roosevelt's; that attached to Roosevelt also . . . and he reaped the political benefit of it."[37]

For all the perceived gains for black Americans, however, the nation was still struggling to recover economically, leaving in question the validity and effectiveness of the New Deal agenda. But politically, the Democratic Party with the Roosevelt coalition in place seemed to offer something for everyone, especially blue-collar workers, blacks and the poor. As Schlesinger later put it, a new, fourth, party system had now emerged, with a task facing FDR "to regulate and humanize the industrial economy" that from the McKinley era had over time brutalized the nation's laboring class.[38] The specter of potential emerging class warfare could readily be seen in the election's voting patterns. A Gallup poll after the 1936 election showed only 42 percent of upper-income voters had gone for Roosevelt, to 60 percent of middle-income voters and 76 percent of those in the lower brackets. Some 80 percent of union members, 81 percent of unskilled workers and 84 percent of workers on relief went Democratic.[39] The party could honestly sing that happy days were here again, and leading the chorus was the ever-smiling and charismatic man in the Oval Office.

But the happy days for Roosevelt were not to last for long. As he embarked on his second term, the threatening shadow of a Supreme Court unconvinced of the constitutionality of the New Deal hung over his plans for a more strenuous assault on the nation's social ills. "I see one-third of a nation ill-housed, ill-clad, ill-nourished," he proclaimed in his second inaugural address.[40] But he was all too aware that by the end of the Court's 1936 term it had heard nine cases dealing with the New Deal and had found seven of them unconstitutional. Three of the verdicts were by votes of 5–4 and two others by 6–3. Conferring with his attorney general, Homer Cummings, FDR decided drastic action was required.

In February 1937 the president suddenly sprang on Congress a proposal for reorganization of the Supreme Court. Contending that its workload had become too great for nine justices to handle, he called for the appointment of an additional justice for each one seventy years old or older, up to a total of six more. Roosevelt was spurred by his knowledge that the Court's four most conservative members were over seventy; his reorganization plan could wipe away the Court's roadblock to existing and future New Deal legislation. Previous presidents had changed the composition of the Supreme Court, after all, and in 1913, Attorney General James C. McReynolds, now ironically sitting on the Court at age seventy-four, had recommended precisely the same scheme to President Wilson.

Conservatives in both parties immediately objected, as well as leading progressive Senators Norris, a Republican, and Burton K. Wheeler, a Democrat. "A liberal cause was never won," Wheeler complained later, "by stacking a deck of cards, by stuffing a ballot box, or packing a court."[41] At first, Republican Party strategists, aware of the rebellion stirring in Democratic ranks, let FDR's own party carry the fight against him. This the Democratic critics did effectively, with Wheeler in the forefront.

Appearing before the Senate Judiciary Committee, he produced a surprise letter from Chief Justice Hughes that challenged Roosevelt's basic assumption. "The Supreme Court is fully abreast of its work," he wrote. "... There is no congestion of cases upon our calendar." Rather than reduce the Court's burden, he said, adding more justices would only mean "more judges to hear, more judges to confer, more judges to discuss, more judges to be convinced and to decide."[42]

Soon afterward the Court further undercut Roosevelt by upholding a state minimum wage law similar to one it had struck down a year earlier on grounds of unconstitutionality, and unanimously upheld two important New Deal bills. Later in the spring it also upheld the Wagner Act and the Social Security Act. Then, a month later, one of the four most conservative justices, seventy-eight-year-old Willis Van Devanter, announced his retirement. Aides urged Roosevelt to declare victory and withdraw his judicial reorganization proposal, but he refused.

There was more irony in the saga. Senator Joe Robinson of Arkansas, who was leading the fight for the Roosevelt plan before the Judiciary Committee, urged the president to accept a compromise of adding a limit of one justice a year for each one over age seventy-five. Robinson was personally interested in that outcome because he had been promised the Court seat to be vacated by Van Devanter. Before Robinson could bring off the compromise, he was found dead in his Capitol Hill apartment, the victim of a heart attack. Democratic senators who had pledged their support for Robinson's compromise felt their commitment no longer existed and Roosevelt's position crumbled.

In a storied account of how FDR was brought to face the music, he was said to have asked Vice President Garner, who had just polled the Senate, "How did you find the Court situation, Jack?" Garner replied: "Do you want it with the bark on or off, Cap'n?" FDR answered: "The rough way." Garner told him: "All right. You are beat. You haven't got the votes."[43] Five and a half months after Roosevelt had presented his plan, it was sent back to committee for a quiet death.

While the whole fiasco was an embarrassing, even humiliating defeat for the president, the Court had changed its view of the New Deal legislation most recently before it. And with the appointment of Senator Hugo Black to the Court to fill the Van Devanter vacancy and subsequent Roosevelt appointments, the president had a Court that was not hostile to further liberal legislation for years to come. The trouble for FDR was that after the Court fiasco, Republicans and conservative Democrats in Congress were more willing and able to undercut or block such legislation from then on. The Democratic unity of the early glory days was slipping away.

At the same time, Roosevelt was encountering other difficulties. The growth of the organized labor movement, greatly expedited by the New Deal legislation protecting and advancing collective bargaining, higher wages and shorter hours, had contributed to a dichotomy in organizational structure. The early development of craft unions, based on workers' skills and disciplines in the American Federation of Labor (AFL) of Samuel Gompers and successors, encountered organizational competition.

In 1936, John L. Lewis, head of the United Mine Workers, created a new Congress of Industrial Organizations (CIO) of unions organized not vertically by craft but horizontally across entire industries. Demands for higher wages and better working conditions produced an increasing number of strikes as CIO unions used the sit-down technique against whole plants. Workers were able to shut them down by sitting at their machines and doing nothing.

By 1937, many of these strikes in such industries as steel and automaking were marked with violence by company-employed thugs, but eventually the strikes led to negotiations and settlements that produced labor peace. The strikes, along with a new recession in late 1937 and into 1938, generated debate within the Roosevelt administration over which path to recovery should be taken—retrenchment and the pursuit of a balanced budget, or boosted federal spending to generate jobs, combat unemployment and jump-start the flagging economy.

The debate, eventually won by the proponents of emergency deficit spending, accompanied the developing split in the Democratic Party—liberals mostly in the North and the cities, conservatives mostly in the South and the towns and farmlands. Unionization was much stronger in the liberal North, capitalizing on increased black and immigrant population gains, and conservative Democrats in the South found increasing common ground with Northern Republicans against New Deal policies. FDR's aspirations of being the president of all the people in all corners of the country had by now atrophied.

A measure of Roosevelt's slippage in his own party came shortly after the Supreme Court fight. A relatively bland proposal for reorganization of the executive branch was killed in its tracks by the Democratic-controlled Congress amid conservatives' concerns that he was seeking dictatorial powers. The president was outraged and decided to show his critics within the party who was boss. To preserve or at least shore up his voting strength in Congress, Roosevelt set out in the 1938 Democratic congressional primaries to reward his friends and, if possible, remove his enemies.

The whole notion of taking an overtly partisan stance, let alone actively seeking to purge fellow Democrats, had been alien to the public Roosevelt as president up to this point. He alluded to this careful public face in a fireside chat in June launching the purge. "As President of the United States," he began, "I am not asking the voters of the country to vote for Democrats next November as opposed to Republicans or members of any other party. Nor am I, as President, taking part in the Democratic primaries."[44]

But then came the transparent contradiction: "As the head of the Democratic Party, however, charged with the responsibility of the definitely liberal declaration of principles set forth in the 1936 Democratic platform, I feel that I have every right to speak in those few instances where there may be a clear issue between candidates for a Democratic nomination involving these principles, or involving a clear misuse of my own name. Do not misunderstand me. I certainly would not indicate a preference in a State primary merely because a candidate, otherwise liberal in outlook, had conscientiously differed with me on any single issue."[45]

Farley, the loyal party man, tried to talk FDR out of the purge. Garner told the party chairman: "The Boss has stirred up a hornet's nest by getting into these primary fights. There are 20 men—Democrats—in the Senate who will vote against anything he wants because they are mad clean through, Jim. I think you ought to take exception to the President's attitude." Farley answered: "John, I just can't do that unless I resign from the Cabinet and the Democratic Committee. I don't like this purge any better than you do, but the situation won't be helped by my breaking with the Boss."[46]

The idea of a purge, as related by Nathan Miller in *FDR: An Intimate History,* had begun in late 1937 in conversations among such liberal Roosevelt insiders as Hopkins, Ickes, Benjamin Cohen, Tommy Corcoran and the president's son Jimmy. They "began meeting informally to consider methods for purging the party of conservative obstructionists and to make certain that the 1940 convention would nominate a liberal presidential candidate."[47]

In the end, the so-called purge met with failure, and instead of increasing New Deal support in the fall elections, the Republicans gained an impressive eighty-one seats in the House and eight in the Senate. As much as the purge, the clinging economic malaise that continued to resist recovery took a political toll on FDR. The results were another political black eye for the president and marked a practical hiatus in the New Deal agenda, a fact that Roosevelt recognized in his State of the Union address to Congress in January 1939. "We have now passed the period of internal conflict in the launching of our program of social reform," he said. "Our full energies may now be released to invigorate the processes of recovery in order to preserve our reforms."[48]

It could not be denied that Roosevelt's policies in his first six years had achieved revolutionary changes in the relationship between government and business, business and labor, and in the growth of a new middle class that embraced many more Americans of both genders and all races and ethnic backgrounds.

In strictly Democratic Party affairs, however, FDR's outspoken self-identification as a man above party until launching the failed purge had hardly been inducive to effective party-building or party cohesion. In shunning Jefferson Day dinners and ordering his cabinet members not to

make campaign speeches he dismissed opportunities to build party loyalty and commitment. Nor did he involve himself in party affairs at the
state and local levels, keeping hands off local feuds and corruptions, especially if the city bosses involved were in his corner. He made little concerted effort to inject his own liberalism into the bloodstream of local and
state Democratic parties, to bolster the liberal vision in the party as a
whole. Any aspirations to bring about a liberal-conservative realignment
of the parties withered accordingly.

FDR's chief political man, Farley, for all his reputation as a party mastermind, presided over a weak Democratic National Committee and was
ineffective in trying to settle intraparty squabbles in the various states. As
James MacGregor Burns noted in *Roosevelt: The Lion and the Fox,* "as a
politician eager to win, Roosevelt was concerned with his own political
and electoral standing at whatever expense to the party. It was much easier to exploit his own political skill than try to improve the rickety,
sprawling party organization."[49]

In Washington, too, two wings in the Democratic Party had evolved—
the liberal presidential and the conservative congressional, which was
effectively putting brakes on the New Deal agenda. In trying to purge
conservative congressional Democrats who were not cordial to the New
Deal, Roosevelt was not simply seeking to break the legislative stalemate;
he was trying at last to bring about that basic liberal-conservative party
realignment he sought. As the 1940 presidential election appeared on the
horizon, he wanted to be certain that his quest to make the national
Democratic Party the vehicle for a solidly liberal agenda would continue
into the future.

Almost from the start of his second term in 1937, speculation had
swirled about the chances that the dynamo from Hyde Park, to see to it
himself that the quest would go on, might buck the two-term tradition set
by George Washington. Now, with only a year to go before the parties
would begin in earnest to decide on their 1940 nominees, the great guess-
ing game intensified. When questions of his intention came up at his
White House press conferences, he would try to josh them away. One
device was to instruct reporters who raised the matter to "put on a dunce
cap and stand in a corner."[50]

In late 1938, when he named Harry Hopkins his new secretary of commerce, the move was taken by many as a way to build Hopkins up with the
business community, nervous about him as administrator of the WPA, as

a possible successor. Others, including Secretary of Agriculture Henry Wallace, Attorney General Robert Jackson and William O. Douglas, then chairman of the Securities and Exchange Commission, also were said to have been encouraged by FDR to consider running. And in January 1939, Roosevelt said he could support only a New Deal Democrat. The country, he said, "would be in a sad state if it had to choose in 1940 between a Democratic Tweedledee and a Republican Tweedledum."[51]

Through all this, the president and the nation found themselves increasingly distracted by ominous events abroad. The strange little man named Adolf Hitler who six years earlier had become chancellor of Germany was now the sole leader, the Fuehrer, and was on the march. In 1936, German troops had moved into the Rhineland; in 1938 into Austria; in March 1939 into Czechoslovakia; and, finally, on September 1 into Poland, precipitating World War II. The future of the Democratic Party suddenly seemed insignificant by comparison.

As the Nazi blitzkrieg rolled into and over Poland, the shocking development half a world away was critical in Roosevelt's deliberations about whether he should break the great American presidential tradition of self-denial that had endured since the beginning of the Republic.

Chapter 19

THE DEMOCRACY FIGHTS FASCISM, 1939–1945

PRIOR TO HITLER'S invasion of Poland, Roosevelt had given indications he intended to honor the two-term tradition and slip easily into retirement. In addition to encouraging Hopkins in early 1939 to run for the 1940 Democratic nomination, he told his secretary of state, Cordell Hull, he hoped Hull would succeed him. He appointed former Indiana Governor Paul V. McNutt head of a new Federal Security Agency to give him greater national visibility and informed Senate Majority Leader Alben W. Barkley of Kentucky that "some of the folks here at the White House" wanted him as the nominee.[1] Others close to the president also thought they were being given encouragement.

At the same time, FDR talked increasingly to intimates of his desire to return to Hyde Park to tend to his new library and "dream house" nearing completion, and to write history. In doing so, however, he did what he always had done in politics: he kept his options open by turning aside all questions about his own intentions for the 1940 election. The situation became a running tilt between FDR and the Washington press corps, to the point that the reporters at their annual Gridiron dinner produced a giant papier-mâché grinning Sphinx puffing on a long cigarette holder.

But the outbreak of World War II in Europe brought a new, serious dimension to Roosevelt's deliberations. In terms of practical domestic politics, it gave him the most persuasive rationale possible for breaking the two-term tradition. He could play the reluctant but steadfast soldier

In seeking his fourth term in 1944, FDR vowed that as commander in chief during wartime he would not engage in partisan speechmaking against Republican challenger Thomas E. Dewey. But in his first speech after renomination, he lashed out at Dewey and the GOP, causing Dewey to strike back in kind. Roosevelt thereupon resumed his lofty posture above the battle and was reelected.

who could not justifiably refuse to continue to serve in time of national crisis—that is, provided the war in Europe was clearly perceived by American voters as such a crisis, and his running for a third term was seen as a genuine draft.

Unlike Wilson in 1914, Roosevelt made no pretense of being neutral in the Second World War, nor did he urge the American people to be so. Two nights after the Nazi invasion of Poland, he told them in a fireside chat he could not "ask that every American remain neutral in thought. . . . Even a neutral cannot be asked to close his mind or his conscience."[2] At the same time, he expressed his "hope the United States will keep out of this war" and assured them that "as long as it remains within my power to prevent, there will be no black-out of peace in the United States."[3]

FDR issued a proclamation of neutrality that carried with it an immediate embargo on the sale of arms and munitions to the belligerent countries, a step required to trigger the executive's emergency powers under existing national defense legislation. But almost at once he set in motion an effort to repeal the embargo to clear the way for aid to the Allies. It was sharply opposed by isolationists in the Senate and other prominent Americans like Hoover and national hero Charles A. Lindbergh, the first man to fly solo across the Atlantic. On November 4, 1939, Congress repealed the embargo after Roosevelt accepted the condition that all arms sales be made on a cash-and-carry basis.

In all this, FDR continued to keep his own counsel about his political future. In January 1940 he signed a contract with *Collier's* magazine to be a contributing editor at $75,000 a year, his salary as president,[4] creating the impression that he planned not to run again. But he also pushed for locating the 1940 Democratic convention in Chicago, where he could be confident boss Ed Kelly would pack the galleries with pro-Roosevelt Democrats. And he dispatched political agents to key states to patch up intramural tiffs with an eye to securing convention delegations favorable to his wishes, whether for his own candidacy or that of another Roosevelt man.

In his own ranks, three men—Hull, Garner and Farley—all opposed Roosevelt breaking the two-term tradition. They continued to consider their own presidential candidacies, ostensibly if not actually encouraged by the Sphinx still holding the job. Hull at sixty-eight was willing to run but unwilling to campaign for the nomination, especially without FDR's blessing. Garner, seventy-one and critical of FDR and the New Deal, seemed more motivated by a determination to block a third term than by a desire for the presidency himself. Farley, only fifty-one, had strong presidential ambitions but was young enough to run after a third Roosevelt term, especially if his boss took him as his running mate in 1940, or even after a Hull or Garner presidency.

According to James MacGregor Burns in *Roosevelt: The Lion and the Fox*, FDR continued to encourage Hull, confident his own silence would freeze his secretary of state from any overt efforts to acquire convention delegates. He dismissed Garner with contempt, Burns wrote, noting "the once cordial relations between the two had turned sour." There was little contact between them except for cabinet meetings "where Garner, red and glowering, occasionally took issue with the President in a truculent manner."[5] As for Farley, Roosevelt strung him along, telling him he didn't intend to run for a third term, not wanting to antagonize the man who had run his two winning presidential campaigns and hoping to keep him aboard.

But Farley, and Garner, increasingly estranged from the president over the game he was playing, entered a select number of the 1940 Democratic primaries. However, wherever FDR's name was placed on the ballot without his bidding, he won overwhelmingly, with or without Farley and/or Garner running. A few states like West Virginia and Ohio chose favorite sons, but Roosevelt easily corralled enough delegates to be nominated if he decided to run, and public opinion polls also strongly favored him. By the eve of the convention, the polls were indicating more than 90 percent backing for the incumbent.

Still, FDR remained convinced that only if a third-term candidacy was widely perceived and accepted as a draft—as an offer he couldn't refuse—could he face the general electorate in the fall with confidence of victory. He was aware that the New Deal had lost much luster with conservative Democrats as well as having incurred the ire of confirmed Republicans, who would look upon a third-term bid as proof of their allegation that he was or intended to be a "dictator."

After months of hiatus in Europe known as "the phony war," Germany resumed in April 1940 with the invasion and conquest of Denmark and Norway, then the Low Countries in May and finally France in June. The fearful events triggered a Roosevelt request to Congress for more than a billion dollars in additional military spending, including a call for the production of fifty thousand aircraft a year. With it, FDR's rationale for a third term acquired stronger impetus, but still he said nothing about his plans, building further interest and pressure for his nomination while boxing in Hull, Garner and Farley.

On the Republican side, the intensified opposition to New Deal policies, the political potential of the third-term issue if Roosevelt were to run again and the absence of a dominant Democratic contender if he didn't, all generated a large field of presidential aspirants. With the candidates relying more on internal party strengths than on the primaries to demonstrate support, there were direct contests involving major hopefuls in only two states, Nebraska and Wisconsin. In both, New York City's anti-racketeering crusader, thirty-eight-year-old District Attorney Thomas E. Dewey, the leader in the polls and an internationalist, defeated Senator Arthur H. Vandenberg of Michigan, a strong isolationist. The result not only boosted Dewey's stock; it raised that of Senator Robert A. Taft of Ohio, fifty-year-old son of the former president, with the party's isolationist wing. Dewey also won primaries in New Jersey, Pennsylvania, Maryland and Illinois without major opposition, and Taft carried his home state of Ohio.

Not represented either in the survey findings or primary results was a fourth figure who finally appeared at 3 percent in the Gallup Poll in early May. A utilities lawyer from Indiana named Wendell L. Willkie had won a reputation as a spokesman for private enterprise in fighting the TVA and as president of the Commonwealth and Southern Corporation. His appearance on the national stage had come only a week or so earlier on the popular radio show *Information Please*. With a well-financed and well-managed campaign he soon climbed to 29 percent in the same poll, while Dewey was dropping from a high of 67 percent to 47. Heading into the Republican convention in Philadelphia in late June, the nomination contest was considered a fight between internationalist Dewey and isolationist Taft. Newcomer Willkie, championed by *Time* magazine publisher Henry R. Luce, was still a long shot but gaining grassroots support.

Only days before the GOP convention, Roosevelt made a dramatic move to give a more bipartisan coloration to his administration. He sought to bring into his cabinet two of the most prominent Republicans, 1936 presidential nominee Alfred Landon and his running mate, Frank Knox. Knox agreed to come aboard as secretary of the navy but Landon, while approving of FDR's bipartisan approach, indicated he could join only if the president agreed to remove "the greatest stumbling block of all"—by declining to seek a third term.[6] This Roosevelt was not prepared to do. Instead, he appointed Henry L. Stimson, late of the cabinets of Taft and Hoover, as secretary of war.

The news jolted the assembled Republicans in Philadelphia as they undertook the task of selecting their nominee. They focused both on the New Deal and Roosevelt's possible bid for a third term. The principal convention speech by Hoover told the delegates "we must recall our people from the flabbiness of the New Deal" and announced that "we Republicans welcome Mr. Roosevelt as a candidate. For this battle must be fought out under the guns of debate. And that debate will be done best with the man who is responsible for it."[7]

As expected, Dewey led through the first three ballots, but with the galleries loudly rooting for and then demanding Willkie, he took the lead on the fourth ballot with Dewey fading to third place behind Taft. On the sixth roll call, most of Michigan's delegation switched to Willkie and put him over the top in one of the greatest upsets in convention history. Senator Charles L. McNary of Oregon, the state's favorite-son candidate for president, was picked by Willkie to be his running mate and was nominated.

Roosevelt followed the Republican convention with interest and had the luxury of awaiting its selection before proceeding with his own plans. Willkie had emerged from Philadelphia greatly strengthened by the dramatic nature of his victory, and he offered the political virtue of being a fresh and exciting face on the political stage. Almost to the eve of the Democratic convention, opening in Chicago on July 15, Roosevelt continued to play games with Hull and Farley. On July 3 he had lunch with Hull, and while repeating his intention not to run, spoke sufficiently about the pressures he faced to do so to convince his secretary of state that he was going to seek a third term.

Four days later, Farley went to Hyde Park for lunch with the president, and the showdown that was inevitable. After a jovial meal, the two men retreated to the library for a private conversation. According to varying accounts in the works of Burns, Frank Freidel and Nathan Miller, Roosevelt informed Farley that the international crisis had finally persuaded him against his intentions not to run, and that it was his duty now to make himself available.

"Jim," the president was reported to have said, "I don't want to run and I'm going to tell the convention so." Farley declined to fold. "If you make it specific," he shot back, according to these accounts, "the convention will not nominate you."[8] He then reiterated his opposition to a third term on principle. There were other good Democrats available, he said, and if the president stepped aside one of them would be nominated. "What would you do in my place?" FDR asked him. "Exactly what General Sherman did many years ago," Farley replied. "Issue a statement saying I would refuse to run and would not serve if elected." Roosevelt answered: "Jim, if nominated and elected, I could not in these times refuse to take the inaugural oath, even if I knew I would be dead within thirty days."[9]

It was clear from all this that Roosevelt's mind was made up, and that his decision would not deter the bitter Farley from having his own name placed in nomination, even though he knew it would be a fruitless gesture. The talk turned to running mates, with several names mentioned but not Farley's. When FDR included Henry Wallace, Farley reminded him that the secretary of agriculture had the image of being "a wild-eyed fellow," but Roosevelt said nothing in reply. Instead, he said only that "the man running with me must be in good health, because there is no telling how long I can hold out. You know, Jim, a man with paralysis can have a breakup at any time. . . . Nothing in this life is certain."[10]

Farley left for Chicago the next day, more committed than ever not to stand by while the charade of an orchestrated draft took place unopposed. As national party chairman, he opened the convention, thanked party workers for the Democratic successes of the past under his chairmanship and praised the administration—without mentioning Roosevelt by name. That was left to Senate Majority Leader Barkley, who ignited a noisy and lengthy floor demonstration when he did pronounce the magic name. Resuming his speech, he closed with a message to the convention "at the specific request and authorization of the President." He read: "The President has never had, and has not today, any desire or purpose to continue in the office of President, to be a candidate for that office, or to be nominated by the convention for that office." The convention delegates listened in hushed silence as Barkley continued: "He wishes in all earnestness and sincerity to make it clear that all of the delegates to this convention are free to vote for any candidate. That is the message I bear to you from the President of the United States."[11]

The convention hall continued in silence for another moment, as delegates pondered the message. Then Ed Kelly's men poured into the aisles, chanting, "We want Roosevelt!" As Barkley hoisted a portrait of FDR over his head, the loudspeakers in the hall suddenly boomed out: "Chicago wants Roosevelt!... Illinois wants Roosevelt!... New York wants Roosevelt!... America wants Roosevelt!"[12] Delegates grabbed their state banners and began a parade through the aisles, and the booming voice was heard again: "Roosevelt! Roosevelt! Roosevelt!" with the delegations shouting along with it. In the basement of the convention hall, Kelly's superintendent of sewers, Thomas D. McGarry, was at the microphone lustily carrying out the assignment from his boss. Henceforth this Chicago minion was known as "the voice from the sewer" that had triggered the FDR "draft."[13]

The balloting was a mere formality, with the president receiving 946 votes to 72 for Farley, 61 for Garner including the full Texas delegation, 9 for Senator Millard E. Tydings, Maryland's favorite son, and 5 for Hull. Only after the roll call, which Roosevelt had hoped would be avoided, did the still-bitter but party loyalist Farley move to declare the president renominated by acclamation.

With Garner off the ticket, the convention moved on to what in both parties had usually been routine, the selection of the vice-presidential nominee. But many delegates were in a disgruntled mood, feeling they had been mere pawns in the presidential nomination. The convention adjourned until the next afternoon. Meanwhile, FDR notified his chief agent at the convention, Harry Hopkins, and other party leaders that, with Hull refusing his offer, he wanted as his running mate Wallace, a reliable liberal who would bring strength to the ticket in the farm belt. Many of the leaders protested, calling Wallace a "mystic," a fuzzy thinker and, especially for the conservatives, too much a New Dealer. But Roosevelt told speechwriter Sam Rosenman: "I won't deliver the acceptance speech until we see whom they nominate."[14]

Rejecting suggestions that he himself go to Chicago, the president persuaded his wife, Eleanor, to fly there to help quell what was shaping up as a revolt. The first thing she did on arrival was to dissuade their son Elliott, a Texas delegate, from putting the name of Texas financier Jesse Jones in nomination, to save his father great embarrassment. But supporters of Farley and Garner, still resentful, attacked Wallace and proposed House Speaker William B. Bankhead for the second spot.

When the convention was called to order that night, a host of names was placed in nomination, including Wallace, Bankhead, Jones, Paul McNutt, Sam Rayburn, Senator Scott Lucas of Illinois and Governor Alva

B. Adams of Colorado. Vice-presidential nominations often were made as mere gestures of respect, with the presidential nominee then making his choice known, to be rubber-stamped by the delegates. But this time it was different. Word having spread that Wallace was Roosevelt's choice, most of the men nominated dropped out, but not Bankhead and McNutt.

Hopkins, from his command post at the Blackstone Hotel, called the White House and told Rosenman: "There is going to be a cat-and-dog fight, but I think that the Boss has enough friends here to put it over." Informed of this report, Roosevelt growled: "Well, damn it to hell, they will go for Wallace or I won't run, and you can jolly well tell them so."[15] The president, playing solitaire at his desk, took pad and pencil and began to write. When he was finished he handed the written sheets to Rosenman and told him: "Sam, take this inside and go to work on it; smooth it out and get it ready for delivery. I may have to deliver it very quickly, so please hurry it up."[16]

Rosenman went out with FDR's secretary, Missy LeHand, and General Edwin "Pa" Watson, his military aide, closely behind. Outside the Oval Office, they read what he had written—a note to the convention delegates telling them that inasmuch as "certain influences pledged to reaction in domestic affairs and to appeasement in foreign affairs have been heavily engaged behind the scenes in the promotion of discord since this convention convened. . . . I cannot in all honor and will not . . . go along with the cheap bargaining and political maneuvering which have brought about party dissension in this convention. . . . It would be best not to straddle ideals. It would be best for America to have the fight out. Therefore, I give the Democratic party the opportunity to make that historic decision. . . . By declining the honor of the nomination for the presidency, I can restore that opportunity to the Convention. I so do."[17]

Watson was beside himself. "Sam, give that damned piece of paper to me," he said to Rosenman. "Let's tear it up. He's all excited in there now—and he'll be sorry about it in the morning. Besides, the country needs him. I don't give a damn who's vice president and neither does the country. The only thing that's important to this country is that fellow in there. There isn't anyone in the United States who can lead this nation for the next four years as well as he can." Rosenman replied: "Pa, I hope he never has to read this speech, but if I know that man inside, he's going to read it if Bankhead gets this nomination, and nobody on earth is going to be able to stop him."[18]

Rosenman wrote later: "Pa Watson was almost in tears, and looked at me angrily for bringing the sheets back [to FDR]. I suppose he had hoped I would run off with them and hide—as if that would have stopped the President. All of us except Missy were opposed to this course and told the President so. But if I ever saw him with his mind made up it was that night."[19]

At the convention hall, meanwhile, Roosevelt agents pressed delegates to go along with the president. When McNutt's name was formally placed in nomination, he asked permission to address the convention and also withdrew, amid catcalls and hisses from the anti-Wallace galleries. Roosevelt, McNutt said, "is my commander in chief. I follow his wishes, and I am here to support his choice for Vice President of the United States." He did not mention Wallace by name. Lucas also pulled out, saying that in light of the demonstrations in the aisles and galleries insisting that FDR "be drafted to run for a third term," and Roosevelt's choice of Wallace, "we should respect his request, because after all, Roosevelt is the individual who is going to carry the load."[20] Seconding speeches for Wallace from labor leader Philip Murray and Rayburn made clear a move was on by the FDR loyalists to assure that the president would have his way.

Mrs. Roosevelt herself capped the effort with an appeal to the delegates, also without naming Wallace, to give her husband a strong right hand in the approaching campaign as he faced presidential burdens increased by the world crisis. "So each and every one of you who give him this responsibility," she declared in her high-pitched voice, "in giving it to him, assume for yourselves a very grave responsibility because you will make the campaign. You will have to rise above considerations which are narrow and partisan. . . . This is no ordinary time, no time for thinking about anything except what we can best do for the country as a whole."[21] The delegates bought the argument and her husband never had to send his message rejecting his own renomination. On the roll call immediately after her speech, Wallace received 626 votes, a clear majority, to 329 for Bankhead and 68 for McNutt despite his withdrawal.

Later that night, Roosevelt addressed the convention by radio as a spotlight shone on a huge picture of him hanging from the rafters. Forgotten were his threats to walk away in a huff, and instead he draped himself in self-sacrificing patriotism. "Lying awake, as I have on many nights," he said, "I have asked myself whether I have the right, as Commander in Chief of the Army and Navy, to call men and women to serve their country or train themselves to serve, and at the same time decline to serve my country in my own personal capacity, if I am called upon to do so by the people of my country.... Today, all private plans, all private lives, have been in a sense repealed by an overriding public danger."²² In spite of his own private plans for retirement, he concluded, "my conscience will not let me turn my back on a call to service." Wallace, the center of the storm just quelled, was not offered the opportunity to express his thanks for his own nomination to the delegates who had had him forced on them.

The Roosevelt "draft" had achieved the ultimate end, but not without cost. The resistance of Garner, Farley and their supporters robbed the event of spontaneity, and the manner of Wallace's selection left many delegates bitter. Republican allegations of "dictatorship" were reinforced by the whole business, and by FDR's third-term bid, undiminished as a GOP argument against him by his rationale that he could not as a patriot stand aside in a period of world crisis.

With the nomination nevertheless safely in hand, Roosevelt turned to the pressing matter of providing all possible aid to England, now under wicked air assaults from the German Luftwaffe, which had debilitated its destroyer fleet. On July 31, Prime Minister Winston Churchill cabled FDR asking for reinforcements through the transfer of old American destroyers. After Willkie complained only that Congress and the public had not been consulted, Roosevelt sent fifty such destroyers to England in a deal that gave the United States ninety-nine-year leases on bases in Newfoundland and the Caribbean. Willkie also went along with a military draft, passed by Congress in August. Such bipartisan cooperation went a way toward reducing foreign policy as a campaign issue, but not entirely and only for a time.

Roosevelt clearly saw his role as commander in chief, rather than as defender of the New Deal, as his strongest argument for defying the two-term tradition. Deftly, he adopted what in the hands of later presidents would come to be known as a "Rose Garden strategy"—staying home and attending to presidential business in lieu of hitting the campaign trail, which by now was more generally accepted by the public. He left stumping for liberal and Democratic votes to Wallace, while installing Ed Flynn as chairman of the national party still split between its liberal presidential and conservative congressional wings. Roosevelt declined to debate Willkie and left it to his acerbic secretary of interior, Harold Ickes, to chide his opponent as "a simple, barefoot Wall Street lawyer,"[23] while the president himself focused on the emerging threat of war.

In September he was obliged to cast an eye on Asia as well as Europe when the Japanese military, with designs on foreign colonies on the continent, took over a relatively moderate government and joined in a tripartite treaty with Germany and Italy. Such developments, FDR explained in his speech accepting his third nomination, would keep him off the campaign trail. "Events move so fast in other parts of the world that it has become my duty to remain either at the White House itself," he said, "or at some nearby point where I can reach Washington and even Europe and Asia by direct telephone, where if need be I can be back at my desk in a space of a very few hours. . . . I shall not have the time or the inclination to engage in purely political debate."[24]

Meanwhile, newcomer Willkie plunged into the fray, whistle-stopping by train across the country, catching the wave of his convention upset and the imagination of voters with his down-to-earth appearance and speaking style. A former Democrat who in 1924 had been a delegate to the party's convention, had voted for FDR in 1932 and as recently as 1938 was calling himself a Democrat, he was a far cry from the old Republican conservative stereotype typified by Hoover. He had been an early supporter of the New Deal before winning fame in the business community with his opposition to the TVA. This history in part obliged Willkie to focus his attack on Roosevelt as a reacher for dictatorial power in bidding for a third term, while failing to restore the economy to health or rearming the country adequately against the threat from fascism abroad. Posters showing Uncle Sam with his thumb down proclaimed: "No Third Term! Democrats for Willkie."

Big and burly, unkempt in comparison to the aristocratic bearing and manner of the squire from Hyde Park, Willkie also offered a contrasting persona to the president, whom he called "The Champ" without a trace of being intimidated. Booth Tarkington described him as "a man wholly natural in manner, a man with no pose, no 'swellness,' no condescension, no clever plausibleness . . . as American as the courthouse yard in the square of an Indiana county seat."[25] But Willkie was no country bumpkin. He worked out of a high-powered New York office and had traveled widely. He was a worthy adversary for Roosevelt, as the polls over the summer indicated.

Yet on the stump he was prone to wild, erratic and impolitic remarks, drawing much heckling from audiences and causing his strong standing in the polls to slip as the campaign unfolded. His slide persuaded him to toughen his stand on FDR's policies toward the war. He finally predicted that if the president were reelected, the country would be a combatant within months. Despite his earlier support of the destroyer deal, he was persuaded by isolationist Vandenberg to denounce it as "the most arbitrary and dictatorial action ever taken by any President in the history of the United States."[26]

At a speech in Joliet, Illinois, he accused FDR of having been an appeaser, charging that "Roosevelt telephoned Mussolini and Hitler and urged them to sell Czechoslovakia down the river at Munich,"[27] only to say later he had misspoken. And in Boston on October 11, he declared that if elected "we shall not undertake to fight anybody else's war. Our boys shall stay out of European wars."[28] Such statements caused his poll numbers to move up again, and to heighten concern in the FDR camp sufficiently to pull the president out of his White House political sanctuary.

In his acceptance speech, Roosevelt had attached a caveat to his statement that he would not engage in purely political debate. "But I shall never be loath to call the attention of the nation," he said, "to deliberate or unwitting falsifications of fact, which are sometimes made by political candidates."[29] Now, in mid-October, concerned about Willkie's climb, he announced he would respond in five campaign speeches, and he took to the stump with his old zest. "I am an old campaigner," he proclaimed to wild cheering in Philadelphia, "and I love a good fight!"[30]

The week before the election at Madison Square Garden, he took on three prominent Republicans who had voted against repeal of the arms embargo and other national defense bills, rhythmically and playfully chiding their names, "Martin, Barton and Fish," until the audience joined in at each chanting reference. The litany became a staple crowd-pleaser in every FDR speech thereafter.

More important, Roosevelt's strategists felt he had to deal more directly with Willkie and his allegation that if the president were reelected he would take the country into the war. Up to this point FDR had always, in denying such intention, included the cautionary words "except in case of attack." Urged by the advisers to drop the phrase, he agreed, and in the Boston speech he declared flatly: "I have said this before, but I shall say it again and again and again: 'Your boys are not going to be sent into foreign wars.' " (When Rosenman before delivery noted the absence of the conditional phrase, FDR replied: "Of course, we'll fight if we're attacked. If somebody attacks us, then it isn't a foreign war, is it?")[31]

After that, Willkie was finished and he knew it. "When I heard the President hang the isolationist votes of Martin, Barton and Fish on me and get away with it," he said later, "I knew I was licked."[32] And as he heard FDR's pledge not to send Americans to war, he was reported to have said to his brother: "That hypocritical son of a bitch! This is going to beat me."[33]

Whatever the voters' specific motivations and qualms about a third term, they elected Roosevelt to it by a popular margin of 27 million votes to 22 million for Willkie, and by 449 electoral votes to only 82 for the likable, rumpled man from Indiana. Once again, the Democratic cities across the country came through for FDR, including millions of lower-income voters still effectively courted by, and believing in, the policies of the New Deal. Willkie accepted defeat graciously. Roosevelt's percentage had dropped from 60.8 percent in 1936 to 54.8 percent, with defections from Democratic ranks among voters of German, Italian and Irish roots resulting from FDR's pro-British policies, but his vote generally remained a strong statement of confidence in him. The threat of war, and an economy showing some signs of recovery at last, overshadowed fears of dictatorship in a third term that Willkie and the Republican Party had sought to nurture.

Now Roosevelt was free to pursue his determination to aid the Allies in whatever ways he could, short of American entry into the war. In January 1941 he asked Congress to enact a law whereby he would be authorized to lend, lease, sell or give all manner of war matériel to the "government of any country whose defense the President deems vital to the defense of the United States."[34] Republican isolationists immediately jumped on the proposal and Democratic Senator Burton Wheeler joined in, calling it "the New Deal's triple A foreign policy." Comparing it to a New Deal farm conservation program, he said "it will plow under every fourth American boy."[35] Despite such opposition, it passed in March, and FDR proclaimed that "our country has determined to do its full part in creating an adequate arsenal of democracy."[36]

Implied in the act was American cooperation in seeing that the matériel arrived safely across the Atlantic. The German regime responded by extending to the coast of Greenland the North Atlantic war zone in which all shipping was subject to attack. This step, in turn, led to a U.S.

agreement with the Danish government-in-exile to station American troops on the huge icebound island, accompanied by American air and sea patrols. Roosevelt's declaration of "an unlimited national emergency" in late May sent Americans to Iceland as well, a move strenuously opposed by Taft as beyond the president's constitutional powers.[37]

The sense of emergency was heightened the next month. Germany, which had entered into a nonaggression pact with the Soviet Union in advance of the Nazi invasion of Poland and was stymied in its designs on Great Britain, suddenly marched into Russia. In mid-July, Japan invaded Indochina and occupied Saigon. FDR froze Japanese assets in the United States and embargoed extremely vital oil shipments to the island empire. Negotiations bogged down over Japan's designs on China, and relations between the United States and Japan steadily disintegrated.

In August, Roosevelt and Churchill met on American and British warships off the coast of Newfoundland and drew up an Atlantic Charter avowing shared objectives for a postwar world. In September, when a German submarine fired on an American destroyer, Roosevelt ordered the navy to shoot on sight any German ships in the American neutrality zone, and after further armed encounters Congress approved of arming U.S. merchant ships. But there hardly was overwhelming support for FDR's war policies there; renewal of the military draft was approved in the House by only a single vote.

In mid-October, General Hideki Tojo, leader of the Japanese war party, took power in Tokyo. A cloud of impending war in the Pacific gathered and finally broke on December 7 with a massive Japanese attack on the American fleet anchored at Pearl Harbor, Hawaii. The fleet was decimated in the worst naval disaster in American history: 265 planes and 2,403 Americans lost and 1,178 wounded. The blow rocked the country, although Roosevelt himself knew the severity of the situation in advance and had alerted American forces in the Pacific. Roosevelt went before Congress the next day and reported on the events of "a date which will live in infamy," concluding with a request that Congress declare since "the unprovoked and dastardly attack by Japan" that "a state of war has existed between the United States and the Japanese Empire."[38]

Three days later the other Axis powers, Germany and Italy, declared war on the United States and Congress reciprocated. A huge national mobilization began under FDR's direct leadership, with more than $100 billion in war contracts placed in the first six months. The economic recovery long sought blossomed virtually overnight as employment soared with the tremendous new demands for production of war goods. Old New Deal agencies geared to spark recovery, such as the Civilian Conservation Corps and the WPA, fell away as new agencies to direct the wartime buildup at home and abroad took their places. Predictably, inflation climbed as the production of domestic goods diminished sharply and the demand increased. War bond sales helped keep prices down somewhat, but price controls inevitably were required.

Although most Americans were against entry into the war up to Pearl Harbor, that sentiment vanished in the wake of the attack. In the new solidarity, investigations of subversives were undertaken, but without the freewheeling extremes exhibited in the Mitchell Palmer era of World War I. A deplorable exception was the internment of more than 100,000 Japanese-Americans from their homes on the Pacific Coast. At the same time, 6.5 million women were brought into the work force for the first time and job opportunities for blacks also rose.

Yet Roosevelt and the Democratic Party received no notable political boost from the advent of the war. The first months and years brought a stream of military setbacks or stalemates, along with dissatisfactions over prices, housing at home and labor strikes. Liberal Democrats groused over FDR's resumption of a nonpartisan posture as the wartime leader, inviting Republican businessmen into his administration and diminishing the party's image as an engine for social reform. In his State of the Union address of 1941, he did talk of the "Four Freedoms," the third of which was "freedom from want," addressing the plight of the New Deal's constituency of the poor. But in the 1942 congressional elections he called for "an end to politics" and did little or nothing to help Democratic candidates.[39]

In a low Democratic turnout, the Republicans gained forty-seven seats in the House and ten in the Senate, facing Roosevelt with the most conservative Congress of his presidency and raising GOP hopes of regaining the White House, whether the war was still on or not, in 1944. Still, Roosevelt more conspicuously than ever distanced himself from a clear partisan posture. In a press conference in December 1943, he declared that he was no longer "Dr. New Deal," and had become "Dr. Win-the-War."[40]

The Allied decision to pursue victory over the Nazis in Europe before dealing with the Japanese required a painful and frustrating holding action in the Pacific, where American forces bore the heaviest responsibility. Lack of progress there produced political impatience at home. But American support of the war never flagged in the nearly four years required to bring victory on both fronts, with Roosevelt in command along with Churchill and their suspicious partner, Joseph Stalin, almost to the end.

After the 1942 congressional elections, the conservatives in Congress continued a piecemeal dismantling of New Deal social agencies. Congress abandoned the National Resources Planning Board in the spring of 1943 and passed the Smith-Connally Act providing new powers for the federal government to act against unions in labor disputes. Roosevelt rationalized the trend, saying in a December press conference that the New Deal had been effective in coping with earlier domestic needs but "at the present time, obviously, the principal emphasis, the overwhelming first emphasis, should be on winning the war."[41]

In his State of the Union address to Congress in January 1944, he proclaimed an "Economic Bill of Rights" to be ensured through expanded social programs, but the reality of the war made it mostly rhetoric. This shift was understandable to FDR's liberal Democratic constituents, but many of them felt he could have done more on the domestic front without sacrifice to the war effort. They were disappointed with his failure to do much for the advancement of the civil rights of blacks, and with his seeming indifference to the plight of Jews in Europe, especially as the scope of their persecution at Nazi hands became better known. Some found solace in the views of Vice President Wallace, who spoke of "the century of the common man,"[42] and others looked to Willkie, whose old liberal colors were now being flown more conspicuously, often in harmony with the Democratic president.

But overall, Roosevelt remained solidly in command politically as the tide of the war began to turn. The Allied invasions of North Africa, Sicily and Italy, the fall of Mussolini and of Rome, and the heavy aerial bombing of Germany gave evidence of tangible progress on the European front. Major naval victories and a steady approach among unfamiliar islands in the Pacific did the same in the war against Japan. Allied diplomats met in Moscow in October 1943 and approved a declaration affirming the need for an international organization to maintain peace after the war. A month later, Roosevelt, Churchill and Stalin held a summit in Teheran to discuss the fate of Germany in the postwar world. And in June 1944,

Allied morale soared with successful landings on the beaches of Normandy.

Through all this, Willkie, by virtue of having been the Republican Party's 1940 presidential nominee, remained its titular head. And despite his liberal positions, in 1944 he set out to capture the nomination again. But with little residual support from party leaders, most of them much more conservative than he, Willkie fell by the wayside. In the most important Republican primary, in Wisconsin, he embarrassingly ran behind not only Dewey, making his second bid for the nomination, but also General Douglas MacArthur and former Governor Harold E. Stassen of Minnesota, and withdrew. Dewey, now only forty-two and having risen to the governorship of New York, was easily nominated on the first ballot at the GOP convention in Chicago in late June. Governor John W. Bricker of Ohio, a conservative, was chosen to balance the ticket.

Willkie, who had repaired his differences with Roosevelt after the 1940 election, entertained thoughts, as did Roosevelt, about party realignment, with liberals in one camp and conservatives in the other. In June he sent liberal Republican Gifford Pinchot, who shared Willkie's dissatisfaction with the conservative wing's isolationism and resistance to change at home, to discuss the possibility with the president. Afterward, Roosevelt told Rosenman: "I agree with him [Willkie] 100 percent and the time is now—right after the election. We ought to have two real parties— one liberal and the other conservative. As it is now, each party is split with dissenters.... We can do it in 1948.... From the liberals of both parties Willkie and I together can form a new, really liberal party in America."[43] But no post-election meeting ever took place; Willkie died in October.

The Democrats, also meeting in Chicago in mid-July, nominated Dr. Win-the-War with no opposition. He dropped the pretenses of 1940 and sent a letter a week before the convention opened, saying he was willing to offer himself one more time. "For myself, I do not want to run," he wrote to Bob Hannegan, who had succeeded Ed Flynn as the national party chairman. "...But as a good soldier...I will accept and serve."[44] The third-term bugaboo having been shattered four years earlier, there was no appreciable objection to Roosevelt staying in office for a fourth, with the job of winning the war unfinished. At sixty-two he was clearly in failing health and looked gaunt after doctors had urged him to lose weight, but by this time he was as close to being the indispensable man as could have been found.

Governor Robert S. Kerr of Oklahoma, the convention's temporary chairman, disposed of the Republican charge that FDR was "a tired old man" by asking: "What would Churchill and Stalin and the Generalissimo [China's Chiang Kai-shek] and the allied leaders think when they learned that he [Dewey] looked upon them as just a group of 'tired old men'?"[45] On the only roll call, Roosevelt received 1,086 votes, to 89 for Senator Harry F. Byrd of Virginia in a Southern gesture of continuing disenchantment with the New Deal, and one for the all-but-forgotten Farley.

The theme of "Don't change horses in the middle of the stream" was pervasive regarding the president, but it did not hold for Vice President Wallace. He drew opposition not only from Southern delegates for his liberal views; many within the FDR inner circle thought he would hurt the Democratic ticket and, aware more than others of the president's declining health, did not want to see Wallace remain a heartbeat from the presidency. Included in this group were city bosses Flynn of the Bronx and Kelly of Chicago, party treasurer Edwin Pauley, Postmaster General Frank Walker, Hannegan, presidential military aide Pa Watson and FDR's press secretary, Steve Early.

In perhaps what proved to be the most significant decision on a running mate up to that time, the opposition to keeping Wallace on the ticket had been at least a year in the making. George Allen, a Roosevelt poker companion and self-described confidant, in his book, *Presidents Who Have Known Me*, described California oil man Pauley as "the Sir Galahad of the righteous band that set out to beat Wallace" in "a conspiracy of the pure in heart."[46] Pauley, Allen wrote, toured the country raising money and urging local party leaders to "mention to Roosevelt, when the opportunities presented themselves, that the Democratic ticket would suffer seriously from the presence of Wallace on it in the 1944 campaign." Then Pauley conspired with Pa Watson to see that these anti-Wallace Democrats got to see Roosevelt when they were in Washington.[47]

In January 1944, Pauley, Hannegan, Walker and Flynn met with Roosevelt and suggested names to him. The first was Senator James F. Byrnes of South Carolina, who had been considered as FDR's running mate in 1940, appointed by him to the Supreme Court and finally coaxed off it to be director of war mobilization. Others on the group's list were Supreme Court Justice William O. Douglas, former Senator Sherman Minton of Indiana, House Speaker Sam Rayburn of Texas and Senators Alben Barkley of Kentucky and Harry S. Truman of Missouri.

Flynn objected to Byrnes on grounds that as a Deep Southerner he would be anathema to Northern blacks and liberals, and would be poison to Catholics because he had left the faith and become a Protestant. Labor would also be opposed, Flynn said, because as war mobilization boss Byrnes had blocked wage demands. According to Allen, "it was the consensus of the conferees that Truman would be the best bet, all things considered. He was making a respected name for himself as chairman of a committee policing war contracts; he was a loyal New Dealer but not a radical; he was from a mid-continental state. The President himself was favorably impressed with Truman's qualifications and said so."[48] But FDR, though high on Byrnes, kept his own counsel, and Truman was saying he wasn't interested.

Meanwhile, Wallace, hoping to stay on the ticket, traveled to the Soviet Union and the Far East building his credentials while an aide, Harold Young, shopped around for delegate support. By this time, Roosevelt had said the convention would be free to make its own choice on a running mate, but given FDR's insistence on Wallace in 1940, that statement did not earn much credibility.

On the night of July 11, eight days before the opening of the Democratic convention, the four conspirators, plus Allen and later John Boettiger, the president's son-in-law, met with Roosevelt upstairs at the White House. A process of elimination took place, according to Allen, first dropping Byrnes and then Barkley because he was older than FDR. The president spoke highly of Douglas for having "a kind of Boy Scout quality," Allen wrote later, and because the president thought "he played an interesting game of poker"![49] But others said Douglas lacked sufficient public support.

That left Truman. Roosevelt praised him, saying he had approved his appointment as chairman of the Senate watchdog committee on defense contracts, and had never regretted the choice. But FDR expressed concern about Truman's age, which he thought was close to sixty, compared to Douglas, who was not yet fifty. In fact, Truman had turned sixty just two months earlier.

Hannegan, also from Missouri and close to Truman, and Pauley, also for him, tried to change the subject of Truman's age, but Roosevelt insisted that his son-in-law find a copy of the *Congressional Directory* to check it. When Boettiger returned with the book, Pauley took it from him and held it closed on his lap. FDR seemed to get the message. According to Allen, he turned to Hannegan and said: "Bob, I think you and everyone else here want Truman."[50] Pauley quickly got up and hustled himself and the other conspirators out of the room before FDR could insist on checking Truman's age and change his mind. On the way out, Roosevelt took Walker aside and, referring to Byrnes, said: "Frank, will you go over tomorrow and tell Jimmy that it's Truman, and that I'm sorry it has to be that way?"[51]

Downstairs, Walker suggested to Hannegan, according to Allen, that "he go back and get Roosevelt's implied approval of Truman in writing.... Hannegan did go back on the pretext of getting his coat ... and got a one-line note penciled on the back of an envelope. It said, 'Bob, I think Truman is the right man. FDR.' " The President promised Hannegan he would provide him a more formal letter expressing his choice.[52]

All those present were aware of Roosevelt's failing health to the point that Allen said they all knew in their hearts that he would not live through another term. Yet the decision was based entirely on the political consideration of which man would most help or hurt the ticket, not which of them would make the best president with the future of the country still at stake in the war. Truman was originally a farmer with only a high school education who had taken some law courses at night, served as a field artillery captain in World War I, and run a failed haberdashery afterward. He was a product of the Tom Pendergast machine in Kansas City who ran, won, lost and then won again for judge of Jackson County before winning his U.S. Senate seat. He was reelected in 1940 with the help of Hannegan, who at that time was boss of the Democratic machine in St. Louis.

Right after the July 11 meeting, Rosenman and Ickes also weighed in against Wallace, and Roosevelt asked Rosenman to break the bad news to his vice president. But Wallace said he would bow out only if FDR personally ordered him to do so. He appealed directly to Roosevelt, reporting that his aide had lined up nearly three hundred delegates for him and that a new Gallup poll would show that 65 percent of Democratic voters wanted him renominated. Roosevelt, still unable to bring himself to tell Wallace to get off the ticket, said, according to Allen, that he hoped to keep "the same team again" and would so inform the convention of his personal preference.

As a result, FDR wrote Senator Samuel Jackson of Indiana, slated to be the convention's permanent chairman, stating his long relationship with Wallace and concluding: "I like him and I respect him and he is my personal friend. For these reasons I personally would vote for his renomination if I were a delegate to the convention. At the same time, I do not wish to appear in any way as dictating to the Convention. Obviously the Convention will do the deciding."[53] It was hardly what could be called a ringing endorsement; it was more like a political kiss of death.

Roosevelt then wrote the letter requested by Hannegan, but what he wrote was not what he had jotted down on that envelope. Instead, it mentioned not simply Truman but also Douglas, adding: "I should, of course, be very glad to run with either of them and believe that either one of them would bring real strength to the ticket. Always sincerely, Franklin Roosevelt."[54] With Hannegan holding the letter privately, supporters of Douglas spread a story that FDR had actually written their man's name before Truman's, and that Hannegan was dismayed because the inclusion of Douglas's name, particularly coming before Truman's, might suggest that Douglas was the president's real preference.

Meanwhile, Byrnes remained under the impression that Roosevelt wanted him, in spite of Hannegan's report that Flynn's objections had cooled off the president. Byrnes wrote later in his autobiography, *All in One Lifetime,* that he called FDR, who told him "you are the best qualified man in the whole outfit and you must not get out of the race. If you stay in, you are sure to win."[55] If so, Roosevelt had now expressed his preference for four men—Wallace, Truman, Douglas and Byrnes. In a second call, Byrnes wrote, FDR told him it was Hannegan and Walker who had said Truman or Douglas would be the safest choice, not him, and he had never said he preferred either. That was good enough for Byrnes. He phoned Hopkins, told him he was running and that the man he was going to ask to place his name in nomination was—Harry Truman! As Truman was quoted later in Merle Miller's oral biography, Byrnes said, " 'Harry, the old man is backing me; I'm going to be the Vice Presidential nominee. Will you make the nominating speech?' I [Truman] said that I'd be happy to."[56]

The next day, according to Byrnes, Kelly called him from Chicago and told him that FDR, reassured by Kelly that Byrnes would not hurt him with the black vote, "has given us the green light to support you and he wants you in Chicago," and Roosevelt had said: "Well, you know Jimmy has been my choice from the very first. Go ahead and name him."[57]

But the president also had said four other words that changed the course of presidential history. He told Hannegan he had better "clear it with Sidney"—Sidney Hillman, president of the Amalgamated Clothing

Workers of America, organizer of the CIO's new political action committee and a prime FDR adviser on labor politics.[58]

When Truman subsequently had breakfast with Hillman and informed him he was going to place Byrnes's name in nomination, the labor leader told him: "Harry, that's a mistake. Labor will never support Byrnes. He's against labor. His whole record proves it." When Truman then asked, "Who the hell do you want then?" Hillman replied: "We're supporting Wallace, but we have a second choice, and I'm looking right at him." Truman had the same conversation with Philip Murray, head of the CIO, and told him, "You needn't be for me. I'm not going to be a candidate."[59]

Meanwhile, Roosevelt's train had arrived in the Chicago yards en route west to visit more military bases. Douglas supporters spread another story that Hannegan had boarded to try to get the president to change the order of names to indicate that Truman was his real choice. Indeed, FDR's secretary, Grace Tully, wrote later that Hannegan "came directly to me [and said] 'Grace, the President wants you to retype this letter and to switch these names so it will read Harry Truman or Bill Douglas,' "[60] and that she did so. But Bruce Allen Murphy in his biography of Douglas, *Wild Bill,* offers documentation that the names were never switched at all, and that the order in FDR's letter was "Harry Truman and Bill Douglas" from the start.

In another meeting with Roosevelt before his train headed west, Flynn and Hillman persuaded the president to forget about Byrnes. When so informed, Truman went to Byrnes and apologetically asked to be relieved of the task of nominating him against the wishes of Roosevelt. Byrnes finally acceded and took himself out of the running. Hannegan then showed Truman the first FDR note saying "Truman is the right man," but he remained unconvinced.

Hannegan and Kelly began spreading the word at the convention that Truman was the man FDR really wanted. His letter saying he would vote for Wallace were he a delegate but reiterating that the choice was up to the convention, they said, was an invitation for the delegates to pick somebody else. Wallace, however, still supported by labor, argued that the letter meant that he was Roosevelt's choice. He flew to Chicago, declaring, "I am in this fight to the finish."[61]

When Roosevelt was placed in nomination, Wallace seconded the call, declaring that the only question before the convention was whether the delegates "believe wholeheartedly in the liberal policies for which Roosevelt has always stood." If so, he implied, they would give him as his running mate the party's most outspoken liberal, Wallace himself.[62] That afternoon, after FDR was nominated, Hannegan asked Truman to come to his suite at the Blackstone, where Flynn, Pauley, Walker and Allen were already gathered. They showed him the "Truman or Douglas" letter, and Hannegan then phoned Roosevelt, whose train had reached San Diego. He held out the phone so that all in the room could hear.

Truman described the scene to Merle Miller in his oral biography: "I was sitting on one twin bed, and Bob was on the other in this room, and Roosevelt said, 'Bob, have you got that guy lined up yet on that Vice Presidency?' Bob said, 'No. He's the contrariest goddamn mule from Missouri I ever saw.' 'Well,' Roosevelt said, 'you tell him if he wants to break up the Democratic Party in the middle of the war and maybe lose that war that's up to him.' Bang. . . . Well, I walked around there for about five minutes, and you should have seen the faces of those birds. They were just worried to beat hell. Finally, I said, 'All right, Bob, if that's the way the old man feels, I'll do it, but who in hell's gonna nominate me now? I've told everybody here that I'm not a candidate, and every member of my committee and everybody else is committed to somebody else.' "[63]

Truman found his Senate colleague from Missouri, Bennett Clark, and he agreed to do it. Meanwhile, Hannegan released the "Truman or Douglas" letter, passing the word that FDR really wanted Truman, who finally declared, "I am a candidate and I will win."[64] But Wallace continued the battle, with Hillman in his corner. Charges of bossism filled the corridors. On the first roll call, Wallace led with 429½ delegates of the 589 needed, to 319½ for Truman, 98 for Bankhead, 61 for Lucas, 49½ for Barkley and a smattering for eleven favorite sons.

As key party bosses for Roosevelt began to apply the screws on the favorite sons, Truman took a narrow lead on the second ballot with 477½ delegates, to 473 for Wallace. Bankhead threw 22 of his votes in Alabama to Truman and McNutt withdrew, whereupon Kelly, who was sitting on the Illinois vote for his senator, Lucas, delivered them to Truman. Flynn did the same with more New York votes, and Truman was over the top.

Roosevelt later told associates that he was astonished that Wallace had run so strongly on the first two ballots. According to Grace Tully, that knowledge would have convinced him to keep Wallace on the ticket, with historic consequences. But Roosevelt, declining in health and occupied with his war responsibilities, let the party bosses shape the outcome of the fight for the vice-presidential nomination, similarly with historic consequences. All this time, the Allied troops in Europe were driving the Nazis back. On July 20 ranking German officers attempted to assassinate Hitler. He was wounded only, but the effort demonstrated the enemy military's eroding resolve. On August 15 the invasion of southern France began, and ten days later the Allied forces that had steadily been moving east from Normandy liberated Paris, amid joyous hysteria. Meanwhile, in the Pacific, American troops leap-frogging from island to island were slowly closing in on Japan, at high human cost.

In the fall election campaign, Dewey was hemmed in from the start by the need to avoid divisive criticism of Roosevelt's handling of the war effort, and by his own stiff personality and arid speaking style compared to the grinning, ebullient president. In a cruel comparison with old spellbinder Bryan, Dewey was called "the Boy Orator of the Platitude," said to be so impressed with himself that he could "strut while sitting down."[65] The contrast between Dewey and the mature, seasoned FDR persuaded Dewey's aides to have him speak about "tired old men" running the country, while encouraging rumors that Roosevelt's health was waning fast. Tales, untrue, of an FDR heart attack or breakdown circulated in Republican circles. But the president did look much older than his sixty-two years, bearing the strains of wartime leadership on his face and his already decimated physique.

Again as in the 1940 campaign, Roosevelt elected not to campaign personally except for an occasional well-staged appearance, such as a radio broadcast from the deck of a destroyer at the Bremerton, Washington, Navy Yard. He left the daily stumping to the energetic Truman. The strategy of offering himself as the engaged, working president, however, did not deter rumors of ill health. Speaking with his son James before one scheduled review of troops at Camp Pendleton near San Diego, FDR suddenly grimaced and turned white. "Jimmy, I don't know if I can make it, I have horrible pains," he whispered. Dissuading his son from calling a doctor, he stretched out on the floor of his train car, obviously in pain, for about ten minutes, then asked his son to help him up to keep his appointment with the troops.[66]

Concern about Roosevelt's health seemed to be spreading among voters. A poll in *Fortune* magazine in late September showed his lead slipping from 9 percent to only 5. The FDR strategists were plainly worried. They didn't have to be. On the night of September 25 at the Statler Hotel in Washington, the old champ stirred himself to give a speech before supporting officials of the Teamsters Union that struck just the right spark with voters.

A Michigan Republican congressman, Harold Knutson, had charged that Roosevelt, on a trip to Alaska, had sent a navy destroyer back to the Aleutian Islands, at huge taxpayer expense, to pick up his Scottie dog, Fala, who had been left behind. Roosevelt was at his playful best, expressing mock indignation: "The Republican leaders have not been content to make personal attacks upon me—or my wife—or my sons; they now include my little dog Fala. Unlike the members of my family, Fala resents this." When the dog learned of what "Republican fiction writers" had said his master had done "at a cost to the taxpayer of two or three or 20 million dollars," FDR intoned in fake high dudgeon, "his Scotch soul was furious. He has not been the same dog since. I am accustomed to hearing falsehoods about myself, but I think I have a right to object to libelous statements about my dog."[67]

In a few deft sentences, Roosevelt pierced the Republican whisperings about his age and health, and in the same breath reminded voters of why they had abandoned the GOP ever since the days of Hoover. "Well, here we are again after four years," he said, "and what years they have been. I am actually four years older, which seems to annoy some people. In fact, millions of us are more than 11 years older than we were when we started in to clean up the mess that was dumped in our laps in 1933." The Republicans' efforts to hang the depression on him, he said, brought to mind the expression: "Never speak of rope in the house of a man who has been hanged."[68]

More than the clever ripostes, Roosevelt's vigorous manner doused cold water on the health rumors and other doubts about his ability to continue to serve. Dewey, markedly restrained to this point, decided he had to turn up the heat. In a speech in Oklahoma City, he charged that FDR had failed to end the depression until war did it for him, and his mismanagement of the war had unnecessarily cost American lives. Republicans took heart, and inspired new allegations of excessive labor influence in the Roosevelt campaign. Indeed, Sidney Hillman's political action committee (PAC) was playing a critical role in registering and rallying union members around the country to vote for the president. Inevitably, the cry of "Clear it with Sidney" was raised to connote a labor—and by inference a communist—takeover of the Democratic campaign. The conservative press, including columnist Westbrook Pegler and publisher William Randolph Hearst, piled on, as Republicans circulated such slogans as "Sidney Hillman and Earl Browder's Communists have registered. Have you?"[69]

Aroused by all this as much as any voter was Roosevelt himself. Abandoning his stay-home strategy, in late October he hit the campaign trail with a vengeance, gathering all his strength and demonstrating it in a windup tour of major cities that impressed voters with his stamina. On one day's tour across New York City's boroughs, he rode through cold and rain in an open car for four hours, stopping only once to change out of his drenched clothes and into dry ones as thousands lined the streets, enduring the elements with him. On election eve, an all-American tribute to him by prominent radio writer Norman Corwin capped a rousing drive to the finish.

The next day, the voters gave Roosevelt his fourth term with 53.5 percent of the popular ballots to 46 percent for Dewey and an overwhelming 432–99 victory in the electoral college. The turnout was nearly 2 million lower than in 1940 and his margin was the lowest of his four presidential campaigns. But there was no doubt that voters would stick with him as long as there was still a war to be won. The Democratic Party too received a vote of confidence, picking up twenty seats in the House while losing just one in the Senate, strengthening FDR's hand in the Democratic Congress for the final push for victory in Europe, and the longer struggle contemplated in the Pacific.

After the election, Roosevelt focused again on discussions with Churchill and Stalin over the shape of the postwar world. In December the German army made a major effort to stem the Allied advance with a furious offensive in the Ardennes Forest, but was thrown back in the Battle of the Bulge. In the Pacific, Manila was liberated from Japanese occupation in February 1945. Roosevelt, Churchill and Stalin met again at Yalta in the Crimea for more specific talks on territorial dispositions after the war and creation of a peacekeeping United Nations organization.

The meeting proved to be grist for endless postwar debates over which leader gained and lost most in the deliberations. Plans were drawn for free elections in liberated Europe; terms of Germany's occupation were laid out; Stalin agreed to enter the war against Japan after the surrender of Germany. Churchill left with high hopes, but later wrote that "our hopeful assumptions were soon to be falsified. Still, they were the only ones possible at the time."[70]

Two weeks after Yalta, American troops reached the Rhine. Soon thereafter the Soviet Union moved into Romania and Poland, causing great trepidation in Roosevelt and Churchill that the Yalta agreements were already being broken. Back in Washington, FDR addressed Congress with a report on Yalta that was well received but accompanied by expressions of concern among the legislators about the president's wan appearance. Weary from his long trip, the president decided to take some time off and went to his vacation White House in Warm Springs, Georgia. On April 11, having shed his antipathy of long ago to partisan Jefferson Day events, he worked on a radio speech marking the occasion to be delivered two days later.

At about one o'clock the next afternoon, April 12, as he was reworking the speech with cousin Daisy Suckley in the room, she looked up from her crocheting and saw the president slumped over in his chair, seemingly looking for something. She went over to him, kneeled down and asked, "Have you dropped your cigarette?" He looked at her, she recalled later, "his forehead furrowed with pain, and tried to smile," then "put his left hand up to the back of his head and said, 'I have a terrific pain in the back of my head.' "[71] His doctor was summoned and immediately diagnosed the trouble as a massive cerebral hemorrhage. The president never regained consciousness, and less than three hours later his momentous and turbulent life was over at age sixty-three and two months.

Vice President Truman was on Capitol Hill that afternoon, and after the Senate had adjourned he dropped by the office of Speaker Sam Rayburn. As he arrived he was told that Steve Early, the president's press secretary, wanted him to call the White House. Early asked him to come there directly. Truman, alone, raced from the House side of the Capitol to the Senate side and his awaiting limousine, and on arrival at 1600 Pennsylvania Avenue he was ushered into the first lady's second-floor study. "Mrs. Roosevelt seemed calm in her characteristic, graceful dignity," Truman wrote later. "She stepped forward and placed her arm gently about my shoulder. 'Harry,' she said quietly, 'the President is dead.' For a moment I could not bring myself to speak.... 'Is there anything I can do for you?' I asked at last. I shall never forget her deeply understanding reply. 'Is there anything we can do for you?' she asked. 'For you are the one in trouble now.' "[72]

Thus ended the longest occupancy of the presidency in the nation's history. But the war to which it could be fairly said Franklin D. Roosevelt had given his life still was going on, with a new Democratic president who had no executive experience thrust into the national leadership.

Chapter 20

TRUMAN: THE BUCK STOPS HERE,
1945–1948

HARRY TRUMAN HAD little time to procrastinate about the hand that destiny had dealt him when, in his own description, "the moon, the stars and all the planets" fell on him.[1] As soon as the oath of office had been administered to him by Chief Justice Harlan F. Stone in the White House, he had his cabinet assembled and asked all members to stay at their jobs. He told them he intended to continue the policies of his predecessor in both domestic and foreign affairs. There was nothing surprising in that; Harry Truman had been a New Deal Democrat from the start, and as a combat veteran of World War I he was committed to the Roosevelt policies abroad as well as at home.

He also found himself automatically the leader of the Democratic Party. Little known at the time, it was a responsibility he had once declined when, as a senator from Missouri, he had been offered the party's chairmanship by FDR. Frank Walker, Roosevelt's postmaster general and political adviser, had extended the offer but Truman had turned it down, arguing he was making a greater contribution to the war effort as chairman of the Senate committee investigating war contracts. Now, he had the responsibility but little time to pay much attention to it, as an incident immediately after his first meeting with his cabinet clearly demonstrated.

As the cabinet members filed out of the room, Secretary of War Stimson remained behind. "He asked to speak to me about a most urgent mat-

From The Herblock Book *(Beacon Press, 1952)*

In 1948, President Harry S. Truman ran for election in his own right against not only the Republican nominee, Thomas E. Dewey, but also "Dixiecrat" nominee J. Strom Thurmond and Progressive Party candidate Henry A. Wallace, and won. This cartoon was captioned "Common to Right of Them, Common to Left of Them."

ter," Truman wrote later in his *Memoirs*. "Stimson told me that he wanted me to know about an immense project that was under way—a project looking to the development of a new explosive of almost unbelievable destructive power. That was all he felt free to say at the time. . . . It was not until the next day that I was told enough to give me some understanding of the almost incredible developments that were under way and the awful power that might soon be placed in our hands."[2]

Thus did the new president of the United States learn for the first time of the greatly advanced plan for the atomic bomb. Months earlier, however, in his capacity as chairman of the Senate investigating committee, he had sent staff members to Tennessee to inquire about very large constructions going on in secret. At that time, Stimson had called on him in his Senate office and told him, Truman wrote later, "I can't tell you what it is, but it is the greatest project in the history of the world. It is most top secret. Many of the people who are actually engaged in the work have no idea what it is, and we who do would appreciate your not going into those plants." Truman replied: "I'll take you at your word. I'll order the investigations into those plants called off."[3]

The fact that as vice president Harry Truman was never informed of the single most significant secret of the Roosevelt administration, known internally as the Manhattan Project, was a sorry commentary on how both the man and his office were regarded by Roosevelt, aware of his own declining health and knowing that Truman at any time might be called on to assume the immense responsibilities of the presidency. That fact probably had more to do than any other, though not immediately, in the informing of future vice presidents about the most important activities of the administration in which they served, and their increased involvement in it.

The revelation about the atom bomb gave special impetus to Truman's imperative focus on foreign policy over domestic political affairs. His first immediate decision as president was to make clear that plans for an international conference in San Francisco to establish a peacekeeping United Nations organization would go forward. Then he had to turn his attention to the conduct of the war in Europe, with particular attention to Russian intentions. Stalin's armies had at last turned back the Nazi onslaught and were now moving into Germany as U.S. and British forces were closing in from the west.

In March, Churchill, concerned over the Soviet advance, had urged that Allied troops move as swiftly as possible to reach Berlin before the Russians got there. But General Eisenhower, concentrating on the destruction of all German forces in the west, and hoping to preserve the cooperative relations with the Soviet Union that had generally existed up to this time, had demurred. New President Truman, sharing Eisenhower's concerns and with the unfinished war in the Pacific and the future United Nations in mind, left the decision on military deployment and objectives to the Allied commander.

As the Russian forces raced westward, the Nazi regime was disintegrating faster and more completely than Eisenhower had contemplated. On April 30, with the Russians already entering Berlin, Hitler committed suicide in his fortified bunker fifty feet below the German Chancellery, along with many of his close associates, including wife Eva Braun. The Fuehrer was found shot in the mouth with his new bride nearby, having taken poison.[4] Three days later the residual German leadership began to give up, and on May 7 at Eisenhower's headquarters in Rheims an unconditional surrender was signed.

By this time, Truman had been advised by Stimson that the new atom bomb would probably be ready for deployment in about four months. On June 1 a special committee on the bomb urged that it be used against Japan as soon as possible, as a means of avoiding a long invasion of the island empire at a huge cost in American lives. A proposal of scientists working on the Manhattan Project suggested that a demonstration of the bomb's mighty power be held in some remote place to convince the Japanese to surrender. But the scheme was rejected on grounds that the bomb might not work, and that only two bombs would be ready by August and should be used for optimum impact on the enemy.[5] A group of scientists importantly involved in atom bomb research wrote a letter to Truman urging that the weapon not be used, but the letter never reached him.

In early July, Truman undertook his first trip abroad as president, aboard the naval cruiser *Augusta,* to meet with Churchill and Stalin at Potsdam, a suburb of Berlin. They were to consider unified steps to bring about the surrender of Japan and address postwar issues in Europe. The day after his arrival, the first atom bomb was successfully tested in the New Mexico desert, but word of the results did not reach Truman for five days. Churchill was then informed, but not Stalin.

The next day, another devastating bomb of a political nature hit Potsdam. Word came that Churchill's Conservative Party had been defeated in

Britain's first postwar election, and he would be succeeded as prime minister by the victorious Labour Party leader, Clement Attlee. The development caused a recess in the talks until Attlee could replace Churchill at the Potsdam table. At the time, the Japanese were seeking to mediate an end to the war through the Russians, but were adamant against meeting the stated terms of unconditional surrender demanded by the Allied side. The result was a rather cryptic Declaration of Potsdam signed by Truman and Attlee calling on Japan to surrender or inviting "the utter devastation of the Japanese homeland."[6] On July 28 the Japanese regime dismissed the demand as "unworthy of public notice,"[7] whereupon Truman gave the American military the go-ahead to use the atom bomb.

On August 6 an American army plane named the *Enola Gay* dropped the first one ever used as a weapon, on the city of Hiroshima. Nearly 100,000 people were killed immediately and an equal number fatally injured in the worst single blow ever delivered to a civilian population. When the Tokyo government failed to surrender, three days later a second bomb was dropped on Nagasaki, with similar deadly results. In a radio address, Truman justified the bomb's development on grounds the Germans had been in pursuit of it, and defended its use "in order to shorten the agony of war, in order to save the lives of thousands and thousands of young Americans."[8] He warned that the bomb would continue to be used until the Japanese surrendered. Five days after the attack on Nagasaki, on August 14, thereafter known as V-J Day, Tokyo accepted the terms of unconditional surrender. The Japanese military had wanted to persevere but Emperor Hirohito personally ordered an end to the slaughter.

At last, World War II was over at a cost of 25 million lives, including 300,000 Americans. The abrupt end, made possible by the use of the atom bomb that eliminated the necessity of a long, drawn-out invasion of Japan, caught planners of the postwar world without an adequate blueprint for reconversion to peacetime. But Truman now could turn to the commitment he had made in taking office, to continue the New Deal policies of FDR. Roosevelt's musings of party realignment, dividing the politics of the country into liberal and conservative camps, were, however, set aside with a new man in the White House and as head of the Democratic Party.

Truman had already begun to shake up his cabinet, first accepting the resignation of Postmaster General Walker, an inside FDR man, and replacing him with Bob Hannegan, his fellow Missourian who, as chairman of the Democratic National Committee, had been importantly involved in persuading Roosevelt to take Truman as his vice president.

Of other changes, the most notable were James Byrnes as secretary of state, replacing Edward Stettinius, and Fred M. Vinson taking over as treasury secretary from Henry Morgenthau Jr. Truman, now serving without a vice president, there being no provision in the Constitution at the time for filling the vacancy, regarded Stettinius as shaky as a potential president in the line of succession then in place. He was strong on the experienced Byrnes, whose own nomination for vice president in 1944 he had been poised to offer until the "conspiracy of the pure in heart" had orchestrated it for Truman himself.

Some liberal intellectuals in the Democratic Party were disturbed at the departure of Morgenthau and the arrival of Byrnes, the Southern Democrat whose Dixie roots had led Ed Flynn to work so hard to derail his vice-presidential prospects. But Truman quickly reassured them and other New Dealers, in a twenty-one-point message to Congress in September, that he was committed to carry out and advance the Roosevelt agenda in the context of converting the nation's economy from war to peace. Adopting FDR's Economic Bill of Rights, he urged the legislators: "Let us make the attainment of those rights the essence of postwar American life."[9]

At the same time, Truman was not a crusader for the New Deal in the way Roosevelt had been. As Robert J. Donovan noted in *Conflict and Crisis,* his book on Truman's first term, "Truman had come to the White House as a practical, not an ordained New Dealer. In the Senate he had been a vote for the New Deal, not a voice, and certainly not an ideological voice. His primary allegiance . . . was to the party, not to an ideology."[10] While he had supported most New Deal policies as a senator, Truman was cool to many of the intellectuals who made up its brain trust, who came from more rarefied Eastern backgrounds, education and social standings. For Truman's comfort level as well as his aspirations for good relations with Congress, his cabinet shake-up brought four members or former members into the administration, led by Vinson, high in Truman's esteem. Some were less enthusiastic about the New Deal than were their predecessors, leading to internal squabbles that complicated Truman's task.

Truman's experience in the Senate made him more conciliatory to congressional leaders than Roosevelt had been. Instead of having White House liaison aides like the aggressive Tommy "The Cork" Corcoran pressuring them and often ruffling feathers, he preferred having his cabinet members send them administration legislative proposals. He was sensitive to the imperative of assistance from moderates like Speaker Sam Rayburn and Senate Majority Leader Scott Lucas in steering such proposals past the shoals of Southern Democratic opposition, represented by Georgians Eugene Cox in the House and Richard Russell in the Senate.

In addition to endorsing FDR's economic package, the new president proposed the expansion of social security and called on Congress for six months in unemployment benefits for workers who had just lost their jobs. On civil rights, about which he had a relatively good record in the Senate, he pushed for creation of a permanent Fair Employment Practices Act, to the chagrin of many Southern Democrats. Coming from segregated Missouri, Truman was not what conservatives would have called a bleeding heart on such issues, but he did come down generally on the liberal side of the ledger in his actions.

Significantly different circumstances existed in mid-1945, however, from those of the prewar halcyon days of the New Deal. They restricted Truman's ability to pursue the old FDR domestic agenda amid the huge challenge of peacetime reconversion. Many influential Democrats disagreed that the New Deal policies should be advanced at all, and many questioned Truman's leadership abilities to do so. With widespread unemployment and inflation anticipated upon the conclusion of the war, they advocated a go-slow approach. Many argued that the best days of the New Deal were already behind it, in terms of meeting the basic needs of the lower strata of the society.

In Congress particularly, conservative Southern Democrats, remembering Roosevelt's failed court-packing effort and the attempted purge in the 1938 elections, remained hostile, especially as organized labor gained a greater voice and influence in party councils. Some intellectuals on the party's left, drawn by the New Deal's ambitious domestic agenda, feared that a postwar concentration on reconversion, and on creating and nurturing the United Nations, would shortchange social welfare policies at home.

The first signs, however, were hopeful for Truman's plans to put the country back on the track FDR had constructed before the war. Peace did not bring, as feared, deep and lasting unemployment and more depression with a sharp decline in government spending. Rather, it saw millions of returning American servicemen and their families engaging in spending sprees for available consumer goods, and in the process pump-priming the economy. The early postwar problem was not joblessness but an inflation of prices and wages.

The Democratic Party that Truman had inherited from Roosevelt had long before expanded from its Southern rural base to Northern cities populated increasingly by Irish, Italian, Polish, Catholic and Jewish immigrants, effectively courted by machine bosses doling out jobs and welfare. Many of the same big-city bosses who had found a political soul mate in FDR warmed to Truman as they recognized not only his loyalty to the New Deal, but also his appreciation of the mutual interest they shared in using federal largesse in effective party-building.

Some of the bosses—Chicago's Ed Kelly, Jersey City's Frank Hague, Pittsburgh's David Lawrence and Ed Flynn of the Bronx—had been for the selection of Truman as FDR's running mate in 1944. As himself a product of the Pendergast machine in Kansas City, though untainted by its excesses, Truman had climbed the political ladder with an appreciation of its help to him, now reciprocated in federal patronage. Beyond that, he understood the value, to himself as to the city bosses, of engaging in true partnerships with them in promoting constructive local projects that would strengthen Democratic constituencies.

Thus, as Sean J. Savage noted in his excellent book *Truman and the Democratic Party,* the president in his 1946 State of the Union address observed that "specifically, the Federal Government should aid state and local governments in planning their own public works programs, in undertaking projects related to Federal programs of regional development, and in constructing such public works as are necessary to carry out the various policies of the Federal Government."[11]

Truman also proposed that his administration give cities technical help in urban planning and renewal as part of what Savage called "cooperative federalism," enabling city machines "to bolster their political longevity by adapting to and exploiting this greater federal intervention rather than resisting it and perceiving it as a threat to their local political power." In Chicago and Pittsburgh particularly, Savage wrote, the machines were not only able "to satisfy the social welfare, public employment and public housing needs of lower-income constituents," but also "meet the demands of home owners and business interests for fewer property-tax increases, urban renewal and structural improvements conducive to commerce and industry."[12]

Truman benefited, too, from the strides that FDR had made in bringing black voters back into the Democratic Party. By 1936, they were switching their allegiance in droves from Republican to a Democratic Party bolstered by the support and active political participation of organized labor on the rise. But as black and labor involvement increased and became more visible, and as FDR articulated a liberal agenda more forcefully in his second term, the prospect for serious erosion in the party's Southern conservative base had also increased. This was especially so after his failed attempt to purge Dixie congressmen.

It was Truman's challenge, therefore, to retain and expand the growth elements in the party without politically debilitating defections from the offended traditional base. In frustration in the fall of 1945, according to Harold Ickes, Truman echoed Roosevelt in saying "he wished that there might be organized a liberal party in the country so that the Southern Democrats could go where they belonged into the conservative Republican Party."[13] But he never acted on that expressed wish.

As it had been in FDR's latter prewar days, Congress loomed as a major problem for its now most illustrious alumnus. From 1936 to 1945 the Democratic Party had seen its once-commanding majorities shrink sharply. In the House, the party's strength had dropped from 333 seats to 243, and in the Senate from 75 to 57.[14] In the fall of 1945, Truman lifted most wartime controls, but when prices and wages climbed in late 1945 and early 1946, fears of soaring inflation caused him to ask Congress to restore them, leading to a long and indecisive battle on Capitol Hill.

Organized labor particularly was incensed about controls, remembering that workers' wages had been held in check throughout the war while industry profited mightily from cost-plus contracts. In late 1945 and into 1946, the country experienced a rash of labor disputes, including strikes against auto- and steelmakers, and most notably a railroad strike in May 1946. When the workers rejected a government wage proposal, Truman called a joint session of Congress and asked for emergency power to draft them into the military. The workers gave in, but not without lasting bitterness toward him. He recovered generally with labor, however, by vetoing a harsh anti-labor bill that the House narrowly failed to override. But this time the veto came at the cost of heavy defections by Southern Democrats. The FDR coalition was proving to be difficult to maintain in the absence of the man who had created it.

In his own official family, too, Truman was confronted with major dissension among old New Deal liberals. Leading figures including Ickes, Chester Bowles and Wilson Wyatt quit, and Henry Wallace, installed by FDR as secretary of commerce and continuing under Truman, broke with him over policy toward the Soviet Union. Wallace, deeply interested in salvaging peaceful relations with Moscow after the wartime collaboration, was distressed over the hardening American posture. The speech of Winston Churchill in March 1946 at Fulton, Missouri, in which he warned that "an Iron Curtain has descended across the Continent" of Europe and signaled a public recognition of the Cold War, had shocked Wallace. He began to make speeches calling for accommodations with the Soviet Union.

In September at a Democratic rally in New York, he criticized American policy at a time Byrnes was meeting with Russian diplomats in Paris, indicating that he had cleared his speech with Truman. Byrnes demanded that the president throttle Wallace, and threatened to resign unless Wallace was fired. Truman complied. By this time Wallace, as the sole original New Dealer in the Truman cabinet, had become the most prominent member of the party's liberal wing, and his departure produced a significant breach in the FDR coalition as the congressional elections approached. Writing to his mother and sister, Truman told them: "Well, I had to fire Henry today, and of course I hated to do it. . . . If Henry had stayed Sec. of Agri. in 1940 as he should have, there'd never have been this controversy, and I would not be here, and wouldn't that be nice? . . . Well, now he's out, and the crackpots are having conniption fits."[15]

Wallace received an outpouring of support from the liberal community, leading him to write to a prominent liberal columnist of the day, Max Lerner: "After recent events I am, in retrospect, very happy. The cause of peace has been strengthened. The chance of war has been lessened. I don't think I could have bought more with less no matter how hard I tried."[16] At the same time, however, critics on the right like FBI Director J. Edgar Hoover were using the Wallace resignation to fan the embers of suspicion already smoldering of possible communist influence in the Democratic Party. Hoover wrote to George Allen: "I thought the President and you would be interested in knowing that national figures affiliated with the Communist Party and its front activities have expressed an opinion that the resignation of Mr. Wallace is a good move for them as it opens the issue of war with Byrnes and peace with Wallace."[17]

Together with the disenchantment of organized labor over wage controls, the defection of prominent liberals was tearing at the roots of the FDR coalition. And at precisely this time the Republicans, after sixteen years in the minority in Congress, were taking dead aim at restoring themselves to majority status in the next congressional elections. Wallace graciously agreed to continue campaigning for Democratic candidates that fall, but the disintegration was obvious. "The New Deal as a driving force is dead within the Truman administration," the *Chicago Sun* observed.[18] Southern disaffection became so bad that after a Jefferson-Jackson Day fund-raising dinner in Little Rock, Arkansas, Governor Ben Laney ruled that, in protest of the Truman leadership, the proceeds would be withheld from the Democratic National Committee.[19]

Republicans gloated over the Democratic president's discomfort. GOP Senator Robert Taft of Ohio, his eye not only on a Republican Congress but also on his party's presidential nomination in 1948, took up the cry against Truman, writing to Thomas Dewey: "If Truman wanted to elect a Republican Congress, he could not be doing a better job."[20] His wife, Martha, was credited with the line "To err is Truman."[21]

Wallace's departure from the cabinet over U.S.-Russian policy not only offended many party liberals; it also gave the Republican opposition a reference point for raising the specter of communism along with general public concern over prices, housing and food shortages, particularly beef products. The GOP adopted as its campaign slogan "Had Enough? Vote Republican." A Republican congressman from Ohio, John Vorys, asked in his stump speeches: "Got enough meat? . . . Got enough houses? . . . Got enough OPA? . . . Got enough inflation? . . . Got enough debt? . . . Got enough strikes? . . . Got enough Communism?"[22]

In California, the communism bugaboo launched the political career of an obscure World War II naval veteran named Richard M. Nixon, who used it effectively to defeat liberal Democratic Congressman Jerry Voorhis, attacking officials "who front for un-American elements, wittingly or otherwise, by advocating increasing Federal controls over the lives of people."[23]

Voorhis's loss proved to be only a small part of a staggering election day defeat for the Democratic Party in Congress and for Truman as the party leader. The Republicans won a fifty-eight-seat majority in the House and a four-seat edge in the Senate. In addition to newcomer Nixon, the GOP gained a Red-hunting senator from Wisconsin named Joseph R. McCarthy, who was destined to be a particular burr in the side of Democrats in the years to come. (Among the Democrats elected to the House was another young navy veteran of twenty-nine from Massachusetts named John F. Kennedy.)

The 1946 congressional results were widely taken as the opening death knell of the political career of Harry Truman, and with him of the New Deal, as he fell in the Gallup poll from 87 percent upon assuming the presidency to a dismal 32 percent. The Republicans looked ahead to the presidential election of 1948 with near-certainty that they would regain the White House as well.

Truman clearly needed a political overhaul simply to be effective in what most thought would be his remaining two years as president. Shortly after the 1946 election, Truman's special counsel, Clark Clifford, James Rowe, an old FDR adviser, and several other cabinet officials and ranking aides began meeting at the apartment of Oscar Ewing, the national committee's vice chairman and administrator of the Federal Security Agency. Calling themselves the Monday Night Group, they considered ways Truman could demonstrate and exploit his liberalism.[24]

For openers, he lifted most wage controls. And the threat of another coal strike led by the tempestuous and generally unpopular United Mine Workers leader John L. Lewis presented the president with an opportunity to cast himself as a hero. Since the previous spring the federal government had been operating the mines under contract with the union, and Clifford and other insiders persuaded the president to take Lewis on. The White House got a court order instructing Lewis to cancel his plans for another strike, and when he declined he was found in contempt. Lewis buckled and Truman was at least temporarily revived politically. He wrote his mother and sister: "Well, John L. had to fold up. He couldn't take the gaff. No bully can."[25] Next, Truman took on the Republicans and conservative Democrats against the anti-labor Taft-Hartley bill, and although it passed over his veto, the very waging of the fight restored much of his old labor support.

Meanwhile, on the foreign policy front, he combated GOP allegations of being soft on communism by unveiling his Truman Doctrine promising aid to countries facing communist domination, starting with Greece and Turkey, and the Marshall Plan for the recovery of Western Europe, the architect of which was his new secretary of state, General George C. Marshall. A policy of containment of the Soviet Union enunciated by State Department expert George F. Kennan became the core of American Cold

War policy; Truman beefed up national security with creation of the Department of Defense, the National Security Agency and the Central Intelligence Agency.

At the same time, Truman initiated a federal loyalty program in which many accused individuals were denied confrontation with their accusers, creating a poisonous atmosphere without discovering any traitors. Among its sharpest critics was Wallace, who continued to express alarm about American policy toward the Soviet Union. He told a New York rally of the Progressive Citizens of America that just as the Truman Doctrine would "turn the world against America," the loyalty program would "turn Americans against each other" and "threaten everything in America that is worth fighting for. Intolerance is aroused. Suspicion is engendered. Men of the highest integrity in public life are besmirched. The president's executive order creates a master index of public servants. From the janitor in the village post office to the cabinet member, they are to be sifted and tested and watched and appraised. Their past and present, the tattle and prattle of their neighbors, are all to be recorded."[26]

In the months after his New York speech, as a new editor of *The New Republic* magazine Wallace denounced the Truman Doctrine as a "global Monroe Doctrine" and, after first praising the Marshall Plan, took issue with it as well.[27] On a speaking tour in England, Wallace charged that he was the victim of a "witch hunt" that was "part of a larger drive to destroy the belief, which I share, that capitalism and communism can resolve their conflicts without resort to war."[28] His comments came as the Senate was passing a $400 million loan to Greece and Turkey as a cornerstone of the Truman Doctrine, and brought the former vice president vehement denunciation from legislators of his own party. Senator J. William Fulbright of Arkansas proclaimed that Wallace's speeches sounded as if they had been penned in Moscow. Truman was reported to have compared Wallace in a private letter to Aaron Burr, the earlier vice president tried for treason.[29]

On his return home, Wallace continued his harangue on another tour around the country that exuded an almost religious fervor. Howard M. Norton of the *Baltimore Sun* said it was "like traveling with a messiah and his disciples," and Edwin A. Lahey of the *Chicago Daily News* wrote that "if fate and a fickle electorate combined to make Henry A. Wallace President of the United States . . . , we would have a John the Baptist in the White House."[30] Such comments were harbingers of trouble to come for Truman within liberal pacifist ranks.

Local elections in 1947, including the only gubernatorial race of the year in Kentucky, did demonstrate, however, some modest Democratic resurgence. From September through November, the Monday Night Group had been working over a long penetrating memorandum by Rowe on how Truman could rejuvenate his political stock with labor, blacks and liberal activists without worrying about alienating the party's Southern base. It did not accept the conventional wisdom that he was a de facto lame duck. In an expanded version of the Rowe memorandum, which in the long run may well have saved and extended the Truman presidency, Clifford wrote:

"The administration should select the issues upon which there will be a conflict with the [Republican] majority in Congress. It [the Truman administration] can assume that it will get no major part of its own program approved. Its tactics must therefore be entirely different than if there were any real point to bargaining and compromises. Its recommendations—in the State of the Union message and elsewhere—must be tailored for the voter, not the Congressman; they must display a label which reads 'no compromise.' " Clifford speculated that "there is little possibility that [Truman] will get much cooperation from the Congress but we want the President to be in position to receive the credit for whatever they do accomplish while also being in position to criticize the Congress for being obstructionists for failing to comply with other recommendations."[31]

Truman immediately embraced the Rowe-Clifford strategy at the opening of the new Congress. He delivered his State of the Union message in person and presented Congress with a shopping list of liberal programs that invited Republican opposition. It was said he regarded the advice from Rowe and Clifford, which also called for beefing up the national committee's research arm, so highly that he kept it in his desk drawer thereafter, and followed it again to good purpose in his 1948 campaign.

As Truman labored to reestablish his liberal credentials with an ambitious agenda before Congress that was tactically designed to draw a sharp line between himself and the Republican majority, Wallace continued to be a threat to cut into the president's liberal support. In December, Senator J. Howard McGrath of Rhode Island, who had just replaced Hannegan as Democratic national chairman, made a direct bid to Wallace to support Truman in the approaching 1948 election. Wallace responded that he could not do so as long as the president continued to push for a peacetime draft. But it was clear now that Wallace's differences with Truman were much broader and unreconcilable.

At month's end, Wallace acceded to the pressures of the Progressive Citizens of America and declared he would be a candidate for president on a third-party ticket. In a national radio address, clinging to his conviction that Truman was putting the country on the path to armed conflict with the Soviet Union, he promised "a positive peace program of abundance and security, not scarcity and war." Arguing that in the coming election there would be "no real fight between a Truman and a Republican," he declared it was time for "a new party to fight these war-makers." To give voters a choice, he said, "we have assembled a Gideon's army—small in number, powerful in conviction, ready for action."[32]

Wallace was not the only political shadow hanging over Truman. Another was General Eisenhower, still in Europe as commander of all Allied forces there, and immensely popular at home as the liberator of Europe and the world from the Nazi peril. Speculation about the general seeking the presidency, or being drafted to run, was widespread, and later reports had it that in 1947 Truman himself, not wanting to run, had told Eisenhower he would back him if he decided to do so.[33] Truman later in his oral biography vehemently denied the reports. "He said I offered him the presidency, which I didn't," Truman told his interviewer, Merle Miller. "In the first place, it wasn't mine to offer ... he assured me he had no intention whatsoever of going into politics. I told him I thought that was the right decision and it was." Truman, who admitted he had no love for Eisenhower, added: "If he'd just stuck to it."[34]

In January 1948 a group of Republicans entered the general's name in the New Hampshire primary, prompting him to ask that it be withdrawn and flatly saying he would not be a candidate. That didn't stop some in the Democratic Party, convinced that Truman could not be elected in his own right in November, from starting a draft-Eisenhower movement, not really knowing whether the general was a Democrat or a Republican. He responded by saying "under no conceivable circumstances" would he run or accept a draft, but the statement didn't deter many in the movement.[35]

Two of FDR's sons, FDR Jr. and Elliott, openly called for the draft and a third, James, then the state Democratic chairman in California, backed it in private, as did their mother, according to Hubert Humphrey, then the liberal mayor of Minneapolis. "Eleanor herself called several times to discuss it," he said later, declaring his own preference for Eisenhower or Bill Douglas.[36] Even the Americans for Democratic Action (ADA), an old FDR fortress, called a special meeting of its board and urged an open convention to consider "men like" Eisenhower and Douglas. At the same time, other Democrats backed away from challenging Truman, with the specter of a late Eisenhower bid still in their minds or imaginations.

All this came in the context of a Gallup poll in March indicating that Truman would lose to any one of four Republicans—Dewey, Stassen, Vandenberg or MacArthur. Truman's departed secretary of interior, Ickes, with characteristically minimal tact, wrote the president urging him not to run: "You have the choice of retiring voluntarily and with dignity, or of being driven out of office by a disillusioned and indignant citizenry. Have you ever seen the ice on a pond suddenly break in every conceivable direction under the rays of a warming spring sun? That is what has happened to the Democratic Party under you, except that your party has not responded to bright sunshine. It has broken up spontaneously."[37]

With such breaches in the liberal wing of the party, Truman continued to propose legislative initiatives designed to address his real or potential political problems looking to the presidential election. With particular focus on black voters, some of whom appeared in 1946 to be drifting back to the Republican camp, he sent Congress a special message on civil rights based on the report of a presidential commission. It focused on racial discrimination, putting the federal government squarely on the side of the victims.

In a speech to the NAACP carried worldwide by radio, he declared: "We cannot be content with a civil liberties program which emphasizes only the need of protection against the possibility of tyranny by the government. . . . The extension of civil rights today means not protection of the people against the government, but protection of the people by the government. We must make the Federal government a friendly, vigilant defender of the rights and equalities of all Americans."[38]

Truman proposed creation of a separate Civil Rights Division in the Justice Department, a permanent presidential Civil Rights Commission, laws against police brutality, lynching and intimidation at voting places, an end to poll taxes, and fair practices in employment, health services, education and housing. The report also recommended the elimination of segregation, but that step obviously was still well down the road. Not all of the others were implemented then or later, but the very statement was historic and achieved much of its political purpose of keeping blacks as Democratic voters.

Predictably, however, it only exacerbated Truman's problems among Southern Democrats. Georgia Congressman Cox wailed that "Harlem is wielding more influence with the administration than the entire white South," and Senator Tom Connally of Texas said the proposal amounted to a "lynching of the Constitution."[39]

Other legislative proposals met with stiff opposition from the Republican majority and conservative Democrats, obliging Truman to veto counterproposals, only to have his vetoes overridden. Within the party, the draft-Eisenhower boom talk continued to simmer, and Wallace was off on his own under the Progressive Party banner. But without active, overt competition for convention delegates, the president's political agents methodically corralled them in state primaries and caucuses, with the Democratic National Committee and Democratic congressional allies pitching in, though frequently without optimism or enthusiasm.

The Republicans observed Truman's intraparty travails with growing expectations of claiming the White House in November. Consequently, they had a large field of presidential aspirants led by Governor Dewey of New York and Senator Taft of Ohio. The Republican primaries served mainly to narrow the field, as voters administered defeats to the other principal contenders. General MacArthur ran weak campaigns in Wisconsin and Nebraska, cooling the conservative boomlet for him. Harold Stassen unwisely took on Taft in the latter's home state and lost, and then was bested by Dewey in Oregon. Meanwhile, Dewey and Taft were busy picking up convention delegates in non-primary states.

Both major party conventions were televised for the first time in 1948, but the audiences were not large and neither party particularly orchestrated its program and events to accommodate, or even pay much attention to, the cameras that would later dominate convention proceedings and news media coverage.

At the Republican convention in Philadelphia in June, temporary chairman Governor Dwight Green of Illinois set the tone by declaring that "the New Deal Party can have no real program because it is no longer a real party. It mustered its majorities from a fantastic partnership of reaction and radicalism. For years," he went on, "this strange alliance was held together by bosses, boodle, buncombe and blarney.... That group of crackpots was never competent to hold responsible office. The lunatic fringe is neither competent to govern nor to let others govern."[40] Former Congresswoman Clare Boothe Luce, wife of the publisher of *Time* magazine, gave Truman short shrift. "Let us waste no time measuring the unfortunate man in the White House against our specifications," she told the GOP convention. "Mr. Truman's time is short; his situation is hopeless. Frankly, he is a gone goose."[41]

Seven names were formally presented to the convention—Dewey, Taft, Stassen, MacArthur, Vandenberg, Governor Earl Warren of California and Raymond Baldwin, a Connecticut favorite son. On the first ballot, twelve candidates got votes, with Dewey in the lead with 434 delegates, 114 short of the required majority. Taft was second with 224 and Stassen third with 157. On the second roll call, Stassen began to crumble, with Dewey garnering most of his delegates and moving to within 33 votes of the nomination. In the course of a recess, the Taft forces folded and Dewey won unanimous support on the next roll call. Governor Warren was selected as his running mate by acclamation. The Republican ticket of the governors of the two most populous states seemed to many to be unbeatable, especially against the beleaguered Truman.

The president approached his own party's convention with major distractions. The year 1948 had marked a continuation of Soviet consolidation of its power in Eastern Europe, capped by a communist coup in Czechoslovakia in February and increasing hostility toward the West through the spring in the wake of congressional approval of the Marshall Plan. In May his recognition of the new state of Israel, even as the United Nations General Assembly was considering trusteeship, spurred controversy. On June 24, the day the Republicans nominated Dewey, Moscow suddenly cut off ground access to Berlin, leading to the initiation by Truman of an airlift of food and other supplies to the city. If the intent was to force the Western powers out of the former German capital city, then jointly governed by the victors of the war, it failed. But it posed a constant source of tension for the American president by then embroiled in turmoil in his own party at home.

Although by convention time the president had no declared rival for the Democratic nomination, the meeting in Philadelphia in mid-July was fraught with political peril for him. The draft-Eisenhower brigade, still led by Jimmy Roosevelt, was persisting. A week before the Democratic convention, he sent telegrams to the 1,592 delegates urging them to pick the "ablest, strongest man available," observing that "no man in these critical days can refuse the call to duty" that the Democratic nomination surely would bring him.[42] Among those who persisted in the Eisenhower draft were bosses Jake Arvey of Chicago and Mayors William O'Dwyer of New York and Frank Hague of Jersey City because they were convinced Truman was a loser who would bring other Democratic candidates down with him. For all of his effective "cooperative federalism" with them, winning the next election from top to bottom remained their primary driving force.

A week before the convention, Hague announced he would deliver New Jersey's thirty-six delegates to Eisenhower. The general responded by stating: "I will not at this time identify myself with any political party and could not accept nomination for any public office or participate in a partisan political contest."[43] Senator Claude Pepper of Florida brushed the statement aside, saying he intended to place Eisenhower's name in nomination anyway. The general sent him a telegram directly: "No matter under what terms, conditions or premises . . . I would refuse to accept. . . . I ask you to accept my refusal as final and complete, which it most emphatically is."[44] The phraseology was not as memorable as General Sherman's famous disclaimer, but just as clear and resolute.

With the Eisenhower problem out of the way, Truman tracked down Justice Douglas on vacation in Oregon and offered him the vice-presidential nomination—an obvious move to placate restless and rebellious party liberals. Douglas declined, reportedly on grounds expressed to old FDR crony Tommy Corcoran that he could not be "a number two man to a number two man."[45] Somewhat surprisingly, Senator Barkley called Truman and asked whether he would object to his seeking the vice presidency. Truman, aware that Barkley at seventy was six years his senior, did not see him as an ideal ticket mate but agreed.

Still to be resolved was a bitter intraparty fight between Northern liberals and Southern conservatives over the convention's civil rights platform plank. A Truman-approved compromise that essentially would have adopted the mild language in the 1944 plank as a conciliatory gesture to Dixie was rejected by the Deep South states. They wanted a clear reaffirmation of states' rights, a thinly veiled cover for continued discriminatory practices toward blacks. When the Southern version prevailed in the platform committee, a group of party liberals took the issue to the convention floor, assuring a major row.

Young ADA leaders Joseph Rauh, Andrew Biemiller and the thirty-seven-year-old mayor of Minneapolis, Hubert Humphrey, prepared a much stronger plank that diplomatically commended Truman "for his courageous stand" on civil rights and called upon Congress to support him in guaranteeing the right of "full and equal political participation . . . equal opportunity of employment . . . security of persons . . . and . . . equal treatment in the service and defense of our Nation."[46] Humphrey, sitting on the convention platform next to a man he had never met—Ed Flynn, the Bronx party boss—nervously told him what his group was about to present. Flynn warmed to the idea and promised to line up other bosses, including Jake Arvey of Illinois and David Lawrence of Pennsylvania.[47] Lawrence, staunchly pro-Truman from the start, proved to be the most loyal and helpful to the incumbent in all aspects of securing the 1948 nomination.

In the end, most of the bosses who had flirted with the draft-Eisenhower movement and shied away from Truman as a prospective loser also fell in behind him once his nomination was assured, with varying degrees of enthusiasm. An exception was Ed Crump, the party boss in Memphis whose own iron grip on his city and much of the rest of Tennessee was not dependent on New Deal largesse. He had opposed Truman for the vice-presidential nomination in 1944 and for the presidential nomination in 1948, even to the point of trying unsuccessfully to get the Tennessee delegation to walk out in the event Truman was chosen.[48]

The debate over civil rights uncovered a new and powerful voice in liberal ranks when Humphrey, then running for the United States Senate, walked to the microphone and electrified the crowd with a soaring speech that met the Southern argument head-on: "There are those who say to you: 'We are rushing this issue of civil rights.' I say we are a hundred and seventy-two years late. There are those who say: 'This issue of civil rights is an infringement on states' rights.' The time has arrived for the Democratic Party to get out of the shadow of states' rights and walk forthrightly into the bright sunshine of human rights."[49]

The mildest of three Southern resolutions was defeated by more than three to one, and two others were turned down by voice vote, whereupon the ADA-authored plank was approved by 651 ½ to 582 ½. Most smaller and border states, apparently fearful of liberal urban power, opposed the plank, and many Northern delegates demonstrated a reluctance to push their Dixie counterparts so far as to trigger a walkout. Nevertheless, when the roll call for the presidential nomination began, with the names of Truman, Senator Richard B. Russell of Georgia, Paul McNutt and William

Julian, an Ohio favorite son, offered, the walkout occurred. The chairman of the Alabama delegation announced that thirteen members of his delegation were leaving in compliance with instructions from the Alabama state convention in the event a civil rights plank unsatisfactory to the South was adopted. He also announced that the full Mississippi delegation was walking out, as did other Dixie delegates.

Amid the furor, and interminable seconding speeches, Truman was easily nominated on the first ballot with 947 ½ votes to 263 for Russell, all from the old Confederacy, where Truman got only North Carolina's 13. For vice president, Russell and Barkley were placed in nomination, but Russell's name was withdrawn and Barkley was declared the nominee.

Because the session dragged on so long, it was nearly two o'clock in the morning when Truman personally addressed the convention. He immediately jolted it out of its doldrums by declaring: "Senator Barkley and I will win this election and make these Republicans like it—don't you forget that!"[50] After a long laundry list of sixteen years of Democratic leadership, Truman firmly addressed the civil rights split in the party that threatened his election. Noting his proposals to Congress on the matter, he explained: "I did that because I believed it to be my duty under the Constitution. Some of the members of my own party disagree with me violently on this matter. But they stand up and do it openly. People can tell where they stand."[51] That, he suggested, was more than could be said for the Republicans, who had failed to act on his proposals on this subject and many others.

Truman went on to rail against "that worst 80th Congress" for lack of achievement, finally unleashing a surprise that was to prove a master political stroke in his bid for another term. "On the 26th of July, which out in Missouri we call 'Turnip Day,' I am going to call Congress back," he declared, "and ask them to pass laws to halt rising prices, to meet the housing crisis, which they are saying they are for in their platform. . . . I shall ask them to act upon vitally needed measures such as aid to education, which they say they are for; for a national health program, civil rights legislation, which they say they are for . . . extension of Social Security and increased benefits, which they say they are for. . . . Now, my friends, if there is any reality behind the Republican platform, we ought to get some action from a short session of the 80th Congress. They can do this job in fifteen days, if they want to do it. They will still have time to go out and run for office."[52]

Truman was invoking the same strategy that Clark Clifford and Jim Rowe had laid out in the memoranda to revive the Truman presidency after the Democratic loss of Congress in 1946. The convention delegates cheered and applauded the challenge to the opposition party. It was a fighting prelude to a predictably unproductive special session against which Truman could and did rave effectively throughout the approaching campaign. An unsigned memo given to Truman by Clifford had noted: "This course may be hazardous politically, but we cannot shut our eyes to the fact that President Truman faces an uphill fight to win the coming election." Later he explained in football jargon: "We had to be bold. If we kept plugging away in moderate terms, the best we could have done would have been to reach midfield when the gun went off. So we had to throw long passes, anything to stir up labor and to get the mass votes of the great cities."[53]

The strategy also kept the national spotlight on Truman, goading the Republican-controlled legislature to do the people's business, and reduced Dewey, at least temporarily, to a bit player in the drama, merely urging Congress to consider carefully the president's proposals. During the special session, Dewey wrote to an aunt: "Mr. Truman's special session is a nuisance but I do not believe it will have much effect on the election."[54] At the end of the session, a reporter asked Truman if he would "say it was a do-nothing session." The president replied: "I would say it was entirely a do-nothing session. I think that's a good name for the Eightieth Congress."[55] Thus was born the label for the attack that fueled his campaign all fall.

On the heels of the Democratic convention, the most vocal states' rights defenders met in Birmingham and nominated their own ticket, popularly known as the Dixiecrats. Governor J. Strom Thurmond of South Carolina was chosen for president and Governor Fielding L. Wright of Mississippi as his running mate. Their platform did not beat about the bush; it demanded "the segregation of the races and the racial integrity of each race."[56] The group's obvious hope was to set itself up as the balance of power in the event no candidate received a majority in the electoral college. It was a possibility they believed to be enhanced by the fact that Henry Wallace was about to be nominated by the Progressive Party at an exuberant convention in Philadelphia.

Wallace, as a result of his attacks on the Truman Doctrine and the Marshall Plan and his expressed sympathies for the Soviet Union, inevitably drew charges of being a communist, and his Progressive Party of being communist-dominated. But Truman and the Democratic Party also found themselves vulnerable to allegations of subversion when former Communist Party members testified before Republican-controlled congressional committees. Elizabeth Bentley, a confessed agent, and Whittaker Chambers, a senior editor for *Time* magazine, accused nine government officials of being involved in spy rings for the Russians, the most prominent of whom was Alger Hiss, a former State Department adviser. Hiss denied Chambers's allegations, but young California Congressman Richard Nixon pressed the accusations, which Truman dismissed as a "red herring." During the campaign, Truman ignored the charges, and the presence of the Wallace campaign may have drawn off much of the political fire on the communism-in-government issue, at least for the time.

When the presidential campaign officially opened on Labor Day, the wide consensus was that nobody—not Truman, not Wallace, not Thurmond, nor any combination thereof—was going to keep Dewey out of the White House in 1949. The Gallup poll in August had the New York governor leading Truman by 48 percent to 37, and that and other polls had Dewey ahead all the way to election day.

Truman had started campaigning even before his nomination, with a whistle-stop train trip to California in June. On Labor Day he made the traditional Democratic bow to the unions in Detroit's Cadillac Square, boosted by the political arms of the AFL and CIO. Dewey didn't set out on his first train trip until the third week in September, confident of victory and secure in the conviction that his best strategy was to remain restrainedly above the fray while the underdog incumbent struggled to gain traction. Dewey had been criticized in 1944 for getting off the high road near the end and making harsh remarks about Roosevelt that appeared to backfire on him. This time around, he was going to avoid that error; indeed, that intent coupled with his natural aloofness, not to say sense of superiority, dictated that Dewey run as if he, not Truman, were the occupant of the Oval Office.

The man who still did sit there, embarking on his first major whistle-stop trip across the country as the Democratic nominee, was given a rousing sendoff from Washington's Union Station on September 17. His running mate, Barkley, urged him to "go out there and mow 'em down!" Truman replied: "I'll mow 'em down, Alben, and I'll give 'em hell!"[57] Those fighting words became his battlefield pledge against Dewey and the Republicans, and before long there was seldom a stop at which somebody in the crowd would fail to call out, "Give 'em hell, Harry!"

In his first major agriculture speech in Dexter, Iowa, he castigated Wall Street manipulators who kept farm prices down, and he reminded listening farmers that "the Republicans [in Congress] gave you that greatest of all depressions" and "stuck a pitchfork in the farmer's back." He went on: "I wonder how many times you have to be hit on the head before you find out who's hitting you. . . . These Republican gluttons of privilege are cold men. . . . What they have taken away from you thus far would only be an appetizer for the economic tapeworm of big business."[58]

Truman continued like that, sunrise to sunset and sometimes beyond, while Dewey adopted a more leisurely and formal pace. At the start of his first whistle-stop trip, the governor had issued a statement backing farm price supports, but it was lost in the Truman harangue charging otherwise. A Republican congressman from Minnesota, August H. Andresen, warned Dewey that Truman was scoring points in the farm states with his attacks. "Many of the farmers are on the fence," he wrote the GOP nominee, "due to remarks made by Truman about Republicans wrecking the farm program."[59] But Dewey continued to take solace in the favorable poll numbers. He declined to respond in kind, nor to defend what Truman now regularly was calling "the do-nothing Eightieth Congress."

In Dewey's opening speech in Des Moines, he promised "an administration which has faith in the American people, a warm understanding of their needs and the competence to meet them. We will rediscover," he droned, "the essential unity of our people and the spiritual strength which make our country great."[60] It was hardly the stuff to set the crowd ablaze, but with the polls reading as they did Dewey seemed content to go along on cruise control. Even the fact that wherever Truman went he was drawing larger and larger crowds did not shake the Dewey campaign's complacency, nor the consensus among reporters on the campaign trail, even those covering Truman, that Dewey was a sure winner.

Compared to the stiff and proper Dewey, however, Truman was the friendly neighbor next door. At stop after stop he would introduce his homebody wife, Bess, to the crowd as "The Boss" and his smiling young daughter as "Miss Margaret." His language was folksy and Main Street and his demeanor benign—until he started out against the Republicans. Then he let himself go, often not letting the facts get in his way. Robert J. Donovan, who rode on the Truman train as a political reporter for the *New York Herald-Tribune,* described the Truman message as "sharp speeches fairly criticizing Republican policy and defending New Deal liberalism, mixed with sophistries, bunkum piled higher than haystacks, and demagoguery tooting merrily down the track."[61]

Truman went so far in Chicago in late October as to imply, to some listeners' ears, that Dewey could be a budding fascist. He warned of "the powerful reactionary forces which are silently undermining our democratic institutions . . . when a few men get control of the economy of a nation, they find a front man to run the country for them." In Germany, he went on, "they put money and influence behind Adolf Hitler. We know the rest of the story."[62] Even this outrageous outburst failed to stir Dewey to angry response.

The only ripple in the smooth sea of Dewey's demeanor came in mid-October when his campaign train, stopped in Beaucoup, Illinois, for a rear-platform speech by the nominee, suddenly lurched backwards in the direction of the crowd packed in close. It quickly stopped before anyone was hurt, but Dewey blurted into the microphone: "That's the first lunatic I have had for an engineer. He probably ought to be shot at sunrise, but I guess we can let him off because no one was hurt."[63]

That remark may have been Dewey's idea of humor, but Truman jumped on it. In a radio criticism of the governor's promise to bring efficiency to Washington, he observed that "Mr. Hoover was an efficiency expert . . . as the Republicans presented him, he was the 'Great Engineer.' We have been hearing about engineers again recently from the Republican candidate. He objects to having engineers back up. He doesn't mention, however, that under the Great Engineer we backed up into the worst depression in our history."[64] Truman was nothing if not relentless.

As the campaign came down to the wire, Truman's crowds got ever bigger and Dewey's lead in the Gallup poll shrank somewhat, to five percentage points. Still, few voices other than Truman's own were giving him a chance. Truman's slight improvement in the polls was attributed to the collapse of the Wallace campaign and the inability of the Dixiecrats to get theirs off the ground. But the Gallup poll, like the others, had stopped surveying voters in mid-October and failed to catch the late rush for the president, who had logged in a remarkable 31,000 miles in an uphill quest for a political miracle.

On election night, after the *Chicago Tribune* had come out with its first edition blaring "DEWEY DEFEATS TRUMAN," the final results gave Truman 2 million more votes than his challenger—49.5 percent of the total to 45 for Dewey and only 2.4 percent each for Wallace and Thurmond. In a four-man race, Truman had come close to achieving a majority, and his electoral college victory was emphatic: 303 to 189 for Dewey and 39 for Thurmond, all in Dixie.

The Democratic Party was the winner too, regaining control of both houses of Congress with a pickup of seventy-five seats in the House and nine in the Senate, where newcomers Paul Douglas of Illinois, Lyndon Johnson of Texas and Estes Kefauver of Tennessee were destined for leadership. Among the new governors was Adlai E. Stevenson II of Illinois, grandson of Grover Cleveland's second vice president.

But the star of the night was Truman. In the most startling presidential election comeback in American history, the commonsense man from Missouri who had never aspired to the presidency, and for some time had said he looked forward to leaving it after one accidental term, had fooled the experts. In his fashion, he had kept the New Deal alive in the face of those in the opposition party and in his own who would have killed it. Now as president in his own right, truly the choice of the people, he had a mandate to give new direction to the party of Jefferson, Jackson and his political benefactor, FDR.

Chapter 21

THE FAIR DEAL, AND END OF AN ERA, 1949–1952

HARRY TRUMAN TOOK his remarkable upset victory over Dewey as a public confirmation that the American people, for all the Republican assaults on his stewardship, wanted to continue the Democratic Party policies embodied in the term "New Deal." In his State of the Union address in January 1949, he gave it a new label, however, by saying, "every segment of our population and every individual has a right to expect from his government a fair deal."[1] It was a phrase he had personally inserted in the speech.

The voters, he said, "have rejected the discredited theory that the fortunes of the nation should be in the hands of a privileged few. Instead, we believe that our economic system should rest on a democratic foundation and that wealth should be created for the benefit of all."[2] His Fair Deal agenda actually went beyond that of the New Deal in proposing at least three major new initiatives in the fields of civil rights, national health insurance and federal aid to public education. Part of giving working Americans a fair deal was Truman's determined effort to win repeal of organized labor's pet hate, the Taft-Hartley law.

For all of Truman's confidence in the voters, his election with only 49.5 percent of the popular vote was hardly a groundswell demand for a more liberal agenda. And while the Democratic Party had achieved narrow control of the Eighty-first Congress, there were enough conservative Democrats holding the balance of power to give the Republicans a work-

In 1952, Governor Adlai E. Stevenson of Illinois ran for president against war-hero General Dwight D. Eisenhower, the Republican nominee, and was snowed under. Here retiring President Harry Truman offers optimism to the beaten Democratic donkey as Stevenson applies smelling salts.

ing majority on a number of issues on which they differed with the Democratic president. Having tasted an unexpected and hence particularly bitter defeat in Dewey's loss, congressional Republicans returned to Capitol Hill determined to resist what many of them came to call Truman's "socialist" policies. Memories of his allegations of the Republican-controlled "do-nothing Eightieth Congress" also added to the hostile climate.

These circumstances made it more important than ever that Truman maintain and nurture cooperative relations with the Democratic congressional leaders, Rayburn in the House and Lucas in the Senate. From the outset, the prospects were not promising for the Fair Deal agenda, despite the election in 1948 of some vigorous new liberals like Humphrey, Douglas and Kefauver to the Senate and a number of Northern and labor members in the House. A liberalization of rules in the House facilitated progress on the agenda there, but failure to weaken the filibuster rule in the Senate became a severe impediment, especially on the civil rights legislation blocked by Dixiecrats. In his second term, Truman sought to deny patronage to conservative Democrats who bucked him, but he was discouraged in the effort by Rayburn and Lucas as being counterproductive.

A month after the election, Truman's critics, probing for more soft spots in the president's political standing, had pounced on the federal indictment of Alger Hiss on two counts of perjury in denying the allegations of spying for the Soviet Union. In a post-election press conference Truman was asked whether he still dismissed the House investigation of Hiss as a "red herring," as he had during the campaign. He replied: "I do." Young Congressman Richard Nixon seized on the answer as a "flagrant flouting of the national interests" and other Republicans soon were labeling the president as soft on communism.

Truman himself seemed unfazed by threats of communism and the Soviet Union perceived by others. Stalin was "Uncle Joe" to him and, secure in American military dominance with sole possession of the atomic bomb, he presided over sharp reductions in the armed forces, to the point that by 1949 the army was down to ten active divisions.

Anticipating a second term of relative tranquility at home and abroad, the president launched an ambitious undertaking to deal with the "revolution of rising expectations" occurring in the Third World, highlighted by a so-called Point Four program of aid to underdeveloped countries to encourage their quest for independence and democracy.[3] After the election General Marshall retired as secretary of state, and Truman put the State Department in the hands of Dean Acheson. With the creation of the North Atlantic Treaty Organization (NATO) in April 1949, the focus of American foreign policy remained on Europe, even as the communists in China drove the nationalist forces of Chiang Kai-shek to Formosa (later called Taiwan) and trouble brewed in Korea, split after World War II into a communist north and democratic south. There, U.S. and Soviet forces that had occupied the divided country since the fall of Japan pulled out in June, amid ambiguous signals concerning the American commitment to a free South Korea. Both MacArthur and Acheson, in drawing a "defensive perimeter" within which U.S. forces stood ready to oppose aggression, failed to include Korea. In the event of an attack, Acheson said, "the initial reliance must be on the people attacked to resist it, and then upon the commitments of the entire civilized world under the Charter of the United Nations."[4]

In September, however, the American leadership was shaken out of its complacency when the Soviet Union successfully tested an atomic bomb. After contentious debate among Truman's scientific and military advisers, the president ordered a start to building an even more lethal hydrogen bomb, while also reviewing American policy toward the Soviet Union. That review came as a much more serious Red scare was emerging than the one of Woodrow Wilson's attorney general, Mitchell Palmer, more than thirty years earlier.

In January 1950, Alger Hiss was found guilty on two counts of lying in denying having passed State Department documents to a Russian agent. Congressman Nixon took to radio to charge "high officials" in the FDR and Truman administrations with having made a "deliberate" effort to cover up what he called the Hiss "conspiracy."[5] Acheson, formerly a close associate of Hiss at the State Department, told reporters in an empathetic if politically imprudent way that "whatever the outcome of any appeal which Mr. Hiss or his lawyers may take in this case, I do not intend to turn my back on Alger Hiss."[6]

In the Senate, Republicans jumped on the remark with unfeigned glee. Chief among the gloaters was Senator Joseph R. McCarthy of Wisconsin, in the process of launching a freewheeling, irresponsible campaign as a Red hunter. A conservative colleague, Karl Mundt of South Dakota, had served on the House committee investigating the Hiss matter before his election to the Senate, and McCarthy asked him if he was aware of Acheson's statement. Mundt replied: "I am not greatly concerned about what influence Alger Hiss has on the position of Dean Acheson's back, but a great many Americans are concerned about the degree of influence Hiss may have had upon the position of Dean Acheson's mind."[7] Whereupon McCarthy rhetorically asked whether Acheson "is also telling the world that he will not turn his back on any of the other Communists in the State Department."[8] That remark was a good example of the McCarthy style, assuming as fact that there were "other Communists" in the department. That afternoon Acheson went to the White House and offered his resignation to the president. Truman refused it and Acheson stayed on as secretary.

But McCarthy did not go away. In early February he launched a Red-baiting campaign in West Virginia in which he said, "I have here in my hand a list" of communists in the State Department "known to the secretary of state" who were "still working and making policy."[9] There was some dispute afterward about the number, but some said later he had put it at 205. At any rate, he then sent Truman this telegram: "In a Lincoln Day speech in Wheeling Thursday night I stated that the State Department harbors a nest of communists and communist sympathizers who are helping to shape our foreign policy. I further stated that I have in my possession the names of 57 communists who are in the State Department at present."[10]

In his telegram McCarthy demanded that Truman give Congress full reports on State Department employees he said were listed by the administration's Loyalty Security Board as poor risks "because of . . . communistic connections," adding that "failure on your part will label the Democratic party of being the bedfellow of international communism."[11] The president disregarded McCarthy's demands out of hand, but the Wisconsin senator repeated his allegations on the Senate floor, where he had immunity from charges of libel and slander.

At one stretch he ranted on over six hours of back-and-forth with other senators, now saying he had the names of eighty-one communists at State, pulling out folders he professed were dossiers of them that later proved to be no such thing, and refusing the requests of colleagues for specific names. He said he was ready to give them to an appropriate committee of the Senate, but never did. Thus was McCarthyism born, eventually igniting public opinion into a frenzy of accusations and division, not only in the Senate but around the country as well. Exasperated, Truman finally called a press conference and labeled McCarthy "the greatest asset that the Kremlin has."[12]

Democratic senators, confident they could bring McCarthy down by exposing his charges as fiction, created a special subcommittee of the Senate Foreign Relations Committee to investigate them. One of the Senate's most prestigious Democrats, Millard Tydings of Maryland, was named chairman. McCarthy attacked the committee, alleging it was really out to uncover his informants "so they can be kicked out of the State Department tomorrow."[13]

Bullying tactics by McCarthy, who at the same time was issuing more unsubstantiated charges without naming a single communist, got Tydings to pressure Truman to release files on loyalty investigations to the committee. A Republican member of the committee, Senator Henry Cabot Lodge Jr. of Massachusetts, reported that a review of eighty-one loyalty files had yielded no evidence of communist affiliation on the part of anyone. The committee declared McCarthy's allegations a "fraud and a hoax . . . perhaps the most nefarious campaign of half-truths and untruth in the history of this republic."[14] But by this time the Wisconsin senator had successfully injected them into the consciousness of millions of Americans still ready to believe them.

Amid this expanding hysteria at home, a National Security Council review in April called for more aggressive military preparation in what was now widely known as the Cold War between the communist and Western worlds. The review recommended a swift buildup not only of nuclear weapons but also of the capability for fighting conventional wars.

The alert came just in time. On June 25 massive forces of the communist puppet regime in North Korea crossed the previously accepted military demarcation at the 38th parallel. Truman immediately ordered American troops under General MacArthur into South Korea to defend it, at the same time calling on the United Nations Security Council to embrace the action. At the time, the Soviet Union was boycotting the council in protest over its refusal to grant a seat to Communist China and hence could not exercise its veto power. Truman rejected demands that he get authorization from Congress, contending it was within his presidential powers to undertake what administration supporters preferred to call a "police action."

The invasion sent South Korean, U.S. and some other UN forces reeling. MacArthur, however, in a brilliant amphibious troop landing behind enemy lines at Inchon, cut off the North Koreans and regained control of most of South Korea. Flush with success, the UN General Assembly authorized the UN command under MacArthur to cross the 38th parallel to establish "a unified, independent, and democratic Korea."[15]

Truman suddenly found himself a president in a major war again, a role he had played only briefly upon succeeding FDR, and this time with mounting political troubles at home as well. Revelations of corruption in the White House centered on Truman's military aide and personal friend, Major General Harry Vaughan, a naïve man who fell prey to exploitative businessmen seeking access. Through him, they bestowed expensive gifts including deep freezers for Mrs. Truman and others in her husband's administration.

Men with such access through Vaughan or other White House aides were discovered to have peddled it for 5 percent of government contracts attained by applicants. The existence and activities of these "five percenters" made juicy newspaper stories and led to congressional investigations that were greatly embarrassing to Truman. Characteristically, he stood steadfastly behind Vaughan's denials of any wrongdoing. In fact, there was nothing illegal about the practice at the time, and Vaughan told a Senate committee: "I do these people a courtesy of putting them in contact with the persons with whom they can tell their story."[16]

Later disclosures coming out of Senate hearings, including the gift of a mink coat to a White House secretary from a firm seeking a government loan, led to a Republican rallying cry against "the mess in Washington" that was to carry over into the next presidential election. Other congressional hearings contributed to Truman's woes and those of the Democratic Party, precipitated by a Democratic maverick, freshman Senator Estes Kefauver of Tennessee, who in the course of investigating organized crime entangled some prominent big-city Democratic politicians.

At the same time, Truman's Fair Deal agenda was being manhandled by Congress. Southern Democrats joined with Republicans to throttle civil rights legislation. They filibustered an anti–poll tax bill, with freshman Texas Senator Lyndon Johnson in his maiden speech calling the parliamentary tool of cloture—stopping debate by vote of a two-thirds majority—"the deadliest weapon in the arsenal of parliamentary procedure."[17] Most significant civil rights reform was detoured, as was Truman's strenuous effort to achieve repeal of the Taft-Hartley law, which, among other things, barred the closed shop—requiring union membership as a condition of hiring—a tremendous organizing tool for labor.

Truman's requests for farm legislation, social security reform, a $4 billion tax increase and more public education funds all bit the dust as well. His only modest legislative achievements were a public housing act and an increase in the minimum wage to 75 cents an hour, and even that was marred by congressional refusal to cover millions of workers exempted from the provision. Truman wrote in his diary: "Trying to make the 81st Congress perform is and has been worse than cussing the 80th.... I've kissed and petted more consarned S.O.B. so-called Democrats and left wing Republicans [than] all the Presidents put together."[18]

At this time Truman had an even more "consarned S.O.B." with whom to deal—General MacArthur. Traveling to the Pacific to discuss the war with him on Wake Island, Truman asked the general how he rated the prospect of Chinese or Soviet intervention on the side of the North Koreans. MacArthur replied he saw "very little" chance of it, adding that with no air force, "if the Chinese tried to get down to Pyongyang [the North Korean capital] there would be the greatest slaughter." If the Soviets joined in, however, that would be different, he said, but he doubted they would.[19]

Truman returned home well pleased with what had been a cordial meeting with the great general, on whom he had bestowed a Distinguished Service Medal at their parting. Two weeks later, after being informed by the CIA in a morning White House meeting that it had been "clearly established" that as many as 15,000 to 20,000 Chinese Communist troops were now in North Korea,[20] he walked across the street to Blair House for lunch and a short nap. He was scheduled to go to Arlington Cemetery in the afternoon for the unveiling of a statue of Field Marshal Sir John Dill, a World War II British general. The residential portion of the White House was under rehabilitation and the Trumans were quartered at the smaller residence on the other side of Pennsylvania Avenue. The temperature was an unseasonably hot 85 degrees in the shade, so he stripped to his underwear and stretched out on a four-poster bed near an open front window looking out on the avenue.

Suddenly gunfire broke out down below, sending Truman scurrying to the open window. "Get back! Get back!" someone below, perhaps one of the Secret Service agents on duty, called to him, and he quickly retreated out of sight. Two men, fanatic Puerto Rican nationalists, had opened fire on the agents in a failed attempt to enter Blair House and kill the president. One defending agent was killed and two others wounded. One of the assailants also was killed and the other, wounded, was later tried, convicted and sentenced to death in the electric chair. Truman, who had always been for Puerto Rican self-determination, later commuted the sentence to life imprisonment, and in 1979 President Jimmy Carter granted the man a pardon.[21]

After the shooting, Truman dressed, left Blair House by a rear exit and proceeded to Arlington Cemetery under heavy guard to keep his appointment. The next day he took his accustomed early morning stroll, with a larger Secret Service contingent in tow. But that was the end of his walking from the White House to Blair House. Thereafter he made the short trip across Pennsylvania Avenue in a bulletproof car.

November brought other jolts to Truman. In the months leading up to the off-year congressional elections, McCarthy had continued his wild allegations of communists in the Truman administration, vengefully focusing on Tydings and two other Democratic members of his investigating committee seeking reelection—Senate Majority Leader Lucas and Brien McMahon of Connecticut. Invading Tydings's state, he declared: "Lucas provided the whitewash when I charged there were communists in high places in government; McMahon brought the bucket; Tydings the brush." The three, he said, "have done more than any others in this nation to shield the traitors, protect the disloyal and confuse Americans in their desperate fight to clean out the communists."[22]

Echoes of McCarthyism also were heard in California, where Congressman Nixon was seeking a Senate seat against Congresswoman Helen Gahagan Douglas. She was, Nixon told one audience, "pink right down to her underwear."[23] On election night, McMahon survived but Tydings, Lucas and Douglas lost, victims of the frenzy whipped up by the pathological loose cannon from Wisconsin. In all, the Democrats lost five Senate seats and thirty in the House, narrowing their majority and further undermining the party's liberal wing.

Even such seemingly entrenched party bosses as Frank Hague in Jersey City and new Tammany Hall leader Carmine DeSapio in New York suffered setbacks. Indeed, bosses in general continued to see their power wane as their old role as distributors of public beneficence was often supplanted by federal social welfare programs. Republicans picked up six governorships and their conservative icon in the Senate, Taft of Ohio, survived an aggressive labor effort to beat him, strengthening his position for the 1952 GOP presidential nomination.

Meanwhile, MacArthur was poised to finish the war in Korea. In late November he announced that his forces were ready to drive north. Two days later, however, Chinese troops swarmed south, splitting the UN forces and pushing them far back into South Korea. Republicans were quick to recall Acheson's statement drawing a "defensive perimeter" in Asia that did not include Korea, implying that it had turned out to be an invitation to the Chinese to move with impunity into South Korea.

MacArthur let it be known that he felt he had been hamstrung by Washington in not having had authority to attack Chinese bases in Manchuria over the North Korean border. Truman, angered, ordered that all commanders in the field—meaning MacArthur—henceforth clear all public comments with Washington. In the meantime, General Matthew B. Ridgway, in charge of the U.S. Eighth Army, fought back and over the next months reestablished control near the 38th parallel. The White House decided to seek a negotiated settlement along the original north-south dividing line.

In late March, however, MacArthur, in violation of Truman's order to clear all statements, and knowing of Truman's intention to negotiate an end to the war, issued what amounted to an ultimatum of his own to China. It said in effect that the Eighth Army's advance had proved that China could not prevail and faced "imminent military collapse" if the United Nations forces were relieved of the restrictions placed upon them.[24]

MacArthur followed that statement with a letter to House Republican leader Joseph Martin agreeing with him that the forces of Chiang Kai-shek on Formosa should be employed to open a second front against China, which would clearly be a widening of the war. MacArthur cast the fight he was waging in Korea in terms of confronting a monolithic Red peril: "If we lose the war to Communism in Asia the fall of Europe is inevitable, win it and Europe most probably would avoid war and yet preserve freedom . . . we must win. There is no substitute for victory."[25] On April 5, Martin read the letter on the House floor. The president, after conferring with his chief military advisers, decided that MacArthur had to be fired.

The announcement of the great warrior's recall created an uproar on Capitol Hill and in the country. Republican members of Congress demanded Truman's own head, with Joe McCarthy predictably being the loudest and most intemperate. He accused the president of being drunk when he made the decision—from "bourbon and Benedictine," adding: "the son of a bitch should be impeached."[26] Nixon, too, chimed in with customary understatement: "The happiest group in the country will be the communists and their stooges. . . . The president has given them what they have always wanted—MacArthur's scalp."[27]

According to Ridgway's diary, when ordered by Truman to replace MacArthur, he called on the deposed commander, who told him he had heard that Truman "was suffering from malignant hypertension . . . characterized by bewilderment and confusion . . . and wouldn't live six months."[28] Invited by Martin to address Congress, the general made the most of the melodramatic opportunity, essentially repeating his military views sharply opposed to those of his commander in chief, and concluding with the memorable line: "Old soldiers never die; they just fade away."[29] In his case, however, MacArthur clung sufficiently to the limelight to seek the presidency later, with feeble result, and the war in Korea dragged on in stalemate without him. Peace talks began in July 1951, but the fighting continued.

With twenty-one months yet to serve in his term, Truman was in political stalemate as well. Congress frustrated him at every turn, and, added to the wide, Republican-fueled perception of a "mess in Washington," his firing of MacArthur caused deep public division. The party's once solid Southern base was eroding and big-city bosses in the North were losing much of their clout. Ironically, the success of the New Deal in reducing the nation's underclass, or at least meeting many of its basic needs through federal programs, diminished the role of many bosses as providers of government largesse. Even in places where Truman's political lieutenants had entered in mutually beneficial partnership with bosses, as with Hague in Jersey City, charges of corruption or voter dissatisfaction were catching up with them. Loyalty programs and processes were running amok, to the chagrin of Truman himself.

In 1952 more scandals broke out in the Bureau of Internal Revenue and even in the Justice Department, culminating in the eventual resignation of Attorney General J. Howard McGrath, not for involvement in corruption himself but for weak policing of it. In April, Truman invoked the same presidential power he had claimed in sending troops to Korea to seize the steel industry, to avert a strike he said would be critically damaging to the war effort. The action triggered no fewer than fourteen congressional resolutions calling for his impeachment.

Labor contracts between the industry and the United Steel Workers of America had expired the previous December, with the union demanding a wage increase. The Taft-Hartley Act provided for an eighty-day cooling-off period, but Truman resisted invoking the law he had tried to repeal, knowing it was anathema to his allies in organized labor. He turned the dispute over to the Wage Stabilization Board and got the union to stay on the job pending its finding. When it came in, however, the industry offered the union much less than the board had called for. Incensed at the steel companies' attitude, Truman decided to rely on inherent constitutional power in a national crisis.

Aware that he could be challenged in court, he took the unusual and probably unethical step of asking his old friend and former treasury secretary Fred Vinson, then Chief Justice of the Supreme Court, for advice. Vinson privately told him to go ahead.[30] When he announced his decision, Philip Murray, head of the CIO, immediately called off the strike and pledged to work for the government as employer. Truman invited Congress to pass legislation that would govern the running of the mills, but was rebuffed. The companies sought and, to Truman's dismay, obtained a restraining order from a district court judge, which the government appealed to the Supreme Court. To the president's further chagrin and humiliation, it ruled his action was unconstitutional, by a vote of 6–3.

Still refusing to use Taft-Hartley, Truman let the strike go on for fifty-three days. On the fifty-first, his secretary of defense, Robert Lovett, declared that the strike had indeed damaged the war effort, and Truman called in both sides, demanding a settlement. They agreed in late July, on terms roughly offered by the companies at the outset.

By this time, beleaguered Harry Truman was a self-proclaimed lame duck. The year before, the states had ratified the Twenty-second Amendment passed by a Republican Congress in protest of FDR's four elections, limiting a president to two terms. It specifically provided, however, that the president in office at the time of ratification—Truman—could seek another term. For most of his second term, he kept his own counsel about his intentions, not revealing that in April 1950, more than ten months before ratification of the amendment, he had written a statement saying flatly he would not run again in 1952: "In my opinion eight years as President is enough and sometimes too much for any man to serve in that capacity."[31] He said he knew he could be elected again but was not going to break the precedent as FDR had done.

In November 1951, Truman informed his closest White House aides of his decision but did not disclose it publicly, no doubt aware that declaring himself a lame duck could diminish his influence with Congress. At that time, he told Fred Vinson he would support him for the Democratic presidential nomination the next year, but Vinson declined. In January of the election year, Truman discussed the presidency with Governor Adlai E. Stevenson of Illinois, not well known to him, but he was impressed and urged Stevenson to seek it. The governor was not persuaded.[32]

Many important Democrats, not knowing of Truman's intentions and fearful that after all the woes of his second term he would be defeated if he ran and would take other party candidates down with him, talked of opposing his renomination. But in New Hampshire, without clearing his actions with anyone, a Manchester lumber dealer took it upon himself to collect enough petitions to enter the president's name in the state's first-in-the-nation Democratic presidential primary. The next day Truman dismissed it, telling a press conference: "All these primaries are just eyewash when the convention meets, as you will find out."[33] He evidently did not take into consideration the growing importance in terms of public awareness and news coverage that such primaries were beginning to acquire.

Truman said he would ask to have his name removed, but it wasn't, and he found himself in a contest, albeit not competing actively in it, with Senator Kefauver. The offbeat Tennessean was now somewhat of a celebrity as a result of the televising of his Senate committee's lively hearings featuring many colorful organized crime figures. He campaigned energetically and diligently in a coonskin cap in New Hampshire, while the president stayed home. Truman's slipping popularity along with Kefauver's folksy appeal and presence produced what was widely seen as a huge upset when the incumbent president was soundly defeated in the primary. A group of Southern Democrats formed a dump-Truman movement and vowed to walk out of the party convention in July if he were renominated.

Truman finally announced on March 29 that he would not seek reelection, leaving the impression that Kefauver's emphatic victory over him in New Hampshire had driven him from the race. Kefauver, for his part, continued on the primary campaign trail, winning in Wisconsin with only token opposition and doing the same or faring well against favorite sons in about ten others. He ran as a confirmed liberal and along the way picked up endorsements from the likes of Paul Douglas, Claude Pepper and Jimmy Roosevelt, while failing to impress party chieftains, who disliked his independence from them.

Others offering themselves as candidates or favorite sons included Senator Richard Russell of Georgia, clearly a regional candidate; W. Averell Harriman, the railroad heir from New York who served in the FDR and Truman administrations; Senator Robert S. Kerr of Oklahoma, a rich and domineering oil man, and seventy-four-year-old Vice President Barkley. Stevenson was being pushed by Illinois machine boss Jake Arvey after running ahead of Truman in his 1948 gubernatorial victory, but Stevenson continued to insist that he wanted only a second term as governor.

In the Republican camp, meanwhile, the man Harry Truman had either urged to run or inquired about as a possible Democratic candidate in 1948, General Eisenhower, had made himself available for a draft. With the conservative Taft already in the race, moderate Senator Lodge in January placed Eisenhower's name in the New Hampshire Republican primary. Thereupon the general dropped his adamant posture of four years earlier against being a candidate, saying from NATO headquarters in France that he would have to yield to a [Republican] "clear-cut call to political duty." The announcement irritated Truman no end, apparently because he had thought the general might agree to be the Democratic nominee.

A month earlier, amid renewed speculation about Eisenhower's political availability as either a Democrat or a Republican, the president had written to him: "My own position is in the balance. If I do what I want to do I'll go back to Missouri and *maybe* run for the Senate. If you decide to finish the European job [as NATO supreme commander] . . . I must keep the isolationists [apparently referring to Taft] out of the White House. I wish you would let me know what you intend to do. It will be between us and no one else."[34]

Eisenhower replied that he, too, had other preferences, "but just as you have decided that circumstances may not permit you to do exactly as you please, so I've found that fervent desire may sometimes have to give way to a conviction of duty."[35] At the same time, he told Truman he thought a draft was "so remote as to be negligible" and that a "policy of complete abstention [from politics] will be meticulously observed by me unless and until extraordinary circumstances would place a mandate upon me" that he couldn't reject.[36]

One aspect of that "mandate" apparently was Eisenhower's concern that Truman or one of his loyalists would run. After the 1952 election, according to Donovan, still covering the White House for the *New York Herald-Tribune*, Eisenhower confided to him and another reporter "that the reason he had run for president was to prevent the Truman administration from continuing in power. He said he would not have run if he had known that Governor Adlai E. Stevenson of Illinois would be the Democratic nominee."[37]

Truman had his own thoughts on the subject. In his memoirs, he wrote: "I am inclined to think that if I had announced early in 1950 or 1951 that I intended to carry the fight myself to a conclusion General Eisenhower would not have been the Republican candidate—and perhaps not the President. I hold to that opinion because I am sure that Eisenhower in 1952 thought that he would have no fight for the election and that perhaps the Democrats would nominate him also."[38]

Truman tried again, in March, to persuade Stevenson to run. When he declined, the president, according to aides, reconsidered for a time his decision not to seek another term, out of concern that Kefauver, for whom he had low regard, might be the party's choice. But in polling his closest staff people, Truman got no urging that he change his mind. Thereupon he gave some pro forma encouragement to Barkley, almost certainly not likely to be nominated because of his age, but the vice president ran into stiff opposition from labor leaders and threatened to withdraw. Truman talked him out of it, but also gave an approving nod to the favorite-son candidacy of Harriman in New York. No matter how many primaries Kefauver won, party regular leaders were not going to buy him, nor would those in the North swallow Russell. Hence the quest for an alternative continued, focusing mostly on the reluctant Stevenson. In the Republican primaries, Taft brought his conservative strength to bear in amassing convention delegates. But the liberal Eastern establishment that had captured the nomination the two previous times for Dewey and then lost the elections was staunchly opposed to him. That fact was a major element in the pressure on Eisenhower to run, with Dewey in the forefront. As Taft and Harold Stassen campaigned aggressively in the primaries and Earl Warren consolidated his support mainly in his home base of California, Eisenhower let Dewey and associates carry the ball for him, remaining above the fray at his post in France.

Their task was not easy, because many convention delegates had committed themselves to Taft, "Mr. Republican," and had to be pried away for a military man whose identity as a Republican had only just been declared. In June the Eisenhower strategists finally persuaded the general to resign as commander of NATO and return home to campaign. He was not a polished orator—the conservative *Chicago Tribune* editorialized that he engaged in "five-star generalities"[39]—but the magnetic and warm personality of the war hero who had beaten Nazism ignited sparks with voters regardless of party.

As the Republican convention opened in Chicago on July 7, Taft came in with a sizable delegate lead and control of the national committee running the show, but Eisenhower was surprisingly strong considering his late start and lack of standing in the party. To close the gap, the Eisenhower forces challenged the credentials of delegates. A group of GOP governors led by Dewey proposed a "fair play" rule that worked to the benefit of Eisenhower in contesting about seventy seats in the Georgia, Louisiana and Texas delegations. Taft had the backing of party organizations in those states and had been awarded their delegates, but the Eisenhower forces had elected rival slates and demanded recognition. When they were rebuffed by the pro-Taft national committee, the general's strategists, in raucous televised debate, pushed through the rule that enabled them to have most of their contested delegates seated.

The strategy paid off. On the first roll call, with the large uncommitted delegations of Michigan and Pennsylvania swinging to Eisenhower, he came within 19 votes of the required majority. Then 19 Stassen votes in Minnesota switched to him, followed by a massive further movement to his column. When it was over he had 845 delegates to only 280 for Taft and 77 for Warren. The forces of the latter two moved to make the vote unanimous, and it was done. Senator Nixon of California, who had been officially committed to Warren as his state's favorite son but had worked behind the scenes with Dewey in the hope of landing on the Eisenhower ticket, was indeed chosen as his running mate, by acclamation. Eisenhower, unaware that the choice was his, accepted the recommendation of Dewey and Herbert Brownell, who in previous years had been Dewey's presidential campaign manager.

Ten days later, also in Chicago, the Democrats met. Stevenson as the host state governor welcomed the delegates, a role that was taken by many as confirmation that he would not agree to be a candidate. His intelligent and witty remarks made many others wish it were not so. The convention passed a platform that essentially endorsed Truman's Fair Deal agenda that had essentially met a dismal fate in Congress. In an attempt to head off another Dixiecrat walkout as in 1948, Northern liberals sought a loyalty oath requiring all delegates to support the nominee, but when key Southerners including Senator Harry Byrd of Virginia and Governor Jimmy Byrnes of South Carolina balked, it was abandoned.

The names of a dozen Democrats were placed in nomination, including that of Stevenson. A draft-Stevenson campaign, organized by a group of Illinois academics and politicians and encouraged by Arvey, was now in full swing. Mayor David Lawrence of Pittsburgh, the Pennsylvania Democratic boss, was aboard, and other state leaders were moving toward the bandwagon. The consensus was that Stevenson's liberal record would win Northern votes without offense to the South, where he was not very well known.

Stevenson apparently was at last convinced. According to Truman in his memoirs, on the fourth day of the convention, the governor suddenly phoned the president "to ask whether it would embarrass me if he allowed his name to be placed in nomination. I replied with a show of exasperation and some rather vigorous words and concluded by saying to Stevenson, 'I have been trying since January to get you to say that. Why would it embarrass me?' "[40] Truman passed the word that Stevenson was his man. A switch to him by the Connecticut delegation "started the swing to Stevenson," Truman wrote, "and my announced open support cinched his nomination."[41]

On the first roll call, Kefauver, on the strength of his primary victories, led with 340 delegates to 273 for Stevenson, 268 for Russell and 123 ½ for Harriman, with the rest scattered among ten others. On the second, Kefauver picked up a handful of votes but Stevenson narrowed his lead, 362 ½ votes to 324 ½, with 294 for Russell. Truman, who had flown to Chicago during the first two roll calls, learned on arrival that Harriman was ready to withdraw in favor of Stevenson, whereupon Truman had aides call favorite sons asking them to release their delegates to Stevenson.[42] It was done; Stevenson was nominated on the third ballot with 617 ½ votes to 275 ½ for Kefauver, 261 for Russell and most of the rest for Barkley. For vice president, Senator John J. Sparkman of Alabama was chosen by acclamation.

Stevenson was a fresh face in national Democratic politics, but he was no match for the war hero, so new to Republican ranks that voters had no trouble seeing him essentially as a nonpartisan, all-American candidate.

Stevenson was obliged to carry the weight of all the difficulties of Truman's second term, from the war in Korea to every real or imagined scandal summed up in the phrase "the mess in Washington." A man of greater intellect, erudition and polish than Truman, Stevenson lacked the common touch of the man from Missouri, appealing more to campus faculty rooms than to Main Street. When he was photographed on a platform showing one shoe with a hole in the sole, the image was seized by campaign strategists as golden, so desperate were they to counter the "egghead" label that their Republican counterparts fastened onto him. It wasn't enough. He also was criticized for having divorced his wife of twenty-one years, an action much frowned upon in the moral climate of the time.

In the first presidential campaign with considerable television coverage and paid television advertising, Eisenhower's beaming countenance and Republican deep pockets gave him an edge that proved to be more than enough for the task of ending twenty years of Democratic rule. Furthermore, Eisenhower was able to campaign in the manner of a movie star on tour, largely holding himself above the fray on the high road while he had the perfect running mate to engage the opposition on the low.

Nixon, having already earned his spurs as a hatchetman in his ugly campaigns against Jerry Voorhis for Congress and Helen Gahagan Douglas for the Senate, hammered away with vitriol and slander. His slashing style was best illustrated in his description of Stevenson as "Adlai the appeaser . . . who got a Ph.D. from Dean Acheson's College of Cowardly Communist Containment."[43]

In fact it was Nixon who provided the only temporary bump on the road to the White House for the Republican ticket. When it was discovered that Nixon had been the recipient of a special fund from supporters and special interests for his own use in advancing his political career, some party leaders feared the disclosure would erode the Republican ability to make capital over the "mess in Washington" issue. Stevenson, too, had received outside financial aid, but nervous Eisenhower aides pressured him to drop Nixon from the ticket. Pleading for a chance to survive, Nixon was given a chance to vindicate himself in a nationwide television talk. Without disavowing the existence of the fund, he deftly if maudlinly defended himself as an honest family man just getting along. With his wife, Pat, dutifully sitting there, he confessed she "doesn't have a mink coat. But she does have a respectable Republican cloth coat, and I always tell her she'd look good in anything."[44]

The highlight of the speech, or lowlight from the Democratic view-point, was a confession that one of his two young daughters had been sent a cocker spaniel named "Checkers" as a gift. Nixon observed that "the kids love that dog, and I just want to say this right now, that regardless of what they say about it, we're going to keep it."[45] At the close, Nixon asked view-ers to call or wire the Republican National Committee and say whether he should stay on the GOP ticket or get off. The reaction was overwhelm-ingly in his favor, and among those persuaded was Eisenhower himself, who afterward had a buoyant reunion with Nixon that basically put the matter to rest.

Meanwhile, Stevenson, probably inadvertently, kept the "mess in Washington" issue on the front pages by repeating a reporter's use of the phrase himself in an interview, angering Truman. "I wondered," he wrote in his memoirs, "if he had been taken in by the Republican fraudulent build-up of flyspecks on our Washington windows into a big blot or 'mess.' "[46] After the election, Truman was also critical of Stevenson's deci-sion to move his campaign headquarters from Washington to Springfield, Illinois, "giving the impression that he was seeking to disassociate himself from the administration in Washington, and perhaps from me."[47] Indeed, Stevenson did not ask Truman to campaign for him until late in the game, at which time the president put aside his grudges and did so with energy. But his stumping was of questionable assistance, inasmuch as his favor-able rating in the Gallup poll, a remarkable 87 percent in the first months of his presidency, would plunge to 31 percent by the end of 1952.[48]

As was now the custom, all the presidential and vice-presidential nominees campaigned far and wide by whistle-stop train and sometimes by plane. Stevenson grumbled about the paid television commercials fashioned by the Republican ad agency people in New York, complaining at one point: "This isn't Ivory Soap versus Palmolive."[49] But in a large sense for many voters it was. The most effective slogan was simply "I Like Ike," seen on campaign buttons everywhere. The hard fact for the Demo-crats was that it was true; it wasn't that they didn't find Stevenson elo-quent and witty; it was just that he wasn't the beloved "Ike." The principal Democratic slogan, by comparison was a loser: "You never had it so good."

The Republicans sloganized the Democrats as the party of "Korea, Communism and Corruption," and Eisenhower sealed the election in late October, bringing his overwhelming military reputation to bear by pledging "I shall go to Korea" to achieve an end to the war.[50] On election night, the results were predictable: Eisenhower nearly 34 million votes (55.1 percent) and 442 electoral votes, Stevenson 27.3 million ballots (44.4 percent) and 89 in the electoral college.

The Democratic run of two decades of the Roosevelt-Truman, New Deal–Fair Deal era was over. Few doubted that had Truman been successful in getting Eisenhower to run as a Democrat, that streak would have remained intact. Instead, the party was left in disarray, without any real sense of how to put the pieces together again. Democrats were no longer singing "Happy Days Are Here Again."

Chapter 22

IN THE SHADOW OF A WAR HERO,
1953–1960

THE EISENHOWER LANDSLIDE left the Democratic Party on the ropes. A net loss of twenty-two seats in the House and two in the Senate also cost the party its leadership of Congress, but there were a few rays of light, not fully appreciated at the time. One was the election to the Senate of a young congressman from Massachusetts named John F. Kennedy. Another was the elevation to the post of Senate minority leader of Lyndon B. Johnson of Texas upon the defeat of the incumbent Democratic leader, Ernest McFarland.

Kennedy won some fame in ousting Boston Brahmin Henry Cabot Lodge but quietly took his seat as a backbencher. Johnson became the sidekick of his Texas mentor and former speaker, Sam Rayburn, still the ranking Democrat in Congress as the House minority leader. Together they ruled the party on Capitol Hill, with Rayburn remaining a revered but often passive figure and Johnson through the force of an aggressive, even pugnacious personality becoming the dominant figure.

The defeated Stevenson, still holding the vague position as the party's titular leader, characteristically did not make much of it. Privately, he sometimes referred to himself as "the hind-tit-ular leader," but also wrote that in that role anyone has "an obligation to wipe out the inevitable debt accumulated by his party during a losing campaign, and also to do what he can to revive, reorganize and rebuild the party."[1] Shortly after the Eisenhower administration took over, however, Stevenson went off on a five-month world tour.

"IT'S ONE OF THE WORST FRACTURES I'VE EVER SEEN!"

After Adlai Stevenson's 1952 loss to Republican Dwight D. Eisenhower, the Democratic Party was sharply split over the 1956 presidential nomination. W. Averell Harriman of New York, backed by former President Harry Truman, emerged as the chief challenger to a second Stevenson nomination. The Illinoisan was chosen nonetheless, but again lost to Eisenhower.

On return, he began to confer with fellow liberals on the future of the party. Among them was economist John Kenneth Galbraith, who in September 1954 wrote that he had been discussing with Harriman and Arthur Schlesinger Jr. "how can we do the most to keep the Democratic party intellectually alert and positive during these years in the wilderness? . . . As the party of the well-to-do, the Republicans do not hesitate to use their dough. As the party of the egg-heads, we should similarly and proudly make use of our brains and experience."² From such deliberations came what was called the Finletter Group, after Thomas K. Finletter, a former State Department special assistant and later secretary of the air force. Other members included diplomats George F. Kennan and Chester Bowles. They wrote and exchanged policy position papers, all with an eye to educating Stevenson toward a possible second try for the presidency. In time they also were said to have been policy seedlings for subsequent Democratic administrations.³

While he did bear the title of titular leader, Stevenson was well aware that influence in the party had inevitably moved to the congressional wing, and he deferred to them. In Congress, Lyndon Johnson carved out much of the Democratic Party posture for the Eisenhower years. As the new session opened in 1953, he made clear he did not intend to break the party's pick or his own on Eisenhower's rock-solid popularity. "We are now in the minority," he proclaimed. "I have never agreed with the statement that it is 'the business of the opposition to oppose.' I do not believe the American people have sent us here merely to obstruct."⁴ That attitude became his trademark as he focused on pulling his tattered party back together, sniping at the Republicans when opportunities arose but always paying deference to the unassailable war hero president. The genial "Ike" played the civilian general, appearing to delegate responsibility in foreign policy to veteran diplomat John Foster Dulles and in domestic affairs to a former New Hampshire governor, Sherman Adams.

Even before his inauguration, Eisenhower had fulfilled his campaign pledge to "go to Korea," and by July an end to the war was negotiated, with the country still partitioned at the 38th parallel. Together with Dulles, he had a full plate dealing with what they saw as an expansionist Soviet Union, a growing competition in nuclear armament and a worldwide threat of communism in an ever-intensifying Cold War that before long reached into Vietnam. The collapse of French colonial forces in Indochina in 1954 led to a north-south partitioning of Vietnam and a first modest involvement of American interests there. Dulles's firm perception of a monolithic communism soon had the Eisenhower administration defending democracy in Europe and Asia alike, with commitments in the Middle East and Latin America as well.

All this reinforced the concept of two superpowers—the United States and the Soviet Union—locked in a fearful struggle for domination short of a shooting war, but with its specter ever hanging over the globe. The Russians' development of a hydrogen bomb, of *Sputnik,* the first earth satellite in space, and the first intercontinental ballistic missile all brought anxiety to the competition, especially with the death of Stalin, a number of internal power struggles within the Soviet Union and the eventual leadership of the bombastic Nikita Khrushchev. The Eisenhower administration moved gradually from a concept of "massive retaliation" to "peaceful coexistence," but always under the shadow of Khrushchev's bellicosity.

Through these years, the Democratic Party's voice was muted on the foreign policy front but cautiously critical on the domestic. Eisenhower started out pursuing what he called "modern Republicanism," but before long gave way to the party's traditional bedrock of fiscal conservatism. His secretary of defense, Charles E. Wilson, late of General Motors, when asked whether he expected his business ties to conflict with his official duties, summed up the administration attitude best. He could not see any conflict, he said, because "for years I thought what was good for our country was good for General Motors, and vice versa."[5] Ike's secretary of interior, Douglas McKay, observed at another point that "we're here in the saddle as an Administration representing business and industry."[6] This philosophy produced two recessions in Eisenhower's first term, and even as he spoke of fiscal responsibility his budgets sometimes dipped into deficit.

Eisenhower also was plagued by McCarthyism, with the power-drunk senator of his own party recklessly throwing charges at the army, including a slander to an honored general as "a disgrace to the uniform."[7] It was reminiscent of another attack by McCarthy in 1951 on General George C. Marshall as part of "a conspiracy so immense and an infamy so black as to dwarf any previous venture in the history of man."[8] In the 1952 campaign, an intimidated Eisenhower deleted praise of his old wartime companion from a speech in McCarthy's home state to avoid offending him.

Now, when the president failed to blow the whistle on McCarthy and defend himself and his party, Stevenson stepped into the breach in early

1954. With a ringing condemnation not only of McCarthy but also of the Republicans cowed by him, he charged that "a group of political plungers has persuaded the President that McCarthyism is the best political formula for political success. . . . A political party divided against itself, half McCarthy and half Eisenhower, cannot produce national unity, cannot govern with confidence and purpose."[9]

The Stevenson speech finally brought a reaction from Eisenhower. He announced through the Republican National Committee that Vice President Nixon, not McCarthy, would respond to Stevenson, and in a press conference he commended Republican Senator Ralph Flanders of Vermont for accusing McCarthy of "doing his best to shatter" the Republican Party.[10] Then Nixon, who to some ears sounded as if he were talking about himself, proclaimed on national radio and television that "men who in the past have done effective work exposing Communists in this country have, by reckless talk and questionable method, made themselves the issue rather than the cause they believe in so deeply."[11] As an attack on McCarthy, who had never exposed a single communist in government, it was a classic Nixon performance, giving the devil much more than his due.

After Stevenson's assault, McCarthy did not last much longer as an intimidating force. The Senate later in the year censured him, and in terms of belling the cat, it was not the President of the United States who played an important role, but the man he had soundly defeated in the 1952 election. After that, McCarthy faded in a blur of alcoholism and incoherence, and died in 1957.

In that sorry episode, Stevenson had given the Democratic Party a strong and assertive voice, but in terms of governance he yielded to elected Democrats on the firing line, foremost of whom were Johnson and Rayburn, and sought smooth relations with them. However, Stevenson and Johnson, were not cut from the same stylistic and cultural cloth, and the relationship was uneasy. Johnson's strategy of accommodation with Eisenhower seemed to be paying off in terms of party revival.

In special elections in 1953, the Democrats picked up seats in New Jersey and Wisconsin, and in the congressional elections of 1954, in spite of Eisenhower's continued public appeal, regained control of Congress with a twenty-nine-seat margin in the House and one in the Senate. Stevenson contributed importantly by making eighty speeches in thirty-three states. With McCarthy in eclipse, Nixon filled the hatchet man void,

Stevenson characterizing his performance as "McCarthyism in a white shirt."[12] The narrow edge in the Senate, resulting from a switch by Senator Wayne Morse of Oregon from the Republican to the Democratic Party, made LBJ the majority leader. The Democrats also picked up nine governorships, including those in the key states of New York, with Averell Harriman, and Pennsylvania, with George Leader. In staunchly Republican Maine, Democrat Edmund S. Muskie was elected.

Perhaps the most momentous event of Eisenhower's first term was the Supreme Court's decision in 1954 in *Brown* v. *Board of Education,* which reversed the legality of "separate but equal" public schools and ordered an end to racial discrimination there—a development that added fuel to the North-South split in the Democratic Party. The Court ordered desegregation of the schools "with all deliberate speed," setting the stage for bitter conflict within the party and an intensification of hostility toward blacks in the South, with intimidating White Citizens Councils springing up across the Deep South.

At the same time, the ruling gave heart to the quest of Southern blacks for an end to segregation. In Montgomery, Alabama, in late 1955, a dynamic young preacher, Dr. Martin Luther King Jr., led a long but ultimately successful boycott of the public bus system, triggered by the refusal of a woman named Rosa Parks, a seamstress, to give up her seat in the rear section designated for blacks to a white man.

In 1956 some ninety Southern Democrats signed a Southern Manifesto condemning the Court's desegregation decision and encouraging defiance and evasion in Dixie. They opposed an Eisenhower proposal to create a bipartisan Civil Rights Commission and a Civil Rights Division in the Justice Department to put teeth in the enforcement of voting rights for blacks. The bill passed the House but never got to the Senate floor for a vote. Some states like Virginia closed schools and for a time conducted private "academies" to educate white students only. Hovering over the Democratic Party was the danger of another Southern walkout at the next national convention of the sort that had produced a Dixiecrat candidate in 1948.

Northern liberal Democrats like Hubert Humphrey champed at the seeming impasse. "The Democratic party is spelling its long-term doom unless it does something," he warned. "Our party ought to be the champion of equal rights—it's morally right and it's politically right."[13] Clarence Mitchell, the Washington director of the NAACP, chimed in:

"Tell those Democrats if they keep a stinking albatross like Senator [James O.] Eastland [of Mississippi, a rabid segregationist] around their necks they can kiss our votes goodbye."[14]

All this time, Stevenson, while resuming a law practice, was busy upgrading his credentials on foreign affairs and preaching party unity, figuring that his best chance for a second nomination was in that Democratic harmony. For that reason, he was not the most forceful spokesman for civil rights, knowing that to put himself in the forefront of that fight was to invite hostility from the party's Southern wing. As a result, some editorialists denigrated his position as "gradualism." Although Stevenson discussed with friends and associates the possibility of skipping another long-shot race against Eisenhower in favor of running in 1960, he never seriously entertained the idea. He knew from the start that the challenge in taking on Eisenhower a second time was not so much in winning as it was in giving voice to his strongly held convictions and direction to a party still floundering in a sea of public adoration of the war hero president.

Unlike 1952, when he was the reluctant candidate, Stevenson determined that if he was going to run again he would be better prepared. The work of the Finletter Group helped make him so. One advantage of Eisenhower's popularity was that it made the Democratic nomination less attractive to others, so Stevenson seemed to have a clear path to it—until September 23, 1955, when Eisenhower, after playing twenty-seven holes of golf in Denver, had a heart attack.

Stevenson was at his home in Libertyville at the time, about to go to Texas for a speech and to meet with Rayburn and Johnson. Before he left he got word from a Harriman associate that the governor had decided to seek the Democratic nomination, and on arrival the two Texans advised Stevenson he would now probably have to run in the primaries. Soon, Humphrey was telling him the same thing.[15] Stevenson did not like the idea of trudging through the states discussing local issues, but he knew he could not leave the impression, either, that he wasn't willing to work for the nomination this time around. Some troublesome signals came his way. Truman, who had pressured him relentlessly in 1952 to run, observed during a trip to New York that if he were a resident there, he would support Harriman. Kefauver also was said to be interested again. There was some talk in the burgeoning Stevenson staff operation that Kefauver might be sidetracked by offering him the second place on the ticket, but Stevenson reportedly was cool to the idea after having been told by Johnson and Rayburn that the maverick from Tennessee was "the most hated man to serve in Congress for many years."[16]

When Stevenson finally declared his candidacy in mid-November, he indicated he would indeed compete in primaries in Illinois, Minnesota, Pennsylvania, Florida and California. The next day he got a telegram from Kefauver saying he was going to join the race, and he did so with zest in Minnesota. Humphrey and Governor Orville Freeman had told Stevenson that he would carry the state with ease. But about three weeks before the March 20 primary he toured the state campaigning not against Kefauver, whom he seldom if ever mentioned, but against Eisenhower, who had just announced his complete recovery and decision to seek a second term. With Republicans in the state urging crossover votes to stop Stevenson, Kefauver upset him with 56 percent of the 300,000-plus votes, claiming 26 of Minnesota's 30 delegates to the national convention. It was an inauspicious start to what earlier had been expected to be a cakewalk.

The result stiffened Stevenson's resolve but also revealed staff disarray. Now he took the fight directly to Kefauver, saying he would stick to his 1952 pledge of offering the same consistent message wherever he campaigned. It "will not be changed," he said in a dig at the wily Tennessean, "to meet the opposition of a candidate who makes it sound in Illinois as though he opposed Federal aid to segregated schools, in Florida as though he favors it, and in Minnesota as though he had not made up his mind."[17] And on that issue, he said, he was unequivocally in support of the Court's desegregation ruling.

Stevenson after his Minnesota defeat committed himself to such a back-breaking schedule that the staff worried about his health and spirit. Weary of the repetition of his speeches, he insisted on retooling them himself, and he continued to complain about the pedestrian nature of subjects he had to address from state to state. "The hardest thing about any political campaign," he said at one point, "is how to win without proving you are unworthy of winning."[18]

Still, he muddled through, winning primaries in Alaska (still a territory, not yet a state), the District of Columbia, New Jersey, Illinois, Oregon on a write-in vote and Florida, where he and Kefauver engaged in the first presidential campaign debate on national radio and television. Finally, in California, he beat Kefauver by nearly two to one. In late July, in advance of the Democratic convention, Kefauver finally dropped out, throwing his support to Stevenson and leaving Harriman, who was seeking delegates in non-primary states, as the chief competitor.

In June, Eisenhower had suffered an attack of ileitis that required surgery, but he recovered quickly and declared himself fit to continue as a candidate. On the eve of the Democratic convention, the Gallup Poll had him far ahead, 61 percent to 37 for Stevenson. On top of that news, Truman formally declared for Harriman, charging that Stevenson lacked the experience to be president. Eleanor Roosevelt, an unabashed Stevenson fan, openly disagreed, saying Stevenson was the better equipped of the two. At the convention in Chicago's International Amphitheatre in mid-August, she personally lobbied state caucuses for him.

The impact of television was obvious as the party planners did their utmost to showcase their most appealing figures and to give exposure to many of their candidates. The convention featured a long documentary of the Democratic Party's history, narrated by freshman Senator Kennedy, and each section of the party platform was read by a different presenter, including several candidates for Congress. Kennedy also put Stevenson's name in nomination and Truman seconded the nomination of Harriman. Senator Warren G. Magnuson of Washington was offered but immediately withdrew his name. Others whose names went before the convention, mostly pro forma recognitions of their contributions to the party, included Lyndon Johnson, Congressman James C. Davis of Georgia, Governor A. B. "Happy" Chandler of Kentucky, Congressman John W. McCormack of Massachusetts, former Governors John S. Battle of Virginia and George Bell Timmerman of South Carolina, and Senator Stuart Symington of Missouri.

Truman's efforts to stop Stevenson, culminated in a press conference calling him a conservative who followed the "counsel of hesitation" and lacked "the kind of fighting spirit we need to win," got nowhere.[19] Stevenson was nominated on the first ballot by the time the roll call reached Pennsylvania, at which point a Harriman supporter motioned for the nomination to be made unanimous and it was done. Before that happened, Stevenson had 905½ delegates to only 210 for Harriman, 80 for Johnson and the rest scattered among six other candidates.

Next came the vice-presidential nomination. Behind the platform at the amphitheater, Stevenson engaged in a heated debate with party leaders over a proposal he was about to make to the convention that had a precedent in 1896, in the hands of William Jennings Bryan. He was going to throw the choice to the delegates as a means of demonstrating the importance of a responsible selection. According to Porter McKeever, a longtime Stevenson associate, in his biography of the man, "for weeks he had been thinking about the vice presidential spot, which had assumed additional symbolic importance in light of Eisenhower's illness. His personal preference was either Humphrey or Kennedy. The latter's religion created problems and, in addition, Speaker Sam Rayburn bitterly opposed 'that little pissant.' Kefauver had strong supporters, but Adlai was not one of them."[20]

Joining Rayburn in opposition to the idea of an open choice were Johnson and the party national chairman, Paul Butler. But other party leaders, including Mayor Richard J. Daley and party boss Jake Arvey of Chicago and Mayor David Lawrence of Pittsburgh, backed Stevenson. Rayburn, unhappy at the nominee's unwillingness to yield, walked out to the podium and introduced him to the surprised convention, "not to make his acceptance speech, but to greet you and make an announcement."[21]

"The American people have the solemn obligation to consider with the utmost care who will be their president if the elected president is prevented by a Higher Will from serving his full term," Stevenson said. He didn't mention the Eisenhower illnesses and the specter of the hated Nixon waiting in the wings, but the message was clear. "It is a sober reminder that seven out of 34 Presidents have served as a result of such indirect selection.... The choice for that office has become almost as important as the choice for the Presidency.... In these circumstances," he went on, "I have concluded to depart from the precedents of the past. I have decided that the selection of the vice-presidential nominee should be made through the free process of this convention so that the Democratic Party's candidate may join me before the nation not as one man's selection but as one chosen by our party as I have been chosen."[22]

The announcement sent the convention into an uproar, just as Stevenson intended, to draw a contrast with the expected routine renomination of Nixon at the approaching Republican convention despite grumblings about him within his own party. Strategists for Kennedy, Kefauver and Humphrey immediately began scurrying for delegate support. Humphrey was undercut by his failure to deliver the Minnesota primary to Stevenson, and the choice came down to Kennedy or Kefauver. Stevenson clearly preferred Kennedy; that was why, he said later, he had chosen him to place his own name in nomination, and expected him to win.[23] Kefauver's opposition in the primaries had soured Stevenson toward him, but the nominee was serious about opening the choice and instructed his staff to steer clear of the competition.

Kennedy was not totally unprepared for the opportunity. He had given thought to running in the New Hampshire presidential primary as a New England favorite son the previous winter, as a stalking horse for Stevenson against Kefauver, who had won the state primary in 1952. He was dissuaded from the idea by Stevenson's campaign manager, James Finnegan, who preferred to have an early Kennedy endorsement, which he gave. But other Democrats in New England, including Senator Abraham Ribicoff of Connecticut and Governor Dennis Roberts of Rhode Island, began to mention Kennedy as a possible Stevenson running mate.

Ted Sorensen, Kennedy's chief Senate aide and speechwriter, prepared a "private" self-serving memorandum laying out statistics that argued that a Catholic would help, not hurt, the ticket in 1956 by luring back urban Democrats who had defected to Eisenhower in 1952. He arranged for the Connecticut party chairman, John Bailey, to accept authorship and circulate what then came to be known as "the Bailey memorandum." The senator's father, Joseph P. Kennedy, was cool to the idea, fearing that if the Democratic ticket lost with his son on it, his Catholicism would be blamed, endangering his chances for the presidency later on. But Sorensen persevered.[24]

Kennedy's brother-in-law Sargent Shriver joined in. On a flight to Chicago shortly before the convention, he met Stevenson and learned that he had seen the Bailey memo but had reservations about the statistics. Stevenson told him, according to James MacGregor Burns in his book *John Kennedy,* that the running mate's qualifications for the presidency were more important than what he might bring to the ticket politically, and that "I hope the convention will give a good deal of deliberation to the vice-presidential question."[25] The remark hinted at the possibility the choice would be thrown to the convention, and Shriver alerted the Kennedy strategists to prepare for that possibility.

There was good reason to think Stevenson was seriously considering Kennedy. Before the convention Sorensen had received a letter from Ken Hechler, Stevenson's research director and later a congressman from West Virginia, asking him to present "the strongest case for Kennedy." Sorensen did so, mentioning his man's political strengths, including his contrast with Nixon, "regardless of Governor Stevenson's need to re-win the Catholic vote."[26] When Kennedy was asked to place Stevenson's name in nomination, his strategists feared it was a consolation prize, but when Stevenson made his announcement handing the choice of his running mate to the delegates, their hopes flickered again.

Upon hearing Stevenson, Kennedy and his advisers moved to the Stockyard Inn just outside the convention hall, where he sprawled out on a bed and watched the fevered activity on the convention floor. Other names placed in nomination included Senator Albert Gore of Tennessee, Governors LeRoy Collins of Florida and Luther Hodges of North Carolina, and Mayor Robert Wagner of New York. On the first ballot, Kefauver led with 483½ votes to 304 for Kennedy, 162½ for Wagner and 134½ for Humphrey. On the second ballot, as Kennedy in his suite soaked a troublesome back in a bathtub, the roll call reached Texas and he heard Lyndon Johnson announce that his state was proudly casting its 56 votes "for that fighting Senator who wears the scars of battle"—all switched from Gore.[27] Kennedy took the lead with 559 votes to 479½ for Kefauver, with 156 votes not cast by states that had passed. If Kennedy could win them all, he would be the nominee, but he didn't. Instead they slightly favored Kefauver, and when they were cast the tally stood at Kennedy 617½, Kefauver 552½, still 68½ short of the required majority.

The delegates on the floor were in a frenzy, state banners being waved wildly for recognition by Rayburn, the convention chairman. He first called on Kentucky, which switched 30 votes to Kennedy, leaving him only 38½ short. The Massachusetts delegation whooped in excitement. But then Gore was recognized and withdrew in favor of Kefauver. Oklahoma thereupon switched its 28 Gore votes to Kefauver and the stampede to him was under way, as Midwestern and Western states, concerned by Kennedy's opposition to high farm supports, broke for the Tennessean. Kennedy dressed quickly, strode over to the convention hall and moved that Kefauver's nomination be made unanimous.

According to Arthur M. Schlesinger Jr. in his *A Thousand Days: John F. Kennedy in the White House,* Kennedy was resentful that Stevenson hadn't chosen him outright, but that Stevenson felt he had given the thirty-nine-year-old senator a spotlight in choosing him to present his name to the convention, and he should have been appreciative of it. "Kennedy instead began to look on Stevenson as indecisive and elusive," Schlesinger wrote. Friendly up to this point, he went on, "their relationship began to take on a slight tinge of mutual exasperation. In later years, however, Kennedy rejoiced that he had lost in Chicago. Had he won the nomination for Vice-President in 1956, he might never have won the nomination for President in 1960."[28]

The Republican National Convention opened in San Francisco three days after the Democratic had adjourned and sped through the renomination of Eisenhower and Nixon without dissent. By this time, Nixon had dodged a vigorous effort by Harold Stassen to have Eisenhower choose another running mate. The president, obviously cool to Nixon and aware of his own mortality after two serious illnesses, had conferred with his controversial vice president about the possibility of leaving the ticket for a cabinet post, ostensibly if preposterously as a better stepping-stone to a future presidential nomination. But Nixon refused to bite, instead holding tenaciously to the status quo. When Eisenhower, peppered with press questions about Nixon's future, said he had asked his vice president "to chart out his own course and tell me what he would like to do," Nixon went to the Oval Office and told him he wanted to run again, and that was that.[29] In the end, Stassen was prevailed upon to put Nixon's name in nomination.

In the fall campaign, Stevenson from the start took dead aim at Nixon as the Achilles' heel of the Republican ticket. In a nationally televised speech, he labeled Eisenhower a part-time president who was no longer "master in his own house," and suggested that in the future the GOP "will depend not on Mr. Eisenhower but on the Republican heir apparent, Mr. Nixon."[30]

Eisenhower began his own campaign with a huge lawn party and picnic for five hundred party leaders at his home in Gettysburg. He affirmed his own physical recovery and Nixon's readiness if he was mistaken about it. "There is no man in the history of America," he proclaimed, "who has had such a careful preparation as has Vice President Nixon for carrying out the duties of the presidency, if that duty should ever fall on him."[31]

With Nixon still aboard to bear the brunt of daily campaigning, Eisenhower was able to focus on his presidential duties. Stevenson, already worn to a frazzle by the strenuous primary campaign to beat back the Kefauver challenge, was not in the best shape for the fall endurance test. Yet part of the Stevenson strategy was to display his vigor and stamina in contrast to the aging Eisenhower. From mid-August to election day he traveled about 55,000 miles, mostly by rail, and gave more than three hundred speeches, insisting almost always in writing or editing them himself, as well as overseeing policy papers put out in his name.

When Stevenson called for unilateral cessation of hydrogen bomb testing and an end to the draft, Eisenhower, as the voice of military experience and expertise, labeled the proposals irresponsible. He called the first proposal "a theatrical national gesture" while weighing the idea himself and said the second "cannot be done under the world conditions of today."[32] When, in the closing days of the campaign, Israel with the aid of Britain and France seized the Suez Canal, and a people's revolution erupted against the Russians in Hungary, Nixon played the Republican trump card. "This is not the moment," he declared, "to replace the greatest Commander-in-chief America has ever had in war or peace with a jittery, inexperienced novice . . . who is utterly unqualified to make the great decisions demanded."[33]

In the end, all Stevenson could do was to play his best card—the Nixon specter hanging over Eisenhower's age and health. "I must say bluntly," he intoned over television on election eve, "that every piece of scientific evidence we have, every lesson of history and experience, indicates that a Republican victory tomorrow would mean that Richard Nixon would probably be president of this country within the next four years. I say frankly as a citizen more than a candidate that I recoil at the prospect of Mr. Nixon as custodian of this nation's future, as guardian of the hydrogen bomb, as representative of America in the world, as commander-in-chief of the United States armed forces."[34]

Stevenson's best card was not nearly good enough. On election day, the Eisenhower-Nixon ticket was resoundingly reelected, winning by a landslide even larger than its 1952 victory: 57.6 percent to 42.1 percent for Stevenson-Kefauver, a popular vote margin of 9.5 million, the widest in history up to that time, and 457 electoral votes to 73. At the same time, however, for the first time in more than a hundred years an incumbent president failed to win at least one of the two houses of Congress. The Democrats held a thirty-two-seat margin in the House and a two-seat edge in the Senate. The outcome made the case that the Republican presidential victory was for the man, not the party, and that the Democratic Party was able to survive the handicap of a failed presidential nominee.

With the Democrats facing four more years as the out party, shortly after the election Democratic national chairman, Paul Butler, announced the formation of a new Democratic Advisory Council (DAC) as an arm of the national committee. Its role would be to give voice to the views and concerns of party leaders and members in addition to those expressed through Democratic members of Congress. The move was widely seen as a declaration of independence by key liberal leaders of the presidential wing of the party from the congressional wing, although its leaders were also invited.

Butler asked twenty Democrats to join—ten from Congress, five state and local leaders and five well-known other party stalwarts. Of these, only Humphrey from the Senate at first signed on. Johnson in the Senate and Rayburn and McCormack in the House leadership declined. Governors Harriman of New York and G. Mennen Williams of Michigan accepted, as did Stevenson, Truman and Kefauver as at-large members. Policy experts such as Acheson and Galbraith agreed to write policy papers and Eleanor Roosevelt would serve as a consultant, but the new group became a source of intraparty friction from the start.

The DAC declared as its purpose "to provide a collective voice for the Democratic Party, representing on a year-long basis the millions of Democrats who may or may not be represented in either House of Congress." It added: "We can win in 1960 only if we begin to hammer out a forceful, coherent policy and keep communicating it to the public."[35] But Johnson feared such action would greatly compound his task of seeking compromise with Republican senators. He wrote Butler that "I trust your group does not go into too much specifics on legislation," and reminded him that "the American people did not elect the Democratic Advisory Committee to pass legislation."[36]

But the liberal DAC was determined, with Johnson functioning more as a conciliator than as a Democratic alternative voice to Eisenhower, to fill the void. LBJ and Rayburn operated on the premise that cooperation with the popular president was best for their own party, and they could point to increasing Democratic membership in Congress as proof. Rayburn, protective of his prerogatives, saw to it that his House Democrats stayed in line. The liberal Americans for Democratic Action (ADA), however, sided with the DAC against Johnson's "moderation," arguing that he was engaged in no more than a "contest of public relations" with the Eisenhower administration.[37] Johnson responded essentially by ignoring Butler. But the chairman's continued criticisms of what at one point he called "very deep cleavages" between "a party that has a national outlook and the congressional leadership whose outlook is highly regionalized" only exacerbated the situation.[38] By 1959, Truman was criticizing Butler for divisive comments and was reported to be pressing for his removal as chairman. At a dinner honoring Eleanor Roosevelt, he assailed "self-appointed guardians of liberal thinking." She responded by saying the party had to be one "where majority rule and where principles are the basis of the party."[39]

In a showdown with Johnson and Rayburn, Butler finally backed off, assuring them he had no intention of usurping their legislative role or splitting the party. In late 1959, however, with fifteen new liberals in the Senate, a Senate Democratic Study Group was formed that pushed Johnson, among other things, to revise the cloture rule on shutting off debate from the required two thirds of the full Senate to two thirds of senators present and voting. The move helped to facilitate passage of new civil rights legislation. One of the new liberals, William Proxmire of Wisconsin, challenged LBJ's brand of personal domination, but to little effect in the long run. As for the DAC, its liberal views were moderated in time by the unifying presence of Truman and, in foreign policy, of the assertive Acheson, often opposed by Stevenson, Chester Bowles and other liberals.[40]

Eisenhower's second term, marked by a sharp recession starting in August 1957 and high unemployment, provided a convenient target for the DAC and the Democratic majority in Congress, which pushed through emergency housing and highway construction bills. The chief achievement was enactment in 1957 of the strongest civil rights bill in nearly a century, creating a federal Civil Rights Commission with broad investigatory powers and authorizing the federal government to bring voting rights cases with penalties for violators. While the bill redounded to Eisenhower's credit, its enactment also was a showcase for Lyndon Johnson's extraordinary legislative skills and persuasive powers.

At the same time, Eisenhower encountered a major political challenge in 1957 when the Democratic governor of Arkansas, Orval Faubus, blocked a court-ordered desegregation of Central High School in Little Rock, employing the National Guard to keep nine black students from enrolling. When Faubus withdrew the troops, a riot broke out, finally persuading Eisenhower to nationalize the guard and dispatch federal paratroopers to escort the students into the school. The DAC was in the forefront of prodding him for action.

On top of this, the Soviet Union's launch of its *Sputnik* space vehicle in October 1957 shocked the country out of its sense of scientific and military superiority, belatedly lending credence to Stevenson's campaign warnings of American slippage in these fields. Also, scandals of corruption finally hit the Eisenhower administration, resulting in the resignation of his secretary of the air force, the Republican national chairman and, above all, the president's right-hand man in the White House, former Governor Sherman Adams. He was found to have received gifts including an expensive Oriental rug and a vicuna coat and free hotel stays from a New England textile manufacturer and old friend, Bernard Goldfine, for whom he interceded with federal regulatory agencies questioning certain business practices. Eisenhower stood by Adams for a time, saying, "I need him," but eventually was forced to yield and accept Adams's resignation.[41]

The leakage in the once-sturdy Eisenhower ship of state brought the Democratic Party a landslide victory in the 1958 off-year congressional elections. Its majority in the House, 129 seats, was the largest since FDR's second-term election, and the party held a 28-seat majority in the Senate. With Eisenhower a lame duck, and with Adams gone from the White House, his administration became increasingly conservative in its last two years, and plagued by foreign policy woes. In South Vietnam, communist and nationalist guerrilla forces known as Viet Cong in 1958 formed a National Liberation Front against the U.S.-backed president, Ngo Dinh Diem. The development led Eisenhower to enunciate a domino theory that was to govern American policy in Southeast Asia, eventually with disastrous result. "The loss of South Vietnam," he said in 1959, "would set in motion a crumbling process that could, as it progressed, have grave consequences for us."[42]

A visit to the United States the same year by Soviet leader Nikita Khrushchev, including a riotous visit to an Iowa farm, a Hollywood movie set and Disneyland, added some comic relief. But the downing of an American U-2 spy plane over the Soviet Union and the capture of the pilot scuttled a planned summit meeting between Eisenhower and Khrushchev in May 1960, and was humiliating.

Closer to home, the entrenchment of a communist state in Cuba only ninety miles from American shores continued to grate on the Eisenhower administration. The president secretly agreed to a CIA plan to arm and train Cuban exiles in Florida for some military foray against the regime of Fidel Castro, even as the CIA undertook planning to assassinate Castro himself. American foreign policy, which Nixon had boasted was in the surest of hands, was in disarray as Eisenhower neared the end of his White

House tenure. After eight years of Republican rule and a Republican president of seemingly unassailable stature in the eyes of American voters, ambitious Democrats looked to Eisenhower's retirement and the 1960 presidential election as a golden opportunity to restore their party to national power.

Stevenson, regardless of his shortcomings, had over the eight years been an intellectual and liberal inspiration for his party, and for many bright and talented young leaders who had begun to emerge. For all the anti–New Deal rhetoric from Republicans in the Eisenhower years, they did little to dismantle the social welfare bedrock of the FDR philosophy. As seen in the 1958 congressional elections, the original New Deal voting coalition had survived and had been nourished over the years by strong infusions of immigrant, labor and black support. By 1960, with the Eisenhower magic spell lifting, the Democratic Party remained a solid base from which to construct a return to the White House.

In this circumstance, no party leaders were more cognizant of the prospect than four senators who had persevered through the dark years of Republican ascendance and saw their own opportunity to occupy the Oval Office: Lyndon Baines Johnson of Texas, Hubert Horatio Humphrey of Minnesota, Stuart Symington of Missouri and John Fitzgerald Kennedy of Massachusetts.

Chapter 23

JFK: THE PARTY BOUNCES BACK, 1960

JOHN KENNEDY'S LOSING bid for the Democratic vice-presidential nomination in 1956 had borne him unexpectedly rich political dividends. In the fall campaign that followed, he had campaigned tirelessly for Stevenson and other Democratic candidates in twenty-four states, covering more than 30,000 miles and making at least 150 speeches over a six-week period.[1] At first, often accompanied only by Sorensen, he had traveled for the most part in commercial planes of all sizes and varieties.

As Kennedy continued the effort in the next three years, his family bought its own converted Convair propeller plane, later named the *Caroline* after his infant daughter, for more comfort and convenience in scheduling. For Christmas 1956, Sorensen had given him a map of the United States showing the states whose delegations had voted for him to be Stevenson's running mate—a graphic illustration of the uphill climb he had west of the Mississippi if he hoped to win the presidential nomination in 1960.[2]

That objective, after Kennedy's burst upon the national scene at the 1956 convention, was publicly low key but privately intensive, as he rode to easy Senate reelection in 1958 and then focused on the approaching presidential election year. Going in, Kennedy had two major hurdles to clear as a candidate—his age (he would be only forty-three at inauguration if elected) and his Catholic religion. There had been a younger president—

Jim Ivey, San Francisco Examiner

The critical event in the 1960 presidential campaign was the first of four televised debates between Democratic Senator John F. Kennedy and Vice President Richard M. Nixon, the Republican nominee. Kennedy's forceful performance demonstrated his ability to deal effectively with the more experienced Nixon, and was widely considered a major factor in his election.

Theodore Roosevelt—but no Catholic had ever attained the White House; Al Smith had tried and failed in 1928.

There was nothing Kennedy could do about his age, but in an interview in *Look* magazine in March 1959 he confronted the religious issue, writing that "whatever one's religion in his private life may be, for the office-holder nothing takes precedence over his oath to uphold the Constitution and all its parts."[3] The comment didn't do much to assuage the doubters, but that fact didn't seem to get Kennedy down. He could joke about the matter, as in a comment at a dinner in New York. He confided that he had asked Francis Cardinal Spellman "what I should say when people ask me whether I believe the Pope is infallible, and the Cardinal replied, 'I don't know, Senator—all I know is he keeps calling me Spillman.' "[4]

Kennedy avidly courted party leaders around the country through 1959, as did the other main contenders, Humphrey, Johnson and Symington. At the same time, he understood that as an unknown political quantity outside his native New England, he needed to demonstrate voter appeal. The vehicle that offered itself was the presidential primary, the tool of political progressives seeking to take over party politics that had flourished in the early 1900s but later waned. In 1952, Kefauver had revived Democratic interest in the primary process by soundly beating an absentee Harry Truman in the New Hampshire party vote, and in 1956 by upsetting Stevenson in the Minnesota primary. In each, the contest was for delegates to the party's national convention, but in small states at least, they were only the incidental prize; more important was the huge national publicity that the primaries drew.

Sixteen states would hold presidential primaries in 1960, and in a key strategy meeting in late October 1959 at the Kennedy family compound at Hyannis Port, the prospective candidate led a discussion of Kennedy insiders on which of the primaries would be contested. The first, in New Hampshire, was a given; after that there was much talk about Wisconsin, where Humphrey doubtless would enter, coming from the neighboring state of Minnesota. There was, according to Theodore H. White's account in his breakthrough book, *The Making of the President, 1960,* only vague discussion of West Virginia, which would turn out to be the critical primary of the election year.[5]

Of the other contenders, Humphrey also was aware of his need to demonstrate grassroots support. His liberalism, worn on his sleeve, and particularly his outspoken advocacy of civil rights, had made him few friends in the South; he, too, would have to enter the presidential primaries to establish his appeal elsewhere. The other two main candidates, Johnson and Symington, were more associated with the party establishment—Johnson as the Senate leader and Symington as a defense specialist with fellow Missourian Truman in his corner.

Johnson strongly believed that his now-dominant presence on Capitol Hill could bring him the nomination through support of party leaders around the country, whom he courted zealously as only the party's master schmoozer and arm-twister could. He elected to remain mostly in Washington through the primary period, using the Senate as the showcase of his talent in getting things done, even with a Republican in the White House. As for Symington, he and his advisers saw his best chance as the compromise "second choice" candidate at a stalemated convention, drawing backing from more moderate Democratic city bosses and other leaders corralled by Truman and his own political mastermind, Clark Clifford.[6]

Thus Johnson and Symington decided to leave the risky primary route to Kennedy, Humphrey and any dark horses who so chose to fight for delegates in the arena of grassroots politicking. A fifth would-be candidate, apparently willing to run again but not to seek the opportunity overtly, was Stevenson, to whom a campaign against someone other than the invincible Eisenhower—that someone assumed to be Nixon—would be appealing. Old stalwarts, aware of Stevenson's thinking, quietly began political research and fund-raising in his behalf, even as he left on a two-month tour of South America.[7]

Kennedy, with his younger brother Robert as campaign manager, formally announced his candidacy on January 2, 1960, in the Senate Caucus Room. He started out in New Hampshire, and Humphrey left the primary there to him, knowing that trying to compete in JFK's backyard would be fruitless and self-defeating. Kennedy won easily there and moved on to the first real test in Wisconsin, where Humphrey had challenged him. Kennedy, believing he needed to sweep all contested primaries he entered, felt he could not afford to duck any challenges.

Kennedy arrived in Wisconsin in full force with a staff that included a professional pollster, Louis Harris, to probe for strong and weak spots in Kennedy strength, enabling the candidate to schedule his speeches accordingly. With no Wisconsin favorite son running, neighbor Humphrey was perceived as the next best thing. The primary was both a threat and an opportunity for Kennedy. He campaigned diligently in every corner of the state, all members of his glamorous family and a host of friends pitching in. Humphrey was quoted at one point as observing: "Beware of these orderly campaigns. They are ordered, bought and paid for. . . . I feel like an independent merchant competing against a chain store."[8]

Humphrey himself worked as he always did, from sunup to sunset and beyond, with his seemingly limitless store of energy and enthusiasm, but he was no match for the Kennedy charisma and earnestness. On the issues of the sky-high unemployment, struggling family farms, the continuing Cold War, there was little to choose in substance between the two men. And although Humphrey was an optimistic man of unwavering good humor, Kennedy's ability to convey a sense of urgency in national purpose provided the electricity of the campaign.

On election night, April 5, Kennedy won about 56 percent of the Democratic primary vote, two thirds of the state's convention delegates and six of the ten congressional districts, narrowly missing in two of the other four. It was well short of late polls and prognostications, and Humphrey buoyantly sought to claim the outcome as a success for him. For Kennedy, it was a victory but not sufficiently strong for a candidate who had to convince the doubters of his electoral firepower. Kennedy did well in the cities and in the eastern part of the state, especially in areas of large Catholic population, Humphrey in areas closest to Minnesota. But Humphrey also won among Catholics who lived near the Minnesota border, so it was difficult to assess the impact of "the religious issue."

That issue was now to be tested in the primary in West Virginia, where Humphrey again challenged Kennedy, who had hoped to stay out of a state that was 95 percent Protestant and only 5 percent Catholic.[9] Even if Humphrey was setting a trap, Kennedy decided he had to walk into it or lose credibility, even though he had already committed to run in the Nebraska primary on the same day, May 10. Humphrey had said earlier that he would withdraw from the race if he failed to win his neighboring state of Wisconsin, but now he vowed to press on in West Virginia.

In retrospect, it was a most fortuitous decision—for Kennedy, although it did not seem so at the time. He had thought and hoped that Humphrey, beaten in a neighboring state to his own, would realize that his chances to be nominated were gone and would bow out gracefully.

Instead, "the religious issue" was being put to the most rigorous possible test for Kennedy short of a primary in the Deep South.

An early Harris poll for the Kennedy campaign in the poor coal-mining state had indicated he would run better than two to one over Humphrey. But in the wake of the Wisconsin primary and all the attention given to the religious issue, Harris came in with a new survey showing Humphrey winning West Virginia by a clear-cut margin of 60 percent to 40.[10] Kennedy had to find ways to deflect concern over his Catholicism, or at least deflect West Virginians' focus on it. "To neutralize the suspicion attached to his faith," Sorensen wrote later, "he emphasized his other attributes, especially his family's war record and patriotism in a state justly proud of its war heroes. To offset the religious issue, he emphasized other issues, especially his efforts for the unemployed, in this most distressed of all states."[11] Indeed, West Virginia ranked at or near the top in states that had lost citizens in foreign wars, and in its jobless and poverty rates.

The Kennedy campaign again poured in human and financial resources on an unprecedented scale, with the candidate himself traveling doggedly from one small city or grizzly coal-mining town to another, morning to night. Humphrey, vastly underfunded, did the same, advertising himself as the true disciple of the beloved FDR. But the spectacle of the young, urbane, wealthy and well-tailored Irish Yankee strolling down countless Main Streets, popping into small groceries and clothing stores, and smilingly introducing himself to staring locals, captured the attention and news coverage. My own clearest memory of the primary as a young traveling reporter was watching Kennedy sitting in an expensive suit on a grimy railroad track leading into a mine shaft, trying to engage blackened-faced miners in conversation about their problems and concerns. They stood nervously back, as if not to sully him with their soot, hesitatingly taking his proffered handshake. Meanwhile, his sisters, in flowery spring frocks, stood self-consciously off to the side as the local country folk gawked at them.

The usually affable Humphrey, already frustrated by the Kennedy wealth and star quality, turned bitter with allegations of vote fraud. "I don't think elections should be bought," he declared amid widespread allegations of Kennedy money being freely passed through receptive local officials and party men. "I can't afford to run through with a checkbook and a little black bag . . . Bobby said if they had to spend a half million to win here they would do it.... Kennedy is the spoiled candidate and he and that young, emotional, juvenile Bobby are spending with wild abandon.... Anyone who gets in the way of... papa's pet is going to be destroyed."[12]

The Kennedy side hit back. Franklin D. Roosevelt Jr., son of the most esteemed president in West Virginia and a Kennedy surrogate campaigner, told an interviewer that Humphrey was "a good Democrat, but I don't know where he was in World War II."[13] The smear, based on correspondence discovered by the Kennedy campaign indicating that Humphrey had sought draft deferments,[14] drew immediate press coverage and editorial condemnation. Both FDR Jr. and Kennedy apologized to Humphrey, but the allegation had found its mark in this super-patriotic state.

Kennedy, meanwhile, seemed genuinely moved, if not shocked, at the depth of poverty and deprivation in West Virginia, and he spoke convincingly about it. But polls continued to indicate that his Catholicism might defeat him in the end. He decided finally that he had to confront the question of his religion head-on once again in this overwhelmingly Protestant state. In a major speech, he gave assurances that "I am not the Catholic candidate for President. I do not speak for the Catholic Church on issues of public policy, and no one in that Church speaks for me."[15] In another, he said: "I will not allow any pope or church to dictate to the president of the United States. There is no conflict between my religion and the obligations of office; should one arise I would resign. I refuse to believe that the people of this state are bigots, guided in this most important choice by prejudice."[16]

At the same time, Sorensen obtained a letter from thirteen nationally prominent Protestant clergymen calling for fellow ministers to preach "charitable moderation and reasoned balance of judgment," and expressing the conviction that "each of the candidates has presented himself before the American people with honesty and independence, and we would think it unjust to discount any one of them because of his chosen faith."[17] The letter was sent to every Protestant minister in West Virginia.

Whatever the reason, West Virginians on election night resoundingly chose Kennedy over the outgunned Humphrey, whether out of positive preference for the man or studied determination to reject the face of religious bigotry that Kennedy's candidacy had threatened to attach to the state and its people. Kennedy trounced Humphrey by 61 percent to 39, carrying 48 of the 55 counties. Charges of vote-buying continued for long after the primary, but the story out of West Virginia was that Kennedy had demolished "the religious issue" in the heavily Protestant state.

Humphrey, receiving news of his defeat in his hotel suite in Charleston, after a brief staff debate decided to withdraw. With Kennedy in Washington, his brother Robert walked in the rain over to Humphrey's hotel, thanked him for his concession, and the two returned together to Kennedy's hotel to greet him on his victorious arrival in Charleston. It was the end to a bitter contest and to Humphrey's presidential hopes in 1960. Kennedy pressed on, running the table in the remaining primaries in Nebraska, Maryland, Oregon and a few other states.

All this while, however, Johnson and Symington were continuing their efforts to collect convention delegates in the non-primary states. Kennedy did the same, being most successful in Michigan, where the courtship of Governor "Soapy" Williams resulted in forty-two of the state's fifty-one delegates going into the Kennedy column. Throughout, the Kennedy camp kept a vigilant eye out for Stevenson, who remained the darling of the party liberals. According to Richard Goodwin in *Remembering America*, after the West Virginia primary Kennedy bid for Stevenson's support by offering to make him secretary of state if elected, but Stevenson declined, still hoping for lightning to strike him a third time.[18]

A late bump in the road for Kennedy before the convention came on July 2, when Truman held a nationally televised press conference and questioned his readiness to be president because of his age. "Senator, are you certain that you are quite ready for the country, or that the country is ready for you in the role of President?" he asked. The nation, he said, needed "a man with the greatest possible maturity and experience.... May I urge you to be patient?"[19] While he was at it, Truman repeated his endorsement of Symington and also put in a good word for Johnson and several other Democrats not running. Kennedy replied, citing his fourteen years in Congress and noting that Truman's age barrier "would have kept Jefferson from writing the Declaration of Independence ... [and] Madison from fathering the Constitution."[20]

On the eve of the convention in Los Angeles opening July 11, a Gallup poll showed Kennedy at 41 percent among rank-and-file Democrats to 25 for Stevenson, 16 for Johnson and 7 for Symington, with the rest scattered. Calculations indicated Kennedy's strength at about 600 delegates, or 161 short of a majority. The question was whether a stop-Kennedy coalition could be put together before he was able to make up the difference.

Johnson, largely occupied running the Senate prior to the convention, had been limited to weekend excursions to states that had Democratic senators committed or at least favorably disposed toward their legislative leader. Whether by the necessity of his Senate duties or gross miscalculation of the manner in which the primary election process was coming to dominate public attention, the man who was larger than life within the Senate had been cut down to life size by Kennedy's political spadework outside it. It was not until July 5, six days before the convention was to open, that LBJ declared his candidacy for the presidential nomination. If he was to succeed, he would have to storm the convention, stop the Kennedy steamroller, deflect the wide sentimental and egghead appeal of Stevenson, and elbow Symington aside. Critical to his strategy was a late-blooming campaign to convey himself not as a Southerner, a breed long shunned in presidential politics, but as a Southwesterner or even a Westerner, stretching the Texas border farther toward the Pacific than it really was.

In Los Angeles, Johnson in desperation took the low road. Before a Washington State caucus, he took a swipe at Kennedy's father, who as ambassador to Britain had been accused of Nazi sympathies. "I was never any Chamberlain umbrella policy man," he said. "I never thought Hitler was right."[21] When Kennedy sent a form letter to all state delegations asking to meet with them, including Texas (inadvertently, according to Sorensen),[22] Johnson challenged Kennedy to debate him before the Texas delegation. Against the advice of some aides, Kennedy agreed on the condition that the debate take place before a joint meeting of the Texas and Massachusetts delegations.

The event immediately assumed the aspect of a showdown at the O.K. Corral, as LBJ touted his own record of Senate leadership and compared it with the Senate absenteeism of "some people." When it was Kennedy's turn to speak, he said of Johnson's allusion to his playing hooky to campaign: "I assume he was talking about some other candidate, not me. . . . I want to commend him for a wonderful record answering all those quorum calls. . . . I was not present on all those occasions. . . . I was not majority leader. . . . So I come here today full of admiration for Senator Johnson, full of affection for him, strongly in support of him—for majority leader."[23]

With that lighthearted squelch, Kennedy pretty much let the air out of the Johnson balloon. But there remained a considerable boomlet for Stevenson both inside and outside the convention hall. While still not declaring his candidacy, Stevenson made a brief appearance on the convention floor, igniting full-throated shouts of "We Want Stevenson!" there and in the packed galleries. They broke out again the next day when Senator Eugene J. McCarthy of Minnesota in a rousing speech offered Stevenson's name in nomination, pleading: "Do not reject this man who has made us all proud to be called Democrats. Do not leave this prophet without honor in his own party."[24]

But if Stevenson had the voices and the hearts of many in the hall, Kennedy had the votes. Still, Robert Kennedy, fearing late defections, whipped his delegate counters to prevent them. "We can't miss a trick in the next twelve hours," he told them, according to Arthur Schlesinger in his book *A Thousand Days*. "If we don't win tonight, we're dead."[25]

Nine names in all were offered to the convention—the aforementioned quartet and five favorite sons. Near the completion of the first and only roll call, Kennedy's hard-earned harvest of delegates reached a majority when Wyoming gave its 15 votes to him. In the end, he had 806 to 409 for Johnson, 86 for Symington, 79½ for Stevenson and 140½ among the favorite sons.

Then came the most dramatic, controversial and, later, historic event of the convention—Kennedy's selection of a running mate. In the customary fashion, prior to his nomination he had shopped around the vice presidency to several Democrats whose support he coveted. Among those he did not approach then was Johnson. A year earlier, in introducing LBJ at a speech in Boston, Kennedy had quipped: "Some people say our speaker might be president in 1960, but frankly I don't see why he should take a demotion."[26] Indeed, the day before the 1960 convention opened, asked about the vice-presidential nomination, Johnson had said: "I wouldn't want to trade a vote for a gavel, and I certainly wouldn't trade the active position of leadership of the greatest deliberative body in the world for the part-time job of vice president."[27]

In a notable bit of irony, Kennedy had also said in an earlier interview he would "select the best man I could get" in the event "my life expectancy was not what I hope it will be." In any event, he added, he did not think it "an enviable prospect for the second man ... to exert influence in the course of events [only] if I should die."[28] Still, the possibility of putting Johnson on the ticket had been broached with Kennedy days before his own nomination for president. Theodore White in *The Making of the President, 1960* wrote that Kennedy in conversation with Philip Graham, the publisher of the *Washington Post,* had said that "if he thought Johnson would accept the vice presidency, he might offer it."[29]

According to a long memorandum for his own files by Graham, he and columnist Joseph Alsop met with Kennedy the next day and pushed the idea of LBJ again. To Graham's surprise, he wrote in his memo, Kennedy bought it so quickly "as to leave me doubting the easy triumph, and I therefore restated the matter, urging him not to count on Johnson's turning it down but to offer the VPship so persuasively as to win Johnson over."[30] Graham passed the word to LBJ through an intermediary but, Schlesinger wrote later, Johnson "dismissed it at once, saying impatiently that he expected the same message was going out to all the candidates."[31] But the offer came, Schlesinger went on, essentially "to restore relations with the Senate leader" on whom a Kennedy legislative agenda would heavily depend, with the expectation in light of LBJ's numerous disavowals of interest, "that there was practically no chance that Johnson would accept."[32]

Kennedy made the offer personally in a visit to Johnson's suite. LBJ, now anticipating it, quickly indicated his interest, but having been counseled against taking the second spot by his mentor, Rayburn, suggested that Kennedy check with the speaker himself. In Schlesinger's account, Kennedy returned to his own suite and told Robert Kennedy with astonishment that Johnson "wants it,"[33] whereupon the two brothers began considering whether the nominee should pull back the offer and, if so, how. However, Kennedy did call on Rayburn, who, relenting, phoned Johnson and now urged him to accept, on grounds he could help beat Nixon, a man Rayburn despised.

By now, all was confusion, so John Kennedy sent his brother to find out once and for all whether Johnson really wanted the job. Robert Kennedy later told Schlesinger that the two brothers had decided to try to get LBJ to withdraw, and as an enticement had offered him, of all things, the chairmanship of the party! Robert Kennedy contended that Johnson had "burst into tears" at the notion and said he really wanted to be on the ticket, whereupon the younger brother had told him that the nominee "wants you to be vice president if you want to be vice president."[34]

Graham wrote in his memo that Johnson, upon summoning him to his suite, "seemed about to jump out of his skin. He shouted at me that

Bobby Kennedy had just come in and told Rayburn and him that there was much opposition and that Lyndon should withdraw for the sake of the party." But Rayburn, he went on, told Graham to call the nominee. He did, repeating what Robert Kennedy had said, whereupon John Kennedy told him: "Oh, . . . that's all right; Bobby's been out of touch and doesn't know what's been happening." Graham handed the phone to Johnson, who was told by Kennedy he really wanted him as his running mate. Robert Kennedy was called in, Graham wrote, "looking dead tired. . . . Bobby took the phone, and as I walked out of the room I heard him say [to his brother], 'Well, it's too late now,' and half slam down the phone."[35]

Whatever the exact sequence of events, the deal was done. Liberals, at first irate at JFK's selection of Johnson, were placated by the argument that LBJ would help the ticket in the South. Kennedy tapped Senator Henry "Scoop" Jackson of Washington State to be Democratic national chairman. Kennedy in his acceptance speech gave a name to his campaign and what would be his administration. "I stand tonight facing west on what was once the last frontier," he said. "Today, some would say . . . that there is no longer an American frontier. But we stand today on the edge of a new frontier—the frontier of the 1960s . . . Woodrow Wilson's New Freedom promised our nation a new political and economic framework. Franklin Roosevelt's New Deal promised security and succor to those in need. But the New Frontier of which I speak is not a set of promises—it is a set of challenges. It sums up not what I intend to offer the American people, but what I intend to ask of them."[36]

Ten days later, the Republican convention opened in the same Chicago convention hall. The only barrier to a first-ballot presidential nomination for Richard Nixon was a late effort by Governor Nelson Rockefeller of New York to inject stronger, more liberal language in the party platform on such issues as national defense and civil rights. Rockefeller, who had no love for Nixon, had been mentioned in 1959 as a possible challenger to him in the primaries, but he had announced late that year, when all the polls indicated an overwhelming preference in the party for Nixon, that he would not be a candidate. To avoid a floor fight, Nixon called on Rockefeller at his Manhattan apartment and struck a "Compact of Fifth Avenue" with him that accepted most of the governor's proposals.

Only one name, that of conservative Senator Barry Goldwater of Arizona, was placed in nomination against Nixon, perceived as a moderate, and Goldwater asked that it be withdrawn, calling on the party to rally behind the Californian in the name of Republican unity. In a dramatic speech that in time would be seen as a clarion call to the party's right wing, Goldwater pleaded: "Let's grow up, conservatives! If we want to take this party back, and I think we can some day, let's get to work!"[37] On the only roll call, Nixon received all but ten votes in Louisiana that went for Goldwater. The convention made Nixon's nomination unanimous, and after a long discussion with party leaders, he chose Henry Cabot Lodge of Massachusetts as his running mate.

Kennedy's two greatest perceived handicaps of the primaries continued to confront him in the fall campaign—his age and his religion. To those was added the question of experience, especially in foreign policy. Nixon, although only four years older than Kennedy, had as vice president for eight years established himself through extensive world travels as heavily experienced in foreign affairs. On a 1959 trip to Moscow, he had engaged in a rather silly "kitchen debate" with Khrushchev over the merits of capitalism and communism that Nixon deftly used to enhance his reputation as a player on the world stage.

The Republican nominee's credentials in governing were less impressive. When, shortly after Nixon's nomination, Eisenhower was asked at a press conference for an example of "a major idea of his you had adopted" during Nixon's vice presidency, the president replied: "If you give me a week, I might think of one. I don't remember."[38] Nevertheless, Nixon ran as the seasoned statesman and veteran politician against the boyish-looking son of a multi-millionaire. As usual, the Republican campaign was the better financed and Nixon led in the polls as the general election campaign got under way. The Democratic strategy was for Kennedy to focus on nine of the largest states while Johnson was dispatched to the South, especially his native Texas. A staff touted somewhat excessively as a well-oiled machine undertook massive voter registration, tapped Harvard brainpower and organized the country state by state under the tutelage of Larry O'Brien, the shrewd Massachusetts operative whose manual for running campaigns became a bible then and in the future. Interfering at first, however, was a special session of Congress that had been orchestrated by Johnson to keep a spotlight on him in erroneous anticipation that he would be the Democratic nominee. Kennedy and Johnson found themselves bogged down in the Senate while Nixon was free to campaign, focusing on the Deep South, where he hoped to capitalize on Kennedy's vulnerability there as a liberal and, some but not Nixon suggested, as a Catholic.

Kennedy, although ailing from a weak back and, not publicly known at the time, afflicted with Addison's disease, was a vigorous and dashing campaigner whose characterization of the country as mired in inertia and whose exhortations to "get this country moving again" struck a responsive chord with voters. Nixon also campaigned energetically, despite an infection in his knee from having bumped it on a car door, hospitalizing him for about ten days in late August and early September. Foolishly, he pledged to visit all fifty states, a decision that obliged him to go to many in which he had little or no chance of winning, needlessly consuming time and energy.

The issue of Kennedy's Catholicism was resurrected almost at once when a new organization of Protestant clergymen calling itself the National Conference of Citizens for Religious Freedom met on September 7 and declared him unacceptable for president. He could not be free, the group said, of the Catholic hierarchy's "determined efforts . . . to breach the wall of separation of church and state."[39] The presiding officer was the Reverend Norman Vincent Peale of New York, the prominent author and lecturer. His celebrity brought publicity to the group's views, much of it negative, leading him to retreat from the group but not from its comments about Kennedy.

Aware of the impact of the issue, Kennedy and his strategists decided to confront it, and the opportunity came in an invitation from the Greater Houston Ministerial Association to address it on September 12. Nixon had already declined a similar invitation. En route to Houston that day, Kennedy was scheduled to speak at the Alamo in San Antonio. He instructed Sorensen to find out how many Catholics had died there in the cause of Texas independence. The best a staff researcher could do was locate some Irish names among the list of the victims, but with no religious affiliation. The Kennedy speech solved the dilemma by noting that "side by side with Bowie and Crockett died McCafferty and Bailey and Carey, but no one knows whether they were Catholics or not. For there was no religious test at the Alamo."[40]

That night in the ballroom of the Rice Hotel in Houston, the atmosphere was tense as Kennedy addressed three hundred Protestant clergymen and three hundred others in the audience, including a host of reporters and a statewide television hookup. "I believe in an America," he said, "where the separation of Church and State is absolute—where no Catholic prelate would tell the President, should he be a Catholic, how to act, and no Protestant minister would tell his parishioners for whom to vote—where no church or church school is granted any public funds or political preference—and where no man is denied public office merely because his religion differs from the President who might appoint him or the people who might elect him."[41] Kennedy said pointedly that if ever a circumstance were to arise pitting his religious conscience against the national interest, he would resign the presidency. He concluded: "I am not the Catholic candidate for President, I am the Democratic Party's candidate for President who happens also to be a Catholic. I do not speak for my church on public matters, and the church does not speak for me."[42]

A round of questions and answers followed, in which Kennedy held his ground. In one response, he said that "if my church attempted to influence me in a way which was improper or which affected adversely my responsibilities as a public servant, sworn to uphold the Constitution," he would reply that he would reject the attempt as "an interference with the American political system."[43] Kennedy's remarks drew heavy applause, and for many Americans they put the issue to rest.

For many others, however, they did not, and Kennedy, while frustrated, bore the matter in good humor. At one point in the campaign Truman, now supporting Kennedy, had injudiciously remarked that Southerners who voted for Nixon could go to hell. When Nixon criticized the former president for the comment, Kennedy said he would send Truman a telegram urging him "that our side try to refrain from raising the religious issue."[44] Many Republicans, including Nixon, said they deplored the airing of Kennedy's Catholicism as an issue, but it did continue throughout the campaign in an array of pamphlets, chain letters and phone calls. Kennedy himself never raised the question again, although he did repeat his position when asked.

The critical phase of the campaign came two weeks after the Houston appearance, when the two candidates faced each other in the first of four nationwide television debates, the first in history. Both candidates and their strategists had come to recognize the power and influence of the new medium of television, and had made maximum use of it, in paid advertising and "free air"—the nightly newscasts. From television sets in 3.2 million homes in 1950, the number had mushroomed to 50 million by 1960, with more households having them than had running water or indoor toilets.⁴⁵ Kennedy particularly was a candidate made for television—handsome, cool, confident and articulate. Nixon, for his part, was an accomplished speaker, especially on world affairs, but somewhat intimidated by the camera and his own suspicions about the news media's attitude toward him.

The way had been cleared for the presidential campaign debates by an action of Congress. It suspended a federal rule requiring the television networks and stations to provide free time to fringe candidates whenever time was offered to major-party candidates. Nixon's strategists advised him, however, not to debate; doing so would only give the lesser-known Kennedy much wider public exposure. But Nixon had weathered a number of television storms in his campaigns for the House and Senate, in the Moscow "kitchen debate" with Khrushchev and, most famously, in his "Checkers" speech defending the Nixon fund. When the networks offered the free time right after the Republican convention, Kennedy immediately accepted and challenged Nixon to do the same, and Nixon, feeling unable to refuse, agreed.

The networks originally offered eight debates, but negotiations between the two candidate camps whittled the number down to four, a week apart from September 26 to October 21. The first was on domestic policy in a CBS studio in Chicago, with a panel of reporters questioning the candidates and Howard K. Smith of CBS News as moderator. As it turned out, this was the only one that really mattered, and it served to elevate the younger and less experienced Kennedy at the expense of Nixon, perceived going into the first debate as an elder statesman.

About seventy million Americans watched or listened to the first debate, the largest audience for a campaign event in history up to that time, and a combination of Kennedy's performance and Nixon's appearance erased overnight the vice president's advantage. Kennedy arrived at his hotel well rested, and after an intense and lengthy briefing by aides who had compiled questions to throw at him, took a three-hour nap, waking refreshed, for a final briefing.

Nixon, on the other hand, had arrived in Chicago late the night before, had given a speech that morning to a hostile union audience and then closeted himself alone in his hotel room all afternoon. On arrival at the television studio for the evening debate, he hit his knee on a car door again, exacerbating the earlier injury from which he had not fully recovered. Kennedy, already well tanned, wore, according to Sorensen, only "a slight trace of makeup."[46] Nixon was given, in the account of Theodore White, "only a light coating of 'Lazy Shave,' a pancake makeup with which a man who has heavy afternoon beard growth may powder his face to conceal the growth."[47]

From the start, it was clear that Kennedy's strategy was to take the debate to Nixon. He opened with a firm and aggressive statement of his conviction that the country, threatened by communism in the Soviet Union and China, was stalled in pursuit of its promise, and that he intended to do something about it. "Are we doing as much as we can do?" he asked. ". . . I do not think we're doing enough . . . I am not satisfied as an American with the progress that we are making. This is a great country, but I think it could be a greater country, and this is a powerful country but I think it could be a more powerful country." Then, chronicling the matters about which "I am not satisfied," he invoked the words that were becoming the heart of his message on the campaign trail: "I think we can do better . . . I think it's time America started moving again."[48]

Nixon seemed determined from the outset to counter his reputation as a slugger and to come across as a man of good will and reasonableness. "The things that Senator Kennedy has said," he began, "many of us can agree with. There is no question but that we cannot discuss our internal affairs in the United States without recognizing that they have a tremendous bearing on our international position. There is no question but that this nation cannot stand still, because we are in a deadly competition . . . not only with the men in the Kremlin but the men in Peking. We're ahead in this competition, as Senator Kennedy, I think, has implied. But when you're in a race, the only way to stay ahead is to move ahead, and I subscribe completely to the spirit that Senator Kennedy has expressed tonight, the spirit that the United States should move ahead." But, he asked, "where then do we disagree?"[49]

Only then did Nixon begin to rebut Kennedy, but always in conciliatory tones: "Senator Kennedy has suggested that he believes he knows the way. I respect the sincerity with which he makes that suggestion. . . . May I indicate that Senator Kennedy and I are not in disagreement as to the aim. . . . I agree with Senator Kennedy completely on that score."[50] And so on.

For ninety minutes, the two presidential candidates discussed a range of issues—from their comparative experience, the farm problem, the federal debt and education to taxes, minimum wage, medical care for the aged and communist subversion. No new or startling views were revealed, but Kennedy's assertiveness and confidence dominated the exchanges with the largely defensive Nixon. He spoke directly to the television audience, turning questions to his own advantage and at times almost ignoring his opponent. The vice president's tone and posture were summed up in an observation early in the debate: "I know Senator Kennedy feels as deeply about these problems as I do, but our disagreement is not about the goals for America but only about the means to reach those goals."[51]

Had the debate taken place in a local town hall somewhere before only the people in the room, Nixon may have fared better. Indeed, in one post-debate poll, a majority of those surveyed who had listened to the exchanges via radio said they thought the vice president had won. On television, however, it was a different story. The camera's close-ups conveyed a somewhat squeamish-looking, heavily perspiring Nixon contrasted by a vigorous and confident Kennedy. Going into the debate, all Kennedy the underdog needed was a public perception that he had held his own; coming out, he was widely accepted as a match or more than a match for the sitting vice president.

The remaining three debates did not change that perception much. Nixon abandoned his deferential manner and became more aggressive against Kennedy, but to little avail. By this time, Kennedy had become a matinee idol playing to larger and larger street crowds that included jumping, squealing young women and girls reaching to touch him. His vivacious young wife, Jacqueline, stayed off the campaign trail most of the time because she was expecting a baby, another fact that added glamour and charm to the Kennedy story. Nixon was left to plod on to fulfill his pledge to visit all fifty states, growing more haggard as he did. He spent valuable hours two days before the election on long flights to and from Alaska, now a state, to make good the promise.

Not until near the end of the campaign did President Eisenhower weigh in for his vice president. On the Democratic side, vice-presidential nominee Johnson was more than carrying his weight campaigning diligently for the ticket in the South. Meanwhile, Kennedy received a boost among black voters when he made a sympathy call to the wife of Martin Luther King Jr., who was jailed in Georgia for a traffic violation in the midst of a civil rights protest, and Robert Kennedy phoned the sentencing judge and got King released.[52] News of these actions swept like wildfire through the black community—with the help of two million pamphlets reporting the interventions distributed outside black churches on the Sunday before the election.[53]

On election eve, the Gallup poll declared the race too close to call, and the poll was right. After a cliffhanger of an election night, the outcome still hung on four states—Michigan, Illinois, Minnesota and California—when Kennedy went to bed shortly before 4 a.m. in the East. When he awoke about five hours later, Sorensen told him he had won all four, which was not quite right. He had lost California, but even without it he had a majority in the electoral college. Nixon later liked to say he could have challenged Kennedy's victory in Illinois on grounds that Mayor Daley of Chicago had caused sufficient illegal Democratic votes to be cast, but he did not want to create a constitutional crisis, so he nobly demurred. But the fact was, Kennedy won the electoral vote without Illinois.

In the end, Kennedy's popular vote was a mere 118,550 more than Nixon's out of 68.3 million cast for the two of them, or 49.9 percent to 49.6 percent, with the remaining 0.5 percent for minor candidates. In the electoral college, however, Kennedy won comfortably, 303–219, with 15 other votes from Alabama, Mississippi and Oklahoma going to Democratic Senator Harry F. Byrd of Virginia. After the eight years in the wilderness of Eisenhower's great personal appeal, the country had returned to the party of the New Deal and Fair Deal, with a vibrant young president, the first born in the twentieth century, promising an exciting exploration of a New Frontier.

President John F. Kennedy in 1962 stared down Soviet Union leader Nikita Khrushchev, seen here with Cuban President Fidel Castro leading the way, in their famous "High Noon" confrontation in the Cuban Missile Crisis. They averted possible nuclear war when the Soviet leader agreed to remove offensive missiles from the island, ninety miles off the U.S. coast.

Chapter 24

THE BEGINNING AND END OF THE NEW FRONTIER, 1961–1963

THE DEMOCRATIC MARGIN of victory in 1960 was narrow. But the enthusiasm with which the young new president took hold of his office and, indeed, the nation's capital infused the government and the country with an air of excitement and buoyancy not seen from the Democratic Party since the best days of the confidently grinning FDR. John Kennedy and his beautiful wife were, without doubt, the most attractive young first couple to grace the White House in years, if not ever. And Kennedy brought with him a new generation of civic-minded and social-minded intellectuals who gave official Washington a mood of joyous urgency.

After eight years of Democratic Party leadership from the congressional wing during the Eisenhower Republican drought, the presidential wing asserted itself. Even as a flood of academics and other liberal eggheads brimming with energy and innovative ideas moved into appointive positions in the executive branch, Kennedy turned the Democratic National Committee over to an old party hack and ally, John Bailey of Connecticut. It was clear from the beginning that the major political decisions would be made in the White House, with the president's brother, now Attorney General Robert Kennedy, and old campaign aides like Kenneth O'Donnell and Larry O'Brien calling the shots.

In Congress, however, the party recapturing the presidency failed for the first time in the century to pick up even a single seat. Only one Democratic senator was defeated but twenty-nine Democrats fell in the House, all of them progressives, to only nine Republican losses. Kennedy's party maintained large majorities in each body on paper—264 Democrats to 174 Republicans in the House, 65 Democrats to 35 Republicans in the Senate. But the unreliability or outright opposition of Southern Democrats imperiled or denied the new president working majorities on much of his liberal legislation.

While the dire domestic circumstances that had midwifed Roosevelt's New Deal agenda in 1933 no longer existed, Kennedy continued to embrace its basic tenets while seeking to turn the nation's attention to its broader role as a power in a world of opportunity and peril. From the start he set a tone of seriousness and challenge with his inaugural address on a bitter-cold January 20: "Let the word go forth from this time and place, to friend and foe alike, that the torch has been passed to a new generation of Americans, born in this century, tempered by war, disciplined by a hard and bitter peace, proud of our ancient heritage, and unwilling to witness or permit the slow undoing of those human rights to which this nation has always been committed, and to which we are committed today at home and around the world. Let every nation know, whether it wishes us well or ill, that we shall pay any price, bear any burden, meet any hardship, support any friend, oppose any foe to assure the survival and the success of liberty."[1]

The speech was short and narrow. Eschewing any shopping list of domestic or foreign objectives, it sent word to Americans at home and friends and adversaries abroad that here was a young president who intended to meet the challenges and responsibilities of a global power with policies rooted in the nation's most basic values and traditions. To the other Cold War power, Kennedy offered cooperation and mutual trust, backed by a quiet reminder of American strength and a will to use it if necessary. "So let us begin anew," he said, "remembering on both sides that civility is not a sign of weakness, and sincerity is always subject to proof. Let us never negotiate out of fear, but let us never fear to negotiate."[2]

Kennedy observed prophetically that the task of achieving enduring peace would not be completed quickly, "nor even perhaps in our lifetime on this planet, but let us begin." He concluded with perhaps his most remembered words: "And so, my fellow Americans, ask not what your country can do for you; ask what you can do for your country. My fellow citizens of the world, ask not what America can do for you, but what together we can do for the freedom of man."[3]

1743 *Th Jefferson* 1826

from the original portrait by Gilbert Stuart in possession
of Bowdoin College–Brunswick, Maine.

Thomas Jefferson of Virginia
Third President of the United States
1801–1809

James Madison of Virginia
Fourth President of the United States
1809–1817

James Monroe of Virginia
Fifth President of the
United States
1817–1825

John Quincy Adams
of Massachusetts
Sixth President of the
United States
1825–1829

Andrew Jackson of Tennessee
Seventh President of the United States
1829–1837

Martin Van Buren of New York
Eighth President of the United States
1837–1841

John Tyler of Virginia
Tenth President of the
United States
1841–1845

James Polk of Tennessee
Eleventh President of
the United States
1845–1849

Franklin Pierce of New Hampshire
Fourteenth President of the United States
1853–1857

From an Ambrotype by Brady.

Expressly for this work.

James Buchanan

James Buchanan of Pennsylvania
Fifteenth President of the United States
1857–1861

ANDREW JOHNSON

Andrew Johnson of Tennessee
Seventeenth President of the United States
1865–1869

Grover Cleveland of New York
Twenty-second and Twenty-fourth President of the United States
1885–1889 and 1893–1897

Woodrow Wilson of New Jersey
Twenty-eighth President of the United States
1913–1921

Library of Congress Prints and Photographs Division; by permission, Perskie Photograph, Baltimore

Franklin D. Roosevelt of New York
Thirty-second President of the United States
1933–1945

Harry S. Truman of Missouri
Thirty-third President of the United States
1945–1953

John F. Kennedy of Massachusetts
Thirty-fifth President of the United States
1961–1963

Lyndon B. Johnson
of Texas
Thirty-sixth President
of the United States
1963–1969

Jimmy Carter of Georgia
Thirty-ninth President
of the United States
1977–1981

Bill Clinton of Arkansas
Forty-second President of the United States
1993–2001

By intent or not, Kennedy thus anticipated that his administration would be one dominated by challenges outside America's borders even as it would often be frustrated by political conflict and stalemate within. His principal campaign cry had been to "get this country moving again," a general statement that was uncomplicated by specific action programs other than an idea borrowed from Hubert Humphrey that he called a Peace Corps. On that concept for volunteer youth service in Third World countries, plus a Food for Peace program and a grand plan for a new partnership with Latin America he labeled the Alliance for Progress, Kennedy acted swiftly upon taking office. All emphasized the theme of selfless American service to other countries and people.

But the new president would soon learn there would be ample developments and pressures at home and abroad of a less benevolent nature that would test his talents and his will. The spirit of youth and gaiety personified by a first couple plunging into a heightened social life of the city belied the heavy burdens that the new president and his advisers would soon face, in a period of repeated confrontation with the Soviet Union.

Kennedy was in office less than three months when a planned foreign policy adventure inherited from the Eisenhower administration blew up in his face. In the final months of Eisenhower's term, a plan had been in the works to send Cuban exiles in the United States into their home country to overthrow communist leader Fidel Castro,[4] and the planning went forward at the CIA into Kennedy's presidency. As president-elect, Kennedy had been briefed that a large force of exiles had been training in secret for months in Guatemala for such an exercise. When the time approached for action, according to Sorensen in his book *Kennedy*, the new president was confronted with a decision either to let the plan go forward or disband the exile group, breed resentment and loose tongues, and trigger more Soviet shipments of arms and planes to Castro. After getting the written endorsement of the Joint Chiefs of Staff and the verbal approval of Secretary of State Dean Rusk and Secretary of Defense Robert McNamara, he gave the go-ahead, on the condition that no American forces were to be used in Cuba.[5]

The invasion at the Bay of Pigs was a disaster. When the approximately fourteen hundred exiles hit the Cuban beach, they soon ran out of ammunition because two supply freighters were sunk by Cuban air force planes. They then were overwhelmed by a defense force of as many as twenty thousand Cuban troops, and ill-conceived plans to destroy the

Cuban planes with unmarked aircraft went awry. The long and short of it was that Kennedy had been ill served by his military advisers, and he should have seen through the stupid and reckless scheme himself, which he later readily admitted to aides. At the very least, the adventure was foolhardy, especially so in the first months of a new administration. The president was on unsure ground and had not sufficiently measured the quality of the military and intelligence officers around him and the advice they were giving him, not to mention the slim chances of keeping the whole operation secret. According to Sorensen, Kennedy berated himself, saying, "How could I have been so far off base? All my life I've known better than to depend on the experts. How could I have been so stupid, to let them go ahead?"[6]

In the end, he faced the music at a news conference. "There's an old saying that victory has a hundred fathers and defeat is an orphan," he said. ". . . I am the responsible officer of the government and that is quite obvious."[7] He took his lumps in the press and in world opinion, but said later he had learned some valuable lessons on procedures and personnel that served him well in later crises. The price he paid at the time, however, was great, in dampening the aura of confidence and exhilaration that had blanketed his first months in office.

Even before the Bay of Pigs fiasco, the luster of Kennedy's sparkling beginning had been eroded by news from Moscow five days earlier that the Soviet Union had successfully put the first man in space and brought him back unharmed. On April 12, 1961, Cosmonaut Yuri Gagarin had completed a full orbital flight around the earth in less than two hours aboard a Russian spacecraft. Like the *Sputnik* satellite before it, the historic manned spaceflight undercut America's sense of technological superiority. Kennedy ordered a comprehensive review of the U.S. space program and, the next month, pledged to put an American astronaut on the moon and return him safely "before this decade is out."[8]

That bold and imaginative initiative, in keeping with Kennedy's proclamation of a New Frontier beyond the physical boundaries of the nation itself, had hardly had its psychological impact when another critical Cold War development forced his attentions back to earth. Shortly before Kennedy's inauguration, Soviet Premier Khrushchev had made an especially bellicose speech in Moscow in which he defended so-called wars of national liberation in places like Cuba, Algeria and now Vietnam, and threw down a gauntlet on continued American presence in Berlin.

The United States, Britain and France, which jointly occupied the western segment of the former German capital deep within what was now Soviet-dominated East Germany, "cannot fail to realize that sooner or later the occupation regime in [West Berlin] must be ended," Khrushchev proclaimed. "It is necessary to go ahead with bringing the aggressive-minded imperialists to their senses, and compelling them to reckon with the real situation. And should they balk, then we will take resolute measures; we will sign a peace treaty with the [East] German Democratic Republic."[9]

Kennedy, hoping to ease tensions with the Soviet Union and curious about his explosive adversary in the Kremlin, after consulting with his Russian experts sent Khrushchev a letter in late February suggesting that they meet in late spring in Vienna or Stockholm. In mid-May, a few weeks after the Bay of Pigs debacle, Khrushchev replied, agreeing to the "summit" between the leaders of the two Cold War superpowers. It was set for early June in Vienna, at a time impoverished and oppressed East Germans were fleeing their country at a rate of four thousand a week. East Germany's population had declined by two million since 1949, and many were lured by the glitz of a prosperous West Berlin. Khrushchev obviously wanted to put a stop to it.

Ted Sorensen, writing later of the two days of meetings in Vienna, reported that the confrontation "was neither a victory nor a defeat for either side. It was, as the American President hoped, useful. It was, as the Soviet Chairman later reported, necessary. It was not, both would have agreed, a turning point of any kind."[10] But James Reston, the distinguished Washington bureau chief of the *New York Times*, who had an interview with Kennedy at the American embassy immediately after the last of the meetings, reported in his memoir, *Deadline*, a different view.

"I remember that Saturday morning very well," he wrote. "He [Kennedy] arrived at the embassy over an hour late, shaken and angry, having been delayed by an unexpected extra meeting with the Soviet leader. He was wearing a hat—unusual for him—and he pushed it down over his forehead, sat down on a couch beside me, and sighed. I said it must have been a rough session. Much rougher than he had expected, he said. Khrushchev had threatened him over Berlin. . . . He had presented Kennedy with an aide-mémoire, setting December 1961 as the deadline for agreement on a Berlin peace treaty. If the United States did not agree to Communist control over access to that city, the Soviet Union would proceed unilaterally to dominate the routes from Western Europe to

Berlin. The president felt this amounted to an ultimatum, and replied that the United States would fight to maintain access to its garrison in Berlin if necessary. The summit meeting ended on that ominous note."

Reston went on: "Kennedy reported this to me quite calmly. He thought he knew, he said, why Khrushchev had taken such a hard line. He felt sure Khrushchev thought that anybody who had made such a mess of the Cuban invasion had no judgment, and any president who had made such a blunder but then didn't see it through had no guts. Now, said the president, we have a problem. Nothing could be resolved with the Soviets, he added, if they thought we would not insist on our rights and would not fight for them. He had tried to convince Khrushchev of U.S. determination but had failed. It was now essential to demonstrate our firmness."[11]

On hearing Khrushchev's declaration that his decision to sign a treaty with East Germany in December was irrevocable, Kennedy, according to Schlesinger in *One Thousand Days,* replied: "It will be a cold winter."[12] In his first speech after the summit, the Soviet leader reiterated his intention of "freeing" West Berlin from its "occupation regime" of the three Western allies "this year."[13] And so the lines were drawn.

On his return to Washington, after weeks of deliberations Kennedy ordered a controlled military buildup and called up 150,000 reservists, but stopped short of declaring a national emergency. The Russians replied with military manpower moves of their own. In late July, Kennedy went on television and told the American people his answer to Khrushchev's bombast. "West Berlin has now become the great testing place of Western courage and will," he said, "a focal point where our solemn commitments . . . and Soviet ambitions now meet in basic confrontation. We cannot and will not permit the Communists to drive us out of Berlin, either gradually or by force. . . . We will at all times be ready to talk, if talk will help. But we must also be ready to resist with force, if force is used upon us."[14]

The Soviet leader's own response came in the early hours of August 13, when East German workers were suddenly ordered to slap up a makeshift barrier of roadblocks and barbed wire between the east and west sections of the city—the beginnings of the infamous Berlin Wall. It wasn't clear at first that the East German regime intended to halt the rising flow from east to west entirely or simply to tighten the monitoring of it. It was not until four days later that construction of a concrete wall was undertaken. It was seen more as a move to control the East German population than as any move against West Berlin, and while the wall shocked the West, it did solve the immediate problem for the communists of the growing population drain.

Kennedy decided, however, that some response was required, and he sent a convoy of fifteen hundred American troops in armored trucks down the Autobahn through East German checkpoints and into West Berlin as a show more of determination than of strength. The Soviets did nothing and Khrushchev subsequently lowered the tension in October by postponing his stated deadline of year's end to sign the treaty with East Germany. A correspondence began between Kennedy and Khrushchev that also helped lower the temperature.

On the other side of the globe, however, a time bomb was ticking in Southeast Asia, where insurgencies brewed in Laos and South Vietnam. The two superpower leaders had agreed in Vienna to work out an accommodation in Laos, but the Western-supported regime in Saigon was under increasing internal pressures. In the spring of 1961, Kennedy had sent Vice President Johnson to Saigon and followed up with a small counterinsurgency force of American Green Berets to advise the military under President Ngo Dinh Diem. In November, Kennedy dispatched General Maxwell Taylor to assess the situation in which the Viet Cong insurgents were further harassing the Diem government. Taylor recommended as many as ten thousand American combat troops be sent to Vietnam, but Kennedy rejected the idea, choosing instead to assign only a cadre of military advisers to the South Vietnamese army.

All these foreign policy demands on the president's time and attention detracted from his New Frontier agenda at home. So did his early awareness that in the face of Khrushchev's belligerence the doctrine of "massive retaliation" with nuclear weapons that had governed U.S. policy in the Eisenhower-Dulles years was too risky. In collaboration with Secretary of Defense McNamara, Kennedy shifted to a "flexible response" that required a major buildup of conventional war forces as well as long-range nuclear missiles to close the "missile gap" with the Soviets that Kennedy as a candidate had insisted existed (but, it turned out, didn't). In September 1961, having thrown cold water in Vienna on Kennedy's efforts to achieve an agreement to ban further nuclear testing, Khrushchev responded by breaking the existing moratorium with extensive testing. At the United Nations, Kennedy challenged the Soviet Union to join in total disarmament, but to no avail, and eventually if reluctantly resumed U.S. testing.

At home, Kennedy successfully kept inflation in check with wage-price guidelines, raised economic growth and lowered unemployment. In a precursor of the War on Poverty, he pushed through Congress an Area Redevelopment Act in 1961 that made a start in the eleven-state rural region of Appalachia from Pennsylvania through Kentucky and into Alabama. Other major domestic initiatives in such areas as aid to education and medical care for the aged were throttled by an effective conservative coalition of Republicans and Southern Democrats. Kennedy's age and own junior status, first in the House and then in the Senate, before reaching the White House left him, according to Sorensen later, "somewhat uncomfortable and perhaps too deferential with these men who the previous year had outranked him."[15]

Southern Democrats holding important committee chairmanships also frustrated Kennedy in his pursuit of anti-discrimination legislation and in their insistence on continued appointment of segregationist judges in the South.[16] At the same time, the peaceful revolution for equal rights there intensified in May 1961 when a group of black and white civil rights leaders undertook what they called a Freedom Ride by one Greyhound and one Trailways bus through Dixie, testing their legal ability to travel as an integrated entity. They got as far as Danville, Virginia, before they were turned away at a bus station, but there were no arrests or violence at that point.

During the ride, Robert Kennedy, who as attorney general had wished the Freedom Riders well, made a strong civil rights speech at the University of Georgia. He candidly told a solemn audience that the Kennedy administration would enforce civil rights statutes on the books, especially in the case of defiance in southern Virginia of *Brown* v. *Board of Education* by maintaining schools for white children only. His straightforwardness was rewarded with sustained applause. The reaction was countered outside the South, however, by a statement by Governor Ernest Vandiver of Georgia that President Kennedy had assured him he would never use federal force to uphold desegregation laws in his state.[17]

Upon entering the Greyhound terminal in Rock Hill, South Carolina, Freedom Rider John Lewis, a black onetime seminary student, was punched and knocked to the ground, and others were also beaten. The Freedom Riders pressed on into Alabama, where outside Anniston one of the buses was firebombed and riders beaten again. At the terminal in Birmingham, members of the Ku Klux Klan were among the hysterical white greeters who again beat the passengers. In Montgomery, the beatings continued and among the victims was John Seigenthaler, a Robert Kennedy deputy sent to try to protect them. When Governor John Patterson reneged on a promise to protect the Freedom Riders, the attorney general sent six hundred deputy U.S. marshals to Montgomery to extricate them and send them on their way. Robert Kennedy later got the Interstate Commerce Commission to require desegregation of all facilities in bus stations used in interstate travel and brought suits against localities that refused.[18]

Kennedy ended his first year as president with a triumphant Latin American trip. He and his Spanish-fluent wife were mobbed by cheering crowds in Caracas and Bogotá as he touted his Alliance for Progress partnership. As Kennedy's second year began, the country got a morale boost from the orbital spaceflight of Marine Colonel John Glenn. But the president's own infectious optimism and witty good cheer were just as important in sustaining the nation's upbeat mood, and his own popularity. All through his first year in office, Kennedy's approval rating in the Gallup poll had never dropped below 72 percent. Ironically, it had surged to 83 percent in the wake of his acceptance of responsibility for the Bay of Pigs fiasco, and by the beginning of 1962 was still at 79 percent.

Problems continued, however, on the domestic front. In Kennedy's efforts to keep inflation in check, in April 1962 he clashed directly and bitterly with the steel industry when its ranking executives bucked his wage-price guidelines and boosted prices after the president had persuaded labor to agree to a noninflationary contract. The chairman of U.S. Steel, Roger Blough, called on Kennedy and handed him a mimeographed statement announcing that his company was raising the price of steel $6 a ton, four times the cost of the wage increase to which the union had agreed. Kennedy was astounded. "I think you're making a mistake," he told Blough, whose regrets were not well received.[19] Upon Blough's departure, the president called several aides into the Oval Office and, after conveying what Blough had told him, remarked heatedly: "My father always told me that steel men were sons-of-bitches, but I never realized till now how right he was."[20]

With other steel companies quickly joining U.S. Steel in the $6 increase, Kennedy reacted with a blistering attack on all of them. In a news conference, he said their "simultaneous and identical actions" were "a wholly unjustifiable and irresponsible defiance of the public interest."

With crisis in Berlin and Americans dying in Vietnam, he said, "the American people will find it hard, as I do, to accept a situation in which a tiny handful of steel executives whose pursuit of private power and profit exceeds their sense of public responsibility can show such utter contempt for the interests of 185 million Americans." He concluded: "Some time ago I asked each American to consider what he would do for his country, and I asked the steel companies. In the last twenty-four hours we had their answer."[21]

Kennedy started turning the screws on the defiant industry chiefs. He ordered McNamara at the Pentagon to shift defense orders to steel companies that had not bought into U.S. Steel's price rise, and his brother at the Justice Department looked into possible anti-trust violations in it. In Congress, Kefauver scheduled another investigation. However, direct pressures on smaller steel producers to hold the line bore fruit. First, Bethlehem Steel, the second-largest producer, rescinded its increase, then U.S. Steel itself. Kennedy's demonstration of toughness and resolve not only rolled back steel prices but also conveyed the strong sense of a chief executive in charge, appreciated particularly by organized labor.

Trouble also brewed again on the civil rights front when James Meredith, a black Mississippian who had applied for admission to the University of Mississippi a year earlier and been turned down, filed suit in federal court. It was dismissed by a federal district judge, but in June 1962 the circuit court of appeals held that Meredith had been rejected "solely because he was a Negro." When Governor Ross Barnett declared that "we will never surrender to the evil and illegal forces of tyranny,"[22] Robert Kennedy stepped in. Unable to dissuade Barnett from resisting, in September he sent federal marshals to accompany Meredith as he sought to register on the Ole Miss campus at Oxford. Barnett, declaring himself an emergency registrar, personally turned Meredith away. Meredith, supported by marshals John Doar and James McShane, kept trying, while Robert Kennedy and the president continued by phone to pressure Barnett, as the tense situation stretched into October.

In the end, with Barnett held in contempt by a federal court, a deal was struck. The buffoonish governor would put on a show of resisting to save face with fellow white Mississippians, but would yield to a stage-managed demonstration of federal force. Once Meredith was brought onto the campus, however, Mississippi highway patrolmen abandoned their posts and violence broke out that had to be quelled by federal troops. Two men were killed and hundreds wounded or otherwise injured before Meredith finally was registered. It was a messy exercise of presidential power, but it succeeded. While it hardened hatred of the Kennedys among racist whites in the Deep South, it again illustrated the young president's fortitude and reinforced his support among blacks everywhere.

As troublesome as the struggle to integrate Ole Miss was, it did not hold a candle to the epic confrontation that presented itself to Kennedy later in October. Back in late August, with the situation in Berlin still a contentious one, Ted Sorensen had lunch with Soviet Ambassador Anatoly Dobrynin. The president's closest aide advised the diplomat that the approaching American congressional elections would not be an inhibition to President Kennedy's ability to respond to any precipitous Soviet action toward the former German capital.[23] In early September, Dobrynin asked Sorensen to come to the Russian embassy, where he conveyed a personal message for Kennedy from Khrushchev. The Soviet leader said he would not take any action before those elections that would complicate, as Sorensen wrote later, "the international situation or aggravate the tension in the relations between our two countries" as long as Kennedy would similarly refrain.[24]

Sorensen replied that tensions had already been aggravated by shipments that summer "of Soviet personnel, arms and equipment into Cuba." According to Sorensen's notes, Dobrynin then emphasized several times, neither confirming nor denying Sorensen's observation, that the Russians "had done nothing new or extraordinary in Cuba." The movements undertaken, he said, "had been taking place somewhat gradually and quietly over a long period of time—and that he stood by his assurances that all these steps were defensive in nature and did not represent any threat to the security of the United States."[25]

American knowledge of the buildup came from aerial surveillance and photography as well as from intelligence reports gathered by the CIA. Kennedy was keeping his eye on the situation, particularly because some Republican members of Congress, notably Senator Kenneth Keating of New York, were reporting from unidentified sources that surface-to-surface missiles were being transported to Cuba. The administration then and later dismissed the reports as rumor or political mischief-making by the Republicans in advance of the off-year elections. But on August 29 aerial photographs for the first time yielded evidence of anti-aircraft surface-to-surface missiles, known as SAMs, on the island, but no signs of offensive missiles of sufficient range to hit the United States. Kennedy in a public statement on September 4 observed that "were it to be otherwise, the gravest issues would arise."[26]

On September 11, amid the speculation, Moscow stated flatly that its missiles had such great range that it wasn't necessary to put them on any foreign soil, including that of Cuba, and that "the armaments and military equipment sent to Cuba are designed exclusively for defensive purposes."[27] Kennedy declared two days later that "if at any time the Communist build-up in Cuba were to endanger or interfere with our security in any way," or if Cuba were to become "an offensive military base of significant capacity for the Soviet Union, then this country will do whatever must be done to protect its own security and that of its allies."[28]

The aerial photography continued into the next month, and on October 14 the first photos spotted the beginnings of a medium-range missile base, with the prospect that it and others would soon be operational. Kennedy quickly assembled some fifteen of his most dependable aides into what eventually was called the Executive Committee of the National Security Council, or Ex Comm, to brainstorm the response under the strictest secrecy. Out of it came Kennedy's decision to turn aside drastic suggestions to launch an invasion or severe aerial bombardment of Cuba, favored by the military chiefs. Instead, he chose a cautious but firm "quarantine" of the island to stop the importing of Soviet missiles and bring about their removal.

In the internal debate, from all accounts, the key figure aside from the president himself was his brother the attorney general, who turned aside the most drastic ideas and kept prodding the group to produce and explore all feasible possibilities. At a critical point, he spoke passionately and persuasively against a sneak attack that would violate the nation's honor. From one account, he said it would be "a Pearl Harbor in reverse" that would "blacken the name of the United States in the pages of history."[29]

It so happened that Soviet Foreign Minister Andrei Gromyko, in this country for a United Nations session, was scheduled to meet with the president before returning to Moscow. It was decided not to disclose to him what Kennedy now knew. Gromyko, accompanied by Dobrynin, talked about Berlin, reiterating that if no agreement was reached on a peace treaty with East Germany, the Soviet Union would proceed on its own. Then he launched a complaint against U.S. actions toward Cuba, reading from notes that the Soviet buildup there was being undertaken "solely [for] the purpose of contributing to the defense capabilities of Cuba and to the development of its peaceful economy" and that "training by Soviet specialists of Cuban nationals in handling defense armaments was by no means offensive."[30] Kennedy received all this deadpan, responding only by reading to Gromyko his earlier warning against the installation of offensive weapons.

On the night of October 22, Kennedy went on nationwide television and dropped on the American people the bombshell of what was going on. He got right to the point about Cuba: "Within the past week, unmistakable evidence has established the fact that a series of offensive missile sites is now in preparation on that imprisoned island. The purpose of these bases can be none other than to provide a nuclear strike capability against the Western Hemisphere." Summarizing the developments, Kennedy called them "a deliberately provocative and unjustified change in the status quo which cannot be accepted by this country" and said "our unswerving objective" regarding the missiles was to "secure their withdrawal or elimination" from the hemisphere. Then he described the "initial" American response—a naval quarantine of Cuba. Some sixteen destroyers, three cruisers, an anti-submarine aircraft carrier and six utility ships were on the picket line, with nearly 150 other ships held in reserve.[31] The decision was now in the Russians' hands.

After an incredibly tense war of nerves played out in the waters north of Cuba, Soviet ships closest to the island suddenly stopped or changed course away from it. After several ships had been passed through the quarantine unsearched, the U.S. forces finally, with Kennedy's approval, halted and boarded a freighter under Soviet charter, inspected it and permitted it to continue. In two days, the Soviet ships themselves had turned around and headed back home. Secretary of State Rusk, a member of Ex Comm, memorably exclaimed: "We're eyeball to eyeball, and I think the other fellow just blinked."[32]

Meanwhile, however, the missile installations in Cuba were moving rapidly toward the operational stage. A letter from Khrushchev to Kennedy received on October 26 indicated the missiles would be removed under UN supervision provided the United States would agree not to invade the island. But before it could be answered, a second, more belligerent letter arrived demanding that American Jupiter missiles based in Turkey be removed as a quid pro quo. Also, news came that a U-2 surveillance plane over Cuba had been shot down and the pilot killed. Deferring a response to that unfortunate complication, and deftly ignoring Khrushchev's second letter, Kennedy elected to respond to the less demanding first communication, and waited.

To the immense relief of all, Khrushchev's response—sent publicly for optimum speed—was positive; he agreed to withdraw the missiles and permit their inspection in return for the American pledge not to invade Cuba, which never was the intention anyway. (Later, it was revealed that an unwritten understanding had been reached that the American missiles in Turkey, which were becoming obsolete, eventually also would be removed, and they were.) Soon after, the Soviet missiles were loaded back on cargo ships and returned to the Soviet Union after aerial inspection by the United States.[33]

Whether as a result of this successful climb back from the brink or not, in November the president's party for the first time since 1934 escaped the usual setback in the off-year elections. Easily retaining control of Congress, the Democrats lost only four seats in the House and gained four in the Senate. Heading into 1963, Kennedy seemed to have more than recovered from his stumbling beginning at the Bay of Pigs. His staring down both the steel industry at home and the Soviet Union in Berlin and Cuba, and his steps to advance the cause of civil rights in the South, gave him the stature as a strong leader of the nation and his party he had lacked on assuming the presidency.

In his third year, Kennedy continued to play aggressively on both the domestic and foreign stages. The civil rights movement, with King now its undisputed leader, pressed the president for greater interventions. In February, Kennedy proposed anti-discrimination legislation strengthening voting rights in the South, but Congress basically ignored it. The target for the year's chief nonviolent protest was Birmingham, Alabama, described by King as "by far the worst big city in race relations in the United States."[34]

King had long planned the effort, but it was delayed until after the city's mayoral election, in which the notoriously racist police commissioner, Eugene "Bull" Connor, was a candidate. The special election on March 5 did not produce a majority winner, however, and Connor was forced into a runoff a month later, which he lost. King then launched a well-planned campaign against stores, restaurants and discriminatory hiring to begin on Good Friday. Connor responded by setting police dogs on the marchers and protesters, including King. When Kennedy failed to intervene aggressively for desegregation as he did in the Meredith case in Mississippi, many civil rights leaders complained. Finally, federal negotiators were sent to argue for more job opportunities and use of public facilities for blacks, and the city's new mayor promised to cooperate. But the night bombing of a black home triggered riots and led to the dispatch of federal troops again. Governor George C. Wallace, a shrewd and publicity-seeking segregationist, took issue with the use of federal forces, insisting that the state police under his direction could handle any violence. Kennedy was not deterred and peace finally was restored.

Soon after, in June, Wallace again put himself on a collision course with the president. Alabama now was the only state that still maintained a segregated state university, and two black students had won court approval for admission, but Wallace declared it would not happen. The Kennedy administration, however, learning from the Ole Miss experience, this time was ready for any eventuality. In a press conference, the president said he hoped federal troops wouldn't be needed but pointed out that the force of law stood behind the admissions. In a show of defiance obviously for local consumption, Wallace stood in the doorway of the University of Alabama registration building and declared the admissions illegal. Kennedy quickly federalized the Alabama National Guard, removing it from Wallace's control, and the governor, having completed his little charade on television, stepped aside and the two students were promptly registered.

Kennedy went on television that night, declaring that "race has no place in American life or law."[35] He announced plans for even stronger civil rights legislation, noting that while "it is better to settle these matters in the courts than on the streets and new laws are needed at every level . . . law alone cannot make men see right. . . . Now the time has come for this nation to fulfill its promise. . . . We face a moral crisis as a country and as a people. It cannot be met by repressive police action. It cannot be left to increased demonstrations in the streets. It cannot be quieted by token moves or talk. It is time to act. . . . Those who do nothing are inviting shame as well as violence. Those who act boldly are recognizing right as well as reality."[36]

A week later, Kennedy introduced the new legislation, which called for an end to discrimination in public accommodations—hotels, restaurants, stores, theaters and the like—and authorized the attorney general to initiate actions to end segregation in public schools when other means were unavailable or ineffective. At the same time, he urged militant civil rights groups to give Congress some breathing room, contending that any massive march on it would only undermine efforts to enact the bill. In fact, Southern senators had already caucused to consider plans to scuttle it.

A major March on Washington for Jobs and Freedom involving King and all the other principal civil rights leaders was already in the making, however, and it went forward. Finally, on August 28, a huge throng estimated at about a quarter of a million blacks and whites crowded around, and some in, the long pool at the base of the Lincoln Memorial to hear orations from its steps, with the giant sitting statue of the Great Emancipator looking down. Although Kennedy had intensified his vocal support for the march's mission, he did not attend, choosing to observe the events via television from his office in the White House only blocks away. His absence caused considerable consternation and criticism from the march's leadership, although King and the others were invited to meet with the president at the White House after the speeches.

Among the less publicized speakers was John Lewis, one of the Freedom Riders who had been beaten and who much later was to become a Democratic member of Congress from Georgia. He pointedly attacked the Democratic Party for its split personality on race and demanded that it take action. "My friends, let us not forget that we are involved in a serious social revolution," he said. "By and large, American politics is dominated by politicians who build their careers on immoral compromises and ally themselves with open forms of political, economic, and social exploitation. There are exceptions, of course. We salute those. But what political leader can stand up and say, 'My party is the party of principles'? For the party of Kennedy is also the party of Eastland. The party of Javits is also the party of Goldwater. Where is *our* party? Where is the political party that will make it unnecessary to march on Washington? Where is the political party that will make it unnecessary to march in the streets of Birmingham?"[37]

The final speaker was King, whose ringing remarks took their place in the annals of the greatest of all American political utterances: "I have a dream that one day on the red hills of Georgia the sons of former slaves and the sons of former slave-owners will be able to sit together at the table of brotherhood. . . . I have a dream that even the state of Mississippi, a state sweltering with the heat of injustice, will be transformed into an oasis of freedom.... I have a dream that one day every valley shall be exalted, every hill and mountain shall be made low, the rough places will be made plain, and the crooked places will be made straight.... When we let freedom ring, when we let it ring from every village and every hamlet, from every state and every city, we will be able to speed up that day when all God's children, black men and white men, Jews and Gentiles, Protestants and Catholics, will be able to join hands and sing in the words of that old Negro spiritual, 'Free at last! Free at last! Thank God Almighty, we are free at last!' "[38]

The speech, and the whole demonstration, stirred the nation. Polls showed that a majority of the nation's white population approved of Kennedy's civil rights legislation, but there were signs of a white backlash in Northern suburbs and, obviously, opposition in the Deep South. Kennedy himself, according to Sorensen later, observed that "obviously it is going to be an important matter" in the 1964 presidential election. "It has caused a good deal of feeling against the administration.... I am not sure that I am the most popular political figure ... today in the South, but that is all right."[39]

Two weeks after the Lincoln Memorial event, racist terror struck Birmingham again, in the Sunday morning bombing of the Sixteenth Street Baptist Church. Four little black girls dressed in white were killed, triggering more riots and tension. Kennedy again dispatched his agents to the city and King cooperated in dampening the outrage in the black community. He spoke at the funeral services for three of the four girls—the family of the fourth preferred a private funeral—and some eight hundred area pastors, white and black, attended in what was the largest interracial gathering of clergymen in Birmingham's history.[40] Racial unrest remained a major social and political problem for the president as he contemplated the approaching election year.

On the international front as well, Kennedy had his hands full. Although the Cuban missile crisis had been resolved peacefully, the president's awareness of the peril of the nuclear age had greatly heightened his determination to achieve a test ban treaty. "I am haunted," he said in March, "by the feeling that by 1970, unless we are successful, there may be ten nuclear powers instead of four, and by 1975 fifteen or twenty."[41] At American University in June, he called for a ban on all atmospheric nuclear tests and the Soviet Union quickly agreed, clearing the way for a treaty ratified by the Senate in September.

The Berlin situation, which seemed so perilous only months before, settled down with continued American access. In late June, Kennedy traveled there to a tumultuous and joyous reception, marked by his memorable declaration from the steps of the city hall: "All free men, wherever they may live, are citizens of Berlin, and therefore, as a free man, I take pride in the words 'Ich bin ein Berliner.' "[42]

Even as the nuclear cloud lifted somewhat, the American effort to shore up the ruling regime in South Vietnam against the communist insurgency was eroding. Confidence in the dictatorial president, Ngo Dinh Diem, a Catholic, was being seriously undermined by corruption in his inner circle and by public unrest, especially among Buddhist leaders who charged religious persecution. In the late summer of 1963, Kennedy wrote Diem warning that unless changes were made to improve the relations of his government with the South Vietnamese people, his regime was in peril and there was only so much the United States could do to help. In a candid television interview in September, Kennedy warned: "I don't think the war can be won unless the people support the effort and, in my opinion, in the last two months the government has gotten out of touch with the people. . . . In the first analysis, it is their war. They are the ones who have to win it or lose it. We can help them, we can give them equipment, we can send our men out there as advisers, but they have to win it, the people of Vietnam."[43]

Despite Kennedy's warnings, the Diem regime continued to damage itself with acts of repression against its people, including the burning of Buddhist temples by forces controlled by Diem's brother Ngo Dinh Nhu. In August, Kennedy sent Republican Henry Cabot Lodge, whom he had defeated for the Senate in 1952, to Saigon as American ambassador. Efforts by Lodge to get Diem to reform his government failed, and a debate ensued in Washington on whether Diem should be forced out. A blizzard of cables flew back and forth between Saigon and Washington relating to the prospect of a coup by dissident generals against Diem, with the Kennedy administration emphasizing at every turn that while it would not explicitly condone such action, neither would it attempt to thwart it. On November 1, Diem was overthrown in the coup and he and Nhu were assassinated. Within a week, the Kennedy administration had recognized the new Saigon regime headed by one of the prime coup plotters, General Duong Van Minh, and Lodge had indicated continued American support.

By this time, more than 16,000 American advisers had been sent to

Vietnam, of whom 73 had been killed. In July, Kennedy had reaffirmed his commitment there, seeming to buy into the theory of falling dominoes by saying "for us to withdraw . . . would mean a collapse not only of South Vietnam but of Southeast Asia."[44] Only a month before the coup, however, he had announced a start to troop withdrawal, reportedly confiding to the Senate majority leader, Mike Mansfield, that his objective was to pull out all American forces, "but I can't do it until 1965—after I'm reelected."[45] Clearly, as the end of 1963 approached, Kennedy's attentions were being drawn more and more to his certain bid for a second term in 1964.

It was with this concern in mind that on November 21 he and his wife boarded Air Force One for a flight to Texas, where a Democratic Party row was going on between two of the state's most prominent politicians, Governor John Connally and U.S. Senator Ralph Yarborough. Kennedy had won Texas by only 46,000 votes in 1960, and he didn't want the intraparty spat to undermine his prospects for the state's twenty-five electoral votes in the next presidential election. So he enlisted the most prominent Texan, Vice President Lyndon Johnson, to use his good offices to try to close the breach.

As a virtually powerless standby, however, LBJ no longer had the political clout he had previously enjoyed as Senate majority leader, even in his home state. The plan was to have the conservative Connally and the liberal Yarborough both appear at Kennedy's side at each stop in the five Texas cities on the two-day schedule.[46] According to William Manchester in his book *The Death of a President,* Connally and aides plotted ways to downstage Yarborough throughout the trip, intensifying rather than alleviating the feud. The feisty liberal senator drew more attention to it by twice conspicuously refusing to take his allocated seat in the car assigned to Johnson, a close Connally friend and former employer. The next day's *Dallas News* trumpeted the hijinks: "YARBOROUGH SNUBS LBJ" and "PRESIDENT'S VISIT SEEN WIDENING STATE DEMOCRATIC SPLIT."[47]

After routine speeches in San Antonio and Houston, where he was well received, Kennedy and party went on to Fort Worth for the night. The next morning, November 22, he spoke at a local Chamber of Commerce breakfast and afterward he ran into Yarborough in the hall. "For Christ's sake, cut it out, Ralph," he demanded, referring to the LBJ snub.[48] Determined to end the farce, Kennedy instructed Larry O'Brien and Kenny O'Donnell to waylay the senator as he came out of the hotel and force him into Johnson's car if necessary. After some cajoling by O'Brien, Yarborough finally agreed. It was a silent ride to the airport, broken only by Mrs. Johnson's friendly chatter.[49]

The plane flew to Love Field in Dallas, where the Kennedys boarded an open limousine, with Connally and his wife, Nellie, in the jump seats, and they headed into downtown. As the car turned onto Elm Street between generally cheerful crowds on either side and rolled past the Texas School Book Depository, Nellie Connally turned to Kennedy in the back seat and observed: "You sure can't say Dallas doesn't love you, Mr. President." Kennedy smiled. "No, you can't," he replied.[50]

Then came the sound of rifle fire, and suddenly the New Frontier was over. The president, mortally wounded, was rushed to a nearby hospital where soon after he was pronounced dead. Connally also was wounded, but not fatally, and recovered. The man apprehended as the assassin, a young drifter named Lee Harvey Oswald, in his flight also shot and killed a police officer before being captured and jailed. Two days later, Oswald himself was shot by Jack Ruby, a nightclub owner, as Oswald was being transferred under police protection from jail. The startling series of events triggered an investigation by a special commission chaired by Chief Justice of the Supreme Court Earl Warren, which ruled that Oswald had acted alone, but conspiracy theories abounded for years thereafter.

On Air Force One at Love Field, after Kennedy's body had been brought aboard, Vice President Johnson was sworn in as the thirty-sixth president by U.S. District Judge Sarah T. Hughes, an old Texas friend, as a stunned Jacqueline Kennedy watched. On return to Washington, Johnson boarded an air force helicopter that took him to the back lawn of the White House. As it landed, he could be seen in animated discussion with Secretary of Defense McNamara, after which he stepped out of the helicopter[51] and, solemn-faced, walked into the presidential residence. There, he made a brief statement on television, expressing the nation's grief and concluding: "I will do my best. That is all I can do. I ask for your help—and God's."[52]

Kennedy's body lay in state in the Capitol rotunda, where thousands of mourners filed by the casket. On the day of burial, Jacqueline Kennedy on foot led a remarkable parade of dignitaries from around the globe, most conspicuously the president of France, General Charles de Gaulle, and Haile Selassie, the emperor of Ethiopia. At Arlington National Cemetery, Kennedy was laid to rest on a quiet hillside just below the Lee-Custis

Mansion. After a flyover by military jets, a rush of autumn leaves descended on the site from a previously clear sky.[53] The nation was left in shock that did not lift for many weeks.

The Kennedy administration, which had begun with great enthusiasm, in considerable degree because of the youth and optimism of its leader, had experienced a stormy term of less than three years that ended more in promise than in achievement. Yet in those 1,037 days Kennedy had demonstrated, after the early stumbling of the Bay of Pigs invasion and an initial tentative response to the civil rights revolution at home, a developing maturity in both foreign and domestic affairs. His death left the country, and his party, in experienced hands; the man he had chosen amid much controversy as vice president, Lyndon Johnson, faced the challenge of finding a place in the hearts of a generation of Americans that in its grief and sense of loss seemed at first to have little place for him.

"There's Money Enough To Support Both Of You —
Now, Doesn't That Make You Feel Better?"

Throughout his presidency, Lyndon B. Johnson insisted the country could have both "guns and butter," that is, conduct the Vietnam War and also meet the pressing needs of the cities at home.

Chapter 25

LBJ: RISE AND FALL OF THE
GREAT SOCIETY, 1963–1968

AT FIRST, LYNDON Baines Johnson wore the crown of American leadership uneasily. "I took the oath, I became President," he later told Doris Kearns [Goodwin], then a former White House fellow assisting him in writing his memoirs. "But for millions of Americans I was still illegitimate, a naked man with no presidential covering, a pretender to the throne, an illegal usurper. And then there was Texas, my home, the home of both the murder and the murder of the murderer. And then there were the bigots and the dividers and the Eastern intellectuals, who were waiting to knock me down before I could even begin to stand up. The whole thing was almost unbearable."[1]

Johnson at fifty-five was a man with a larger-than-life ego who at the same time struggled with a sense of cultural inferiority in comparison with the urbane Massachusetts aristocrat he succeeded in office. In his first gesture as president, he asked all the key Kennedy men to remain in their government posts to help him through the turbulent first days and months of his unexpected presidency. He pointedly included Robert Kennedy, the grief-stricken brother of the slain president, who agreed to stay on as attorney general, though listlessly for many months thereafter. Johnson later told Kearns: "I needed that [Kennedy] White House staff. Without them I would have lost my link to John Kennedy, and without that I would have had absolutely no chance of gaining the support of the media or the Easterners or the intellectuals. And without that support I would have had absolutely no chance of governing the country."[2]

Johnson, who had served loyally if unhappily as vice president to a former Senate junior colleague, moved almost at once to reassure a shocked capital city and nation that he would pursue the most important objectives of John Kennedy with all intensity. In a stirring speech to Congress on November 27, only five days after the tragedy in Dallas, the new president expressed that commitment.

"All I have I would have given gladly not to be standing here today," he offered at the start. He recalled that Kennedy in his inaugural address had observed that all his aims would not be achieved in the life of his administration nor even perhaps in his lifetime, but had added, "let us begin." Johnson picked up on that plea: "Today, in this moment of new resolve, I would say to all my fellow Americans, let us continue[3] ... the ideas and the ideals which he so nobly represented must and will be translated into effective action.... In this critical moment, it is our duty, yours and mine, to do away with uncertainty and delay and doubt, and to show that we are capable of decisive action, that from the brutal loss of our leader we will derive not weakness but strength, that we can and will act and act now.... John Kennedy's death commands what his life conveyed—that America must move forward."[4]

Johnson was true to his word. He immediately picked up and pushed to enactment an $11 billion tax cut to stimulate the economy, and a civil rights bill barring discrimination in public accommodations that had been in the works at the time of Kennedy's death. In May 1964, in a speech at the University of Michigan in Ann Arbor, LBJ spoke at length about a "Great Society" in which national wealth would not be a goal in itself, but a means of spreading not only physical but also cultural and aesthetic well-being to every corner of the land. A blizzard of domestic legislation ensued that embraced farm aid, food stamps, urban mass transit, federal airport aid, anti-crime bills, a housing act, federal employee health benefits and more.

LBJ later said he thought of the Great Society "as an extension of the Bill of Rights.... In our time a broadened concept of freedom requires that every American have the right to a healthy body, a full education, a decent home, and the opportunity to develop to the best of his talents.... I saw it as a program of action to clear up an agenda of social reform almost as old as this century and to begin the urgent work of preparing the agenda for tomorrow."[5]

The Great Society was, indeed, far more than a continuation of the

New Frontier in both its scope and social welfare outlook. It sought to put the country, and the Democratic Party, more solidly on the course of the old New Deal. Beyond that, it sought to tap into the growing national wealth to benefit not merely the disadvantaged targets of the FDR agenda, but also the middle class that had emerged as a beneficiary of it.

A centerpiece was Johnson's self-proclaimed War on Poverty, with the ambitious if unrealistic objective of wiping it out. He created a new Office of Economic Opportunity under the direction of Sargent Shriver, a Kennedy brother-in-law who at the time was head of the Peace Corps. It cast a wide net, including subagencies like the Job Corps for school dropouts, a Neighborhood Youth Corps for other jobless teenagers, Head Start for preschool children, Volunteers in Service to America (VISTA) as a sort of domestic Peace Corps in economically deprived areas, and a Community Action Program.

The last, which aimed to achieve "maximum feasible participation" of the poor themselves in planning anti-poverty programs at the local level, stirred up a storm among city officials who feared their traditional role in administering social welfare was being usurped. Prominent community organizers like Saul Alinsky of Chicago used the War on Poverty to help local citizens in poor neighborhoods "fight city hall" to win social programs that would be run by them. Under Johnson, non-defense spending climbed, and eventually the number of Americans living below the poverty line as calculated by the government was nearly halved. Despite considerable achievements, the program was constantly under attack by conservatives as wasteful and ineffective.

Looming over Johnson's ambitious domestic agenda was the war in Vietnam, which he sought to contain without detriment to his Great Society plans. With 1964 a presidential election year and LBJ running for election to a term in his own right, he hoped to hold that limited conflict at bay while he busily constructed the framework of his domestic initiatives. But the overthrow of Diem did not bring stability to the successor regime in Saigon, and as the strength of Viet Cong guerrillas approached an estimated 100,000, Johnson scrapped President Kennedy's earlier plans to pull back. Instead he inaugurated a program known as A-34 to make periodic secret attacks against North Vietnam, further complicating the American commitment.[6]

Politically at home, Johnson had achieved such swift and impressive success in picking up the reins of power and assuaging public apprehensions about his leadership that his nomination in 1964 was soon a certainty. The only temporary irritant was a protest candidacy in several Democratic primaries by Alabama's Governor Wallace, who made himself the embodiment of opposition in the South to LBJ's civil rights agenda. Wallace's theatrics in his failed effort to resist the desegregation of the University of Alabama had given him national exposure; he capitalized on it by making respectable showings against Democratic stand-in candidates for Johnson in Indiana (29.8 percent), Wisconsin (33.8 percent) and Maryland (a rather astonishing 42.8 percent).[7] Race riots in Northern cities fanned a white backlash, even as the need for civil rights enforcement was being reemphasized by continued violence against blacks in the Deep South, most notably in the murder of three civil rights workers from the North in Philadelphia, Mississippi, in June.

The only open question about LBJ's candidacy was the identity of his running mate, and in resolving it he confirmed the biggest open secret of his administration—the continued enmity between himself and Robert Kennedy. The mutual antagonism went back at least to John Kennedy's selection of Johnson to be his running mate at the 1960 Democratic convention. It was exacerbated by Robert Kennedy's coldness toward LBJ as vice president, elevated to anger and bitterness upon Johnson's ascendancy to the Oval Office in place of the slain president and brother.

For his part, Johnson was super-sensitive to what he saw as personal affronts, as when "Bobby," as LBJ called him, ran immediately to the side of his shocked sister-in-law Jacqueline on the arrival in Washington of Air Force One bearing the body of his brother from Dallas.[8] When Johnson asked and Robert Kennedy agreed to stay on as attorney general, Kennedy was a sullen, silent presence most of the time.

As he pondered his future through the gloom and haze of his brother's assassination, Robert Kennedy began to consider the possibility of an eventual restoration of the New Frontier through the vice presidency. If Johnson were to take him as his running mate in 1964, Kennedy obviously would be in a strong position for the Democratic presidential nomination in 1968 if Johnson did not run, or in 1972 if he did. He began to be pressured by friends and followers to go after the vice-presidential nomination as much as it was possible to do so, considering the choice would be in the hands of a mortal enemy.

One friend, William Dunfey, the Democratic national committeeman from New Hampshire, encouraged a self-starting write-in campaign for him in the state's March primary. Kennedy issued a statement saying the president "should be free to select his own running mate," stopping short of asking that the campaign be closed down. On primary day, Kennedy got 25,900 write-ins for vice president to 29,600 for LBJ for president.[9]

Johnson's own feelings at the outset were not clear. According to Kenneth O'Donnell, LBJ told him shortly after becoming president: "I don't want history to say I was elected to this office because I had Bobby on the ticket with me. But I'll take him if I need him."[10] His own brother, Sam Houston Johnson, said, however, that the president would never take RFK: "The reasons were quite obvious: a) Lyndon hated Bobby. b) Bobby hated Lyndon."[11] Kennedy was under no illusions about Johnson's thinking. He knew that only if LBJ calculated that he needed him on the ticket was it going to happen. He told interviewer John Bartlow Martin: "The one thing Lyndon Johnson doesn't want is me as Vice President, and he's concerned about whether he's going to be forced into that.... He's hysterical about how he's going to ... avoid having me or having to ask me."[12]

Meanwhile, the Republicans were undergoing a fierce ideological struggle between their conservative and moderate-to-liberal wings over their presidential nomination. Following Nixon's narrow loss to Kennedy in 1960, he might have been considered a likely prospect for a second try in 1964, but he chose in the meantime to run for governor of California in 1962 and was defeated by Democratic Governor Edmund G. "Pat" Brown. Afterward, Nixon famously declared to assembled reporters that "you won't have Nixon to kick around anymore because, gentlemen, this is my last press conference"[13] and was considered washed up in national politics.

In the same cycle, Governor Rockefeller was easily reelected in New York and was regarded as the likely choice of the liberals. In the first three months of 1964, however, Nixon still led in the Gallup polls of Republican voters. Neither he nor his 1960 running mate, Henry Cabot Lodge, contested in the GOP primaries against Rockefeller and the conservative candidate, Senator Goldwater. Surprisingly, Lodge won the New Hampshire contest in March as a write-in candidate, even as he was serving as the American ambassador in Saigon, and led in the Gallup poll into June.

The primaries after New Hampshire only confused the Republican picture. Goldwater won in Illinois, Indiana and Texas, Governor William W. Scranton in his home state of Pennsylvania and Rockefeller in Oregon, where he campaigned on the slogan "He Cared Enough to Come" when

Goldwater decided to skip the state. Nixon, who had agreed to have his name on the ballot, finished fourth behind Lodge and Goldwater. The decision came down to California, where Goldwater campaigned hard and narrowly beat the New Yorker. The defeat was attributed by many to the fact that Rockefeller's second wife delivered a son only three days before the primary, reminding voters of his messy divorce a year earlier, and he left California on the final weekend to be with them.

At the Republican convention in San Francisco in mid-July, a late effort to stop Goldwater by supporters of Scranton fizzled and the Arizonian was nominated on the first ballot. He chose Congressman William E. Miller of New York, a hack politician tied to upstate utility interests and a fiercely partisan campaigner who was then Republican national chairman. Goldwater explained that he had picked Miller because "he drives Lyndon Johnson nuts."[14]

In a defiant acceptance speech, Goldwater, rather than holding out an olive branch to the defeated Rockefeller and Scranton forces, essentially invited them to take a walk in the fall election if they could not buy into his ultra-conservative views. "Anyone who joins us in all sincerity," he intoned, "we welcome. Those who do not care for our cause, we don't expect to enter our ranks in any case.... I would remind you that extremism in the defense of liberty is no vice. And let me remind you also that moderation in the pursuit of justice is no virtue."[15] The words set off a wild demonstration in the Cow Palace—and wholesale liberal defections from the Republican Party in November.

The Democrats were elated that Goldwater had been nominated, believing that his reputation as a loose cannon and extremist, reaffirmed by his own acceptance speech, would make him easy to beat. That judgment, in turn, removed the last vestiges of the argument that Johnson would need Kennedy on the ticket to be elected. Two weeks after Goldwater's nomination, Johnson summoned Kennedy to the Oval Office to break the news. In advance, the president had Clark Clifford prepare a memorandum on his decision, which he literally read to his visitor.

It was an artful concoction. The memo did not include Johnson's subsequent public explanation that he had concluded "it would be inadvisable for me to recommend to the convention any member of my cabinet or any of those who meet regularly with the cabinet."[16] Nor did it say as in his later memoir that he was excluding them because he wanted them "to do their jobs, without consideration—in their minds or anyone else's—of how their performances would affect their political fortunes."[17] It was in reference to this rationale that Kennedy later wryly remarked that his only regret was that "I had to take so many nice fellows over the side with me."[18]

In the memo Johnson read to him, he argued that "the nomination of Senator Goldwater is the decisive factor," not because he believed he could beat him without Kennedy on the ticket. Rather, he wrote, he couldn't take Kennedy because "Goldwater's strength will be in the South, the Southwest and possibly in the Middle West" as well as the border states. Therefore, he went on, the ticket "should be so constituted as to create as little an adverse reaction as possible upon the Southern States,"[19] implying (probably correctly) that Kennedy would hurt the ticket in Dixie and not help it elsewhere.

The memo tried to throw Kennedy a bone by suggesting "important governmental assignments and missions" would be open to him as well as "the possibility of an opening occurring in the position of this country's representative to the United Nations." He invited Kennedy to talk to him about it again "when you are ready to discuss it."[20] Obviously, that time would never come and Johnson had to know it. Thus ended Kennedy's vice-presidential aspirations. Three weeks later he announced his candidacy for the United States Senate from the state of New York, his birthplace.

Right after LBJ made his statement that he would choose no cabinet member, he instructed old New Deal stalwart Jim Rowe to inform Adlai Stevenson, then UN ambassador, that he was off the list as one who regularly sat with the cabinet, and to tell Hubert Humphrey that he was still his favorite. As early as the previous March, Johnson had called Humphrey in and in the course of discussing legislation had told him that "if I just had my choice, I'd like to have you as my vice president."[21] The "Bobby problem" was still alive at the time and Humphrey, whose national ambitions had seemed buried in the 1960 West Virginia primary, took the remark as a signal to go out and prove himself loyal and qualified for the job. Now, he phoned Johnson with assurances that if chosen, he would be the soul of fealty and support. At the same time, Johnson told aide Walter Jenkins to advise the junior Minnesota senator, Gene McCarthy, that he remained in the running, presumably as a Catholic to counter Goldwater's choice of Miller, also a Catholic.

On the night after Johnson informed Kennedy he would not be his running mate, half a world away four patrol boats containing South Vietnamese commandos, operating under the A-34 plan, conducted raids along the North Vietnamese coast from the Gulf of Tonkin, in an exercise that would lead to far-reaching manifestations for Johnson's war policy. The next day, an American destroyer, the *Maddox,* began patrolling in the same area in international waters. On the morning of Sunday, August 2, three North Vietnamese torpedo boats made a hapless run at the *Maddox,* firing torpedoes but missing. The *Maddox* radioed a nearby American carrier, the *Ticonderoga,* for air support, and its planes sank one of the attacking boats and damaged the others.[22]

Johnson, from all reports, decided to lowball the episode, but the Joint Chiefs of Staff ordered another carrier, the *Constellation,* into the South China Sea, along with a second destroyer, the *C. Turner Joy.* On the night of August 4, an inexperienced sonar operator on the *Maddox* reported what he thought were torpedoes fired at the ship, and word to that effect was flashed to the Pentagon and on to the president. The commander of the *Maddox,* Captain John J. Herrick, had intercepted radio messages that had given him the "impression" that an attack by the enemy patrol boats was imminent, but he later reported that the "entire action leaves many doubts."[23]

Navy Commander James B. Stockdale, the pilot leader of the American aircraft dispatched from the *Ticonderoga* in response, later reported that he had had "the best seat in the house" over the reported attack. When a briefing officer asked him whether he had seen enemy patrol boats, he answered: "Not a one. No boats, no boat wakes, no ricochets off boats, no boat gunfire, no torpedo wakes—nothing but black sea and American firepower."[24] Although it was widely disputed long thereafter that such an attack had ever occurred, Johnson used the reported episode as his rationale to go to Congress for what many interpreted as a blank check for escalating the American role in the war. Much earlier, Walt Rostow, head of the policy and planning staff at the State Department, had urged the drafting of a congressional resolution that would empower LBJ short of a formal declaration of war to launch attacks on North Vietnam. William P. Bundy, the assistant secretary of defense, by now had ordered the drafting. The dual purpose was to commit Congress specifically to the war policy and counter any charges from Republican superhawks like Goldwater that LBJ was not pursuing the war aggressively enough. The resolution had been ready since June, but Johnson had decided to hold off.[25]

As Stanley Karnow wrote in his excellent history of the Vietnam War: "Though the situation in South Vietnam was deteriorating, it did not yet look sufficiently critical for him to court the risk of appearing like a warmonger to American voters. Nor did he have the hard evidence to prove that North Vietnam merited the bombing. He could probably get his resolution, but only at the cost of damaging the image of moderation he was striving to project. Better to wait until after the November election."[26]

Now, however, he had "the hard evidence"—or at least what could be presented to Congress as such. As Karnow also wrote: "Subsequent research by both official and unofficial investigators has indicated with almost total certainty that the second Communist attack in the Tonkin Gulf never happened. It had not been deliberately faked, but Johnson and his staff, desperately seeking a pretext to act vigorously, had seized upon a fuzzy set of circumstances to fulfill a contingency plan."[27]

In any event, after conferring with congressional leaders and talking directly with Goldwater, LBJ went on television and told the American people that "a number of hostile vessels [had attacked] two U.S. destroyers" and he was asking Congress to authorize the appropriate response.[28] Invoking the Constitution, the Charter of the United Nations and U.S. obligations under the SEATO Treaty, the resolution declared the United States "prepared, as the President determines, to take all necessary steps, including the use of armed force," to assist requesting countries in defense of their freedom.[29] Both the House and Senate rushed it through with less than two and a half hours of committee hearings; the House passed it by 416–0 and the Senate by 88–2, with the only dissenters Wayne Morse of Oregon and Ernest Gruening of Alaska. Both men were subsequently subject to continuing browbeating from Johnson directly and personal attacks behind their backs.[30]

Johnson authorized retaliation in response to the alleged patrol boat attacks. Stockdale, ordered to lead them, reacted by asking: "Reprisal for what? . . . How do I get in touch with the President? He's going off half-cocked."[31] But thereafter Johnson held off further escalation, determined to downplay the war as an issue until after the November election. Understandably, he preferred to keep the public focus on his spectacular Great Society agenda and legislative successes. Before the year was out, forty-five of fifty-two major initiatives would be enacted, a remarkable rate of 87 percent.[32]

At the end of August, the Democrats held their national convention in Atlantic City, presumably chosen earlier by John Kennedy out of his love for ocean breezes. Only two events disturbed the harmonious mood in advance of Johnson's nomination—a dispute over the Mississippi delegation and LBJ's choice of a running mate in the wake of his exclusion of Robert Kennedy. Earlier in the year, a determined group of Mississippi blacks and some white allies calling themselves the Mississippi Freedom Democratic Party had formed a rival delegation to the national convention to dispute the legitimacy of the all-white composition of the regular state party. Before the convention's credentials committee, the delegation presented witnesses who testified that they had experienced physical violence and suffered economic deprivations when they attempted to register to vote, and other barriers to exercising the franchise. They also argued that the Mississippi regular party had been disloyal to the national party in 1960 by choosing unpledged electors who voted against the Kennedy-Johnson ticket. But the regular party had followed state law in putting together its delegation.

The clash threatened to be a major embarrassment to Johnson and the party in the midst of the drive for civil rights as a centerpiece of the Great Society agenda. Johnson had aides call on Humphrey to work out a settlement, an assignment that was both an opportunity and a peril for him as he earnestly hoped to be LBJ's choice as his running mate. The outcome was to seat the regular Mississippi Democrats delegation on the condition they support the 1964 ticket and work to have the Mississippi presidential electors vote for it after the election.

Two leaders of the Freedom Democrats, Dr. Aaron Henry and the Reverend Edwin King, were to be seated as "delegates-at-large to the whole convention" and the others would be seated as honored guests. But the Freedom Democrats rejected the proposal and all except four Mississippians in the regular delegation, refusing to sign the loyalty oath, walked out. The convention, however, ratified the deal by a voice vote. The Alabama delegation, which had been chosen unpledged to Johnson, also was required to sign a loyalty oath, resulting in a split and walkout. Neither of these circumstances impeded LBJ's nomination.[33]

There remained the matter of his running mate. Although Robert Kennedy had been told directly by Johnson that he would not be on the ticket, a boomlet began at the convention to draft him for vice president regardless of LBJ's wishes. In his Atlantic City hotel suite, Kennedy found himself besieged by mischievous aides to make a surprise appearance on

the convention floor before the roll call on the vice-presidential nomination. Doing so, they argued, could stampede the convention, or at a minimum cause Johnson great discomfort. For a time, Kennedy seemed
intrigued by the possibility but unconvinced by it. As a just-declared candidate for the Senate from New York, he knew he already had his hands
full politically, so in the end he rejected the idea. He settled for a scheduled appearance on the floor after the vice-presidential roll call, to introduce a film tribute to his late brother John.[34]

Meanwhile, in Washington, Johnson was staging a bizarre drama in
finally unveiling his choice of a running mate. He let the word be spread
that he was continuing to consider both Minnesota senators, Humphrey
and McCarthy. At one point, under a blazing sun, he led sweating White
House reporters on a fast walk around the South Lawn as he speculated
and tantalized on his possible choice and the qualifications he sought.
Humphrey seemed better to meet them, but Johnson insisted he still had
not made up his mind. In any event, the Johnson yardsticks for vice-
presidential service were well publicized in the next day's newspapers, as
the president knew they would be. While the Mississippi delegation compromise was being negotiated in Atlantic City, LBJ finally instructed Jim
Rowe to take Humphrey aside there and tell him he was the president's
choice, provided he would accept all conditions imposed, with loyalty at
the top of the list. Humphrey quickly agreed and was told to return to
Washington at once but not to say anything to anyone, even his wife, as to
why he was going. Naturally, as LBJ also knew it would, this secrecy
fanned the speculation.

At the same time, McCarthy also was asked to go back to Washington,
but seeing himself cast in Johnson's little drama as a pawn to be used and
eventually discarded, he decided to pre-empt him. He sent a telegram to
the president jilting him before LBJ could leave him at the altar. While he
himself had "not been indifferent" to LBJ's choice, McCarthy wired, in his
opinion the conditions he had set "would be met most admirably by Senator Humphrey."[35] McCarthy saw to it that the press got the text of the
telegram before it got to Johnson.

Humphrey was elated, but the resourceful LBJ was not finished. On
another ambulatory press conference around the South Lawn, he let the
chasing reporters know that Humphrey had been asked to come to the
White House. When the Minnesotan arrived at the Atlantic City airport
for the flight to Washington, he found he was to have a traveling com-

panion—Senator Thomas Dodd of Connecticut, also summoned to the White House. Dodd, a political hack later censured by the Senate for converting campaign contributions to personal use, certainly couldn't be LBJ's surprise choice—or could he? When their plane landed, a limousine from the White House picked them up together and drove them there, where they were obliged to sit for half an hour before the president came out and escorted them to the residence. At the door, he took Dodd inside, leaving Humphrey outside to cool his heels a bit longer as reporters surrounded him and rain began to fall. As LBJ-crafted humiliations went, this one was a masterpiece.

Only then, when Dodd had departed, Johnson called Humphrey into the Oval Office and offered him the vice-presidential nomination, which he quickly accepted. Later, Humphrey recalled LBJ telling him: "If you didn't know you were going to be vice president a month ago, you're too damn dumb to have the office."[36] Thus was the Democratic ticket settled, giving the hapless Humphrey a foretaste of what it would be like playing understudy to the calculating, overbearing Johnson.

Johnson and Humphrey were routinely nominated by acclamation, and on the final night of the convention, as LBJ slouched imperially in the president's box on his fifty-sixth birthday, he also was subjected to some uncomfortable moments. The appearance on the convention rostrum below of Robert Kennedy, there to introduce the heavily nostalgic film eulogizing his late brother, set off a remarkable outpouring of emotion and affection from the delegates. So intense was it as to make one wonder whether the draft boomlet for him might have succeeded after all, at least in creating temporary chaos on the floor. The sighting of him, sad-faced, drooping as he came to the microphone, brought an eruption of cheers and applause that went on and on—for twenty-two full minutes, as Kennedy repeatedly tried to begin his remarks, only to give way to the acclaim each time with a wry, sorrowful half-smile. Finally, when he could speak, his quote from Shakespeare's *Romeo and Juliet* in recollection of his brother brought tears to many in the hall, not excluding otherwise hard-bitten reporters: "When he shall die / Take him and cut him out in little stars / And he will make the face of heaven so fine / That all the world will be in love with night / And pay no worship to the garish sun."[37]

After the emotion had run its course at last, the JFK film was shown and an overwhelmed Robert Kennedy left the platform, Humphrey delivered an acceptance speech that brought the convention back to its immediate purpose. As LBJ continued to slouch in real or feigned boredom, his running mate recited the long list of social welfare bills proposed by Johnson and supported by congressional Democrats—"but not Senator Goldwater!" He repeated the phrase with each reference, with the delegates in loud unison joining in. Johnson in his own acceptance speech called for broad support "not just to preside over a finished program" but to begin again "to build a Great Society" providing "every American the fullest life which he can hope for."[38]

The fall campaign was an anticlimax, with the rigidly conservative and jingoistic Goldwater caricatured by the Democrats as a warmonger who could not be trusted with his finger on the nuclear button. The most devastating Democratic advertisement, aired only once and then pulled for fear of a backlash, showed a little girl plucking petals from a daisy as a deep voice intoned a countdown from ten to zero. The view of the little girl faded and dissolved into a nuclear mushroom cloud as Johnson was heard saying: "These are the stakes. To make a world in which all of God's children can live, or go into the dark. We must either love each other or we must die."[39]

Other negative ads against Goldwater reminded voters of his impolitic suggestions about making participation in the social security program voluntary and turning the highly successful Tennessee Valley Authority over to private enterprise. "Barry" was an easy target, and he made himself easier for the Democrats with quirky behavior. Always photographed wearing his trademark black-rimmed glasses, on one occasion he removed them and poked his finger through one side, demonstrating it had no lens and he didn't really need them. A cartoonist responded by showing Goldwater poking his finger in one ear and out the other to portray the emptiness therein.

The Goldwater campaign offered its candidate as an undiluted alternative to the Great Society, captured in the slogan "A Choice, Not an Echo," and sought to capitalize on his blunt and straightforward manner with billboards that said "In Your Heart You Know He's Right." The Democrats countered with bumper stickers reading "In Your Gut You Know He's Nuts."[40] Johnson's power of incumbency, his effective pursuit of the Kennedy agenda and legacy, and his own extension of it in his Great Society proved far too much for Goldwater to overcome.

The only real political vulnerability for Johnson was his conduct of the Vietnam War. The Tonkin Gulf resolution buttressed him in Congress, and he responded to Goldwater's hawkishness by assuring American voters that he was on a moderate, sensible course. His pledge during the campaign that "we are not going to send American boys away from home to do what Asian boys should be doing for themselves"[41] was consoling to the home front, if deceptive.

On election day, Johnson won overwhelmingly, with 61.1 percent of the popular vote to only 38.5 percent for Goldwater, the largest margin in a presidential election up to that time, and 486 electoral votes to 52. The Democrats also widened their control in the Senate, 68 seats to 32 for the Republicans, and in the House, 295 to 140. Among the Senate winners was Robert Kennedy, who—no doubt to Johnson's satisfaction—ran behind LBJ in New York. Progressives now had a clear working majority in Congress and a high point for Democratic liberalism, signaling even greater progress toward Johnson's concept of the Great Society—if only he could manage to eradicate the troublesome war in Vietnam.

In 1965 the parade of new social welfare programs marched on: Medicare, aid to secondary and higher education, low-income housing with rent supplements, the Model Cities Act, a new Voting Rights Act further barring discrimination and empowering the federal government to register black voters in Southern states that declined to do so. New Departments of Housing and Urban Development, with the first black secretary, Robert C. Weaver, and Transportation were created, and a new farm program. The list went on and on, as federal spending gradually shifted from its former emphasis on defense to welfare-related expenditures. Johnson, convinced that he could pursue his Great Society while meeting the demands of the Vietnam War, continued to buy both "guns and butter."

With the election behind him and having reaffirmed his leadership of the Democratic Party, he moved to assert it even more aggressively by pulling the levers of political power more securely into the White House. He diminished the role and influence of the Democratic National Committee, cutting its budget in half, reducing its staff by two thirds and even having its long-distance phone lines taken out. His chief White House aides took over patronage, with old Texas friend Marvin Watson as chief liaison with the committee.[42]

Like FDR before him, Johnson sought to broaden his appeal beyond party lines. He saw the Democratic Party as a vehicle for service beyond the old petitioners and disadvantaged to whom the early New Deal had addressed its most strenuous social-welfare initiatives. In spite of this, however, the Johnson program, especially the War on Poverty, was increasingly seen as one for the special constituencies of poor and minority Americans.

This perception came amid growing militancy in black America and consequent white apprehension. As the struggle for racial equality extended beyond legal battles to campaigns for economic justice in the North as well as the South, younger black leaders, impatient with the nonviolent approach of King and others to improve life in black ghettos, put a harder edge on the movement. The Black Muslims, led by Elijah Muhammad and his most eloquent spokesman, Malcolm X, preached black separatism and self-defense. But after Malcolm eventually came out for "a working unity among all peoples, black and white," he was murdered in February 1965, in what apparently was an internal Muslim power clash.[43]

In March, a voter registration trek to the Alabama state capital in Montgomery led by King was confronted by Governor Wallace's state troopers as the marchers crossed the Edmund Pettus Bridge in Selma. Young organizer John Lewis and nearly sixty other marchers were beaten and tear-gassed in what was dubbed "Bloody Sunday." It drew national television attention and was a factor later in the year in the enactment of the landmark Voting Rights Act. A race riot in Watts, a black section of Los Angeles, in August led to thirty-four deaths before the National Guard was called in to quell it in an escalating trend toward violent protest.

Meantime, the war in Vietnam remained mired in military stalemate and governmental corruption in Saigon. The communist-backed National Liberation Front, the political organization of the Viet Cong, showed no sign of weakening. The guerrillas jolted Washington in February 1965 with a daring mortar attack on a U.S. base outside the Central Highlands town of Pleiku. Eight American Special Forces advisers were killed and more than a hundred others wounded. Johnson's national security adviser, McGeorge Bundy, was in Vietnam at the time and called LBJ recommending immediate air strikes on North Vietnam. According to Stanley Karnow in his Vietnam history, Humphrey dissented, whereupon Johnson "banished Humphrey from Vietnam deliberations for the next year, and quietly rehabilitated him only after Humphrey pledged to subscribe to the official administration line."[44]

Johnson did order the reprisal raids and continued them as part of a Rolling Thunder campaign against the North. They were designed to underscore the American commitment to stay the course in Vietnam and thus break North Vietnamese and Viet Cong morale. The American press in Saigon was becoming increasingly critical of American policy, to the point that the Defense Department flew members of the Pentagon press corps to South Vietnam in the hopes, not fully realized, of getting contrary views from them.[45]

As the bombing escalation failed to shake the enemy's resolve, Johnson agreed to send combat troops to the South, to little effect. In July, after five months of bombing, McNamara presented the president with three options on Vietnam: cut losses and pull out, maintain the existing level of effort and escalate. Johnson chose the third, and by the end of 1965 more than 184,000 Americans were there, and the defense share of federal spending was mushrooming.

This buildup brought to the fore a student and radical protest against the war, and against the older generations, that had been simmering at least since 1962. Then, a group calling itself Students for a Democratic Society (SDS) met in Port Huron, Michigan, and declared independence from the pursuit of the materialism of their predecessors. "We are people of this generation," the *Port Huron Statement* authored by University of Michigan student Tom Hayden and others said, "bred in at least modest comfort, housed now in universities, looking uncomfortably to the world we inherit. Our work is guided by the sense that we may be the last generation in the experiment with living. . . . We would replace power rooted in possession, privilege or circumstances by power and uniqueness rooted in love, reflectiveness, reason and creativity. As a social system, we seek the establishment of a democracy of individual participation. . . . If we appear to seek the unattainable . . . then let it be known that we do so to avoid the unimaginable."[46]

Out of this declaration came a campaign for "participatory democracy" that soon established itself on college campuses across the country and in alternative liberal and radical political groups. This "New Left" reached into the Democratic Party as well. As early as 1964, before the American presence in Vietnam was very large, SDS and other groups began debating the wisdom and justice of the American involvement, especially the unilateral decision-making about it in the White House.

At first, leading SDS members and other radicals talked of responses short of American withdrawal, but by late 1964 and early 1965 plans were under way for a major March on Washington to End the War in Vietnam. On April 17, 1965, an estimated 20,000 to 25,000 marchers converged on Washington and the White House in what Todd Gitlin, one of the SDS leaders, called "the largest peace march in American history."[47] A new slogan, "Make Love, Not War," summed up the platform of what eventually came to be known as the counterculture.[48]

One of the speakers, Paul Potter, put the Vietnam War in the context of a sweeping rebellion against "the system." SDS, he proclaimed, "must end that system. We must name it, describe it, analyze it, understand it and change it. For it is only when that system is changed and brought under control that there can be any hope for stopping the forces that create a war in Vietnam today or a murder in the South tomorrow, or all the incalculable, innumerable more subtle atrocities that are worked on people all over, all the time."[49]

This vision was not at all what Lyndon Johnson had in mind for a Great Society, and thus "the movement" was on a collision course with him on much more than the war. It would not be long before it was grappling with him not only on Vietnam but also on his very stewardship of the country as he sought to meet America's needs at home and its other threats from abroad.

Still, Johnson continued to add to the Great Society roster of domestic achievements: in 1966 a Teachers Corps, traffic, highway and mine safety programs, a new GI Bill, child nutrition and clean rivers programs and more. Throughout, he rationalized that to protect his ambitious domestic agenda he had to shield from Congress and the American public the lack of military progress in Vietnam and its immense cost.

Among those on Capitol Hill with concerns about Johnson's conduct of the war, Robert Kennedy was emerging as a principal spokesman. He had instantly become more than the usual freshman senator by virtue of his lineage, and a general awareness of the LBJ-RFK feud. Because of it, Kennedy through 1965 had taken great care to avoid public criticisms of the president, but in February 1966 he broke openly with him over the Vietnam War.

He declared that admission of the National Liberation Front "to a share of power and responsibility" in the Saigon government was "at the heart of the hope for a negotiated settlement." Vice President Humphrey mocked Kennedy's suggestion, comparing it to "putting a fox in the chicken coop; soon there wouldn't be any chickens left."[50] But Kennedy persevered in calling for an end to the bombing of North Vietnam and a start to broader peace talks, even as Johnson denounced "nervous nellies" who would "turn on their own leaders, and their country, and on our fighting men."[51]

In the off-year congressional election campaign that fall, Kennedy campaigned hard for fellow Democrats while always making the point that he intended to support Johnson for reelection in 1968, especially when calls came from the crowd for him to run himself. After a civil rights speech at the University of California at Berkeley, just as Johnson was to meet with then–South Vietnamese Premier Nguyen Cao Ky in Manila, Kennedy responded to a question by saying he didn't think the people of South Vietnam wanted Ky as their leader. Afterward, recognizing that his remark might undercut LBJ at his meeting with Ky, he came into the press room and tried, unsuccessfully, to dissuade reporters from writing about it rather than his civil rights theme.

Throughout 1966 the society that Johnson so strove to perfect was being torn apart from within. More race riots erupted in Chicago and smaller cities, fanned by the emergence that summer of new leaders like Stokely Carmichael preaching "Black Power" uninhibited by Dr. King's adherence to the nonviolent principles and tactics of Gandhi. A burgeoning feminist movement also was gaining impressive strength, with the creation of the National Organization for Women (NOW). It was bipartisan but dominated by Democrats who looked to their own party for relief from social and particularly economic discrimination by gender. Together with the growing anti-war movement, these forces were major distractions for LBJ in his crusade for the Great Society.

Johnson's growing petulance with his critics peaked that fall when he lashed out at Richard Nixon, campaigning diligently for Republican congressional candidates in the first step of his comeback attempt. When the Johnson-Ky meeting in Manila produced an offer to North Vietnam for a mutual withdrawal of troops and an end to infiltration from the north, Nixon criticized it. Thereupon an irate LBJ called a press conference and lambasted him as "a chronic campaigner" who was using the war "in the hope that he can pick up a precinct or two, or a ward or two."[52]

Unwittingly, Johnson's remarks anointed Nixon as the chief GOP spokesman. When the Republicans picked up a whopping forty-seven House seats that fall, Nixon, who had campaigned for sixty-six House candidates and forty-four won, emerged the party's hero. That Democratic defeat was widely interpreted as a rejection of LBJ's Great Society, inasmuch as public support for the war remained firm, despite the growing protest against it on American campuses.

In 1967, however, Johnson continued to press on with his ambitious domestic agenda: an education act, air pollution control, increases in social security, an age discrimination bill, urban fellowships and research, Vietnam veterans' benefits, anti-racketeering legislation. But his domestic programs did little to stem the racial turmoil, with more riots in Detroit, Newark, Atlanta, Tampa, Cincinnati and elsewhere that year. In an effort to determine the root causes, LBJ appointed a presidential Commission on Civil Disorders chaired by Governor Otto Kerner of Illinois.

Meanwhile, Black Panther leader Huey P. Newton stated the case for violent Black Power. Writing in July 1967, he said of white leadership that "the oppressor has no rights that the oppressed is bound to respect. Kill the slavemaster, destroy him utterly, move against him with implacable fortitude."[53] Dr. King responded that "the problem with hatred and violence is that they intensify the fears of the white majority, and leave them less ashamed of their prejudices toward Negroes. In the guilt and confusion confronting our society, violence only adds to the chaos."[54]

Either way, many white voters blamed Johnson for unrealistically stirring up expectations with his grandiose plans for social improvement. As for King, while saying at an August Conference for the New Politics in Chicago that the 1968 election should be made a referendum on the Vietnam War, he cold-shouldered an idea that he head a third-party ticket with peace protester Benjamin Spock, the prominent pediatrician.

More than the racial climate, however, Johnson's conduct of the war was now the root cause of his political problems within his own party. The New Left was becoming more aggressive in taking its opposition to the campuses and to the streets, and some amateur political operators began to think what was then the unthinkable: opposing and possibly even deposing a sitting president. In the spring of 1967, one such amateur, Dr. Martin Shephard of New York, pushed the idea of entering a ticket of Robert Kennedy and war critic Senator J. William Fulbright of Arkansas in the 1968 New York primary, but was dissuaded by Kennedy.

Also in the spring, two Democratic alumni of the University of North Carolina—Allard K. Lowenstein, thirty-eight, and Curtis Gans, thirty—got the notion that Johnson, repudiated in the 1966 elections, could be denied their party's nomination. Lowenstein, a lawyer who was a Kennedy ally in New York Democratic reform politics, approached the new senator directly about leading a dump-Johnson effort within the Democratic Party. Flying to California with him in August, Lowenstein discussed various ways the deed could be done. Kennedy was skeptical. "He took it as seriously as the idea of a priest in Bogota deposing the Pope," Lowenstein said later.[55]

Unable to land Kennedy for the scheme, Lowenstein tried others, starting with retired army general James M. Gavin, proponent of an "enclave" theory of maintaining an American presence in Vietnam while negotiating peace. Gavin turned out to be a Republican. Lowenstein talked to Harvard professor and former ambassador to India John Kenneth Galbraith, who informed him that his Canadian birth of Canadian parents ruled him out. A consensus of like-minded Democrats suggested two other Democratic senators—George McGovern of South Dakota and McCarthy of Minnesota. McGovern was sympathetic to the idea but was focusing on his own reelection to the Senate in 1968. He also mentioned McCarthy as better known. But when Lowenstein first approached McCarthy, the senator told him, "I think Bobby should do it."[56]

On October 15, Lowenstein was co-chairman at a Conference of Concerned Democrats in Chicago at which McGovern, McCarthy and Senators Frank Church of Idaho and Vance Hartke of Indiana all were proposed as possible anti-Johnson candidates. Lowenstein kept in touch with Kennedy on the matter but increasingly focused on McCarthy as a foe of the war who might be willing to take direct action. Finally, on the Senate floor one day, McCarthy told McGovern: "You know those people you sent over to me? I may just do that."[57] Kennedy continued to consider the idea as well, but the weight of his feud with LBJ persuaded him then that such a campaign would be seen as no more than a personal vendetta. It would split the party, he argued, and deliver the presidency to Nixon, who was already emerging as a likely Republican nominee.

The war protest, while still representing a minority view in the country, was picking up steam by now. On October 21, by some estimates as many as 200,000 war critics marched to the Lincoln Memorial and then, for many, on to the Pentagon. Marchers burned their draft cards, and others bearing flowers stuffed them in the gun barrels of anti-riot troops who kept them from the building. The next day, attempts to storm it were met with tear gas; more than 40 demonstrators were injured and 681 arrested and later released. Johnson condemned "storm-trooper bullying" and "rowdyism" by the mostly peaceable demonstrators.[58] By this time, the American presence in Vietnam had mushroomed to an incredible 486,000 troops; 15,000 Americans had died there, 60 percent of them in 1967.[59]

Johnson was finding it difficult to travel anywhere except on well-secured military installations where friendly receptions could be guaranteed. His support among the nation's governors was also evaporating. At a bizarre National Governors Conference aboard a cruise ship to the Virgin Islands, an LBJ effort to strong-arm the governors into passing a pro-war resolution blew up in his face. A Republican functionary intercepted a telegram to LBJ's agent telling him in no uncertain terms to turn the screws on recalcitrant Republicans. Soon copies of the wire were all over the ship, to Johnson's great embarrassment, scuttling the resolution and a visit by Johnson to the conference in the Virgin Islands.

On November 1, Defense Secretary McNamara sent Johnson a crucial memorandum that signaled his break with administration policy. He said he was convinced that "continuing on our present course will not bring us by the end of 1968 enough closer to success, in the eyes of the American public, to prevent the continued erosion of popular support for our involvement in Vietnam." He estimated "10,900 to 15,000 additional American dead and 30,000 to 45,000 additional wounded requiring hospitalization," and recommended a bombing halt by the end of the year and gradually turning over all military tasks to the South Vietnamese.[60] Johnson, now convinced that McNamara was under the influence of his good friend Robert Kennedy on the war, dumped him by nominating him, at his request, to be head of the World Bank.

McCarthy, frustrated by the Senate's inability to affect the direction of the war, also decided it was time for a new course. Later in November he called Kennedy and told him he was agreeable to making the race but would not if Kennedy himself decided to take up the challenge. Kennedy again said he wouldn't, so on November 30, McCarthy declared his candidacy, noting that he had waited "a decent period of time for others to indicate" they would take on LBJ. Of Kennedy specifically, he told a questioner, "I would have been glad ... to have had him move early. I think if he had, there would have been no need for me to do anything."[61]

Asked whether he thought Kennedy might jump in if he made "a significant showing," McCarthy said he might, and it would not be "illegal or contrary to American politics" if it happened. Well, would he step aside if it did? McCarthy wryly observed that "it may be less voluntary than that. But I don't see that as a great disaster, let me tell you, if it should happen that way."[62]

At the time, McCarthy was clearly focused only on dumping Johnson as a means of ending the war, but that casual attitude would soon change. When some of his young supporters complained, he wrote in *Look* magazine that if Kennedy were to let him wage the fight in the primaries and then try to step in, "he will have a fight on his hands to see who has the most strength. I will not step aside voluntarily."[63]

At first McCarthy appeared ready to duck 1968's first-in-the-nation primary in New Hampshire. The state Democratic organization was solidly in the hands of pro-Johnson party regulars, starting with Governor John W. King. When McCarthy finally decided to compete, what drew him in was the regulars' decision to run the president as a write-in candidate, and he didn't start to campaign in earnest until late January, in his laid-back fashion. He spoke as if on a lecture tour, seldom raising his voice, and never declaring a desire to be president, only a willingness to serve. He spoke of the indecency of the war and hardly ever about himself, a style that appealed to his mostly youthful, idealistic supporters who began to drop out of college in droves to work for him. A young speechwriter, Jeremy Larner, described them as "the kids who reacted against the violent anti-Americanism of the New Left, whom they far outnumbered. Though they hated the war and the draft, they still believed that America could be beautiful—if it would live up to its own principles."[64]

Soon these young college students were flooding New Hampshire, shedding their trappings of the new counterculture, cutting their long hair and shaving their beards so that they could hit the state's doorsteps "Clean for Gene" without offending the staid New Hampshirites. A young Harvard divinity student, Sam Brown, headed the college volunteers, soon known as McCarthy's Kiddie Corps. In the ranks were Ann Hart, daughter of Democratic Senator Philip Hart of Michigan, a Johnson supporter, and McCarthy's own daughter Mary, a freshman at Radcliffe. The candidate's press secretary was a frenetic dynamo named Seymour Hersh, who eventually was to play a key role in generating opposition to the Vietnam War as a freelance reporter, when he broke a story of American massacres of Vietnamese civilians in the hamlet of My Lai.

At first the Johnson White House paid little attention to the political guerrilla effort being waged in New Hampshire, occupied as it was with more bad news from the Far East. A major American base in Vietnam was under siege, and off the coast of North Korea, patrol boats seized the U.S.S. *Pueblo,* an American navy intelligence-gathering ship, with eighty-three crewmen aboard. The commander surrendered and followed the North Korean patrol boats into the North Korean port of Wonsan, drawing cries of outrage from Congress, and from Nixon, who called the incident "an incredible blunder."[65] With Nixon running well ahead in the New Hampshire primary against Michigan Governor George Romney, the White House was keeping an eye on him.

Kennedy, meanwhile, was more focused on what McCarthy was doing in the first primary state. Having made the decision not to challenge Johnson, he remained uncomfortable with it and continued to worry that decision in his own mind and with his closest political advisers, including his brother and Senate colleague, Ted Kennedy. On January 29 (January 30 in Saigon) he met with reporters for breakfast at the National Press Club in Washington and under heavy questioning said he couldn't see of "any foreseeable circumstances" in which he would change his mind.

What, he was asked, if Johnson were not to seek reelection after all? "You're talking about an act of God," he said dismissively.[66] Kennedy said he feared his entry into the race would severely split the Democratic Party and lead to the election of the despised Nixon. He alleged that McCarthy's challenge was only helping Johnson and, in his opinion, was not "able to tap the unrest in the country."[67] Nor did he think his endorsing McCarthy would help him—a view obviously not held in the McCarthy camp.

At one point, reporter Peter Lisagor of the *Chicago Daily News* leaned over and handed Kennedy a wire service story just received. It told of a serious outbreak of Viet Cong attacks on major cities in South Vietnam, including Saigon, where the American embassy itself was breached. It was the Tet offensive that would shatter any American illusions about progress in the war and deal a major psychological blow to confidence at home. The White House and the generals later insisted that in turning back the assaults the American and South Vietnamese forces had delivered a body blow to the enemy and had achieved a great victory, but it was not seen nor reported that way at home. LBJ's pursuit of the war seemed to its critics all the more a course of folly. McCarthy jumped on the news, chiding the president for "hollow claims of progress and victories." He noted that "only six months ago we were told that 65 percent of the population was secure. Now we know that even the American Embassy is not secure."[68] As for Kennedy, he recognized at once that the Tet attacks marked a turning point in the war, at least in the perception of it in the United States. The news set him to more agonizing about his decision. In its wake, he said in another speech that the events of Tet "have taught us something.... For the sake of those young Americans who are fighting today, if for no other reason, the time has come to take a new look at the war in Vietnam; not by cursing the past but by using it to illuminate the future."[69] He reiterated his call for negotiations to give the National Liberation Front a voice in a new Saigon regime.

McCarthy, who was trailing Johnson by 70 percent to 18 in the Gallup Poll in New Hampshire at the time of Tet, began to climb. Even as Johnson ordered the bombing of North Vietnam resumed, more unrest was plaguing his administration at home. His decision to wipe out all graduate school deferments except for medical students sent campuses reeling. Racial disturbances erupted at the all-black South Carolina State and Claflin Colleges in Orangeburg, at Alcorn A&M in Mississippi and at two high schools in New Haven.

At Columbia University in New York, protests over construction at a park bordering on Harlem raised tensions, and in Memphis, black sanitation workers struck the city for a pay raise, with police wielding nightsticks and anti-riot guns to break up a march. And on top of all this, George Wallace announced that he would run for president again, this time as an independent, with unpredictable ramifications for the Democratic vote in the South. Kennedy was particularly irate over Johnson's silence on a report by the Kerner Commission warning that "our nation is moving toward two societies, one black, one white—separate and unequal." It urged a "massive and sustained" national commitment to combat this trend, which obviously would have to take a back seat as long as the Vietnam War was being financed at the level it had now reached. In fact, Westmoreland at this point was asking for a whopping 206,000 more troops. Clark Clifford, now installed as Johnson's secretary of defense, called for a complete review of the war policy. Having supported it in the past, he could be persuasive with Johnson. The Gallup Poll was now finding that 49 percent of those interviewed thought sending American troops to Vietnam had been a mistake, and 69 percent favored training more South Vietnamese so that the Americans could withdraw and leave the fighting to them.

In New Hampshire, more and more college students were pouring in to canvass for McCarthy. The candidate himself remained personally cool and detached but passionate in his message against the war. He was an ideal candidate, said Richard Goodwin, an LBJ defector in the ranks, because "his cause was pure, the issues cleanly drawn and unstained by personal ambition."[70]

The pro-Johnson forces in the state, meanwhile, played into the opposition's hands. They sent out coded cards to all registered Democratic voters in the state requesting them to pledge, with name and address, to support Johnson, and informing them one part of the card would be sent to the White House and another to the state committee. McCarthy charged that the device came "closest to denying a people their right to a secret ballot" than anything he had ever seen, thus playing on New Hampshirites' celebrated independence. Governor King foolishly responded by saying there would be "dancing in the streets of Hanoi" if McCarthy won in New Hampshire.[71]

The state was now a frenzy of political activity. On the Republican side, Romney's campaign collapsed, persuading him less than two weeks before the voting to abandon his candidacy and assuring an easy Nixon primary victory. Nelson Rockefeller, who had been a strong Romney supporter, questioned Nixon's ability to win Democratic votes. While saying he wasn't going to create dissension in the party by jumping into the race, he said he was "ready and willing to serve the American people if called."[72] Eager to assist him was Governor Spiro T. Agnew of Maryland, who promptly formed a one-man draft-Rockefeller effort. A confident Nixon goaded Rockefeller to join the primary chase with a classic Nixon needle: "I admire men who get into the arena. Some of the others have not."[73]

The gibe was meant for Rockefeller but it applied just as well to Kennedy, especially in his own mind. Tortured by his own indecision, he finally resolved after another round of discussions with his associates that he would run after all. The question was whether to jump in before the New Hampshire primary amid reports of a McCarthy surge and appear to be pulling the rug out from under him, or to wait until after the vote and risk seeming to be capitalizing on his expected success. The latter was chosen as the better alternative, because if McCarthy could demonstrate LBJ's vulnerability, Kennedy could say it was not he who was splitting the Democratic Party.

On election day, a typical New England winter snowstorm hit New Hampshire, putting a premium on getting voters to the polls, and the zeal in doing so was all on the side of McCarthy's energetic Kiddie Corps. They did not quite overcome the regular party strength, but they came close enough; the heretofore little-known McCarthy won an amazing 42.2 percent of the vote to 49.4 percent for the sitting president of the United States on write-ins. When Republican write-ins for McCarthy were added in, he trailed Johnson by a mere 230 votes. Beyond that, the Johnson operatives had foolishly permitted forty-five filings for the available twenty-four national-convention delegate seats, while the disciplined McCarthyites filed a single slate of twenty-four and won twenty of the delegates to four for LBJ.

A triumphant McCarthy told his jubilant children's crusade: "People have remarked that this campaign has brought young people back into the system. But it's the other way around."[74] The *Boston Globe* headline the next morning proclaimed: "McCARTHY'S N.H. DREAM BECOMES LBJ'S NIGHTMARE." On the Republican side, a basically unopposed Nixon won 79 percent of the vote and seemed on his way to nomination unimpeded.

Kennedy was now ready to move. He met McCarthy, who told him flatly he wasn't going to be chased out and said he hoped Kennedy would leave the primaries to him. Subsequently, there were conversations about splitting up the remaining primaries against Johnson to inflict as much political damage on him as possible by not dividing the anti-war vote. Thereafter, they could face each other in a decisive final major primary in California in June. But the deal never came off. Ted Kennedy took a late-night flight to Wisconsin, site of the next primary, to give McCarthy advance notice of his brother's announcement of candidacy and possibly discuss cooperation against LBJ. But the post-midnight meeting was so icy, according to Curtis Gans, who was present, the idea "never made it into the dialogue."[75]

Kennedy also met with Johnson in a last attempt to persuade him to appoint a blue-ribbon review panel on the war policy and to learn what he had in mind to respond to the grim Kerner Commission report on racial division in the country. Getting nowhere, he finally declared his candidacy in the same ornate Senate Caucus Room where his brother had entered the 1960 race. McCarthy's "remarkable New Hampshire campaign," Kennedy said defensively, "has proven how deep are the present divisions within our party and country. Until that was publicly clear, my presence in the race would have been seen as a clash of personalities rather than issues. But now that the fight is one over policies which I have long been challenging, I must enter that race. The fight is just beginning, and I believe that I can win."[76]

Allegations of more "ruthlessness" on his part were heard at once, especially from young campaign workers for McCarthy. But the Minnesota senator had one more opportunity to take on Johnson alone, in Wisconsin, whose filing date had passed, keeping Kennedy out and obliging him to point to Indiana, the next primary on the calendar available to him. In a Gallup poll released on the day of his announcement, however, Kennedy was already running basically even with Johnson. And as he hit the campaign trail with a frenzied visit to Kansas, delirious crowds surged around him. At the airport in Topeka, a farmer named Stan Mitchell summed up the feeling among the crowd about RFK jumping into the race on the heels of McCarthy's success. "I don't care how he got in," he said, "just so he got in."[77]

Kennedy's entry also caused Rockefeller to reconsider his own recent decision to stay out of the Republican race, while holding himself available. After a flurry of meetings, rumor spread in New York that he had changed his mind and was going to run an active campaign against Nixon after all. Agnew, rejoicing in Annapolis, called the Maryland statehouse reporters into his office to watch the momentous declaration on television with him—and was shocked when Rockefeller again said, for all the buildup, that he still was going to stay out of the race after all. An appalled and irate Agnew did not forget, with major ramifications to come.

In Wisconsin, where McCarthy pointedly had told Kennedy he didn't need or want his help, the Minnesotan made the most of his last solo chance against Johnson. In a state where anti-war sentiment already was fired up, especially in liberal Madison, McCarthy had a head of steam. Larner wrote later that "a mad joy prevailed. Kids . . . worked all night on peanut butter, getting out transcripts and information. Managers held meetings all day long, researchers rushed up corridors in their underwear, everyone stayed up drinking and talking and fooling around. We were heady with history, which we knew was driving us on to win in Wisconsin."[78]

The Johnson organization, meanwhile, was in a panic after New Hampshire. With LBJ dismissing that vote as meaningless and not deigning to campaign himself, key cabinet members were rushed to Wisconsin as surrogate speakers, to little effect. The president's most trusted political operative, Larry O'Brien, made a flying trip into the state and returned with bad news for him. "How bad?" LBJ asked, O'Brien wrote later. " 'Sixty-forty,' I told him. 'Maybe two to one.' "[79]

On March 31, the Sunday night before the primary, Johnson went on national television to speak about the war. That day his public support had sunk to 36 percent in the Gallup poll. From the Oval Office, he spoke for about forty-five minutes, renewing an offer to stop the bombing of North Vietnam if Hanoi would enter into "productive discussions" toward peace. Meanwhile, he said, he would be sending 13,500 more American troops over the next five months, some of whom would be called-up reserves, and spending $2.5 billion more equipping South Vietnamese troops.

Then, in closing, Johnson looked directly into the camera and, recalling the unity that had come out of the traumatic circumstances of his assumption of the presidency in 1963, said: "What we won when all of our people united just must not now be lost in suspicion and distrust and selfishness and politics among any of our people. And believing this as I do, I have concluded that I should not permit the presidency to become involved in the partisan divisions that are developing in this political year. With America's sons in the fields far away, with America's future under challenge right here at home, with our hopes and the world's hopes for peace in the balance every day, I do not believe that I should devote an hour or a day of my time to any personal partisan causes, or to any duties other than the awesome duties of this office, the presidency of your country. Accordingly, I shall not seek, and I will not accept, the nomination of my party for another term as your president."[80]

With those words, Lyndon B. Johnson shocked the nation and, for all practical purposes, brought an end to his Great Society dream. Although he would persevere in its pursuit over the ten months left to him in office, the war to which he had now pledged his full attention was destined to consume him, and that dream. And the country and his Democratic Party, for all of his personal self-sacrifice, were about to embark on one of the stormiest and most divisive periods in their history.

Chapter 26

DEMOCRATIC CATACLYSM, 1968

THE PIPE-DREAM CHALLENGE to an incumbent president that drove him out of contention for another term was only the first jolt of an unprecedented, unpredictable and violent year. Lyndon Johnson's bombshell withdrawal from the 1968 race reached Eugene McCarthy at Carroll College in Waukesha, Wisconsin, where he had just finished addressing a large indoor rally. When reporters rushed down the center aisle and broke the news to him, he conveyed it at once to the overflow crowd, setting off a wild demonstration. Then he quickly returned to his Milwaukee hotel and a news conference at which he proclaimed that Johnson "now has cleared the way for the reconciliation of our people."[1]

McCarthy was asked whether he thought Hubert Humphrey would now enter the race. He said he didn't know, "but I think if you look closely, you might see a slight cloud on the horizon tomorrow morning." As for Kennedy, McCarthy said, "I have not been seeking a knock-down, drag-out battle with him up to this point," but "on the other hand, I have not been seeking an accommodation." In other words, he would be pressing on, no matter the opposition.[2]

Humphrey, having dinner in Mexico City with Mexican President Gustavo Díaz Ordaz at the residence of American Ambassador Fulton Freeman, had received a phone call from Marvin Watson telling him what the president was about to do. Humphrey suggested the party retire to the library to watch LBJ on television. After the startling news, Humphrey and

War Casualty

The deep divisions in the Democratic Party over the Vietnam War turned its 1968 national convention into chaos, severely crippling the party's chances for election in that stormy year.

party returned to dinner, with the vice president offering no public comment on his own plans.

At the time Kennedy was flying from Arizona to New York. On arrival at Kennedy Airport, the New York Democratic Party chairman, John Burns, boarded the plane and blurted the news to him. Kennedy left the plane and silently pushed his way through a crowd in the terminal, as a woman screamed to him: "You're going to be our next president!" En route to Manhattan, in the car with his wife, Ethel, political adviser Fred Dutton and a reporter, he mused: "I wonder if he'd have done this if I hadn't come in."[3]

In any event, Johnson's withdrawal from the race generated even more enthusiasm in Kennedy's crowds. For himself, LBJ's action produced a new appreciation for his old foe; Kennedy said at one stop in the Philadelphia area: "We take pride in President Johnson, who brought to final fulfillment the policies of thirty years, and who yesterday sacrificed personal considerations to win the peace for which all Americans yearn."[4]

That night, the Democratic voters of Wisconsin expressed their view by giving McCarthy 56.2 percent of the primary vote and 52 of the 60 convention delegates at stake. Nixon did even better among the Republicans, winning 79.4 percent to 11 for Ronald Reagan, an absentee candidate whose supporters ran television ads for him over the final weekend.

The next day, Johnson met with Kennedy and Humphrey separately, telling each—somewhat incredibly from his vice president's point of view—that he would not take sides in the Democratic fight to succeed him. He even went so far as to say, according to aide Joseph Califano, that he wanted none of his cabinet members involved, and instructed Califano to tell them to "stay out of the race or get out of the government."[5]

The next primary, in Indiana, gave Kennedy his first opportunity to demonstrate his political strength, but without the prime target against whom he had reluctantly and tardily entered the race. Had Kennedy had his choice, he probably would not have picked conservative Indiana, but it was the next state where filing for the primary was still open. In a state with a black population of 9 percent and a sizable white, blue-collar vote in the industrial north, Kennedy's challenge was to fashion an effective black–blue collar coalition. Therefore he preached racial justice along with toughness on crime, found disproportionately in the black sections of the major cities. He talked about equality, but also about welfare reform and law and order. Larry O'Brien, who joined the RFK campaign after LBJ's withdrawal, wrote later: "Some purists in our camp saw this as a sellout, but it was the only sensible politics by a man who was running a serious campaign for the presidency."[6]

McCarthy, meanwhile, seemed curiously reluctant to engage, and Humphrey continued to ponder his political plans. Indiana's Democratic governor, Roger Branigan, who was on the ballot as a stand-in for Johnson, now was seen to be assuming that role for Humphrey. All this heightened Kennedy's difficulty in crafting his most effective focus in a conservative state. He continued, however, to talk about racial conflict, and when a student at Ball State asked him about it, he replied that while there were extremists among both whites and blacks in the country, "most people in America want to do the decent thing."[7]

Putting that optimistic viewpoint to a test at this time in Memphis was Martin Luther King Jr., who had joined in the strike of predominantly black sanitation workers. On the previous night, he had told a capacity crowd at the Mason Temple that there always were death threats against him. "Well, I don't know what will happen now," he had said, "but it really doesn't matter with me now. Because I've been to the mountaintop. I won't mind. Like anybody, I would like to live a long life. Longevity has its place. But I'm not concerned about that now. I just want to do God's will. . . . And He's allowed me to go up to the mountain. And I've looked over, and I've seen the promised land. I may not get there with you, but I want you to know tonight that we as a people will get to the promised land. So I'm happy tonight. I'm not worried about anything. I'm not fearing any man."[8]

Early the next evening, April 4, as King rested in his room at the Lorraine Motel before dinner at the home of a local minister, he stepped out onto the small balcony and joked with friends standing below. A single rifle shot rang out from a cheap rooming house across the way, tearing into his face and dropping him amid a pool of blood. He was rushed to nearby St. Joseph's Hospital, but the wound was fatal. He was thirty-nine years old. The assailant, later identified as James Earl Ray, forty, white, fled but was apprehended, convicted of murder after a guilty plea and sentenced to ninety-nine years in prison. Kennedy was in Muncie, Indiana, sitting in a chartered plane when a reporter rushed aboard and told him the news. His informant did not know at the time that King was dead, but it was confirmed when the plane reached Indianapolis.

It so happened that Kennedy was scheduled to speak at a rally in a black section of the city, and when he arrived a festive air prevailed in the crowd of about a thousand people who were unaware of the tragic news. In a somber voice, he told them: "I have some bad news for you, for all our fellow citizens, and people who love peace all over the world. And that is that Martin Luther King was shot and killed tonight."[9] As the crowd gasped, Kennedy continued speaking from notes hurriedly scribbled en route to the rally, pleading for racial conciliation in that hour of shock and grief and concluding with what was for him a most unusual personal reference.

Informing the crowd that the assailant was probably white, he said: "For those of you who are black and are tempted to be filled with hatred and distrust at the injustice of such an act, against all white people, I can only say that I feel in my own heart the same kind of feeling. I had a member of my family killed, but he was killed by a white man. But we have to make an effort in the United States, we have to make an effort to understand, to go beyond these rather difficult times. My favorite poet was Aeschylus. He wrote: 'In our sleep, pain which cannot forget falls drop by drop upon the heart until, in our own despair, against our will, comes wisdom through the awful grace of God.' . . . Let us dedicate ourselves to what the Greeks wrote so many years ago: to tame the savageness of man and to make gentle the life of this world. Let us dedicate ourselves to that, and say a prayer for our country and for our people."[10]

Kennedy's plea, however, was ignored in major cities across the country. That night and the next morning, racial disturbances and rioting broke out in Washington, Boston, New York, Newark, Trenton, Baltimore, Pittsburgh, Cincinnati, Detroit, Chicago, Nashville, Memphis, Kansas City and Oakland, and in more than a hundred smaller cities and towns. Some forty-six deaths were reported and hundreds more people were injured. Johnson called out 4,000 federal troops, and more than 20,000 regular army and 34,000 national guardsmen were summoned to anti-riot duty before order was restored. Kennedy flew to Washington, where he walked the troubled streets of one of the city's black sections.

A few days later, Kennedy, along with McCarthy, Humphrey and Nixon, attended the King funeral in Atlanta. Absent among the declared or prospective presidential candidates, not surprisingly, was Wallace, still pursuing his independent quest for voter support. In Baltimore, particularly hard-hit by riots, Governor Agnew summoned the city's black leaders and read them a riot act of his own for what he perceived as their failure to quell the disturbances. Word of his harangue got back to Nixon and led him to start thinking more favorably about Agnew, who earlier had been an unsuccessful one-man draft-Rockefeller campaign.

Around the same time, Rockefeller himself was doing some more rethinking. At the end of April, he announced that he would after all enter the Republican presidential race, but not as a combatant against Nixon in the remaining primaries. Rather, his strategy was to use his personal celebrity, charisma and—not least—wealth in a public relations effort to sell himself as the only Republican who could attract enough Democrats and independents to win the election. His plan, simply put, was to try to drive up his numbers in the major public opinion polls to make a persuasive case to the GOP convention that summer that Nixon was a sure loser and he the party's best hope for victory. Agnew, left once at the altar by Rockefeller, was no longer interested; his political affections were gradually turning to Nixon.

When the Democratic campaign resumed in Indiana, Kennedy continued to strike conservative themes but also did not neglect to tweak the privileged about their responsibilities to the less well off. At the Indiana University Medical Center, when a student asked him, "Where are you going to get all the money for these federally subsidized programs you're talking about?" Kennedy stared at him and shot back: "From you." He went on: "I look around this room and I don't see many black faces who will become doctors. You can talk about where the money will come from.... You don't see many people coming out of the ghettos or off the Indian reservations to medical school. You are the privileged ones here. It's easy to sit back and say it's the fault of the federal government, but it's our responsibility too.... You sit here as white medical students, while black people carry the burden of the fighting in Vietnam."[11]

There were many other memorable moments as Kennedy regained his rhythm on the stump and increasingly tapped into the Camelot nostalgia that built among the crowds with each passing day. Perhaps the most remarkable swing of the entire campaign came on the day before the Indiana primary across the northwestern corner of the state, from South Bend to Gary and into Chicago. For nine exhausting hours, the Kennedy motorcade rolled west through crowds that lined not only the city streets along the route but also the highways in between. Standing on the back seat of his open convertible, with aide and bodyguard Bill Barry, a former Kent State football star and FBI agent, holding him about the waist for dear life, Kennedy shook thousands of hands as other hands reached out just to touch him or grab articles of his clothing. Sometimes he would reach down and take a child with him and then hand him back to a parent, or play catch with a basketball-bearing kid for several blocks en route. From city to suburbia to city again, Kennedy encountered the black-blue coalition on which he based his hopes for victory.

The next night it came to him, with 42.3 percent of the Indiana vote to 30.7 for Branigan, standing in for Humphrey. McCarthy managed only 27 percent, with Kennedy winning ten of the state's eleven congressional districts. Having anticipated the defeat, McCarthy dismissed as insignificant not only the vote but also the state that delivered it. "They kept talking about the poet out there," he said later. "I asked if they were talking about Shakespeare or even my friend Robert Lowell. But it was James Whitcomb Riley. You could hardly expect to win under those circumstances."[12]

McCarthy essentially conceded the next Democratic primary state, Nebraska, to Kennedy, who won there with 51.5 percent of the vote to 31 for McCarthy. Days before the vote McCarthy had moved on to Oregon, where he would make his stand, having built an early organization on the basis of a strong anti-war sentiment in the state. His national campaign seemed in disarray after the Indiana and Nebraska setbacks, with dissension in the ranks between older and younger workers, and some dissatisfaction among both groups with their candidate's often aloof and sometimes petulant manner.

But the political landscape and demographics of Oregon gave McCarthy grounds for optimism. For one thing, the state had a very small black population and a limited number of blue-collar industrial workers of the sort that had formed Kennedy's winning coalition in Indiana. For another, Oregon was largely a contented suburbia relatively untouched by the social concerns that were at the heart of the Kennedy pitch.

At the same time, the Kennedy strategists had taken the state more or less for granted and had focused instead on the approaching California primary a week after the Oregon voting, sending their most experienced operatives there. Steve Smith, the Kennedy brother-in-law running the campaign, said later that Oregon "was something of a stepchild, and when you recognized the problem it was almost too late."[13] When a late-arriving Kennedy man asked whether the campaign had "the ghettos organized," Congresswoman Edith Green replied indignantly, "There are no ghettos in

Oregon."[14] As Kennedy himself told one reporter, "Let's face it, I appeal best to people who have problems."[15]

Beyond that, the Kennedy campaign, eager to put McCarthy's candidacy behind it, began to adopt a somewhat cavalier attitude toward him, training its guns instead on Humphrey, still not officially in the race but sounding more like a candidate and heir to the regular party backing relinquished by Johnson. It proved to be a tactical mistake. Many McCarthy supporters already resented Kennedy for leaping into the race on McCarthy's back; the dismissing of their man's chances made them more so.

Humphrey for his part had elected to avoid the pitfalls of the remaining state primaries, content to garner the substantial regular party leadership support that had been committed to Johnson. Still, Kennedy focused on him, choosing to say little about McCarthy in hopes of yet luring his anti-war stalwarts into his own camp. Speaking one day in the city of Eugene, Kennedy got cutesy with his listeners, calling their home "the Eugene I like best in the country."[16] He got some laughter, but also some boos for his little joke.

McCarthy meanwhile played on Oregon's self-image, observing one day in Corvallis that the public opinion polls "seem to prove that [Kennedy] is running ahead of me among the less intelligent and less well-educated voters of the country. On that basis," he said loftily, "I don't think we're going to have to apologize or explain away the results in the state of Oregon."[17]

He was right. On election night, McCarthy administered the first election defeat ever suffered by the Kennedy clan, winning 44.7 percent of the Democratic primary vote to 38.8 for Kennedy and the rest for Johnson and Humphrey. McCarthy was quietly exultant. "Every wagon train gets as far as the Missouri River," he said, "but the real test starts up the Oregon Trail. . . . The next test is the California trail and we're on to California."[18]

Kennedy was notably gracious in defeat, thanking his tearful supporters and the people of Oregon, then reading his concession wire to McCarthy. In a quiet postmortem in his hotel suite, he accepted blame for the loss and conferred with aides about the changed situation, deciding he would now have to accept the debate challenge McCarthy had been making and he had been ignoring.

The first Kennedy defeat came at a time the whole country was being set back on its heels by widespread campus unrest and growing racial and anti-war sentiment. At Columbia, Princeton, the University of Chicago, Northwestern and a number of smaller colleges, protests ranging from mild marches and demonstrations to a takeover of the campus at Columbia reflected the national unease. From Memphis into Mississippi and then northward toward Washington, a Poor People's March on foot, bus and train set out for an encampment off the Mall called Resurrection City, U.S.A., and by mid-May more than 1,500 had arrived. Almost daily, smaller groups marched to Capitol Hill and various federal agencies, staging sit-ins in some of them, to dramatize the protest against government neglect of the plight of the poor. And although Vietnam peace talks began in Paris, the war intensified with more Viet Cong raids on Saigon and other cities in the South. A record 562 Americans were killed in the first week of May, raising the total of U.S. dead to nearly 23,000. Before the month was out, Johnson asked Congress for another $4 billion to continue the war effort.

As the campaign for the Democratic nomination moved into California, Kennedy and entourage landed in Los Angeles, which gave him a tumultuous welcome. Now a defeated candidate for the first time in his life, he kicked off his drive for the state's 174 delegates—second then only to New York's 190—with a noontime motorcade through downtown, where he was swarmed by well-wishers with the black and brown faces of his special constituency. The crowd seemed to resuscitate him as hands reached out by the thousands to pull at him or just touch him as his open convertible rolled by. At a rally of campaign workers at the Beverly Hilton, Kennedy summed up his feelings: "If I died in Oregon, I hope Los Angeles is Resurrection City."[19]

The major new development was the scheduling of a Kennedy-McCarthy debate. No longer able to ignore the Minnesotan, Kennedy on a whistle-stop tour of the Central Valley told his crowds he was the first of the present candidates to speak out against Johnson's course in Vietnam. True as that may have been, it was McCarthy who had first put himself on the line on the issue as a candidate. On the eve of the debate, as Kennedy advisers huddled in preparation, McCarthy characteristically set the campaign aside and went to a baseball game.

The next morning, Kennedy rose late in his hotel suite in San Francisco and undertook two hours of intensive debate preparation. Meanwhile, McCarthy campaigned up the California coast and checked into the same hotel, where, after reviewing debate material, he was joined by a few literary friends—poet Robert Lowell, writers Shana Alexander and Mary McGrory—for some relaxation and the singing of old Irish songs. Such outsiders were disdained by the staff as "the astrologers," but they seemed to fit well with the candidate's mood and demeanor.

In the debate, Kennedy strove to emulate his late brother in his famous 1960 debates with Nixon, seeking to demonstrate that despite his comparative youth he was a match, or more than a match, for his older, presumably more experienced opponent. The first questioner asked McCarthy what he would do "to bring peace to Vietnam" that Johnson wasn't doing. He replied that a "new government in South Vietnam" would have to include the National Liberation Front "as a prerequisite to any kind of negotiations ... [on] what the nature of that new government would be."[20] Kennedy pounced on the answer, saying he would oppose "forcing a coalition on the government of Saigon, a coalition with the Communists, even before we begin the negotiations."[21]

Kennedy's remark was a misrepresentation of what McCarthy had said, but in the theater of television debate, the chemistry counted for as much as the words, and viewers saw an aggressive younger man taking the contest to his opponent. McCarthy responded rather lamely: "I didn't say I was going to force a coalition government on South Vietnam. I said we should make it clear that we are willing to accept that."[22]

The most telling exchange, however, dealt with a domestic issue—economic opportunity in the inner cities. When Kennedy called for more public housing there, McCarthy gave his opponent an opening to score points with a critical constituency in the state—white suburbanites not normally seen as strong for Kennedy. "I would say we have to get into the suburbs, too, with this kind of housing," McCarthy said.[23] Again Kennedy pounced. While saying he was "all in favor of moving people out of the ghettos," he pointedly said to McCarthy: "You say you are going to take ten thousand black people and move them into Orange County." Kennedy expressed concern about taking undereducated blacks and placing them "in the suburbs where they can't afford the housing, where their children can't keep up with the schools, and where they don't have the skills for the jobs." Such a move, he declared, "is just going to be catastrophic," because ghetto children needed to be trained before any such exodus.[24]

To many, Kennedy's remarks had the ring of demagoguery, especially the reference to Orange County, famous as a mecca of conservatism and, to some, of white superiority and racial hostility. But once again

McCarthy gave a benign response. Had the debate been a prizefight, there would have been no knockout, but Kennedy probably would have been given a close decision for his engagement and aggressiveness. McCarthy seemed more interested in getting the debate over with. Thomas Finney, his campaign manager at the time, was overheard afterward complaining: "He flubbed it! Blew it! Threw it away! How can you get him elected?"[25] Kennedy declared himself "satisfied"; McCarthy dismissed the whole affair as "a kind of no-decision bout with three referees and sixteen-ounce gloves."[26]

In any event, Kennedy acted as though he had won, suggesting that after the California primary he and McCarthy might "somehow join and try to bring together" all the anti-war, anti–LBJ-HHH forces. At the same time, Kennedy operatives resumed courting young McCarthyites to defect to their side if Kennedy won the primary. As for the increasingly bitter McCarthy, he declared on a television show that "under no circumstances would I join with Kennedy to stop Hubert Humphrey."[27] Tardily, he said Kennedy's remarks about moving blacks into Orange County were "scare tactics" that "could increase suspicion and mistrust among the races," and "a crude distortion" of his position.[28]

On the day before the primary, Kennedy campaigned by motorcade through San Francisco's Chinatown, his wife, Ethel, joining him standing on the rear seat of their open convertible. Crowds jammed the narrow street when suddenly six rapid-fire claps were heard. Ethel jumped down and hunched over, but her husband remained standing, waving and holding on to outstretched hands to brace himself. The noise turned out to be the igniting of a string of large firecrackers, not an unusual event in that neighborhood. At Kennedy's direction, an aide climbed into the back seat to steady Ethel.

Kennedy's long day ended with a frenetic fly-around to California's main media markets, concluding with an airport reception in San Diego and a rally at a downtown hotel at which Kennedy momentarily faltered before resuming his final speech of the primary with his trademark ending: "Some men see things as they are and say, 'Why?' I dream things that never were and say, 'Why not?' "[29] McCarthy wound up his day in Los Angeles, where the Kennedy party also bedded down for the night; the Kennedys themselves went out to the beachfront home of a friend in Malibu to spend primary day with six of their children. As Californians went to the polls that day, Kennedy relaxed on the beach, his solitude disturbed only by a scare when his twelve-year-old son was caught in an undertow. The candidate plunged into the ocean and pulled the boy to safety.

That night, the Kennedys were driven into town to the Ambassador Hotel to await the returns, and McCarthy waited at the Beverly Hilton. The exit polls indicated Kennedy was ahead, and even before a final result was in, McCarthy sought to explain away defeat in a television interview. "We made our real test in Oregon where there were no [minority] bloc votes," he said, "and we made the case as clear as we could there, neglecting California in order to run in Oregon, and expected it would go about like this." He emphasized his appeal to independents, saying, "We're demonstrating what we said we would, that I can get votes no other Democrat can get."[30]

In the Kennedy suite, talk about what needed to be done after California dominated. According to Richard Goodwin, now with Kennedy, the candidate at one point took him aside and whispered, "I think we should tell him [McCarthy] if he withdraws now and supports me, I'll make him secretary of state." Goodwin wrote later that he had suggested the move earlier but Kennedy had rejected it. "But now," Goodwin wrote, "McCarthy could prove a fatal obstacle. The goal was well worth the price."[31]

Finally, with returns indicating a Kennedy victory, the candidate and his wife took a service elevator down to the ballroom floor, then walked through the kitchen area and out to address his cheering supporters. Kennedy was in a playful mood, thanking brother-in-law Steve Smith for being so "ruthless" in running the campaign, and others including "my dog Freckles—I'm not doing this in order of importance; I also want to thank my wife, Ethel." He said his victory in largely urban California and in rural South Dakota on the same night made him confident the country could end its divisions over race and the war. He called for a debate between himself and Humphrey, who had not entered a single primary but had now amassed a majority of the delegates. He concluded with "my thanks to all of you, and on to Chicago, and let's win there."[32]

Then Kennedy turned and was about to go through the crowd and down some stairs to a spillover reception where closed-circuit television had carried his remarks. But a press conference had been scheduled and it was past midnight, California time, crowding deadlines in the East, so instead he went back the way he had come into the ballroom, through the kitchen area toward the press room beyond. He was less than halfway through the kitchen when there was a quick "pop" like a firecracker or a boy's cap pistol going off, then a pause and a rapid volley of more pops, sounding like the firecrackers during the Chinatown motorcade on the previous day. Kennedy fell back, arms over his bleeding head, his eyes open, conscious but grievously wounded. Two muscular athletes in the Kennedy entourage spied the assailant, a small, dark-skinned young man with a pistol in his hand. They lunged for him and needed what seemed like minutes to get the gun from him as they tried to pin him to a kitchen steam table. Finally the gun was wrenched free, as others administered to the fallen candidate and rushed him to the nearby Hospital of the Good Samaritan.[33] Five others had been hit in the hail of bullets, none fatally.

Outside the hospital, hundreds set up an all-night vigil that stretched into the next day as surgery was performed on Robert Kennedy. Three bullets had struck him, the critical one passing the mastoid bone in his head and lodging in the midline of his brain. President Johnson expressed the nation's grief and ordered Secret Service protection at once for all presidential and vice-presidential candidates. He had asked Congress for it when King was assassinated but nothing had been done; now he acted on his own.

McCarthy called on the family at the hospital, then left Los Angeles for Washington. The assailant was identified as Sirhan Bishara Sirhan, twenty-four, a Jordanian born in Jerusalem who had lived in Los Angeles since 1957. He was charged with six counts of assault with intent to murder, with bail set at $250,000. Later, two notebooks were found in his home in Pasadena indicating his intention to kill Kennedy before the first anniversary of the six-day Arab-Israeli war, on June 5. About two hours past midnight on June 6, Kennedy's press secretary, Frank Mankiewicz, entered the makeshift press room at the hospital and announced that Kennedy had died. Johnson again expressed the nation's grief and declared the next Sunday a national day of mourning.

Kennedy's body was flown back to New York and placed in state in St. Patrick's Cathedral, where mourners stood for hours in lines winding down the streets nearby until they could file by the casket. At the funeral, his brother Ted eulogized him: "My brother need not be idealized, or enlarged in death beyond what he was in life; to be remembered simply as a good and decent man, who saw wrong and tried to right it, saw suffering and tried to heal it, saw war and tried to stop it."[34] Afterward, seven hundred invited guests boarded a twenty-one-car train to Washington as thousands of Americans lined the tracks en route, with Ethel Kennedy as hostess staunchly consoling others. A trip that should have taken no more than four hours lasted nearly twice as long, and the burial took place in the still summer darkness, at the same site in Arlington Cemetery where John Kennedy lay.

In two short months, the leading representatives of the protests against racial injustice and war had been killed. Early in 1969, Sirhan was convicted of murdering Kennedy and of attempted murder of the other victims. The jury voted the death penalty, ignoring a letter from Ted Kennedy saying his brother "would not have wanted his death to be a cause for the taking of another life."[35] The sentence was changed to life imprisonment, however, after the California Supreme Court outlawed capital punishment.

While the assassination of a second Kennedy did not ignite the widespread riots that had followed the killing of King, anti-war and other protests expressing Kennedy's sentiments grew in intensity. Draft resisters were arrested in Eastern cities; Resurrection City marchers continued to petition and harass federal agencies; a fourteen-wagon mule train from Mississippi en route to Washington was halted by state troopers in Georgia and all 130 riders arrested; a national convention of student war protesters in New York ended in a walkout over a power struggle. Even in the Republican Party, tempers were being frayed as Rockefeller stepped up his quixotic campaign to persuade his party to reject Nixon, already well over the top in delegates needed for the nomination.

As for McCarthy, whatever spark had survived from his New Hampshire victory seemed all but extinguished. As his speechwriter, Jeremy Larner, wrote later: "McCarthy did not resign his candidacy; he left his lottery ticket in the big barrel to await the hand of God. . . . He stood all summer passive and self-absorbed in the winding-down of his campaign. . . . Now in the heat of a lost, hot, vacant summer, while millions hoped for him and waited, Gene McCarthy regressed to his balanced presentation of self, to the sacred ceremony of his personality."[36]

McCarthy rather halfheartedly called on Humphrey to debate him then or at the convention itself. But Humphrey wanted no part of any exchange that certainly would focus on the Vietnam War, forcing the vice president either to defend the Johnson policy and thereby alienate himself further from the war protesters or put distance between himself and LBJ and bring down the wrath of that more earthly god in the Oval Office.

In a speech in mid-June, the vice president made a feeble stab at independence by declaring himself "a man of change" who, if elected, would not seek to "relive the Johnson administration." But he immediately trimmed the observation by saying, "one does not repudiate his family in order to establish his own identity."[37]

The two remaining Democratic candidates stumbled through the last of the presidential primaries with no change in their relative positions. In New York, McCarthy won 62 of the state's 123 elected convention delegates to 30 for Kennedy and only 12 for Humphrey. One of his supporters, Paul O'Dwyer, won the Democratic nomination for the Senate and Allard Lowenstein, "the man who dumped Johnson," won a place on the ticket from a Long Island congressional district. In Minnesota, Humphrey won the bulk of the at-large delegates chosen at the Democratic state convention, and a moderate Vietnam plank backed by him carried over McCarthy's call for withdrawal of all American troops. At state party conventions in New York, Illinois and Connecticut, the McCarthy forces were similarly rebuked. The *New York Times* reported that by its reckoning Humphrey now had 1,600 delegates pledged to him, with only 1,312 needed for nomination.

Once again Lowenstein took the lead in opposition to the Johnson war policy. In late June in Chicago, he organized a Coalition for an Open Convention of McCarthy and former Kennedy supporters that unanimously adopted a resolution opposing Humphrey's nomination; it mapped plans for platform and credentials fights at the approaching convention in the same city. Also, SDS leaders Tom Hayden and Rennie Davis announced plans for anti-war demonstrations there, as the Paris peace talks dragged on, their urgency underscored by continued rocket attacks on Saigon. By this time, there were an astounding 534,000 American forces in Vietnam, with a toll since 1961 of more than 25,000 dead and 83,000 wounded. Johnson, finally conceding that the country could not afford both guns and butter, signed a new 10 percent tax increase to finance the escalating costs of the war. The federal budget deficit was now at $25.4 billion for fiscal 1968, the largest since World War II.

Also in Washington, after more protests and demonstrations around town, more than a thousand police surrounded Resurrection City, now a ragged, squalid encampment, and closed it down. That night, riots broke out in a twenty-block area, persuading Mayor Walter Washington to call out 450 members of the District of Columbia National Guard and impose an overnight curfew. The Poor People's Campaign leader, Ralph Aber-nathy, was arrested and sentenced to twenty days in jail, along with other protesters. George Wallace, pursuing his independent campaign and seiz-ing the opportunity, called the nation's capital "a jungle . . . where you can't walk safely with your wife and children in the shadow of the White House."[38]

On the stump, McCarthy was attracting large crowds and Humphrey was encountering increasing heckling as he sought in vain to be his own man while hewing to the basic Johnson policy on Vietnam. He continued to play the inside political game of pressuring regular party loyalists in non-primary states to a point, Lowenstein said later, that further alienated McCarthy Democrats. "They were acting as if every single vote they could get was important at a time when they could have acted with largeness of spirit," he wrote. The Humphrey forces, he said, "rode roughshod over the opposition in a way where what was building up was a feeling that no matter what happened, he's not going to get my vote."[39]

Urged to put distance between himself and Johnson on the war, Humphrey asked fifteen foreign policy experts to draft a Vietnam plank for him, which he showed to the president. LBJ rejected it, telling him, "Hubert, I have two sons-in-law over there, and I consider this proposal to be a direct slap at their safety and at what they are trying to do."[40] Humphrey dutifully shelved it.

In late July the Republicans held their convention in Miami Beach and routinely nominated Nixon despite the last-minute formal candidacy of Reagan. Rockefeller's hugely expensive effort to convince fellow Republicans of Nixon's unelectability and his own ability to win, based on heavy television advertising around the country designed to drive up his standing in the polls, was a miserable failure. After having campaigned in forty-four states, Rockefeller was buried by his own strategy. The final Gallup poll before the convention had Nixon leading Humphrey by two percentage points and McCarthy by five, and Rockefeller running only even against Humphrey and one point ahead of McCarthy. Other polls came up with contrary findings, but in the absence of clear affirmation of Rockefeller's basic premise that Nixon was a sure loser and he was a win-ner, his stop-Nixon effort collapsed like the house of cards it was.

The only surprise at the Republican convention was Nixon's choice of a running mate. He had chosen Governor Agnew of Maryland to place his name in nomination, but when he picked him to be the party's vice-presidential nominee, the question "Spiro who?" reverberated through the hall. Nixon had made a pro forma survey of leading Republicans on the choice and nobody had mentioned Agnew. But internal polls had indicated there was no Republican who would bring Nixon votes, so essentially he picked a nobody. Nixon also was taken by Agnew's hard law-and-order line after the Baltimore riots in the wake of King's slaying. It was a choice that in the end would have historic ramifications, with the eventual resignations in disgrace of one administration's vice president and president. At a press party after the convention, Nixon the philosopher said of his choice of Agnew: "There is a mysticism about men. There is a quiet confidence. You look a man in the eye and you know he's got it—brains. This guy has got it. If he doesn't, Nixon has made a bum choice."[41]

The Democrats now headed toward their August convention in Chicago with a sense of dread. The Lowenstein group was unable to wed the McCarthy and old Kennedy forces or find an alternative candidate. In early August, Senator George McGovern was persuaded to become a candidate as a rallying point for the Kennedy supporters. Humphrey, meanwhile, flew to the LBJ ranch with another Vietnam speech draft for the president's clearance. Again Johnson balked, telling him, "You can get a headline with this, Hubert, and it will please you and some of your friends. But if you just let me work for peace, you'll have a better chance for election than by any speech you're going to make."[42] Humphrey discarded the draft.

In the week before the convention opened, the anti-Humphrey forces focused on credentials, rules and platform committee hearings, seeking a wedge into his delegate strength, to little avail. In a rare show of unity, a challenging Mississippi delegation led by black civil rights leaders Aaron Henry and Charles Evers won broad support to be seated, as did challengers to Alabama's pro-Wallace delegation. But McCarthy credentials challenges in other states were rejected.

In the rules committee, Humphrey sought abolition of the unit rule, generating fierce opposition from Governor John Connally of Texas, who saw the move as an attack on his own power. He hinted that he might deny Humphrey Texas votes, and that Johnson himself might decide to come to Chicago demanding another term after all. Doris Kearns (Goodwin), then a sounding board for LBJ on her anti-war generation, later told Tom Hayden: "He wanted them to fete his accomplishments and, if the convention fell apart, crazy as it seems, he would be there, available."[43]

Larry O'Brien wrote later that Connally had told him that "if Humphrey wasn't careful, Lyndon Johnson's name would be entered in nomination. I took that for the bluff that it was . . . but it underscored the uncertainty of Humphrey's position."[44] In the end, Humphrey backed off trying to abolish the unit rule and assured Connally he wouldn't waver from Johnson's policy on the war.

The Democratic convention opened amid a siege mentality on the part of Chicago Mayor Richard J. Daley. "As long as I am mayor of this town," he declared in welcoming the delegates, "there will be law and order in Chicago."[45] The International Amphitheatre near the Chicago stockyards was encircled by barbed wire and a long, high chain-link fence with entry monitored closely by city police. With estimates of expected demonstrators as high as 100,000, Daley put all 11,000 officers on twelve-hour shifts and at his request Governor Samuel Shapiro called up 5,600 Illinois national guardsmen, with 7,500 regular army troops on standby.

Phony warnings of dumping LSD in the city water supply played on the fears of city officials; various street theater hijinks were promised by young protesters calling themselves Yippies; ordinary young anti-war protesters poured into the city's parks to rally and sleep, sending Daley to extreme lengths to maintain security. On the night of August 22, a seventeen-year-old Native American in hippie garb named Jerome Johnson was shot and killed near Lincoln Park by police who said he had fired on them. As more demonstrators streamed into this and other city parks, two anti-war chants were heard over and over: "Hey, hey, LBJ, how many kids have you killed today?" and "Dump the Hump!"

Humphrey and McCarthy meanwhile met for breakfast amid speculation that McCarthy might at last give in and agree to be his fellow Minnesotan's running mate. McCarthy quickly squelched the idea, saying, "If I were to go on the ticket with Hubert it would be kind of like the captain of a ship getting in the first lifeboat and waving to those still on board, saying, 'I hope it doesn't sink.' "[46] It was clear that there would be a fight, not for the nomination but over the position the party would adopt on Vietnam in its platform.

The battle stirred Ted Kennedy, who had been in isolation ever since his brother Robert's death, to reenter the fray. He called for halting all bombing of North Vietnam unconditionally and negotiating with Hanoi for the mutual withdrawal of all foreign troops from South Vietnam.

Already talk had begun about drafting him for the presidential nomination, but he declared that while "like my three brothers before me I pick up a fallen standard," he was not available as a candidate.[47] Nevertheless, Mayor Daley, entertaining strong doubts about Humphrey's electability, phoned Kennedy and urged him to change his mind. Around the same time, Steve Smith met with McCarthy, who offered to ask his delegates to vote for Kennedy, but Kennedy adhered to his decision not to be a candidate, and that was that.

In the fight over the Vietnam plank, the anti-Humphrey forces pushed for an immediate end to the bombing, a negotiated withdrawal of all foreign troops and a negotiated government coalition including the National Liberation Front. The platform committee version supported by the administration (Humphrey) side wanted a bombing halt only if it "would not endanger the lives of our troops in the field," withdrawal after the end of the war and internationally supervised free elections in the South.[48] A heated and tumultuous debate ensued in the hall as thousands of demonstrators moved into Grant Park and were charged by police wielding nightsticks, clubbed to the ground and thrown into awaiting paddy wagons.

Three hours after the debate on the plank began, interrupted frequently by shouts of "Stop the war!" from McCarthy and McGovern delegates, the administration plank was adopted by 1,527¾ votes to 1,041¼ against. Word of the result flowed quickly out of the hall to the downtown streets of Chicago, raising the level of the protest higher than ever, and along with it the violent response of the police. Soon television cameras were capturing scenes of such brutality toward the unarmed demonstrators that a review commission later branded what had happened in the streets as a "police riot."

Back in the hall, the delegates were just learning what was going on downtown. A telephone strike had delayed transmission of live television, and only when tapes and film of the rioting were seen in the hall was the scope of the turmoil apparent. Delegates gawked at the screens as speeches nominating the candidates droned on. Senator Abraham Ribicoff of Connecticut, placing McGovern's name before the convention, brought it to a frenzy when he said, "With George McGovern as president . . . we wouldn't have to have Gestapo tactics in the streets of Chicago."[49] With that, Daley leaped to his feet directly in front of Ribicoff, shaking his fists and shouting through the din on the floor, according to witnesses adept at lipreading, a crude sexual accusation toward the Connecticut senator.

When the roll call of the states finally got under way, it was anticlimactic. Humphrey won easily, with 1,761¾ votes to 601 for McCarthy, 146½ for McGovern and 67½ for the Reverend Channing E. Phillips of the District of Columbia, the first black ever placed in presidential nomination in a major party. Humphrey's first choice to be his running mate, Ted Kennedy, said no, so Humphrey turned to Senator Edmund S. Muskie of Maine, who was routinely selected. The only opposition, of a symbolic nature, came from civil rights and anti-war protester Julian Bond, at twenty-eight not yet old enough to qualify for the office. As in 1964 when Robert Kennedy introduced a film on John F. Kennedy amid a huge outpouring of emotion from the convention delegates, Ted Kennedy in a taped message introduced a similar film about his brother Robert, with the same tearful reaction from the 1968 delegates.

Humphrey, in his acceptance speech, struggled to do justice to his reputation as "the happy warrior." He expressed "deep sadness" over what was going on in Chicago's streets, observing that "surely we have now learned the lesson that violence breeds counterviolence and it cannot be condoned, whatever the source." The observation did not win him new friends in the hall, nor did a concluding reference to Johnson: "I truly believe that history will surely record the greatness of his contribution to the people of this land, and tonight to you, Mr. President, I say thank you."[50]

Afterward, more mayhem took place, this time with many young McCarthy volunteers as the victims. Police and national guardsmen invaded a farewell party in a fifteenth-floor room at the Conrad Hilton, alleging that the volunteers had thrown objects down on them in the street. The authorities clubbed them with nightsticks and dragged them into the hotel lobby. McCarthy, notified by a volunteer, went to the fifteenth floor and then to the lobby and demanded that the prisoners be released. The scene was a sorry coda to a convention that left the Democratic Party in shreds, well before the presidential election in which Humphrey would have to face Richard Nixon and a united and well-heeled Republican Party, as well as the threat of major Southern defections in the candidacy of George Wallace.

Humphrey was so unprepared for the fall campaign that his strategy was conceived only on the way home from Chicago and on the first campaign swings in September. In the party's dire straits, Larry O'Brien agreed not only to run the Humphrey campaign but also to assume the chairmanship of the Democratic National Committee to assure optimum coordination through the November election.

The Nixon campaign, meanwhile, had prepared in leisure and with the lessons of Nixon's narrow 1960 defeat clearly in mind. Then, an uncertain and often ailing nominee, foolishly committed to campaign in every state, had stretched himself thin to the point of exhaustion. This time he would run a much more controlled campaign, limited wherever possible to carefully crafted and scripted appearances designed to show him at his rested best. While Humphrey was racing full tilt from dawn to midnight, as was his style as well as his perceived need, Nixon would avoid the spontaneous with its pitfalls and thus be seen in person and on camera only as he chose to be seen. As he had done in the basically uncontested primaries, he would run as if he already were president, emphasizing his experience and saying little controversial—especially about how he would deal with the war in Vietnam, which already had Humphrey in a box.

Experts in the art of television as much as in the art of politics would play a leading role this time around, and the slashing Nixon of old would be played in 1968 by his running mate, Agnew, who soon proved he was more than up to the task. He started by comparing Humphrey to Neville Chamberlain, calling him "squishy soft" on communism, and went down from there. In the Nixon-Agnew campaign, "law and order" became the theme, played against the Democrats on the general premise that the country had lost its way under their leadership, falling into the hands of anarchists, criminals and political cowards.

Nixon's new campaign style enabled him to dodge most of the partisan arrows fired at him, especially as he adopted as his mantra that discussing what he would do about Vietnam if elected would only assist the enemy. Humphrey had no such easy out. The rising protest against the war increasingly targeted his inability or unwillingness to break with the Johnson policy. Everywhere he went that fall, cries of "Dump the Hump!" and "Stop the war!" hounded him. A low point came in Seattle in late September when a heckler with a bullhorn charged him with "murder," saying, "We have come not to talk with you, Mr. Humphrey. We have come to arrest you."[51] It was clear to his advisers that unless he made a clear break with LBJ on the war, he had no chance.

Reluctantly, Humphrey finally gave in. In a speech in Salt Lake City on

September 30, about which he advised LBJ but did not ask his approval, he said: "As president, I would stop the bombing of North Vietnam as an acceptable risk for peace, because I believe it could lead to success in the negotiations and a shorter war." As a sweetener to the hawks, he added: "If the government of North Vietnam were to show bad faith I would reserve the right to resume the bombing."[52] It was not that different from what LBJ was saying, except that Humphrey would make his bombing halt unconditional. Nevertheless, Califano wrote later, "Johnson never forgave him for it."[53]

The very next day, in Nashville, Humphrey's crowds turned more friendly. One sign said: "IF YOU MEAN IT, WE'RE WITH YOU." He was now campaigning not as vice president, he said, but as a man on his own. The speech, with the airtime bought by the campaign, had carried a pitch for money, and it began to stream in. But Nixon, while not willing himself to spell out his Vietnam position, did not hesitate to jump on Humphrey, implying he might be "undercutting the United States position in Paris." He piously hoped his opponent would "not pull the rug out from under the negotiators and take away the trump card [the bombing halt] the negotiators have."[54]

Through all this, George Wallace campaigned in areas of racial unrest and crime, North and South, peddling his special brand of fear and hate that complemented the Nixon-Agnew law-and-order offensive. His campaign ran television ads playing on voter concerns over school busing and safety in the streets, while in person he never ceased to make sneering, malicious remarks about liberals and other protesters that never failed to raise the spirits and venom of his listeners. For all the transparent nature of his appeal, Wallace's threat to win enough electoral votes in Dixie to throw a close race between Nixon and Humphrey into the House of Representatives worried both major party nominees.

On October 3 in Pittsburgh, however, Wallace made a move that diminished that concern. He unveiled as his running mate retired Air Force Chief of Staff General Curtis LeMay, former commander of the Strategic Air Command, and in so doing shot a huge hole in his own campaign. Exposed to an inquiring press, LeMay was naturally asked about his position on the use of nuclear weapons. Ridiculing what he called "a phobia" about them, he called the Bomb "just another weapon in the arsenal," adding, "I don't believe the world would end if we exploded a nuclear weapon."

As Wallace stood by aghast and appalled as even he grasped the political fallout that would rain down on his campaign as a result, LeMay went on to describe positive aspects that countered all the "propaganda" about the danger of a nuclear explosion. At the test grounds in the Pacific, he said, "the fish are all back in the lagoons, the coconut trees are growing coconuts, the guava bushes have fruit on them, the birds are back. As a matter of fact, everything is about the same except the land crabs. They get minerals from the soil, I guess, through their shells, and there's a little question about whether you should eat a land crab or not."

The rats on the Bikini atoll, he said reassuringly, were "bigger, fatter and healthier than they ever were before." There was no difference between being killed by "a rusty knife" and a nuclear weapon, he blissfully continued. "As a matter of fact, if I had a choice I'd rather be killed by a nuclear weapon."[55] Wallace stepped in, saying neither he nor LeMay advocated using nuclear weapons, but LeMay kept on in the same mode, burying himself and the Wallace campaign under a thick layer of nuclear dust.

More significant now than LeMay's rantings about the Bomb were the political ramifications of Humphrey's Salt Lake City call for an unconditional end to the conventional bombing of North Vietnam. Before the speech, he was trailing Nixon by 43 percent to 28 in the Gallup poll, and now seemed to be making a mild recovery. Old campaign lieutenants of McCarthy, Kennedy and McGovern in early October organized a New Democratic Coalition seeking, among other things, to rally liberal support to Humphrey. They hoped at last to persuade McCarthy to endorse Humphrey, and to that end got McCarthy to set conditions for that move. He said he wanted, in addition to an unconditional bombing halt, free elections in Vietnam with participation of the National Liberation Front, draft law reform and Democratic Party reform, "so that we shall not have another Chicago." It got Humphrey's back up; he was, he said, "not prone to start meeting conditions" from McCarthy. So nothing happened right then.[56] Not until a week before the election did McCarthy finally relent and give Humphrey a halfhearted blessing, saying that although Humphrey "falls far short" of what he wanted on foreign policy, he was better than Nixon on domestic issues.[57]

In late October, another Gallup poll showed Humphrey creeping up: Nixon 44 percent, Humphrey 36, Wallace 15, with Humphrey getting the bulk of the Wallace slippage. With the election now two weeks away, there was one possible development both sides understood had the potential of closing the gap, and one fear among the Nixonites: a break-through in the Paris peace talks. A major stumbling block was Hanoi's insistence that the National Liberation Front be admitted to the talks and Saigon's unwillingness to agree. Johnson strategists feared that Saigon believed it would get a better deal under a Nixon administration and was stalling until after the election.

Indeed, Johnson had reason to believe that Nixon agents were in con-tact with the Saigon regime through a Chinese-born American citizen, Anna Chennault, widow of a celebrated World War II American military leader, who was close to Nixon. He had ordered FBI and CIA surveillance of the South Vietnamese embassy in Washington, which had intercepted incriminating cables. Specifically, one such cable dated October 27 from South Vietnamese Ambassador Bui Diem to South Vietnamese President Nguyen Van Thieu quoted in Bui Diem's book, *In the Jaws of History,* said: "The longer the present situation continues, the more we are favored. . . . I am regularly in touch with the Nixon entourage." By "Nixon entourage," he wrote later, "I meant John Mitchell [Nixon's campaign manager] and Senator John Tower [a Nixon ally]."[58] As a result of this cable, Califano also wrote later, "LBJ now suspected that Nixon had acted on Chennault's advice [to urge Thieu to stall] and treasonably, to his thinking, subverted his own government in order to win the election."[59]

On the night of October 31, Johnson suddenly went on television and announced that he had decided to halt the bombing of North Vietnam "on the basis of the developments in the Paris talks."[60] He said the Hanoi regime had agreed to the participation of the Saigon government at the talks in Paris and the United States had approved a role for the NLF. Humphrey was jubilant over the news; Nixon greeted it cautiously and pledged that neither he nor Agnew "will destroy the chance of peace. We want peace."[61]

Two days later, however, the Saturday before the American election, Thieu suddenly told the South Vietnamese National Assembly that his regime was boycotting the Paris talks, because including the NLF "would just be another trick toward a coalition government with the Commu-nists." Saigon, he said, would talk only to the Hanoi regime.[62] Johnson was furious, Humphrey deflated and Nixon relieved.

Johnson realized that release of the cables and other material gath-ered by his intelligence agencies could scuttle Nixon on the eve of the election. But not wanting to reveal that he had acquired the information through sensitive intelligence sources he wanted to protect, he sent it over to Humphrey as a lifeline to his campaign. By this time he had also ordered intelligence surveillance of Chennault, seen frequently going in and out of the South Vietnamese embassy. To Johnson's further ire, Humphrey balked. According to Larry O'Brien, Humphrey "expressed deep concern" about the information, asking, "What kind of a guy could engage in something like this?"[63] To others long familiar with Nixon's record of political skulduggery, it may have seemed a strange question to ask. In any event, Humphrey declined to make the information public, a decision that may well have cost him the presidency.

On election night, Nixon squeezed through by seven tenths of one percent of the vote, 43.4 percent to 42.7 for Humphrey, 13.5 percent for Wallace and the rest scattered. The winner had 302 electoral votes, 31 more than he needed to keep the election out of the House, to 191 for Humphrey and 46 for Wallace. The Democratic Party was out in the cold again, losing an election it might have won, on several counts.

Beyond Humphrey's failure to disclose the strongly suspected meddling of Nixon in the Paris peace talks, there was also his failure until too late in the campaign to separate himself from Johnson and his Vietnam policy. Had he fought harder for the Vietnam peace plank at the Democratic convention, he might have swung enough anti-war votes from the McCarthy, McGovern and Kennedy campaigns to edge Nixon. And had McCarthy himself endorsed Humphrey earlier and with more enthusiasm, that might have made the difference in Humphrey's favor. If there was one Republican who should have been able to unify the Democrats, it was the despised Nixon.

Instead, a year filled with horrors for the Democratic Party—the deaths of Martin Luther King and Robert Kennedy, a disastrous national convention that left a stamp of disarray and bitterness toward it in the minds of millions of television-viewing Americans, its sitting president and his ambitious Great Society in tatters—came to an end on the sour note of seeing Nixon on the doorstep of the White House, with the Paris peace talks stalled once more.

The war now would be his problem, and might also bring him down, as it had Johnson. That, at least, was the Democratic hope. Instead, the Vietnam War and the other cataclysmic events of 1968 were to provide the ingredients for a concerted Republican effort to cast the Democratic Party as the root of all the nation's ills—and a rationale for a new, dominant conservatism in the country.

The Hartford Times

Ed Valtman '72

THE OLD MAN AND THE SEA

In 1972, Democratic presidential nominee George S. McGovern ran as a strong protest candidate against the war in Vietnam. He was pilloried by his opponent, Republican President Richard M. Nixon, and soundly defeated in spite of the Watergate affair of the same year.

Chapter 27

REFORM, BUT NOT REVIVAL, 1968–1974

GENERALLY OVERLOOKED AMID the chaos in Chicago in 1968 was a critical action that paved the way for a major revitalization of the Democratic Party. The national convention's disorder and division underscored its inadequacy as a truly democratic vehicle for expressing the will of the men and women who made up the contemporary party. Its one constructive achievement was in providing the means to achieve imperative internal change.

The catalyst was widespread dissatisfaction among Democratic women, liberals and minority groups that the existing system shut them out by undemocratically delegating excessive power to party bosses and other old-guard leaders. In July 1968 the vice chairman of the Connecticut McCarthy for President Committee, Anne Wexler, played a leading role in the creation of an Ad Hoc Commission to look into the problem. It was needed, she wrote then, "because delegates are selected in at least 20 different ways and the method of deciding how they should vote may be both illegal and unconstitutional."[1]

The Ad Hoc Commission was formally established the next month with then Governor Harold Hughes of Iowa as its chairman. It rapidly undertook an extensive examination of the party's political processes that encompassed everything from the role of presidential primaries to the functions and authority of the convention itself. A paper entitled "The Democratic Choice," presented to the 1968 convention, opened with a

prophetic warning: "This Convention is on trial."[2] It offered specific recommendations to the delegates gathering in Chicago and provided a
framework for discussions in the convention credentials committee,
chaired by Governor Richard Hughes of New Jersey.

After reporting on various 1968 challenges before his committee, Hughes begged the convention's indulgence to offer some "further
thoughts." His committee wanted, he said, to "encourage appropriate
revisions in the delegate selection process to assure the fullest possible
participation and to make the Democratic Party completely representative
of grass root sentiment."[3] He urged the convention to create a special committee to recommend remedies to the Democratic National Committee.

Thereupon the full convention approved a call to the 1972 convention providing that all Democrats have "meaningful and timely opportunities to participate fully" in the selection of delegates and alternates who
would choose the next Democratic presidential and vice-presidential
nominees.[4] Considering the contentiousness of the Chicago gathering and
the far-reaching potential of the proposal, surprisingly there was no
debate whatever on it and no minority report of any kind filed.[5] Nor did
the press pay much attention to it, or to a resolution to review party rules,
which also passed.

Out of the shambles of Humphrey's bitterly narrow defeat, the
national party sought to regroup under the leadership of a new national
chairman, Senator Fred Harris of Oklahoma. Harris, a liberal only two
years in the Senate, had co-chaired Humphrey's campaign for the 1968
nomination along with Ed Muskie and had hoped to be Humphrey's running mate. After the election, as a sort of consolation prize, Humphrey
gave Harris the party chairmanship. He revitalized the national committee
staff and appointed his Senate colleague George McGovern as chair of a
Committee on Party Structure and Delegate Selection. Harold Hughes,
just elected to the Senate, had seemed the obvious choice for the job and
wanted it, but Harris balked. McGovern, who took the post reluctantly,
insisted that Hughes be vice chairman. Three of the strongest voices in the
commission deliberations came from member Fred Dutton of the 1968
Robert Kennedy campaign and staffers Eli Segal and Ken Bode of the 1968
McCarthy team.[6]

Harris also picked Congressman James O'Hara of Michigan, a prominent New Deal liberal, to lead a Commission on Rules tasked with writing
new regulations and procedures for the 1972 convention. Creation of

these groups constituted a major step toward giving the party back to the rank and file as opposed to the old party power-wielders, whose whims and dictates had manipulated the rules over the years to maintain their own political fiefdoms and agendas.

At the first public hearing, Hubert Humphrey, the beneficiary in 1968 of the old ways of doing things, somewhat surprisingly said: "I come here with a very simple message. There are two Democratic parties in this country. One is the Democratic Party of the people; the people who work and vote and sacrifice for it, the people who look to it for leadership and assistance, the people who decide whether it will sit in the seats of power. The other Democratic Party is a collection of offices and machinery, with fancy titles. It issues press releases. It was, in 1968, completely and thoroughly separated from the people of the real Democratic Party. It is still separate today. It is your job to return the machinery to the control of those who are its rightful owners."[7] McGovern was more pointed: "When parties have been given the choice of reform or death in the past, they have always chosen death. We are going to be the first to live."[8]

More hearings in Washington and around the country in the spring and summer of 1969 drew large numbers of party activists. The party long had been accustomed to function mostly through local and state entities, with Democrats meeting as a national body only once every four years. Now the reexamination of how delegates to the national convention were chosen and what rules applied to their deliberations provided more of a national focus, and required state parties to review their own rules as well. Under the two new commissions, the party would be obliged to function continually from one presidential year to the next rather than coming together only once every four years to pick its national ticket.

The selection of delegates, often by party leaders and in some states more than a year before the national convention, was challenged. So were the varying procedures from state to state for choosing them through presidential primaries, once again on the rise with a renewed interest in giving voice to grassroots sentiments. Surprisingly, one of the strongest calls for grassroots participation through presidential primaries came from Mayor Daley, who advocated that all states be required to hold them. Any candidate who failed to enter at least one third of the primaries, he argued, would be ineligible for the party nomination—a condition that would have disqualified Humphrey in 1968.[9] The commission was not ready to go that far.

Questioned was the fairness of the winner-take-all primary, wherein the top vote-getter received all the delegates, as in California. There was no true national framework for the pre-convention activities, nor firm rules governing the role and authority of the national convention. Some states, particularly in the South, continued to cling to state primacy in party affairs.

One McGovern Commission member, Will Davis of Texas, observed at one point: "If you want a national Democratic party superceding [sic] state party sovereignty, then let us say so."[10] Another, Aaron Henry, the black civil rights leader from Mississippi, pleaded for a national focus: "We cannot endorse racist, reactionary state candidates; either we are a part of a national party or we have to cease being Democrats."[11]

Among the major changes in delegate selection was a decision to standardize the state delegations by using the same formula to calculate their size. A state's electoral college votes and Democratic voting in the three previous presidential elections would now determine how many delegates the state was entitled to send to the national convention. All delegates had to be selected through their state's primary election, state convention or committee procedures, and within the calendar year of the national convention and election. Automatic appointment as delegates by local and state party kingpins was prohibited, requiring even party office-holders and elected officials to win their seats in open competition. In states selecting delegates by convention, at least 75 percent had to be chosen at the congressional district level or below; no more than 10 percent of any state delegation was to be selected by party committee. Procedures were set for challenging delegates in open meetings.

A more difficult task was addressing demands of women, minorities and youth for a voice in the party more proportionate to their numbers. The notion of explicit quotas clashed with the party's principles and image, but a major complaint about the 1968 convention was that these Democrats, many of them against the war, had been severely underrepresented on the convention floor. After much debate, the commission required that each state party take "affirmative steps" to provide representation to women, minorities and youth in its convention delegation in "reasonable relationship" to their percentage of the state population.[12]

Concerning party rules, the commission called for written, stable, open and well-publicized procedures for delegate selection without modification or discretionary abuse by party officials.[13] Proxy voting was outlawed, and the commission also "ratified" elimination of the unit rule, already thrown out at the 1948 convention, but it dodged the question of the winner-take-all primary.

All these new regulations met with considerable opposition from some state parties, especially in the South, as dictation from the national party, and from organized labor. Although AFL-CIO leaders were named to the reform commissions, they essentially boycotted them and warned that the new rules would undercut the old party power structure, of which they were a part, and open the door to greater liberal influence.

According to William J. Crotty in his comprehensive study of the reform commissions, *Decision for the Democrats: Reforming the Party Structure,* organized labor "never bothered to master the content or spirit of the changes, yet they remained determined to increase their representation at the national convention. Employing the old ways, the aging federation leadership was deeply offended when its well-financed 'uncommitted' slates repeatedly fell to delegates tied to specific nominees. It was infuriated when state officials insisted on running in support of one of the real contenders [for party nomination] rather than cooperating in the old tactic of putting themselves forward as favorite-son candidates intended to insure the AFL-CIO a block of delegates to barter at the convention."[14]

The Democratic National Committee itself, as a conservative reflection of the old ways of doing business, was regarded as a threat by some reform commission members and was sidestepped whenever possible. In early 1970, Fred Harris stepped down as chairman and Larry O'Brien was prevailed upon to return to the post. Reformers feared that the chairmanship of this old party pro would be a barrier to effective implementation of the commission guidelines, but those fears were unfounded.

In a critical move, O'Brien called on Joseph Califano, the party's legal counsel, for an opinion as to whether the commission guidelines were binding on the state and national parties. Califano ruled that "the guidelines should be respected by the state parties as their guide in assuring that the delegate selection processes within each state provide all Democrats with a fully meaningful and timely opportunity to participate" in the process.[15] Thereafter O'Brien was a strong supporter of the reforms, and the national committee itself included the guidelines in its preliminary call to the 1972 convention. Some twenty state parties were obliged to seek legislative remedies to comply with certain of the guidelines. In the end, according to Crotty, "an incredible 97 percent of the guidelines had been enforced, an unequalled record of success."[16]

As he also noted, "the commission's approach in establishing national rules and requiring their enactment constituted a radical departure. The regulations themselves were not significantly obtrusive. They did not destroy the integrity of the reigning system. Rather, the guidelines were intended as minimal guarantees to people who wished to participate in delegate selection that safeguarded their rights. For this reason, they were difficult to oppose in principle."[17]

The O'Hara Commission, assigned the task of reforming the national convention itself after the Chicago fiasco of 1968, approved rules calling for larger convention committees with membership divided equally among men and women, "giving due regard to the race and age of the men and women elected." All meetings were required to be open and to meet prior to the convention. All demonstrations during candidate nominations were banned; favorite-son nominations were discouraged; times allotted for speeches were limited. But nothing was done that might have restored the national convention to the status of decision-maker on the party's national ticket it had before the proliferation of delegate-selecting primaries.

As all these reforms were being debated and shaped, the depth of the Democratic Party's fall from power was accentuated by ascendancy to the presidency of its longtime bête noire, Richard Nixon. He was elected in 1968 in part because he had left the impression he had a "secret plan" to end the Vietnam War, but he had no such plan. Instead, he sought to lower the temperature of American protest at home with a policy of "Vietnamization," gradual withdrawal of American troops and turning the ground fighting over to the South Vietnamese, with U.S. advisory and material support. At the same time, early in 1969 he launched secret B-52 raids into Cambodia and in April 1970 authorized an "incursion" into that country to "clean out major enemy sanctuaries. If the world's most powerful nation . . . acts like a pitiful helpless giant," he said, ". . . all other nations will be on notice that despite its overwhelming power the United States when a real crisis comes will be found wanting."[18]

Rather than quelling domestic protest, the Cambodian action ignited campus demonstrations across the country, highlighted by Ohio national guardsmen firing on a crowd of students at Kent State University, killing four and wounding nine others, and police killing two black students and wounding a dozen more at Jackson State College in Mississippi. An aroused Democratic-controlled Congress repealed the Gulf of Tonkin resolution that Lyndon Johnson had used as a blank check to pursue the Vietnam War, and the Democrats hoped to rebound in the 1970 congressional elections.

But Nixon claimed to be the voice of a "silent majority" that supported the war. He characterized student protesters as "bums," and his vice president, Spiro Agnew, played off the public memory of the 1968 Democratic convention fiasco to demonize the Democratic Party as the captive of long-haired radicals. With Agnew daily castigating Democratic candidates as radical liberals (shortened on the stump to "radic-libs") and their supporters as "an effete corps of impudent snobs," he labored with some success at painting the party as disloyal, even anarchistic.[19]

On election night, the Democrats picked up nine House seats but lost two in the Senate, a showing that was well below the traditional off-year gains of the out-party. They did, however, win eleven governorships, indicating that for all the recollections of 1968 and the Nixon-Agnew battering, the party of Jefferson and Jackson was hanging on. Among the prominent Democratic winners was Humphrey, regaining a Senate seat from Minnesota as the start of a possible return presidential bid in 1972. His 1968 running mate, Muskie, drew attention and praise for an election-eve national television address that also projected him into the early speculation on the party's next presidential nominee.

After the 1968 election, Ted Kennedy was again prominently mentioned, but in July 1969 a tragic auto accident on Chappaquiddick Island off Cape Cod eliminated him from contention. After a late party of former campaign workers for Robert Kennedy, Ted Kennedy, accompanied by a female passenger, drove his car off a bridge. He escaped, but the young woman drowned. He said later he had tried to rescue her but could not, and finally swam to nearby Martha's Vineyard, but did not report the accident until the next morning. He escaped serious charges but the episode tarred him.

In January 1971, McGovern, well schooled in the new delegate-selecting procedures, resigned as chairman of the committee that authored them and was replaced by Congressman Donald Fraser of Minnesota. Later in the month McGovern declared his candidacy for the 1972 Democratic nomination. His brief service as a stand-in for the Robert Kennedy presidential campaign in 1968 gave him a modest cadre of supporters. His home-state base of South Dakota made him a long shot, at 3 percent among Democratic voters in an early poll,[20] albeit one with some potential as one of the party's most outspoken opponents of the war in Vietnam. McGovern's campaign manager was a thirty-four-year-old Denver lawyer named Gary Hart, whose own story in the annals of Democratic presidential politics was yet to be written.

Official deceptions in the conduct of the war revealed in the Pentagon Papers in 1971 heightened public concern, as did word of the My Lai massacres of 1968, wherein American troops were reported to have shot Vietnamese villagers in cold blood. While a public opinion poll now found that 65 percent of Americans surveyed thought it "morally wrong" for their countrymen to be fighting in Vietnam, a majority still backed Nixon's view that South Vietnam should not be allowed to fall to communism.[21]

Starting early in part to head off a candidacy by Mayor John Lindsay of New York, a liberal Republican on the verge of switching party allegiance, McGovern all through 1971 toiled diligently as the liberal standard-bearer, hammering away at the immorality and folly of the war. He began by stitching together the remnants of the 1968 Robert Kennedy and Eugene McCarthy anti-war forces. Muskie, however, emerged as the early front-runner on the basis of his appealing vice-presidential candidacy in 1968 and that election-eve television speech in 1970. He undertook an extensive tour in 1971 to Western Europe, the Soviet Union, Egypt and Israel to bolster his foreign policy credentials and seemed on his way to nomination as the party's centrist candidate.

But like George Romney before him, Muskie stumbled over the issue of Vietnam. He could not express with clarity where he stood on the war, and as a result he offered a muddled message to a Democratic electorate that was increasingly weary of the morass in which the country was mired. He was also deliberative to a fault; it took him forever to make up his mind on other issues as well, and beneath a serene appearance and manner he had a hot temper and a deficiency of patience.[22] In an effort to occupy the center of the political spectrum, he came across to many voters as indistinct. Muskie depended heavily on big-name endorsements in the party, giving his campaign at first a veneer of inevitability.

A host of other Democrats entered the race, hoping to pick up the pieces of the broken party: Governor Wallace of Alabama; Mayor Lindsay of New York, now a convert from the GOP; six senators—Henry "Scoop"

Jackson of Washington State, Birch Bayh and Vance Hartke of Indiana, former national party chairman Fred Harris, and Harold Hughes of Iowa and William Proxmire of Wisconsin (early dropouts); and three House members—the first black woman candidate, Shirley Chisholm of New York, Patsy Mink of Hawaii and William R. Anderson of Tennessee. Others competed with varying degrees of intensity and hope—McCarthy, former Governor Terry Sanford of North Carolina, Los Angeles Mayor Sam Yorty and Governor Lester Maddox of Georgia. Nixon led them all in the polls, except for a dip from November 1970 to March 1971 when Muskie pulled even.

In the wake of the McGovern-Fraser Commission reforms, twenty-two states and the District of Columbia scheduled primaries in 1972 that would select nearly two thirds of all national convention delegates. For the first time with no appointed delegates, high-profile officeholders were obliged to compete to gain voting seats on the convention floor. By tradition, the first primary was in New Hampshire in early March, with Muskie of Maine the favorite as a result of his New England ties and personal efforts to build the Democratic Party there. He won, but his 46.4 percent of the vote compared to 37.2 for anti-war candidate McGovern in a five-candidate race was deemed not particularly impressive. One of Muskie's state campaign managers had injudiciously said she would "eat my hat" if he failed to win a majority.[23]

Not known at the time, Muskie may have been undercut by political dirty tricks played in New Hampshire by the Nixon political operation, called the Committee to Re-elect the President and soon known by its acronym, CREEP. Nixon strategists deemed Muskie the strongest prospective Democratic nominee and unleashed freewheeling enlistees to smear him. Later disclosures revealed that CREEP had placed spies in the Muskie campaign, and anonymous callers affecting exaggerated African-American accents phoned New Hampshirites late at night urging them to vote for Muskie as an advocate of school busing.

Other Nixon operatives were found to have dispatched what came to be known as "the Canuck letter." In it, Jane Muskie, the candidate's wife, was said to have made a disparaging remark about French Canadians, an important segment of the New Hampshire electorate: while Maine did not have many blacks, "we have 'Cannocks' [*sic*]." The viciously right-wing publisher of the *Manchester Union Leader,* William Loeb, ran the letter and an editorial declaring "Sen. Muskie Insults Franco-Americans."[24]

The senator drew negative comment when, shortly before the vote, he stood on a flatbed truck in a snowstorm outside the newspaper's building and emotionally defended his wife against an editorial smear by Loeb, appearing to some to be crying. Others saw the moisture on his cheek as melted snow, but the episode was widely interpreted as evidence of Muskie cracking under pressure.

A week later, Muskie stumbled badly in the Florida primary, where more CREEP dirty tricks were orchestrated against him, again portraying him as a strong liberal advocate of school busing, anathema to many Floridians. Humphrey, who by now had allied himself with the Senate doves on Vietnam, and pro-war Jackson made their first serious bids there, but all three finished behind Wallace, with Muskie running a dismal fourth with only 8.9 percent of the vote. Wallace had 41.6 percent in his native region; Humphrey was a weak second with 18.6 percent and Jackson third with 13.5 percent. McGovern, with only 6.2 percent, trailed all of them.

The following week, Muskie rebounded slightly, winning a lightly contested two-man race against a low-profile effort by McCarthy in Illinois that most other candidates skipped, with a majority of the delegates elected as uncommitted under the thumb of Mayor Daley. But Muskie's star was already plunging.

McGovern, who had steadily been building a grassroots organization of anti-war and good-government liberals with an emphasis on the young, got his breakthrough in Wisconsin on April 4. Under the leadership of twenty-five-year-old Gene Pokorny, already a veteran of the civil rights and anti–Vietnam War movements, McGovern won with 29.6 percent over Wallace's 22.1 percent, 20.7 for Humphrey and 10.3 for Muskie, who was effectively finished off three weeks later in Pennsylvania by Humphrey and in Massachusetts by McGovern, and shelved his campaign.

That left Humphrey, Wallace and McGovern, and each picked his spots carefully. McGovern labored under a politically ill-advised welfare reform proposal that would have given a thousand dollars to every American and was immediately attacked as a fuzzy-headed liberal giveaway. Humphrey defeated McGovern in Ohio and Wallace in Indiana and West Virginia; Wallace won Tennessee and North Carolina; but McGovern beat Humphrey and Wallace in Nebraska.

On May 15, Wallace was gunned down by an unbalanced stalker as he addressed a crowd outside a shopping center in Laurel, Maryland, and was left paralyzed. Surprise Wallace victories the next day in Michigan and Maryland went for naught, although they did reflect the northward creeping of racial bias as a political force. The loss of labor-dominated Michigan was a particular blow to Humphrey, but he pressed on. McGovern, now riding the tide of anti-war sentiment and leading a growing army of liberal activists, swept the remaining seven primaries. He concluded by capturing winner-take-all California, but a dispute over more than half the delegates he had won carried into the convention in Miami Beach in the last battle of 1972 between the party's new and old politics.

McGovern carried the Golden State by only 44.3 percent to 39.2 for Humphrey, but under the winner-take-all rules he collected 271 delegates, as well as a total of 98 more in other primaries on the same June 6 in New Jersey, South Dakota and New Mexico. He was within 40 votes of the 1,509 needed for nomination. Two weeks later in New York, amid a fragmented state Democratic Party and no substantial opposition, McGovern collected another 230 to 256 delegates, which seemed more than enough to assure his nomination.

In New York as in all other states, many of the leading Democrats who had stayed on the sidelines or committed themselves to candidates other than McGovern found themselves on the outside looking in at the Miami Beach convention. Under the new rules of the McGovern-Fraser Commission, Democrats who wanted to go to the convention had to be elected in their states' primaries or delegate-selecting conventions; many of them rode the wrong candidate horse and never got there, at least not as voting delegates. As a result, the Democratic gathering in Miami Beach in mid-July looked in some respect more like an anti-war protest of the long-haired and jean-clad than the fun-loving romps of the party elite of yore.

Three nights before the New York primary, however, a mysterious episode occurred at the Democratic National Committee headquarters in the Watergate building complex in Washington that was destined to have immense political ramifications, though not—unfortunately for the Democratic Party—in the 1972 election cycle. Police foiled a break-in at the headquarters, catching five men red-handed in the midst of a burglary of the office of party chairman O'Brien.

In short order it became known that the five were all in the pay of Nixon's CREEP, and diligent gum-shoeing by a pair of young city-side *Washington Post* reporters, Bob Woodward and Carl Bernstein, began peeling away the political story of the century. Nixon and his closest aides denied any direct involvement in the break-in just as the Democrats were about to choose the nominee who would oppose the Republican occupant of the White House. The five men were arrested and held for trial on criminal charges of illegal bugging along with two CREEP officials, E. Howard Hunt and G. Gordon Liddy. All five were indicted in mid-September but, in light of the obvious political implications, two district court judges ordered the trial delayed until after the November election.

McGovern was now on the brink of becoming the Democratic nominee, but first he had to overcome the Humphrey campaign's eleventh-hour challenge to his apparent sweep of the California delegation. A week before the convention opened, forty-five state delegations were ruled in full compliance of the new rules and the rest in substantial compliance. With the "reasonable representation" yardstick applied, black delegates made up 15 percent of the total and women 40 percent, both triple the 1968 figures, and youth under age thirty constituted 21 percent, quadruple that of 1968. The California challenge was one of eighty-two raised before the convention's credentials committee and one of twenty-three that went to the floor for resolution.[25]

Winner-take-all primaries had not been outlawed by the commission rules accepted by the full national committee. But Humphrey strategists argued that, in keeping with the spirit of open and fair allocation in the commission guidelines, California's 271 delegates should be split in proportion to the actual primary vote. The credentials committee's hearing examiner ruled against the challenge, but the full committee, controlled by old-guard Democrats, reversed the decision and gave 151 California delegates to Humphrey, keeping McGovern short of a majority. His strategists appealed to the judiciary, and a district court first upheld the committee, but a court of appeals ordered that McGovern be given back the 151 delegates. The Supreme Court then stayed that order and kicked the decision back to the convention, where deft maneuvering and a favorable procedural ruling from party chairman O'Brien won the day for McGovern. The convention's rules committee, however, pushed through the abolition of the winner-take-all primary for 1976.[26]

In a stormy sideshow that underscored how the McGovern-Fraser guidelines had changed the power quotient in the party, the credentials committee voted to deny seats to Mayor Daley and fifty-eight other Cook County delegates on grounds their election in the Illinois primary violated the guidelines, especially in underrepresentation of minorities. Court action by Daley failed, and compromise efforts by the McGovern strategists to appease Daley but not imperil McGovern's nomination were rejected by the outraged Chicago mayor.[27]

Before the presidential roll call the next afternoon, Humphrey released his delegates and Muskie withdrew and endorsed McGovern. There followed a flood of platform proposals that produced much heat and little light. A constitutional amendment for equal rights for women was backed, and abortion and gay rights planks were rejected in debates that underscored before television cameras the dichotomy in the party on such privacy issues. With floor demonstrations outlawed by the new rules, the convention heard five short nominating speeches and McGovern was chosen on the first ballot with 1,864 votes to 485 for Jackson, 377 for Wallace, 101 for Chisholm and 69 for Sanford.

The excitement, however, was not over. McGovern still had to select his running mate. He had already been turned down by his first choice, Ted Kennedy, but had held off, hoping Kennedy might change his mind. Then all the controversy over the California challenge had robbed him of time to think about others. The next morning, McGovern met with Hart and other top aides who offered him seven names: Senators Walter Mondale, Abe Ribicoff and Tom Eagleton, Governor Pat Lucey of Wisconsin, Larry O'Brien, Sargent Shriver and Mayor Kevin White of Boston. Afterward, a larger meeting of his staff was called; it was "maximum feasible participation," the byword of the reformers, in spades. At the closed meeting around a long green-felt table, the staff members debated and each wrote lists of possible choices in order of preference. Eagleton's name was not prominent on them.[28]

McGovern wrote later that he had considered Muskie until the Maine senator declined to endorse him before the California challenge, which McGovern thought might have averted it. He made his first offer, he said, to Mondale, who didn't want to risk his Senate seat. White and Eagleton had considerable backing among the insiders, and McGovern sounded out White without making an offer, but objections from the Massachusetts delegation through John Kenneth Galbraith dissuaded him. He then urged his old colleague Senator Gaylord Nelson of Wisconsin to be his running mate, who in turn suggested Eagleton, already recommended by Kennedy and Mondale.[29]

In his autobiography, *Grassroots,* McGovern later wrote: "I knew that

Tom fervently wanted the nomination. None of those who knew him best in the Senate had even hinted at anything other than his ideal qualifications. Rather than asking him any questions, I simply said I wanted him to be my running mate and that I hoped he would accept. 'George, I'm going to say yes before you change your mind,' he said jubilantly." McGovern handed the phone to Frank Mankiewicz, the nominee wrote. "He assured Frank that there was nothing in his background that would be embarrassing to the national ticket."[30]

McGovern subsequently wrote that the "final element" in the eventual demise of his candidacy occurred "the moment I selected Missouri's attractive young senator, Tom Eagleton, as my vice presidential running mate. From that moment on, the 1972 presidential results were determined. Richard Nixon and Spiro Agnew were home free."[31] The political circus over the vice-presidential nomination that followed without doubt seriously tarnished McGovern's image for decisiveness and leadership.

Eagleton was easily nominated by the convention, but long floor wrangles over a proposal for a new national party charter, a constitutional amendment for equal rights for women, enlargement of the national committee and a midterm national party conference in 1974 stretched the proceedings into the wee hours, depriving McGovern of an optimum television audience for his acceptance speech. The convention had been intended to erase the public's bad memories of the Chicago convention of four years earlier. Instead, it created new impressions of a disorganized party in the hands of the sorts of liberal rabble-rousers of whom Nixon and Agnew were already effectively warning in their concerted demonization of the opposition.

Nor was the matter of McGovern's running mate at an end. After the convention had adjourned, rumors and reports of Eagleton's medical problems began to reach the vacationing McGovern camp. Gary Hart and Frank Mankiewicz met with Eagleton, and under questioning he owned up to having been hospitalized three times and twice undergone shock therapy. He agreed to have all his medical records produced for the campaign and to meet with McGovern.[32]

The two men conferred in Custer, South Dakota, where McGovern was vacationing, and held a joint press conference in which Eagleton revealed his medical history. Beforehand, however, Eagleton convinced McGovern that his medical problems had been resolved and, according to McGovern, vowed to withdraw on his own at any indication that his candidacy would hurt the ticket's chances of election. Thereupon McGovern announced that Eagleton would remain on the ticket.[33]

Almost at once, protests started pouring in to McGovern from key supporters. Keeping on the ticket a man who had misled him and whose mental health would continue to feed negative speculation, they said, was going to mean sure defeat in November. When one story appeared under a headline proclaiming that McGovern was reconsidering his decision on Eagleton, McGovern authorized an aide to say he was backing Eagleton "a thousand percent," figuring anything less would doom the ticket's chances.[34]

Eagleton, for his part, dug in his heels, saying he was not going to be chased out of the race. The pressures on McGovern mounted from some of his most trusted friends and colleagues, to the point that he finally informed Eagleton by phone that they would have to meet again and decide what to do. But Eagleton, who earlier had assured McGovern he would go quietly if staying on would jeopardize the ticket, told reporters in San Francisco: "My decision to stay on the ticket is irrevocable."[35] Another report from columnist Jack Anderson alleging that Eagleton had been arrested several times in Missouri for drunken driving, subsequently retracted, enabled Eagleton to switch from offender to victim, and he made the most of it.

McGovern, boxed in by his pledge of "a thousand percent" support of Eagleton, finally conceived of a way he might nudge his troublesome ticket mate out the door. At this time, Eagleton was making a speech in Hawaii and would be returning to the West Coast in the morning. I was in Custer at the time covering the McGovern campaign for the *Los Angeles Times,* and I was called to the nominee's cabin for a background discussion of the situation. McGovern told me of his dilemma: He wanted Eagleton off the ticket but wanted him to jump before he had to be pushed. Assuming Eagleton would be reading my newspaper as soon as he landed in Los Angeles, he hoped word of his feelings would persuade Eagleton to take him off the hook. To cover his bases, McGovern later strolled into the dining room where other reporters were having dinner and repeated his lament.

My lead story in the *Times* the next morning began: "CUSTER, S.D.– Public and political reaction to Senator Thomas F. Eagleton's disclosure of past hospitalization for nervous disorders has been so negative that Senator George S. McGovern is convinced that Eagleton must withdraw from the Democratic ticket, the *Times* has learned. At the same time, McGovern is determined to leave the initiative to Eagleton, convinced that when his running mate, just back from Hawaii, takes his own soundings he will reach the same conclusion."[36]

But Eagleton declined to take the hint, until McGovern finally had a showdown meeting with him in Washington. He agreed then to step aside only on the condition that McGovern say it was not Eagleton's mental health but the disruption that the controversy caused that had dictated the decision. McGovern, who later wrote he had indeed heard unreassuring assessments from Eagleton's doctors, reluctantly agreed to end the matter. "I did what I had to," McGovern wrote, "but the Eagleton matter ended whatever chance there was to defeat Richard Nixon in 1972."[37]

An embarrassingly long search ensued for Eagleton's replacement, with one prominent Democrat after another—Kennedy, Ribicoff, Humphrey, Muskie—being approached and turning down the offer to be the caboose on a train going nowhere. Sargent Shriver, as a loyal soldier in the ranks, finally agreed and was accepted by a special meeting of the Democratic National Committee. The fiasco once again underscored the cavalier nature of the vice-presidential selection process, especially when undertaken under severe time pressures, and McGovern's credibility never recovered.

In the third week of August, the Republicans also met in Miami Beach and routinely renominated Nixon and Agnew. Primary challenges to Nixon from Congressman Paul N. "Pete" McCloskey, a critic of the president's war policy, and Congressman John M. Ashbrook of Ohio, a champion of the party's ultra-right, had gotten nowhere. The main interest centered on efforts by former Eisenhower administration official and Minnesota Governor Harold Stassen to have Nixon drop Agnew from the ticket, but they also got nowhere. Nixon was known to prefer his secretary of treasury, former Democrat John B. Connally, as his running mate for a second term,[38] to the point that he even considered appointing Agnew to the Supreme Court as a way of opening the path for Connally.[39] But Agnew would have none of it, and stayed on the ticket. The Republican convention, a model of discipline and polish, provided a contrast to the earlier Democratic circus that only deepened the hole in which McGovern found himself.

The Democratic nominee proceeded to dig it even deeper with the appointment of Jean Westwood, a liberal activist from Utah, as national party chairman replacing O'Brien. The veteran Democratic professional had told McGovern earlier he wanted to step aside after the convention and McGovern proceeded on that basis. But he learned the morning after the convention had adjourned that O'Brien was reconsidering under pressure from other party stalwarts. A compromise for Westwood and O'Brien to share the chairmanship through the fall campaign did not pan out, and even as the campaign began bad feelings caused divisions and griping. O'Brien accepted the title of chairman of the fall campaign but did not play the central role that his experience and political knowledge warranted.

Nixon meanwhile was basking in the glow of foreign policy successes. Earlier in the year he had made a historic opening to China with a personal visit there and had signed an agreement with the Soviet Union signaling détente in Europe, and also a new arms control agreement. Most American troops were out of Vietnam by the time of the Republican convention and Nixon's secretary of state, Henry Kissinger, was hard at work to bring about a negotiated settlement of that long and debilitating war. One poll indicated Americans by 49 percent to 33 thought Nixon more likely to bring peace in Vietnam than McGovern, castigated by the Republicans as an appeaser, or worse.

McGovern campaigned valiantly against all odds. As the saga of the break-in of Democratic headquarters at the Watergate continued to unfold in the *Washington Post* and a relatively few other newspapers, he sought to tap into it as evidence of Nixonian deception and abuse of power. In a television speech, he labeled the Nixon administration the most corrupt in the nation's history. But the Nixon White House continued to disavow direct involvement and McGovern found himself relying essentially on newspaper reports of further evidence of criminal misbehavior by agents of the president's reelection campaign. It was a futile effort. Many newspapers thought the *Post* was climbing out on a limb that was bound to break with its relentless investigative stories by Woodward and Bernstein tightening the noose around the corrupt Nixon crowd.

Meanwhile, the Nixon strategists turned hatchet man Agnew loose on McGovern, who made an easy target for his definition of a "radic-lib." Nixon himself played the statesman on the world stage, above the uneven domestic political fray, not deigning to debate the hapless McGovern while slyly questioning his loyalty and patriotism. It was often observed during the campaign that Agnew was "Nixon's Nixon," but the original version was also intermittently at work.

As a final blow, less than two weeks before the election in November, Kissinger grandly declared that talks with North Vietnam in Paris were on the brink of fruition and that "peace is at hand." It wasn't, but the false prediction further deflated McGovern's anti-war rhetoric in the waning days of the campaign. On election day it was a rout: Nixon captured 60.7 percent of the vote to 37.5 for McGovern and compiled a Republican popular-vote margin of 18 million, the largest in history.

For all the internal reforms, the Democratic Party remained on its knees. Nixon carried every state except liberal Massachusetts, plus the District of Columbia, and cemented his Southern strategy. Remarkably for a Republican, he won more labor votes, more Catholic votes and even boosted the GOP tally among blacks and Jewish voters. There seemed nothing in sight to put the Democratic Party back on its feet, not even a Christmastime bombing of Hanoi and Haiphong that triggered Democratic outrage in Congress.

But as Nixon and Agnew embarked on their second term, that prospect began to change. Nine days before their inauguration, the trial of the Watergate break-in burglars had at last gotten under way in U.S. District Court. Judge John Sirica pressured the defendants to say whether any higher-ups in the Nixon campaign committee or administration had been involved and they all flatly denied any were. Five of the accused pleaded guilty, and two others, CREEP operatives Liddy and James McCord, were convicted on January 30, 1973, their lips still sealed. A deeply dissatisfied Sirica, hoping to loosen their tongues, delayed sentencing, to no immediate avail.

But McCord, a former CIA operative, finally cracked. He wrote a letter to Sirica telling him, among other things, that "there was political pressure applied to the defendants to plead guilty and remain silent," perjury had been committed in the trial, and others not yet identified were involved in the break-in plot.[40] The McCord letter was an icebreaker in the conspiracy of silence, which later was revealed to have been achieved by the paying of hush money from the White House in a continuing cover-up involving the president himself.

Hearings through much of 1973 chaired by Democratic Senator Sam Ervin of North Carolina, accompanied by continued newspaper sleuthing by the *Washington Post* team of Woodward and Bernstein and by other news organizations, steadily unraveled the sordid story of deceit and corruption at the highest levels. At the same time, Attorney General Elliot L. Richardson appointed esteemed Harvard Law School professor Archibald Cox as a special prosecutor to investigate the whole Watergate matter.

At the core, the Nixon strategists, their campaign treasury bursting with money and driven by a steely determination to annihilate the political opposition, had resorted to the Watergate burglaries and assorted other crimes to discredit and defeat Muskie and then McGovern, in a reelection campaign Nixon was already near-certain to win. All through 1973, new revelations and the efforts of Nixon and his operatives to cover up or defend themselves dominated the Washington scene. Although Democrats like Ervin led the inquiry, Republicans as well were drawn in. The impeccable reputations of Richardson and Cox gave credibility to the Justice Department investigation, although before long Cox became a target of White House allegations of liberal witch-hunting.

On Friday, July 13, which turned out to be a very unlucky day for Nixon, a former White House aide, Alexander Butterfield, disclosed the existence of an automatic voice-recording system in the Oval Office. The news triggered a bitter fight between Nixon and the Senate committee over release of the tapes. As the walls were closing in on a defiant Nixon, the ashes of the Democratic defeat of 1972 were beginning to emit a faint glow.

At the same time, the Republican administration suffered another political blow that summer with allegations that Agnew had accepted payoffs from Maryland contractors as governor and then vice president. The charges led to his resignation in October, orchestrated by the Nixon Justice Department to remove him from the line of presidential succession even as Nixon's own tenure in office appeared increasingly shaky. Agnew agreed to plead nolo contendere to a charge of income-tax evasion and to step down to escape a prison sentence. Nixon recommended House Minority Leader Gerald R. Ford Jr. as Agnew's successor and Congress accepted the nomination of one of its own.

Ten days after Agnew's resignation, another blow fell on Nixon. Frustrated by Cox's pursuit of White House tapes that might shed light on the Watergate affair, the president on Saturday, October 20, ordered Richardson to fire Cox. Richardson refused and resigned, as did his deputy, William D. Ruckelshaus, in what came to be known as "the Saturday Night Massacre." The third in line in the Justice hierarchy, Solicitor General Robert J. Bork, finally complied, amid an uproar of press and public criticism that Nixon was behaving like the dictator of a banana republic. His credibility was shrinking by the hour, and with it rose the Democrats' hopes of a political resurrection looking to the 1976 presidential election. Reeling, Nixon defensively appointed another special prosecutor, Leon Jaworski of Texas, who proceeded to pick up where Cox had left off.

In February 1974 the House authorized its Judiciary Committee, chaired by Democratic Congressman Peter Rodino of New Jersey, to investigate the president's conduct in the Watergate fiasco, starting with an inquiry into what constituted an impeachable offense. As more and more information was gleaned from the White House tapes and further testimony, the unthinkable became commonplace—that the president of the United States faced possible removal from office.

The final blows came on July 24 when the Supreme Court ruled by an 8–0 vote that sixty-four White House tapes subpoenaed by the special prosecutor had to be turned over. Among them was the "smoking gun" tape of June 23, 1972, six days after the break-in, in which Nixon was heard ordering his chief of staff, Bob Haldeman, to have the CIA tell the FBI: "Don't go any further into this case, period!"[41] The tape was explicit confirmation of his personal role in the cover-up. Three days later, the House Judiciary Committee began voting articles of impeachment against Nixon. On August 9, 1974, after Republican senators had informed him that he did not have the votes to escape conviction, he resigned. Suddenly the Democratic prospects for a return to the White House that had seemed so dismal on the night of George McGovern's defeat in 1972 took on a definite luster.

Chapter 28

POST-WATERGATE INTERLUDE,
1974–1980

THE WATERGATE SCANDAL and Nixon's resignation had so discredited the Republican Party that a host of Democratic presidential prospects for 1976 soon emerged. The new president, Gerald Ford, was not generally regarded as politically formidable for a White House term on his own, as he himself had suggested in becoming vice president only eight months earlier: "I am a Ford, not a Lincoln."[1] While he immediately won praise for offering normalcy upon the conclusion of what he termed "our long national nightmare,"[2] Ford quickly eroded much of that good will one month after taking office by granting Nixon a highly controversial total pardon. Democratic strategists entertained visions of a return to national power two and a half years hence, with no radical change in the party's essentially liberal message, yet cautious about feeding an image of radicalism that had been so widely perceived—and effectively peddled by the Republicans—in the McGovern candidacy.

No one Democrat of White House ambition or qualification by experience or age was a major architect of the Nixon fall, and thus able to lay claim as a particular political beneficiary of the scandal. The chairman of the special Senate committee that had investigated the affair, Sam Ervin of North Carolina, was too old; the chairman of the House Judiciary Committee that had voted articles of impeachment, Peter Rodino of New Jersey, was a journeyman legislator with low name recognition.

Senator Ted Kennedy, still tarnished politically by the Chappaquid-

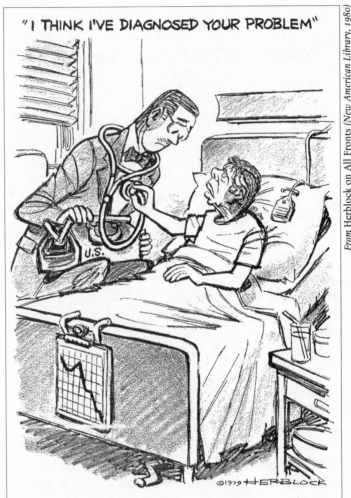

"I THINK I'VE DIAGNOSED YOUR PROBLEM"

As President Jimmy Carter struggled through his one term amid foreign and domestic troubles, he finally told the American people the problem could be found in their own lack of confidence in the country.

dick car accident of five years earlier but still the party's most prominent liberal, categorically said barely a month after Nixon's resignation that he would accept neither the nomination nor a draft. Citing family responsibilities, he declared: "There is absolutely no circumstance or event that will alter the decision."[3] A couple of months later, Senator Walter F. Mondale of Minnesota, another liberal who had already visited thirty states and spent about $100,000 in an exploration of his presidential prospects, followed suit. "Basically I found I did not have the overwhelming desire to be president which is essential for the kind of campaign that is required," he said. "I don't think anyone should be president who is not willing to go through fire."[4] Later, he refined his reluctance to the prospect of a year of "sleeping in Holiday Inns."[5]

A third liberal, Congressman Morris K. Udall of Arizona, was the first Democrat to demonstrate that willingness a few days after Mondale bowed out, and ten others eventually followed. For all of Ford's vulnerabilities, however, the sorry shape of the Democratic Party after McGovern's overwhelming defeat, and the continuing division between mostly liberal young party activists and mostly moderate-to-conservative old warriors, gave the party little assurance that the Nixon resignation and pardon constituted a sure return ticket to the Oval Office.

Dissatisfaction within the party over the McGovern-Fraser delegate-selection rules, especially the shutting out of party officials and office-holders who failed to be elected as delegates in 1972, had brought about appointment of another commission headed by Barbara Mikulski, a city councilwoman in Baltimore who later became a U.S. senator from Maryland. Among other things, it provided for such party leaders to be extended convention "privileges" but not voting rights. It also permitted certain proxy voting in state delegations and set a formula for proportional representation of delegates pledged to a particular presidential candidate. A Compliance Review Commission was created to monitor states' adherence to the rules.[6]

Also established through a mandate of the 1972 party convention was a new commission chaired by former Governor Terry Sanford of North Carolina, a man of reason and compromise, to write an unprecedented charter for the party. Under a new national chairman, Robert S. Strauss of Texas, previously a formidable national party treasurer, the Charter Commission undertook the difficult task of writing a document that would please both reformers and party regulars, including leaders of the AFL-

CIO still chafing at the McGovern-Fraser reforms. Strauss, elected chairman with the strong support of organized labor, started as a staunch defender of the party regulars, but eventually became an effective instrument of compromise, driven by his desire, above all else, to bring a unified party into the 1976 presidential election.

The commission approved a draft charter in March 1974, but a meeting in Kansas City in August erupted in an open fight when the party regulars and labor leaders, strengthened in numbers by new Strauss appointments, softened affirmative action provisions in delegate selection. California Assemblyman Willie Brown, a leader of the commission's black caucus, charged that the changes were "driving blacks and women out of the party," and a walkout ensued. Sanford blamed "mistakes of judgment" by Strauss, and a compromise shifted the dispute to an approaching national party mini-convention, itself opposed by many regulars as a likely vehicle for reformers' mischief.[7]

For all this dissension, the Democrats demonstrated some recovery in the congressional elections that November, strengthening their control of both houses. They picked up forty-nine House seats and five in the Senate, as well as four more governorships, giving them power bases in eight of the ten largest states. Ford had already encountered an energy crisis that helped plunge the country into recession, with inflation and unemployment rising.

At the party's first midterm convention, in Kansas City in December, delegate-selection and charter reform were the main issues. Even McGovern agreed that the 1972 reform requiring all delegates to be elected had gone too far in barring automatic convention participation by important officeholders and party officials, many of whom ran as delegates for losing presidential candidates. Now states were given the option of selecting 25 percent of future national-convention delegates through the party apparatus, thus assuring most state officials a free ride. Strauss, for his part, recognized the need for unity and took a more conciliatory posture, to the distress of labor.[8]

The mini-convention, in a move to mollify women and minorities that irritated the AFL-CIO and its president, George Meany, accepted a resolution prohibiting mandatory quotas but requiring every state to adopt and implement an affirmative action plan to assure these Democrats full participation in the delegate-selecting process. Meany's political chief, Alexander Barkan, proclaimed that the AFL-CIO would go its own way.[9]

John Hennings, president of the California federation, warned: "Union labor will no longer suffer sophisticated discrimination in the highest councils of the Democratic Party. We say to Mr. Strauss and we hope he is listening: he stands with us or this party will go down to division and ruin in the election of 1976." Strauss reassured labor of its key role in the party, at the same time proclaiming that "we have institutionalized due process. . . . Together we have brought the national Democratic Party back to political life."[10] But McGovern stirred the reformers by urging them not to brush differences under the party rug. "To avoid issues is to invite disaster," he said. ". . . We cannot be bland in what we say and blind to the evils before us. If we are, we will be united but defeated; we will be in the center, but a dead center." It was a proposition that would be directly challenged in the party in the future.[11]

In any event, the mini-convention provided a showcase for the horde of presidential aspirants who came to Kansas City. Among them was the one-term governor of Georgia, James Earl Carter Jr., who preferred the familiar Jimmy, with a country-boy manner to match. Not yet a declared candidate, he courted delegations from important presidential primary states like New Hampshire, inviting them to his small room in the local Holiday Inn for private, soft-spoken but sincere chats. After the scourge of Watergate, contrary to McGovern's warning, he offered himself as a centrist, and as an outsider to the political evils of Washington and a pious straight shooter to boot. The first impression he left with many was of a strange if serious dreamer with an open heart if not an open purse in the traditional New Deal fashion.

Others who attended, or entered the early competition for the Democratic nomination, included a liberal contingent of Sanford, Senator Birch Bayh of Indiana, 1972 vice-presidential nominee Sargent Shriver, Governor Milton J. Shapp of Pennsylvania, and former senator and party chairman Fred Harris. Joining Carter as candidates of the center were Senators Henry Jackson of Washington State and Lloyd Bentsen of Texas, and on the right, now in a wheelchair, was George Wallace.

The mini-convention forum continued to leave a bad taste in the mouths of labor leaders. In February 1975, Meany declared the AFL-CIO's independence from the Democratic Party in terms of presidential candidate selection, saying it was "not the business of the AFL-CIO." The federation would await the result of the nominating process, he said, before throwing its weight into the fray. In congressional races, he said, the AFL-

CIO's political arm would "try to elect labor's friends to the House and to the Senate and to the state legislatures, irrespective of political parties."[12]

By this time, Carter had already embarked on his active bid for the Democratic presidential nomination. In late February, now a former governor, he and aide Jody Powell drove to Le Mars, Iowa, just north of Sioux City, for a testimonial dinner for the Plymouth County recorder, Marie Jahn, the only Democratic event to which he had been invited at the time. "I think they may have asked a couple of other people first," Powell said later.[13] From the start, Carter and his chief strategist, fellow Georgian Hamilton Jordan, had eyed Iowa, the first state that would hold a process for the selection of national convention delegates, as a foothold for his candidacy.

Although the New Hampshire primary was better known as the kick-off event in delegate selection, the process actually began every four years in Iowa at precinct caucuses across the state. Local Democrats met on an early Monday night of the election year, discussed the candidates and then physically gathered in groups according to presidential preference and voted. In this way, precinct Democrats elected delegates to the county and state levels in support of preferred candidates, with delegates to the party's national convention eventually chosen. By dint of sheer hard work and organization over a year's time, while other candidates were just beginning to evaluate the political landscape and focusing on New Hampshire, Carter zeroed in on Iowa.

With a young organizer named Tim Kraft moving into the state, and Carter paying repeated visits to its byways, the little-known Georgian pulled a modest surprise in late summer by finishing first in a straw poll of 5,762 attendees at practice precinct caucuses. He won a mere 9.9 percent of the votes, which was more than runner-up Sargent Shriver pulled, but far behind the 34 percent who said they were uncommitted. Nevertheless, it was an indication to those relatively few political observers watching that this fellow Carter could not be ignored. In late October he scored a breakthrough at the state party's annual Jefferson-Jackson dinner at Iowa State University in Ames to which all the prospective presidential candidates were invited. With Kraft packing the hall, Carter again ran first, this time with 23 percent of 1,094 attendees. Tickets for the event were $50 a couple but seats in the balcony went for $2, and a Kraft memo to Carter backers informed them that the two bucks "gets you everything but the chicken dinner." The memo further advised that "one could probably drift down from the balcony onto the floor and vote" in the straw poll.[14] Once again "uncommitted" led the voting, but Carter headed the active field and the next day newspapers across the country reported him as the surprise victor. Bayh, Harris and Udall were put down as also-rans. Udall, focusing on New Hampshire, made hardly any effort in Iowa.

By the time of the real Iowa precinct caucuses in mid-January 1976, Carter had logged in 260 days on the road, many of them in Iowa. And he made a point of taking his time with voters, responding to their concerns at length, often asking them, "Have I answered your question?"[15] In the wake of Watergate, he sold his own goodness, promising, "I will never lie to you" and "a government as good and kind and honest and decent, and as filled with love, as are the American people."[16]

On the night of January 19, in 2,530 precincts across Iowa, the Carter magic worked again. About 37 percent of the delegate vote was cast either as undecideds or for minor candidates, but Carter again was the top vote-getter, with 27.6 percent, more than twice the vote of the runner-up, Bayh. Once more the story went out across the nation's news wires: long-shot Jimmy Carter was a winner.

The next major stop was New Hampshire's first-in-the-nation primary and the first political event that really pulled out all elements of the news media, not just the political junkies who had trekked early to and around Iowa. No candidate up to this time had ever won the presidency without winning the New Hampshire primary in one party or the other. Once again Carter benefited from the head of steam he had built in Iowa, and from the fact that as a moderate he was running against a field largely made up of liberals. Since January planeloads of Georgians had flooded the state preaching in Southern drawl the gospel of their homegrown saint, "Jimmeh." Other candidates shipped workers in, but none could outdo the Carter organization, or the candidate himself, in enthusiasm and diligence. He won 30 percent of the Democratic vote and 13 convention delegates to 24 percent and 4 delegates for Udall, with the others far behind.

In Massachusetts, Scoop Jackson, who had skipped Iowa and New Hampshire, hoped to ambush Carter there, and Wallace sought to tap into racial unrest in Boston. Both succeeded to a degree, with Jackson winning the primary, but with only 23 percent of the vote. Udall was second with 18, Wallace third with 17 and Carter trailing with 14. Jackson, with a well-financed effort, cut into Carter's centrist vote and Udall into liberal support. But by now the focus was on the approaching Florida primary, which would test Carter in his own region against Wallace. His victory over the feisty Alabamian, by 34 percent to 31, with Jackson third at 24, deflated both Wallace and Jackson. In a showdown between Carter and Udall in liberal Wisconsin, a crippled Harris debated dropping out, leaving the liberal vote to Udall in that liberal state. But in the end he made one last try there and possibly cost Udall his only victory of the campaign. Carter beat Udall by only 7,449 votes out of 740,528 cast, with Harris drawing 8,185, enough to have made Udall the winner.

Jackson, who now needed an impressive victory in New York, where he diligently courted the Jewish vote, won but not strongly enough to derail Carter, who beat him in Pennsylvania by twelve percentage points and captured the bulk of delegates committed to a candidate. Carter seemed to have a clear field to the nomination until two other Democrats, Governor Edmund G. "Jerry" Brown Jr. of California and Senator Frank Church of Idaho, jumped into the race. Concern was growing in the party that it had made a major mistake in putting an unknown on the verge of its biggest prize. The concern even tempted Hubert Humphrey to join the chase, but in the end he declined.

For Church and Brown, it was a question of one candidate too many and too late. Between them, they won eight of the remaining eleven contested primaries with Carter, but neither one emerged strong enough against an early-running candidate who in the end won eighteen of the thirty primaries he entered. In the process, Carter managed by running nearly everywhere to post at least one victory on every primary day, countering the publicity given to the Church and Brown victories.

On the final primary date, Brown won his home state and New Jersey, but Carter came back in Ohio by drubbing Udall and Church there, benefiting also from a statement by Mayor Daley prior to that vote affirming Carter's right to the nomination. "This man, Carter," he said, "has fought in every primary, and if he wins in Ohio, he'll walk in under his own power."[17] In a party that had expended so much time and energy adopting reforms to enhance democracy in its own practices, Daley's argument was quite persuasive, if not politically comforting about the fall outcome. Many fellow Democrats saw in Carter a weak candidate who might well give away the party's golden chance to regain power in the first post-Watergate election.

Prior to the convention Carter, having learned from the sorry experience of McGovern's 1972 selection of Eagleton as his running mate, conducted an open and deliberative exploration of the best choice. After having aide Jordan rate the likeliest prospects, Carter interviewed seven men—Senators Muskie, Mondale, Jackson, Church, John Glenn and Adlai Stevenson III, and House Judiciary Committee chairman Peter Rodino. He settled on Mondale, a man with the Washington experience Carter lacked, who arrived at the interview with impressive questions about how Carter's vice president should and would be used. The Carter process for making the most important decision in the hands of a presidential nominee provided a blueprint of how an intelligent choice should be made— one sometimes but not always followed thereafter. Carter's first-ballot nomination at the party convention in New York was routine, with Udall releasing his delegates and Brown announcing that all of California's delegates would go to Carter. Strauss's efforts to bring unity to a contentious party were finally realized.

In mid-August in Kansas City, President Ford, plagued all spring and into the summer by a challenge from former Governor Ronald Reagan of California, finally beat it back and was nominated for a term in his own right on the first Republican ballot. After an erratic start over the party primary course, Reagan had recovered and by convention time had enough delegate support to threaten Ford if some of the latter's support could be shaken loose. But Reagan campaign efforts to pry them away fell short and Ford chose Senator Bob Dole of Kansas as his running mate.

As Carter had done all year, he continued in the fall to campaign as a Washington outsider, keeping his national campaign operation in Atlanta. Ford, for his part, was advised by candid strategists that because he was not the most forceful or effective candidate on the stump, it would be best for him to stay off the campaign trail until closer to the election. He would be better served, they told him, by occupying himself with presidential duties that would show him to best advantage. In this first presidential campaign to be conducted under post-Watergate campaign finance law, providing a federal subsidy to each major party nominee provided he eschewed fund-raising, both candidates would be spared the burden of soliciting money.

Ford as the incumbent was not supposed to give a little-known opponent equal billing in debate. But he was well aware that, as an unelected vice president who had become an unelected president, it was uncertain whether he had a constituency to call his own. More important, having pardoned Nixon and governing during a time of economic distress, Ford was uncomfortably trailing Carter by fifteen percentage points in the Gallup Poll as the fall campaign began. His strategists agreed that he had better risk debates.

Negotiations dragged into September, effectively causing both camps to mark time until the first one on September 23. Carter aides complained, as had McGovern aides before them about Nixon, that Ford adopting a Rose Garden strategy gave him as the incumbent an unfair advantage, inhibiting news media criticism and interchange with the candidate that occurred more easily on the campaign trail. Each candidate had a public impression to protect or change. Ford's was that he was a lightweight; Lyndon Johnson had once questioned whether he could "walk and chew gum at the same time." With Carter it was his extravagant righteousness and piety, reflected in his promise never to lie, coupled with a talent for evasive or exaggerated claims. In short order, both impressions would become campaign fodder.

Carter's was the first to undergo public scrutiny. In an interview with *Playboy* magazine shortly before the first debate, he was grilled on his religiosity and whether his views on morality might affect his secular decisions as president. In defense, he offered the following: "I try not to commit a deliberate sin. I recognize that I'm going to do it anyhow, because I'm human and I'm tempted. And Christ set some impossible standards for us. Christ said, 'I tell you that anyone who looks on a woman with lust has in his heart already committed adultery.' I've looked at a lot of women with lust. I've committed adultery in my heart many times. This is something that God recognizes I will do—and I have done it—and God forgives me for it. But that doesn't mean I condemn someone who not only looks on a woman with lust but leaves his wife and shacks up with somebody out of wedlock. Christ says don't consider yourself better than someone else because one guy screws a whole bunch of women while the other guy is loyal to his wife."[18]

Carter went on in that vein, concluding with a self-serving comment about how his own religious beliefs would keep him on the straight and narrow in both his private and public life. "But I don't think I would ever take on the same frame of mind that Nixon or Johnson did," he said, "lying, cheating and distorting the truth. Not taking into consideration my hope for strength of character, I think that my religious beliefs alone would prevent that from happening to me. I have that confidence. I hope it's justified."[19]

The interview immediately got many in the religious community howling—and the traveling press corps composing and singing. To the tune of "Heart of My Heart," the first stanza began: "Lust in my heart, how I love adultery; Lust in my heart, that's my theology; When I was young at the Plains First Baptist Church, I would preach and sermonize—but oh, how I would fantasize."[20]

Carter's *Playboy* interview provided ridiculing background chatter for the first of his debates with Ford. The highlight of that one, bizarrely, was a technical breakdown in the sound equipment that left the two presidential nominees standing in silence, saying not a word to each other, for an incredible twenty-seven minutes. In advance of the debate, Carter led Ford in the Gallup poll, 54 percent to 36. Afterward, his lead had shrunk, inexplicably, to 50–42; the *Playboy* interview had not been mentioned once, but by that time it was common knowledge.

Carter, seeking to capitalize on public dismay toward Ford's pardon of Nixon, took to referring to "the Nixon-Ford administration." But a more telling blow to Nixon's handpicked successor came from Ford's own mouth in the second debate, on foreign policy, a field in which Carter had practically no experience. A questioner observed that as a result of an agreement with the Soviet Union signed in Helsinki, "the Russians have dominance in Eastern Europe." Ford pounced, insisting that "there is no Soviet domination of Eastern Europe, and there never will be under a Ford administration." When the unbelieving questioner, Max Frankel of the *New York Times*, gave Ford an opportunity to correct himself, Ford only dug himself a deeper hole, listing the Yugoslavians, Romanians and Poles, all living in satellite states, among those he didn't believe "consider themselves dominated by the Soviet Union."[21] He apparently meant to say they didn't accept domination, but the answer came off as unknowing—reinforcing the image of Ford as a dim bulb.

Ford's strategists immediately recognized they had a problem. The answer was bad enough; the worst part was that it threw the Ford campaign on the defensive and consumed valuable time in damage control as election day approached, especially as the news media chewed over the gaffe. What's more, Ford alluded to it two days later in citing his visit to Poland a year earlier and observing that the Poles "don't believe that they are going to be forever dominated, if they are, by the Soviet Union."[22]

Despite staff urging, Ford would not concede that he had misspoken until five days after the debate.

The Ford campaign's debate woes were not over. In a face-off between the vice-presidential nominees, Bob Dole and Walter Mondale, Dole's apparent bitterness over his old war wounds, and a cavalier attitude toward debate preparation and performance, also brought criticism of the Republican ticket. Moving from light banter to harsh invective, Dole denigrated the Nixon pardon as a campaign issue, saying it wasn't a very good one, "any more than the Vietnam war would be, or World War One or World War Two or the Korean War—all Democrat wars, all in this century." Noting that he carried wounds of the Second World War, he added: "I figured up the other day if we added up all the killed and wounded in Democrat wars in this century, it would be about 1.6 million Americans, enough to fill the city of Detroit."[23]

Mondale leaped in: "I think that Senator Dole has richly earned his reputation as a hatchet man tonight. Does he really mean that there was partisan difference over our involvement in the fight against Nazi Germany?"[24] As Dole continued his flippant manner, the Ford strategists yearned for the debate to end, but their Democratic counterparts rejoiced. Afterward, the Carter camp authored and ran a television ad that pictured Dole and Mondale with a voice-over that said: "What kind of men are they? When you know that four out of the last six vice presidents have wound up as presidents, who would you like to see a heartbeat away from the presidency?"[25]

In the final days, amid a blizzard of negative campaigning on both sides, the Republican consulting team of Doug Bailey and John Deardourff produced a brilliant upbeat commercial featuring a marching band playing the campaign theme song, "I'm Feeling Good About America." It had Ford talking about trust at a rally at his alma mater, the University of Michigan in Ann Arbor. Suddenly a sharp report was heard and Ford was seen ducking, and then resuming his speech. The camera next showed Ford in a motorcade in Dallas as the voice-over said, "When a limousine can parade openly through the streets of Dallas, there's a change that's come over America. The people and their president are back together again."[26] The effect was electrifying—but the ad was never used; it was judged too unsettling, especially for viewing in Texas, which Ford lost, and the election as well.

Narrowly, the Democrats were back in the White House after an eight-year absence. Carter won 50.1 percent of the vote to 47.9 for the incumbent, and 297 electoral votes to 240. Gene McCarthy's quixotic campaign as an independent brought him less than one percent of the vote. The winner could thank several factors: the Nixon pardon, Ford's Eastern Europe mistake in the second debate, Dole's boorish behavior and words in the third, a weak economy during Ford's brief White House tenure. And Carter himself could take credit for offering the voters a clear contrast—not with Ford but with Nixon, after the dark days of Watergate and assorted other crimes. His pledge that "I'll never lie to you" took root in political soil made fertile for such an appeal by the Nixon years. At the same time, his centrist posture on most issues provided a contrast with the liberal, New Deal predecessor candidates of his own party going back to FDR.

Carter took the presidential oath of office in 1977 on a gracious note, thanking Ford "for all he has done to heal our land" and pausing to shake his hand.[27] But almost at once, the new president was plunged into a sea of controversy, a condition from which he never really recovered in a troubled four-year tenure. Along with Carter's personal political woes, the Democratic Party slipped over the next twelve years into a quagmire of lost purpose and lost confidence. Without the old firm allegiance to the New Deal concept of government as an aggressive engine of constructive change, its moorings were steadily being eroded by a new conservatism in the Republican Party. The embers of the Goldwater movement of the 1960s, smoldering in the GOP through the Nixon-Ford years, found oxygen in the emergence of Ronald Reagan as a national figure, as a presidential candidate in 1976 and 1980, and as a popular president through most of the eighties.

But the trouble began with Carter, whose unfamiliarity with Washington and with the affairs of state at home and abroad cast him as an uncertain and indecisive figure from the start of his presidency. He was perceived not only as alien to the nation's capital but also, in many ways, to his own party, with its frayed but still existing New Deal roots and outlook. At the outset he and his wife, Rosalynn, charmed the country by hopping out of their inauguration parade limousine and walking down Pennsylvania Avenue to their new home. With the cost of home heating rising, he took to wearing a sweater in the Oval Office and urging his fellow Americans to do the same in their places of work and at home, rather than turning up their thermostats.

After only three months in office, Carter addressed the nation on television and announced in the starkest terms a new policy to avert "a national catastrophe" of energy shortages. "With the exception of preventing war," he said, "this is the greatest challenge that our country will face during our lifetimes," and called meeting it with conservation measures "the moral equivalent of war."[28] At the same time, with an eye to protecting American oil interests in the Middle East, he urged a resolution of a continuing Arab-Israeli dispute and courted both Saudi Arabia and Iran. In late 1977 he visited Teheran and praised Shah Mohammed Riza Pahlavi for "the admiration and love which your people give to you,"[29] a naïve observation Carter would live to regret.

At home, he pleased women by appointing three to his cabinet and minorities by putting more of them in key federal jobs than any previous president had done. But a reliance on old Georgia friends to staff the White House brought criticism and, sometimes, ridicule. Their unfamiliarity with Washington was illustrated when a leading Japanese-American member of Congress from Carter's own party, Norman Mineta, was not invited to a White House state dinner for the Japanese prime minister because a staff aide assumed from the congressman's name that he was Italian.[30]

Carter got into hot water early with Western congressmen by trying to scuttle pork-barrel water projects in their states, and with key leaders on Capitol Hill by not playing ball to their satisfaction on job appointments. The Senate cooled off his urgent energy proposals, and after sending a host of other legislative initiatives to Capitol Hill, Carter was obliged to slow the pace. "We now know better when the Congress can move rapidly and when they can't," he said.[31]

Liberals like George McGovern openly criticized Carter's conservative economic proposals, including an income tax cut, on grounds they did not address rising unemployment and welfare, energy and tax reform needs. When Carter rejected the complaints as coming from a left fringe of the party, McGovern replied that the critics were "not a handful of liberal malcontents but the mainstream of the Democratic Party. . . . I don't think there's anything very leftish about my position. It's just old-fashioned Democratic philosophy. It's the present administration that's out of step."[32] At the same time, early dabblings in foreign policy were unimpressive. Arms-limitation treaty talks with the Soviet Union begun by Ford became stalled even as Carter was claiming that the United States was at last free of "inordinate fear of communism."[33]

Carter's second year was no better, as the economy struggled under climbing inflation and interest rates. In his State of the Union address, he conspicuously rejected the New Deal philosophy of bigger and more benevolent government as the costs of entitlement programs like social security and Medicare, indexed for inflation, dominated and busted the federal budget. "Government cannot solve our problems," he said, in what sounded to his own party's liberals like Republican rhetoric, and a pointed repudiation of the very core of the New Deal. "It can't set our goals. It cannot define our vision. Government cannot eliminate poverty or provide a bountiful economy or reduce inflation, or save our cities, or cure illiteracy, or provide energy. And government cannot mandate goodness. . . . Those of us who govern can sometimes inspire. And we can identify needs and marshal resources. But we simply cannot be the managers of everything and everybody."[34]

An America that had been accustomed to seeing its standard of living rise with each new generation seemed to be in a stall, and Carter bore the political brunt of it. Repeated staff mixups were laid to a president inexperienced in the ways of Washington, along with his own disinclination to feed domestic political considerations into decision-making as well as what he rigidly believed was the right course.

For all that, Carter, by sheer grit, determination and unexpected diplomatic skill, achieved in September 1978 a remarkable breakthrough in the long impasse between Israel and Egypt, bringing their leaders together at Camp David. For two weeks, Carter held Israeli Prime Minister Menachem Begin and Egyptian President Anwar el-Sadat virtual house prisoners as he pressured them to sign an agreement known as the Camp David Accords. In March 1979 a peace treaty was signed after thirty years of intermittent war. Israel agreed to return the Sinai Peninsula to Egypt and eventually to permit Palestinian autonomy in the West Bank and the Gaza Strip.

Carter had other successes over the first two years, some of them controversial. He signed the treaties turning over the Panama Canal to Panama, worked toward normalizing relations with China and put a human rights stamp on his policies toward Central America, plagued by revolutionary movements. But at home his image as hesitant and indecisive in the face of mushrooming economic woes was symbolized in the public mind with ever-lengthening lines at the nation's gasoline pumps. In the off-year congressional elections, the Democratic Party lost twelve seats in the House and three in the Senate.

All this fueled extensive mutterings of I-told-you-so among old New Dealers who abhorred Carter's lack of passion for the old party commitment to government as an engine of progressive, imaginative change. Many still yearned for a return, if not to the days of FDR and Truman, at least to Camelot, through Ted Kennedy. The polls reflected a general agreement among voters. In a Harris survey in September 1978, Kennedy led Carter by 40 percent to 21. From time to time, the heir to the legend would tantalize his faithful with criticisms of Carter, on one occasion accusing him of "a failure of leadership" for not pushing for broad national health insurance.

At the party's mini-convention in Memphis in December, Kennedy delivered a stem-winding pitch for a national program and an end to social welfare cuts made under Carter, and he seldom passed other opportunities to be critical. Yet whenever prodded about challenging him, Kennedy would give his "E, E and I" answer—that he expected Carter to be renominated, that he expected he'd be reelected, and that he intended to support him.[35] Carter himself told a news conference his differences with Kennedy were "minor" on how to achieve "the same ultimate goals," and that "I don't consider there is a schism, a growing schism in the Democratic Party at all."[36]

Nevertheless, in early 1979 key Kennedy advisers—a mixture of kin and old family friends—began to meet at his home in northern Virginia for private assessments of the political terrain. Notably, insiders said later, the discussions always focused on whether to run, not on how to do it—a distinction that was to have pertinence later. Separately, draft-Kennedy groups got active in New Hampshire, Iowa and Ohio. In April 1979, when Carter proposed a modest windfall profits tax on oil, Kennedy attacked it as "a transparent fig leaf over the vast new profits the industry will reap." Carter's response was a weak "that's a lot of baloney."[37] Still, Kennedy kept his own counsel while continuing to take soundings with his inner circle.

The president and his wife, after attending an international economic conference in Tokyo and a stopover in Seoul in June, were planning a rest stop of a few days in Hawaii. His chief political advisers, Jordan and Powell, sensitive to how pictures of a president vacationing under the palms would play back home to average Americans sweating out the long gas lines, persuaded him to cut his vacation short and return to Washington. In early July it was announced that Carter would shortly make a major televised speech to the nation on energy. The day before the speech was due, however, Carter reviewed a draft at Camp David, was not satisfied with it and decided the situation called for a much broader assessment of where the country stood under his watch, and where he wanted to take it. The networks were notified that the speech would be postponed.

The delay caused considerable public and press consternation. It grew as the president over the next days, stretching beyond a week, invited what amounted to a parade of unofficial advisers and kibitzers to Camp David, summoned to give their suggestions on what needed to be said and done. "Once you got into sort of having people up," Powell said later, "you can't make an arbitrary decision. You've got to think about who you're leaving out."[38] Before the farce was over, nearly 150 assorted politicians, economists, labor leaders, businessmen and others had been flown up to the mountainside cabin.

Some said a consensus emerged that Carter had to make himself better understood to the public. Veteran Washington wise man Clark Clifford, for one, said of Carter: "I think he believes, as I do, that he's not getting across to people."[39] In other words, the problem was not the substance, but the communication of it. But, the country seemed to be asking, what is the substance? One thing did come out of the episode: widespread ridicule in the press and an augmented picture of a president who didn't know where he was going.

When Carter finally returned to Washington and delivered the speech, it was an embarrassing mea culpa in which he quoted actual criticisms of some of his visitors, admitted mistakes, offered the outlines of an energy policy and, finally, blamed the American people. He spoke of "a crisis of confidence . . . that strikes at the very heart and soul and spirit of our national will." The message came to be known as "the malaise speech," although Carter did not use that word. Subsequently, he pledged to "come to you throughout America with fresh proposals. Some will involve the traditional government, some will not. Above all, I will defend our common national purpose against those narrow special interests who often forget the overriding needs of America."[40]

After a brief rise in the Gallup poll, however, and a wholesale call for cabinet-level resignations meant to signal a fresh start, Carter found himself back in the same hole again. The Camp David extravaganza was widely seen as no more than a failed public relations effort, serving to bring more attention to Carter's own political malaise.

Among those who saw and were deeply disturbed was Ted Kennedy. In an interview later, Kennedy said: "I thought his assessment of the country, its spirit, its direction, its ability to cope with the problems of our time, whether it was the economy or energy or foreign policy, just ran so contrary to everything I believe in and that I was brought up to believe in, that it added impetus to the thinking I was giving [to running] at that time."[41]

Through the fall, the inner circle discussions continued, with Kennedy himself finally agreeing to announce his candidacy in early November. At the time, the Gallup poll was showing Carter's public approval collapsing to 29 percent and Kennedy leading him by two to one for the Democratic nomination.

Three nights before the senator was to make his declaration, CBS News broadcast a one-hour television documentary written and narrated by Roger Mudd. It included two lengthy interviews with Kennedy, touching on all major controversies surrounding him, including the Chappaquiddick tragedy. For Kennedy, the show was a disaster, but not so much because of his evasive and repetitive answers to questions about that and other matters of a personal nature. Rather, it was a rambling, inarticulate response to Mudd's simple inquiry: "Why do you want to be president?"[42] What it suggested more than anything else was that Kennedy had been so focused on the question of whether to run that he never addressed what it was he wanted to do if elected. Certainly a man in public life so long, and so effective in advancing liberal legislation, had solid motivations for running, but he simply was unable to express them clearly and effectively. Staff aides later conceded that the interview probably undermined confidence in Kennedy among an indeterminate number of voters—and many more who read scathingly negative "reviews" about it in the press afterward.

Hamilton Jordan, in his later book, *Crisis: The Last Year of the Carter Presidency,* wrote of Kennedy's answer to the question of why he wanted to be president: "He started out, in a halting, rambling, almost incoherent way, to mouth a series of clichés and half sentences. Senator Kennedy did not have an answer. . . . He was running because he wanted to be President. That was not such an unusual motive, but most aspirants figure out a way to disguise it better."[43]

In any event, the television show and interview provided an unfortunate backdrop for Kennedy's formal announcement of candidacy in

Boston on November 7, in which he more effectively said he would work "to release the native energy of the people" that Carter had failed to tap. "The only thing that paralyzes us today," he said in a thinly veiled reference to Carter's malaise speech, "is the myth that we cannot move. If Americans are pessimistic, it is because they are also realistic. They have made a fair judgment on how government is doing—and they are demanding something better."[44]

Kennedy's press secretary at the time, Tom Southwick, later said Mudd's interview was probably "the most important" element in Kennedy's ultimate failure to wrest the Democratic nomination from Carter, with one exception.[45] That was an event that occurred half a world away on the same day the Mudd interview was broadcast, when a mob stormed the American embassy in Teheran and seized more than sixty Americans as hostage, eventually holding fifty. Carter suddenly found himself to be the functional equivalent of a wartime president, with all the obligations—and patriotic support of his countrymen—entailed in a war.

In January 1979, the shah of Iran, said by Carter earlier to have "the admiration and love" of his people, had been forced to flee his country when it was taken over by a radical Islamic regime led by the fanatical Ayatollah Ruhollah Khomeini. Taking temporary refuge in Egypt, Morocco and finally Mexico, the shah had sought admission into the United States, a prospect that split Carter's chief foreign policy advisers. Zbigniew Brzezinski, the president's national security adviser, had favored admitting him; Secretary of State Cyrus Vance wanted to bar him and focus on getting along with the new regime. In late October, with the shah ailing, Carter had reluctantly agreed to admit him for emergency treatment of cancer and gallstones—a move that a week later triggered the seizure of the American embassy and the taking of American hostages.

That night, it so happened that the Democrats in Iowa were again holding the annual Jefferson-Jackson dinner at which Carter four years earlier had made his dramatic breakthrough by running first in its straw poll. This time around, as the incumbent president he was considered a shoo-in, with the only interest the question of how much support Kennedy, on the verge of declaring his candidacy, would receive. After all, he led the president in the national polls, Iowa had a progressive Democratic Party, and key labor leaders were behind a draft-Kennedy effort. The senator himself did not attend but Ethel Kennedy and her eldest son, Joe, did. Carter won 70.6 percent of the straw vote to only 26 percent for

Kennedy and less than one percent for Jerry Brown, the only other Democrat on the ballot.

Domestic politics was shunted to a back burner by the Iranian crisis—and with it any active campaign by Carter in the Iowa caucuses. Hoping to resolve the crisis quickly, the president left the campaign trail to Kennedy, who was unable to take full advantage as he encountered the usual growing pains of a presidential run amid unusually high expectations. At the same time, Americans rallied around the president. An AP-NBC News poll indicated seven of ten Americans believed he was doing all he could to extricate the hostages, and that he should not force the shah to go back to Iran. In late November a Harris survey showed Carter moving ahead of Kennedy, 48 percent to 46, for the first time. Kennedy blundered by publicly criticizing the shah; while accurately talking of "the repressive dictatorship of the shah," he left himself open to the accusation of jeopardizing the lives of the American hostages and, for political gain, undercutting Carter's efforts to free them.[46]

Prior to the hostage-taking, a debate in Iowa among Carter, Kennedy and Brown, who had begun stumping in the state, had been arranged by the *Des Moines Register and Tribune.* But now Carter notified the paper that the crisis would prevent him from participating. The Kennedy and Brown campaigns complained loudly, but there was nothing they could do when the president painted his withdrawal in terms of the national interest. Thus was born Carter's "Rose Garden strategy" that enabled him to "campaign" from the White House with all the trappings of power and nonpolitical national purpose.

The insulation of the presidency proved to be so effective that even when Carter ordered an embargo on American shipments of grain to the Soviet Union in response to its military effort in Afghanistan, it did him no harm in agricultural Iowa. When Kennedy criticized the embargo, Vice President Mondale flew into Des Moines and said Kennedy had to make up his mind "whether to do the political thing or the thing that best serves this nation."[47] A furious Kennedy reminded him of his family's service to the country, including the loss of three brothers, and said he didn't need a lecture on patriotism from anyone. But Mondale's remark alerted Kennedy to the political peril of criticizing Carter during the crisis. On caucus night in Iowa, the president trounced Kennedy, 59 percent to 31, but the senator decided to press on, in the approaching New Hampshire primary in his native New England.

Having so decided, Kennedy realized he would have to confront Carter and risk the fallout. In a major speech at Georgetown University, he defended the right and imperative to criticize a president in time of crisis. "If the Vietnam war taught us anything," he said, "it is precisely that when we do not debate our foreign policy, we may drift into further trouble. . . . The silence that has descended across foreign policy has also stifled the debate on other essential issues. The political process has been held hostage here at home as surely as our diplomats abroad."[48] And at Harvard he declared that "no president should be reelected because he happened to be standing there when his foreign policy collapsed around him."[49]

Kennedy's efforts to force Carter out of his Rose Garden strategy got nowhere. The president responded by charging that his opponent's remarks were "very damaging to our country . . . and to the achievement of our goals to keep the peace and get our hostages released."[50] The fires of patriotism continued to burn bright at home, a reality demonstrated in the public frenzy that accompanied the upset victory of the American Olympic hockey team over the Soviet Union and its subsequent capture of the gold medal at Lake Placid, New York. On the eve of the New Hampshire primary, Carter entertained the winners at the White House amid much fanfare, and the next day Carter defeated Kennedy soundly, 49 percent to 38, in his own New England backyard.

Carter primary victories in states across the South and in Illinois put Kennedy on the ropes. He made a mild comeback with victories in New York and Connecticut but lost in Kansas and Wisconsin—the Wisconsin result possibly helped by an early-morning Carter statement from the Oval Office of a possible breakthrough in the hostage crisis that never materialized. As the crisis dragged on, it appeared that Kennedy would never get Carter out of the Rose Garden.

But Carter's patience with the hostage impasse had worn thin. In late April he decided to go ahead with a Pentagon plan to extricate the hostages in a daring helicopter raid on Teheran. It ended in disaster in the Iranian desert, with one helicopter colliding on the ground with a transport plane that was part of the mission, causing a fire that killed eight men and burned four others. Carter accepted the blame and, once again, the American people rallied around their president—no doubt to Kennedy's further frustration.

Kennedy managed to edge Carter in the Pennsylvania primary and in caucuses in Michigan, and the president finally had to abandon his Rose Garden strategy as Kennedy developed into the formidable candidate his liberal supporters had yearned for. In the final eight primaries on June 3, he won five, but Carter accumulated enough delegates to claim the nomination. A gambit by the Kennedy camp to "open" the party's national convention in New York, aimed at freeing Carter delegates from their previous commitments to him, fizzled. But Kennedy stirred the hall with a call on his liberal followers to persist, in itself an indictment of centrist Carter: "For all those whose cares have been our concern, the work goes on, the cause endures, the hope still lives, and the dream shall never die."[51]

The president was renominated on the first ballot, as was Mondale, but there was one final humiliation for Carter. At the convention's close, with all of the party's leading lights assembled on the platform with the president, Kennedy made a conspicuously late appearance, and Carter was obliged to chase him around the stage for the ceremonial raised hands. It seemed another signal to liberals to abandon Carter in the general election.

By now that task seemed almost insurmountable. The Republicans culminated a heavily contested primary season by nominating former California Governor Reagan in Detroit. After a shaky start in losing the Iowa caucuses to jack-of-all-political-trades George Bush, Reagan recovered in subsequent primaries and swept to first-ballot selection, with Bush as his running mate after a farcical flirtation with former President Ford to be on the ticket with him. Reagan, no longer dismissed as a joke as a former grade-B movie actor, led Carter in trial runs by as much as twenty-five percentage points.

The Democratic nominee, wounded by a dismal economy, the long lines at the gas pumps, inflation in double figures and the unresolved hostage crisis, also had been damaged by Kennedy in the primaries, as he demonstrated how alien Carter had become to liberal orthodoxy. An independent candidacy by Republican Congressman John B. Anderson of Illinois was a wild card in the equation, his presence denying Carter a clean shot at the conservative Reagan. Carter badly wanted to debate Reagan but declined to take part in a three-way debate. That was fine with the Reagan camp, with its man leading so comfortably in the polls. Reagan did, however, agree to face Anderson alone. It was an indecisive affair but was generally judged to be a plus for Reagan simply by showing he could handle himself in such a confrontation. Also, Anderson began dropping in the polls, diminishing the rationale for including him in further debates.

Carter as a campaigner ignored Anderson and focused on Reagan, playing transparently on the Democratic-encouraged public concern that Reagan, like Goldwater before him on the right, was an uninformed loose cannon not to be trusted with his finger on the nuclear button. Carter in stump speeches cast the election in terms of "whether we will have peace or war."[52] In one Los Angeles television interview he observed that Reagan had a "repeated habit" of advocating the use of force "to address problems that arise diplomatically between nations. I don't know what he would do if he were in the Oval Office."[53]

Reagan's answer was that "every time you talk about national security and restoring the margin of safety that for 30 years after World War II this country had, there are those who say that's warlike, that this is the fellow who wants to take us into war. I think to accuse that anyone would deliberately want a war is beneath decency."[54] When Carter began to draw press criticism for the harshness of his remarks, he backed off to the degree of saying, "I'm not accusing Reagan of wanting a war. But I do know that in a troubled world, on the closest margins of decision, there is the option of the use of weapons or the commitment to try to resolve a dispute peacefully. That is a judgment the American people will have to make."[55]

There were other Carter observations as well that the Reagan camp complained implied racism on their man's part. Reagan the old actor effectively played the role of the unjustly injured party, while for the first time questioning why the hostages in Iran had been left in captivity for nearly a year.

The polls were beginning to tighten now, and in mid-October both sides finally agreed to a debate, one on one. It took place in Cleveland on October 28 and came down to a series of prepared rhetorical questions posed by Reagan in his summation that focused the election squarely on Carter's stewardship in the White House. He asked the audience: "Are you better off than you were four years ago? Is it easier for you to go and buy things in the stores than it was four years ago? Is there more or less unemployment in the country than there was four years ago? Is America as respected throughout the world as it was? Do you feel that our security is as safe, that we're as strong as we were four years ago?"[56]

That was the election right there. The only remaining concern in the

Reagan camp was that Carter might spring an "October Surprise" by arranging a release of the hostages before election day, but it never happened. Reagan was elected by a landslide, 50.9 percent to 41.2 percent for Carter and 7.9 percent for Anderson, with Reagan winning 489 electoral votes to only 49 for the Democratic incumbent. The result ushered in what soon became known as the Reagan Revolution—a new era of conservatism during which the demonization of Democratic liberalism, begun by Nixon, was resumed and reached new depths in the hands of ideological opposites.

Chapter 29

BUCKING THE REAGAN REVOLUTION,
1981–1984

TO DEMOCRATS WHO had resisted the siren song of Ronald Reagan (many had not), his inauguration in January 1981 was a particularly bitter one. Their defeated nominee, now former President Jimmy Carter, was obliged to sit quietly on the inaugural platform, for the first time facing west down the Mall toward the Washington Monument, to witness the oath-taking of his Republican successor. More dismaying, Carter had to sit there even as the first news came that the American hostages whose release he had sought for 444 days were at this very hour being given their freedom. By design or not, it seemed a final humiliation, tempered only by his relief that they would no longer be in bondage.

In another sense, however, Carter may have been the least distressed of Democrats by what Reagan said to the country as he took office. In an echo of Carter's 1978 State of the Union observation that "government cannot solve our problems," the new Republican president proclaimed: "Government is not the solution to our problem. Government is the problem."[1] The words ushered in an era of retrenchment in the role of government as an agent of change that had been the hallmark of the New Deal from its birth under FDR, slowed perhaps by Carter but not abandoned.

What came to be called Reaganomics started with the doctrinaire conservative Californian's cockeyed idea that taxes could be cut deeply and defense spending boosted sharply while achieving a balanced budget. In the 1980 Republican primaries, rival George Bush had rightly ridiculed

"LET'S FACE IT, FRITZ...YOU'RE NO HARRY TRUMAN AND I'M NO LAUREN BACALL!"

In 1984, Democratic presidential nominee Walter Mondale, running well behind Republican President Ronald Reagan, gambled with the selection of little-known Congresswoman Geraldine Ferraro as his running mate and lost badly. This cartoon is a play on a famous photo of Harry Truman playing the piano for actress Lauren Bacall.

the idea as "voodoo economics,"[2] a phrase he first denied having uttered and then disowned when Reagan reluctantly chose him as his running mate. Reaganomics produced record deficits that Reagan's advisers then cited to justify sharp cutbacks in social welfare programs, in effect tearing a large hole in the social "safety net" for the poor that had been a staple of the New Deal philosophy. Reagan pledged to maintain such a net for "the truly needy,"[3] setting off a loud debate with Democrats over what constituted true need.

George Gilder, a conservative economics theoretician who became an influential voice in the Reagan ranks, suggested that hardship would be an effective catalyst in driving the working poor to keep themselves above water. "In order to succeed," he wrote, "the poor need most of all the spur of their poverty."[4] Reagan himself, however, never spoke in such harsh terms. Rather, he spread a veneer of good cheer and good will over policies that hit hardest at the working poor, cutting back on such government largesse as food stamps, school lunches and job training for the unemployed.[5] Under Reaganomics, many federal programs were subjected to means tests—a demonstrable proof that recipients were "truly needy." At the same time, Reagan policy pushed for deregulation by the federal government in a range of areas, from food and highway safety to use of public land for private exploitation, to the dismay of the environmental community.[6]

In foreign policy, Reagan also challenged, rhetorically at least, the long-standing Democratic posture of containment along with accommodation where possible toward the Soviet Union. He cast the competition in the starkest terms of good against evil. He called the communist regime in Moscow "the evil empire" and "the focus of evil in the modern world."[7] He used this moralistic outlook to justify the largest peacetime military buildup in the nation's history, including expanding the nuclear arsenal, claiming the United States through Democratic neglect had fallen behind the Soviet Union in military preparedness. He supported arming right-wing exiles, called Contras, against the leftist Sandinista regime in Nicaragua and invaded tiny Grenada in the Caribbean. To cap it all off, in early 1983 he called for development of a program of missile defense in space, immediately derided by opponents, including many in the Democratic Party, as "Star Wars."

All this awakened the Democratic faithful to the earthshaking change that this happy-go-lucky former movie star had brought to Washington, and the depth of the challenge he posed to old Democratic ideals and policies. Although Reagan's victory was in considerable part the electorate's rejection of Carter, the new president's personal style brought him popularity and support on his own, and both shot up with a failed assassination attempt against him barely two months after he had taken office. A young man named John Hinckley, later ruled to have been insane at the time, fired a bullet to within an inch of Reagan's heart. Immediate surgery saved his life. Conscious on admittance to the hospital, he said to his surgeons, "I hope all you fellas are Republicans," further adding to his reputation for good humor.[8]

Congress quickly passed Reagan's budget, which for all his rhetoric about balanced budgets was $37.6 billion in deficit. Democrats in Congress soon learned that what Reagan said and what he did often were two different things, but making voters care about it was another matter. Congress also passed a $25 billion tax cut over three years, the largest in history, with enough Democratic support to carry it, coaxed by a Reagan pledge not to campaign in 1982 against Democrats who voted for it.

Yet Democrats saw signs of hope for the party as Reagan's first year in the Oval Office ended. The federal deficit was climbing and unemployment reached 8.9 percent. Reagan's approval rate in the Gallup poll dipped to 49 percent from 68 percent in the previous May, upon his recovery from the shooting. By May 1982 the jobless rate was 9.5 percent, the highest in forty years. The congressional Democrats, who had rolled over for his first budget, refused to do so for his second unbalanced one.

At the same time, stories abounded about how Reagan's cuts in social welfare programs were punishing the poor. The Census Bureau reported in July that 14 percent of American families were living in poverty, the highest in fifteen years. In October, with the off-year congressional elections around the corner, the jobless rate reached 10.1 percent.

In foreign policy, no progress had been made on nuclear arms control and relations with the Soviet Union were growing colder. The president, campaigning for fellow Republicans, urged voters to "stay the course" and assured them the country was "recovery-bound." He called on them to "vote your hopes," but in his terms many didn't.[9] The Republicans kept their 54–46 majority in the Senate but lost twenty-six House seats to the Democrats, enough to break Reagan's working majority there of Republicans and Southern "boll weevil" Democrats who had delivered for him in his first year. The Democrats also picked up eight governorships, fanning their own hopes to terminate the Reagan Revolution in 1984.

These results, and one other development, led to a bumper crop of Democratic presidential hopefuls willing to be the vehicle for that undertaking. The other development was an announcement by Ted Kennedy a month after the off-year elections that an "overriding obligation" to his three children and the rest of the Kennedy family brood had persuaded him not to make another try for the White House in 1984.[10] The decision was met with disappointment by many liberals but with a sense of relief by other Democrats who feared Kennedy's liberalism, and his baggage—the Chappaquiddick incident of nearly fifteen years before—would bring him and the party defeat.

With Kennedy taking himself out of the running, former Vice President Mondale became the immediate front-runner. He seemed advantageously positioned as an effective vice president given more responsibilities than previous holders of the office, with support beyond the Carter circle to the party's liberal core, and with organized labor. Indeed, his strategists set about casting Mondale's nomination as inevitable. Others who indicated their availability included Governor Reubin Askew of Florida and four senators: former astronaut John Glenn of Ohio, Alan Cranston of California, Fritz Hollings of South Carolina and Gary Hart of Colorado, who had used his job as McGovern's campaign manager in 1972 as a launching pad to election to the Senate.

Once again the party created a commission to review and make adjustments in the delegate-selection rules. This time it was chaired by Governor James B. Hunt Jr. of North Carolina, a representative of the moderate New South in Democratic politics. With many party regulars still not satisfied with their role at the national convention, the Hunt Commission created for the first time a class of "super-delegates." They would be officeholders and party officials who would not have to be elected and would remain uncommitted until the convention. Then they would function as political wise men to confirm the choice of primary voters if it was deemed a satisfactory one, or to weigh in against it if that choice, in their judgment, was leading the party to defeat in the fall. More than one proponent of the super-delegate scheme may have had Jimmy Carter retrospectively in mind.

Giving these party leaders this special role obviously was seen as advantageous to the most prominent and best-known candidates. So were other commission changes increasing the threshold of votes a candidate had to acquire to receive a share of delegates to the national convention from a state or congressional district. Finally, the commission recommended creation of a thirteen-week "window" from late winter to spring in which all delegate-selecting primaries and caucuses would have to be held. Exceptions were given to Iowa's precinct caucuses and New Hampshire's primary to hold their events prior to the window, to preserve their traditional roles as the kickoff events of the process.

The idea behind all this was to compress the nomination period and produce the party standard-bearer as early as possible, to reduce intraparty friction and provide more time for the prospective nominee, in advance of the confirming nomination, to gear up for the general election. Once again, the move was seen as most likely to benefit veteran, well-known Democrats. In practical terms, creation of the window was an inducement for states to move their delegate-selecting events forward on the calendar, to assure that their voices would count in the choice of the nominee. Such "front-loading" was an immediate product of this commission decision.

In a practical sense, however, the campaigns were going to be just as long. To qualify for the federal subsidy available under the post-Watergate campaign finance laws, candidates had to demonstrate a minimum fundraising ability of their own in the twelve months prior to the presidential election year. This provision obliged prospective candidates to hit the campaign trail well in advance of the election year. In early February 1983, Cranston announced his candidacy and the others followed soon after.

In attempts to gain an edge on the field, most of the 1984 candidates were drawn to a number of state party conferences or dinners at which they had an opportunity to speak and otherwise sell themselves to the faithful—and not incidentally, to garner free publicity on local and occasionally national television. These "cattle shows" often were accompanied by straw votes of party attendees that provided a rough reading on the pecking order of candidates. They cost their campaigns considerable amounts of money to court the straw voters.

Cranston, a long shot, made a particularly lavish effort at a Wisconsin Democratic convention and surprisingly beat Mondale in the straw poll. The result shook up the complacent Mondale campaign in one of his neighboring states and raised modest questions about his front-runner status, but it meant nothing for Cranston in the long run. Mondale persevered in other straw votes and basically shored up his position at the front of the pecking order, while also picking up important endorsements from the AFL-CIO and the National Education Association.

As the election year approached and with it the first real delegate-selection tests in the Iowa precinct caucuses, Mondale remained the front-runner, with his most likely challenger considered to be Glenn, if only because of his celebrity and the second-largest campaign treasury behind Mondale. Of the other Democratic candidates, the Southerners—Askew and Hollings—apparently were too reminiscent of Carter to be taken seriously. That left Hart, who at that time was pretty much a blank page to Democratic voters, and two late entries who had missed most of the 1983 preliminaries—1972 nominee George McGovern and civil rights leader and black preacher nonpareil Jesse Jackson.

McGovern had continued after his defeat to be a liberal thorn in Jimmy Carter's side, prodding him without much success to remain faithful to the liberal New Deal creed. McGovern had lost his Senate seat in 1980 in the Reagan landslide and was back in the picture as the voice of liberal conscience. As for Jackson, there was obvious appeal for black voters in his candidacy, but also some reserve among other black leaders who were not ready to concede political leadership to him in their community. Jackson became an immediate threat to Mondale—not to wrest the nomination from him, but to draw away enough black voters to permit someone else to slip in, or at the least to imperil Mondale's support from the black community as the Democratic nominee. The first concern was how a Jackson candidacy might undermine Mondale's chances in a string of Southern primaries including Georgia, Alabama and Florida on what was being called Super Tuesday in mid-March. The Mondale strategy for the primaries was for an early knockout of the other candidates, and Super Tuesday was considered a key.

Jackson, in character, jumped into the race with both feet, touring the country addressing large audiences, black and white, with his sermon on social and economic justice. His campaign was driven both by his determination to elevate the voice of black America in the nation's political conversation and to cement his position as its political leader. In a characteristic bit of diplomatic freelancing, he flew to Syria in late December and negotiated the release of a twenty-seven-year-old black navy flier, Lieutenant Robert O. Goodman, whose plane had been shot down in Lebanon earlier that month. He flew back to the United States with Goodman in tow and appeared on television from the White House, accepting Reagan's thanks for "a personal mission of mercy" for which "he has earned our gratitude and admiration."[11] When it came to capturing the spotlight, there was no one like Jesse Jackson, and if he was not going to be the Democratic nominee for president, neither could he be ignored with impunity, especially by Mondale.

The serious campaign business started in mid-February 1984 with the Iowa caucuses. Mondale won with 49 percent, but because that result was expected the news spotlight fell on the distant runner-up, Hart. His 16.5 percent provided what passed for a surprise, unless it was Glenn's woeful fifth-place finish with 3.5 percent behind McGovern (10 percent) and Cranston (7) and just ahead of Askew, Jackson and Hollings. Hart, the old McGovern campaign manager who was in New Hampshire that night, knew how to make the most of it. He talked by phone to the press room in Des Moines, where his Iowa campaign manager relayed questions from reporters and he answered them. Hart, calling for new ideas and direction in the party, had worked the Iowa rural vote and got just enough of it to make himself suddenly Mondale's chief challenger.

Eight days later in the New Hampshire primary, Hart, riding the crest of extensive news coverage out of his Iowa "triumph" and his campaign funds swelled by it, defeated Mondale outright. He won 39 percent of the vote to 27 for the former vice president, 12 for Glenn and 5 or less for each of the others. Rain, snow and sleet cut down the turnout, which should have favored the establishment candidate; instead, the result revealed a deficiency of passion for Mondale. At the same time, Hart, the young Westerner with a Marlboro cowboy look, was striking a chord by calling for a break from the failed past. Cranston, Hollings and Askew all withdrew then or shortly afterward, but Glenn hung on, hoping for better luck in the Southern primaries. It was, however, now for all practical purposes a two-man race between Mondale and Hart, with Mondale needing some way to spark his campaign—or bring Hart's down to earth.

But five days later in Democratic town caucuses in Maine, Hart won again, with 50.7 percent of the vote to 43.7 percent for Mondale, who had the state's party establishment behind him. Two nights later in Vermont, Hart beat Mondale again. It was now only a week until the three Southern primaries and six others elsewhere on Super Tuesday that the Mondale camp had earlier thought could mark the end of the Glenn campaign, and a free ride the rest of the way to the convention for Mondale. Instead, his aides were talking seriously to him about the possibility that he might have to withdraw if he couldn't stop the Hart tide in Dixie. Late polls in Massachusetts and Rhode Island indicated Hart victories in both. Mondale had established himself long ago as a doctrinaire liberal of the old school and it was too late for him to take on a new persona. If he could not be further built up, the obvious political tactic was to tear the opposition down, and that was what the Mondale campaign proceeded to do.

On the Sunday before Super Tuesday, Mondale debated Hart in Atlanta and sought to paint him as a candidate devoid of substantive ideas, although Hart had offered a host of them over the previous year. It was true, however, that Hart had emerged from Iowa as a sort of matinee idol, catapulted into prominence more by his surprise showing and resultant favorable publicity in the news media than by any ideas. Mondale, to make that point, at an aide's suggestion, borrowed a catchphrase from a popular television commercial in which an old woman complained about a skimpy hamburger. Listening to Hart, Mondale suddenly said to him: "You know, when I hear your ideas, I'm reminded of that ad, 'Where's the beef?' "[12]

As the debate audience laughed, Hart gamely sought to respond in a serious vein, but Mondale had successfully served up the kind of one-liner that was certain to make the network television shows that night or the next morning. At the same time, Hart was suffering from some imprecisions in his personal biography, which now was getting closer scrutiny. There were discrepancies about his date of birth, his religion, his signature, his military record and his real name, which turned out to have been shortened from the original "Hartpence."

Suddenly Mondale's question of "Where's the beef?" had been broadened by the news media, best capsulized by the opening of a report on him on Super Tuesday eve by John Dancy of NBC News: "Who is Gary Hart, anyway, and what does he believe?" Mondale himself chipped in on CBS, observing: "The fact of it is that up until now, Americans do not know what Mr. Hart believes and who he is."[13]

For all these newly floated uncertainties, on Super Tuesday, Hart still won six of the nine contests, including Florida, the largest, to only two for Mondale and one, Hawaii, going to an uncommitted slate over Mondale's. By any reasonable yardstick, that result could have been expected to be another major boost for Hart and to bury Mondale. But in a clever bit of self-preservation, the Mondale camp cast his victories in Alabama and

Georgia as his resurrection, and it worked. With the two New England states already conceded to Hart and the results from the other states not yet in, the television network anchors played up Mondale's victories in two of the three Southern states. Mondale himself fed the story line in interviews in which he said the results meant he and Hart were headed for a "marathon" run for the nomination.[14] The night turned out to be a missed opportunity for Hart by his failing to manage the expectations and interpretation game adequately.

In the next weeks, Mondale recovered with victories in Michigan, Arkansas, Illinois, Pennsylvania and New York, capturing the major northern industrial states in spite of a major vote drainoff in them for Jackson. Hart, whose early success had come so fast that his campaign had not sufficiently slated delegates in the last three states, could not match the work of the party organizations for Mondale. Still, Hart persevered into the final round of primaries, more distinctly defining Mondale as the candidate of the party's losing past, of Humphrey and Carter, and setting himself as the voice of the young and newly affluent middle class. "Do we really want to offer the voters a referendum on the politics which they rejected in 1980?" he asked. "If we do, then they'll decide in 1984 that the policies which did not work for Carter-Mondale will not work for Walter Mondale."[15]

Hart managed to bounce back in primaries in Ohio and Indiana, but Mondale kept moving toward the nomination by winning in Maryland and North Carolina, with decisive primaries slated on the first Tuesday of June in delegate-rich California and New Jersey. Hart needed both to have a chance at the convention; he won the first but lost the second after an attempt at humor backfired on him. Campaigning with his wife, Lee, in the Golden State, he told a private cocktail party crowd that he and Lee usually campaigned separately. "That's the bad news," he said. "The good news for her is that she campaigns in California and I campaign in New Jersey." When Lee remarked that she got to hold a koala bear in California, her husband broke in: "I won't tell you what I got to hold—samples from a toxic dump."[16] The crack got a good laugh—in California. In New Jersey, where the natives were tired of "Jersey jokes," Hart's remarks pushed his more thoughtful observations out of the news for several critical days. Only some late scrambling and calculating enabled the Mondale camp the morning after the final primary day to claim it had a majority of delegates needed for the nomination.

Prior to the Democratic convention, Hart and Mondale met in New York for a unity meeting after which Hart said he and Mondale "have agreed to do everything within our power to see that Ronald Reagan does not have a second term in the White House."[17] Afterward, Hart flew to New Hampshire for a rally of his supporters, thanking them and pointedly telling them he would be back in four years. In losing, Hart had built a strong case for another presidential try, and for his basic contention that the Democratic Party needed to turn away from New Deal thinking; that it had to address the changes occurring in the society that demanded more attention be paid to the needs and desires of a mushrooming middle class, increasingly spilling out of the cities into suburbia.

In advance of the Democratic convention in San Francisco in July, the main interest in the party was in Mondale's selection of a running mate, and he made history by choosing a woman for the first time, little-known Congresswoman Geraldine Ferraro of New York. He used the same basic interview and vetting process that Carter had employed in picking him in 1976. But equally important in Mondale's deliberations was his own dismal standing in the polls against Reagan. In June, Gallup had him trailing the incumbent by nineteen percentage points, and his advisers agreed on the wisdom of making a startling selection. Picking a woman certainly was that; taking one who had served a mere three terms in the House with no particular distinction was more so. In announcing her choice, Mondale clung to the position that her gender was not the deciding factor. "I looked for the best vice president and I found her in Gerry Ferraro," he said.[18] But there was no doubt that, looking at the polls, he had decided to "throw the long bomb" in a bid to find among women voters the lift he would need against Reagan.

As the convention opened, the Ferraro selection dominated all talk, but almost at once it was overtaken by another Mondale blockbuster. The national chairman, Charles Manatt, was a Californian who had taken great pride in bringing the party convention to his state. Traditionally, the new nominee had the right to install his own chairman, but customarily only after the convention, so that the outgoing chairman could have his days in the spotlight. But Manatt, a conspicuously ambitious Kiwanis glad-handing type, was no favorite within Mondale's inner circle and it was decided he would have to go—before the convention began.

Adding insult to injury, the Democrat chosen to replace him was an old Jimmy Carter crony from Georgia, Bert Lance, who had served as the

Carter administration's budget director until allegations of bank irregularities in Georgia forced his resignation in 1977 and led to his indictment in 1979. A year later he was acquitted of most of the charges and the rest were dropped, but he was regarded, nonetheless, as a political negative. As Mondale had not chosen a Southerner as his running mate, key aides argued that a bone should be tossed to Dixie in the form of the party chairmanship. Lance had been one of Mondale's strongest, most loyal friends and advisers in the fight for the nomination, and Mondale decided to reward him.

When word got out of the Lance-for-Manatt deal, all hell broke loose at the convention, and, to make matters worse, Manatt balked at being the sacrificial lamb. He dug his heels in as state party chairmen rallied to his support and other Democrats openly decried the stupidity of the proposed move. In the end of what Mondale himself called a "firestorm," he backed down, made Lance general chairman of his campaign, not of the national party, and left Manatt in place as party chairman. All Mondale accomplished was to give the party and the country a demonstration of his judgment that only further undercut his credibility as a candidate.

Nevertheless, Mondale and then Ferraro were nominated on the first ballot. In accepting, Mondale made a fighting speech with a candor that first stirred the convention hall and then shocked it. Deploring the state of the economy under Reagan's policy of tax cuts and deficits, he said: "Here is the truth about the future. We are living on borrowed money and borrowed time. These deficits hike interest rates, clobber exports, stunt investment, kill jobs, undermine growth, cheat our kids and shrink our future. Whoever is inaugurated in January, the American people will have to pay Mr. Reagan's bills. The budget will be squeezed. Taxes will go up. And anyone who says they won't is not telling the truth to the American people. I mean business. By the end of my first term, I will reduce the Reagan budget deficit by two thirds. Let's tell the truth. . . . Mr. Reagan will raise taxes and so will I. He won't tell you. I just did."[19]

The spectacle of a presidential nominee telling voters right out of the gate that if elected he would raise their taxes startled his fellow Democrats and overjoyed his Republican foes. GOP pollster Robert Teeter said of Mondale's candor: "All it did was reinforce the stereotype of Mondale. It was perfect. It did for us what we couldn't have done with advertising. . . . He just proved himself to be the classic, big-spending, liberal, New Deal, old-time Democrat."[20]

To persistent press questions about whether he might indeed have to raise taxes in a second term, Reagan finally gave a categorical answer. "Walter Mondale is not telling the truth," he said. "I've said before and I will say it again and no matter how many of you try to put in a hedging line, we have no plans for, nor will I allow any plans for, a tax increase. Period." And a few days later: "My opponent has spent his political life supporting more taxes and more spending. For him, raising taxes is a first resort. For me, it is a last resort."[21]

Meeting in Dallas a month later, the Republicans quickly renominated Reagan and Bush amid sky-high optimism. As the fall campaign began, Mondale had already put himself on the defensive with his acknowledgment that he would raise taxes, and Ferraro's candidacy had inadvertently added to the Democratic woes with the surfacing of stories about financial difficulties involving her husband. A further irritant was Jesse Jackson, who toyed with Mondale over endorsing him.

Efforts by Mondale to goad Reagan into a debate on the economy, the need for taxes and other issues were at first rebuffed. When Mondale released a detailed plan on new taxes putting most of the burden on the rich, Reagan told a rally: "The American people aren't undertaxed. The government is overfed. The main difference between ourselves and the other side is that we see an America where every day is the Fourth of July. They see an America where every day is April Fifteenth."[22]

At the same time, the Reagan campaign filled the nation's television screen with upbeat, patriotic commercials. One called "America Is Back" and another called "It's Morning Again" showed placid and happy scenes of Americans of all ages at work and play. The first ended with the narrator saying: "Now that our country is turning around, why would we ever turn back?" The second, recalling Reagan's decisive line in his 1980 debate with Jimmy Carter, concluded: "Why would we ever want to return to where we were less than four short years ago?"[23]

Meanwhile, Mondale, definitely not a creature of the television age, staunchly resisted packaging by his aides. Instead, he railed against the Reagan "feel good" ads that tapped into American success at the Olympics. He said in one campus speech: "This crowd doesn't want you to think about the stakes in this contest. They want to trivialize it. That is arrogance. We are in an American presidential election. . . . This election is not about country music and birthday cakes. It is about old people who can't pay for medicine. This election is not about the Olympic torch. It is about the civil-rights laws that opened athletics to women and minorities who won those gold medals."[24] It was vintage Mondale; vintage New Deal rhetoric.

Reagan's advisers finally agreed to two debates with Mondale and one between Bush and Ferraro. In the first televised confrontation between the presidential nominees, Reagan at times sounded so confused and disoriented that his performance immediately gave rise to press speculation that his age—now seventy-three—was finally catching up with him. Soon the airwaves were flooded with old clips of Reagan dozing off at meetings or being prompted by his wife, Nancy, as he tried to dodge a question. The Mondale strategists suddenly saw a ray of light in the previously dark outlook for their man, and they looked forward to the second encounter.

After the vice-presidential debate, in which Ferraro scored effectively by turning a rather condescending manner by Bush back against him, Mondale and Reagan met again before the television cameras. The key question came from Henry Trewhitt of the *Baltimore Sun*. Reminding the aging Reagan of the extreme pressure under which President Kennedy had to function during the Cuban missile crisis, Trewhitt asked him whether "you would be able to function in such circumstances." Reagan, in a mock-serious tone, replied: "I will not make age an issue in this campaign. I am not going to exploit, for political purposes, my opponent's youth and inexperience."[25]

The audience howled with laughter, as Mondale stood with an appreciative grin on his face. "I knew when I walked off that platform after the second debate," he said later, "that the election was over."[26] Reagan, in his closing comments, offered another rambling, almost incoherent monologue about the beauty of the California coastline, but it didn't matter. With that prepared one-liner about age, he had reminded voters of the old Reagan sparkle that had won them in the first place, and he was home free.

On election day, Reagan won a second term with 59 percent of the vote to 41 percent for Mondale. He also routed him in the electoral college, with 525 votes to only 13 for the Minnesotan, who managed to carry only his own state and the heavily Democratic District of Columbia.

Once again, a Democratic candidate offering basically the New Deal formula for righting the nation's ills was rejected, and emphatically this time, in preference for a charismatic figure whose charm and wit counted for more with voters than a disastrous economic policy.

The country seemed no longer to be listening to appeals in behalf of its most downtrodden and disadvantaged, which had been the bedrock of Democratic politics for more than three decades. America had become more middle class, more suburban, more affluent, its citizenry more self-centered, even more self-aggrandizing. And if that was so, the Democratic Party could no longer hope for political success by playing Robin Hood. Meanwhile, it had to endure four more years of the Reagan Revolution that, in Democratic minds, transfixed the country with wrongheaded economic nostrums and public relations magic.

When front-running Senator Gary Hart of Colorado saw his campaign for the 1988 Democratic presidential nomination crumble in the wake of a womanizing scandal, Governor Michael S. Dukakis of Massachusetts moved into the void. With ample funds and the support of the party's strong liberal wing, he was nominated, but he proved to be an inept campaigner and lost in November to the Republican nominee, Vice President George H. W. Bush.

Chapter 30

A TIME FOR PARTY SOUL-SEARCHING,
1985–1991

DEMOCRATS GREETED THE second Reagan term with mixed feelings. On one hand, the enormity of his victory over Mondale demoralized the party and gave Reagan a clearer mandate than ever to inject his conservative ideology into the nation's political mainstream. It also provided a green light for continuing his confrontational approach to dealing with what he styled "the evil empire" directed from Moscow. On the other hand, the Democrats knew that in four more years Reagan would be gone from the White House, thanks to that product of Republican hatred of FDR, the constitutional two-term limit.

In any event, the depth of the 1984 defeat signaled a soul-searching within the party about the face it had been showing to the nation's voters, and what needed to be done to establish a winning and defensible posture before the next presidential election. It was easy to write off the Mondale defeat on the grounds that he had been Jimmy Carter's man and voters wanted no more of that troubled era. Mondale, in his own right, was an easy target as an old New Dealer controlled by and often intimidated by the interest groups that still dominated the party, from organized labor and blacks to women. And finally there was that bizarre promise to raise taxes.

Among many Southern Democrats, Mondale was hardly viewed as Jimmy Carter's man. Rather, they saw him as another of the old New Deal liberals whose candidacy had put the party back on the philosophical road that had meant defeat behind Humphrey and the "New Politics" of McGovern in the presidential elections of 1968 and 1972. Ever since the Republican Southern strategy authored by Nixon and augmented by Reagan had changed the political environment of Dixie, they had deplored their region's decline in party influence from the days of the Democratic Solid South to being a stepchild of the Northern-dominant "national party."

Among those who first decided to do something about it was Congressman Gillis Long of Louisiana, chairman of the House Democratic Caucus. He sought without success to give a more Southern coloration to the party and its 1984 presidential nominee before and during the primaries that ultimately produced Mondale and his New York running mate. After the election, Long, with the assistance of a young aide named Al From, brought together a group of moderate Democratic governors and members of Congress, largely but not exclusively from the South and border states, to continue the quest.[1]

In January 1985, From wrote a memorandum called "Saving the Democratic Party," in which he attacked its strategy of "making blatant appeals to liberal and minority interest groups in hopes of building a winning coalition where a majority under normal circumstances simply does not exist. It simply does not understand that winning coalitions must be forged around ideas, not constituency groups." With liberal and labor activists dominant in the Democratic National Committee, From continued, "elected officials must either take control of, or find ways to go around, the DNC." He proposed they form "on their own authority . . . a governing council for the Democratic Party, independent of the DNC."[2]

In late February such a group, calling itself the Democratic Leadership Council (DLC), came into being. It consisted at first of ten governors including Charles Robb of Virginia, Lyndon Johnson's son-in-law, and Bill Clinton of Arkansas; fourteen senators including Sam Nunn of Georgia and Al Gore of Tennessee, and seventeen House members including Long and Richard Gephardt of Missouri, the group's first chairman.[3] Nunn's role gave the new organization a defense-oriented image at first as, according to one early observer, "the Cold War wing of the Democratic Party."[4]

Its membership, eventually known as New Democrats, did not sit well with the party's new national chairman elected after the 1984 debacle, Paul Kirk, a longtime close aide to Ted Kennedy. Kirk had already created a Democratic Policy Commission to chart a new party course; he was not enthusiastic for a separate body functioning outside his authority, reminiscent of the controversial Democratic Advisory Council of the 1950s.

Yet Kirk moved quickly to heal old wounds and promote party unity, creating a "fairness commission" to examine complaints from Jesse Jackson and others about inequities in convention delegate selection. Also, harkening to the DLC argument that the party needed to put less emphasis on its coalition of special interest groups like labor, minorities and women, Kirk eliminated their caucuses within the DNC. He scrapped the midterm party conferences, which in the three prior off-years had become occasions for intraparty squabbling.[5]

Jackson meanwhile took dead aim at the DLC as a retreat from core liberal Democratic values, deriding it as "Democrats for the Leisure Class" who "didn't march in the sixties and won't stand up in the eighties."[6] To counter such assaults, the DLC moved to broaden its own composition even as it sought to promote its interests against the dominant old party power-wielders from Northern states and the largest cities. From an early narrow base it defensively adopted a "big tent" approach to attract not only party conservatives and centrists but also liberals willing to join out of collegiality or hopes of party unity. The price of doing so was diminution of its distinction from the DNC, a price it eventually decided not to pay.

Other efforts were going forward to elevate the South's role in presidential party politics. As early as the 1970s some Democratic state legislators had discussed the advisability of creating a Southern regional primary—grouping several state contests on a single day—as a means of advancing a Southern candidate or obliging other candidates to pay more attention to Southern issues and interests. But the nomination and election of Carter in 1976 cooled off the idea, only to be resurrected upon his defeat in 1980. The Southern Legislative Conference (SLC) passed a resolution in 1984 recommending it, but too late to implement in that election year. After Mondale's defeat, it was revived in 1985 under the leadership of Governor Bob Graham of Florida, chairman of the Southern Governors' Association[7] and a representative of the more moderate and progressive New South.

The notion held promise not just for the South but for the whole party. The Democratic vote in Dixie had been falling precipitously, especially among whites, to the point that even native Carter had failed to win a majority of the white vote in 1976, and Mondale had won a pathetic 28 percent in 1984. Anything that could make the Democratic Party competitive again in the region would be beneficial across the board, and a Southern regional primary found much enthusiasm in the new DLC.

The three Southern states that had constituted a sort of mini–Super Tuesday in 1984–Florida, Georgia and Alabama–were scheduled to vote on the same day again in 1988, and eleven other states from Maryland and Virginia to Texas and Oklahoma joined the parade. Outside the South, nine more states also chose the day for primaries or caucuses, or twenty in all. March 8, 1988, would be a true Super Tuesday on which, the architects envisioned, the Democratic presidential nominee would emerge from the South, or at least be acceptable to the region.

With Reagan not eligible to seek reelection in 1988, there was no shortage of eager Democratic candidates, especially when his second term produced a Republican scandal of major proportions. As Reagan, in fits and starts, sought arms control agreements with a new Soviet leader, Mikhail Gorbachev, he also pushed what came to be known as the Reagan Doctrine, the active if often covert opposition to Soviet subversion of other countries. "We must not break faith," he said in 1985, "with those who are risking their lives on every continent, from Afghanistan to Nicaragua, to defy Soviet-supported aggression."[8]

In keeping with that resolve, it came to light in late 1986 that the Reagan administration had been secretly selling arms to Iran in the hope of obtaining release of American hostages in Lebanon, after having declared it would never do business with terrorists or Iran under Ayatollah Khomeini. Furthermore, it was discovered that proceeds from the sale had been diverted to the Contra rebels in Nicaragua seeking to oust the Sandinista regime, in direct contravention of a congressional ban on such aid. At first Reagan had categorically denied any such swap of arms for hostages, but investigation revealed that Reagan's national security adviser, Admiral John Poindexter, in league with a devious freelancer on the NSC staff, Marine Lieutenant Colonel Oliver North, and CIA director William Casey, had indeed carried out such a deal. The perpetrators denied that Reagan knew about their actions or authorized them, but in any event the scandal brought new vulnerability to the Republican Party in advance of the 1988 presidential election.[9]

So did the ramifications of Reaganomics, which led to heavy foreign borrowing and unprecedented peacetime budget deficits. October 19,

1987, saw the worst stock market collapse since 1929, with prices nose-diving 22.6 percent at a cost to investors of more than $1 trillion.[10] The "truly needy" who were to have been protected by the shredded safety net of the Reagan years multiplied.

All this, and the Democratic recapture of the Senate in 1986, boosted Democratic hopes of a return to the White House in 1988, and a bumper crop of presidential hopefuls, especially when Ted Kennedy announced again that he would not seek the Democratic nomination. Leading the pack was Gary Hart, whose surprise performance in the 1984 campaign had brought him a faithful and enthusiastic following. As the self-proclaimed candidate of new ideas, he sold himself as the party's antidote to the old look that had brought Mondale to such an overwhelming defeat. At the same time, he benefited among liberals from his old identity as manager of the 1972 McGovern campaign. In the Senate, he had established himself as an innovative thinker in the realms of military defense and Soviet relations, and after the 1984 election had burnished those credentials with a visit to Moscow and a three-hour conversation with Gorbachev. As he approached the 1988 election, while not a DLC member, he struck many as the different kind of Democrat who could put a new face on the party.

At the same time, Hart was plagued with a hangover from his 1984 presidential run—what was regarded as "the character issue." Beyond all the questions about his age, his real name and all the rest that had lent an air of mystery and evasion about him, there was a subterranean issue often whispered but never written about for lack of accusation or definite proof—that he was a womanizer.

In the spring of 1987, the matter went beyond whispering, to the point that he was openly asked by reporters about the rumors. He invited a *New York Times* reporter to follow him, and a tip to a newspaper, the *Miami Herald,* led to the staking out of Hart's apartment in Washington. It was discovered he had entertained a young woman named Donna Rice there overnight, the details of which were uncertain. That was enough to start the ball rolling in earnest, and when evocative photos of Hart with the woman were printed in a supermarket gossip tabloid, Hart was thrown into a desperate effort at political damage control. Despite his denials of impropriety, he was driven from the presidential race well in advance of the election year.[11]

Hart's departure left the Democratic contest wide open. Of all the prospective candidates only one, Jesse Jackson, had a substantial national reputation, and his was one of such controversy that his chances of gaining the nomination were regarded as nil, even by the most realistic leaders of his black constituency. The others included Senators Joseph Biden of Delaware, chairman of the Senate Judiciary Committee, Paul Simon of Illinois and Albert Gore Jr. of Tennessee; Governor Michael Dukakis of Massachusetts and former Governor Bruce Babbitt of Arizona; and Congressman Gephardt, a rising star in the House leadership, and Congresswoman Patricia Schroeder of Colorado, who soon dropped out. Others mentioned but not committing were Governor Mario Cuomo of New York and Senator Bill Bradley of New Jersey.

With party chairman Kirk persuading state parties to abandon the pre-election-year straw polls that consumed much candidate money for meaningless return, the candidates instead engaged in a marathon of debates in 1987, and some slippery campaign practices that damaged some of the candidates. Biden, accused of plagiarizing in some of his speeches, pleaded innocence but was forced to the sidelines. Dukakis was tarnished but not eliminated when a close aide acknowledged having given the press evidence of Biden's misdeed.[12] The Massachusetts governor was saved by a posture of incorruptibility and a fat campaign treasury that enabled him to overcome this and later setbacks in early primaries.

The first of them came in the Iowa caucuses, won by Gephardt from neighboring Missouri after diligent campaigning. He captured 31 percent of all precinct delegates elected, to 26.7 percent for Simon and 22.1 for Dukakis in spite of a strong effort. But Dukakis quickly recovered in the primary in his neighboring state of New Hampshire, with 36 percent of the vote to 20 for Gephardt, 17 for Simon and the others, as in Iowa, trailing far behind. Next, Dukakis won Minnesota and Gephardt took South Dakota, setting the stage for what was expected to be the decisive round of primaries and caucuses, most of them in the South, two weeks later on Super Tuesday. Then, more than half the delegates needed for nomination were to be chosen.

That brief time, and the proliferation of primary states, combined to undermine the purpose of Super Tuesday—heavy candidate and media attention to the participating states and their special provincial concerns. In a campaign for national office, the candidates couldn't afford to be bogged down by regional issues or to spend any appreciable time in the smaller states. Instead of producing a Southern nominee, Super Tuesday worked to the advantage of two Northern liberals, Dukakis of Massachusetts and Jackson of Illinois (by way of South Carolina). The Dukakis campaign bankroll gave him an advantage in the two largest competing states, Texas and Florida, and Jackson benefited from a heavy black vote across the South.

Super Tuesday brought Dukakis victory in eight states, including Texas and Florida in Dixie, 26 percent of the total vote and 356 national convention delegates. Jackson won five states, all in the South, also with 26 percent of the vote and 355 delegates. Close behind was Gore, who had done nothing in the previous contests but was helped by his Tennessee and DLC connections, and probably also by Jackson's drawing black votes from liberal Dukakis. Gore won in five Southern states and Nevada with just under 26 percent of the vote, picking up 318 delegates—and a temporary lifeline, fading thereafter. The big loser was Gephardt, who won only his own state of Missouri, 13 percent of the vote and 94 delegates.

That left Dukakis, Jackson and, barely, Gephardt. While Super Tuesday had worked to a degree in bringing more candidates to the South for more days of campaigning and boosted voter turnout in the region, it failed to project a Southern candidate into serious contention for the Democratic nomination. In the next key state, Michigan, where labor was dominant in the party, Gephardt had hoped to bounce back with an endorsement from the AFL-CIO. But none was given and his candidacy was finished. Meanwhile, Dukakis was blindsided by Jackson, who rode a heavy black and blue-collar vote to a victory of nearly two to one, carrying 10 of Michigan's 18 congressional districts and 74 of 137 delegates elected.

Suddenly, the Democratic fight was a two-man race, and with the controversial Jackson as one of the two, the other one, Dukakis, was on his way to the party nomination. With plenty of campaign money left and Jackson as his prime opponent, Dukakis won Wisconsin with 47 percent of the vote to 28 for Jackson and 17 for Gore. Simon, trailing badly again, dropped out, but Gore hung on heading to the New York primary. There, Dukakis won 51 percent to 37 for Jackson and 10 for Gore, despite—or perhaps because of—the endorsement of bombastic New York Mayor Ed Koch. The rest of the way, through Pennsylvania, Oregon and California, was a mop-up operation for Dukakis.

Assured of enough delegates to win the nomination in June, Dukakis went back to Massachusetts and resumed his duties as governor in his trademark all-business fashion. In July he was nominated on the first ballot at the party national convention in Atlanta, promising cheering delegates that "the Reagan era is over and a new era is about to begin."[13] Touting himself as an effective administrator while jabbing at the right-wing framework of the Reagan Revolution, Dukakis declared at one point: "This election is not about ideology, it's about competence."[14] After turning aside pressure by Jackson for the vice-presidential nomination, Dukakis chose Senator Lloyd Bentsen of Texas as his running mate and came out of the convention riding high. He headed back to Massachusetts again to resume his gubernatorial duties.

Other newly anointed presidential nominees might have gone off on vacation or plunged into preparations for the fall campaign or even begun it, but not the super-conscientious Dukakis, still the servant of the citizens of his state. It was an unwise decision, because in the weeks between the adjournment of the Democratic convention and the opening of the Republican gathering in New Orleans, Dukakis's lead of seventeen percentage points over Republican front-runner George Bush in an NBC News poll had all but vanished.

The GOP nomination contest meanwhile had essentially been a challenge to Vice President Bush to project himself as his own man after eight years of silent fealty to Reagan, who had plucked him from political oblivion by choosing him as his ticket mate in 1980. Tagged by the news media as a "wimp" and hounded for clarification of the role of a key aide and possibly himself in the Iran-Contra scandal, Bush stonewalled through the 1984 Republican primaries. He ran a poor third in the Iowa caucuses behind Bob Dole and television evangelist Pat Robertson, but recovered in New Hampshire, wounding Dole with eleventh-hour television ads casting him (inaccurately) as a tax-raiser in that strongly anti-tax state. He went on to carry sixteen states on Super Tuesday and wrap up the Republican nomination.

At the party's national convention, Bush acted in two ways on aides' advice to move decisively out of Reagan's shadow. The first was a forceful acceptance speech after his first-ballot nomination in which he made a memorable pledge. Borrowing a trademark phrase of Hollywood tough guy Clint Eastwood, he declared: "Read my lips: No new taxes."[15] It was a commitment that he would come to regret. The second was his stunning choice of a young and unimpressive senator from Indiana, Dan Quayle, as his running mate. That choice, too, caused Bush considerable regret, as the news media immediately subjected Quayle to a round of questioning about his earlier service in the Indiana National Guard that had saved him from the rigors and dangers of Vietnam.

With the Democrats and the news media assailing Bush on his selection of Quayle and, more importantly, on his role in the Iran-Contra affair, Bush's strategists decided to force Dukakis onto the defensive with a barrage of negative advertising and campaigning. One obvious and old line of fire was painting him as an old-fashioned liberal. Another was challenging his claim as the candidate of competence. A third was questioning his patriotism and commitment to a strong national defense. A fourth was implying illness. And finally, a fifth was playing the race card by capitalizing on a Dukakis program of work release for Massachusetts convicts—probably the most politically effective of all. In all these, Dukakis proved to be a willing accomplice by turning the other cheek to all the accusations against him, naïvely believing the truth would be apparent to the voters.

That he was a liberal was undeniable. His competence was attacked by Bush personally and through a television ad charging pollution in Boston harbor. His patriotism was questioned by raising as an issue his veto of a state law requiring public school teachers to lead students in the pledge of allegiance to the flag, which legal advisers had told him was unconstitutional. To counter the suggestion that he was weak on defense, Dukakis went to a Michigan plant that made army tanks and permitted himself to be filmed and photographed with his head popping out of a turret wearing a helmet that made him look like a turtle. The image had nothing to do with his support of the military but became a source of ridicule unmercifully exploited by the Republicans.

More seriously, Dukakis's health was questioned in a rumor, untrue, that he had undergone psychiatric treatment. But most damaging of all was a television ad that referred to a prison furlough program, initiated by a previous Republican governor of Massachusetts and continued by Dukakis. It showed men leaving a jail through a revolving gate while a narrator said: "Governor Michael Dukakis vetoed mandatory sentences for drug dealers. He vetoed the death penalty. His revolving-door prison policy gave weekend furloughs to first-degree murderers not eligible for parole. While out, many committed other crimes like kidnapping and rape and many are still at large. Now Michael Dukakis says he wants to do for America what he has done for Massachusetts. America can't afford that risk."[16]

The ad clearly referred to, but did not mention or depict, a Massachusetts prisoner named Willie Horton, a black man convicted of murder who was released on a weekend furlough, fled and raped a woman in Maryland. However, flyers circulated by some Bush state committees or ostensibly independent groups did name and display a photo of Horton, all of them disavowed by the national Bush campaign. In all of these attacks, Dukakis either offered legalistic responses or ignored them, leaving himself vulnerable, according to the old political axiom that a charge unanswered is a charge proved, or at least believed by voters.

A seeming confirmation of Dukakis's insensitivity to the allegations of indifference leveled against him by the Republicans came in a debate with Bush. The moderator, Bernard Shaw of CNN, opened with a pointed if hypothetical question to the Democratic nominee. "Governor," he was asked, "if Kitty Dukakis [his wife] were raped and murdered, would you favor an irrevocable death penalty for the killer?"[17] The question obviously had been posed to gauge the personal reaction of a man who had been accused of lack of emotion. Instead of answering in the words of an outraged husband, Dukakis proceeded to defend his stand against the death penalty, saying, "I don't see any evidence that it's a deterrent."[18] His flat, bloodless answer shocked many as much as had the jarring question, and the response was in a real sense a metaphor for the whole campaign, with Dukakis brutally attacked and turning the other cheek.

The only comparably notable exchange of the campaign came in the vice-presidential debate between Bentsen and Quayle, when the Republican nominee compared his congressional service with that of John F. Kennedy and Bentsen stiffly told him: "Senator, I served with Jack Kennedy. I knew Jack Kennedy. Jack Kennedy was a friend of mine. Senator, you are no Jack Kennedy."[19] The comment, though memorable, had no appreciable impact on the campaign's outcome. Even carrying Quayle on his back, Bush won the election comfortably, with 53.9 percent of the vote to 46.1 for Dukakis, winning 40 states and 426 electoral votes to 10 and the District of Columbia and only 111 in the electoral college for the Democratic nominee. One Democratic elector from West Virginia gave his presidential vote to Bentsen and his vice-presidential vote to Dukakis.

Once again, for the twelfth time in fourteen elections, except for

Carter in 1976 and 1980, the Democratic Party had offered the electorate a liberal nominee, and for the fourth time in the last five, had seen him defeated, the moderate Carter in 1976 again the exception. For members of the Democratic Leadership Council, whose hopes for the nomination of a non-liberal had been dashed, the time had come to take more concerted and determined action to find one of their own to change the party's direction, and its fortunes, at the presidential level.

At its core, the DLC believed that Democrats had to shed the liberal image that had been so effectively demonized by the Republicans ever since Nixon had used the tactic against Humphrey in 1968 and McGovern in 1972. This time around, Bush had shaped the debate to his advantage by harping on cultural issues and "values" while Dukakis had peddled his "competence" in administering Democratic programs often pegged excessively to the poor—or so the Republicans argued. In spite of Dukakis's insistence to the contrary, "ideology" did count with the voters in 1988. As a young governor of Arkansas and DLC member named Bill Clinton put it in an election postmortem: "No matter how popular your programs may be, you must be considered in the mainstream on shared values of the American people, the ability to defend the nation and the strength to enforce its laws."[20]

To bring the party around to focus on values rather than programs as manifested for years in New Deal liberalism, some in the DLC leadership thought for a time after the Dukakis defeat that the best avenue to accomplish that end might be to elect a DLC stalwart as the national party chairman. The New Democrats would take over the party itself rather than simply trying to accommodate with it. With the support of Sam Nunn, then the DLC chairman, Bruce Babbitt ran against the prime liberal candidate, Ron Brown, former DNC deputy chairman, successful Washington lawyer and a key figure in the 1980 Ted Kennedy and 1984 Jesse Jackson campaigns. But Brown proved so strong with institutional DNC members that Babbitt and other contenders dropped out and Brown was elected in February 1989, becoming the DNC's first black chairman.

From said later that the DLC had no real support within the DNC and decided it could better use its resources in developing a winning philosophy and policy agenda, which the DNC, focusing on election mechanics, did not do to any effective degree. "While there was an initial conversation about taking over the party," one DLC policy strategist, Elaine Kamarck, recalled later, "it was also clear there was a vacuum on issues in the party, and that institutionally if you filled the ideas vacuum, you didn't need to take over the DNC."[21]

At the outset, Brown as a consensus builder sought to work with the DLC, and in the process keep it in line. But as the DLC adopted more contrary positions, friction inevitably developed. At one point, Brown needled the DLC by observing that "the last thing we need in this country is two Republican parties. One is plenty."[22]

Still on the outside looking in, the DLC began to draw the line more sharply, with more outspoken criticism of the DNC. DLC leaders concluded that if their views were to prevail, two things were needed: a carefully crafted philosophy and agenda, and a presidential candidate to sell and eventually implement them. Thus was a DLC think tank called the Progressive Policy Institute born in late 1988 under another veteran House Democratic Caucus staffer, Will Marshall, as From led the quest for a DLC candidate.[23]

In creating the think tank, From said later, "I think we helped put the party into the information age. We made ideas more important. In the seventies and eighties, we really lost the battle of ideas. When Reagan won in '80, the Republicans seized the ideas initiatives; they had something to say and we didn't have anything to say. We as a party thought all we had to do was get the vote out, but our vote was eroding. . . . The country was moving in one direction and the Democratic Party was moving in the other. We tried to reconnect the party with the country while still holding to the values of the old party."[24]

The search for a candidate took From to Little Rock in April 1989, where he pressed Bill Clinton to become chairman of an expanded DLC, from which he could make an effective run for the Democratic presidential nomination in 1992. Part of the scheme, Clinton was told, would be the opening of DLC state chapters around the country, giving him a rationale for extensive travel that would bring him greater name recognition and an active base in the party. It took a year of persuading, but Clinton finally came around and replaced Nunn as DLC chairman.[25]

Meanwhile, intraparty frictions had intensified. At a DLC meeting in 1989, a shouting match between Robb, a New Democrat, and Jackson, speaking for the party's liberal wing, spotlighted the growing ideological division. Two party theorists, Kamarck and William Galston, wrote a paper called "The Politics of Evasion: Democrats and the Presidency" that sharply criticized the DNC and the national party for its approaches to the lost 1988 presidential campaign. It took issue with the notion that inadequate mechanics and candidates had cost the Democrats the White House in recent elections. It also argued against the idea that the party's nominees had to be more liberal rather than less to win, and that the party would remain strong as long as its congressional base remained so.[26]

The confrontation with the established party was intentional. "Only by going out and saying, 'This party is seriously screwed up,'" Kamarck said later, "could we get attention. Only by having a fight could you get the voters to understand that something new was happening. After '88, we really needed a second look on the part of the voters, because in '80 and '84, everybody chalked it up to 'Oh, Ronald Reagan, he's so charismatic.' But George Bush [in 1988] wasn't charismatic at all, and he beat us. And we needed substance behind that second look. We realized after the 1984 campaign that the New Deal way of looking at the electorate was dead, and the 1984 Mondale campaign was really the end of the New Deal coalition." Soon new ideas like charter schools, welfare reform, community policing and reinventing government, she said, were laying out what came to be called a "third way" to govern.[27]

In March 1990 a DLC conference in New Orleans produced a declaration that the party's "fundamental mission is to expand opportunity, not government," a direct slap at old liberal orthodoxy. In calling for reductions in government spending and opposition to tax increases, it proposed replacing "the politics of entitlement with a new politics of reciprocal responsibility."[28]

As the new DLC chairman, Clinton joined the chapter-building effort already begun, and by the time of the organization's major convention in Cleveland in May 1991, most states were represented. In a parade of would-be 1992 presidential aspirants, Clinton clearly outshone the field with a brilliant speech from a few notes that marked him as among the strongest contenders, although he had not yet declared an intention to run.

Clinton said the party's electoral problem at the presidential level was that middle-class and working-class Americans had "not trusted us in national elections to defend our national interests abroad, to put values into our social policy at home, or take tax money and spend it with discipline." He pitched the new DLC philosophy as "opportunity, responsibility, choice, a government that works, a belief in community."[29]

In all this, Clinton's criticism of the old liberalism was more deftly

crafted than one that came from Congressman David McCurdy of Oklahoma, who assailed "the forces which took command of the Democratic
Party in 1972 and . . . have paralyzed many of our government and social
institutions."[30] Either way, it was clear that the DLC was now bent on taking over the party with a new agenda and, it hoped, a presidential candidate of its own.

Jesse Jackson, given a forum at previous DLC conferences, had sought
to blur and thus undermine the organization's efforts to build an identity
separate from the DNC, proclaiming in New Orleans that he was
"delighted that we are so united."[31] Hence he was not invited to the Cleveland convention, a move that brought accusations of racism from Jackson
and personal pressure from him on black members of the DLC. His exclusion exposed divisions within the organization about how much further it
should go in moving away from a big-tent concept and becoming a narrow advocate of centrist positions. Ron Brown as chairman of the DNC
threatened not to address the convention, and when he finally did so he
emphasized the imperative of the DLC to be "inclusive"[32] for the sake of
party harmony.

One consequence of the DLC's increasing independence, and the
derogation of old liberalism by some of its members, was the formation of
a new Coalition for Democratic Values headed by liberal Senator Howard
Metzenbaum of Ohio. He said the new CDV was being formed to counter
the DLC's efforts to "move the party to the right," adding, "the future of
the Democratic Party does not lie in the fine-tuning of Reaganism."[33]

Although Bush had defeated Dukakis handily in 1988, Democratic
professionals of all stripes were optimistic that he could be beaten the
next time around. For one thing, the man himself was not impressive; for
another, he was vulnerable within his own party. Despite his declaration
that he was his "own man," his 1988 candidacy had been seen by many
voters as a way to continue the Reagan era without Reagan. At the same
time, Bush was never accepted as a true Reaganite in its dominant right
wing, but rather a closet moderate who had swallowed his own views in
subservience to the man who had made him vice president. Bush and his
political advisers were well aware of this fact, and it was one reason he
had thrown red meat to the right wing in his 1988 acceptance speech
pledge of "no new taxes."

On taking office, however, Bush did not hesitate to put his own men
in key positions, starting with James Baker as secretary of state and

Richard Darman, the bête noire of the right wing, as budget director. Both were considered foxes in the chicken coop by old Reaganites, although both had worked in the Reagan administration. Indeed, it was because the conservatives believed it was the team of Baker and Darman who had sold Reagan himself on tax increases that they eyed both with suspicion in the highest reaches of the Bush administration.

It was for this reason that Bush's "no new taxes" pledge was so critical to keeping the Republican right wing at bay during his White House tenure. Darman in his confirmation hearings went out of his way to reassure the fiscal conservatives by saying he would apply "the duck test" to any proposal that might even remotely appear to be a tax increase. "If it looks like a duck, walks like a duck and quacks like a duck," he explained, "it's a duck. If it looks like a tax, it's a tax. Ducks are off the table."[34]

Indeed, Bush was determined to adhere to Darman's duck test, as was his chief political adviser, Lee Atwater, who had been his campaign manager of record in 1988 and now was Republican national chairman. Atwater took on the task of placating the right wing about Bush whenever events warranted. He calmed down the party critics in the first year when they blamed Bush for the rejection of John Tower to be secretary of defense and for not taking some unspecified tougher action toward the Chinese suppression of Tiananmen Square demonstrations in Beijing. He stroked them in October when they were upset over a conciliatory summit Bush had held at Malta with Gorbachev, still the head of Reagan's "evil empire" as far as they were concerned.

Bush's standing on the right sharply improved in late December, however, when he ordered an invasion of Panama that led to the surrender of dictator Mañuel Noriega, and when he embraced such right-wing icons as a constitutional amendment banning flag-burning. After his first year in office, Bush had a 79 percent approval rating in a poll by the *Washington Post* and ABC News, higher than John Kennedy's rating at the end of his first year.

Yet Bush's support in his own party was always dependent on his fealty to the no-new-taxes pledge. As the federal budget deficit resulting from Reagan's borrow-and-spend policies continued to rise and the economy slowed, threatening recession, the foxes in the chicken coop like Darman began to mention the unmentionable. But Atwater was always there to remind Bush of the pledge, while reassuring the party base on the right.

In March 1990, however, Atwater collapsed and was diagnosed as having a brain tumor that ultimately cost him his life. The White House chief of staff, John Sununu, an arrogant man with a political tin ear to boot, tried ineffectively to play the Atwater role with Bush. Meanwhile, the economy continued to go south. Pressures mounted from Democratic leaders in Congress for a remedial tax increase, but they were not about to go over that politically risky cliff without Bush going hand in hand with them. Any discussions on a budget compromise, Senate Majority Leader George Mitchell flatly informed Bush, would have to be held "without preconditions," meaning new taxes could not be put off the table.[35] Alarmed House Republicans sent their president a letter reminding him of the pledge, but the congressional Democrats dug in their heels, insisting that he as president call for new taxes.

Incredibly to the Republican right wing, in late June 1990, Bush finally yielded to the proddings of Mitchell and House Speaker Thomas Foley, and a helpful shove from Darman. As evidence of the White House's awareness of the political significance and peril of the decision, no verbal announcement was made. Instead, White House press secretary Marlin Fitzwater tacked a brief statement on the press room bulletin board in which Bush said it was "clear to me that both the size of the deficit problem and the need for a package that can be enacted" required several actions, one of which, tucked into the list without fanfare, was "tax revenue increases."[36]

The note also said that "the bipartisan leadership [in Congress] agrees with me," which hardly took the curse off as far as the Republican right wing was concerned.[37] Darman's duck had come waddling out of the Oval Office, and holding him on a leash was George Bush. Immediately, eighty-nine Republican House members signed a letter to him saying they were "stunned by your announcement" and declaring a tax increase "unacceptable."[38]

In a subsequent news conference, Bush argued that "new facts" on the economic situation required him to break the pledge. "I'm doing like Lincoln did, think anew," he said, in an almost comic defense, referring to Lincoln's urging Congress in 1862 to "think anew" about the issue of slavery.[39] But his party's right wing was not thinking Great Emancipator right then. Instead, they saw Bush as the Great Prevaricator or worse, and they were never going to forget or forgive what he had just done.

William Kristol, who was chief of staff to Vice President Quayle at the time, later explained why Bush's action was so devastating to him politically. "He put all his chips on the no-tax pledge," he said. "It was not so much breaking it, but the way he broke it, the almost cavalier way he announced it; his clear failure, and the failure of those around him, to see what it meant in terms of his personal word, especially with the conservative Republicans. It seemed to reveal, perhaps somewhat unfairly, that there was no core of belief there."[40]

In any event, Bush's reneging on taxes gave the Democratic Party a major political opportunity, not widely perceived at first, because another event was occurring as the budget negotiations proceeded that would for a time give Bush political cover. That August, Iraqi forces invaded the tiny but oil-rich state of Kuwait, catching Bush by surprise but igniting him into a forceful response. He slapped a strict trade embargo on Iraq and froze all Iraqi and Kuwaiti assets in the United States. When the UN Security Council also voted a trade embargo on Iraq, its dictator, Saddam Hussein, annexed Kuwait, leading Bush to undertake Operation Desert Shield, an immense military buildup in the Persian Gulf area, at the same time mobilizing an impressive international alliance through the United Nations to force an Iraqi withdrawal.

Meanwhile at home, Bush had suffered politically from the poor economy and, within his party, from breaking the no-tax pledge. His rating of 79 percent in the *Washington Post*/ABC News poll at the year's start fell to 65 percent in July as unemployment rose, and when in September Bush agreed to a five-year deficit-reduction plan that included new taxes, the grumbling on the right began anew. House Republicans rejected the plan in a slap at their own president, before another compromise was finally struck. Evidence of how severely Bush was hurt by his tax flip-flop came in a letter from Ed Rollins, then chairman of the National Republican Congressional Committee, to Republican House candidates. He advised them to distance themselves from Bush on the budget-deficit reduction issue and take a no-new-taxes pledge themselves if they hoped to be elected. Bush was furious, but Rollins held his ground.[41]

Now Bush's approval rate in the same poll was down to 56 percent, and even support for his dispatch of troops to the Persian Gulf did not raise it much. In the off-year elections in November, the Democrats took one Senate and eight House seats from the Republicans, and the losers blamed Bush's abandonment of the no-new-taxes pledge. His lame response was to warn the Democrats in Congress that he would veto any further tax increases they might seek, and the bombastic Sununu went further, basically saying Congress could go home for all he cared. "There's not another single piece of legislation that needs to be passed in the next two years for this president," he said defiantly. "In fact, if Congress wants to come together, adjourn and leave, it's all right with us. We don't need them."[42]

All this was music to Democratic ears, but soon after, in mid-January 1991, it was drowned out by the sound of American air and ground power in the Persian Gulf. When Saddam would not budge from Kuwait and all U.S. and allied preparations were completed, Bush launched Operation Desert Storm, a lightning-swift aerial assault on Iraq followed by a massive land force that drove what was left of the Iraqi forces out of Kuwait. The successful war gave Bush an immense political as well as military victory that overnight boosted his popularity at home. Two days after the first bombs fell, his approval rate was back up to 79 percent and his reelection in 1992 seemed assured. At the same time, the startling collapse of the Soviet Union after a failed coup against Gorbachev, his subsequent resignation as head of the Soviet Communist Party and his replacement by Boris Yeltsin as president of the Russian Republic brought a general euphoria in the country.

But a recession that Bush for a long time refused to acknowledge deepened and, after a brief upturn over the summer, dipped again. His political advisers began to get nervous and urged him to begin planning for his reelection campaign and to get out around the country. But he preferred attending to presidential duties and pleasures and put it off. The victory in the Gulf, he seemed to believe, was all he needed to be reelected the next year. When near-depression hit New Hampshire, a state that helped him win the 1988 Republican nomination and whose residents he had vowed afterward he would never forget, he sent Quayle with a feeble message of "I care."

One political event in the fall of 1991 gave the Democrats a modicum of hope. In a special election for a vacancy in the U.S. Senate in Pennsylvania, their candidate, Harris Wofford, an old Kennedyite appointed by Democratic Governor Robert Casey to a brief interim term, upset former Republican Governor Richard Thornburgh, who had stepped down as Bush's attorney general to run. Architects of Wofford's campaign, in which he stumped relentlessly for national health insurance, were two little-known Democratic political operatives named Paul Begala and James Carville, later to become celebrities in their own right. The fact that

Thornburgh had been a part of the Bush administration enabled some Democrats to see Wofford's victory as a repudiation of the president, although it was a stretch to so conclude.

Nevertheless, few prominent Democrats were yet willing to take on the hero of the Persian Gulf war. The first to declare his bid for the 1992 Democratic presidential nomination was a long shot, former Senator Paul Tsongas of Massachusetts. He was well liked and well respected, but had been forced in 1984 to retire from the Senate with cancer. He was said to have been cured, but doubts lingered.

Others held back, even as national party chairman Brown set to work organizing the DNC for the 1992 general election. He wanted to have machinery in place for the eventual party presidential nominee, including better coordination with statewide candidates and their campaigns. By the summer of 1991, three of the more prominently mentioned possible candidates, House Majority Leader Gephardt and Senators Al Gore and Jay Rockefeller, all had announced that they would not run.

Soon after Labor Day, however, four other Democrats joined Tsongas in the contest for the Democratic nomination—former Governors Douglas Wilder of Virginia and Jerry Brown of California and Senators Tom Harkin of Iowa and Bob Kerrey of Nebraska. Harkin's decision to run as a clear-cut liberal and champion of labor effectively erased Iowa's traditionally leadoff precinct caucuses as an important factor in the Democratic competition for 1992, and elevated New Hampshire's first-in-the-nation primary. Consequently the candidates beat a path there through late 1991.

Bill Clinton was not yet a candidate, but he had won high marks in preliminary joustings at party meetings for his ability to deliver stem-winding speeches without text or notes. He was always a great talker, Arkansas Democrats avowed. To win their approval of a presidential bid in 1992, in fact, he had been obliged to talk his way out of a pledge he had made to Arkansas voters in seeking reelection for governor in 1990 that if reelected he would complete the four-year term. So he had to go back to them in 1991, "asking" whether he should go after the Democratic presidential nomination after all. To nobody's surprise, he read their reply as a "yes."

At the outset, according to Kamarck, Clinton first considered running in 1992 primarily with the objective of giving greater national exposure to the DLC agenda and to himself as a different kind of Democrat, with an eye to making his real bid for the Democratic nomination in 1996. At a meeting at Boston's Logan Airport in the summer of 1991, Kamarck recalled later, Clinton mused about a quick venture into presidential waters in the coming winter and being able to return to the governorship by March if lightning failed to strike him.[43]

Through the next months, the DLC continued to send Clinton as chairman around the country, scheduling him and paying for his out-of-state travel expenses, all with an eye to pushing him into declared presidential candidacy. On October 3, in front of the Old State House in Little Rock, he finally made it official, laying out his proposed agenda as the candidate of the New Democrats. He pledged to work for "the forgotten middle class" and deftly dodged the demonized liberal label as well as the conservative, saying, "the change we must make isn't liberal or conservative. It's both and it's different."[44] With the DLC strongly behind him, he embarked on an adventure that was destined to change the shape, and some would say the soul, of the Democratic Party.

The field now had six declared candidates, often derisively dismissed as the "Six-pack," just as the 1988 field of Democratic presidential aspirants had been ridiculed as "the Seven Dwarfs." There remained, however, one other prominent Democrat many in the party hoped would run and thought could win—Governor Mario Cuomo of New York, who continued to tantalize the political community. Ever since delivering an electrifying speech calling the party back to its New Deal roots and objectives at the 1984 Democratic National Convention in San Francisco, Cuomo had been the answer to liberal Democrats' dreams as a national candidate. They yearned for him to say at last he would run.

Cuomo was a threat to all the other candidates, but he posed a particular potential challenge to Clinton as chairman of the DLC, which Cuomo held in low regard. He saw the organization as breaking ranks from the party's time-honored aggressive posture on the left and positioning itself safely in the center. In May 1991 the New York governor had taken the DLC to task for what he called its "implicit position that we have something we have to apologize for, and now we have to move to the middle."[45] A Cuomo-Clinton confrontation, however, was not in the cards. At the very hour of the filing deadline for the New Hampshire primary in mid-December, Cuomo announced he would remain as governor in Albany. Without Cuomo, the Democratic field did not seem all that imposing.

Clinton nevertheless continued to impress national Democrats with his speeches following his declaration of candidacy. As the election year of 1992 began and before a single primary vote had been cast, he found himself anointed the consensus front-runner for the Democratic presidential nomination. What was more, the DLC now had one of its own in an advantageous position to change the party's direction away from the left-of-center positions that had brought it to defeat so often over the previous thirty-four years. But he was not there yet. In addition to fighting off the other Democratic candidates, Bill Clinton had demons of his own to conquer, or at least talk away.

In 1992, Governor Bill Clinton of Arkansas, seeking the Democratic presidential nomination, was plagued by reports of womanizing, but overcame them and was elected.

Chapter 31

A DIFFERENT KIND OF DEMOCRAT, 1992

BY ALL NORMAL political standards, Arkansas Governor Bill Clinton should have had a smooth ride to the 1992 Democratic presidential nomination. The only true liberals in the "Six-pack" of declared candidates, Tom Harkin and Jerry Brown, each had a serious drawback: Harkin was regarded essentially and narrowly as labor's man in the field, and Brown's previous erratic runs, most recently a loss in a bid for a U.S. Senate seat, diminished his political reputation. Besides, after the defeats of Mondale and Dukakis, the liberal credential had lost much of its luster as Democratic leaders sought a winning formula for a return to the White House. Cuomo's decision not to run was the final blow to the party's left.

The one black candidate in the field, Douglas Wilder, reconsidered and dropped out of the race as the election year got under way, and Jesse Jackson was on the defensive in his continuing effort to keep the party on the liberal path. The two remaining contenders, Paul Tsongas and Bob Kerrey, also had handicaps—Tsongas, a history of ill health and a certain quirkiness of appearance and style, and Kerrey, a blunt manner and lack of clearly identified campaign theme and purpose.

From the start, Tsongas made a strong bid for the party's center with thoughtful position papers and a book calling on fellow Democrats to shed the anti-business reputation their party had acquired through the New Deal years. While Tsongas was a virtual unknown nationally and derided as "another Greek from Massachusetts," Democrats in his neighboring state of New Hampshire were familiar with him, and therein was Tsongas's best entry portal to wider publicity and potential success. He made the most of it, and the nation's first primary there soon became basically a contest between Tsongas and Clinton.

It was during the New Hampshire primary when Clinton's personal drawbacks as a national candidate first surfaced, but within his inner circle there had long been concern that it might happen. In 1990 a disgruntled former state employee had held a press conference in Little Rock announcing he was filing a lawsuit against Clinton. He claimed he had been fired and charged that the young Arkansas governor had used state funds in pursuit of five women, one of them identified as Gennifer Flowers, a former television reporter and later local nightclub singer. The case got little press attention at the time, as local reporters wrote off the employee as a chronic crank.

In the summer of 1991 the conservative *Washington Times* had reported unverified rumors that Clinton had had "extramarital affairs, illegitimate children and [had] used drugs." Similar indirect references had shown up in *The New Republic* and the column of conservative polemicist George Will.[1] To all this, Clinton reassured his political aides there was nothing to worry about.

The same was the case with staff concerns about the governor's lack of military service during the Vietnam War. He told aides that while he had opposed the war, he didn't duck service but was saved from serving by having received a high lottery number. Nevertheless, Clinton's political strategists, with the earlier Gary Hart experience clearly in mind, decided that to pre-empt troublesome questions later, it would be wise for him to find a forum in which to deal with various rumors. He chose a popular breakfast meeting of reporters organized by the *Christian Science Monitor* bureau chief in Washington, Godfrey Sperling, which Clinton's wife, Hillary, also attended.

Primed for the womanizing question planted by an aide, Clinton said all the rumors stemmed from the disgruntled employee's lawsuit and again called them "false." Then, as planned, he told the reporters "what you need to know about Hillary and me is that we've been together nearly twenty years. It has not been perfect or free from problems, but we're committed to our marriage and its obligations—to our child [a daughter, Chelsea] and to each other. We love each other very much." And that, he said, "ought to be enough" to satisfy the press on the whole matter.[2]

Shortly after Clinton's declaration of candidacy, *Penthouse* magazine bought and ran an interview with a self-styled rock-star groupie from Arkansas named Connie Hamzy, in which she alleged a near-encounter with Clinton at a Little Rock hotel in 1984. CNN Headline News briefly picked up the story but then dropped it after Clinton aides swiftly controlled the damage, submitting affidavits from witnesses who said the woman had approached Clinton and he had quickly rebuffed her.

None of this had any effect on his campaign in New Hampshire, where a sixty-second television ad in which Clinton directly laid out a persuasive plan for economic recovery shot him into the lead over Tsongas in an internal campaign poll. In mid-January, however, the womanizer rumors resurfaced, first with a regurgitation of the lawsuit in a supermarket tabloid, then in a televised debate among the Democratic candidates and finally in the same gossip tabloid again. This time it ran a first-person account by Flowers providing vivid details of repeated Clinton visits to her Little Rock apartment, backed up by audiotapes, produced at a subsequent news conference. They purported to have Clinton saying to her of their liaison, "If they ever hit you with it, just say no and go on. . . . If everybody is on record denying it, no problem."[3]

On a dismal, rainy day at a paintbrush plant in Claremont, New Hampshire, Clinton was confronted by the traveling press corps with the story, which he had already been told about by Mark Halperin, an ABC News producer. Again he denied it, while saying he had talked to Flowers and had advised her "to just tell the truth" if asked about a relationship with him.[4] After quickly touring the plant, Clinton closeted himself with aides George Stephanopoulos and Paul Begala to decide what course to take. "We were trying to figure out how deep the wound was," Stephanopoulos said later, "and whether we had to go for radical surgery right away, or if we had time to stabilize the patient and keep moving."[5]

By breaking off the day's campaigning, however, Clinton assured that the traveling reporters of the so-called mainstream press would be obliged to explain why, thus finding themselves in the position of having the tail of American journalism—the supermarket tabloid—wagging the dog. Some newspapers, like the *New York Times,* buried the story well inside their pages, but most trumpeted it and the local television station in Manchester showed the frenzy around Clinton at the plant in Claremont.

Instead of going on television himself, Clinton cut off campaigning.

He flew back to Little Rock to deal with eleventh-hour appeals to stay the scheduled execution of the convicted killer of a police officer, which in the end he rejected. On Super Bowl Sunday, Clinton and his wife submitted to a taped interview on the popular CBS News show *60 Minutes* to discuss the womanizing matter. Shown immediately after the game to an audience of thirty-four million, the show produced further denials by Clinton about an affair with Flowers and a strong defense of him by his wife. He acknowledged without specificity that he had been responsible for "wrongdoing" and "causing pain in my marriage," but balked at a question about having committed adultery.[6]

"I think most Americans who are watching this tonight," he said near the end, "they'll know what we're saying, they'll get it, and they'll feel that we have been more candid." His wife added: "I don't think being any more specific about what's happened in the privacy of our life together is relevant to anybody besides us."[7]

Upon Clinton's return to New Hampshire shortly before the Democratic primary, another story broke that kept him and his campaign on the defensive—not from some sleazy supermarket tabloid this time but from the staid, respectable, mainstream *Wall Street Journal*. It quoted a former army recruiter in Arkansas saying Clinton in 1969 had signed up for the Reserve Officers Training Corps (ROTC) at the University of Arkansas Law School to avoid the draft and stay out of Vietnam, and then "was able to manipulate things so that he didn't have to go in."[8]

At the time Clinton had been at Oxford on a Rhodes Scholarship, and by signing up for the ROTC program, he had obtained a deferment to finish his scholarship before entering law school back home. By that time, however, he had put himself back in the draft, had drawn a lottery number too high to be called and decided to go to Yale Law School instead of Arkansas.

Again damage control was required. Clinton, again mobbed by reporters in a hotel lobby in Nashua, insisted, "I was not seeking to avoid military service" by signing up for the reserve training. When he decided instead to take his chances with the draft, he said, he had not had any way of knowing he would subsequently receive a high draft lottery number that would save him from being called.[9] Clinton and his campaign party once more retreated to Little Rock to assess the political fallout. It was severe, as measured by the campaign's pollster, Stan Greenberg: Clinton's support in New Hampshire had plunged from 37 percent of voters surveyed to 17, and a *Boston Globe* poll showed Tsongas pulling even with him.

Matters grew worse when Clinton and party returned to New Hampshire, where Halperin of ABC News handed Stephanopoulos a copy of a December 1969 letter from Clinton to the Arkansas draft official thanking him "for saving me from the draft" and explaining why he was withdrawing from the ROTC. The letter included a strong denunciation of the Vietnam War. The draft, Clinton also wrote, was "illegitimate" in forcing American citizens to "fight and kill and die in a war they may oppose, a war which even possibly may be wrong, a war which, in any case, does not involve immediately the peace and freedom of the nation."[10]

Most pointedly for Clinton's political future, he praised two Oxford friends for becoming conscientious objectors and said he had considered the same option but "decided to accept the draft in spite of my beliefs for one reason: to maintain my political viability within the system." He had prepared himself for "a political life," he wrote, and was not going to jeopardize his chances with later charges that he had dodged the draft.[11]

Younger Clinton advisers feared that the letter, and particularly the latter reference, had doomed their man's candidacy. But James Carville, now Clinton's chief political strategist and like him a member of the Vietnam generation, saw it otherwise. Telling Clinton the letter was "your best friend," Carville concocted the strategy of selling it as an honest reflection of a young man's deep turmoil over a war with which he disagreed, and his decision in the final analysis to face his draft obligation. In the end, Clinton appeared on the ABC News program *Nightline,* where Ted Koppel read the letter in full and Clinton called it "a true reflection of the deep and conflicted feelings of a just-turned-twenty-three-year-old young man."[12]

Deftly, the Clinton campaign now cast its candidate as the beleaguered underdog against Tsongas. Clinton in person and on television threw himself vigorously into the closing days of the New Hampshire primary. Vietnam hero Kerrey, while saying the war was not an issue, ran ads questioning Clinton's electability in light of the furor. All Clinton campaign operatives of importance were moved from Little Rock to New Hampshire, led by campaign chairman Mickey Kantor, working with a sense that unless Clinton made a respectable showing there, his candidacy could be finished before it had really begun.

On election day, Tsongas, as expected, won, with 33 percent of the

Democratic vote. Clinton was second with 25 percent, Kerrey with 11 and the others far behind. Accentuating the positive, Clinton proclaimed himself "The Comeback Kid" in a primary he had been expected to win until the womanizing and draft-dodger stories had obliged him to pull himself back from the brink. At the same time, the whole matter of Clinton's credibility had been shaken by the revelations, and his candidacy proceeded under a cloud of uncertainty about what new allegations might yet derail him.

In the Republican primary, President Bush also won New Hampshire despite his early neglect of the state, but only after a telling indication of his vulnerability. His 53 percent of the GOP vote drew more public attention and surprise than the 37 percent won by his challenger, former Nixon and Reagan operative, newspaper columnist and television commentator Patrick J. Buchanan. Incensed at what he saw as Bush's abandonment of Reaganite principles in his tax increase and other matters, Buchanan proclaimed to his followers: "Tonight we began as a little rebellion that has emerged into a full-fledged middle-American revolution. We are going to take our party back from those who have walked away from us and forgotten us."[13]

Another figure aligned with neither party had the same basic idea, but of "taking back" the whole country. As the Republican and Democratic primary fights went forward, a Texas billionaire of distinctly independent streak named Ross Perot decided to launch a third-party bid, ostensibly at the behest of millions of dissatisfied voters that only he seemed to hear calling his name. On the cable news program of talk-show host Larry King, Perot said he would run if voters put him on the ballot in all fifty states.[14] They responded by flooding the telephone lines, and he took the plunge, pumping his own money and energy into the effort. His populist pitch, delivered with a heavy Texas twang, put him at the disposal of "the owners" of the country under the banner "United We Stand." They, in turn, engaged in a remarkable self-starting effort to put Perot on the ballot in their states, and by April a *Washington Post*/ABC News poll had him in serious contention: Bush 36 percent, Clinton 31 percent, Perot 30 percent.

Here was a wild card whose impact on the election of 1992 was not to be dismissed out of hand. As a challenger to the Bush status quo, the Perot candidacy threatened to split the anti-Bush vote, to the detriment of the eventual Democratic nominee. Beyond that, it underscored a critical development in presidential campaigning—the bypassing of the traditional press corps in favor of direct communication with the voters via television. As John Chancellor, one of the medium's most astute observers, wrote later: "The candidates preferred to talk politics with less-experienced interrogators on early-morning talk shows. Candidates had intimate chats with voters on telephone lines while other voters listened in. Talk-show America became party-line America."[15] In all this time, Chancellor also noted, Perot had not bought a single television commercial in "a classic hostile-takeover bid, conceived and executed by an audacious entrepreneur."[16]

Meanwhile, Buchanan's strong showing in New Hampshire against Bush encouraged Democrats to believe they could beat the Republican incumbent, especially if the challenge from the right in his own party continued and deepened GOP divisions. Having himself survived in New Hampshire on the Democratic side, Clinton now benefited greatly from the calendar, the front-loading of primaries dominated by those in the South starting two weeks later in Georgia, and then in an expanded Super Tuesday thereafter.

Tsongas maintained his position by running essentially even with Jerry Brown in Maine at 30 percent and comparing that vote with Clinton's 15 percent there. Meanwhile, a basically unopposed Harkin had carried the caucuses in his own state of Iowa, and Kerrey won the meaningless primary in South Dakota. He then headed south to Georgia, determined to derail Clinton there. In Atlanta, he said Clinton could not win and if nominated was "going to be opened up like a soft peanut" by the Republicans in the fall, alluding to his already identified vulnerabilities.[17] While vowing not to inject Vietnam service as an issue, Kerrey lamented at one point that "it was the men and women who went to Vietnam who suffered when they came home, and all of a sudden all the sympathy in this campaign is flowing to somebody who didn't go."[18]

Tsongas, clinging to his position as front-runner, meanwhile was being ganged up on by the other candidates struggling to stay alive. Their actions benefited Clinton, who already was casting the nomination race as a two-man event between himself and Tsongas. He readily joined the pack against Tsongas, ridiculing his pro-business stance. In one remark in Colorado, the site of another early primary, Clinton compared Tsongas's economic recovery ideas with the New Deal that had brought the country out of the 1930s depression. "Franklin Roosevelt didn't get this country off its back," he observed, "by saying the only thing we have to fear is lack of venture capital."[19]

The dam began to break for Clinton in the Georgia primary, when he won 57 percent of the vote in a field of five, with only 24 percent for Tsongas. In Maryland, Utah and Washington, Tsongas hung on, and Brown narrowly edged Clinton in Colorado, but Georgia was the key test on that Tuesday. Four days later, Clinton won in South Carolina and on Super Tuesday, March 10, when eight states held primaries and three held caucuses, Clinton won eight of the eleven, including Florida, which Tsongas had hoped to salvage. There, Clinton carried 51 percent of the vote to 35 for Tsongas, who on the same day managed to take only his own Massachusetts, Rhode Island and Delaware.

The goal of the Southern governors and the Democratic Leadership Council to give the South a stronger if not dominant voice in presidential nomination selection had produced the desired effect. Thereafter Clinton began a mop-up exercise in Illinois and Michigan, scoring his first major victories outside the South and driving Tsongas to end his campaign, leaving only Jerry Brown, who narrowly won Connecticut after Tsongas's withdrawal, barely in contention.

Meanwhile, there was some grumbling among DLC leaders that their former chairman, the man they saw as their handpicked candidate for president, had not pushed the DLC agenda sufficiently in the drive to take over control of the party. Yet Clinton often wove the DLC theme into his speeches, and never more notably than in a pitch in Macomb County, outside Detroit, known as "the home of the Reagan Democrats." First he told a predominantly white suburban audience concerning racial divisions: "This is a crisis of economics, of values. It has nothing to do with race.... The one thing that it's going to take to bring this country together is somebody's got to come back to the so-called Reagan Democratic area and say, 'Look, I'll give you your values back, I'll restore the economic leadership, I'll help you build the middle class back.' But you've got to say, 'Okay, let's do it with everybody in this country.' "[20]

The next morning, before a black congregation in a Baptist church in Detroit, he recalled what he had said in white Macomb County and went on: "I come here to challenge you to reach out your hand to them, for we have been divided for too long.... On [election day], tell the people of Macomb County, 'If you'll give up your race feelings, we'll say we want empowerment, not entitlement, we want opportunity but we accept responsibility, we're going to help be a part of the change.' "[21]

The only bump in the road thereafter came briefly during the New

York primary, when the credibility question against Clinton surfaced again in a debate with Brown. A panelist asked Clinton about possible past drug use and he gave his standard answer: "I have never broken the laws of my country." By this time, Clinton's reputation for the cute evasion was well known, so the reporter pressed him: what about breaking a state law or a law of another country, for instance when he was a student at Oxford? Clinton replied: "I've never broken any state laws, and when I was in England, I experimented with marijuana a time or two." Then, after a pause: "And I didn't like it, and I didn't inhale, and I didn't try it again."[22]

The artful dodging brought Clinton more ridicule, but didn't slow his march toward the nomination, nailed down in the final major primaries in New York, Pennsylvania and California. Still, a *Washington Post* poll after the New York primary found 55 percent of voters surveyed saying they lacked confidence in Clinton's honesty and integrity to be president.

At the national convention in New York, chairman Ron Brown saw to it that a rare harmony prevailed, with a platform that reflected the new influence of the DLC and of the New Democrat to be nominated. One plank noted the change in the party platform going back to New Deal days. It said: "We offer a new social contract based neither on callous, do-nothing Republican neglect nor on an outdated faith in programs as the solution to every problem."[23]

After a Carter-like deliberative process, Clinton selected a fellow DLC member, Senator Al Gore, to be his running mate, a man who shared not only his regional identity but also his core philosophy. The choice gave a distinctly young look to the new Democratic team, which they later exploited to great effect on several joint bus tours across various states, deploring the stagnant state of the economy under Bush.

On the eve of Clinton's acceptance speech, Ross Perot suddenly stole the spotlight by announcing he was quitting the presidential campaign. He told aides his reason was that his children were being adversely affected by it, but the public rationale he gave, preposterously, was that "now that the Democratic Party has revitalized itself, I have concluded that we cannot win in November."[24] His continued candidacy would deprive anyone of a majority in the electoral college, he said, and thus throw the election into the House of Representatives, delaying the presidential choice. Clinton placed a call to Perot and in his speech called on the shocked Perot volunteer army "to join us in our efforts to change our country and give our government back to the people."[25] However, it was not the last that would be heard from the feisty independent from Texas.

Immediately after the Democratic convention, Clinton and Gore developed a politically effective traveling road show, complete with a routine climaxed by a Gore Q-and-A with the greatly amused crowd. "It's time for Bush and Quayle to go!" he would proclaim. Then he would yell: "What time is it?" And the shouted reply would come: "It's time for them to go!"[26]

Before long, large roadside gatherings would await the bus cavalcade in small towns as a political and personal bonding between the two Democratic candidates developed. Each had his own bus, but Gore often would ride with Clinton in his, frequently slowing the trip with long private gabfests. It got to the point where weary traveling reporters, at the end of a grueling day, would rock Clinton's bus to break up the schmoozing or call out to the two new best buddies: "What time is it? It's time for us to go!"[27] Voters seemed to like the new team. On the heels of the Democratic convention, the *Washington Post*/ABC News poll had Clinton leading Bush by a whopping 60 percent to 34.

While Clinton and Gore were thus cavorting, the Republican National Convention met in Houston to rubber-stamp the renomination of Bush and Quayle, the challenge to Bush from Buchanan by this time having petered out. For some time during the Bush term, however, there had been considerable speculation that Quayle would be dumped from the ticket in 1992. Although for the most part he had kept an even course as vice president, his penchant for verbal gaffes demonstrated in the 1988 campaign occasionally had been on display again.

Quayle, for example, went to El Salvador and proclaimed that the United States was committed to "work toward the elimination of human rights" in the region. In a speech to the United Negro College Fund, whose motto was "A mind is a terrible thing to waste," Quayle mangled it so that it came out: "What a waste it is to lose one's mind, or not to have a mind, is being very wasteful. How true that is."[28] After erroneously coaching a young student in a spelling bee, signs on the campaign trail greeted Quayle as "Mr. Potatoe Head." And so on.

The vice president nevertheless proved to be a prolific fund-raiser for his party, but every time Bush caught a cold the talk of replacing him was heard anew. Bush campaign chairman and veteran pollster Robert Teeter had a poll taken measuring how Quayle and other possible running mates might affect the Republican ticket. The results were inconclusive, so he stayed on.

The dominant aspect of the Republican convention was its harsh conservative tone, highlighted not by Bush's acceptance speech but by a slashing attack on the Democrats and Clinton by Buchanan. In what was only a thinly veiled notice of his own intentions to take over the party, he tossed red meat to the religious fundamentalists, declaring: "There is a religious war going on in this country for the soul of America. It is a cultural war as critical to the kind of nation we shall be as the Cold War itself. And in that struggle for the soul of America, [Bill] Clinton and [Hillary] Clinton are on the other side and George Bush is on our side."[29] The convention boosted Bush's poll numbers, narrowing Clinton's lead over him in the *Post*/ABC poll to 49 percent to 40.

The fall campaign saw a continuation of personal attacks on Clinton by Bush operatives including his campaign's distaff pit bull, Mary Matalin, whose way of denying she had attacked Clinton personally was to tell a reporter: "The larger issue is that he's evasive and slick. We've never said to the press that he's a philandering, pot-smoking draft dodger."[30] At the same time, the Clinton campaign missed no opportunity to remind voters of the Bush campaign's use of the Willie Horton case against Dukakis in 1988, suggesting that when it came to going negative, the Republican leopard had not changed its spots. Bush himself stayed mostly on the high road, letting surrogates attack Clinton's "character."

Meanwhile, the Clinton campaign hammered away at Bush's record on the stalled economy. Carville in Little Rock ran a "war room" where daily strategy and "rapid response" to all allegations from the opposition were shaped. A sign on the wall reminded the troops of three themes to be struck: "Change vs. more of the same," "The economy, stupid," and "Don't forget health care."[31]

Clinton television ads charged "years of Republican neglect" and "the worst economic record since the Great Depression," and trumpeted the new face Clinton was putting on his own party. "They're a new generation of Democrats, Bill Clinton and Al Gore," one proclaimed. "And they don't think the way the old Democratic Party did. They've called for an end to welfare as we know it, so welfare can be a second chance, not a way of life. They've sent a strong signal to criminals by supporting the death penalty. And they've rejected the old tax-and-spend politics."[32]

In the last days of September, Perot suddenly dangled his considerable support before the Clinton and Bush campaigns, inviting their leaders to Dallas to present their platforms to the state leaders of his United We Stand organization. Mickey Kantor led the Clinton delegation and Bob Teeter the Republican, and each group was given two hours to make its pitch for support, but they turned out to be mere props for another Perot surprise. The next day he reported that his toll-free telephone number, still in operation, had received a million and a half calls urging him to get back into the race. Two days later he did so, announcing he was "honored to accept their request."[33] The wild card was back again, this time pouring his millions into television "infomercials" featuring himself talking at length. It was anybody's guess what the effect would be.

One tangible result was the decision of the Commission on Presidential Debates to include Perot in three presidential sessions with Clinton and Bush. Perot's running mate, retired Navy Admiral James Stockdale, was scheduled for one vice-presidential debate against Gore and Quayle. Although conventional wisdom dictated that an incumbent decline to debate, Bush agreed because he was trailing Clinton in the polls.

The critical confrontation came at the University of Richmond, in a town-meeting format in which the three candidates faced voters selected because they had identified themselves as undecided. Although this sort of format was often derided by the press as inviting softball questions, this time it worked, as complaints were raised from the audience about the substance and tone of the campaign.

Of the three candidates, Clinton was by far the most effective, responding directly to the questioners, giving them detailed answers in terms of their own lives and concerns. By contrast, Bush, intent on attacking the front-running Clinton, often seemed confused and unable to grasp the substance of some questions and the tactical dynamic of the debate. Pressed on how he as a wealthy man could understand the problems of the average voter, Bush suggested that it was like saying "you haven't had cancer, therefore you don't know what it's like"—precisely the questioner's point.[34] Later, the all-seeing television eye caught Bush glancing at his wristwatch, leaving the immediate impression that he wished the whole business would be over.

The debates only served to solidify Clinton's support and help give Perot the visibility he needed to remain a factor. On election night, Clinton returned the Democratic Party to the White House as a plurality president, with 43 percent and 370 electoral votes to 37 percent and 168 electoral votes for Bush. Perot won a very respectable 19 percent, a record for an independent candidate, but no votes in the electoral college. Clinton's percentage, however, was the lowest posted by a winning candidate in eighty years, and the Democrats lost nine seats in the House, leaving them with their lowest number, 258, since the first Eisenhower administration.

One bright spot was a notable rise in voter turnout for the first time in thirty-two years, to 55.2 percent of the eligible voting-age population from 50.1 percent four years earlier. Clinton, with his centrist pitch, recaptured the Reagan Democrats by two to one over Bush, and led comfortably among young and first-time voters, while holding on to the old Democratic coalition with strong support from the black, Jewish and Latino constituencies.

In a broader sense, change was the winner, with the candidates of change, Clinton and Perot, together burying the incumbent Republican. Even Clinton's struggles with the womanizing and draft-dodging issues did not bring him down because voters were more focused on their own problems. His pitch to middle-income as well as lower-income Americans resonated with them, as questions about Bush's commitment to them, and about Perot's stability, remained.

The New Democrats of the DLC rejoiced in what they perceived as their victory, not only in electing Clinton but in the process moving closer toward taking over the direction and agenda of the Democratic Party. But that perception would soon be open to question. While embracing the main themes of the DLC, often agitating liberals, Clinton had continued to speak out more emphatically than the DLC did in support of social issues like abortion rights and civil rights dear to old liberal hearts.[35] Bill Clinton was a New Democrat, to be sure, but not without conspicuous liberal stripes, as he entered the White House in 1993.

President Bill Clinton, on taking office in 1993, issued an executive order removing the ban on military service by homosexuals, a decision that outraged many top brass, who were already alienated from Clinton because he avoided the draft during the Vietnam War.

Chapter 32

LOOKING LIKE AMERICA, 1993–1996

NEWLY ELECTED PRESIDENT Clinton had pledged as a candidate that he would appoint a cabinet and run an administration that would "look like America." That is, his appointments would reflect the gender, racial, ethnic and religious composition of the nation at large—a measure of his determination to create an inclusive government that would address the needs and aspirations of all Americans.

It was a noble-sounding notion on which the first Democratic president in twelve years would begin his White House tenure. But it did not exactly square with the New Democrat philosophy he also espoused—the DLC credo wherein opportunity would be extended to all without regard to sex, race, ethnicity or religion, in return for acceptance of individual responsibility. As Kenneth S. Baer noted in his book *Reinventing Democrats,* this focus on a cabinet that looked like America "painted Clinton as a societal liberal" and his "commitment to diversity over other criteria such as ideology, internal policy cohesion and factional loyalty inevitably disadvantaged New Democrats."[1]

In the country at large as well, Clinton, even before he took office, expressed his intention to extend this inclusiveness to homosexuals in the military, another campaign pledge that had drawn little attention and for which there was no great groundswell of popular demand. As an opening gambit for a new administration, it proved to be a hornet's nest, generating a controversy and a confrontation with the Pentagon and important members of Congress that he did not need.

The proposal put Clinton in immediate conflict with his fellow DLC member, Chairman Sam Nunn of the Senate Armed Services Committee, and with General Colin Powell, chairman of the Joint Chiefs of Staff.[2] In light of Clinton's history of draft avoidance during the Vietnam War, he already was in bad odor with many in the military and their congressional supporters. Senate Republican leader Bob Dole chipped in with an observation that the new president, having never shared a foxhole with anyone, could not understand what such a move would mean in terms of military morale.[3] This was hardly the optimum note on which to launch the Clinton presidency, and particularly mindless inasmuch as there had been no conspicuous pressure from gay America for such early action. A compromise policy eventually was adopted called "don't ask, don't tell," meaning that the sexual orientation of gay members of the armed forces was not to be subject to interrogation as long as they kept it their own business.

At the same time, Clinton stumbled out of the gate in his insistence on putting an inclusive face on his cabinet, particularly in terms of gender. An urgent and diligent search for a woman to be his attorney general led to an embarrassing series of missteps that sent a message that another Southern governor, like Jimmy Carter, had been elected when he wasn't ready for the challenges of national office.

Clinton's first choice to head the Department of Justice was a high-powered New York corporate lawyer named Zoe Baird who also happened to be a goddaughter of his new secretary of state, Warren Christopher.[4] She and her Yale law professor husband were discovered to have hired an illegal immigrant Peruvian couple as nanny and chauffeur for less than minimum wage plus board, and without paying social security or taxes for them until just before her appointment had been announced.[5] Bernard Nussbaum, the newly selected White House counsel, advised Clinton to keep Baird on and ride out the storm, but aide George Stephanopoulos insisted the "nanny" story would hang on, so it was better for Clinton to cut his losses quickly.[6] The Baird nomination was withdrawn.

Next, determined to choose a woman for the post, Clinton approached a federal district court judge, Kimba Wood, wife of then *Time* magazine writer Michael Kramer, who also turned out to have a somewhat similar "nanny" problem. The woman hired was also an illegal alien but Wood had paid her social security taxes and had initiated action to obtain legal residency for her. Before the nomination was made, however, it was leaked to the press and Wood withdrew, leaving Clinton with more egg on his face.[7]

The search for a female attorney general went on, with Clinton finally settling on Janet Reno, the district attorney in Miami. That appointment, too, brought questions about Clinton's judgment, and Reno's, when shortly afterward the siege of a compound of the Branch Davidian cult at Waco, Texas, by agents of the Bureau of Alcohol, Tobacco and Firearms, ended in the fiery death of more than eighty members, including women and children.

Clinton also ran into trouble with the DLC over the nomination of old friend and civil rights activist Lani Guinier, a law professor at the University of Pennsylvania, to be assistant attorney general for civil rights, and with his black and liberal constituencies when he withdrew it under conservative fire. Guinier, a schoolmate of Clinton's at Yale Law School, provided ammunition for Republican and other conservative critics in academic writings in which she questioned "simple-minded notions of majority rule" that she suggested punished racial minorities. Clinton caved in with the alibi that "at the time of the nomination I had not read her writings,"[8] thus sacrificing what chips he had won from blacks and liberals for the appointment, and dismaying other loyal "Friends of Bill."

The New Democrats were not happy with the new president for whose election they took credit. In addition to pushing gays in the military early, Clinton also had signed executive orders lifting federal restrictions on funding and access to abortions, among his first presidential decisions. Such actions prompted Senator John Breaux of Louisiana, a DLC chairman, to call on Clinton to break away from "lifestyle and entitlement liberalism" and govern more like a New Democrat.[9] Others in the DLC, while not expecting Clinton to abandon his more liberal inclinations, hoped he would make them less conspicuous.

His first budget also disappointed the New Democrats. With congressional Republicans declining to cooperate on such proposals as a middle-class tax cut, Clinton was obliged to court old Democrats with social spending accommodations and at the same time massage the New Democrats with a start on deficit reduction. He ended up pleasing neither faction. He squeezed his budget through without a single Republican vote, but an economic stimulus package was rejected by the Senate.

More significant to the DLC, its hopes of Clinton being its vehicle for remaking the Democratic Party and taking it over from the old liberal congressional leadership were going aglimmering. His early concept of a "New Covenant" pairing opportunity with responsibility as a departure from the New Deal, the Fair Deal, the New Frontier and the Great Society became a forgotten theme song. Early talk of a Clinton "first hundred days" of bold initiatives comparable to that of FDR in 1933 evaporated. *Time* magazine ran a cover story entitled "The Incredible Shrinking Presidency,"[10] and other publications and commentators echoed the sentiment.

The crunch came in Clinton's decision to make health care reform the centerpiece of his first-year agenda. The New Democrats wanted him to tackle welfare reform first, in keeping with his campaign objective to "end welfare as we know it." But with Hillary Clinton espousing health reform and liberals in Congress arguing it must go first, changing the welfare system was put on hold. At a state governors' national conference in Washington, however, the new president told them: "We must begin now to plan for a time when people will ultimately be able to work for the check they get, whether the check comes from a private employer or the U.S. taxpayer."[11]

The policy choice went to the heart of the division between the old Democrats and the new, and opened Clinton to the old Republican criticism of Democratic "tax and spend liberalism" that he had labored so hard to counter as a different kind of Democrat.

Not only the priority choice but also the implementation of the health reform campaign under Hillary Clinton's leadership proved disastrous. She assembled a large task force of experts and social theoreticians that met in secret at the White House, angering many congressional Democrats and mobilizing the health-care insurance industry against it. After months of deliberations, Clinton unveiled a complex scheme of managed care, with multiple choices covering all Americans through new health alliances run by the government and paid largely by employers. It became an easy target for opponents, including small insurance companies, who ran a television ad showing a middle-aged couple, "Harry and Louise," expressing concerns over "a new army of government bureaucrats," and whether under the Clinton plan they would lose their right to choose their doctor.[12]

For all of Hillary Clinton's tenacity, at congressional hearings and around the country, she began to be perceived not as the first lady but as a fierce political player in a way that diminished her stature with the public. Her role in her husband's administration had been unique from the start, as it had been throughout his political career. During his 1992 presidential campaign, he had touted her as a kind of bonus for the voters, cheerily referring to her political talents by telling them that by voting for him they were getting "two for the price of one." But she had not been elected by the people, and all those who didn't care for her or this special role hardened into a substantial anti-Hillary core.

The president's wife also became the center of an early-term controversy over the firing of longtime officials in the White House travel office amid allegations of misuse of funds, and their replacement by a Little Rock travel agency with Clinton connections. Later she was embroiled in a questionable real-estate deal in Arkansas known as Whitewater, leading to appointment of an independent counsel to conduct an investigation that haunted the Clintons throughout their White House tenure. It ensnared some Clinton associates but eventually came to naught concerning the Clintons themselves, though with significant collateral developments.

A sad side story to the case was the suicide in July 1993 of Vincent Foster, an old Hillary Clinton law firm friend and associate assigned at the White House to deal with the Whitewater and other personal Clinton family matters. His death generated Republican allegations of cover-up and foul play that also came to nothing. In sum, Hillary Clinton as an ex-officio administration power was as much a distraction as a bonus, at least in her husband's first presidential years.

Yet Bill Clinton managed in many ways to navigate a productive course through all the shoals. He launched a program of voluntary national social service, at first ridiculed, that won many Republican supporters. A "reinventing government" project placed under Vice President Gore achieved a substantial reduction in the federal work force. Most notably, Clinton pushed through a North American Free Trade Agreement that was anathema to labor, Ross Perot and liberals, enlisting a wily political operative, William Daley, brother of Chicago's mayor, to help achieve its passage.

Still, the Republicans and some New Democrats were able to sustain their criticism of him as a liberal as a result of the health-care reform initiative, the attempted Lani Guinier nomination, his support of government-mandated family leave, and so on. Cartoonist Garry Trudeau drew Clinton in his *Doonesbury* comic strip as a waffle, representing his ability to take either side, or none, on any issue, depending on the circumstances and his political imperative at the time.

As a national party leader, Clinton demonstrated no coattails. In the off-year elections of 1993, Democrats lost the mayoral races in Los Angeles and New York, Senate races in Texas and Georgia, and governorships in New Jersey and Virginia. Calls for the head of his handpicked Democratic National Committee chairman, David Wilhelm, were heard and eventually satisfied. At the same time, however, an impressive 88 percent of the legislation Clinton sent to Congress in that first year passed, albeit often by narrow margins.[13]

The mixed perceptions of Clinton were not the least of his problems as his first year in the Oval Office ended. Once more the allegations of womanizing surfaced in a right-wing magazine article quoting Arkansas state troopers saying they had facilitated and witnessed numerous Clinton extramarital affairs when he was governor. In February 1994 one of the women allegedly involved, Paula Corbin Jones, publicly accused Clinton of having propositioned her in a Little Rock hotel room in 1991 and began legal action against him, bankrolled by conservative groups. It was an accusation that would follow him through the rest of his presidency, with politically debilitating results.

In his 1994 State of the Union address, Clinton again wore both his liberal and his conservative New Democrat hats. He pressed his case for his wife's universal health insurance plan, warning opponents he would not take no for an answer. "Hear me clearly," he intoned. "If the legislation you send me does not guarantee every American private health insurance that can never be taken away, I will take this pen [brandishing the prop], veto that legislation, and we'll come right back here and start again."[14]

Clinton also seized upon anti-crime legislation to counteract the customary Republican allegation of Democratic softness toward criminals and, not accidentally, to assuage New Democrat gripes. He called for a policy of "three strikes and you're out"—three convictions for violent crimes would result in a life sentence[15]—and proposed putting up to 100,000 more police on the streets of American cities. The plan was criticized by the Congressional Black Caucus, however, again illustrating his inherent political problem in trying to appeal to and accommodate various constituencies.

Clinton's perceived vacillations were reflected in slipping poll figures. At the end of 1993, he had received an approval rating of only 50 percent in the Harris survey; by May it had dropped to 42 percent and to 40 percent in July. The Whitewater investigation continued, with its first inde-

pendent counsel, Robert Fiske, replaced by Kenneth Starr, who would figure large for most of the rest of the Clinton presidency.

In June 1994, Clinton dropped old Arkansas friend Mack McLarty as
his White House chief of staff and replaced him with his budget director,
Leon Panetta, a congressional veteran. He also made changes at the top at
the Pentagon and CIA. On Capitol Hill, fifty-eight Democrats in the
House voted against his crime bill and only herculean efforts saved it.
Hillary Clinton's health care reform died before her husband even had the
chance to exercise his threatened veto.

The bottom finally fell out for Clinton in the congressional elections
that November, when a concerted Republican effort led by House Republican Whip Newt Gingrich successfully "nationalized" them, making the
House and Senate races a referendum on the Clinton leadership. With
unparalleled partisanship and the skillful melding of a new crop of Southern conservatives into a personal army behind him, Gingrich and allies
proclaimed the goal of an "Opportunity Society" and authored a "Contract With America"[16] signed by 367 Republicans. Its provisions included
a balanced budget amendment to the Constitution, term limits for members of Congress, capital gains tax cuts, barring of U.S. troops under UN
command and other right-wing litmus-test positions. At the same time,
the Republican congressional leadership dug in against all Clinton legislative efforts, to demonstrate his political impotency.

The strategy worked with a vengeance. For the first time in forty
years, on election day the Republicans took control of both houses of
Congress, picking up an astounding fifty-three seats in the House and
nine in the Senate. Not a single Republican incumbent was defeated. Two
Democratic senators, Richard Shelby of Alabama and Ben Nighthorse
Campbell of Colorado, subsequently switched parties, enlarging the
Republican margin in the Senate even more. The huge Republican victory
was fashioned chiefly by the rejection of Democratic candidates by white
voters, and males particularly, especially in the South. Meanwhile, women,
blacks and other minorities salvaged what remained of Democratic
strength.[17] In the new Congress, Gingrich was installed as Speaker of the
House, with his target nothing less than demolishing what he reveled in
calling "the welfare state," and the Clinton presidency with it.

Key New Democrats also were lost in the GOP avalanche, including
Congressman David McCurdy of Oklahoma, a DLC chairman who turned
bitterly against Clinton on grounds he had abandoned New Democratic

principles and objectives. Clinton himself was humbled by the election outcome. He seemed to buy into the analysis that his failure to adhere to those principles and objectives had enabled the Republicans to demonize him as just another tax-and-spend liberal.

Al From, one of the DLC architects, was quick to dance on the grave of the departed, declaring that "this election said the New Deal coalition is Humpty Dumpty, and it isn't going to be put back together again."[18] The DLC rushed out with a "Mainstream Contract" to counter what was now called the Gingrich Revolution, and to lead the errant Clinton out of the wilderness and back to the straight path.

In another tract, called the "New Progressive Declaration," the New Democrats broke directly with the New Deal gospel of big government as the engine of constructive and beneficent change. It declared that "the presumption for democratic action must be reversed. Citizens and local institutions, rather than distant government agencies, should be the public problem-solvers of first recourse."[19]

Clinton quickly got the message. He proposed a "Middle Class Bill of Rights" that included plans for a middle-income tax cut, and his recovery was greatly assisted by characteristic overreaching by Gingrich and his troops. Their extreme proposals, pushed through the Republican-controlled Congress, made it easier for Clinton to rally liberals and New Democrats to opposition. In one of the longest State of the Union addresses ever, he incorporated many New Democrat themes, even as Gingrich peddled his "Contract With America." Labor and other liberal critics demeaned it as a sort of Mafia hit on the country, calling it the GOP "Contract on America." But an even more inflated Gingrich crowed that he and his conservative cohorts were remaking the face of American politics.

To climb out of the deep hole in which Clinton found himself after the loss of Congress, he reached out to an old political adviser, a calculating consultant named Dick Morris, who had worked for him in his Arkansas gubernatorial comeback but was now toiling mostly for Republicans, including Senator Trent Lott of Mississippi. Morris was a pragmatic thinker who immediately grasped Clinton's dilemma. He saw the president as caught between the liberal congressional Democrats on the left and the conservative congressional Republicans on the right. His solution was to position the president out of the line of fire between the two and above them as a third force. He called it "triangulation," and made sure it was publicized with his name attached. But as a practical matter it closely coincided with the centrist New Democrat posture, which sought to de-emphasize liberal reliance on big government and focus on the DLC mantra of individual "opportunity with responsibility."

Gingrich's "Contract With America" sailed through the House in what he grandly proclaimed "the first hundred days," modestly comparing himself to FDR, only to meet a dead end in the Senate. The real confrontation between him and Clinton came over the fiscal 1996 budget. The new House speaker won agreement from the Senate majority leader, Bob Dole, not simply to push for a balanced budget but also to seek a constitutional amendment mandating it. The amendment effort failed by one vote in the Senate but the pair pressed on, determined to balance the budget for the next fiscal year, despite considerable misgivings on the Senate side.

Clinton, with a near-invisible Morris at his elbow, resisted the old Democratic approach of attacking Republican cuts, especially in social security and Medicare, or playing the class card of poor against rich. Instead, he offered a balanced-budget plan of his own as a counter to the GOP's anti-Democratic mantra of tax-and-spend.[20]

The House and Senate Republicans had proposed spending cuts of more than $1 trillion over seven years to achieve their balanced budget, and also, in the House, tax cuts of $353 billion and increased defense spending. Clinton responded with proposed spending cuts of $1.1 trillion over ten years and a tax cut for middle-class wage earners only, in keeping with the new Democrat gospel.[21] It did not sit well with key congressional Democrats who felt they could win reelection simply fighting Republican Medicare cuts, but Clinton would not be deterred.

The battle lines were drawn. Gingrich, feeling his oats, behaved as if he were not simply the Speaker of the House but the president, treating Clinton with transparent disdain that only magnified his own arrogance. In so doing, he made himself an ideal target for Clinton, now cast in the underdog's role against a hostile Republican Congress. Clinton felt obliged to respond to a press conference question about his diminished clout by insisting that "the president is relevant here."[22]

Just as the Republicans had painted the Democrats for years with broad brush strokes as liberal extremists, Clinton cast the Gingrich Revolution as an attempted seizure of the government by extremists of the right. This effort coincided with the bombing in mid-April of a federal office building in Oklahoma City in which 167 persons were killed. Clinton quickly put partisan posture aside and presented himself to the American people as chief mourner and unifier. He also went on television to discuss new laws to deal with terrorism. Under the circumstances, it was harder for Gingrich and company to wage partisan combat against him over anything, including the budget.

Clinton's strategy of agreeing on the balanced-budget principle but arguing over the details enabled him to focus on the most unpopular of the Republican cuts, not only in Medicare but also in other government services that Americans cherished. Popular programs for the poor such as food stamps, school lunches and foster care felt the cut of the Republican knife.[23] Gingrich, already caricatured as the congressional Darth Vader, the wicked villain of the *Star Wars* films, found himself playing an unwilling but still resolute pawn to the president in his assumed role as public defender in the battle of the budget.

In all this, the figures of Dick Morris and Bill Curry, a political ally now on the White House staff, were prominent in pursuing the triangulation strategy, placing Clinton above and out of the line of fire between congressional Republicans and Democrats. In the process, the president began to climb back in the public opinion polls, and Gingrich to slide. A Gallup poll for CNN and *USA Today* in July had Clinton leading Dole, the prospective 1996 Republican nominee, by 50 percent to 44. An NBC/*Wall Street Journal* poll the next month showed 42 percent of voters surveyed had a negative opinion of Gingrich, compared to 31 percent the previous January.[24]

A key to Clinton's revival was an extensive and costly television advertising campaign recommended and engineered by Morris and implemented by media consultant Bob Squier. It trumpeted the president's accomplishments in pulling the economy out of recession and onto a path of growth and prosperity, while painting the Republicans as obstructionists. The burden of financing the ads, which were opposed by anti-Morris liberals in the White House, set both Clinton and Gore to prodigious fund-raising efforts that later proved politically embarrassing to both.

The showdown with Gingrich over the budget came near the end of 1995 when Clinton threatened the closing of various government functions rather than accept Republican social spending cuts. Gingrich, badly misjudging the public mood, dug in his heels and Clinton called his bluff. "The Republican Congress has failed to pass most of its spending bills," he declared, "but instead has sought to impose some of its most objection-able proposals on the American people by attaching them to bills to raise the debt limit and to keep the government running."[25] He vetoed the debt limit request and proceeded to send home about 800,000 federal workers, first for a few days and then for three weeks, the longest such shutdown in history. National parks were forced to close, along with federal monu-ments and other sightseeing attractions.

Clinton successfully cast the petulant Gingrich and the Republican leadership as petty, rigid and insensitive, and they took the heat for the closedowns. Dole, much more willing to deal than Gingrich by tempera-ment and a prospective 1996 presidential candidate, was chagrined at the outcome.

The year 1995 ended with the Gingrich Revolution in tatters and Clin-ton on the mend politically. In the course of the year, while defending lib-eral spending programs against the Gingrich onslaught, he had moved closer to his identity as a New Democrat. At the same time, after a shaky first year in foreign policy in which American power and prestige were embarrassed in Somalia, Haiti and Bosnia, where Serbian "ethnic cleans-ing" continued, Clinton helped broker peace negotiations in Ireland and the Middle East.

But the arena of most importance and testing for Clinton came at home. In his State of the Union message in January 1996, he heartened his old DLC comrades and vexed party liberals by declaring: "The era of big government is over."[26] Yet he had won the key battle of the budget against the Republicans. By this time, rumblings within the DLC about abandon-ing Clinton and finding another candidate, or even breaking off as a third party as a "third way," had come and gone.[27] He was the New Democrat candidate, unquestionably, for 1996.

During the election year, two new subgroups to the DLC were formed, a political action committee called the New Democrat Network in June created by Senators Joseph Lieberman and Breaux, to help fund congressional candidates, and a New Democratic Coalition in November, an outgrowth of the House Democratic Caucus.[28]

Through the first half of 1996, the Clintons continued to function under the cloud of the Whitewater investigation, and the sexual harass-ment suit of Paula Jones continued as an irritant. But the president's renomination in August was never in doubt, nor Gore's either.

On the Republican side, Bob Dole was the front-runner from the start

against a field of eight others, including Malcolm S. "Steve" Forbes Jr., heir
to the *Fortune* magazine empire; Senator Phil Gramm of Texas; commentator Pat Buchanan; former Governor Lamar Alexander of Tennessee and,
briefly, Governor Pete Wilson of California.

Forbes poured millions of dollars into a television advertising campaign in the Iowa caucuses that cut deeply into Dole's lead, but Dole survived. In New Hampshire, however, he was upset by Buchanan, who had
thrown a scare into George Bush there four years earlier. Dole, well
financed and a sentimental choice because of his long party service,
recovered smartly, swept the remaining primaries and was nominated in
San Diego in mid-August. Before then he resigned from the Senate to
focus on what clearly was an uphill campaign. He chose former Congressman Jack Kemp of New York as his running mate.

Clinton's popularity, after he took the measure of Gingrich, continued to rise. Shortly before the Democratic National Convention in
August, after a bitter fight within the White House between the New
Democrats and the liberals, the president took the step that most significantly tied him to the centrists. He agreed to sign a welfare reform bill
that diverged sharply from the longtime Democratic notion of a firm and
lasting "safety net" beneath the poor. Presented a bill passed in the Senate
with enough votes to override a veto, Clinton signed it, causing an uproar
in liberal circles.

The new law included "workfare" provisions designed to move welfare recipients into the workplace and cut those who didn't do so from
the relief rolls after five years. Clinton had promised in 1992 to "end welfare as we know it," and this legislation certainly did that. Marian Wright
Edelman, head of the Children's Defense Fund and a Yale Law School
friend of Hillary Clinton, led the vocal protest. A government study indicated some 1.5 million children would be forced into poverty because 75
percent of all families on welfare were on more than five years.[29]

At the convention in Chicago, however, New Democratic dominance
was evident in a party platform that supported Clinton on the welfare legislation as well as deficit reduction, tougher anti-crime measures, middle-
class tax cuts and a balanced budget, while protecting Medicare,
Medicaid, education and the environment. The platform called for a
"smaller, more effective, more efficient, less bureaucratic government" for
all Americans that would not "interfere with their lives but enhances their
quality of life."[30] Shying from the New Deal litany of government as the

engine of change, the platform declared that "today's Democratic Party knows that the private sector is the engine of economic growth."[31]

The only strong reminder at the convention of earlier Democratic days was the party's celebration of a return to Chicago for the first time since the disastrous convention of 1968 there, when anti–Vietnam War protesters filled the streets and Mayor Richard J. Daley's police pummeled them into submission. Now the mayor's son Richard M. was running the city and everything went off smoothly for Clinton's coronation. The only brief disturbance was the disclosure that Dick Morris, the self-proclaimed architect of the latest Clinton comeback, had been involved with a prostitute in a seamy story that forced his resignation from the Clinton campaign. He acknowledged he had permitted the woman in question to listen in on phone conversations he was having with the president. It was not the sort of story Clinton needed at this point, smacking of his own earlier womanizing problems.

Dole had greater problems that had nothing to do with sexual conduct, although a story did eventually surface about a long-ago affair. For one thing, Ross Perot, who had won 19 percent of the national vote in 1992, was back in the picture as the self-anointed nominee of his new Reform Party after a rigged vote at a rigged convention in Valley Forge, Pennsylvania. Potentially, he could cut into the anti-Clinton vote, to Dole's detriment. Beyond that, the veteran Dole was running like a dry creek, and a high-risk proposal from him for a 15 percent tax cut across the board, coupled with a pledge to balance the budget, was not believable. A poll for the *New York Times* in early September found that 64 percent of voters surveyed said they didn't believe he could pull it off.[32]

There were also lingering questions about his age. He was seventy-three going into the election, four years older than Ronald Reagan was when he was elected to his first term. The generational gap between Dole and Clinton was obvious, and debilitating for Dole. On the stump, he talked about the good old days; Clinton buoyantly campaigned about using his second term to build "a bridge to the 21st Century."[33]

For most of the campaign, Clinton adopted a "presidential" posture, above the fray, as Dole struggled to get a foothold. In his last hope to turn the campaign around, the aging senator was no match for Clinton in their two nationally televised debates, nor was Kemp in his one encounter against Gore. In the final days, Dole hammered at reports of improper fund-raising by Clinton and Gore, to no avail. As a last gasp, Dole over the campaign's final weekend set out on a nonstop swing of 96 hours that covered more than 10,000 miles across 20 states, but the effort was fruitless.[34] On election night, Clinton was assured a second White House term with 49 percent of the vote to 41 percent for Dole and 8 percent for Perot. Clinton beat Dole in the electoral college, 379 votes to 159. The only sour note for Clinton and the Democrats was their failure to regain control of either house of Congress.

Clinton's first term had been a roller coaster but had ended with the promise of a smoother ride through the second. At home, the economy was getting healthier and politically he had co-opted the Republicans. Abroad, he had helped achieve a cease-fire and peace agreement in the Balkans and the ouster of a dictatorship in Haiti, and was looking more like a leader. Most of all, his segue from New Deal to New Democrat politics by the end of the first term persuaded many centrists in the party that indeed they had found a president willing and able to remake it in their image. They had no idea what troubles were in store, either for the man or the party, in the four years ahead.

Chapter 33

DEMOCRATIC PHOENIX, 1997–1999

BILL CLINTON'S SECOND term began amid high hopes for the Democratic Party. The economy was booming to the extent that the president's goal of deficit reduction finally seemed more than a pipe dream. With a $22.6 billion federal deficit for 1997, the lowest in three years, economists began forecasting a surplus. New and old Democrats, while still sparring, accepted the president as their leader as the party aimed at regaining control of Congress in the off-year elections of 1998.

The Democratic Leadership Council reveled in Clinton's reelection, taking it as a confirmation of its effort and strategy. Also, of forty-one new Democratic congressmen, twenty-eight identified themselves as New Democrats. Clinton gave the centrist wing further representation in his second term, making Erskine Bowles his chief of staff, Bruce Reed his domestic policy adviser, Robert Shapiro undersecretary of commerce and Governor Roy Romer of Colorado, vice chairman of the DLC, chairman of the Democratic National Committee.[1]

But the core constituencies of the party, most notably organized labor, had continued to play a critical role in electing the top of the Democratic ticket and congressional candidates as well. The AFL-CIO had poured $35 million into the latter effort, and the National Education Association's political action committee alone gave $5.4 million.[2]

The intraparty friction, however, endured, with liberals still dominant in Congress and labor leaders expressing chagrin at the centrist drift of

Reprinted with permission, Kevin Kallagher (KAL), Baltimore Sun, 1998

President Clinton, accused of having a sexual affair with a White House intern, Monica Lewinsky, flatly denied the allegation, but the charge, later in effect admitted, led to his impeachment by the House of Representatives, although he was acquitted by the Senate and served out his second term.

the party under Clinton. The budget deal that he struck with Republicans to balance the budget by fiscal 2002, countering new domestic spending with tax and entitlement cuts, disappointed House Democratic leader Richard Gephardt, the DLC's first chairman who had fallen away in his increasing courtship of organized labor. He called it "a deficit of principle, a deficit of fairness, a deficit of tax justice and, worst of all, a deficit of dollars."[3]

The party's factions locked horns over Clinton's request to Congress to renew fast-track negotiating power on trade agreements, inhibiting congressional amendments. Labor and liberals fought it vociferously, with the DLC weighing in on the president's side, to no avail. In November, Clinton pulled the legislation before it was rejected.[4] In a speech at Harvard at year's end, Gephardt blasted his old colleagues by saying New Democrats were those "who set their compass only off the direction of others—who talk about the political center but fail to understand that if it is only defined by others it lacks core values, and who too often market a political strategy masquerading as policy."[5]

But there was no question that Clinton was holding a winning hand against the Republicans. In January the House had formally reprimanded Gingrich on ethics and campaign-finance violations and fined him $300,000. Clinton's attorney general, Janet Reno, declined under Republican pressure to appoint an independent counsel to look into allegations of fund-raising improprieties by the president and vice president in connection with their successful reelection campaign. Inflation and unemployment both continued down.

On the foreign policy front, with the end of the Cold War, the dissolution of the Soviet Union and China still struggling to overcome its immense economic challenges, the United States could indisputably lay claim to being the world's remaining superpower. Accordingly, Clinton's voice and presence on the world stage became dominant. He played a stronger hand in cooling off the Balkans while leading in the expansion of NATO to three former members of the Soviet bloc, Hungary, Poland and the Czech Republic.[6]

Still, the shadow of Clinton's personal life, and allegations of financial and sexual misconduct, continued to hang over him and his party. The Republican congressional leadership kept the Clintons in their political sights, even as Gingrich's power and influence steadily eroded in the wake of his crumbling revolution and personal woes. The investigation of the

Clintons' Whitewater and other business dealings by an independent counsel, Kenneth Starr, pressed on with minor indictments of others but yielding nothing conclusive against them. The Paula Jones accusations, however, persisted, and in May 1997 the Supreme Court ruled that the president could be sued while he was still in office, saying such legal action would not unduly burden him—a judgment that would prove in time to be woefully off the mark.[7]

Through 1997 and into the new year, Clinton was indeed able to function without major distractions caused by any complications in his personal life—until the morning of January 21, 1998. Then, the *Washington Post* and ABC News broke a story that would haunt the remainder of his presidency. Starr, the independent counsel, was investigating allegations that the president of the United States had been engaged in a sexual relationship with a young White House intern from late 1995 until the spring of 1997 in the environs of the Oval Office itself.

Three days earlier, a skeletal report of the affair had first appeared on the Internet but it was the news stories that caused the combustion. The revelations naturally threw the White House into a state of chaos and gloom. Only six days later, Clinton was to deliver the first State of the Union address of his second term. To the amazement of staff aides, he seemed able to steel himself against the swirling scandal and work diligently on the speech through all the turmoil of the next days.

The stories identified the young woman as Monica Lewinsky, the twenty-four-year-old daughter of a well-off Beverly Hills doctor and his wife, who had just graduated from Lewis and Clark College in Oregon before landing the internship through the father's connections. Her name and the story had come to Starr's attention in connection with the Paula Jones sexual harassment suit, in which Lewinsky was listed as a potential witness regarding Clinton. Only two weeks before the story broke, Lewinsky had signed an affidavit denying having had a sexual relationship with him.[8]

But a few days later, a onetime friend and working associate named Linda Tripp contacted Starr and revealed to him details of the affair as related to her by Lewinsky. Starr sought and obtained authorization to expand his investigation to look into possible perjury or obstruction of justice. His staff quickly organized a "sting" operation wherein Tripp wore a recording device to a lunch with Lewinsky that produced incriminating information involving the president. At Starr's instruction, Tripp invited

Lewinsky to another lunch at a Washington area hotel, where his investigators were waiting. They interrogated Lewinsky at length to determine
whether she had suborned perjury or obstructed justice in her affidavit.[9]

The next day, January 17, four days before the story broke, Clinton
gave his deposition in the Jones case via videotaping, and denied any sexual relationship with the former White House intern. On the day the story
surfaced, the president quickly repeated the denial in a number of interviews, including one with Jim Lehrer on the PBS show *The NewsHour.* But
given Clinton's history of rumored or real sexual misconduct, and Starr's
continuing investigation, the Lewinsky story would not die. In a major
exercise in damage control, the president went before television cameras
in the White House on the day before his State of the Union speech and
repeated his denial. Peering intently into the cameras, Clinton declared: "I
am going to say this again: I did not have sexual relations with that
woman—Miss Lewinsky."[10]

The next morning, the president's wife jumped to his defense, denouncing on a television show what she called "a vast right-wing conspiracy" to
bring her husband down. That night, as he entered the House chamber,
Democrats on the floor put on a brave front, applauding his arrival for the
traditional, and always positive, report card on the condition of the country. With no reference whatever to the scandal, Clinton spelled out his
achievements for his first five years: "We have fourteen million new jobs;
the lowest unemployment in twenty-four years; the lowest core inflation
in thirty years; incomes are rising and we have the highest home ownership in history. Crime has dropped for a record five years in a row. And the
welfare rolls are at their lowest levels in twenty-seven years. Our leadership in the world is unrivaled. Ladies and gentlemen, the state of our
union is strong."[11]

With his fellow Democrats loyally cheering him on as if nothing
untoward hovered over his televised appearance, Clinton put a label on
the course he had so far successfully trod, between the old liberal Democratic path of bigger and more engaged government and the conservative
Republican retreat from governmental problem-solving. "We have moved
past the sterile debate of those who say government is the enemy and
those who say government is the answer," he said. "My fellow Americans,
we have found a Third Way. We have the smallest government in thirty-
five years, but a more progressive one. We have a smaller government, but
a stronger nation."[12]

Clinton's third way already was sending ripples out to London and other Western capitals, but now the concept was all but lost in the intensifying public fever over his personal scandal. Even his declaration that the humming economy his administration had generated would produce what had been unthinkable—an end to the huge federal deficit and a surplus to be used to salvage the beleaguered social security system—could not veil the enormity of the peril to his presidency.

As later revealed, Clinton had begun a clandestine relationship with Lewinsky in the White House in November 1995. When aides became concerned about what was seen as her intrusive behavior, she was transferred the following April to the Pentagon, where she became friendly with Tripp. In the months thereafter, she sought the president's help in getting a job again in the White House or, eventually, in New York, where her mother lived.[13]

In November 1997 Lewinsky received but turned down an offer to work there for United Nations Ambassador Bill Richardson. Through Betty Currie, Clinton's personal secretary, she met with Washington power lawyer Vernon Jordan, a close Clinton friend, who agreed to help her, with Clinton's knowledge, in her job search.[14]

Meanwhile, Lewinsky had confided in Tripp about her relationship with Clinton and Tripp had secretly taped some of the conversations. She so informed lawyers for Paula Jones, and in early December, Lewinsky was listed by Jones's lawyers among those to be deposed about Clinton's private life. When Clinton learned of it he advised Lewinsky by phone that she might avoid being deposed by filing an affidavit in which she could say she had been in the Oval Office only to deliver documents. She did so and subsequently, through Jordan, received and accepted a job offer from a cosmetics company in New York.[15]

It was around this time that Tripp informed Starr's office of the tapes in her possession and the unraveling of the sordid story began. At first Lewinsky balked at cooperating with Starr, seeking full legal immunity. But she finally agreed and told all, including that she had performed oral sex on the president in an Oval Office anteroom. She produced a dress purporting to bear a stain of semen that subsequently, through DNA testing, proved to be Clinton's.[16]

By this time, the Jones suit had been dismissed by the court, but her lawyers said they would appeal. Clinton meanwhile was subpoenaed by Starr in July to testify before a grand jury exploring possible perjury or obstruction of justice. After much dodging, the president finally agreed to give testimony on August 17 by way of closed-circuit television from the White House. Despite artful semantic dodging over what constituted "sexual relations," and saying only that he and Lewinsky had engaged in "inappropriate intimate contact" and "inappropriate sexual banter,"[17] it was clear he was acknowledging some sexual intimacy with Lewinsky. Yet he and his lawyers continued to deny that he had lied, either in his deposition in the Jones case or before the grand jury, or that he had tried to buy Lewinsky's silence with a job offer or gifts he had given her.

Speaking to the nation on television, Clinton continued his artful dodging. "While my answers were legally accurate," he insisted, "I did not volunteer information. Indeed, I did have a relationship with Miss Lewinsky that was not appropriate." However, he said, "at no time did I ask anyone to lie, to hide or destroy evidence, or to take any other unlawful action." But, he went on, "I misled people, including even my wife. I deeply regret that."[18]

From that point, Clinton proceeded to a thinly veiled attack on his interrogators, saying the questions asked of him arose from "a politically inspired lawsuit, which has since been dismissed." It was, he said, "time to stop the pursuit of personal destruction and the prying into private lives and get on with our national life."[19] At the same time, however, a campaign was under way among Clinton aides and supporters to discredit both Lewinsky and Starr, the former as a "stalker" and the latter as a right-wing fanatic bent on destroying the president.

On August 20, three days after Clinton's television quasi-confession and diatribe against the investigations, he authorized air attacks "at terrorist-related facilities in Afghanistan and Sudan because of the threat they present to our national security."[20] The target in Sudan was a suspected chemical weapons facility, but it turned out to be a pharmaceutical factory. Immediately Republican Senator Arlen Specter questioned whether there was "any diversionary" motivation in the assaults, and comparisons were made to a recent movie, *Wag the Dog,* in which a president ordered a make-believe war to divert attention from a sex scandal.[21]

By now, demands were being heard from Republicans in Congress for Clinton's impeachment or his resignation. The House Republican whip, Congressman Tom DeLay of Texas, declared: "For the good of the country, and to put this scandal behind us, the president should resign. It is bad enough that our president is guilty of having an extramarital relationship with one of his young interns. But it is much more damaging that this president looked the American people in the eye and knowingly lied to us."[22] The statement amounted to a Republican declaration of war against Clinton from perhaps the most partisan political brawler in the opposition party.

Some Democrats joined in denouncing the president. Senator Joseph Lieberman of Connecticut took the Senate floor and labeled Clinton's conduct "immoral" and "deserving of rebuke." Fellow Democratic Senators Daniel Patrick Moynihan of New York and Bob Kerrey of Nebraska associated themselves with Lieberman's remarks.[23] Many Democrats in Congress had been unhappy with Clinton long before the Lewinsky affair. He had few credits with them to cash in, but he did remain a Democratic president, and the zeal with which DeLay and others, as well as Starr, were going after him persuaded the Democrats that they had to defend one of their own regardless of their personal feelings.

In early September, Starr released to Congress a voluminous report on his findings, and the Republican-controlled House, with many Democrats agreeing, overwhelmingly voted for its release. It spared no details in recounting the sordid affair, leading Democratic defenders to accuse Starr of intentional overkill to "get" the president. The Democratic leaders in Congress, Senator Thomas A. Daschle and Gephardt, called on Clinton, however, to desist from hiding behind legalisms and "hairsplitting" over words.[24] Shortly afterward, the videotape of Clinton's grand jury testimony was released, showing his transparent evasions, including a memorable observation that "it depends on what your definition of 'is' is."[25] In early October the House voted, 258–176, for an impeachment inquiry by its Judiciary Committee.

Meanwhile, the 1996 Democratic campaign fund-raising scandal continued under investigation by the Justice Department, with fourteen indictments brought against party fund-raisers without touching Clinton or Gore. Attorney General Reno continued her refusal to seek an independent counsel, to the anger of Republican critics.

Through all this, the DLC had pursued its objective of solidifying the New Democratic philosophy in the party at the congressional level. The New Democrat Network and the New Democratic Coalition stepped up their fund-raising efforts with an eye to electing more of their members in the approaching 1998 off-year elections. At the same time, the DLC launched a new quarterly magazine called *Blueprint: Ideas for a New Cen-*

tury in which William Galston and Elaine Kamarck elaborated on their concept of how better-educated Americans—"wired workers" of the computer age—were creating a new political target for the party. It was, they wrote, a "mistake to believe that Democrats can construct majorities based on a swelling pool of poor and near-poor Americans waiting to be mobilized by an old-fashioned politics of redistribution"—the fading New Deal construct.[26]

In the congressional elections in November, for all the scandals, the party of the president lost no seats in Congress for the first time in sixty-four years, holding the line in the Senate and, in fact, picking up five House seats, and three governorships including California. Organized labor fell short in its drive to regain control of the House, but its financial and manpower support, an estimated $20 million, contributed mightily to narrowing the gap with the Republicans. Soon afterward, the AFL-CIO authorized a budget of $46 million to complete the job of retaking the House in 2000.[27] Its power assured a strong voice in Congress and in the party against what labor leaders often saw as the New Democrat heresy.

The results of the congressional elections were a severe blow to Speaker Gingrich, who had predicted a Republican pickup of twenty seats. Facing a leadership challenge within his own party, he suddenly announced he was stepping down as speaker. The news jolted the GOP leadership in the House, which was soon rocked again when the man expected to succeed him, Congressman Bob Livingston of Louisiana, chairman of the House Appropriations Committee, disclosed earlier sexual indiscretions of his own.

In mid-November, Clinton agreed to settle the still-troublesome Paula Jones harassment suit for $850,000, without making an admission of guilt or any apology. But the House Judiciary Committee pressed on, releasing twenty-two hours of taped conversations between Lewinsky and Tripp and hearing directly from Starr about the president's relationship with the former intern, and his efforts to cover it up. The independent counsel took the occasion to report that he had uncovered no impeachable offenses by either of the Clintons in his long Whitewater investigation and other inquiries into alleged misconduct in the White House. The first family declared vindication but the impeachment inquiry went on. The committee submitted eighty-one questions to Clinton, whose written answers were dismissed by Republican members as evasive and insufficient.[28]

In December, at the DLC's annual convention in Washington, Clinton looked past his legal and ethical problems to the future, and his own legacy. "The real test of our ideas," he said, "is whether they outlive this presidency; whether they are bigger than any candidate, any speech, any campaign and debate."[29] The meeting provided a forum for party presidential hopefuls, including Gore's espousal of a course of "practical idealism," which fit snugly into the moderate New Democrat formula for political success.[30]

Even as Clinton was speaking of his legacy, however, his legal defense team was desperately defending his past. White House special counsel Gregory Craig, while acknowledging that the president's conduct in the Lewinsky affair had been "maddening," argued strenuously that it had not been impeachable.[31] The Clinton defenders contended that the private behavior cited did not rise to the level of an offense requiring his removal from public office, and in that contention public opinion polls offered strong support. Again and again, they found that while most Americans deplored their president's private conduct and moral weakness, they did not want him removed from office before his second term expired. A *Washington Post*/ABC News poll on December 15 found that while 56 percent of those surveyed said they had an "unfavorable impression of Clinton as a person," only 39 percent favored his impeachment, to 60 percent opposed. By 57 percent to 36, they favored censure over impeachment.

Nevertheless, the Republican-led committee pressed on, approving four articles of impeachment against Clinton after turning back a Democratic proposal simply to censure him. On basic party-line votes, the committee accused him of committing perjury before the grand jury and in his deposition in the Jones case, obstruction of justice and abuse of power. In the midst of these deliberations, the president ordered missile attacks on Iraq in response to dictator Saddam Hussein's interference with United Nations weapons inspectors—a deployment that raised more suspicions of political timing and motivation among Clinton critics. Some Democrats called for a hiatus in the impeachment deliberations while the attacks were still going on, but the Republicans refused and debate in the House proceeded.

The speakers on both sides spoke for the most part at cross-purposes. The Republican prosecutors, called "managers," argued the clear illegality of the chief officer of the land violating his oath by lying; the defending

Democrats cast the accusations against the president as a political vendetta. In the midst of all this, the prospective speaker, Livingston, announced that in calling on Clinton to resign he, as a similar sexual transgressor, could do no less himself. Bedlam ensued on the floor. Gephardt, seizing on Livingston's decision to step aside, called on the House to "stop destroying imperfect people at the altar of an unobtainable morality."[32] Obviously referring to Clinton as well as to Livingston, he urged the Republicans to join the Democrats in voting censure of the president rather than impeachment. The plea fell on deaf ears.

On December 19, 1998, the House impeached Clinton on two of the four articles, the allegations of perjury before the grand jury and obstruction of justice in "corruptly" encouraging Lewinsky to give "perjurious, false, and misleading testimony" in the Jones case, in supporting "a scheme to conceal evidence" subpoenaed, in helping Lewinsky get a job to prevent her "truthful testimony" and other "false and misleading" statements in his Jones deposition and grand jury testimony.[33]

After the votes Clinton, maintaining a bold front, gathered the Democratic Party's congressional leadership, his wife and his White House staff on the South Lawn and couched his unsuccessful fight against impeachment in terms of defending not himself but the American Constitution. He thanked Gephardt, standing behind him, and "the few brave Republicans who withstood enormous pressures to stand with [the Democrats] for the plain meaning of the Constitution and for the proposition that we need to pull together, to move beyond partisanship, to get on with the business of our country."[34]

Casting his own partisan attack on the Republicans as a plea for an end to partisan warfare, he said: "We must stop the politics of personal destruction. We must get rid of the poisonous venom of excessive partisanship, obsessive animosity, and uncontrolled anger." To meet the challenges ahead, he said, "we have to have some atmosphere of decency and civility, some presumption of good faith, some sense of proportionality and balance in bringing judgment against those who are in different parties."[35] Vice President Gore, the ever-loyal subordinate, added icing to the cake by predicting that Clinton would go down in history as one of the nation's greatest presidents.

Clinton's remarks conveyed his conviction, or at least his rationale, that Starr and the Republican congressional "managers" who handled the prosecution against him in the House, and would argue their case in the

Senate, were motivated principally, even solely, by partisanship or irrational distaste and ire toward his conduct. His self-description as a defender of the Constitution was more artful dodging. His lawyers questioned whether his sexual misconduct rose to the level of an impeachable offense, but the chief officer of the country had plainly lied to a grand jury. The basic position that no American is above the law was squarely at stake. This was not to say that there was no personal venom involved among the prosecutors. The straitlaced Starr and some of the Republican House managers obviously disapproved bitterly of Clinton, his morals and his politics. But attributing their prosecution of him, and the zeal with which they pursued it, only to that disapproval was to diminish the seriousness of his offense.

On January 7, 1999, the impeachment process moved to the Senate for trial, with Chief Justice of the United States William H. Rehnquist presiding. From the outset, it was clear that the Democrats had the votes for acquittal. The Constitution requires a two-thirds vote of all senators present, or sixty-seven when all one hundred take part, to convict, and the Democrats had more than the thirty-four votes to block conviction. The only question was whether enough Democrats would swallow their disgust at the behavior of the president of their own party to save him from the disgrace of being the first occupant of the Oval Office ever to be forced from office by a vote of the Senate. Balanced against Clinton's conduct, and his obvious lying in his deposition and testimony before the grand jury, was what many of these Democratic senators perceived as a partisan and moralistic Republican witch-hunt.

Much wrangling took place over the possibility of averting a trial with an agreement to censure Clinton or, if that could not be done, over the calling of witnesses. Two former presidents, Democrat Jimmy Carter and Republican Gerald Ford, jointly proposed a censure on the condition that Clinton would admit he had lied under oath, provided the statement would not be used against him in any subsequent criminal court procedure.[36] Veteran Democratic Senator Robert Byrd of West Virginia called for some alternative devised by the Senate in which the White House would play no part. But all such suggestions failed to derail the public spectacle of a president being tried, with his presidency at stake.

That Clinton would survive became certain on January 27, when the Senate voted by 56–44 against dismissing the case. Only one senator, Democrat Russell Feingold of Wisconsin, crossed party lines, breaking with his president by joining all Senate Republicans to go forward with the trial.[37]

For two days, arguments on both sides were heard and senators posed questions. Only three witnesses—Lewinsky, Jordan and a White House aide, Sidney Blumenthal—were questioned in private by selected House managers. For the first time in history, television monitors were placed in the Senate chamber and parts of the videotaped testimony were shown to all senators and the public. By a vote of 70–30, the Senate voted against calling Lewinsky to testify in person. By now, the details of the whole sordid business were well known, as well as Clinton's transparent evasions and dizzying circumlocutions.

A senior Republican known for his fairness and integrity, Senator Richard Lugar of Indiana, stated the case this way: "The impeachment trial of President Clinton is not about adultery. The impeachment trial involves the President's illegal efforts to deny a fair result in the suit brought by Ms. Paula Jones. I have no doubt that the President worked deliberately to deny justice in this suit. In doing so, he lied to a federal grand jury and worked to induce others to give false testimony, thus obstructing justice. Ms. Jones has often been described as a small person in our judicial system. In contrast, the President, who at the time of his inaugural takes a solemn oath to preserve and protect equal justice under the law for even the most humble of Americans, is a giant figure. As senators who also take a solemn oath, we must ask ourselves the fundamental question: 'Is any man or woman above the law?' "[38]

Tom Daschle, the Senate minority leader, took the opposite tack, excoriating the impeachment process involved, but he also concluded with a personal condemnation of the president. He deplored "an investigation by an independent counsel which exceeded the bounds of propriety; a decision by the Supreme Court subjecting sitting Presidents to civil suits . . . a deeply flawed proceeding in the House Judiciary Committee, which in an unprecedented fashion effectively relinquished its obligation to independently weigh the case for impeachment, the disappointing decision to deny members of the Senate and the House the opportunity to vote on a censure resolution, even though I believe it would be supported by a majority in both houses; and finally, the bitterly partisan nature of all the actions taken by the House of Representatives in handling this case.

"But as deeply disappointed as I am with the process," Daschle said, "it pales in comparison to the disappointment I feel toward this President.

Maybe it is because I had such high expectations. Maybe it is because he holds so many dreams and aspirations that I hold about our country. Maybe it is because he is my friend, I have never been, nor ever expect to be, so bitterly disappointed again."[39]

In the impeachment inquiry against Richard Nixon, his collusion in bribing the Watergate burglars and covering up his abuse of presidential power were so blatant as to rule out partisanship. In the case against Clinton, bipartisanship was impossible, with the Republicans determined to get rid of a Democratic president and the Democrats equally determined to save him. The Republicans prevailed in the House, where majority votes were all that were required to impeach. The Democrats prevailed in the Senate, where one third of the chamber plus one was enough to acquit. On February 12 the Senate found Clinton not guilty of both articles of impeachment before it. The vote was 55–45 on committing perjury and 50–50 on obstruction of justice, both short of the required two thirds.[40]

Clinton, speaking from the Rose Garden, dispensed with the accusatory language he had used after the House vote to impeach. "Now that the Senate has fulfilled its constitutional responsibility, bringing this process to a conclusion," he said, "I want to say again to the American people how profoundly sorry I am for what I said and did to trigger these events and the great burden they have imposed on the Congress and the American people." Now, he concluded, "this can be and this must be a time of reconciliation and renewal for America."[41]

As the president turned to leave, an ABC News correspondent, Sam Donaldson, called out: "In your heart, sir, can you forgive and forget?" Clinton paused, then turned back to the microphones and said: "I believe any person who asks for forgiveness has to be prepared to give it."[42] But if Starr was waiting for any direct statement of forgiveness from the president for his zealous pursuit over the previous years, from the fruitless Whitewater investigation through the scathing report on which the House managers sought and achieved impeachment, he had an endless wait. Clinton in a television interview in January 2000 said he did not regret fighting a "completely overboard" independent counsel by "defending the Constitution and the presidency."[43]

If any group deserved special thanks from Clinton, beyond the "millions of Americans" he cited in his brief Rose Garden remarks, it was the forty-five Democratic senators, including a reluctant Feingold, who voted against both counts, assuring the president's acquittal. Many others, cha-grined that Clinton had forced them to vote on his unseemly behavior at all, did so in his favor while figuratively holding their noses. They recog-nized that their party as well as their president had a stake in his acquit-tal, and there were all those public opinion polls indicating that voters didn't want him removed from office. For all the furor over the Lewinsky scandal, Clinton was presiding over a booming economy and, except for the irritant of Saddam Hussein in Iraq that had dictated the missile strikes during the House inquiry, there was no major conflict abroad.

With nearly two years to go in his second term, Clinton set out to put the scandals behind him and build a legacy of achievement that might diminish if not erase those scandals from the history books. The economy continued to flourish and he made substantial incremental gains in health care and education. In foreign policy he added luster to his reputation in moving in conjunction with NATO to combat with air strikes the "ethnic cleansing" by Serbian forces against the Albanian minority in Kosovo.[44] But suspicions lingered that he had timed these attacks and earlier ones on Sudan, Afghanistan and Iraq as diversions from his personal troubles.

At the same time, Clinton was not quite out of the woods regarding the scandals. In mid-February a woman named Juanita Broaddrick gave an interview to the *Wall Street Journal* accusing Clinton of having raped her in 1978, and followed it up with another interview with NBC News. Asked about the charge at a news conference, Clinton referred the question to his lawyer, David Kendall, who declared the allegation to be "absolutely false," and there the matter rested.[45]

In April 1999 the judge in the Paula Jones case, Susan Webber Wright, found Clinton in contempt of court as a result of "clear and convincing evidence" that he had been guilty of "false, misleading and evasive answers that were designed to obstruct the judicial process" in his depo-sition.[46] She specifically chastised him for saying he had never been alone with Lewinsky and for playing evasive word games over what constituted sexual relations.[47] She instructed him to pay $90,000 in legal costs incurred by Jones's lawyers in connection with that deposition. The ruling also imperiled his license to practice law in Arkansas, and in 2000 the license was suspended by order of the state supreme court.

In October, as Starr prepared to step aside as independent counsel, he called his staff together to consider whether his successor should seek a criminal indictment against the president. The staff had gathered evidence against the possibility that such a decision would be made, one that would require a stronger case for conviction than in impeachment proceedings. It reported that four charges—perjury, subornation of perjury, conspiracy and obstruction of justice—could be brought. Some argued that Clinton had been punished enough; others felt justice had not yet been served. Starr himself departed merely urging the president to "get right with the law," a demand justified, he said, by Judge Wright's contempt ruling.[48]

Among those at the meeting was Robert W. Ray, later selected as Starr's replacement to wrap up the Clinton investigation. He remained silent on the question of indictment until the spring of 2000, when he suggested he might indict Clinton after he left office. The president responded in addressing a newspaper editors' conference, saying he was proud to have fought impeachment "because I think we saved the Constitution of the United States."[49] Once again, he cast the fight of his life for political survival in terms of noble patriotism.

With Congress still in Republican hands, Clinton spent most of the rest of his presidency unsuccessfully seeking patients' rights legislation, stronger gun controls and, with more rhetoric than action, a ban on unregulated "soft" money to political parties in federal elections. He continued to buck Republican proposals to cut taxes, vetoing in September 1999 a GOP bill that would have reduced taxes by $792 billion over ten years, arguing that deficit reduction and salvaging social security had to come first.

Crowding in on Clinton by this time was the developing 2000 campaign to choose his successor. Gore was the Democratic front-runner from the start. Throughout his White House years, Clinton had made him a partner more than any previous vice president had been, giving him significant assignments and bringing him into his inner councils in politics as well as policy. In the year leading up to the next presidential election, Clinton repaid him for his outspoken and vigorous support throughout the ordeal with a wholehearted endorsement and a declaration that Gore was the best vice president in American history, effectively throttling most prospective challengers.

In the end, only one other Democrat—former Senator Bill Bradley of New Jersey, the onetime Princeton and professional basketball star with a reputation for serious politics—elected to vie with Gore for the Democratic presidential nomination in 2000. A moderate in his own right,

Bradley was generally considered a "neoliberal" and for all practical purposes gave the New Democrats two horses in the race.

In bequeathing the record of the Clinton-Gore years to his vice president, Clinton handed him a mixed bag. The achievement of prosperity at home and peace abroad was all that a vice president could have asked as the basis for a successful presidential campaign. But the bitter memories of the scandals made Clinton himself a questionable commodity on the campaign trail, in spite of his unparalleled talent as a public speaker and persuader of voters. Overall, however, the president's blessing seemed an advantage, within the Democratic Party at least, as Gore approached 2000 in the hope of extending the party's occupancy of the White House, and the New Democrat philosophy, for another four to eight years.

Reprinted with permission, Kevin Kallagher (KAL), Baltimore Sun, 1999

In the 2000 presidential campaign, Vice President Al Gore sought to distance himself from the scandal-ridden President Clinton but was willing to take some credit for the strong economic record of the Clinton-Gore administration.

Chapter 34

CALAMITY IN 2000

WITH PRESIDENT CLINTON completing eight years in the Oval Office and hence unable to succeed himself, Vice President Gore was free to make an early start in pursuit of the 2000 Democratic nomination. He did so with the encouragement of Clinton and the Democratic Leadership Council, of which he was a charter member. And when House Minority Leader Gephardt announced in February 1999 that he would not run, Gore garnered considerable support from organized labor as well.

Three other early Democratic prospects, Senators Bob Kerrey of Nebraska, Paul Wellstone of Minnesota and John Kerry of Massachusetts, also decided well in advance of the next presidential election year not to contest for their party's nomination. That left only former Senator Bradley, already campaigning informally, standing in Gore's way as a likely challenger.

Even before the vice president's formal declaration of candidacy, his campaign came under criticism. He sought to associate himself with the economic boom times of the Clinton-Gore years while running as his own man, standing at a distance from the Clinton sex scandals. At the same time, his fund-raising activities in 1995 and 1996 in behalf of the Clinton-Gore reelection campaign continued to plague him, especially his presence at a Buddhist temple luncheon in Los Angeles which he first denied was a fund-raiser and then described as "finance-related."

At one point in May, Clinton reacted to reports about the Gore campaign in early disarray by phoning a *New York Times* political writer and expressing his concern, while saying he was confident Gore would be the Democratic nominee. He told the reporter he had advised Gore to loosen up and be more approachable to crowds, to combat his reputation for stiffness. It was "smart" for Gore to play down his association with him, he added, and emphasize his independence. Gore aides reported that the vice president was not happy about the president's phone call and observations.[1]

In mid-June, Gore formally declared his candidacy, boasting that he and Clinton had produced the "strongest economy in the history of the United States," adding, "I want to keep our prosperity going, and I know how to do it."[2] At the same time, however, he also pledged to bring "moral leadership" to the nation, and in a remark seen as a reference to Clinton's misconduct, he observed: "I say to every parent in America: It is our own lives that we must master if we are to have the moral authority to guide our children."[3] That night, in a network television interview, he labeled Clinton's behavior in the Lewinsky affair "inexcusable" and, speaking as a father, "terribly wrong."[4]

Ignoring Bradley in his announcement speech, Gore focused on the front-running Republican candidate, Governor George W. Bush of Texas, son of the former president, who four days earlier had kicked off his campaign in Iowa on a platform of "compassionate conservatism." Gore declared that the poor needed more than "crumbs of compassion," and alluded to Bush's lack of experience in foreign policy compared to his own.

Right after Labor Day, Bradley entered the race, identifying himself as more liberal than his moderate record in eighteen years in the Senate usually cast him. Proposing his own version of universal health care, he called on the country to use its "unprecedented prosperity" to address this need and to reduce child poverty. "The economy soars," he said, "but some of us are left behind."[5] Two earlier prospective candidates, Kerrey and Wellstone, endorsed him, but few other prominent Democrats. Former basketball stars, however, such as Michael Jordan and Phil Jackson, a teammate with the New York Knicks and later coach of the Chicago Bulls and Los Angeles Lakers, came out for him and helped raise campaign money, which at the outset helped Bradley be competitive with Gore. At the time, though, a *Washington Post*/ABC News poll had Gore leading Bradley by nearly three to one.

The former New Jersey senator vowed to seek the presidency "in a different way"—on the high road—by conducting a positive campaign of "big ideas," and he invited Gore to accompany him on that road. But the vice president brushed aside the invitation. At the annual Iowa Democratic Party Jefferson-Jackson dinner in Des Moines a month later, with both men attending, Gore accused Bradley of having failed the party in its two "most defining moments of the last 20 years." He cited his opponent's Senate votes for Ronald Reagan's "slashing budget cuts" in 1981 that "threatened decency and social justice," and assailed Bradley's subsequent retirement from Congress. "When Newt Gingrich took over Congress and tried to reinforce Reaganomics [with] deep cuts in Medicare and Medicaid, I didn't walk away," Gore said. "I decided to stay and fight!"[6] Bradley had retired after his third term, observing that "politics is broken."

Bradley in his dinner remarks ignored Gore's attack and called for a friendly competition between them similar to that going on between home-run hitters Mark McGwire and Sammy Sosa, pushing each other to greater accomplishments. Gore immediately responded by challenging Bradley to debate him weekly in Iowa. "What about it, Bill?" he asked. "If the answer is yes, stand up."[7] Bradley, smiling, remained seated, refusing to take the bait.

In mid-January of the election year, Bradley did debate Gore in Iowa, with disastrous results for him. He had already been under fire in Iowa for having opposed federal funds for developing ethanol, a fuel alternative made from corn, and then switching his opposition. He explained that in the first instance he had viewed the issue from the perspective of his New Jersey constituency, but later saw it as a "national" solution. The rationale did not sit well with many Iowa farmers.

The Gore campaign jumped on this vulnerability. Its opposition-research team discovered an obscure Bradley vote in the Senate on flood relief, which the vice president deftly and aggressively used to paint his opponent as uncaring toward the plight of farmers in one of the Midwest's most agricultural states. In advance of the debate, an aide to Senator Tom Harkin of Iowa, a Gore supporter, found that in 1993, after severe floods had hit Iowa farmland, Bradley voted, with the Senate Democratic leadership, against a Harkin-sponsored amendment to add about $1 billion to a $4.7 billion disaster relief bill. Earlier he had voted for the larger amount.[8]

The Gore campaign planted in the debate audience an Iowa farmer who had lost three hundred acres to flooding that year. Gore introduced him to Bradley, citing "many other disasters facing farmers where you were one of a handful who didn't help the farmers." Bradley, instead of saying he had supported the much larger flood relief bill, sought to divert the question. The debate, he said, "is not about the past; this is about the future."[9] The answer was weak and evasive. Only later did Bradley say he had voted for the larger relief bill but against the amendment "because it was relief not just for farmers, but it was for relief generally."[10] That response didn't help him much either. From then on, it was an uphill fight for Missouri-born Bradley, who had spent his adult life in the East.

In an effort to recover, Bradley began to attack Gore's voting record in Congress. At a Des Moines elementary school where he warned students of the dangers of cigarette smoking, he charged that in 1988 Gore had voted against curbs on tobacco advertising and in 1985 against efforts to prevent a tobacco tax cut. Gore, playing on an earlier Bradley complaint that the vice president was "hammering me on my agricultural votes of 15 years ago," needled his opponent. Bradley's charge, he said, "smacks of desperate, negative campaigning. . . . It sounds like he's gone back 15 years to pick out some amendment that had other things connected to it."[11]

Bradley's offensive in Iowa was too late. Gore, backed strongly by most of the Iowa Democratic Party establishment and organized labor, won the state's precinct caucus vote, 63 percent to 35, in spite of Bradley spending an estimated $2.2 million there.[12]

The two pressed on to the New Hampshire primary eight days later. Bradley had fielded an impressive grassroots volunteer organization there and hoped to engage in campaign debate beyond farm issues in which he was only modestly grounded. He was running strongly in the state until his weak showing in Iowa, which persuaded him to be more aggressive. In a debate in Manchester, Bradley accused Gore of misrepresenting his record, asking: "If you can't trust people to tell them the truth in a campaign, how are they going to trust you as president?" Gore merely parried the attack by questioning how Bradley could deplore negative campaign attacks "while in the next breath launching real negative attacks."[13] Bradley, generally aloof, observed: "When Al accuses me of negative campaigning, he reminds me of Richard Nixon. He would chop down a tree, stand on a stump and give a speech about conservation,"[14] a line borrowed from a Stevenson speech in the 1950s. And so it went.

Bradley made a much stronger showing in New Hampshire, but Gore beat him again, 52 percent to 48, in the first presidential primary of 2000.[15] One contributing factor may have been the presence of Senator John McCain of Arizona, running against Texas Governor Bush in the Republican primary. McCain had bypassed the Iowa GOP caucuses, won easily by Bush, in favor of concentrating on the party primary in New Hampshire, where its large segment of independent voters could cast ballots in either party contest. McCain upset Bush there, drawing a heavy independent vote that might otherwise have gone to the centrist Bradley in the Democratic primary, or so Bradley's advocates argued.

Bradley vowed to fight on, characterizing his New Hampshire showing as a "remarkable turnaround" after his one-sided loss to Gore in Iowa.[16] But the McCain phenomenon haunted his campaign. While the Republicans dominated news coverage for the next month with a running battle between Bush and McCain in primaries or caucuses in South Carolina, Michigan and other states, the Democratic presidential stage was essentially dark. After a minor Democratic primary in Delaware on February 5 won by Gore, national party rules prohibited all delegate-selection processes until Super Tuesday, March 7, when Democrats in sixteen states including California and New York would choose about 60 percent of the delegates needed for nomination. That meant that for all intents, Bradley was off the nation's television screens for more than a full month as the Republican contest drew the spotlight. It proved to be an unfortunate position for a candidate who had been beaten in the first two Democratic tests and needed a quick comeback to avoid a loser image setting in.

In an effort to put his campaign back on the tracks and draw positive national news media attention, Bradley spent the last week in February campaigning in Washington State, in a Democratic presidential preference primary, or "beauty contest," in which no convention delegates were at stake. Again he was beaten by Gore, by more than two to one. The following week he was shut out in the Super Tuesday pack of state primaries and caucuses and withdrew from the race.

Bradley's determination to campaign "in a different way" that would elevate politics had been frustrated by the rough-and-tumble of electoral combat with a give-no-quarter opponent in Gore. The vice president's attacks on Bradley's voting record in the Senate and his decision to leave it drew more resentment than response from Bradley at first, until the primary defeats and his anger prodded him to hit back. "He took the blows for a long time before he finally said, 'I can't take this anymore,' " an aide later observed.[17] To many voters, Bradley seemed as a result not to be such a different kind of candidate after all. And then there was the pull of McCain's candidacy to independent voters who might in his absence have made Bradley a more formidable foe against Gore.

For his part, the vice president proceeded with a delegate mop-up operation in the remaining primary states, sweeping them all while keeping an eye on the Republican presidential competition. McCain had more successes in New England states and Michigan where there were substantial numbers of independent voters and state election laws permitting them to vote in the GOP primaries. But he finally hit a stone wall in Republican-only primary states and fell to Bush. The Texas governor, opting out of federal campaign finance laws limiting how much he could raise and spend, drummed up an unprecedented $37 million for the primaries and, for all practical purposes, drove a dozen GOP challengers for the nomination to the sidelines.[18] By the conclusion of Super Tuesday, it was already established that Gore and Bush would be the major-party standard-bearers in the fall campaign.

Third-party efforts, however, continued to seek a place in the electoral equation by tapping into the same voter discontent that had fueled the independent candidacies of Ross Perot in 1992 and 1996, and of lesser known long shots and parties. Perot's self-fashioned movement, now known as the Reform Party with Perot himself playing coy about a possible candidacy, endured internal struggles and finally emerged at a stormy convention in Long Beach, California, with a renegade Republican, former Nixon and Reagan White House aide and television commentator Pat Buchanan, as its nominee.

Also, veteran consumer advocate Ralph Nader, declaring at the environmentalist Green Party's convention in Denver that there was no difference between the Democrats and Republicans, decided to take on the political status quo with another wild-card candidacy. Unlike his symbolic bid in 1996, he entered the campaign with $1 million and vowed to be an important factor in the race. Few took him very seriously at the time, but it seemed clear that whatever votes he won he would take away from Gore, whose environmental record was much superior to that of Bush.

With the nominations of Bush and Gore only formalities to be played out at the Republican and Democratic conventions, the rest of the spring and early summer were given over to speculations about their running mates. Bush asked his father's former secretary of defense, Richard Cheney, to undertake his search, and for a time McCain's name was prominently mentioned in the press. But much animosity had developed between Bush and McCain in their primaries competition, and McCain remained insistent that he was not interested. Bush finally created a mild surprise in advance of the GOP convention in Philadelphia by choosing Cheney, saying later that he had gradually realized that "the person who was best qualified to be my vice-presidential nominee was working by my side."[19]

Similarly, Gore called on an esteemed former cabinet member, Clinton Secretary of State Warren Christopher, who had led Clinton's vice-presidential search that chose Gore, to head his quest for a running mate. Trailing Bush by as much as seventeen percentage points in some polls after the Republican convention, Gore decided on a bold move. He chose Senator Joseph Lieberman of Connecticut, making him the first member of the Jewish faith, and an orthodox one at that, to run on a major-party national ticket. The choice was received enthusiastically among not only Jewish Democrats but also the DLC faithful. Recalling the election of John F. Kennedy in 1960 as the country's first Catholic president, Gore declared: "We'll make history again. We will tear down an old wall of division once again."[20]

At the Democratic convention in Los Angeles, both Gore and Lieberman were routinely nominated. In his acceptance speech, the vice president struck a populist theme that was more in keeping with the old liberals than with the New Democrats. "The difference in this election," he said, "is they're for the powerful. We're for the people."[21] And he seemed to go out of his way to emphasize he did not intend to run on Clinton's coattails. "This election is not an award for past performance," he said. "I'm not asking you to vote for me on the basis of the economy we have. Tonight, I ask for your support on the basis of the better, fairer, more prosperous America we can build together."[22] It was a distinction that foreshadowed his attitude on the stump in the fall campaign, to the chagrin of many of his supporters who believed his best chance at election was to remind voters of the prosperity of the Clinton years.

Gore and Lieberman opened their campaign by emulating the successful Clinton-Gore bus tours of 1992, with a variation. They traveled the Mississippi River by boat, stopping at various points for rallies. The immediate post-convention polls indicated that Gore had narrowed the gap between Bush and himself, and he got good news in the decision of Attorney General Reno to reject again Republican calls for an independent counsel to investigate the vice president's 1995–96 fund-raising activities. Asked about the ruling from the Justice Department run by Gore's party, Bush lumped him in with Clinton by responding that "the best way to put all these scandals and investigations behind us is to elect someone new."[23]

Once again, a debate over having debates occupied the first month of the general election campaign. The very prospect of them served to put the campaign on hold, or at least to reduce the comings and goings of Gore, Bush and their running mates to "gaffe watches"—the press monitoring of the candidates for any misstep or misstatement that would affect the public perceptions of them. Bush and Gore finally agreed to three debates and a fourth between their running mates. The vice president was widely expected to have the upper hand on the strength of past debate performances, and low expectations of Bush's ability to hold his own. Those attitudes proved to be critical in how the debates themselves were later assessed.

In the first debate, on the Boston campus of the University of Massachusetts on October 3, the two presidential nominees exchanged criticisms on proposed tax cuts, prescription drug benefits for the elderly and dependence on foreign oil, taking predictable positions. Gore accused Bush of planning to waste much of the federal surplus by giving the largest tax cuts to the wealthy; Bush countered by saying he wanted to "send one-quarter of the surplus back to the people who pay the bills."[24] Bush said he favored a prescription drug plan through private-sector insurance; Gore warned Bush's plan would deny such benefits for most elderly recipients for several years. Gore called for tax incentives to spur development of more energy-efficient vehicles; Bush proposed oil exploration in the Arctic National Wildlife Refuge in Alaska.

More than the substantive aspects of their responses, the two nominees' debating styles and demeanors dominated most of the post-debate analyses. Gore, aggressive and armed with statistics throughout, seemed almost to bully the less specific and defensive Bush. Some of Bush's answers brought smirks, audible sighs of impatience and raised eyebrows from Gore, reactions that drew critical comments from television and print analysts and voters interviewed afterward.

In their second debate eight days later at Wake Forest University in

Winston-Salem, North Carolina, most notable in retrospect was Bush's reiteration of earlier strong opposition to American involvement in "nation-building" in trouble spots abroad. Gore, for his part, conspicuously sought to soften the impression of weary superiority over Bush he had left in the first debate with his visible and audible responses to his opponent's comments. Asked about allegations that he was given to using factual errors and untrue anecdotes to make his points, Gore contritely promised to be more precise and, in keeping with his revised demeanor, was almost deferential to Bush in contrast with his first-debate performance. This change also was duly noted by the critics. But each campaign resumed attacking the other for misstating facts and exaggerating.

The third presidential debate at Washington University in St. Louis did not significantly change the overall impression that Gore had a firmer grasp on the intricacies of domestic and especially foreign policy. But Bush continued to benefit from the low expectations about him at the outset of the debates, presenting modest evidence that he had a sufficient knowledge to handle the presidency if elected. The one lively and substantive debate between vice-presidential nominees Joseph Lieberman and Richard Cheney at Centre College in Kentucky produced many post-debate comments that the two should have been at the top of their tickets.

With about two weeks to go, opinion surveys indicated an extremely close race. An ABC News tracking poll gave Bush 47 percent, Gore 46 percent, Green Party nominee Nader 4 percent and the Reform Party's Buchanan 1 percent, and other polls were similar. Surveys in six traditionally Democratic states indicated that Nader was drawing enough Democratic votes from Gore to give Bush a chance of carrying them. To counter this possibility, liberal political groups supporting such issues as abortion, gay and civil rights and environmentalism toured these states in the hope of weaning Nader voters back into the Gore column.[25]

Some enterprising voters initiated an Internet scheme whereby Gore and Nader supporters could swap their votes to mutual advantage. A Nader objective in the election was achieving 5 percent of the popular vote, which would qualify his Green Party for federal campaign funds in 2004. The scheme urged Gore supporters to vote for Nader in states where Gore was far ahead, and for Nader voters to back Gore in states where he needed help to beat Bush. State officials, however, ordered Web sites in California and Oregon proposing the swap to shut down.

At the same time, Republican groups began to air television ads quoting Nader making critical comments about Gore—without mentioning his similar derogations of Bush. Nader himself brushed aside Democratic warnings that his vote in some states could give the election to Bush, and pleas that he withdraw from the race. "Al Gore has to earn his votes, just like all of us," he said in the closing days.[26]

Through all this, Gore kept his political partner of the previous eight years, President Clinton, at a distance. He made no joint appearances with him and, at the urging of his advisers in closely contested swing states, asked him not to campaign there, obviously fearing a voter backlash over Clinton's personal misconduct in office. Clinton himself, expressing concern that Gore was not making optimum use of the achievements of the Clinton-Gore years, did visit other states, reminding voters of that record and warning of what a change in the Oval Office would mean. Five days before the election, Clinton said in a radio interview that since he couldn't run for a third term, electing Gore was "the next best thing."[27] The observation did not sit well with Gore aides who believed the reminder of the Clinton-Gore connection was not helpful, and condescending as well.

On November 2, two television stations in Maine reported that Bush had been arrested in 1976 for driving under the influence of alcohol. They said he had failed a roadside sobriety test when police pulled his car over after he had left a bar near the Bush family home in Kennebunkport. Bush had pleaded guilty to a misdemeanor and paid a $150 fine. The story resurrected tales about an earlier drinking problem, leading him to repeat that he had given up alcohol on his fortieth birthday. He said he was "not proud" of the incident and had not revealed it because he wanted to remain a role model for his twin daughters. The Gore campaign said it had had nothing to do with the late-breaking story, but Bush called its appearance "dirty politics."[28] Another story in the *Boston Globe* raised questions about apparent Bush lapses in fulfilling Air National Guard obligations in 1972 and 1973.

In the final days, the two major candidates zeroed in on key swing states, repeatedly visiting Florida and Middle West battlegrounds. Gore felt obliged to return to his home state of Tennessee and Bush visited West Virginia, a traditional Democratic stronghold where Gore's strong environmentalist and gun-control positions put the state in jeopardy for him. On the day before the election, Bush campaigned in Tennessee and Gore completed a thirty-hour blitz over four Midwest states and Florida before returning to Tennessee to vote.

Not long after the polls opened across the country, a major controversy had already surfaced in Palm Beach County, Florida. Voters began to complain of a confusing ballot wherein the names of Gore and Reform Party nominee Buchanan were improperly aligned on computer punch cards, leading many voters who had intended to vote for Gore to punch holes that gave their votes to Buchanan. As a result, Buchanan was accumulating many times more votes on these "butterfly" ballots in the county, a Democratic stronghold, than there were registered members of the Reform Party.

It turned out that the misleading alignment of names and boxes to mark resulted from an unintentional gaffe by the county elections official, Theresa LePore, a Democrat. Because there were so many elderly voters in the county, she decided, the names of all ten presidential candidates and their running mates would be printed in larger type on the ballot punch cards. The larger type consequently produced the misalignment.[29] Hundreds of voters flooded the local board of elections office with complaints; those who tried to correct their mistake by punching the card twice had their ballots thrown out. LePore dispatched a memo to all precincts in the county alerting poll workers to remind voters "that they are to vote only for one (1) presidential candidate and that they are to punch the hole next to the arrow next to the number next to the candidate they wish to vote for."[30] Still, the protests continued all day until closing time at the polls.

Through the day, the Voter News Service, a vote-counting collaboration of five television networks and the Associated Press, gathered data from agents asking voters about their choices as they left the polls. At 2:09 p.m. Eastern time, these exit polls were flashed to subscribing television outlets and newspapers, projecting a squeaker—Bush 49 percent in the earliest accounting, Gore 48 percent. In Florida, it was Gore 50, Bush 47. The Republican nominee himself phoned the Fox News decision desk in New York, manned, interestingly, by his cousin John Ellis. The Bush dynasty, it seemed, reached into other inner sanctums beyond the governor's mansion in Tallahassee, where the candidate's brother Jeb lived. Cousin George asked about the exit polls and Cousin John complied, assuring him not to worry about such early findings.[31]

Election night was a nightmare. As actual returns came in from the

East, the expectations of a close result were being realized. Beginning at 7:49 p.m. Eastern time, on the basis of exit polls and early returns, the television networks and the Associated Press surprisingly projected Gore as the winner in Florida, deemed essential to Bush's chances of election. As more votes poured in from late-reporting precincts, however, at 10:13 p.m. the Voter News Service pulled back the projection, labeling the state too close to call. Meanwhile, returns from other states across the country were coming in. Gore was winning most of the New England and Middle Atlantic states, much of the upper Midwest, Washington and California. Bush was sweeping the South and most of the Plains and Rocky Mountain states. It became clear that the election's outcome would rest on Florida's twenty-five electoral votes.

Around 2 a.m., cousin John Ellis at Fox News, reviewing VNS numbers showing Cousin George leading in Florida by 51,433 votes, called him in Austin and gave him the news. Then, at 2:16 a.m. on November 8, Fox News anchorman Brit Hume declared the state for Bush, and thus the presidency. "I feel a little bit apprehensive about the whole thing," he confessed to his viewers. "I have no reason to doubt our decision desk [manned by Bush's cousin] but there it is."[32] Shortly afterward, the other networks followed suit.

At 2:30 a.m., with the networks now saying Gore was behind in Florida by about 50,000 votes, the crestfallen Democratic nominee decided to concede, and instructed his campaign chairman, Bill Daley, to phone Donald Evans, his counterpart in the Bush campaign, to inform him of his candidate's intention. Then, without bothering to confer with his chief operative in Florida, Michael Whouley, on the state of play there, Gore instructed a speechwriter to touch up an already prepared concession speech. Afterward he headed for what was to have been a victory rally in Nashville, convinced he had lost. But first he would call Bush directly and congratulate him.[33]

By this time the networks were reporting that Gore had informed Bush that he would concede. Hearing this, the Florida attorney general, Democrat Bob Butterworth, called the Gore bunker in Tallahassee. Gore must not concede, he said, because Bush's margin in the state had fallen to 6,000 votes and under Florida law there would be an automatic recount. Whouley contacted Daley, riding in the motorcade behind Gore's car, and urged him to stop Gore before he formally conceded. Daley got the word to an astonished Gore and then phoned Evans again and told him there would be a further delay in Gore calling his candidate.[34]

Gore, on the advice of his political aides, decided to make no public statement and instead Daley told the crowd that the election was still in doubt. Meanwhile, Gore picked up a phone and called Bush in Austin, where the Bush family awaited a formal Gore concession before going to his own victory celebration. It was now after 3 a.m. in the East. Gore told him: "Circumstances have changed dramatically since I first called you. The state of Florida is too close to call." Bush was astonished. "Are you saying what I think you're saying?" he asked, obviously irritated. "Let me make sure I understand. You're calling back to retract that concession?" Gore shot back: "Don't get snippy about it."[35] If Bush was finally the winner, he said, he would bow out and support the new president-elect, but the issue was still in doubt.

Jeb Bush was standing at his brother's side at the time and had been repeatedly checking his own Florida sources. "My little brother says it's all over," George Bush informed Gore, who coolly observed: "I don't think this is something your little brother gets to decide." An exasperated Bush told him, "Do what you have to do," and hung up.[36]

The first "final" count in Florida gave Bush a lead of only 1,784 votes out of approximately 5.8 million, well within the margin of one half of one percent of the total cast required to trigger a statewide machine recount under state law. The recount began at once, even as thousands of absentee ballots from Floridians abroad were still to come by the legal deadline of November 17. Recounts also were indicated in Oregon and New Mexico, but their combined twelve electoral votes were not enough in themselves to decide the election's outcome. It was already clear, however, that Nader's presence on the ballot in Florida had been pivotal. Returns gave him 100,000 votes in the state, more than enough to have swung it into the Gore column had Nader not been on the ballot there. Exit polls had indicated that the bulk of Nader voters said they would have voted for him had Nader not been an alternative.[37]

In the congressional elections, the Democrats made gains but not enough to wrest control of either the House or Senate, which had been a major objective of organized labor. The most notable Democratic victory was that of first lady Hillary Clinton for the Senate seat in New York over Republican Rick Lazio.

While the Florida recount went forward, two women voters in Palm

Beach County filed a lawsuit and won an injunction against final certification of the results in the county, contending that the so-called butterfly
ballot used had unfairly led them to cast their votes for Buchanan rather
than Gore. Also, amid complaints that black as well as Jewish voters were
being recorded as having voted for Buchanan or blocked from voting at
all, the Reverend Jesse Jackson rushed to Palm Beach, and Miami as well,
organizing protests. "Once again," he proclaimed, "sons and daughters of
slavery and Holocaust survivors are bound together in a shared agenda,
bound by their hopes and their fears about national public policy."[38] Nevertheless, the black turnout was huge, and more than 90 percent for Gore.

To deal with these and other subsequent challenges, the Gore campaign rushed a team of lawyers to Florida to observe possible recounts
and map strategy, and Jeb Bush mobilized the state's Republican law community to do the same. Both camps chose former secretaries of state, Warren Christopher for Gore and James A. Baker III for Bush, to lead their
efforts. For the next thirty-five days, a political and judicial tug-of-war
ensued amid repeated charges and countercharges of election malfea-
sance, chicanery, outright fraud and legal legerdemain, reaching finally to
the Supreme Court of the United States.

Under state law, each candidate could demand hand recounts, either
statewide or in selected counties. With Bush narrowly ahead, his lawyers
chose to stand pat with his lead and requested none, choosing to argue
that the votes had already been counted and recounted by machine, and
those results should stand. Gore's managers, concerned that the nation's
voters would grow impatient with a statewide recount, instead asked for
hand recounts in four counties—Palm Beach, Broward, Volusia and
Miami-Dade. All four were strongly Democratic areas where they hoped
to pick up the votes they needed to overtake Bush.

Time was a distinct if not immediate factor in the matter of vote
recounting because of an old federal law, called a "safe-harbor" provision.
It said that if a state legislature certified a slate of presidential electors by
December 12, that certification would be sheltered—that is, not subject to
challenge in Congress when all electoral votes were reported, on December 18 under the law. From the start the Bush strategy was to try to stall
recounts until December 12 in the expectation that Bush's lead would still
hold up and his slate would be certified by the Florida legislature. In any
event, the Republican-controlled legislature was prepared to name Bush
electors on its own if their certification through normal procedures had

not occurred by that date. So the Bush team held at the outset that the matter was one for the legislature, not the judiciary, to decide.

Therefore, the Gore strategists had to push for recounts with that December 12 legislative "safe harbor" deadline hanging over them. The provision was not mandatory, however, and arguments were made that certification could be made as late as December 18, or even beyond. That had happened in the 1960 presidential election, when Hawaii presented two slates of presidential electors and Congress did not accept the prevailing one until early January 1961.

In any event, canvassing boards in the four Gore-selected counties quickly began sample precinct hand recounts to assess whether enough missed or incorrect votes could be found to warrant a full hand recount. These included ballots in which no clear preference was made, called "undervotes," and those in which more than one preference was indicated, called "overvotes." Election officials in Volusia and, after much haggling, in Palm Beach voted for full hand recounts. In Palm Beach, the officials agreed to use a "sunshine rule" in deciding whether a valid vote was cast—that is, if a ballot let light through when held up to the sunlight, it was valid. But other debates went forward over the validity of various "chads"—the small pieces of the ballot card that were to be punched out: categorized as hanging, dimpled, one-, two- or three-cornered. Broward and Miami-Dade election officials voted against a full hand recount, but the Gore campaign pushed for reconsideration.

By now, Florida election officials statewide were reporting that Bush's lead had been cut nearly in half, to only 960 votes, with all but one of the state's sixty-seven counties reporting. A separate AP survey found Bush ahead by only 327 votes with all counties in.[39] Looking ahead, the Bush strategists decided that if they had to go to court at all, they would take the federal route, convinced that the Florida Supreme Court was too strongly Democratic to risk its decisions. This strategy would conflict sharply with traditional Republican ideology. But at this point, it was decided, ideology would have to take a back seat to practical politics.[40]

On November 11, therefore, the Bush team became the first to go to court, despite its early insistence that the matter was not the business of the judicial branch. The Bush lawyers filed a request in U.S. District Court to stop all hand counts, but was turned down the next day. The judge, a Democrat, lauded the American system of "decentralization"—another way of saying it was best to have state courts deal with state election conflicts.[41]

By now, the Florida secretary of state, Katherine Harris, who also happened to be a co-chair of the Bush-for-President campaign in the state, had said she would not extend the deadline for delivering recount results, specified under state law as seven days after the election. The Florida Democratic Party and the Gore campaign asked a judge to force an extension, but he refused, while telling Harris she was not to rule out late-arriving returns "arbitrarily." Nevertheless, she informed the Palm Beach officials that they lacked the legal authority to proceed, and the hand counts were suspended.[42]

While professing neutrality, Harris never left any doubt about which side she was on. On November 14 she reported that certified returns from all sixty-seven counties showed Bush with a lead of 300 votes. She called for written explanations of why she should accept any late returns, with a 2 p.m. deadline of the next day. She specified that only mechanical error in the voting machines would warrant accepting them. None was reported, although later—too late—officials did find malfunctionings as a result of jamming, resulting from chads never having been cleaned out from previous elections. Upon receiving the written requests for an extension, Harris summarily rejected all of them and said she intended to certify the final election results on the next Saturday, November 18, when all overseas absentee ballots had to be in and counted.

Next, Harris asked the Florida Supreme Court to stop all hand counts. The state high court, which had a majority of Democrats, refused. The Bush legal team made the same request to a federal district court but was also turned down. The Gore campaign rejoiced at this latter decision, believing it indicated federal judges would adhere to the long-held view that state elections were in the purview of state courts.

But Gore knew time was beginning to become more of a factor, in light of the safe-harbor deadline. He went on television and proposed to Bush that if he would accept the manual recounts in the four counties, Gore would drop all legal challenges, including contesting the butterfly ballots (in which he had little chance of winning anyway). He also offered to have a full statewide recount, including those counties strongest for his opponent, and called for a meeting between the two. It was an offer Gore had to know Bush would refuse, and he did, rejecting it out of hand; he was still ahead and would ride on his lead.

Bush's chief supporter in the state elections office, Harris, continued to say she would not include any manual recounts submitted after the original deadline. But the Florida Supreme Court, without being asked, stepped in, ordering her not to certify the election results until it had heard arguments in the case.[43] The Bush lawyers figured they had the state's highest court pegged correctly as sympathetic to Gore. If Bush had friends in Florida, his strategists reasoned, they were not ultimately on the state supreme court but in the Republican-controlled legislature, which was already poised to choose Bush electors on its own if necessary. And then there were the federal courts, especially the Rehnquist Court in Washington, dominated by Republican conservatives. But first the Bush team had to find a legitimate federal issue with which to gain admission before it. The obvious one was Article II of the Constitution, which specified that the power to choose presidential electors resided with the state legislatures.

Meanwhile, completion of the overseas ballot-counting on November 18 raised Bush's lead to 930 votes. When Democrats complained that many of the overseas ballots lacked postal marking indicating they had been mailed within the deadline, the Bush campaign cried foul, accusing the Gore campaign of trying to deny men and women in uniform of their rights. Indeed, a Gore campaign memo fell into enemy hands saying the rigid legal standard should be insisted upon, requiring an election-day postmark or overseas votes would be invalid. But by now, the core Gore mantra was "Count Every Vote," and any appearance of trying to block such votes was an embarrassment to the Gore cause, especially with the Bush camp playing the patriotism card for all it was worth.

When Bush supporters publicized the memo, the Gore campaign, apparently fearing a backlash, assigned Senator Lieberman to put out the fire. But when Lieberman got on the NBC News program *Meet the Press* that Sunday morning, he only added fuel to it. "If I was there," he said in response to a question about the memo, "I would give the benefit of the doubt to ballots coming in from military personnel generally. . . . Go back and take another look. Because, again, Al Gore and I don't want to ever be part of anything that would put an extra burden on the military personnel abroad who want to vote."[44] Lieberman sounded as if he were out of the Gore strategy loop.

On November 21, after hearing from both sides, the Florida Supreme Court ruled unanimously that hand-recounted votes were to be accepted, and extended the deadline for five days. In a direct rebuke to the unbending Harris, the judges ruled that "the will of the people, not a hypertechnical reliance upon statutory provisions, should be our guiding principle in election cases,"[45] which sounded to the Gore camp like "Count Every Vote."

Although the extension was clearly inadequate, the Gore campaign grasped it. The next day, however, Bush charged that the Florida Supreme Court was trying to "usurp" the power of the state legislature and asked the U.S. Supreme Court to declare the hand recounts in the four Gore-selected counties unconstitutional. In another blow to the Gore camp, election officials in Miami-Dade County voted on November 22 to stop their recount, deciding that the November 26 deadline made it impossible for them to complete the task in time.[46]

Faced with a gargantuan job of counting an estimated 650,000 ballots in four days, the canvassers had decided at first to count only the undervotes, of which there were about 10,750. To facilitate the process, the counters moved to another room one floor up, a move that agitated a group of Republicans watching the process. About thirty or forty of them tried to get on the elevator and then demanded entry into the new counting room, calling for the tabulations to stop and charging fraud. One Democratic Party official holding a sample ballot was accused by the crowd of trying to steal a ballot and fled in fear. It turned out that many in the crowd were Republican staffers from Washington, helpfully identified by Democrats from news photographs of the "riot."[47] The Miami-Dade canvassers finally threw up their hands and abandoned the count as hopeless, to the extreme dismay of the Gore camp.

All this time, recounts from other counties and overseas trickled in. Gore picked up 567 additional votes from Broward County and Bush smaller numbers elsewhere by the time the November 26 deadline arrived. Palm Beach missed it narrowly, and asked Harris for a short extension and meanwhile submitted the recounts it had made. Predictably, she refused, but canvassers pressed on, finally completing their task two hours and five minutes after the deadline. But the resolute secretary of state declined the complete as well as the timely filed partial recounts. Thereupon she certified Bush as the winner of Florida's twenty-five electoral votes with an edge of only 537 ballots out of 5.825 million between the two major candidates, and hence the winner of the presidency.

Bush promptly went on television and declared himself president-elect.[48] The next day, Gore on television asked the nation to be patient while the whole matter was played out in the courts. "Ignoring votes means ignoring democracy itself," he pleaded. All he had ever asked, he said, was "a complete count of all the votes cast in Florida—not recount after recount, as some have charged, but a single full and accurate count. We haven't had that yet."[49]

Once the certification was made, Gore still had a chance in a second, "contest," phase in which state law permitted the loser to challenge the certification by questioning aspects of the election. The next day, his team went into Leon County Circuit Court in Tallahassee and did so, saying failure to recount all the ballots had deprived the Democratic nominee of victory. The Gore lawyers asked Judge N. Sanders Sauls to order 14,000 disputed ballots from Palm Beach and Miami-Dade recounted.

On November 28, Sauls turned down a request for an immediate recount of the disputed ballots but ordered that they be delivered to his courthouse for possible examination. The next day, he ordered that all ballots from the two counties—more than a million—be brought to Tallahassee, initiating a bizarre shipment by truck and police escort north and west across the state over the weekend.

On December 1 the U.S. Supreme Court heard arguments on the Bush call for a review of the Florida Supreme Court's ruling permitting the hand recounts to go forward. That action alone unnerved the Gore team, aware that the high court in Washington traditionally viewed controversies over state elections as matters to be handled by state courts.

On December 2, Sauls took testimony in his court on whether the undervotes should be looked at, and on December 4, without having examined a single one, astonishingly ruled there was no "credible" evidence of a "reasonable probability" that a recount could change the outcome.[50] The election was already a virtual deadlock, and Gore's lawyer, David Boies, maintained that it was self-evident that a recount could produce that change. The Gore team decided to appeal Sauls's ruling before the Florida Supreme Court.

On the same day the U.S. Supreme Court, in an unsigned opinion, set aside the Florida court's decision to extend the deadline on hand recounts and sent the case back for clarification. In effect it punted, expressing "considerable uncertainty as to the precise grounds" for the Florida decision.[51] Bush's lawyers argued that the state high court had usurped the state legislature's role of selecting presidential electors, provided in Article II of the U.S. Constitution, by creating new rules for counting and certifying votes. The lawyers also argued that "the use of arbitrary, standardless, and selective manual recounts" violated the equal protection and due process clauses of the Constitution.[52]

The federal court's action dismayed the Gore team, but it kept seeking a way to survive. On December 7 it argued against Sauls's sweeping rejection of ballot recounts before the Florida Supreme Court, and the next day the state high court threw the vice president a lifeline. By a 4–3 vote, it overruled Sauls and ordered an immediate statewide recount. "While we agree that practical difficulties may well end up controlling the outcome of the election," the majority wrote, "we vigorously disagree that we should therefore abandon our responsibility to resolve this election dispute under the rule of law. We can only do the best we can. . . . We are confident that with the cooperation of the officials in all the counties, the remaining under-votes in these counties can be accomplished within the required time frame." The judges fell back on the existing standard that a legal vote would be one providing "clear indication of the intent of the voter."[53] The court also ruled that 383 votes counted earlier but not included in totals be given to Gore, cutting Bush's lead to a mere 154 ballots. The Gore team was euphoric.

The Bush lawyers, led by Theodore Olson, a veteran conservative litigator, immediately appealed that decision to the U.S. Supreme Court. On Saturday, December 9, even as the recounts ordered by the state high court had begun, the U.S. Supreme Court by a 5–4 vote announced a stay. It scheduled a hearing on the Bush motion for Monday, December 11, one scant day before the safe-harbor provision would trigger in, protecting Florida's certification of presidential electors. The vote was a clear conservative-liberal split, with Chief Justice Rehnquist, Antonin Scalia, Clarence Thomas, Anthony Kennedy and Sandra Day O'Connor in the majority and John Paul Stevens, Ruth Bader Ginsburg, Stephen Breyer and David Souter in the minority.

To grant a stay, the Court supposedly was required to find that the petitioner—Bush—faced "irreparable harm" if it was not given. But the one most likely to be dealt irreparable harm by the recount not going forward was Gore. Scalia argued that "the counting of votes that are of questionable integrity" did threaten harm to Bush "by casting a cloud upon what [Bush] claims to be the legitimacy of his election."[54] But Stevens for the minority contended that "preventing a recount from being completed will inevitably cast a cloud on the legitimacy of the election."[55]

The timing was as devastating for Gore as the stay itself, as the Gore lawyers realized, leaving little or no time for the recount because of the safe-harbor deadline even if the Supreme Court ruled in their favor. Scalia drove home the point by noting that the mere granting of the stay indicated there was a "substantial probability" that Bush's appeal would prevail.[56] Boies, who had referred to the December 12 safe-harbor deadline for completion of recounts in his argument before Sauls, now had reason to regret it.

After another feverish weekend of legal preparations, the two sides presented their arguments to the Supreme Court as scheduled on December 11. For ninety minutes the debate went forward on whether the state supreme court had acted within its rights by ordering the recounts or, as the Bush team argued, in doing so had changed the law in ways that encroached on the power of the state legislature, and violated voters' equal protection under the law. Then, as reporters waited outside, a court spokesman announced that there would be no decision forthcoming that night.

As a result, on the next day, December 12, the broad sidewalk outside the Court on Capitol Hill was jammed with television cameramen and newspaper reporters, as well as protesters, in an all-day vigil extending past nightfall as the justices deliberated. Finally, shortly after 10 p.m., less than two hours before the safe harbor would vanish, the word came in a sixty-five-page argument and decision that the reporters read on the fly, trying to decipher the outcome. It was confusing, but the speed-readers soon ascertained in all the verbiage that the election was over at last. The Court, its conservative bloc holding firm, by a 5–4 vote had slammed the door on further vote recounts and handed the election to Bush.

Incredibly to the Gore camp and many legal experts, the majority had turned its back on the Court's traditional position of leaving state election controversies to state courts. It ruled that the Florida Supreme Court in authorizing hand counts had established new standards for the state election law after the election, in violation of Article II. By a second, 7–2, vote that was widely read as a smoke screen to mitigate the ideological split in the Court, the justices also accepted the argument that the recounts denied equal protection of the law to Florida voters whose votes were not challenged. Earlier, the Bush campaign had offered the equal protection argument almost halfheartedly, not believing it could carry.

For the first time in history, an American president in effect had been elected not by the voters but by the nation's ranking jurists, and by a margin of one, with the majority casting its lot with a member of its own party. In being given Florida's twenty-five electoral votes, Bush had just one more than was required to gain the presidency, while losing the popular vote to Gore, eventually by 539,947 ballots.[57]

The critical decision came "per curiam," meaning by the whole court, with no names attached. Concurring and dissenting opinions made clear, however, that the same ideological division that had stayed the Florida Supreme Court decision on the previous Saturday had held firm, just as Scalia had foretold. In a remarkable acknowledgment that the Court was detouring from its devotion to federalism and its past precedent in leaving election matters to the state courts, the no-name decision noted: "Our consideration is limited to the present circumstances, for the problem of equal protection in election processes generally presents many complexities."[58] In other words, the high court whose responsibility was to guide lower courts on the interpretation and application of laws through its decisions was saying to them: don't take this one as a precedent.

The decision, while making the Court the final arbiter in selecting the president, concluded with a disclaimer of any desire to be so. "None are more conscious of the vital limits on judicial authority than are the members of this Court," it said, "and none stand more in admiration of the Constitution's design to leave the selection of the President to the people, through their legislatures, and to the political sphere. When contending parties invoke the process of the courts, however, it becomes our unsought responsibility to resolve the federal and constitutional issues the judicial system has been forced to confront."[59] Unsought responsibility? The Court could easily have followed precedent and left the whole matter to the Florida judiciary, which the dissenters vigorously argued should have been done.

Rehnquist, in his concurring opinion, joined by Scalia and Thomas, acknowledged that "in most cases, comity and respect for federalism compel us to defer to the decisions of state courts on issues of state law. That practice reflects our understanding that the decisions of state courts are definitive pronouncements of the will of the States as sovereigns."[60] But because a question of "federal constitutional law" was raised in application of Article II and the equal protection clause, the Chief Justice wrote, an exception had to be made. To respect the state legislature's election powers, he said, "we must ensure that post-election state-court actions do not frustrate the legislative desire to attain the 'safe harbor' provided by [federal law]."[61]

Rehnquist also argued that "in light of the legislative intent identified by the Florida Supreme Court to bring Florida within the 'safe harbor' provision . . . the remedy prescribed by the Supreme Court of Florida [a statewide recount] cannot be deemed an 'appropriate' one" because it "could not be completed by December 12."[62] By the time the decision had been hastily digested by press and public, December 12 was only minutes from being history. James Baker's strategy of stalling and running out the clock had prevailed, thanks to the creative reasoning of the five Republican justices.

Justice Stevens, with fellow Democrats Ginsburg and Breyer concurring, countered: "The Constitution assigns to the States the primary responsibility for determining the manner of selecting the Presidential electors. . . . When questions arise about the meaning of state laws, including election laws, it is our settled practice to accept the opinions of the highest courts of the States as providing the final answers. On rare occasions, however, either federal statutes or the Federal Constitution may require federal judicial intervention in state elections. This is not such an occasion. The federal questions that ultimately emerged in this case were not substantial." There was nothing mandatory about the safe-harbor provision, they said, and neither that nor Article II "grants federal judges any special authority to substitute their views for those of the state judiciary on matters of state law."[63]

As for the differing standards that the majority said violated the equal protection clause, Stevens cited an old case in which the reviewing court wrote: "We must remember that the machinery of government would not work if it were not allowed a little play in its joints."[64] If the majority truly believed that more specific instructions for vote counting than determining "the intent of the voter" were required, he wrote, instead of halting the recounts it should have remanded the case again to Florida to achieve that end, and provided adequate time for it to happen. He noted that the safe-harbor provision was not compulsory, citing the Hawaii experience when Congress did not accept its presidential electors until two weeks before John F. Kennedy's inauguration. Even if an equal protection issue could be validly raised, Stevens wrote, the majority could have ordered "relief appropriate to remedy that violation without depriving Florida voters of their right to have their votes counted."[65]

In his most pointed and devastating comment on the majority decision, Stevens said: "What must underlie petitioners' [the Bush lawyers] entire federal assault on the Florida election procedures is an unstated lack of confidence in the impartiality and capacity of the state judges who would make the critical decisions if the vote count were to proceed. Otherwise, their position is wholly without merit. The endorsement of that position by the majority of this Court can only lend credence to the most cynical appraisal of the work of judges throughout the land. It is confidence in the men and women who administer the judicial systems that is the true backbone of the rule of law.

"Time will one day heal the wound to that confidence that will be inflicted by today's decision," Stevens concluded. "One thing, however, is certain. Although we may never know with complete certainty the identity of the winner of this year's Presidential election, the identity of the loser is perfectly clear. It is the Nation's confidence in the judge as an impartial guardian of the rule of law."[66]

Justice Souter, the Court's sole moderate Republican, in a separate dissent joined by Breyer and in part by Stevens and Ginsburg, said the Court should not have reviewed the case nor stopped the recount of undervotes. If it hadn't, he wrote, and had allowed the Florida high court to work its will, "it is entirely possible that there would ultimately have been no issue requiring our review, and political tension could have worked itself out in the Congress . . . our customary respect for state interpretations of state law counsels against rejection of the Florida court's determination in this case."[67] Souter said the case should have been sent back to Florida with instructions "to establish uniform standards for evaluating the several types of ballots that have prompted differing treatments," to be used in whatever recounting might be ordered by the state high court.[68]

Justice Ginsburg, in an equally stinging dissent, targeted the majority's Catch-22 of stopping the recounts and then arguing that there wasn't enough time to complete them. Arguing that the safe-harbor provision was no barrier, she wrote: "The Court's conclusion that a constitutionally adequate recount is impractical is a prophecy the Court's own judgment will not allow to be tested. Such an untested prophecy should not decide the Presidency of the United States." She concluded by omitting the customary "respectfully" and wrote simply, "I dissent."[69]

Breyer, in his own dissent, was blunt. "The Court was wrong to take this case," he wrote. "It was wrong to grant a stay. It should now vacate the stay and permit the Florida Supreme Court to decide whether the recount should resume. The political implications of this case for the country are momentous. But the federal legal questions presented, with one exception, are insubstantial."[70] Finally, Breyer argued: "Above all, in this highly politicized matter, the appearance of a split decision runs the risk of undermining the public's confidence in the Court itself.... What it does today, the Court should have left undone. I would repair the damage done as best we now can, by permitting the Florida recount to continue under uniform standards."[71]

Formally, the Court had remanded the case to the Florida court, but without allowing time to do what the minority suggested, the election was over, by judicial fiat. The next night, after phoning Bush, Gore went on television and said: "Now the U.S. Supreme Court has spoken. Let there be no doubt, while I strongly disagree with the court's decision, I accept it. I accept the finality of this outcome, which will be ratified next Monday in the electoral college. And tonight, for the sake of our unity of the people and the strength of our democracy, I offer my concession."[72]

It was a gracious bowing out, one that could shore up his political viability for a second try if that proved to be his desire in 2004. Gore was widely criticized in many quarters, including within the Democratic Party, for continuing his challenge of the result for more than a month, but he did not buckle under in his legitimate quest for fairness. The justice of that result, if not its constitutional validity under the flawed electoral college system, deserves to remain under a cloud in history in light of the Supreme Court's tortured reasoning, its apparent political bias and the role of Bush's brother and other Florida allies like Katherine Harris in the post-election maneuvering.

A later review of 175,010 ballots previously uncounted by hand in all sixty-seven Florida counties by a consortium of major news organizations did not resolve the issue clearly. More than a year after the election, it contended that had the limited recounts in the four counties selected by the Gore campaign or of the undervotes statewide ordered by the Florida Supreme Court gone forward, Bush likely would have maintained his slim lead. But the inquiry also found that had all ballots uncounted by hand been reviewed under the broad standard of indicating the intent of the voter, Gore likely would have been narrowly elected.[73]

Gore's last official function as vice president, and his final personal agony, was his attendance at the swearing-in of President George W. Bush on January 20, 2001. After eight years of Democratic administration, the direction of the country was turned over to a Republican. Criticism from Democratic quarters continued to rain down on the defeated Democratic nominee, who despite winning half a million more popular votes than his opponent, had failed to hold on to the presidency for his party. Many said his campaign had been a disaster, failing to make the most of the achievements of the Clinton years and especially failing to make optimum use of one of history's most popular, if often simultaneously defiled, Democratic presidents.

The bridge to the twenty-first century, which Clinton in the 1996 campaign had so optimistically proclaimed as the route to greater Democratic dreams and realities, had led instead to political disaster in the 2000 campaign. Clinton had played only a bit part in that campaign and saw his anointed heir apparent lose a presidency that earlier had seemed well within his grasp. The outlook not only for Al Gore, but also for the whole Democratic Party, was glumly uncertain as the new century was unfolding.

THE DEMOCRATIC ROAD AHEAD

THE CLOUD THAT hung over the Democratic Party in the wake of the 2000 election debacle did not quickly dissipate. Compounding the depression of defeat was a widespread sense among party leaders and rank and file alike not only that the new Republican president was unjustly anointed but also that he was unfit intellectually and culturally for the job.

At least in many Democratic eyes, George W. Bush came off as a cocky, swaggering cowboy who was much more attitude than substance. As in the campaign that had brought him to the White House, he was unpolished in speech and manner, and in the vernacular of the day grammatically challenged, particularly in contrast with the departed Clinton. Bush's predecessor, like him, had been given to the country idiom of the South and West, but Clinton had the erudition of the well-schooled mind and a masterful ability to articulate extemporaneously. Bush in his first months as president was scripted for nearly every observation of substance he made.

His practice of leaning heavily on his vice president, Dick Cheney, a man experienced in the ways of Washington as a former White House chief of staff, congressional leader and secretary of defense, quickly generated jokes. When Cheney suffered a mild heart attack early in his vice presidency, wags suggested that if he died, Bush would succeed him as president.

Although Bush had campaigned on a pledge to "change the tone" of partisanship in Congress, almost at once he invited more of the same with a conservative agenda that had little accommodation in it. He called for a huge tax cut of $1.35 trillion, weighted in favor of the rich, at first arguing as he had in the campaign that the surplus built up in the Clinton-Gore years warranted it. But as an economic slide rapidly began to erode that surplus, Bush switched his rationale for the tax cut, saying it was required as a stimulus to the worsening economy. Eventually he rammed it through Congress largely on a partisan vote.

The Democrats in Congress remained in the minority, but they pointed to the next midterm elections in 2002, hoping to gain majority status, having picked up Senate and House seats in 2000. They could argue that the country was evenly divided, what with Gore having won the popular vote over Bush.

The nadir for the new president came in June 2001, when a disgruntled Republican, James M. Jeffords of Vermont, the most moderate member of his party in the Senate, suddenly jumped GOP ranks and declared himself an Independent who would vote with the Democrats to organize the Senate. The move was a severe blow to Bush and gave the Democrats control there by a single vote.

In light of Bush's unimpressive beginning, Democratic hopes were rising that he would be a one-term president when, as Harry Truman had said on another occasion, "the moon and the stars and all the planets" suddenly fell on him on the morning of September 11, 2001. In an incredibly audacious attack, nineteen Middle East terrorists hijacked four American jet planes in Boston and Washington, flew two of them into the twin towers of New York's World Trade Center, causing their complete collapse, and another into the Pentagon in Washington. The fourth plane crashed in the Pennsylvania countryside, after a struggle aboard, as it headed toward Washington and apparently the U.S. Capitol. Nearly 3,000 persons perished in the New York assault and 184 at the Pentagon.

The tragic attack transformed the country, and Bush's political fortunes. It was soon determined that the terrorism was the work of an anti-Western, anti-American network called Al Qaeda, directed by fanatic Islamic fundamentalist Osama bin Laden. His organization, with training camps in Afghanistan, was known in the West but little publicized until then in the United States. Clinton as president had tried to destroy him and his operation earlier but had failed.

Bush, at first jolted and uncertain in the wake of the startling attacks and the dimensions of the damage, soon recovered and seized the situation, declaring a "war on terrorism" that produced a swift and deadly attack on Al Qaeda positions in Afghanistan. It routed the ruling Taliban government there that supported and gave refuge to bin Laden and his operation, but did not eradicate the terrorist network itself. Yet Bush's determined words and actions rallied a shocked nation; political partisanship fell away as he took on the mantle of a wartime president against an enemy that had no easily identifiable national base or standing military entity.

An understandable wave of American patriotism swept over the country, elevating the Republican president above concerns and partisan disagreements that now were obliterated just as the twin towers themselves had been. Bush's popularity soared to unprecedented heights for any American president and stayed there into the next year, as he directed this equally unprecedented war against a phantom foe who had brought fear of foreign attack as never before experienced at home.

But the moratorium on Democratic criticism of Bush did not last. While the party was largely silenced on his conduct of the war on terrorism, even as bin Laden apparently eluded death or capture, other developments at home encouraged some Democrats to speak out.

For one thing, the economic slide that had seen the surplus of the Clinton-Gore years steadily evaporate and turn to huge federal deficits came amid shocking disclosures of corporate corruption and greed. The Democrats jumped on them, reminding voters of Bush's own close ties to corporate America as a former Texas oil executive. Bush responded with pledges to hold perpetrators accountable, calling for "corporate responsibility," but the Democrats increasingly thought they had in the scandals an avenue of successful attack on him.

At the same time, the stock market went into a nosedive, causing investors large and small to lose millions in their retirement plans. The Democrats seized on Bush's advocacy of "personal investment accounts" financed in part with social security payroll taxes, calling the scheme "privatization of Social Security" and warning seniors against "gambling your retirement on the stock market."

Bush, however, deftly kept the nation's focus on the war on terrorism, which continued to dominate public fears and concerns. A wave of anthrax germ mailings shortly after the September 11 attacks, thought at first to be the work of terrorists but not established, intensified the public apprehension. So did seemingly random sniper attacks in the Washington, D.C., area that literally drove the region under cover for nearly a month in the fall of 2002.

Through all this, Bush pushed for a new Department of Homeland Security that would pull together security-related government employees from a host of agencies—an idea, ironically, first suggested by Democrats in Congress and rejected by the Republican president. When Bush finally embraced it, the scheme came under increasing scrutiny concerning its practicality, as well as stiff opposition from organized labor and some civil liberties groups on grounds the consolidation would come at the cost of workers' job protection and civil rights. Politically, with nonpartisanship fading rapidly, Republicans began to use failure to achieve the new department as grounds to question the Democrats' patriotism.

As the war on terrorism dragged on, Bush turned to another front that reinforced his image as a wartime president—unfinished business in Iraq. The Persian Gulf war of a decade earlier, orchestrated by his father, the first President Bush, had driven Iraqi strongman Saddam Hussein out of Kuwait but left him in power. The junior Bush, determined to remove him, set as his objective "regime change," justified by an alleged Iraqi buildup of "weapons of mass destruction"—chemical and biological—and efforts to build nuclear weapons.

The Bush administration began to talk of pre-emptive action against Iraq under a doctrine of "anticipatory self-defense." It argued that the threat from such weapons to U.S. nationals and property, as well as the rest of the West if they were to reach terrorist hands, justified striking first, and unilaterally. The argument was supported by a new and sweeping administration "national security strategy" that said America's position as the world's only remaining superpower imposed a "responsibility" to use its strength to prevent any catastrophic use of such weapons of mass destruction.

Efforts by the Bush administration to establish a link between Iraq and the Al Qaeda terrorist organization were at best unconvincing and at worst deceptive. Nevertheless Bush insisted that time was running out on the West. He threatened to go it alone against Iraq if the United Nations, whose repeated resolutions demanding disarmament continued to be ignored by Saddam Hussein, declined to join in military action.

In the face of what seemed like an inexorable march to war against

Iraq, the Democratic leadership in Congress shied from opposition while urging Bush to press his case in the United Nations. There, delegates committed to collective action against threats to peace, the bedrock of the UN charter, were particularly dismayed about the new American assumption of a unilateral right to invade another country, and how it could break down the whole framework of the international rule of law.

Faced with internal disputes among his own State and Defense Departments, Bush finally was prevailed upon to seek broader UN support for military action against Iraq. As the first midterm congressional elections on Bush's watch approached, he sought a resolution from Congress authorizing use of American military force if necessary to disarm Saddam Hussein, arguing that such legislative support would help achieve similar UN backing.

The Democratic leaders on Capitol Hill, fearful that opposition to the foreign policy of the wartime president would hurt their party in the midterm elections, urged fellow Democrats to vote for the resolution as a means of getting the war issue "off the table." After that, they reasoned, they could focus the elections on what they saw as Bush's vulnerabilities—the vanishing budget surplus, the corporate scandals, increasing unemployment and the stock market slide.

Two weeks before those elections, enough Democrats voted for the Bush war resolution to achieve its passage. History gave the Democrats some hope that if they could indeed switch the subject away from the prospective war against Iraq and onto Bush's domestic woes, they could regain control of the House and broaden their one-seat margin in the Senate. Every Republican president since Theodore Roosevelt in 1902 had lost congressional seats in the first midterm elections of his tenure; the party of the people looked to the voters to put them back on the road to power.

But Bush, counseled by his chief political adviser, fellow Texan Karl Rove, agreed to invest his political capital as a popular wartime leader to buck that history. For most of the last month before election day, he campaigned tirelessly across the country urging voters to send more Republicans to Congress to support his war on terrorism. On election night, Bush's aggressive campaigning punctured the Democrats' dreams of takeover of Congress. Instead of regaining control, they lost both houses; their strategy of giving Bush his war resolution to "get it off the table" proved to be naïve. The Democrats remained a strong minority numerically on Capitol Hill, but psychologically they were left demoralized and adrift.

A few days after the balloting, the UN Security Council by a 15–0 vote adopted Bush's war resolution calling on Saddam Hussein to disclose and destroy chemical and biological weapons of mass destruction in his possession or suffer "serious consequences." UN inspectors were given unprecedented access to possible storage places but failed to uncover any such weapons. Bush, impatient with the pace of the inspections and repeatedly accusing Iraq of stalling and deception, pressed the UN Security Council to pass a second use-of-force resolution in effect authorizing an invasion of Iraq. With Council member France in the lead, however, an anti-war bloc repulsed him, in possibly the most embarrassing defeat for American diplomacy in the fifty-seven-year history of the world organization.

But Bush was undeterred. With only Great Britain among the leading powers at his side, the American president launched the nation's first major preemptive war, amid street protests around the globe and in the United States as well against his decision to go to war without formal UN sanction. Polls at home, however, found strong support for Bush's action and left a growing field of Democratic presidential hopefuls for 2004 (not including Gore, who said he would not run) in a political sea of uncertainty, as what Bush called his "coalition of the willing" slugged its way to Baghdad and eventual victory. Some domestic dissent and questions continued about his new doctrine of preemption in dealing with the global terrorist threat, but the Democrats seemed in no shape to take advantage of whatever concerns existed.

Still, they could derive some hope from the fact that after the Gulf war of 1991, President George Bush the elder had seemed so certain of reelection that Democratic presidential prospects like Governor Mario Cuomo of New York had chosen not to run, leaving to a field of lesser lights, including Governor Clinton of Arkansas, on what many then believed to be a fool's errand.

Democrats could reflect, too, on the fact that after President Clinton's first midterm congressional elections, he was considered a goner for a second term in light of the Gingrich revolution that had put the Republicans in control of the House for the first time in forty years. So political miracles occasionally did happen.

Over the more than two hundred years of the Democratic Party's existence, after all, there had been many unpredictable twists and turns. The party had begun as an underdog against the Federalists, as an agrarian-based political force driven by egalitarian convictions under Jefferson and Madison. It had taken on a populist coloration under Jackson and then found itself nearly undone by the peculiar institution of slavery in the South, which in the process helped give birth to the rival Republican Party. After nearly half a century in the political wilderness following the Civil War, broken only by Cleveland's two nonconsecutive terms, the party emerged from one world war under Wilson as a reluctant international player, and from a second as a bastion of social and liberal reform and a global superpower.

From a dominant white, rural base in the South, the party's strength in time had expanded to the major industrial cities of the Northeast and Midwest. There, a diverse base of blue-collar and minority workers was fed by an increasing stream of immigrants drawn to American shores by the promise of religious and political freedom and job opportunity. Wilson's New Freedom, arguing for stronger governmental regulation of the workplace, helped attract labor to that base.

Under FDR's New Deal in the 1930s and 1940s, liberal government and big-city bosses successfully courted this constituency with social services and new welfare programs, most importantly including social security and Medicare. After the defeat of fascism in Europe and Japan, postwar recovery and prosperity broadened a middle class that sustained government growth, sheltered by Truman's Cold War containment of communism. And Kennedy, in resisting Soviet efforts to pressure the United States out of Berlin and upset the balance of power with the introduction of missiles into Cuba, bolstered that containment policy.

In the civil rights movement of the 1950s and 1960s, the Democratic Party shed much of its Southern segregationist and discriminatory past and became the champion of racial justice. But resultant frictions and resentments within a broader multiracial society, compounded by the divisive Vietnam War, impaired Lyndon Johnson's Great Society ambitions, opening the door in the 1970s and 1980s to a swelling Republican conservatism.

In time, effective Republican demonizing of liberalism eroded the Democratic Party's majority status and drove the party to seek safer centrist ground, which it found in the 1990s under Clinton. In 2000 the party seemed on the brink of cementing a new and politically effective "third way" beyond the old liberal-conservative dichotomy that had dominated the American political scene ever since the end of World War I. But the narrow electoral-college defeat of Al Gore, and then the events of September 11, 2001, vastly overshadowed the domestic issues on which the Democratic Party had hoped to rebound in 2002, leaving it with an identity crisis and a dilemma. Furthermore, the preemptive war in Iraq, in conflict with American principle and tradition, likewise detracted from the party's trademark focus on economic and social problems at home.

The opening of the new century therefore demanded serious soul-searching in the party, amid much internal squabbling. Many liberal and progressive Democrats, now under an umbrella organization known as the Campaign for America's Future, called for the party to return to its roots—to the old idealistic principles and many of the old programs that sought to make government a more aggressive engine for social progress. Other groups like the Democratic Leadership Council insisted that Democrats had to press on with the centrist approach, eschewing the old confrontational class warfare in favor of a new, enlightened and pragmatic partnership between toilers and entrepreneurs, in an era of massive technological and informational change.

Yet there remained in both camps the same commitment to social and economic justice that had marked the earliest days when Jefferson and then Jackson struggled to create and sustain a political entity that could truly call itself the party of the people.

NOTES

Chapter 1: AN UNWANTED PREGNANCY, 1775–1792

1. Arthur M. Schlesinger Jr., Introduction to *History of U.S. Political Parties* (New York: Chelsea House, 1973), 1:xxxiv.
2. Joseph J. Ellis, *Founding Brothers: The Revolutionary Generation* (New York: Knopf, 2001), p. 22.
3. Claude G. Bowers, *Jefferson and Hamilton: The Struggle for Democracy in America* (Boston: Houghton Mifflin, 1953), pp. 23, 35.
4. Ibid., p. 95.
5. William E. Dodd, *The Statesmen of the Old South* (New York, 1911), p. 23.
6. Bowers, pp. 92, 108–109.
7. Wilfred E. Binkley, *American Political Parties: Their Natural History* (New York: Knopf, 1962), p. 53.
8. Ibid., p. 6.
9. Bowers, p. 30.
10. Ibid., p. 98.
11. Binkley, p. 13.
12. James Madison, *The Federalist Papers, No. 10.*
13. John M. Blum et al., *The National Experience: A History of the United States,* 7th ed. (New York: Harcourt Brace Jovanovich, 1989), p. 129.
14. Bowers, p. 102.
15. Ibid., p. 29.
16. Joseph Charles, *The Origins of the American Party System* (Williamsburg, VA: Institution of Early American History and Culture, 1956), p. 11.
17. Reginald Horsman, in *Running for President: The Candidates and Their Images,* ed. Arthur M. Schlesinger Jr. (New York: Simon & Schuster, 1994), 1:4, 7.
18. Binkley, p. 19.
19. Linda K. Kerber, "The Federalist Party," in *History of U.S. Political Parties,* 1:10.
20. Bowers, p. 35.

21. Ibid., pp. 53–54.
22. Ellis, p. 49.
23. Ibid.
24. Ibid.
25. *History of U.S. Political Parties*, 1:284.
26. Bowers, p. 67.
27. Ibid.
28. Ibid.
29. Ibid., p. 88.
30. Ibid., p. 76.
31. Ibid., p. 78.
32. Ibid., pp. 82–83; David McCullough, *John Adams* (New York: Simon & Schuster, 2001), p. 429.
33. Bowers, p. 86.
34. Ibid., p. 167.
35. Ibid., p. 169.
36. Ibid., pp. 169–70.
37. Letter from Hamilton to Edward Carrington, May 26, 1792, in *History of U.S. Political Parties*, 1:277.
38. Ibid.
39. Ibid., 1:278, 279, 281.
40. Ibid., 1:280.
41. Ibid.
42. Ibid., 1:280–81.
43. Noble E. Cunningham Jr., "The Jeffersonian Republican Party," in *History of U.S. Political Parties*, 1:243.
44. Ibid.
45. Letter from Jefferson to Washington, Sept. 9, 1792, in *History of U.S. Political Parties*, 1:286.
46. Ibid., 1:284.
47. Ibid., 1:287.
48. McCullough, p. 442.
49. Ibid., p. 288.
50. Nathan Schachner, *Thomas Jefferson: A Biography* (New York: Yosselof, 1957), pp. 409–10.
51. Pauline Maier, in *Of the People: The 200-Year History of the Democratic Party* (Los Angeles: General Publishing Group, 1992), p. 27.
52. Bowers, pp. 173–74.
53. Maier, p. 27.

Chapter 2: THE NEW PARTY IS BORN, 1792–1796

1. Claude G. Bowers, *Jefferson and Hamilton: The Struggle for Democracy in America* (Boston: Houghton Mifflin, 1953), p. 178.
2. Ibid., p. 181.
3. Ibid.
4. Ibid., p. 183.

5. Arthur M. Schlesinger Jr., Introduction to *History of U.S. Political Parties* (New York: Chelsea House, 1973), 1:xxxiv–xxxv.
6. Charles A. Beard, *The American Party Battle* (New York: Macmillan, 1928), p. 36.
7. Bowers, pp. 144–50.
8. Ibid., p. 108.
9. Ibid., p. 154.
10. Anne T. Dowling, ed., Preamble to *A History of the Democratic Party: Official Report of Proceedings of the Democratic National Convention, 1964* (Washington, DC: Democratic National Committee, 1968), p. 7; Frank R. Kent, *The Democratic Party: A History* (New York: Century, 1928), p. 13. Kent gives the date as May 12, contrary to other accounts.
11. Ibid., p. 14.
12. Arthur M. Schlesinger Jr., in *Of the People: The 200-Year History of the Democratic Party* (Los Angeles: General Publishing Group, 1992), p. 14.
13. Kent, p. 15.
14. Bowers, pp. 214–17; Thomas S. Pancake, *Thomas Jefferson and Alexander Hamilton: Shapers of History* (Woodbury, NY: Barron's Educational Series, 1974), pp. 199–204.
15. Bowers, p. 216.
16. Ibid.
17. Nathan Schachner, *Thomas Jefferson: A Biography* (New York: Yosselof, 1957), p. 485.
18. Bowers, p. 216.
19. Ibid., pp. 225–26.
20. Ibid., p. 218.
21. Schachner, p. 492.
22. Pancake, p. 204.
23. Ibid.
24. Ibid., pp. 204–206; Schachner, p. 499.
25. Pancake, p. 201.
26. Bowers, p. 229.
27. Pauline Maier, in *Of the People*, p. 28.
28. Bowers, p. 230.
29. Noble E. Cunningham Jr., in *The Jeffersonian Republicans, 1789–1801* (Chapel Hill: University of North Carolina Press, 1957), p. 71.
30. Ibid., p. 76.
31. Bowers, p. 257.
32. Ibid.
33. Pancake, p. 215.
34. Bowers, pp. 247–48.
35. David McCullough, *John Adams* (New York: Simon & Schuster, 2001), p. 456.
36. Bowers, pp. 254–56.
37. Ibid., pp. 261–62.
38. Ibid.
39. Ibid., pp. 271–76.
40. Ibid., pp. 276–79.
41. Stephen G. Kurtz, *The Presidency of John Adams: The Collapse of Federalism, 1795–1800* (Philadelphia: University of Pennsylvania Press, 1957), p. 19.

42. Ibid., p. 20.
43. Ibid., p. 21.
44. Ibid., p. 23.
45. Ibid., p. 31.
46. Ibid., p. 32.
47. Bowers, pp. 294–97.
48. Cunningham, "The Jeffersonian Republican Party," in *History of U.S. Political Parties* (New York: Chelsea House, 1973), 1:247.
49. Kurtz, p. 46.
50. Ibid.
51. Ibid., p. 47.
52. Bowers, pp. 305–306.
53. Kurtz, p. 74.
54. Ibid.
55. Ibid., p. 75.
56. Ibid., p. 87.
57. Ibid.
58. Noble E. Cunningham Jr., in *The Jeffersonian Republicans*, p. 93.
59. Washington's Farewell Address, 1796.
60. Bowers, p. 309.
61. McCullough, p. 463.
62. Cunningham, "The Jeffersonian Republican Party," 1:249.
63. Ibid., 1:248–49.
64. Edmund Berkeley and Dorothy Berkeley, *John Beckley: Partisan in a Nation Divided* (Philadelphia: American Philosophical Society, 1973), p. 280.
65. Ibid., p. 285.
66. Schlesinger, *History of Political Parties*, 1:xxxv.
67. Kurtz, p. 200.
68. Ibid., p. 194.
69. Cunningham, in *The Jeffersonian Republicans*, p. 98.
70. Kurtz, pp. 112–13.
71. Bowers, pp. 312–13.

Chapter 3: A HEARTBEAT FROM POWER, 1797–1800

1. Pauline Maier, in *Of the People: The 200-Year History of the Democratic Party* (Los Angeles: General Publishing Group, 1992), p. 30.
2. Claude G. Bowers, *Jefferson and Hamilton: The Struggle for Democracy in America* (Boston: Houghton Mifflin, 1953), p. 313.
3. Stephen G. Kurtz, *The Presidency of John Adams: The Collapse of Federalism, 1795–1800* (Philadelphia: University of Pennsylvania Press, 1957), pp. 209–10.
4. Ibid., p. 221.
5. Ibid., p. 222.
6. Ibid., p. 215.
7. Ibid.
8. Bowers, p. 313; David McCullough, *John Adams* (New York: Simon & Schuster, 2001), p. 466.
9. Kurtz, p. 212.

10. Thomas S. Pancake, *Thomas Jefferson and Alexander Hamilton: Shapers of History* (Woodbury, NY: Barron's Educational Series, 1974), p. 237.
11. Bowers, p. 344.
12. Kurtz, p. 229.
13. Pancake, p. 240.
14. Nathan Schachner, *Thomas Jefferson: A Biography* (New York: Yosselof, 1957), p. 581; Pancake, p. 241.
15. Pancake, pp. 241–42.
16. Ibid., p. 243; McCullough, pp. 493–94.
17. Pancake, p. 246; McCullough, pp. 495–96.
18. Bowers, p. 366.
19. Ibid., pp. 364–66; Wilfred E. Binkley, *American Political Parties: Their Natural History* (New York: Knopf, 1962), p. 79.
20. Bowers, p. 365.
21. Pancake, p. 262.
22. Bowers, p. 373.
23. Kurtz, p. 299.
24. Ibid., p. 309.
25. Ibid., p. 311.
26. Ibid., p. 312.
27. Pancake, p. 249; Bowers, p. 376; McCullough, pp. 504–506.
28. Bowers, p. 376.
29. Ibid., p. 378.
30. Pancake, pp. 249–50.
31. Bowers, p. 377.
32. Pancake, p. 250.
33. Ibid.
34. Ibid., pp. 250–51.
35. Noble E. Cunningham Jr., in *The Jefferson Republicans, 1789–1801* (Chapel Hill: University of North Carolina Press, 1957), pp. 126–29; Pancake, pp. 252–55.
36. Bowers, pp. 416–17.
37. Kurtz, p. 328.
38. Pancake, p. 263.
39. Noble E. Cunningham Jr., "The Jeffersonian Republican Party," in *History of U.S. Political Parties*, ed. Arthur Schlesinger Jr. (New York: Chelsea House, 1973), 1:253.
40. Ibid.; McCullough, p. 536.
41. Bowers, pp. 456–57.
42. Kurtz, p. 395.

Chapter 4: THE NEW PARTY TAKES OVER, 1800–1801

1. Noble E. Cunningham Jr., in *Running for President: The Candidates and Their Images*, ed. Arthur M. Schlesinger Jr. (New York: Simon & Schuster, 1994), 1:34–35.
2. Cunningham, in *The Jeffersonian Republicans, 1789–1801* (Chapel Hill: University of North Carolina Press, 1957), p. 154.
3. Ibid., p. 155.

4. Ibid., p. 157.
5. Ibid., p. 191.
6. Ibid., p. 250.
7. Ibid., p. 252.
8. Ibid., p. 162.
9. Ibid., p. 165.
10. Ibid., p. 166.
11. Ibid., p. 176.
12. Ibid., p. 254.
13. Ibid.
14. Ibid., p. 168.
15. Ibid., p. 171.
16. Nathan Schachner, *Thomas Jefferson: A Biography* (New York: Yosselof, 1957), p. 608.
17. *History of U.S. Political Parties,* ed. Arthur M. Schlesinger Jr. (New York: Chelsea House, 1973), 1:94–95.
18. Ibid., p. 95.
19. Cunningham, in *Running for President,* 1:34.
20. Cunningham, in *The Jeffersonian Republicans,* p. 202.
21. Ibid., p. 186; David McCullough, *John Adams* (New York: Simon & Schuster, 2001), p. 545.
22. Cunningham, in *The Jeffersonian Republicans,* p. 186.
23. Cunningham, in *Running for President,* 1:31.
24. Ibid., p. 30.
25. Ibid., p. 31.
26. Ibid., p. 32.
27. Ibid.
28. Thomas S. Pancake, *Thomas Jefferson and Alexander Hamilton: Shapers of History* (Woodbury, NY: Barron's Educational Series, 1974), p. 275.
29. Schachner, p. 648.
30. Cunningham, in *The Jeffersonian Republicans,* p. 232.
31. Ibid., p. 240.
32. Ibid.
33. Schachner, p. 650.
34. Cunningham, in *The Jeffersonian Republicans,* p. 241.
35. Ibid.
36. Schachner, pp. 651–52.
37. Ibid., p. 652.
38. Ibid.
39. Ibid.
40. Ibid., p. 653.
41. Ibid.
42. Ibid., p. 654.
43. Ibid., p. 656.
44. Ibid., p. 657.
45. Ibid., p. 658.
46. Ibid.
47. Cunningham, in *The Jeffersonian Republicans,* pp. 260–61.

Chapter 5: THE JEFFERSONIAN ERA BEGINS, 1801–1809

1. *History of U.S. Political Parties,* ed. Arthur M. Schlesinger Jr. (New York: Chelsea House, 1973), 1:294.
2. Ibid., 1:293.
3. Nathan Schachner, *Thomas Jefferson: A Biography* (New York: Yosselof, 1957), p. 662.
4. Ibid.
5. Noble E. Cunningham Jr., *The Jeffersonian Republicans in Power* (Chapel Hill: University of North Carolina Press, 1963), p. 8.
6. Schachner, pp. 670–71.
7. Claude G. Bowers, *Jefferson in Power: The Death Struggle of the Federalists* (Boston: Houghton Mifflin, 1936), pp. 94–95.
8. Ibid., p. 146.
9. John M. Blum et al., *The National Experience: A History of the United States,* 7th ed. (New York: Harcourt Brace Jovanovich, 1989), p. 161.
10. *History of U.S. Political Parties,* 1:293.
11. Lance Banning, "The Jeffersonians in Power: 1801–1824," in *Of the People: The 200-Year History of the Democratic Party* (Los Angeles: General Publishing Group, 1992), p. 38.
12. *History of U.S. Political Parties,* 1:294.
13. Cunningham, *The Jeffersonian Republicans in Power,* p. 203.
14. Bowers, p. 124.
15. Cunningham, *The Jeffersonian Republicans in Power,* p. 205.
16. Ibid.
17. Ibid.
18. Ibid., p. 206.
19. Ibid.
20. Ibid., p. 207.
21. Ibid., p. 209.
22. Ibid., p. 210.
23. Schachner, p. 723.
24. Cunningham, p. 77.
25. Norman K. Risjord, *Old Republicans: Southern Conservatism in the Age of Jefferson* (New York: Columbia University Press, 1965), pp. 30, 41–42; Marshall Smelser, *The Democratic Republic, 1801–1815* (New York: Harper & Row, 1968), pp. 234–36.
26. Blum, p. 166.
27. *History of U.S. Political Parties,* 1:295.
28. Blum, p. 168.
29. Ibid., p. 164.
30. Ibid.
31. Ibid., p. 165.
32. Schachner, pp. 741–49.
33. Noble E. Cunningham Jr., in *Running for President: The Candidates and Their Images,* ed. Arthur M. Schlesinger Jr. (New York: Simon & Schuster, 1994), 1:47.
34. Ibid., p. 43.
35. Ibid., p. 44.

36. Cunningham, *The Jeffersonian Republicans in Power*, p. 105.
37. Ibid., p. 106.
38. Ibid., pp. 106–107.
39. Ibid., p. 107.
40. Ibid., pp. 107–108.
41. Bowers, p. 236.
42. Ibid.
43. Ibid., p. 222.
44. Ibid., p. 229.
45. Cunningham, *The Jeffersonian Republicans in Power*, pp. 212–13.
46. Ibid., pp. 213–14.
47. Bowers, p. 253.
48. Joseph J. Ellis, *Founding Brothers: The Revolutionary Generation* (New York: Knopf, 2001), p. 32.
49. Ibid., p. 33.
50. Ibid., p. 34.
51. Ibid., p. 35.
52. *History of U.S. Political Parties*, 1:97–98.
53. Smelser, pp. 119–23.
54. Cunningham, *The Jeffersonian Republicans in Power*, p. 214.
55. Ibid., p. 215.
56. Ibid., p. 216.
57. Ibid., pp. 216–17.
58. Ibid., p. 218.
59. Bowers, pp. 266–67.
60. Smelser, p. 82.
61. Risjord, pp. 44–45.
62. Ibid., p. 47.
63. Ibid., p. 46.
64. Ibid., p. 67.
65. Ibid., p. 52.
66. Ibid., p. 54.
67. Cunningham, *The Jeffersonian Republicans in Power*, p. 82.
68. Ibid.
69. Risjord, p. 54.
70. Ibid., p. 55.
71. Cunningham, *The Jeffersonian Republicans in Power*, p. 90.
72. Risjord, p. 56.
73. Cunningham, *The Jeffersonian Republicans in Power*, pp. 83–84.
74. Ibid.
75. Ibid., pp. 84–85.
76. Ibid., p. 85.
77. Risjord, p. 57.
78. Ibid., p. 61.
79. Ibid., p. 63.
80. Ibid., pp. 79–80.
81. Cunningham, *The Jeffersonian Republicans in Power*, p. 222.
82. Smelser, p. 182.

83. Cunningham, *The Jeffersonian Republicans in Power*, p. 94.

84. Risjord, pp. 79–80; Irving Brant, *The Fourth President: A Life of James Madison* (Indianapolis: Bobbs-Merrill, 1970), p. 383.

85. Brant, pp. 391–92.

86. Bowers, pp. 485–86.

87. Risjord, p. 64.

88. Cunningham, *The Jeffersonian Republicans in Power*, p. 222.

89. Ibid., p. 303.

Chapter 6: THE PARTY STANDS ALONE, 1809–1827

1. Norman K. Risjord, *Old Republicans: Southern Conservatism in the Age of Jefferson* (New York: Columbia University Press, 1965), p. 116.

2. Henry Adams, *History of the United States of America During the Administrations of James Madison* (New York: Library of America, 1986), p. 11.

3. Edgar E. Robinson, *The Evolution of American Political Parties* (New York: Harcourt, Brace, 1924), p. 86.

4. Adams, p. 15.

5. Irving Brant, *The Fourth President: A Life of James Madison* (Indianapolis: Bobbs-Merrill, 1970), p. 439.

6. Ibid., p. 445.

7. Ibid., pp. 445–46.

8. John M. Blum, et al., *The National Experience: A History of the United States*, 7th ed. (New York: Harcourt Brace Jovanovich, 1989), p. 170.

9. Ibid., p. 171.

10. Ibid.

11. Ibid., p. 172.

12. Adams, p. 430.

13. Gaillard Hunt, *The Life of James Madison* (New York: Doubleday, Page, 1902), p. 323.

14. Blum, p. 172.

15. Ibid., p. 174.

16. Ibid., p. 176.

17. Ibid.

18. Brant, p. 597.

19. Blum, p. 182.

20. Noble E. Cunningham Jr., *The Presidency of James Monroe* (Lawrence: University Press of Kansas, 1996), p. 19; Wilfred E. Binkley, *American Political Parties: Their Natural History* (New York: Knopf, 1962), p. 99.

21. Cunningham, p. 20.

22. Ibid., p. 21.

23. Brant, p. 598.

24. William N. Chambers, *Political Parties in a New Nation* (New York: Oxford University Press, 1963), p. 198.

25. Blum, p. 197.

26. Ibid.

27. Cunningham, p. 104.

28. Blum, p. 197.
29. Cunningham, p. 104.
30. Blum, p. 197.
31. Cunningham, p. 189.
32. Blum, p. 188.
33. Marie B. Hecht, *John Quincy Adams: A Personal History of an Independent Man* (New York: Macmillan, 1972), p. 371.
34. Ibid., p. 374.
35. Ibid., p. 403.
36. Ibid., p. 408.
37. Ibid., p. 407.
38. Robert V. Remini, "Years of Triumph, 1825–1848," in *Of the People: The 200-Year History of the Democratic Party* (Los Angeles: General Publishing Group, 1992), p. 49.
39. Hecht, p. 408.
40. Ibid., p. 410.
41. Ibid., p. 411.
42. Ibid., p. 412.
43. Blum, p. 209.
44. Ibid.
45. Hecht, p. 453.

Chapter 7: JACKSONIAN DEMOCRACY, 1828–1836

1. Robert V. Remini, in *Running for President: The Candidates and Their Images,* ed. Arthur M. Schlesinger Jr. (New York: Simon & Schuster, 1994), 2:103–104.
2. Wilfred E. Binkley, *American Political Parties: Their Natural History* (New York: Knopf, 1962), p. 117.
3. Arthur M. Schlesinger Jr., *The Age of Jackson: Politics and Government, 1829–1837* (Boston: Little, Brown, 1945), p. 12.
4. Remini, 2:104.
5. John M. Blum, et al., *The National Experience: A History of the United States,* 7th ed. (New York: Harcourt Brace Jovanovich, 1989), p. 209.
6. Schlesinger, p. 51.
7. Robert V. Remini, in *Of the People: The 200-Year History of the Democratic Party* (Los Angeles: General Publishing Group, 1992), p. 52.
8. Blum, p. 205.
9. Remini, in *Running for President,* 2:109.
10. Ibid., p. 110.
11. Ibid.
12. Ibid., p. 111.
13. Marvin Meyers, *The Jacksonian Persuasion* (Stanford, CA: Stanford University Press, 1957), p. 15.
14. Ibid.
15. Ibid., p. 2.
16. Blum, p. 210.
17. Ibid., p. 211.

18. Ibid., p. 214.
19. Ibid., p. 215.
20. Ibid., pp. 216–17.
21. Ibid., pp. 217–18.
22. Schlesinger, p. 54.
23. Ibid., p. 55.
24. Blum, p. 215.
25. Ibid., p. 218.
26. Ibid., p. 219.
27. Ibid., p. 218.
28. Ibid., p. 219.
29. Ibid.
30. Ibid., p. 220.
31. Ibid.
32. Schlesinger, p. 81.
33. Ibid., p. 87.
34. Ibid., p. 89.
35. Meyers, p. 14.
36. Blum, p. 212.
37. Ibid., p. 220.
38. Schlesinger, p. 92.
39. Blum, p. 221.
40. Ibid., p. 222.
41. Daniel Feller, in *Running for President*, 2:133–34.
42. Robert V. Remini, *Martin Van Buren and the Making of the Democratic Party* (New York: Columbia University Press, 1959), p. 11.
43. Ibid.
44. Feller, p. 134.
45. Ibid., p. 136.
46. Ibid., p. 138.
47. Ibid., p. 139.
48. Schlesinger, p. 214.

Chapter 8: JACKSONIANISM WITHOUT JACKSON, 1837–1844

1. Jackson's Farewell Address, 1837.
2. John M. Blum, et al., *The National Experience: A History of the United States,* 7th ed. (New York: Harcourt Brace Jovanovich, 1989), p. 223.
3. Ibid., p. 224.
4. Ibid., p. 225.
5. Sean Wilentz, in *Running for President: The Candidates and Their Images,* ed. Arthur M. Schlesinger Jr. (New York: Simon & Schuster, 1994), 1:148.
6. Ibid., p. 150.
7. Ibid., p. 152.
8. Robert V. Remini, in *Of the People: The 200-Year History of the Democratic Party* (Los Angeles: General Publishing Group, 1992), p. 56.
9. Wilentz, p. 149.

10. Ibid., p. 151.
11. Ibid., pp. 151–52.
12. Blum, p. 242.
13. Ibid., p. 243.
14. Ibid., p. 244.
15. Ibid., p. 247.
16. Ibid.
17. Ibid., p. 246.
18. Marie B. Hecht, *John Quincy Adams: A Personal History of an Independent Man* (New York: Macmillan, 1972), pp. 544–46.
19. Ralph M. Goldman, *Dilemma and Destiny: The Democratic Party in America* (Lanham, MD: Madison Books, 1986), p. 57.
20. Ibid., p. 61.
21. U.S. Constitution, Article II, Section 1.
22. Jules Witcover, *Crapshoot: Rolling the Dice on the Vice Presidency* (New York: Crown, 1992), p. 36.
23. Arthur M. Schlesinger Jr., *The Age of Jackson: Politics and Government, 1829–1837* (Boston: Little, Brown, 1945), p. 396.
24. Blum, p. 256.
25. Ibid., p. 247.
26. Ibid., pp. 258–59.
27. Richard C. Bain and Judith H. Parris, *Convention Decisions and Voting Records* (Washington, DC: Brookings Institution, 1973), p. 35.
28. Ibid., p. 34.
29. Schlesinger, p. 459.
30. Blum, p. 260.
31. Remini, in *Running for President*, 2:169.
32. Ibid., p. 170.
33. Ibid.
34. Ibid.

Chapter 9: MANIFEST DESTINY, WAR AND COMPROMISE, 1845–1852

1. Arthur M. Schlesinger Jr., *The Age of Jackson: Politics and Government, 1829–1837* (Boston: Little, Brown, 1945), pp. 444–45.
2. Ibid., pp. 397–98.
3. John M. Blum et al., *The National Experience: A History of the United States,* 7th ed. (New York: Harcourt Brace Jovanovich, 1989), p. 260.
4. Ibid., p. 261.
5. Ibid., p. 262.
6. Ibid.
7. Ibid., p. 261.
8. Ibid.
9. Ibid.
10. Ibid., p. 263.
11. Ibid., p. 264.
12. Ibid.

13. Glyndon G. Van Deusen, "The Whig Party," in *History of U.S. Political Parties*, ed. Arthur M. Schlesinger Jr. (New York: Chelsea House, 1973), 1:355.

14. Michael F. Holt, "The Democratic Party, 1828–1860," in *History of U.S. Political Parties*, 1:520.

15. Blum, p. 264.

16. Robert V. Remini, in *Of the People: The 200-Year History of the Democratic Party* (Los Angeles: General Publishing Group, 1992), p. 61.

17. Blum, p. 265.

18. Saul Braun, revised by Robert A. Rutland, in Michael Beschloss, ed., *American Heritage Illustrated History of the Presidents* (New York: Crown, 2000), p. 149.

19. Blum, p. 265.

20. Ibid.

21. Holt, 1:522.

22. Richard C. Bain and Judith H. Parris, *Convention Decisions and Voting Records* (Washington, DC: Brookings Institution, 1973), p. 39.

23. Ibid., p. 40.

24. Wilfred E. Binkley, *American Political Parties: Their Natural History* (New York: Knopf, 1962), p. 150.

25. Eugene H. Roseboom, *A History of Presidential Elections* (New York: Macmillan, 1964), pp. 140–41.

26. Gil Troy in *Running for President: The Candidates and Their Images*, ed. Arthur M. Schlesinger Jr. (New York: Simon & Schuster, 1994), 1:188.

27. Ibid., p. 187.

28. Ibid., p. 188.

29. Roseboom, p. 139.

30. Troy, p. 189.

31. Ibid., p. 191.

32. Ibid., p. 193.

33. Blum, p. 267.

34. Ibid., p. 268.

35. Ibid.

36. Ibid., p. 269.

37. Ibid., p. 270.

38. Ibid., pp. 270–71; Van Deusen, 1:354–55.

39. Roseboom, p. 144.

40. Blum, p. 271.

41. Ibid.

42. Holt, 1:525.

Chapter 10: THE PARTY SELF-DESTRUCTS, 1853–1860

1. Arthur M. Schlesinger Jr., *The Age of Jackson: Politics and Government, 1829–1837* (Boston: Little, Brown, 1945), p. 480.

2. Ibid.

3. Ibid., p. 481.

4. John M. Blum, et al., *The National Experience: A History of the United States*, 7th ed. (New York: Harcourt Brace Jovanovich, 1989), pp. 272–73, 297.

5. David M. Potter, *The Impending Crisis, 1848–1861* (New York: Harper & Row, 1976), p. 155.
6. Blum, p. 298.
7. Wilfred E. Binkley, *American Political Parties: Their Natural History* (New York: Knopf, 1962), p. 193.
8. Blum, p. 300; Eugene H. Roseboom, *A History of Presidential Elections* (New York: Macmillan, 1964), p. 153.
9. Roseboom, p. 155.
10. Ibid.
11. Ibid., p. 159.
12. Blum, p. 301.
13. Ibid., p. 302.
14. Richard C. Bain and Judith H. Parris, *Convention Decisions and Voting Records* (Washington, DC: Brookings Institution, 1973), p. 57.
15. Ibid., pp. 59–60.
16. Ibid., p. 53.
17. Blum, p. 305.
18. Ibid.
19. Roseboom, p. 169.
20. Blum, pp. 307–308.
21. Ibid., p. 308.
22. Michael F. Holt, "The Democratic Party, 1828–1860," in *History of U.S. Political Parties*, ed. Arthur M. Schlesinger Jr. (New York: Chelsea House, 1973), 1:532.
23. Ibid., 1:533.
24. Blum, p. 311.
25. Ibid., p. 310.
26. Ibid., p. 313.
27. Ibid.
28. Binkley, p. 202.
29. Ibid., pp. 203–204.
30. Bain and Parris, p. 71.
31. Ibid., p. 75.
32. Roseboom, p. 175.
33. Blum, p. 315.
34. Binkley, p. 205.
35. Potter, p. 519.
36. Ibid., p. 520.
37. Ibid., p. 523.
38. Ibid., p. 524.
39. Ibid., p. 525.
40. Blum, p. 317.
41. Ibid.; Bain and Parris, p. 53.

Chapter 11: CIVIL WAR AND PEACE DEMOCRATS, 1861–1868

1. John M. Blum, et al., *The National Experience: A History of the United States*, 7th ed. (New York: Harcourt Brace Jovanovich, 1989), p. 317.

2. David M. Potter, *The Impending Crisis, 1848–1861* (New York: Harper & Row, 1976), p. 549.
3. Ibid., p. 567.
4. Ibid.
5. Ibid.
6. Ibid., pp. 567–68.
7. Ibid., p. 568.
8. Joel H. Silbey, *A Respectable Minority: The Democratic Party in the Civil War Era, 1860–1868* (New York: Norton, 1977), pp. 28–29.
9. Wilfred E. Binkley, *American Political Parties: Their Natural History* (New York: Knopf, 1962), p. 239.
10. Leon Friedman, "The Democratic Party, 1860–1884," in *History of U.S. Political Parties,* ed. Arthur M. Schlesinger Jr. (New York: Chelsea House, 1973), 2:888.
11. Christopher Dell, *Lincoln and the War Democrats: The Grand Erosion of Conservative Tradition* (Cranbury, NJ, and London: Associated University Presses, 1975), p. 60.
12. Binkley, p. 260.
13. Ibid., p. 269.
14. Silbey, pp. 54–55.
15. Ibid., p. 102.
16. Blum, p. 338.
17. Jean Baker, "In the Wilderness, 1849–1872," in *Of the People: The 200-Year History of the Democratic Party* (Los Angeles: General Publishing Group, 1992), p. 73.
18. Blum, p. 339.
19. Eugene H. Roseboom, *A History of Presidential Elections* (New York: Macmillan, 1964), p. 190.
20. Friedman, 2:890.
21. Blum, p. 340.
22. Binkley, p. 267.
23. Silbey, p. 103.
24. Ibid.
25. Dell, p. 215.
26. Ibid., p. 216.
27. Silbey, p. 112.
28. Binkley, p. 248.
29. Blum, p. 347.
30. Richard C. Bain and Judith H. Parris, *Convention Decisions and Voting Records* (Washington, DC: Brookings Institution, 1973), p. 83.
31. Ibid., p. 348.
32. Binkley, p. 270.
33. *History of U.S. Political Parties,* 2:914.
34. Friedman, 2:891–92.
35. Jules Witcover, *Crapshoot: Rolling the Dice on the Vice Presidency* (New York: Crown, 1992), p. 43.
36. Eric L. McKitrick, *Andrew Johnson and Reconstruction* (New York: Oxford University Press, 1988), p. 69.
37. Ibid., p. 74.
38. Ibid., p. 78.

39. Ibid., p. 80.
40. Ibid.
41. Ibid., pp. 70–71.
42. Ibid., p. 74.
43. Silbey, p. 185.
44. Ibid., p. 177.
45. Ibid.
46. Roseboom, p. 208.
47. Arthur M. Schlesinger Jr., ed., *Running for President: The Candidates and Their Images* (New York: Simon & Schuster, 1994), 2:xiv.
48. Hans L. Trefousse, in *Running for President*, p. 285.
49. Binkley, p. 276.
50. Ibid.
51. Friedman, 2:886.
52. Trefousse, p. 290.

Chapter 12: THE WILDERNESS YEARS, 1869–1880

1. Leon Friedman, "The Democratic Party, 1860–1884," in *History of U.S. Political Parties*, ed. Arthur M. Schlesinger Jr. (New York: Chelsea House, 1973), 2:898.
2. Ibid., 2:898–99.
3. Michael Perman, *The Road to Redemption: Southern Politics, 1869–1879* (Chapel Hill: University of North Carolina Press, 1984), p. 78.
4. Ibid., p. 79.
5. Ibid.
6. Ibid., p. 64.
7. John M. Blum et al., *The National Experience: A History of the United States*, 7th ed. (New York: Harcourt Brace Jovanovich, 1989), p. 371.
8. Richard C. Bain and Judith H. Parris, *Convention Decisions and Voting Records* (Washington, DC: Brookings Institution, 1973), p. 94.
9. Friedman, 2:887.
10. Bain and Parris, p. 97.
11. Ibid., p. 95.
12. Ibid., p. 96.
13. William S. McFeely, in *Running for President: The Candidates and Their Images*, ed. Arthur M. Schlesinger Jr. (New York: Simon & Schuster, 1994), 1:306.
14. Ibid., p. 308.
15. Ibid., p. 311.
16. Friedman, 2:895.
17. Donald A. Ritchie, in *Running for President*, 1:325.
18. Friedman, 2:895–96.
19. Bain and Parris, p. 102.
20. Eugene H. Roseboom, *A History of Presidential Elections* (New York: Macmillan, 1964), p. 241.
21. Bain and Parris, p. 107.
22. Ritchie, p. 326.
23. Ibid.

24. Ibid., p. 328.
25. Friedman, 2:901; Ritchie, p. 329.
26. C. Vann Woodward, *Reunion and Reaction: The Compromise of 1877 and the End of Reconstruction* (New York: Oxford University Press, 1966), p. 18.
27. Roseboom, pp. 243–45.
28. Ibid., p. 246.
29. Ritchie, p. 330.
30. Roseboom, p. 247; Ritchie, p. 331.
31. Ritchie, p. 331.
32. Abram S. Hewitt, "Secret History of the Disputed Election, 1876–77," in *History of U.S. Political Parties*, 2:958–66.
33. Ritchie, p. 332.
34. Friedman, 2:902.
35. Woodward, p. 8.
36. Ibid., p. 10.
37. Roseboom, p. 250.
38. Ibid.
39. Ibid., p. 251.
40. Bain and Parris, pp. 115–16.
41. Ibid., pp. 119–20.
42. Leonard Dinnerstein, in *Running for President*, 1:347.
43. Ibid., p. 349.
44. Ibid., p. 350.

Chapter 13: ON THE ROAD TO PARTY RECOVERY, 1881–1896

1. John M. Blum et al., *The National Experience: A History of the United States*, 7th ed. (New York: Harcourt Brace Jovanovich, 1989), p. 461.
2. Eugene H. Roseboom, *A History of Presidential Elections* (New York: Macmillan, 1964), p. 263.
3. Ibid., p. 265.
4. Richard C. Bain and Judith H. Parris, *Convention Decisions and Voting Records* (Washington, DC: Brookings Institution, 1973), pp. 121, 125.
5. Roseboom, p. 266.
6. Lewis L. Gould, in *Running for President: The Candidates and Their Images*, ed. Arthur M. Schlesinger Jr. (New York: Simon & Schuster, 1994), 1:367.
7. Bain and Parris, p. 128.
8. Ibid.
9. Ibid.
10. Ibid.
11. Ibid.
12. Ibid., p. 130.
13. Roseboom, p. 269.
14. Gould, p. 367.
15. Allan Nevins, *Grover Cleveland: A Study in Courage* (New York: Dodd, Mead, 1932), pp. 162–66.
16. Ibid., pp. 166–67.

17. Ibid., p. 177.
18. Roseboom, p. 271.
19. Gould, p. 371; Nevins, p. 182.
20. Gould, p. 373.
21. Ibid.
22. Ibid.
23. Roseboom, p. 273.
24. Nevins, p. 82.
25. Paolo E. Coletta, "The Democratic Party, 1884–1910," in *History of U.S. Political Parties,* ed. Arthur M. Schlesinger Jr. (New York: Chelsea House, 1973), 2:990.
26. Roseboom, p. 276.
27. Nevins, pp. 203–205.
28. Bain and Parris, p. 135.
29. Roseboom, p. 279.
30. Gould, p. 391.
31. Ibid., p. 394.
32. Ibid., p. 396.
33. Ibid., p. 398.
34. Roseboom, p. 284.
35. Gould, p. 399.
36. Wilfred E. Binkley, *American Political Parties: Their Natural History* (New York: Knopf, 1962), pp. 310–11.
37. Nevins, p. 440.
38. Robert A. Fratkin, in *Running for President,* 1:411.
39. Blum, p. 464.
40. Ibid., p. 465.
41. Ibid.
42. Ibid., pp. 468–69.
43. Coletta, 2:995.
44. Ibid.
45. Ibid.
46. Bain and Parris, p. 145.
47. Ibid., p. 148.
48. Ibid.
49. Fratkin, p. 415.
50. Blum, p. 471.
51. Nevins, p. 540.
52. H. Wayne Morgan, *From Hayes to McKinley: National Party Politics, 1877–1896* (Syracuse, NY: Syracuse University Press, 1969), p. 454.
53. Michael McGerr, "The Gilded Age: 1873–1896," in *Of the People: The 200-Year History of the Democratic Party* (Los Angeles: General Publishing Group, 1992), p. 91.
54. Morgan, p. 481.
55. Blum, p. 471.
56. Ibid.
57. Edgar E. Robinson, *The Evolution of American Political Parties* (New York: Harcourt Brace, 1924), p. 239.
58. Coletta, 2:1000.

Chapter 14: THE BRYAN ERA, 1896–1912

1. Richard C. Bain and Judith H. Parris, *Convention Decisions and Voting Records* (Washington, DC: Brookings Institution, 1973), p. 150.
2. Ibid., p. 156.
3. Ibid., p. 155.
4. Ibid., pp. 155–56.
5. H. Wayne Morgan, *From Hayes to McKinley: National Party Politics, 1877–1896* (Syracuse, NY: Syracuse University Press, 1969), p. 496.
6. Paolo E. Coletta, "The Democratic Party, 1884–1910," in *History of U.S. Political Parties,* ed. Arthur M. Schlesinger Jr. (New York: Chelsea House, 1973), 2:1002.
7. Morgan, p. 388.
8. Ibid., p. 497.
9. Ibid.
10. Ibid.
11. Eugene H. Roseboom, *A History of Presidential Elections* (New York: Macmillan, 1964), p. 305.
12. *History of U.S. Political Parties,* 2:1080–85.
13. Donald A. Ritchie, in *Running for President: The Candidates and Their Images,* ed. Arthur M. Schlesinger Jr. (New York: Simon & Schuster, 1994), 1:428.
14. Roseboom, p. 309.
15. Edgar E. Robinson, *The Evolution of American Political Parties* (New York: Harcourt Brace, 1924), p. 248.
16. Roseboom, p. 312.
17. Ritchie, p. 429.
18. Ibid., p. 430.
19. Ibid., p. 431.
20. Ibid., p. 433.
21. John Milton Cooper Jr., "The Best . . . and Worst of Times, 1897–1920," in *Of the People: The 200-Year History of the Democratic Party* (Los Angeles: General Publishing Group, 1992), p. 97.
22. Bain and Parris, p. 158.
23. Jules Witcover, *Crapshoot: Rolling the Dice on the Vice Presidency* (New York: Crown, 1992), p. 54.
24. Ibid.
25. Ibid.
26. Roseboom, p. 325.
27. Donald Young, *American Roulette: The History and Dilemma of the Vice Presidency* (New York: Viking, 1974), p. 116.
28. Ibid., p. 118.
29. Bain and Parris, p. 163.
30. J. Rogers Hollingsworth, *The Whirligig of Politics: The Democracy of Cleveland and Bryan* (Chicago: University of Chicago Press, 1963), p. 173.
31. Coletta, 2:1006.
32. Hollingsworth, p. 188.
33. Roseboom, p. 333.
34. Coletta, 2:1008–1009.
35. Hollingsworth, p. 218.

36. Roseboom, p. 341.
37. Ibid.
38. Ibid., p. 342.
39. Edmund Morris, *Theodore Rex* (New York: Random House, 2001), pp. 362–63.
40. Ibid., p. 364.
41. Coletta, 2:1013.
42. Roseboom, p. 354.
43. Arthur S. Link, *Woodrow Wilson and the Progressive Era* (New York: Harper & Bros., 1954), pp. 7–8.

Chapter 15: WILSON AND THE NEW FREEDOM, 1912–1915

1. George C. Rapport, *The Statesman and the Boss* (New York: Vantage, 1961), pp. 36–37.
2. Ibid., pp. 37–38.
3. Edmund Ions, *Woodrow Wilson: The Politics of Peace and War* (London/New York: Macdonald/American Heritage, 1972), p. 23; Ray Stannard Baker, *Woodrow Wilson: Life and Letters, Governor, 1910–1913* (New York: Scribner's, 1946), pp. 43–47.
4. Rapport, pp. 44–45.
5. Ibid., p. 46.
6. John M. Blum, *Woodrow Wilson and the Politics of Morality* (Boston: Little, Brown, 1956), p. 43.
7. Rapport, p. 57.
8. Ibid., pp. 58–59.
9. Ibid., pp. 62–63.
10. Arthur S. Link, *Wilson: The Road to the White House* (Princeton: Princeton University Press, 1947), p. 353.
11. Ibid., p. 356.
12. Eugene H. Roseboom, *A History of Presidential Elections* (New York: Macmillan, 1964), p. 363.
13. Ibid., p. 370.
14. Richard C. Bain and Judith H. Parris, *Convention Decisions and Voting Records* (Washington, DC: Brookings Institution, 1973), p. 188.
15. Ibid.
16. Ibid., p. 189.
17. Ibid., pp. 190–91.
18. Ibid., pp. 191–92.
19. John M. Blum et al., *The National Experience: A History of the United States,* 7th ed. (New York: Harcourt Brace Jovanovich, 1989), p. 527.
20. Ibid., p. 530.
21. Blum, *Woodrow Wilson and the Politics of Morality,* p. 61.
22. Blum, *The National Experience,* p. 530.
23. August Heckscher, in *Running for President: The Candidates and Their Images,* ed. Arthur M. Schlesinger Jr. (New York: Simon & Schuster, 1994), 2:75.
24. Ibid.
25. Arthur S. Link, *Woodrow Wilson and the Progressive Era* (New York: Harper & Bros., 1954), p. 26.

26. Blum, *The National Experience*, p. 531.
27. Ibid., p. 534.
28. Link, pp. 64–66.
29. Blum, *The National Experience*, p. 537.
30. Ions, pp. 52–54.
31. Jules Witcover, *Sabotage at Black Tom* (Chapel Hill, NC: Algonquin, 1989), pp. 39–41.
32. Blum, *The National Experience*, p. 539.
33. Witcover, p. 101.
34. Ibid., p. 102.
35. Ibid., p. 104.
36. Blum, *The National Experience*, p. 539.
37. Ibid., p. 540.
38. Ibid.
39. John Milton Cooper Jr., "The Best . . . and Worst of Times, 1897–1920," in *Of the People: The 200-Year History of the Democratic Party* (Los Angeles: General Publishing Group, 1992), p. 107.

Chapter 16: THE GREAT WAR TESTS THE PARTY, 1916–1920

1. John M. Blum et al., *The National Experience: A History of the United States,* 7th ed. (New York: Harcourt Brace Jovanovich, 1989), p. 542.
2. Richard C. Bain and Judith H. Parris, *Convention Decisions and Voting Records* (Washington, DC: Brookings Institution, 1973), p. 194.
3. Eugene H. Roseboom, *A History of Presidential Elections* (New York: Macmillan, 1964), p. 382.
4. Ibid., p. 383.
5. Bain and Parris, p. 198.
6. August Heckscher, in *Running for President: The Candidates and Their Images,* ed. Arthur M. Schlesinger Jr. (New York: Simon & Schuster, 1994), 2:92.
7. Arthur S. Link, *Woodrow Wilson and the Progressive Era* (New York: Harper & Bros., 1954), p. 244.
8. Heckscher, 2:94.
9. Roseboom, p. 386.
10. Link, p. 265.
11. Ibid., p. 268.
12. Ibid.; Jules Witcover, *Sabotage at Black Tom* (Chapel Hill, NC: Algonquin, 1989), p. 102.
13. Witcover, p. 221.
14. Link, p. 274.
15. Ibid., p. 282.
16. Blum, p. 550.
17. Ibid., p. 553.
18. Ibid.
19. Ibid., p. 556.
20. Ibid.
21. Ibid., p. 558.
22. Ibid., pp. 558–59.

23. John Milton Cooper Jr., *Breaking the Heart of the World: Woodrow Wilson and the Fight for the League of Nations* (Cambridge, Eng.: Cambridge University Press, 2001), p. 188; Edwin A. Weinstein, *Woodrow Wilson: A Medical and Psychological Biography* (Princeton: Princeton University Press, 1981), p. xiii.
24. Edmund Ions, *Woodrow Wilson: The Politics of Peace and War* (London/New York: Macdonald/American Heritage, 1972), p. 111.
25. Jules Witcover, *Crapshoot: Rolling the Dice on the Vice Presidency* (New York: Crown, 1992), p. 62.
26. Ibid.
27. Ibid., p. 63.
28. Ibid., pp. 63–64.
29. Blum, p. 563.
30. Ions, p. 114.
31. Blum, pp. 556–57.
32. Ibid., p. 568.

Chapter 17: THE SIDEWALKS OF NEW YORK, 1920–1933

1. William E. Leuchtenburg, *The Perils of Prosperity, 1914–32* (Chicago: University of Chicago Press, 1958), p. 89.
2. Ibid., p. 87.
3. Ibid., p. 88.
4. Edmund Ions, *Woodrow Wilson: The Politics of Peace and War* (London/New York: Macdonald/American Heritage, 1972), p. 117.
5. Eugene H. Roseboom, *A History of Presidential Elections* (New York: Macmillan, 1964), p. 404.
6. David Burner, "The Democratic Party, 1910–1932," in *History of U.S. Political Parties,* ed. Arthur M. Schlesinger Jr. (New York: Chelsea House, 1973), 3:1826.
7. Leuchtenburg, p. 91.
8. Arthur M. Schlesinger Jr., *The Crisis of the Old Order, 1919–1933* (Boston: Houghton Mifflin, 1959), p. 51.
9. Ibid., p. 57.
10. Roseboom, p. 411.
11. Ibid., p. 412.
12. Burner, 3:1826.
13. Ibid., 3:1823.
14. Schlesinger, p. 98.
15. Ibid., p. 99.
16. Ibid.
17. Ibid., p. 100.
18. Burner, 3:1824.
19. Nathan Miller, *FDR: An Intimate History* (Garden City, NY: Doubleday, 1983), p. 217.
20. Schlesinger, p. 103.
21. Ibid., p. 104.
22. Roseboom, p. 418.
23. Schlesinger, p. 127.
24. Roseboom, p. 424.

25. Ibid., p. 425.
26. Henry F. Graff, in *Running for President: The Candidates and Their Images,* ed. Arthur M. Schlesinger Jr. (New York: Simon & Schuster, 1994), 2:150.
27. John M. Blum et al., *The National Experience: A History of the United States,* 7th ed. (New York: Harcourt Brace Jovanovich, 1989), p. 597.
28. Burner, 3:1829.
29. Schlesinger, p. 127.
30. Burner, 3:1828.
31. Blum, p. 601.
32. Ibid., p. 602.
33. Ibid., p. 603.
34. Ibid., p. 604.
35. Ibid., p. 606.
36. Ibid., p. 612.
37. Ibid.
38. James MacGregor Burns, *Roosevelt: The Lion and the Fox* (New York: Harcourt, Brace, 1956), p. 127.
39. Frank Freidel, *Franklin D. Roosevelt: A Rendezvous with Destiny* (Boston: Little, Brown, 1990), pp. 67–68.
40. Burns, p. 133.
41. Ibid.
42. Ibid.
43. Frank Freidel, in *Running for President,* 2:163.
44. Ibid., 2:164.
45. Schlesinger, p. 413.
46. Burns, p. 135.
47. Freidel, *Franklin D. Roosevelt,* p. 72.
48. Richard C. Bain and Judith H. Parris, *Convention Decisions and Voting Records* (Washington, DC: Brookings Institution, 1973), p. 243.
49. Schlesinger, p. 403.
50. Burns, p. 140.
51. Schlesinger, p. 264.
52. Ibid., p. 265.
53. Freidel, *Franklin D. Roosevelt,* p. 76.
54. Schlesinger, p. 416.
55. Burns, p. 144.
56. Freidel, in *Running for President,* 2:169.
57. Schlesinger, p. 435.
58. Ibid., pp. 465–66.

Chapter 18: FDR AND THE NEW DEAL, 1933–1939

1. James MacGregor Burns, *Roosevelt: The Lion and the Fox* (New York: Harcourt, Brace, 1956), p. 7.
2. Ibid., p. 36.
3. John M. Blum et al., *The National Experience: A History of the United States,* 7th ed. (New York: Harcourt Brace Jovanovich, 1989), p. 619.
4. Burns, p. 163.

5. Ibid., p. 164.
6. Nathan Miller, *FDR: An Intimate History* (Garden City, NY: Doubleday, 1983), p. 309.
7. Ibid., p. 310.
8. Ibid., p. 311.
9. Ibid.
10. Burns, p. 179.
11. Ibid., p. 183.
12. Ibid., p. 184.
13. Arthur M. Schlesinger Jr., *The Age of Roosevelt: The Coming of the New Deal* (Boston: Houghton Mifflin, 1958), p. 504.
14. Burns, p. 206.
15. Schlesinger, p. 486.
16. Ibid., pp. 489–90.
17. Ibid., p. 495.
18. Ibid., p. 497.
19. Ibid., p. 503.
20. Frank Freidel, *Franklin D. Roosevelt: A Rendezvous with Destiny* (Boston: Little, Brown, 1990), p. 141.
21. Schlesinger, p. 506.
22. Otis L. Graham Jr., "The Democratic Party, 1932–1945," in *History of U.S. Political Parties,* ed. Arthur M. Schlesinger Jr. (New York: Chelsea House, 1973), 3:1943.
23. Freidel, p. 161.
24. Ibid., p. 163.
25. Ibid.
26. Miller, p. 373.
27. Blum, p. 634.
28. Richard C. Bain and Judith H. Parris, *Convention Decisions and Voting Records* (Washington, DC: Brookings Institution, 1973), p. 247.
29. Ibid., p. 248.
30. Alan Brinkley, in *Running for President: The Candidates and Their Images,* ed. Arthur M. Schlesinger Jr. (New York: Simon & Schuster, 1994), 2:184–85.
31. Ibid., p. 185.
32. Blum, p. 634.
33. Brinkley, 2:191.
34. Nancy J. Weiss, *Farewell to the Party of Lincoln: Black Politics in the Age of FDR* (Princeton: Princeton University Press, 1983), p. 94.
35. Ibid., p. 221.
36. Ibid., pp. 212, 214.
37. Ibid., p. 222.
38. Arthur M. Schlesinger Jr., Introduction to *History of U.S. Political Parties* (New York: Chelsea House, 1973), p. xi.
39. Graham, 3:1947.
40. Burns, p. 292.
41. Miller, p. 398.
42. Ibid., p. 401.
43. Ibid., p. 404.

44. Burns, p. 360.
45. Ibid., pp. 360–61.
46. Miller, p. 413.
47. Ibid., p. 412.
48. Ibid., p. 416.
49. Burns, p. 380.
50. Miller, p. 443.
51. Ibid., p. 445.

Chapter 19: THE DEMOCRACY FIGHTS FASCISM, 1939–1945

1. James MacGregor Burns, *Roosevelt: The Lion and the Fox* (New York: Harcourt, Brace, 1956), p. 412.
2. John M. Blum et al., *The National Experience: A History of the United States,* 7th ed. (New York: Harcourt Brace Jovanovich, 1989), p. 655.
3. Frank Freidel, *Franklin D. Roosevelt: A Rendezvous with Destiny* (Boston: Little, Brown, 1990), p. 322.
4. Nathan Miller, *FDR: An Intimate History* (Garden City, NY: Doubleday, 1983), p. 445.
5. Burns, p. 414.
6. Freidel, p. 322.
7. Richard C. Bain and Judith H. Parris, *Convention Decisions and Voting Records* (Washington, DC: Brookings Institution, 1973), p. 254.
8. Burns, p. 425; Miller, p. 449.
9. Burns, p. 425.
10. Miller, p. 449.
11. Bain and Parris, p. 258; Burns, p. 427.
12. Miller, p. 450.
13. Bain and Parris, p. 258; Miller, p. 450.
14. Burns, p. 428.
15. Miller, p. 451.
16. Jules Witcover, *Crapshoot: Rolling the Dice on the Vice Presidency* (New York: Crown, 1992), p. 79.
17. Ibid.; Miller, p. 452; Kenneth S. Davis, *FDR: Into the Storm, 1937–1940* (New York: Random House, 1993), p. 601.
18. Witcover, pp. 79–80.
19. Ibid., p. 80.
20. Bain and Parris, p. 260.
21. Witcover, p. 80; Doris Kearns Goodwin, *No Ordinary Time: Franklin and Eleanor Roosevelt: The Home Front in World War II* (New York: Simon & Schuster, 1994), p. 133.
22. Miller, p. 453.
23. Justus D. Doenecke, in *Running for President: The Candidates and Their Images,* ed. Arthur M. Schlesinger Jr. (New York: Simon & Schuster, 1994), 2:205.
24. Burns, p. 435.
25. Ibid., p. 433.
26. Freidel, p. 352.

27. Ibid., p. 354.
28. Ibid.
29. Burns, p. 435.
30. Ibid., p. 446.
31. Freidel, p. 355.
32. Miller, p. 457.
33. Freidel, p. 355.
34. Blum, p. 658.
35. Ibid.
36. Ibid.
37. Ibid., p. 659.
38. Miller, p. 480.
39. Otis L. Graham Jr., "The Democratic Party, 1932–1945," in *History of U.S. Political Parties*, ed. Arthur M. Schlesinger Jr. (New York: Chelsea House, 1973), 3:1954–55.
40. Ibid., p. 1955.
41. Blum, p. 682.
42. Ibid.
43. Graham, 3:1962.
44. Blum, p. 682.
45. Bain and Parris, pp. 264–65.
46. Witcover, pp. 84–85.
47. Ibid., p. 85.
48. Ibid.
49. Ibid., p. 86.
50. Ibid.
51. Ibid., p. 87.
52. Ibid.
53. Ibid., p. 89; Bain and Parris, pp. 266–67.
54. Witcover, p. 90.
55. Ibid., pp. 91–92.
56. Merle Miller, *Plain Speaking: An Oral Biography of Harry S. Truman* (New York: Putnam, 1974), p. 175.
57. Witcover, p. 93.
58. Freidel, p. 536.
59. M. Miller, p. 181.
60. Witcover, p. 94.
61. Ibid., p. 96.
62. Ibid.
63. M. Miller, pp. 181–82.
64. Witcover, p. 97.
65. Steven Fraser in *Running for President*, 2:219–20.
66. N. Miller, p. 501.
67. Fraser, 2:225.
68. Ibid., 2:226.
69. Ibid., 2:228.
70. Blum, p. 689.
71. N. Miller, pp. 509–10.

72. Harry S. Truman, *Memoirs,* vol. 1, *Year of Decisions* (Garden City, NY: Doubleday, 1955), p. 5.

Chapter 20: TRUMAN: THE BUCK STOPS HERE, 1945–1948

1. Merle Miller, *Plain Speaking: An Oral Biography of Harry S. Truman* (New York: Putnam, 1980), p. 193.
2. Harry S. Truman, *Memoirs, vol.* 1, *Year of Decisions* (Garden City, NY: Doubleday, 1955), p. 10.
3. Ibid., pp. 10–11.
4. William L. Shirer, *The Rise and Fall of the Third Reich: A History of Nazi Germany* (New York: Simon & Schuster, 1960), p. 1133.
5. John M. Blum et al., *The National Experience: A History of the United States,* 7th ed. (New York: Harcourt Brace Jovanovich, 1989), p. 691.
6. Ibid., p. 692.
7. Ibid.
8. Ibid., p. 693.
9. Robert J. Donovan, *Conflict and Crisis: The Presidency of Harry S. Truman, 1945–1948* (New York: Norton, 1977), p. 113.
10. Ibid., p. 26.
11. Sean J. Savage, *Truman and the Democratic Party* (Lexington: University Press of Kentucky, 1997), pp. 27–28.
12. Ibid., p. 28.
13. Donovan, p. 123.
14. Davis R.B. Ross, "The Democratic Party, 1945–1960," in *History of U.S. Political Parties,* ed. Arthur M. Schlesinger Jr. (New York: Chelsea House, 1973), 4:2676.
15. Truman, p. 560; Donovan, p. 229.
16. John C. Culver and John Hyde, *American Dreamer: The Life and Times of Henry A. Wallace* (New York: Norton, 2000), pp. 428–29.
17. Donovan, p. 228.
18. Culver and Hyde, p. 429.
19. Donovan, p. 230.
20. Ibid.
21. Ibid.; David McCullough, *Truman* (New York: Simon & Schuster, 1992), p. 493.
22. Donovan, p. 231.
23. Ibid.
24. Savage, pp. 113–16; Donovan, pp. 271–72.
25. Donovan, p. 242.
26. Culver and Hyde, p. 438.
27. Donovan, p. 342.
28. Culver and Hyde, p. 440.
29. Ibid., p. 441.
30. Ibid., p. 444.
31. Bert Cochran, *Harry Truman and the Crisis Presidency* (New York: Funk & Wagnall's, 1973), pp. 217–18; Irwin Ross, in *Running for President: The Candidates and Their Images,* ed. Arthur M. Schlesinger Jr. (New York: Simon & Schuster,

1994), 2:239–41; Savage, pp. 113–16; McCullough, pp. 589–93. (There was some later dispute over how influential the Rowe-Clifford memo was with Truman. See McCullough, pp. 592–93.)

32. Donovan, p. 343.
33. Ibid., p. 338. Donovan reported three close Truman sources—John Snyder, Sam Rosenman and John Steelman—all recalling Truman telling them he would step aside for Eisenhower in 1948.
34. M. Miller, pp. 338–39.
35. Donovan, p. 389.
36. Ibid., p. 388.
37. Ibid., pp. 388–89.
38. Ibid., p. 334.
39. Ibid., p. 354; D. Ross, 4:2685.
40. Richard C. Bain and Judith H. Parris, *Convention Decisions and Voting Records* (Washington, DC: Brookings Institution, 1973), p. 269.
41. Donovan, p. 402.
42. McCullough, p. 633.
43. Donovan, p. 404.
44. Ibid.
45. Ibid., p. 405.
46. Bain and Parris, p. 275.
47. Hubert H. Humphrey, *Beyond Civil Rights: A New Day of Equality* (New York: Random House, 1968), pp. 34–35.
48. Savage, p. 31.
49. Humphrey, p. 37.
50. McCullough, p. 642; Donovan, p. 407.
51. McCullough, p. 643.
52. Ibid.; Donovan, p. 407.
53. Cochran, p. 229.
54. Donovan, p. 415.
55. Ibid.
56. McCullough, p. 645.
57. Donovan, p. 420.
58. I. Ross, p. 243.
59. Donovan, p. 423.
60. McCullough, p. 669.
61. Donovan, p. 425.
62. I. Ross, p. 243.
63. Donovan, p. 427.
64. Ibid.

Chapter 21: THE FAIR DEAL, AND END OF AN ERA, 1949–1952

1. John M. Blum et al., *The National Experience: A History of the United States,* 7th ed. (New York: Harcourt Brace Jovanovich, 1989), p. 709.
2. Ibid.
3. Ibid.

4. Robert J. Donovan, *Tumultuous Years: The Presidency of Harry S. Truman, 1949–1953* (New York: Norton, 1982), p. 137.
5. David McCullough, *Truman* (New York: Simon & Schuster, 1992), p. 759.
6. Ibid.
7. Donovan, p. 136.
8. Ibid.
9. Blum, p. 717.
10. Donovan, p. 162.
11. Ibid., p. 163.
12. McCullough, p. 768.
13. Ibid., p. 766.
14. Donovan, p. 295.
15. Blum, p. 713.
16. McCullough, p. 745.
17. Donovan, p. 119.
18. Ibid., pp. 126–27.
19. Blum, p. 713.
20. McCullough, p. 808.
21. Ibid., p. 812; Donovan, p. 294.
22. Donovan, pp. 296–97.
23. Ibid., p. 296.
24. McCullough, p. 836.
25. Donovan, p. 352.
26. Ibid., p. 359.
27. Ibid.
28. Ibid., p. 360.
29. McCullough, p. 851.
30. Donovan, p. 386; McCullough, p. 897.
31. McCullough, p. 771.
32. Donovan, p. 395.
33. Ibid., p. 396.
34. McCullough, p. 888; Donovan, p. 393.
35. McCullough, pp. 888–89.
36. Donovan, p. 393.
37. Ibid., pp. 393–94.
38. Harry S. Truman, *Memoirs,* vol. 2, *Years of Trial and Hope* (Garden City, NY: Doubleday, 1956), p. 493.
39. Eugene H. Roseboom, *A History of Presidential Elections* (New York: Macmillan, 1964), p. 509.
40. Truman, *Memoirs,* 2:496.
41. Kenneth S. Davis, *The Politics of Honor: A Biography of Adlai E. Stevenson* (New York: Putnam, 1967), p. 271.
42. John Bartlow Martin, *Adlai Stevenson of Illinois* (Garden City, NY: Doubleday, 1976), pp. 598–99.
43. Blum, p. 719.
44. Jules Witcover, *Crapshoot: Rolling the Dice on the Vice Presidency* (New York: Crown, 1992), p. 119.
45. Ibid.

46. Truman, *Memoirs*, 2:498.
47. Ibid.
48. Sean J. Savage, *Truman and the Democratic Party* (Lexington: University Press of Kentucky, 1997), p. 203.
49. Alonzo L. Hamby, in *Running for President: The Candidates and Their Images*, ed. Arthur M. Schlesinger Jr. (New York: Simon & Schuster, 1994), 2:262.
50. Ibid.; McCullough, p. 912.

Chapter 22: IN THE SHADOW OF A WAR HERO, 1953–1960

1. Porter McKeever, *Adlai Stevenson: His Life and Legacy* (New York: Morrow, 1989), p. 313.
2. Ibid., p. 315.
3. Ibid., p. 316.
4. Davis R.B. Ross, "The Democratic Party, 1945–1960," in *History of U.S. Political Parties*, ed. Arthur M. Schlesinger Jr. (New York: Chelsea House, 1973), 4:2696.
5. John M. Blum, et al., *The National Experience: A History of the United States*, 7th ed. (New York: Harcourt Brace Jovanovich, 1989), p. 733.
6. Ibid.
7. McKeever, p. 323.
8. Blum, p. 733.
9. McKeever, p. 324; Kenneth S. Davis, *The Politics of Honor: A Biography of Adlai E. Stevenson* (New York: Putnam, 1967), p. 299.
10. McKeever, p. 325.
11. Ibid.
12. Ibid., p. 328.
13. Ross, 4:2698.
14. Ibid.
15. McKeever, p. 356.
16. Ibid., p. 357.
17. Ibid., p. 369.
18. Ibid., p. 373.
19. Davis, p. 332; McKeever, p. 376.
20. McKeever, p. 376.
21. Ibid.
22. Davis, p. 333; McKeever, p. 377.
23. Jules Witcover, *Crapshoot: Rolling the Dice on the Vice Presidency* (New York: Crown, 1992), p. 141.
24. Ibid.; Theodore C. Sorensen, *Kennedy* (New York: Harper & Row, 1965), p. 83.
25. James MacGregor Burns, *John Kennedy* (New York: Harcourt, Brace and World, 1961), p. 184.
26. Witcover, p. 142; Sorensen, p. 84.
27. Sorensen, pp. 89–90.
28. Arthur M. Schlesinger Jr., *A Thousand Days: John F. Kennedy in the White House* (Boston: Houghton Mifflin, 1965), p. 9.
29. Herbert S. Parmet, *Eisenhower and the American Crusades* (New York: Macmillan, 1972), p. 433.
30. George Gallup Jr. and Alec M. Gallup, in *Running for President: The Candidates*

and Their Images, ed. Arthur M. Schlesinger Jr. (New York: Simon & Schuster, 1994), 2:275.

31. Ibid., pp. 275–76.
32. McKeever, p. 382.
33. Ross, 4:2700.
34. Witcover, pp. 132–33.
35. Arlene Lazarowitz, *Years in Exile: The Liberal Democrats, 1950–1959* (New York: Garland, 1988), p. 120.
36. Ibid., p. 121.
37. Ibid., p. 125.
38. Ibid., pp. 128–29.
39. Ibid., pp. 130–31.
40. Ibid., pp. 141–43.
41. Parmet, p. 522.
42. Blum, p. 729.

Chapter 23: JFK: THE PARTY BOUNCES BACK, 1960

1. Theodore C. Sorensen, *Kennedy* (New York: Harper & Row, 1965), p. 100.
2. Ibid., p. 102.
3. Ibid., p. 109.
4. Ibid., p. 113.
5. Theodore H. White, *The Making of the President, 1960* (New York: Atheneum, 1961), p. 56.
6. Ibid., p. 42.
7. Ibid., p. 49.
8. Sorensen, p. 135; Richard N. Goodwin, *Remembering America: A Voice from the Sixties* (Boston: Little, Brown, 1988), p. 82.
9. White, p. 100.
10. Sorensen, p. 139.
11. Ibid.
12. Goodwin, p. 88.
13. Sorensen, p. 142.
14. Goodwin, p. 88.
15. Sorensen, p. 142.
16. Goodwin, p. 87.
17. Sorensen, p. 144.
18. Goodwin, p. 90.
19. Sorensen, p. 152.
20. Ibid.
21. Jules Witcover, *Crapshoot: Rolling the Dice on the Vice Presidency* (New York: Crown, 1992), p. 146.
22. Sorensen, p. 156.
23. Witcover, p. 146.
24. Richard C. Bain and Judith H. Parris, *Convention Decisions and Voting Records* (Washington, DC: Brookings Institution, 1973), p. 305.
25. Arthur M. Schlesinger Jr., *A Thousand Days: JFK in the White House* (Boston: Houghton Mifflin, 1965), p. 39.

26. Witcover, p. 147.
27. Ibid.
28. Sorensen, p. 162.
29. White, p. 173.
30. Witcover, p. 149.
31. Schlesinger, p. 43.
32. Ibid., p. 45.
33. Ibid., p. 49.
34. Witcover, p. 156.
35. Ibid., p. 157.
36. Bain and Parris, p. 306; Richard C. Wade, "The Democratic Party, 1960–1972," in *History of U.S. Political Parties,* ed. Arthur M. Schlesinger Jr. (New York: Chelsea House, 1973), 4:2832.
37. Bain and Parris, p. 308.
38. Witcover, p. 138.
39. Sorensen, p. 188.
40. Ibid., pp. 189–90.
41. White, pp. 391–93.
42. Sorensen, p. 191.
43. White, p. 261.
44. Sorensen, p. 193.
45. John M. Blum et al., *The National Experience: A History of the United States,* 7th ed. (New York: Harcourt Brace Jovanovich, 1989), p. 737.
46. Sorensen, p. 198.
47. White, p. 286.
48. U.S. Senate Commerce Committee, *Freedom of Communications,* Part 3, *Presidential Debates of 1960* (Washington, DC: U.S. Government Printing Office, 1961), pp. 73–74.
49. Ibid., p. 75.
50. Ibid., pp. 76–77, 90.
51. Ibid., p. 78.
52. Taylor Branch, *Parting the Waters: America in the King Years, 1954–1963* (New York: Simon & Schuster, 1988), pp. 362–67; White, pp. 332–33.
53. Sorensen, p. 216.

Chapter 24: THE BEGINNING AND END OF THE NEW FRONTIER, 1961–1963

1. Theodore C. Sorensen, *Kennedy* (New York: Harper & Row, 1965), pp. 245–46.
2. Ibid., p. 247.
3. Ibid., p. 248.
4. The subject of the Eisenhower plan to overthrow Castro had come up in the fourth Kennedy-Nixon debate in 1960. Kennedy, not aware of Eisenhower's plan, had proposed the idea himself, and although Nixon knew of the plan and approved, he castigated Kennedy for proposing it. He called it "probably the most dangerously irresponsible" recommendation of the campaign and said it "would be an open invitation to Khrushchev to come in [and] . . . engage us in what would be a civil war and possibly even worse than that." Later, Nixon, in his

book *Six Crises* (Garden City, NY: Doubleday, 1962), defended this sham. "There was only one thing I could do," he wrote. "The covert operation had to be protected at all costs. . . . I had to go to the other extreme: I must attack the Kennedy proposal [which he really supported] . . . as wrong and irresponsible." Years later, when I asked Nixon in an interview why he couldn't just have said nothing in the debate, he replied that his attack "was the only political position that was salvageable. I couldn't say what we were actually doing and what I was advocating in the government. . . . Kennedy was taking a highly popular position, and to simply say you were against it would not have been enough politically. I had to give the reasons it was wrong." So much for Nixon's credibility.

5. Sorensen, pp. 295–96.
6. Ibid., p. 309.
7. Ibid., p. 308.
8. Ibid., p. 525.
9. Arthur M. Schlesinger Jr., *A Thousand Days: John F. Kennedy in the White House* (Boston: Houghton Mifflin, 1965), p. 303.
10. Sorensen, p. 543.
11. James Reston, *Deadline: A Memoir* (New York: Random House, 1991), pp. 290–91.
12. Schlesinger, p. 374.
13. Sorensen, p. 586.
14. Ibid., p. 592.
15. Ibid., p. 345.
16. John M. Blum et al., *The National Experience: A History of the United States*, 7th ed. (New York: Harcourt Brace Jovanovich, 1989), p. 754.
17. Taylor Branch, *Parting the Waters: America in the King Years, 1954–63* (New York: Simon & Schuster, 1988), p. 415.
18. Schlesinger, p. 936.
19. Sorensen, p. 448.
20. Ibid., pp. 448–49; Schlesinger, p. 635.
21. Sorensen, pp. 450–51; Schlesinger, p. 636.
22. Schlesinger, p. 941.
23. Sorensen, p. 667.
24. Ibid.
25. Ibid., p. 668.
26. Ibid., p. 670.
27. Ibid., p. 668.
28. Ibid., p. 671.
29. Ibid., p. 684. In Kennedy's own account of the Cuban missile crisis, *Thirteen Days* (New York: Norton, 1969), he wrote: "Listening to the proposals, I passed a note to the president: 'I now know how Tojo felt when he was planning Pearl Harbor.'"
30. Sorensen, p. 690.
31. Ibid., pp. 703–704.
32. Blum, p. 752.
33. By mutual agreement, the U.S. Navy flew planes low over the missile-bearing ships at an appointed location in the Atlantic, north of Puerto Rico. Russian seamen pulled back tarpaulin covers from the missiles so their identification could be verified. As a Pentagon pool reporter on one of the planes, I was able to witness this unusual bit of history.

34. Branch, p. 684.
35. Blum, p. 754.
36. Sorensen, p. 495.
37. Branch, p. 880.
38. Schlesinger, p. 972; Todd Gitlin, *The Sixties: Years of Hope, Days of Rage* (New York: Bantam, 1993), p. 145; Branch, pp. 882–83.
39. Sorensen, p. 505.
40. Branch, p. 892.
41. Blum, p. 752.
42. Sorensen, p. 601.
43. Ibid., pp. 658–59.
44. Blum, p. 749.
45. Ibid.
46. William Manchester, *The Death of a President* (New York: Harper & Row, 1967), p. 3.
47. Ibid., pp. 24–25, 67, 78–79, 113–14.
48. Ibid., p. 116.
49. Ibid., p. 124.
50. Ibid., p. 153.
51. Observation by author.
52. Manchester, pp. 344–45.
53. Observation by author. There was no explanation later for this odd and striking phenomenon.

Chapter 25: LBJ: RISE AND FALL OF THE GREAT SOCIETY, 1963–1968

1. Doris Kearns, *Lyndon Johnson & the American Dream* (New York: Harper & Row, 1976), p. 170.
2. Ibid., pp. 177–78.
3. Irving Bernstein, *Guns or Butter: The Presidency of Lyndon Johnson* (New York: Oxford University Press, 1996), p. 24.
4. Kearns, pp. 173–74.
5. Lyndon B. Johnson, *The Vantage Point: Perspectives of the Presidency, 1963–1969* (New York: Holt, Rinehart and Winston, 1971), p. 104.
6. John M. Blum et al., *The National Experience: A History of the United States,* 7th ed. (New York: Harcourt Brace Jovanovich, 1989), p. 757.
7. Richard C. Bain and Judith W. Parris, *Convention Decisions and Voting Records* (Washington, DC: Brookings Institution, 1973), p. 314.
8. Jeff Sheshol, *Mutual Contempt* (New York: Norton, 1997), pp. 115–16. Sometime later, in an interview with Walter Cronkite, Johnson professed not to remember the snub. "I would have thought that the natural thing to do was go as quickly as you could to the widow, Mrs. Kennedy, and try to console her and give her strength," he said. "I would have found nothing improper in it."
9. Arthur M. Schlesinger Jr., *Robert Kennedy and His Times* (Boston: Houghton Mifflin, 1978), p. 652.
10. Jules Witcover, *Crapshoot: Rolling the Dice on the Vice Presidency* (New York: Crown, 1992), p. 175.
11. Schlesinger, p. 650.

12. Robert Dallek, *Flawed Giant: Lyndon Johnson and His Times, 1961–1973* (New York: Oxford University Press, 1998), p. 138; Schlesinger, p. 653.

13. Jules Witcover, *The Resurrection of Richard Nixon* (New York: Putnam, 1970), p. 22.

14. Witcover, *Crapshoot*, p. 179.

15. Bain and Parris, p. 314.

16. Witcover, *Crapshoot*, p. 180.

17. Johnson, p. 98.

18. Witcover, *Crapshoot*, p. 180.

19. Johnson, p. 576.

20. Ibid., pp. 576–77.

21. Witcover, *Crapshoot*, p. 185.

22. Dallek, pp. 247–48; Bernstein, pp. 335–36; Stanley Karnow, *Vietnam: A History* (New York: Viking, 1983), pp. 367–68.

23. Karnow, pp. 370–71.

24. Bernstein, p. 336.

25. Karnow, pp. 358–62.

26. Ibid., p. 362.

27. Ibid., p. 373.

28. Dallek, p. 153.

29. Bernstein, p. 338.

30. Author's interview with Gruening.

31. Bernstein, p. 337.

32. Theodore H. White, *The Making of the President, 1964* (New York: Signet, 1965), p. 328.

33. Bain and Parris, p. 315.

34. Witcover, *Crapshoot*, p. 181.

35. Ibid., p. 191.

36. Ibid., p. 193.

37. White, p. 348.

38. Bain and Parris, pp. 316–17.

39. Robert Dallek, in *Running for President: The Candidates and Their Images*, ed. Arthur M. Schlesinger Jr. (New York: Simon & Schuster, 1994), 2:313.

40. Ibid., p. 310.

41. Ibid., p. 314.

42. Kearns, p. 245; Dallek, *Flawed Giant*, p. 295.

43. Blum, p. 763.

44. Karnow, p. 413.

45. Covering the Pentagon at the time, I was among those flown to Saigon for briefings by the American command, including General William Westmoreland, and visits to Pleiku, Danang and other locales of U.S. participation. The trip produced mixed reports on American progress. On a return flight from Danang to Saigon, I shared a cargo plane with a body bag containing the remains of one of the first American marines killed in Vietnam.

46. Tom Hayden, *Reunion: A Memoir* (New York: Random House, 1988), p. ix; Jules Witcover, *The Year the Dream Died: Revisiting 1968 in America* (New York: Warner, 1997), p. 3.

47. Todd Gitlin, *The Sixties: Years of Hope, Days of Rage* (New York: Bantam, 1993), p. 183.

48. Blum, p. 764.
49. Gitlin, p. 184.
50. Jules Witcover, *85 Days: The Last Campaign of Robert Kennedy* (New York: Putnam, 1968), p. 19; Schlesinger, p. 736.
51. Blum, p. 760.
52. Witcover, *The Resurrection of Richard Nixon,* p. 165.
53. Blum, p. 762.
54. Ibid., p. 763.
55. Witcover, *85 Days,* p. 28.
56. Ibid.
57. Ibid., p. 29.
58. Witcover, *The Year the Dream Died,* p. 34.
59. Gitlin, p. 242.
60. Robert S. McNamara, *In Retrospect: The Tragedy and Lessons of Vietnam* (New York: Times Books, 1995), pp. 307–309. It was characteristic of the precise McNamara, whom I covered for three years as a reporter at the Pentagon during his watch, that he would list as a "best estimate" that "10,900" Americans, not 11,000, would die.
61. Witcover, *85 Days,* p. 35.
62. Ibid.
63. Ibid.
64. Jeremy Larner, *Nobody Knows: Reflections on the McCarthy Campaign of 1968* (New York: Macmillan, 1969), p. 37.
65. Witcover, *The Year the Dream Died,* p. 60.
66. Witcover, *85 Days,* p. 15.
67. Witcover, *The Year the Dream Died,* p. 65.
68. Ibid., p. 73.
69. Ibid.
70. Richard Goodwin, *Remembering America: A Voice from the Sixties* (Boston: Little, Brown, 1988), p. 492.
71. Witcover, *The Year the Dream Died,* p. 93.
72. Ibid., p. 88.
73. Ibid., p. 89.
74. Ibid., p. 100.
75. Author's interview with Gans.
76. Witcover, *The Year the Dream Died,* p. 107.
77. Ibid., p. 115.
78. Larner, p. 47.
79. Lawrence F. O'Brien, *No Final Victories: A Life in Politics from John F. Kennedy to Watergate* (Garden City, NY: Doubleday, 1974), p. 229.
80. Johnson, p. 435; Witcover, *The Year the Dream Died,* pp. 141–42.

Chapter 26: DEMOCRATIC CATACLYSM, 1968

1. Jules Witcover, *The Year the Dream Died: Revisiting 1968 in America* (New York: Warner, 1997), p. 142.
2. Ibid.

3. Author's interview with Dutton.

4. Witcover, p. 146.

5. Joseph A. Califano Jr., *The Triumph & Tragedy of Lyndon Johnson* (New York: Simon & Schuster, 1991), p. 292.

6. Lawrence F. O'Brien, *No Final Victories: A Life in Politics from John F. Kennedy to Watergate* (Garden City, NY: Doubleday, 1974), p. 238.

7. Witcover, p. 151.

8. David L. Lewis, *King: A Critical Biography* (New York: Praeger, 1970), p. 387; Witcover, p. 152.

9. Witcover, p. 154; Schlesinger, *Robert Kennedy and His Times* (Boston: Houghton Mifflin, 1978), p. 874.

10. Schlesinger, p. 875; Witcover, pp. 154–55.

11. Witcover, p. 177.

12. Ibid., p. 201.

13. Author's interview with Smith.

14. Author's interview with Dutton.

15. Witcover, p. 218.

16. Ibid., p. 217.

17. Ibid., p. 219.

18. Ibid., pp. 225–26.

19. Ibid., p. 235.

20. Ibid., p. 240.

21. Ibid.

22. Ibid.

23. Ibid., p. 242.

24. Ibid.

25. Albert Eisele, *Almost to the Presidency: A Biography of Two American Politicians* (Blue Earth, MN: Piper, 1972), p. 320.

26. Witcover, p. 243.

27. Ibid., p. 244.

28. Ibid.

29. Ibid., p. 247.

30. Ibid., p. 249.

31. Richard N. Goodwin, *Remembering America: A Voice from the Sixties* (Boston: Little, Brown, 1988), p. 537.

32. Witcover, p. 252.

33. Author's observations. Informed by a Kennedy aide that the candidate would be holding a news conference in a room on the opposite side of the kitchen pantry, I left the ballroom platform and preceded Kennedy into the pantry, where I was perhaps twenty feet ahead of him when the first shots rang out.

34. Witcover, p. 261.

35. Ibid., p. 263.

36. Jeremy Larner, *Nobody Knows: Reflections on the McCarthy Campaign of 1968* (New York: Macmillan, 1969), p. 124.

37. Witcover, pp. 272–73.

38. Ibid., p. 280.

39. McCarthy Historical Project Archive, Georgetown University.

40. Eisele, p. 336.

41. Witcover, p. 307.
42. Eisele, p. 337.
43. Tom Hayden, *Reunion: A Memoir* (New York: Random House, 1988), p. 293.
44. O'Brien, p. 251.
45. Richard C. Bain and Judith H. Parris, *Convention Decisions and Voting Records* (Washington, DC: Brookings Institution, 1973), p. 323.
46. Witcover, p. 321.
47. Ibid., pp. 321–22.
48. Hubert H. Humphrey, *The Education of a Public Man: My Life in Politics* (Minneapolis: University of Minnesota Press, 1991), p. 390; Bain and Parris, p. 323.
49. Witcover, p. 336.
50. Ibid., p. 342.
51. Ibid., p. 375.
52. O'Brien, p. 261.
53. Califano, p. 325.
54. Witcover, p. 380.
55. Ibid., p. 385.
56. Ibid., p. 390.
57. Ibid., p. 416.
58. Bui Diem, with David Chanoff, *In the Jaws of History* (Boston: Houghton Mifflin, 1987), p. 244.
59. Califano, p. 327.
60. Witcover, p. 417.
61. Ibid., p. 418.
62. Ibid., p. 421.
63. O'Brien Oral History Collection, LBJ Library.

Chapter 27: REFORM, BUT NOT REVIVAL, 1968–1974

1. William J. Crotty, *Decision for the Democrats: Reforming the Party Structure* (Baltimore: Johns Hopkins University Press, 1978), p. 15.
2. Ibid., p. 16.
3. Ibid., p. 13.
4. Ibid.
5. Ibid., p. 14.
6. Robert Sam Anson, *McGovern: A Biography* (New York: Holt, Rinehart and Winston, 1972), pp. 246–48.
7. Crotty, p. 58.
8. Anson, p. 248.
9. Ibid., p. 251; Richard C. Wade, "The Democratic Party, 1960–1972," in *History of U.S. Political Parties,* ed. Arthur M. Schlesinger Jr. (New York: Chelsea House, 1973), 4:2844.
10. Wade, 4:2845.
11. Ibid.
12. Ibid., 4:2846.
13. Crotty, p. 83.
14. Ibid., p. 111.
15. Ibid., p. 115.

16. Ibid., p. 147.
17. Ibid., p. 145.
18. John M. Blum et al., *The National Experience: A History of the United States,* 7th ed. (New York: Harcourt Brace Jovanovich, 1989), p. 774.
19. Jules Witcover, *White Knight: The Rise of Spiro Agnew* (New York: Random House, 1972), p. 305.
20. Richard C. Bain and Judith H. Parris, *Convention Decisions and Voting Records* (Washington, DC: Brookings Institution, 1973), p. 230.
21. Blum, p. 774.
22. Author's observation of Muskie over many months in 1971–72.
23. Interview with Maria Carrier in New Hampshire, February 1972.
24. Herbert S. Parmet, in *Running for President: The Candidates and Their Images,* ed. Arthur M. Schlesinger Jr. (New York: Simon & Schuster, 1994), 2:348.
25. Bain and Parris, p. 332.
26. Ibid., pp. 332–34.
27. Ibid., pp. 333–34.
28. Jules Witcover, *Crapshoot: Rolling the Dice on the Vice Presidency* (New York: Crown, 1992), pp. 245–46.
29. George S. McGovern, *Grassroots: The Autobiography of George McGovern* (New York: Random House, 1977), p. 198.
30. Ibid., p. 199.
31. Ibid., p. 187.
32. Ibid., pp. 202–203.
33. Ibid., pp. 204–207.
34. Ibid., p. 211.
35. Ibid.
36. Witcover, *Crapshoot,* p. 247.
37. McGovern, p. 215.
38. H. R. Haldeman, *Haldeman Diaries: Inside the Nixon White House* (New York: Putnam, 1994), pp. 317, 324–25.
39. Author's telephone interview with John Ehrlichman, assistant to President Nixon for domestic affairs, upon publication of the *Haldeman Diaries,* 1994.
40. J. Anthony Lukas, *Nightmare: The Underside of the Nixon Years* (New York: Viking, 1976), p. 303.
41. Ibid., p. 231.

Chapter 28: POST-WATERGATE INTERLUDE, 1974–1980

1. James M. Blum et al., *The National Experience: A History of the United States,* 7th ed. (New York: Harcourt Brace Jovanovich, 1989), p. 794.
2. Jules Witcover, *Marathon: The Pursuit of the Presidency, 1972–1976* (New York: Viking, 1977), p. 41.
3. Ibid., p. 125; *Facts on File,* 1974, p. 791.
4. Witcover, *Marathon,* p. 126.
5. Ibid., p. 127.
6. William J. Crotty, *Political Reform and the American Experiment* (New York: Crowell, 1977), pp. 246–47.
7. Ibid., pp. 250–51.

8. *Facts on File,* 1974, pp. 1021–22.
9. Witcover, *Marathon,* p. 130.
10. *Facts on File,* 1974, p. 1022.
11. Ibid.
12. *Facts on File,* 1975, p. 139.
13. Witcover, *Marathon,* p. 194.
14. Ibid., p. 201.
15. Ibid., p. 210.
16. Ibid., p. 232.
17. Ibid., p. 349.
18. Ibid., pp. 565–66.
19. Ibid.
20. Ibid., p. 568.
21. Ibid., pp. 597–98.
22. Ibid., p. 603.
23. Ibid., p. 614.
24. Ibid.
25. Ibid, p. 616. Actually, it was four out of seven. Ford, Nixon, Johnson and Truman all became president. Agnew, Humphrey and Barkley did not.
26. Ibid., pp. 638–39.
27. Leo P. Ribuffo in *Running for President: The Candidates and Their Images,* ed. Arthur M. Schlesinger Jr. (New York: Simon & Schuster, 1994), 2:373.
28. Blum, p. 807.
29. Ibid., p. 802.
30. Jack W. Germond and Jules Witcover, *Blue Smoke and Mirrors: How Reagan Won and Why Carter Lost the Election of 1980* (New York: Viking, 1981), p. 25.
31. *Facts on File,* 1977, p. 976.
32. Ibid., p. 381.
33. Blum, p. 800.
34. *Facts on File,* 1978, p. 30.
35. Germond and Witcover, *Blue Smoke and Mirrors,* p. 49.
36. *Facts on File,* 1978, p. 956.
37. Germond and Witcover, *Blue Smoke and Mirrors,* pp. 50–51.
38. Ibid., p. 32.
39. Ibid., p. 33.
40. Ibid., pp. 36–37.
41. Ibid., p. 52.
42. Ibid., p. 69.
43. Hamilton Jordan, *Crisis: The Last Year of the Carter Presidency* (New York: Random House, 1982), p. 21.
44. Germond and Witcover, *Blue Smoke and Mirrors,* p. 78.
45. Ibid.
46. Ibid., p. 88.
47. Ibid., p. 142.
48. Ibid., pp. 146–47.
49. Ibid., p. 148.
50. Ibid.
51. Ibid., p. 202.

52. Ibid., p. 245.
53. Ibid., p. 247.
54. Ibid.
55. Ibid., p. 253.
56. Ibid., p. 281.

Chapter 29: BUCKING THE REAGAN REVOLUTION, 1981–1984

1. John M. Blum et al., *The National Experience: A History of the United States,* 7th ed. (New York: Harcourt Brace Jovanovich, 1989), p. 810.
2. Ibid.
3. Ibid., p. 812.
4. Ibid., p. 813.
5. Ibid., p. 812.
6. Ibid., p. 813.
7. Ibid., p. 814.
8. Jack W. Germond and Jules Witcover, *Wake Us When It's Over: Presidential Politics of 1984* (New York: Macmillan, 1985), p. 32.
9. Ibid., p. 35.
10. Ibid., p. 36.
11. Ibid., p. 84.
12. Ibid., p. 188.
13. Ibid., pp. 193–94.
14. Ibid., p. 199.
15. Ibid., p. 304.
16. Ibid., p. 314.
17. Ibid., p. 349.
18. Ibid., p. 366.
19. Ibid., p. 409.
20. Author's interview with Bob Teeter.
21. Germond and Witcover, pp. 417–18.
22. Ibid., p. 471.
23. Ibid., p. 478.
24. Ibid., pp. 484–85.
25. Ibid., p. 533.
26. Steven M. Gillon in *Running for President: The Candidates and Their Images,* ed. Arthur M. Schlesinger Jr. (New York: Simon & Schuster, 1994), 2:411.

Chapter 30: A TIME FOR PARTY SOUL-SEARCHING, 1985–1991

1. Kenneth S. Baer, *Reinventing Democrats: The Politics of Liberalism from Reagan to Clinton* (Lawrence: University Press of Kansas, 2000), p. 7.
2. Al From memorandum, "Saving the Democratic Party," Jan. 2, 1985.
3. Jack W. Germond and Jules Witcover, *Whose Broad Stripes and Bright Stars? The Trivial Pursuit of the Presidency, 1988* (New York: Warner, 1989), pp. 40–41.
4. Interview with Elaine Kamarck, July 2002.

5. Germond and Witcover, p. 40.
6. Ibid., p. 45.
7. Ibid., p. 41.
8. John M. Blum et al., *The National Experience: A History of the United States,* 7th ed. (New York: Harcourt Brace Jovanovich, 1989), p. 821.
9. Ibid., p. 822.
10. Ibid., p. 825.
11. Germond and Witcover, pp. 211–12.
12. Ibid., pp. 230–43.
13. Ibid., p. 354.
14. Ibid.
15. Jack W. Germond and Jules Witcover, *Mad as Hell: Revolt at the Ballot Box, 1992* (New York: Warner, 1993), p. 22.
16. Germond and Witcover, *Whose Broad Stripes and Bright Stars?,* p. 11.
17. Ibid., p. 5.
18. Ibid.
19. Ibid., p. 440.
20. Baer, p. 126.
21. Interview with Kamarck.
22. Ibid., p. 128.
23. Ibid., pp. 134–37.
24. Interview with Al From, June 2002.
25. Baer, p. 136.
26. Ibid., pp. 129–32.
27. Interview with Kamarck.
28. Baer, pp. 168–69.
29. Ibid., pp. 178–79.
30. Ibid., p. 178.
31. Ibid., p. 183.
32. Ibid., p. 187.
33. Ibid., p. 184.
34. Germond and Witcover, *Mad as Hell,* p. 26.
35. Ibid., p. 31.
36. Ibid., pp. 33–34.
37. Ibid., p. 34.
38. Ibid.
39. Ibid., p. 36.
40. Ibid., p. 37.
41. Ibid., p. 44.
42. Ibid., p. 46.
43. Interview with Kamarck.
44. Baer, p. 191.
45. Germond and Witcover, *Mad as Hell,* pp. 115–16.

Chapter 31: A DIFFERENT KIND OF DEMOCRAT, 1992

1. Jack W. Germond and Jules Witcover, *Mad as Hell: Revolt at the Ballot Box, 1992* (New York: Warner, 1993), p. 166.

2. Ibid., pp. 169–70.
3. Ibid., p. 176.
4. Ibid., p. 179.
5. Ibid.
6. Ibid., pp. 185–86.
7. Ibid.
8. Ibid., p. 191.
9. Ibid., p. 193.
10. Ibid., p. 196.
11. Ibid., pp. 196–97.
12. Ibid., p. 204.
13. Ibid., p. 151.
14. Gerald Posner, *Citizen Perot: His Life & Times* (New York: Random House, 1996), p. 246.
15. John Chancellor, in *Running for President: The Candidates and Their Images,* ed. Arthur M. Schlesinger Jr. (New York: Simon & Schuster, 1994), 2:439.
16. Ibid., 2:440.
17. Germond and Witcover, p. 251.
18. Ibid., p. 252.
19. Ibid., p. 255.
20. Ibid., p. 264.
21. Ibid.
22. Ibid., p. 273.
23. Ibid., p. 343.
24. Posner, p. 285.
25. Germond and Witcover, p. 372.
26. Ibid., p. 383.
27. Ibid., p. 384.
28. Ibid., p. 392.
29. Ibid., p. 410.
30. Ibid., p. 420.
31. Ibid., p. 432.
32. Ibid., p. 442; Kenneth S. Baer, *Reinventing Democrats: The Politics of Liberalism from Reagan to Clinton* (Lawrence: University Press of Kansas, 2000), p. 204.
33. Posner, p. 290.
34. Germond and Witcover, p. 10.
35. Baer, pp. 206–207.

Chapter 32: LOOKING LIKE AMERICA, 1993–1996

1. Kenneth S. Baer, *Reinventing Democrats: The Politics of Liberalism from Reagan to Clinton* (Lawrence: University Press of Kansas, 2000), p. 222.
2. Martin Walker, *The President We Deserve: Bill Clinton: His Rise, Falls and Comebacks* (New York: Crown, 1996), p. 178.
3. Ibid., p. 179.
4. James B. Stewart, *Blood Sport: The President and His Adversaries* (New York: Touchstone, 1996), p. 245.
5. Walker, p. 179.
6. Stewart, pp. 245–46.

7. Ibid., p. 250.
8. Walker, p. 311.
9. Baer, pp. 212–13.
10. Walker, p. 201.
11. Ibid., p. 183.
12. Ibid., p. 222.
13. Ibid., p. 317.
14. Ibid., p. 320.
15. Ibid., p. 318.
16. Lewis L. Gould, in *American Heritage Illustrated History of the Presidents* (New York: Crown, 2000), p. 505; Baer, p. 232.
17. Walker, pp. 329–30; Baer, p. 232.
18. Baer, p. 233.
19. Ibid., p. 235.
20. Ibid., p. 239.
21. Elizabeth Drew, *Showdown: The Struggle Between the Gingrich Congress and the Clinton White House* (New York: Simon & Schuster, 1996), pp. 208, 234.
22. Walker, p. 338; Drew, p. 194.
23. Drew, p. 327.
24. Ibid., p. 284.
25. Ibid., pp. 325–26.
26. Baer, p. 240; Drew, p. 376.
27. Baer, p. 244.
28. Ibid., p. 246.
29. Bob Woodward, *The Choice* (New York: Simon & Schuster, 1996), p. 352.
30. Baer, p. 249.
31. Ibid.
32. Ibid., p. 247.
33. Ibid.
34. Evan Thomas and *Newsweek* Team, *Back from the Dead: How Clinton Survived the Republican Revolution* (New York: Atlantic Monthly Press, 1997), p. 198.

Chapter 33: DEMOCRATIC PHOENIX, 1997–1999

1. Kenneth S. Baer, *Reinventing Democrats: The Politics of Liberalism from Reagan to Clinton* (Lawrence: University Press of Kansas, 2000), p. 252.
2. Ibid., p. 251.
3. Ibid., p. 252.
4. Ibid., p. 253.
5. Ibid., p. 252.
6. Lewis L. Gould, in *American Heritage Illustrated History of the Presidents* (New York: Crown, 2000), pp. 507–508.
7. Ibid., p. 508.
8. Jeffrey Toobin, *A Vast Conspiracy: The Real Story of the Sex Scandal That Nearly Brought Down a President* (New York: Random House, 1999), p. 195.
9. Ibid.
10. Joe Klein, *The Natural: The Misunderstood Presidency of Bill Clinton* (New York: Doubleday, 2002), p. 11.

11. Ibid., pp. 16–17.
12. Ibid., p. 17.
13. Richard A. Posner, *An Affair of State: The Investigation, Impeachment, and Trial of President Clinton* (Cambridge, MA: Harvard University Press, 1999), p. 19.
14. Ibid.
15. Ibid., p. 22.
16. Ibid., p. 28.
17. Peter Baker, *The Breach: Inside the Impeachment and Trial of William Jefferson Clinton* (New York: Scribner, 2000), p. 28.
18. Ibid., p. 433.
19. Klein, p. 170; Baker, pp. 433–34.
20. Baker, p. 50.
21. Klein, p. 175; Baker, p. 50.
22. Baker, p. 44.
23. Ibid., p. 427.
24. Ibid.
25. Klein, p. 177.
26. Baer, p. 257.
27. Ibid., p. 263.
28. Baker, p. 429.
29. Baer, p. 256.
30. Ibid., p. 261.
31. Baker, p. 430.
32. Ibid., p. 250.
33. Ibid., pp. 438–41.
34. Ibid., p. 435.
35. Ibid., p. 436.
36. Ibid., p. 263.
37. Ibid., p. 432.
38. *Facts on File,* 1999, p. 110.
39. Ibid.
40. Baker, p. 432.
41. Ibid., p. 414.
42. Ibid.
43. Susan Schmidt and Michael Weisskopf, *Truth at Any Cost: Ken Starr and the Unmaking of Bill Clinton* (New York: HarperCollins, 2000), p. 278.
44. Gould, p. 510.
45. Baker, pp. 415–16.
46. Schmidt and Weisskopf, p. 277.
47. Baker, p. 416.
48. Schmidt and Weisskopf, pp. 277–78.
49. Baker, p. 417.

Chapter 34: CALAMITY IN 2000

1. *Facts on File,* 1999, pp. 433–34.
2. Ibid., p. 433.
3. Ibid.

4. Ibid.
5. Ibid., p. 650.
6. Jules Witcover, "Candidates Waging War of Styles in Iowa," *Baltimore Sun*, Oct. 11, 1999.
7. Ibid.
8. Jules Witcover, "Bradley Put on Defensive on Farm Voting Record," *Baltimore Sun*, Jan. 13, 2000.
9. Ibid.
10. Ibid.
11. Ibid.
12. *Facts on File*, 2000, p. 49.
13. Jules Witcover, "Bradley Questions Gore's Truthfulness," *Baltimore Sun*, Jan. 28, 2000.
14. Jack W. Germond and Jules Witcover, "Clock Winding Down, Bradley Takes Shot," *Baltimore Sun*, Jan. 31, 2000.
15. *Facts on File*, 2000, p. 59.
16. Jules Witcover, "Bradley 'Turnaround' Raises His Hopes for Super Tuesday," *Baltimore Sun*, Feb. 2, 2000.
17. Author's interview with aide, March 8, 2000.
18. Jules Witcover, *No Way to Pick a President: How Hired Guns and Money Have Debased American Elections* (New York: Farrar, Straus and Giroux, 1999), p. 9.
19. *Facts on File*, 2000, p. 517.
20. *Baltimore Sun*, Aug. 9, 2000.
21. *Facts on File*, 2000, p. 581.
22. Ibid., p. 583.
23. Ibid., p. 623.
24. Ibid., p. 732.
25. Ibid., p. 819.
26. Ibid., p. 820.
27. Ibid., p. 842.
28. Ibid., p. 841.
29. *Washington Post* Political Staff, *Deadlock: The Inside Story of America's Closest Election* (New York: PublicAffairs, 2001), pp. 66–67.
30. Ibid., p. 69.
31. Ibid., pp. 31–32.
32. Ibid., p. 43.
33. Ibid., pp. 20, 44–45.
34. Ibid., pp. 47–48.
35. Ibid., p. 49. Others in the room reported hearing Gore's response as: "With all due respect to your little brother, he is not the final arbiter of who wins Florida" (ibid.) and "Your younger brother is not the ultimate authority on this" (*Facts on File*, 2000, p. 838).
36. *Washington Post* Political Staff, p. 49.
37. *Facts on File*, 2000, pp. 837–40.
38. *Washington Post* Political Staff, p. 75.
39. Ibid., p. viii.
40. Ibid., pp. 82, 162.
41. Ibid., pp. 102–03.

42. Ibid., p. ix.
43. Ibid., p. x.
44. Ibid., p. 131.
45. Ibid., pp. 113–14.
46. Ibid., p. xi.
47. Ibid., pp. 138–41.
48. Ibid., p. xii.
49. Ibid., p. 161.
50. Ibid., pp. xiii, 171.
51. Ibid., p. 172.
52. Ibid., p. 162.
53. Ibid., p. 200.
54. Ibid., p. 212.
55. Ibid., pp. 211–12.
56. Ibid., p. 212.
57. Associated Press, Jan. 19, 2001.
58. E. J. Dionne and William Kristol, eds., *Bush v. Gore: The Court Cases and the Commentary* (Washington, DC: Brookings, 2001), p. 107.
59. Ibid., p. 108.
60. Ibid., p. 109.
61. Ibid., p. 110.
62. Ibid., p. 117.
63. Ibid., pp. 117–18.
64. Ibid., p. 119.
65. Ibid., p. 120.
66. Ibid., p. 121.
67. Ibid., pp. 121, 124.
68. Ibid., p. 125.
69. Ibid., p. 132.
70. Ibid., pp. 132–33.
71. Dionne and Kristol, pp. 142–43.
72. *Washington Post* Political Staff, p. 239.
73. Dan Keating and Dan Balz, "Florida Recounts Would Have Favored Bush," *Washington Post*, Nov. 12, 2001.

BIBLIOGRAPHY

Adams, Henry. *History of the United States of America During the Administrations of James Madison*. New York: Library of America, 1986.

Allen, Frederick Lewis. *Only Yesterday: An Informal History of the 1920s*. New York: Harper & Row, 1931.

Anson, Robert Sam. *McGovern: A Biography*. New York: Holt, Rinehart and Winston, 1972.

Baer, Kenneth S. *Reinventing Democrats: The Politics of Liberalism from Reagan to Clinton*. Lawrence: University Press of Kansas, 2000.

Bain, Richard C., and Judith H. Parris. *Convention Decisions and Voting Records*. Washington, DC: Brookings Institution, 1973.

Baker, Jean H. *Affairs of Party: The Political Culture of Northern Democrats in the Mid-19th Century*. New York: Fordham University Press, 1998.

——. *The Stevensons: A Biography of an American Family*. New York: Norton, 1996.

Baker, Leonard. *John Marshall: A Life in Law*. New York: Macmillan, 1974.

——. *The Johnson Eclipse: A President's Vice Presidency*. New York: Macmillan, 1966.

Baker, Peter. *The Breach: Inside the Impeachment and Trial of William Jefferson Clinton*. New York: Scribner, 2000.

Baker, Ray Stannard. *Woodrow Wilson: Life and Letters, Governor, 1910–1913*. New York: Scribner's, 1946.

Beard, Charles A. *The American Party Battle*. New York: Macmillan, 1928.

Berkeley, Edmund, and Dorothy Berkeley. *John Beckley: Partisan in a Nation Divided*. Philadelphia: American Philosophical Society, 1973.

Berman, Edgar. *Hubert: The Triumph and Tragedy of the Humphrey I Knew*. New York: Putnam, 1979.

Bernstein, Barton J., and Allen J. Matusow. *The Truman Administration: A Documentary History*. New York: Harper & Row, 1966.

Bernstein, Carl, and Bob Woodward. *All the President's Men*. New York: Simon & Schuster, 1974.

Bernstein, Irving. *Guns or Butter: The Presidency of Lyndon Johnson.* New York: Oxford University Press, 1996.

Beschloss, Michael, ed. *American Heritage Illustrated History of the Presidents.* New York: Crown, 2000.

———. *Taking Charge: The Johnson White House Tapes, 1963–1964.* New York: Simon & Schuster, 1997.

Best, Gary Dean. *FDR and the Bonus Marchers, 1933–1935.* Westport, CT: Praeger, 1992.

Binkley, Wilfred E. *American Political Parties: Their Natural History.* New York: Knopf, 1962.

Blum, John M. *Woodrow Wilson and the Politics of Morality.* Boston: Little, Brown, 1956.

Blum, John M., et al. *The National Experience: A History of the United States,* 7th ed. New York: Harcourt Brace Jovanovich, 1989.

Bollens, John C., and G. Robert Williams. *Jerry Brown: In a Plain Brown Wrapper.* Pacific Palisades, CA: Palisades, 1972.

Bowers, Claude G. *Jefferson and Hamilton: The Struggle for Democracy in America.* Boston: Houghton Mifflin, 1953.

———. *Jefferson in Power: The Death Struggle of the Federalists.* Boston: Houghton Mifflin, 1936.

Branch, Taylor. *Parting the Waters: America in the King Years, 1954–63.* New York: Simon & Schuster, 1988.

Brant, Irving. *The Fourth President: A Life of James Madison.* Indianapolis: Bobbs-Merrill, 1970.

Bruce, Harold R. *American Parties and Politics.* New York: Holt, 1936.

Bui Diem, with David Chanoff. *In the Jaws of History.* Boston: Houghton Mifflin, 1987.

Burner, David. *The Politics of Provincialism: The Democratic Party in Transition, 1918–1932.* New York: Knopf, 1968.

Burns, James MacGregor. *John Kennedy.* New York: Harcourt, Brace and World, 1961.

———. *Roosevelt: The Lion and the Fox.* New York: Harcourt, Brace, 1956.

Byrnes, James F. *All in One Lifetime.* New York: Harper & Row, 1958.

Califano, Joseph A., Jr. *The Triumph & Tragedy of Lyndon Johnson: The White House Years.* New York: Simon & Schuster, 1991.

Caro, Robert A. *The Path to Power: The Years of Lyndon Johnson.* New York: Vintage, 1983.

Carter, Dan T. *When the War Was Over.* Baton Rouge: Louisiana State University Press, 1985.

Carter, Jimmy. *Turning Point: A Candidate, a State, and a Nation Come of Age.* New York: Times Books, 1992.

Chambers, William N. *The Democrats in American Politics: A Short History of a Popular Party.* New York: Van Nostrand, 1972.

———. *Political Parties in a New Nation.* New York: Oxford University Press, 1963.

Charles, Joseph. *The Origins of the American Party System.* Williamsburg, VA: Institution of Early American History and Culture, 1956.

Chase, James S. *Emergence of the Presidential Nominating Convention, 1789–1832.* Urbana: University of Illinois Press, 1973.

Clancy, Herbert J., S.J. *The Democratic Party: Jefferson to Jackson.* New York: Fordham University Press, 1962.

Cochran, Bert. *Adlai Stevenson: Patrician Among the Politicians.* New York: Funk & Wagnall's, 1969.

——. *Harry Truman and the Crisis Presidency.* New York: Funk & Wagnall's, 1973.

Coletta, Paolo. *William Jennings Bryan.* Lincoln: University of Nebraska Press, 1964.

Connally, John, with Mickey Herskowitz. *In History's Shadow: An American Odyssey.* New York: Hyperion, 1993.

Cook, Blanche Wiesen. *Eleanor Roosevelt,* vol 2: *1933–1938.* New York: Viking, 1999.

Cooper, John Milton, Jr. *Breaking the Heart of the World: Woodrow Wilson and the Fight for the League of Nations.* Cambridge, Eng.: Cambridge University Press, 2001.

——. *Pivotal Decades: The United States, 1900–1920.* New York: Norton, 1990.

——. *The Warrior and the Priest: Woodrow Wilson and Theodore Roosevelt.* Cambridge, MA.: Belknap Press, 1983.

Cotter, Cornelius, and Bernard Hennessy. *Politics Without Power: The National Committees.* New York: Atherton, 1964.

Crotty, William J. *Decision for the Democrats: Reforming the Party Structure.* Baltimore: Johns Hopkins University Press, 1978.

——. *Political Reform and the American Experiment.* New York: Crowell, 1977.

Culver, John S., and John Hyde. *American Dreamer: The Life and Times of Henry A. Wallace.* New York: Norton, 2000.

Cunningham, Noble E., Jr. *The Jeffersonian Republicans, 1789–1801.* Chapel Hill: University of North Carolina Press, 1957.

——. *The Jeffersonian Republicans in Power.* Chapel Hill: University of North Carolina Press, 1963.

——. *The Presidency of James Monroe.* Lawrence: University Press of Kansas, 1996.

Dallek, Robert. *Flawed Giant: Lyndon Johnson and His Times, 1961–1973.* New York: Oxford University Press, 1998.

Dangerfield, George. *The Era of Good Feelings.* New York: Harcourt, Brace, 1952.

Dauer, Manning J. *The Adams Federalists.* Westport, CT: Greenwood, 1968.

Davis, Kenneth S. *FDR: The New Deal Years, 1933–1937.* New York: Random House, 1979.

——. *FDR: Into the Storm, 1937–1940.* New York: Random House, 1993.

——. *FDR: The War President.* New York: Random House, 2000.

——. *The Politics of Honor: A Biography of Adlai E. Stevenson.* New York: Putnam, 1967.

Dell, Christopher. *Lincoln and the War Democrats: The Grand Erosion of Conservative Tradition.* Cranbury, NJ, and London: Associated University Presses, 1975.

Dershowitz, Alan M. *Supreme Injustice: How the High Court Hijacked Election 2000.* New York: Oxford University Press, 2001.

DeSantis, Vincent P. *The Gilded Age, 1877–1896.* Northbrook, IL: AHM, 1973.

——. *Republicans Face the Southern Question: The New Departure Years, 1877–1897.* Baltimore: Johns Hopkins Press, 1959.

Dionne, E. J., and William Kristol, eds. *Bush v. Gore: The Court Cases and the Commentary.* Washington, DC: Brookings, 2001.

Dole, Bob, and Elizabeth Dole. *Unlimited Partners: Our American Story.* New York: Simon & Schuster, 1996.

Donovan, Robert J. *Conflict and Crisis: The Presidency of Harry S. Truman, 1945–1948.* New York: Norton, 1977.

——. *Tumultuous Years: The Presidency of Harry S. Truman, 1949–1953.* New York: Norton, 1982.

Dorsett, Lyle W. *Franklin D. Roosevelt and the City Bosses.* Port Washington, NY: Kennikat, 1977.

Dougherty, Richard. *Goodbye, Mr. Christian: A Personal Account of McGovern's Rise and Fall.* Garden City, NY: Doubleday, 1973.

Dowling, Anne T., ed. *A History of the Democratic Party: Official Report of Proceedings of the Democratic National Convention, 1964.* Washington, DC: Democratic National Committee, 1968.

Doyle, James. *Not Above the Law: The Battles of Watergate Prosecutors Cox and Jaworski.* New York: Morrow, 1977.

Drew, Elizabeth. *Showdown: The Struggle Between the Gingrich Congress and the Clinton White House.* New York: Simon & Schuster, 1996.

Duffy, Michael, and Dan Goodgame. *Marching in Place: The Status Quo Presidency of George Bush.* New York: Simon & Schuster, 1992.

Eisele, Albert. *Almost to the Presidency: A Biography of Two American Presidents.* Blue Earth, MN: Piper, 1972.

Eisenhower, Milton S. *The President Is Calling.* Garden City, NY: Doubleday, 1974.

Emery, Fred. *Watergate: The Corruption of American Politics and the Fall of Richard Nixon.* New York: Touchstone, 1995.

Evans, Rowland, and Robert Novak. *Lyndon B. Johnson: The Exercise of Power.* New York: Signet, 1966.

Freidel, Frank. *Franklin D. Roosevelt: A Rendezvous with Destiny.* Boston: Little, Brown, 1990.

Germond, Jack W., and Jules Witcover. *Blue Smoke and Mirrors: How Reagan Won and Why Carter Lost the Election of 1980.* New York: Viking, 1981.

——. *Mad as Hell: Revolt at the Ballot Box, 1992.* New York: Warner, 1993.

——. *Wake Us When It's Over: Presidential Politics of 1984.* New York: Macmillan, 1985.

——. *Whose Broad Stripes and Bright Stars?: The Trivial Pursuit of the Presidency, 1988.* New York: Warner, 1989.

Gillman, Howard. *The Votes That Counted: How the Court Decided the 2000 Presidential Election.* Chicago: University of Chicago Press, 2001.

Gitlin, Todd. *The Sixties: Years of Hope, Days of Rage.* New York: Bantam, 1993.

Glad, Paul W. *McKinley, Bryan and the People.* Philadelphia: Lippincott, 1964.

Goldman, Eric F. *The Tragedy of Lyndon Johnson.* New York: Knopf, 1969.

Goldman, Ralph M. *The Democratic Party in American Politics.* New York: Macmillan, 1966.

——. *Search for Consensus: The Story of the Democratic Party.* Philadelphia: Temple University Press, 1979.

Goldwater, Barry M. *With No Apologies: The Personal and Political Memoirs of United States Senator Barry M. Goldwater.* New York: Morrow, 1979.

——. *Why Not Victory: A Fresh Look at American Foreign Policy.* New York: McGraw-Hill, 1962.

Goodwin, Doris Kearns, *No Ordinary Time: Franklin and Eleanor Roosevelt: The Home Front in World War II.* New York: Simon & Schuster, 1994.

Goodwin, Richard N. *Remembering America: A Voice from the Sixties.* Boston: Little, Brown, 1988.

Gosnell, Harold F. *Truman's Crises: A Political Biography of Harry S. Truman.* Westport, CT: Greenwood, 1980.

Gould, Lewis L. *Progressives and Prohibitionists: Texas Democrats in the Wilson Era.* Austin: University of Texas Press, 1973.

——. *Reform and Regulation: American Politics from Roosevelt to Wilson.* Prospect Heights, IL: Waveland, 1996.

Harris, Fred R. *Potomac Fever.* New York: Norton, 1977.

Hayden, Tom. *Reunion: A Memoir.* New York: Random House, 1988.

Hecht, Marie B. *John Quincy Adams: A Personal History of an Independent Man.* New York: Macmillan, 1972.

Hicks, John D. *Republican Ascendancy, 1921–1933.* New York: Harper & Bros., 1960.

Hofstadter, Richard. *The Age of Reform: From Bryan to FDR.* New York: Knopf, 1955.

Hollingsworth, J. Rogers. *The Whirligig of Politics: The Democracy of Cleveland and Bryan.* Chicago: University of Chicago Press, 1963.

Humphrey, Hubert H. *Beyond Civil Rights: A New Day of Equality.* New York: Random House, 1968.

——. *The Education of a Public Man: My Life in Politics.* Minneapolis: University of Minnesota Press, 1991.

Hunt, Gaillard. *The Life of James Madison.* New York: Doubleday, Page, 1902.

Ions, Edmund. *Woodrow Wilson: The Politics of Peace and War.* London/New York: Macdonald/American Heritage, 1972.

Jenkins, Roy. *Truman.* New York: Harper & Row, 1986.

Johnson, Haynes. *The Best of Times: America in the Clinton Years.* New York: Harcourt, 2001.

Johnson, Lady Bird. *A White House Diary.* New York: Holt, Rinehart and Winston, 1970.

Johnson, Lyndon Baines. *The Vantage Point: Perspectives of the Presidency, 1963–1969.* New York: Holt, Rinehart and Winston, 1971.

Jordan, Hamilton. *Crisis: The Last Year of the Carter Presidency.* New York: Putnam, 1982.

Karabell, Zachary. *The Last Campaign: How Harry Truman Won the 1948 Election.* New York: Knopf, 2000.

Karnow, Stanley. *Vietnam: A History.* New York: Viking, 1983.

Kearns, Doris. *Lyndon Johnson & the American Dream.* New York: Harper & Row, 1976.

Kennedy, Robert F. *Thirteen Days: A Memoir of the Cuban Missile Crisis.* New York: Norton, 1969.

Kent, Frank R. *The Democratic Party: A History.* New York: Century, 1928.

Kessel, John H. *The Goldwater Coalition: Republican Strategies in 1964.* Indianapolis: Bobbs-Merrill, 1968.

Key, V. O., Jr. *Southern Politics in State and Nation.* Knoxville: University of Tennessee Press, 1977.

Klein, Joe. *The Natural: The Misunderstood Presidency of Bill Clinton.* New York: Doubleday, 2002.

Kleppner, Paul. *The Third Electoral System: Parties, Voters and Political Cultures, 1853–1892.* Chapel Hill: University of North Carolina Press, 1979.

Kousser, J. Morgan. *The Shaping of Southern Politics: Suffrage Restriction and the*

Establishment of the One-Party South, 1880–1910. New Haven: Yale University Press, 1974.

Kurtz, Stephen G. *The Presidency of John Adams: The Collapse of Federalism, 1795–1800.* Philadelphia: University of Pennsylvania Press, 1957.

Larner, Jeremy. *Nobody Knows: Reflections on the McCarthy Campaign of 1968.* New York: Macmillan, 1969.

Leuchtenburg, William E. *The FDR Years: On Roosevelt and His Legacy.* New York: Columbia University Press, 1995.

——. *The Perils of Prosperity, 1914–32.* Chicago: University of Chicago Press, 1958.

Levine, Lawrence W. *Defender of the Faith: William Jennings Bryan: The Last Decade, 1915–1925.* New York: Oxford University Press, 1965.

Lewis, David L. *King: A Critical Biography.* New York: Praeger, 1970.

Lewis, Finlay. *Mondale: Portrait of an American Politician.* New York: Harper & Row, 1980.

Lichtman, Allan J. *Prejudice and the Old Politics: The Presidential Election of 1928.* Chapel Hill: University of North Carolina Press, 1979.

Link, Arthur S. *Woodrow Wilson and the Progressive Era.* New York: Harper & Bros., 1954.

——. *Wilson: The Road to the White House.* Princeton: Princeton University Press, 1947.

Livermore, Shaw, Jr. *The Twilight of Federalism: The Disintegration of the Federalist Party, 1815–1830.* New York: Gordion, 1972.

Lomask, Milton. *Aaron Burr: The Years from Princeton to Vice President, 1756–1805.* New York: Farrar, Straus and Giroux, 1979.

Lorenz, J. D. *Jerry Brown: The Man on the White Horse.* Boston: Houghton Mifflin, 1978.

Lukas, J. Anthony. *Nightmare: The Underside of the Nixon Years.* New York: Viking, 1976.

McCarthy, Eugene J. *The Year of the People.* Garden City, NY: Doubleday, 1969.

McCormick, Richard P. *The Presidential Game: The Origins of American Presidential Politics.* New York: Oxford University Press, 1982.

——. *The Second American Party System: Party Formation in the Jacksonian Era.* New York: Norton, 1973.

McCoy, Donald R. *The Presidency of Harry S. Truman.* Lawrence: University Press of Kansas, 1984.

McCullough, David. *John Adams.* New York: Simon & Schuster, 2001.

——. *Truman.* New York: Simon & Schuster, 1992.

McFarland, G. *Mugwumps, Morals and Politics, 1884–1920.* Amherst: University of Massachusetts Press, 1975.

McGovern, George. *An American Journey.* New York: Random House, 1974.

——. *Grassroots: The Autobiography of George McGovern.* New York: Random House, 1977.

McKeever, Porter. *Adlai Stevenson: His Life and Legacy.* New York: Morrow, 1989.

McKitrick, Eric L. *Andrew Johnson and Reconstruction.* New York: Oxford University Press, 1988.

McNamara, Robert S. *In Retrospect: The Tragedy and Lessons of Vietnam.* New York: Times Books, 1995.

Manchester, William. *The Death of a President.* New York: Harper & Row, 1967.

Maraniss, David. *First in His Class: The Biography of Bill Clinton*. New York: Touchstone, 1995.

Martin, John Bartlow. *Adlai Stevenson of Illinois*. Garden City, NY: Doubleday, 1976.

——. *Adlai Stevenson and the World*. New York: Anchor, 1978.

Martin, Ralph G. *A Hero for Our Time: An Intimate Story of the Kennedy Years*. New York: Macmillan, 1983.

Merriam, Charles E., and Harold Foote Gosnell. *The American Party System*. New York: Macmillan, 1949.

Milbank, Dana. *Smashmouth: Two Years in the Gutter with Al Gore and George W. Bush—Notes from the 2000 Campaign Trail*. New York: BasicBooks, 2001.

Miller, Merle. *Lyndon: An Oral Biography*. New York: Putnam, 1980.

——. *Plain Speaking: An Oral Biography of Harry S. Truman*. New York: Putnam, 1974.

Miller, Nathan. *FDR: An Intimate History*. Garden City, NY: Doubleday, 1983.

Morgan, H. Wayne. *From Hayes to McKinley: National Party Politics, 1877–1896*. Syracuse, NY: Syracuse University Press, 1969.

Morris, Dick. *Behind the Oval Office: Winning the Presidency in the Nineties*. New York: Random House, 1997.

Morris, Edmund. *Theodore Rex*. New York: Random House, 2001.

Morris, Roger. *Partners in Power: The Clintons and Their America*. New York: Holt, 1996.

Murphy, Bruce Allen. *Wild Bill: The Legend and Life of William O. Douglas*. New York: Random House, 2003.

Muskie, Edmund S. *Journeys*. Garden City, NY: Doubleday, 1972.

Nevin, David. *Muskie of Maine*. New York: Random House, 1972.

Nevins, Allan. *Grover Cleveland: A Study in Courage*. New York: Dodd, Mead, 1932.

——, ed. *Polk: The Diary of a President, 1845–1849*. New York: Longmans, Green, 1929.

Nichols, Roy F. *The Disruption of American Democracy*. New York: Macmillan, 1948.

O'Brien, Lawrence F. *No Final Victories: A Life in Politics from John F. Kennedy to Watergate*. Garden City, NY: Doubleday, 1974.

Pancake, Thomas S. *Thomas Jefferson and Alexander Hamilton: Shapers of History*. Woodbury, NY: Barron's Educational Series, 1974.

Parmet, Herbert S. *Eisenhower and the American Crusades*. New York: Macmillan, 1972.

——. *JFK: The Presidency of John F. Kennedy*. New York: Dial, 1983.

Patterson, James T. *Grand Expectations: The United States, 1945–1974*. New York: Oxford University Press, 1996.

Perman, Michael. *Reunion Without Compromise: The South and Reconstruction, 1865–1868*. Cambridge, Eng.: Cambridge University Press, 1973.

——. *The Road to Redemption: Southern Politics, 1869–1879*. Chapel Hill: University of North Carolina Press, 1984.

Perry, Elisabeth Israels. *Belle Moskowitz: Feminine Politics and the Exercise of Power in the Age of Alfred E. Smith*. New York: Oxford University Press, 1987.

Phillips, Cabell. *The Truman Presidency: The History of a Triumphant Succession*. New York: Macmillan, 1966.

Polsby, Nelson W. *Consequences of Party Reform*. New York: Oxford University Press, 1983.

Posner, Gerald. *Citizen Perot: His Life & Times*. New York: Random House, 1996.

Posner, Richard A. *An Affair of State: The Investigation, Impeachment, and Trial of President Clinton*. Cambridge, MA: Harvard University Press, 1999.

Potter, David M. *The Impending Crisis, 1848–1861.* New York: Harper & Row, 1976.

Prescott, Frederick C. *Alexander Hamilton and Thomas Jefferson.* New York: American Book, 1934.

Rakove, Jack N., ed. *The Unfinished Election of 2000.* New York: Basic Books, 2001.

Rapport, George C. *The Statesman and the Boss.* New York: Vantage, 1961.

Reeves, Richard. *President Kennedy: Profile of Power.* New York: Touchstone, 1993.

Reeves, Thomas C. *A Question of Character: A Life of John F. Kennedy.* New York: Free Press, 1991.

Remini, Robert V. *Andrew Jackson and the Course of American Democracy, 1833–1845.* New York: Harper & Row, 1984.

——. *Martin Van Buren and the Making of the Democratic Party.* New York: Columbia University Press, 1959.

Reston, James. *Deadline: A Memoir.* New York: Random House, 1991.

Risjord, Norman K. *Old Republicans: Southern Conservatism in the Age of Jefferson.* New York: Columbia University Press, 1965.

Robinson, Edgar E. *The Evolution of American Political Parties.* New York: Harcourt, Brace, 1924.

Roseboom, Eugene H. *A History of Presidential Elections.* New York: Macmillan, 1964.

Ross, Irwin. *The Loneliest Campaign.* New York: New American Library, 1968.

Ross, Lillian. *Adlai Stevenson.* Philadelphia: Lippincott, 1966.

Rutland, Robert Allen. *The Presidency of James Madison.* Lawrence: University Press of Kansas, 1990.

Sait, Edward McC. *American Parties and Elections.* New York: Appleton-Century, 1939.

Salinger, Pierre. *With Kennedy.* Garden City, NY: Doubleday, 1966.

Savage, Sean J. *Roosevelt: The Party Leader.* Lexington: University Press of Kentucky, 1991.

Schachner, Nathan. *Thomas Jefferson: A Biography.* New York: Yosseloff, 1957.

Schandler, Herbert Y. *The Unmaking of a President: Lyndon Johnson and Vietnam.* Princeton, NJ: Princeton University Press, 1977.

Schell, Orville. *Brown.* New York: Random House, 1978.

Schlesinger, Arthur M., Jr. *The Age of Jackson: Politics and Government, 1829–1837.* Boston: Little, Brown, 1945.

——. *The Age of Roosevelt: The Crisis of the Old Order, 1919–1933.* Boston: Houghton Mifflin, 1957.

——. *The Age of Roosevelt: The Coming of the New Deal.* Boston: Houghton Mifflin, 1958.

——. *Robert Kennedy and His Times.* Boston: Houghton Mifflin, 1978.

——. *A Thousand Days: John F. Kennedy in the White House.* Boston: Houghton Mifflin, 1965.

——, ed. *History of U.S. Political Parties,* vols. 1–4. New York: Chelsea House, 1973.

——, ed. *Running for President: The Candidates and Their Images,* vols. 1 and 2. New York: Simon & Schuster, 1994.

Schmidt, Susan, and Michael Weisskopf. *Truth at Any Cost: Ken Starr and the Unmaking of Bill Clinton.* New York: HarperCollins, 2000.

Sheshol, Jeff. *Mutual Contempt.* New York: Norton, 1997.

Shirer, William L. *The Rise and Fall of the Third Reich: A History of Nazi Germany.* New York: Simon & Schuster, 1960.

Silbey, Joel H. *A Respectable Minority: The Democratic Party in the Civil War Era, 1860–1868.* New York: Norton, 1977.

Smelser, Marshall. *The Democratic Republic, 1801–1815.* New York: Harper & Row, 1968.

Solberg, Carl. *Hubert Humphrey: A Biography.* New York: Norton, 1984.

Sorensen, Theodore C. *Kennedy.* New York: Harper & Row, 1965.

——. *The Kennedy Legacy.* New York: Macmillan, 1969.

Steffens, Lincoln. *The Shame of the Cities.* New York: Hill and Wang, 1904.

Stephanopoulos, George. *All Too Human.* Boston: Little, Brown, 1999.

Stewart, James B. *Blood Sport: The President and His Adversaries.* New York: Touchstone, 1996.

Tapper, Jake. *Down and Dirty: The Plot to Steal the Presidency.* Boston: Little, Brown, 2001.

Thomas, Evan. *Robert Kennedy: His Life.* New York: Simon & Schuster, 2000.

Thomas, Evan, and *Newsweek* Team. *Back from the Dead: How Clinton Survived the Republican Revolution.* New York: Atlantic Monthly Press, 1997.

Toobin, Jeffrey. *A Vast Conspiracy: The Real Story of the Sex Scandal That Nearly Brought Down a President.* New York: Random House, 1999.

Truman, Harry S. *Memoirs,* vols. 1 and 2. Garden City, NY: Doubleday, 1955, 1956.

Tugwell, Rexford. *The Democratic Roosevelt.* Garden City, NY: Doubleday, 1957.

U.S. Senate Commerce Committee. *Freedom of Communications,* Part 3, *Presidential Debates of 1960.* Washington, DC: U.S. Government Printing Office, 1961.

Walker, Martin. *The President We Deserve: Bill Clinton: His Rise, Falls, and Comebacks.* New York: Crown, 1996.

Washington Post Political Staff, David von Drehle, writer. *Deadlock: The Inside Story of America's Closest Election.* New York: PublicAffairs, 2001.

Weinstein, Edwin A. *Woodrow Wilson: A Medical and Psychological Biography.* Princeton: Princeton University Press, 1981.

Weiss, Nancy J. *Farewell to the Party of Lincoln: Black Politics in the Age of FDR.* Princeton: Princeton University Press, 1983.

White, F. Clifton, and William J. Gill. *Why Reagan Won: The Conservative Movement, 1964–1981.* Chicago: Regnery Gateway, 1981.

White, Theodore H. *The Making of the President, 1960.* New York: Atheneum, 1961.

——. *The Making of the President, 1964.* New York: Signet, 1965.

——. *The Making of the President, 1972.* New York: Atheneum, 1973.

Witcover, Jules. *Crapshoot: Rolling the Dice on the Vice Presidency.* New York: Crown, 1992.

——. *85 Days: The Last Campaign of Robert Kennedy.* New York: Putnam, 1969.

——. *Marathon: The Pursuit of the Presidency, 1972–1976.* New York: Viking, 1977.

——. *No Way to Pick a President: How Money and Hired Guns Have Debased American Elections.* New York: Farrar Straus Giroux, 1999.

——. *The Resurrection of Richard Nixon.* New York: Putnam, 1970.

——. *The Year the Dream Died: Revisiting 1968 in America.* New York: Warner, 1997.

Wofford, Harris. *Of Kennedys and Kings: Making Sense of the Sixties.* New York: Farrar Straus Giroux, 1980.

Woodward, Bob. *The Choice.* New York: Simon & Schuster, 1996.

——. *Shadow: Five Presidents and the Legacy of Watergate.* New York: Simon & Schuster, 1999.

Woodward, C. Vann. *Reunion and Reaction: The Compromise of 1877 and the End of Reconstruction.* New York: Oxford University Press, 1966.

Young, Donald. *American Roulette: The History and Dilemma of the Vice Presidency.* New York: Viking, 1974.

Zieger, Henry A. *Lyndon B. Johnson: Man and President.* New York: Popular Library, 1963.

INDEX

Page numbers in *italics* refer to illustrations

ABOUT THE AUTHOR

JULES WITCOVER has covered American politics, and the Democratic Party, for more than half a century as a reporter, syndicated columnist, and author. He has written ten books on politics and history, including a novel, and is coauthor of five other political books. Witcover has also attended every Democratic National Convention since 1964, when the party nominated Lyndon B. Johnson in Atlantic City. After writing *85 Days*, the definitive account of the last campaign of Robert Kennedy in 1968, he chronicled every presidential campaign from 1976 to 1992 and then offered a seething critique of the process in 1999 in *No Way to Pick a President*. A recipient of the Sigma Delta Chi Award for Washington correspondents, Witcover has written on national politics for the Newhouse Newspapers, the *Los Angeles Times, The Washington Post,* and *The Washington Star,* and since 1981 he has been a political columnist for the Baltimore *Sun*. He lives with his wife, Marion Elizabeth Rodgers, in Washington.

ABOUT THE TYPE

This book is set in Läckö, a typeface named after a seventeenth-century Baroque castle, now a museum, situated near Lidköping, Sweden. Designer Bo Berndal, asked to provide a typeface appropriate for the museum's exhibition signs and printed matter, drew inspiration from typefaces used in early-eighteenth-century French and Swedish books in the Rococo style; the present face, with its clean lines and prominent weight, shows a mixture of influences and the designer's own touches.